Transmedial Narratology and Contemporary Media Culture

Frontiers of
Narrative

SERIES EDITOR
Jesse E. Matz, Kenyon College

Transmedial Narratology and Contemporary Media Culture

JAN-NOËL THON

University of Nebraska Press | Lincoln and London

© 2016 by the Board of Regents of the University of Nebraska

Acknowledgments for the use of copyrighted material appear on pages xiv–xvi, which constitute an extension of the copyright page.

All rights reserved

Library of Congress Cataloging-in-Publication Data
Thon, Jan-Noël.
Transmedial narratology and contemporary media culture / Jan-Noël Thon.
pages cm — (Frontiers of narrative)
Includes bibliographical references and index.
ISBN 978-0-8032-7720-5 (cloth: alk. paper)
ISBN 978-1-4962-0770-8 (paper: alk. paper)
ISBN 978-0-8032-8837-9 (epub)
ISBN 978-0-8032-8838-6 (mobi)
ISBN 978-0-8032-8839-3 (pdf)
1. Narration (Rhetoric) 2. Storytelling in mass media. 3. Discourse analysis, Narrative. I. Title.
P96.N35T48 2015
302.2301'4—dc23
2015024270

Set in Minion by Westchester Publishing Services

Contents

List of Illustrations   vii
Acknowledgments   xiii
Introduction   xvii

1 Toward a Transmedial Narratology   1

PART 1. STORYWORLDS ACROSS MEDIA

2 The Storyworld as a Transmedial Concept   35
3 Narrative Representation across Media   71

PART 2. NARRATORS ACROSS MEDIA

4 The Narrator as a Transmedial Concept   125
5 Narratorial Representation across Media   167

PART 3. SUBJECTIVITY ACROSS MEDIA

6 Subjectivity as a Transmedial Concept   223
7 Subjective Representation across Media   265

Conclusion   327

Notes   333
Works Cited   425
Index   493

Illustrations

1. Animated picture in *Run Lola Run*   88
2. Anthropomorphic cats and mice in "Maus"   92
3. Metaphorically represented Germans and Jews in *Maus*   92
4. Metaphorical pig masks in *Maus*   93
5. Jimmy and the delivery van in *Jimmy Corrigan: The Smartest Kid on Earth*   97
6. Faded turquoise color scheme and other markers of subjectivity in *Jimmy Corrigan*   98
7. Jimmy remembering Thanksgiving in *Jimmy Corrigan*   99
8. Pictorial representation and verbal narration in *Neverwinter Nights*   108
9. Verbal-pictorial representation and verbal narration in *Max Payne*   109
10. A backpack full of plate armor in *Dragon Age: Origins*   113
11. Introductory sequence in *Run Lola Run*   169
12. Intertitle "UND DANN" ("subsequently") in *Run Lola Run*   170
13. Metaleptically hesitant expression of the experiencing I in *Fight Club*   175
14. The narrating I telling an extradiegetic narratee "a little bit about Tyler Durden" in *Fight Club*   176
15. Tyler Durden pointing at the "cigarette burn" on the film picture in *Fight Club*   176
16. Tyler Durden inserting a pornographic picture into a family film in *Fight Club*   177
17. The diegetic Charlie Kaufman dictating parts of his script in *Adaptation.*   181

18 The diegetic Charlie Kaufman typing parts of his script in *Adaptation.* 181
19 Subjective narration boxes in *Batman: The Dark Knight Returns* 184
20 Subjective frameless narration boxes in *Jimmy Corrigan: The Smartest Kid on Earth* 185
21 Extradiegetic heterodiegetic narrator in *The League of Extraordinary Gentlemen* 186
22 Extradiegetic heterodiegetic narrator in *The Sandman: Preludes and Nocturnes* 186
23 Dodola functioning as an extradiegetic homodiegetic narrator in *Habibi* 188
24 Dodola functioning as an intradiegetic heterodiegetic narrator in *Habibi* 190
25 Black frames marking the "mood" of the story in *Habibi* 191
26 The representation of writing blurring the lines of authorship in *Habibi* 192
27 The representation of maps blurring the lines of authorship in *Habibi* 193
28 Initial representation of Dream's internal voice in *The Sandman: Preludes and Nocturnes* 194
29 Indeterminacy of the narrator's diegetic status in *The Sandman: Preludes and Nocturnes* 196
30 The narratorial representation's switch to the past tense in *The Sandman: Preludes and Nocturnes* 197
31 Intradiegetic homodiegetic narrator in *The Sandman: Preludes and Nocturnes* 198
32 Narration in an intradiegetic letter in *The League of Extraordinary Gentlemen* 199
33 Art Spiegelman's self-representation in *Maus* 201
34 Art Spiegelman's "authoring I" wearing a metaphorical mask in *Maus* 201
35 Intradiegetic homodiegetic framing narrator in *Maus* 202
36 Intradiegetic homodiegetic nonframing narrator in *Maus* 203

37 Art taping Vladek's verbal narration in *Maus*   203
38 Oscillation between different "historical truths" in *Maus*   206
39 The narrator is revealed to be Sandy Bravitor in *DeathSpank: Thongs of Virtue*   212
40 DeathSpank takes up the narratorial duties in *DeathSpank: Thongs of Virtue*   214
41 Interactive narrator in *Bastion*   216
42 Ludic unreliability of the narrator in *Bastion*   217
43 First "full-fledged" nonnarratorial representation of James Cole's dream in *12 Monkeys*   267
44 A highly conventionalized a posteriori contextual content marker in *12 Monkeys*   267
45 Tyler Durden talking to the unnamed experiencing I in *Fight Club*   272
46 The unnamed experiencing I talking to himself in *Fight Club*   272
47 Tyler Durden dragging the experiencing I around in *Fight Club*   273
48 The experiencing I dragging himself around in *Fight Club*   273
49 John Nash's (quasi-)perception of rays of light in *A Beautiful Mind*   275
50 John Nash's (quasi-)perception of his colleague's tie in *A Beautiful Mind*   275
51 (Quasi-)perceptual overlay of bats in *Fear and Loathing in Las Vegas*   279
52 Distorted face of the parking attendant in *Fear and Loathing in Las Vegas*   280
53 Anthropomorphic reptiles in a bar in *Fear and Loathing in Las Vegas*   281
54 Switch to (quasi-)perceptual overlay in *Fear and Loathing in Las Vegas*   281
55 A priori contextual content marker in *The Sandman: Season of Mists*   284
56 A posteriori contextual content marker in *The Sandman: Season of Mists*   285

57 A priori contextual content marker of the memory sequence in *The Arrival*   286
58 Nonnarratorial representation of the old man's memories in *The Arrival*   287
59 Mr. Griffin applying makeup in *The League of Extraordinary Gentlemen*   289
60 Mr. Hyde "seeing" temperature in *The League of Extraordinary Gentlemen*   290
61 Nonnarratorial representation of the "contents" of Wallace's mind in *Sin City: Hell and Back*   294
62 Onset of Wallace's hallucinations in *Sin City: Hell and Back*   295
63 Wallace's hallucinations "cooling off" in *Sin City: Hell and Back*   296
64 Narratorial representation of (quasi-)perceptions in *Sin City: Hell and Back*   297
65 Nonnarratorial representation of Chris's dream in *Black Hole*   299
66 Vertical (inter)subjective representation in *Black Hole*   300
67 Horizontal (inter)subjective representation in *Black Hole*   301
68 Chris's experiencing I finishing her narrating I's sentence in *Black Hole*   303
69 Chris functioning as an intradiegetic thinking narrator in *Black Hole*   304
70 Spatial point-of-view sequence in *F.E.A.R.*   307
71 The player-controlled character's first encounter with Alma in *F.E.A.R.*   310
72 Intersubjective representation in *Batman: Arkham Asylum*   314
73 "Detective mode" in *Batman: Arkham Asylum*   314
74 The first Scarecrow sequence in *Batman: Arkham Asylum*   316
75 Batman imagining himself as the Scarecrow in *Batman: Arkham Asylum*   317
76 A hall transforming into a back alley in *Batman: Arkham Asylum*   318

77 Batman imagining himself as the young Bruce in *Batman: Arkham Asylum*   318
78 "Fake crash" before the third Scarecrow sequence in *Batman: Arkham Asylum*   319
79 "Game over" before the third Scarecrow sequence in *Batman: Arkham Asylum*   320
80 Extrafictional directions and other elements of the interface in *Alan Wake*   323

Acknowledgments

There are a great many colleagues and friends who have, in one way or another, contributed to my narratological thinking during the many years it took me to write this book. The sheer number of people to whom I feel indebted presents me with a problem, though, as trying to name them all would necessarily entail forgetting to name some. Hence, I will limit myself to explicitly thanking only the comparatively few who have provided specific feedback on parts of the manuscript in its various stages of production, yet promise to thank the countless others to whom I feel more vaguely but no less sincerely indebted in person, should the opportunity arise.

First and foremost, the project has been tirelessly supported, both intellectually and institutionally, by Jens Eder, Jan Christoph Meister, Marie-Laure Ryan, and Klaus Sachs-Hombach. Moreover, Benjamin Beil, Franziska Bergmann, Stephan Packard, Daniel Punday, Maike Sarah Reinerth, Felix Schröter, Daniel Stein, and Werner Wolf have provided valuable feedback, either during the peer review process or in various less formal settings. Finally, David Herman and Jesse E. Matz as well as Kristen E. Rowley and the editorial team at the University of Nebraska Press have made the publication process a thoroughly pleasurable experience. To all of them, as well as to the many others who will have to remain unnamed for now, my deepest gratitude!

The present book is a shortened and slightly revised version of my PhD thesis in media and communication studies, which was granted the highest distinction (summa cum laude) by the University of Mannheim on March 27, 2014, and subsequently received the Foundation for Communication and Media Studies' award for outstanding research achievements. Work on this thesis has been generously supported by a PhD scholarship from the German National Academic Foundation, which I hereby gratefully acknowledge.

Earlier versions of parts of the argument presented in this book have previously been published, and while most of the material has been substantially revised and expanded since its initial publication, I am grateful for permission to draw on it here:

> Thon, Jan-Noël. "Converging Worlds: From Transmedial Storyworlds to Transmedial Universes." *Storyworlds: A Journal of Narrative Studies* 7.2 (2015): 21–53. Print.
>
> Thon, Jan-Noël. "Narratives across Media and the Outlines of a Media-Conscious Narratology." *Handbook of Intermediality: Literature—Image—Sound—Music*. Ed. Gabriele Rippl. Berlin: De Gruyter, 2015. 439–456. Print.
>
> Thon, Jan-Noël. "Game Studies und Narratologie." *Game Studies: Aktuelle Ansätze der Computerspielforschung*. Ed. Klaus Sachs-Hombach and Jan-Noël Thon. Cologne: Herbert von Halem, 2015. 104–164. Print.
>
> Stein, Daniel, and Jan-Noël Thon. "Introduction: From Comic Strips to Graphic Novels." *From Comic Strips to Graphic Novels: Contributions to the Theory and History of Graphic Narrative*. 2nd ed. Ed. Daniel Stein and Jan-Noël Thon. Berlin: De Gruyter, 2015. 1–23. Print.
>
> Thon, Jan-Noël. "Who's Telling the Tale? Authors and Narrators in Graphic Narrative." *From Comic Strips to Graphic Novels: Contributions to the Theory and History of Graphic Narrative*. 2nd ed. Ed. Daniel Stein and Jan-Noël Thon. Berlin: De Gruyter, 2015. 67–99. Print.
>
> Thon, Jan-Noël. "Fiktionalität in Film- und Medienwissenschaft." *Fiktionalität: Ein interdisziplinäres Handbuch*. Ed. Tobias Klauk and Tilmann Köppe. Berlin: De Gruyter, 2014. 443–466. Print.
>
> Thon, Jan-Noël. "Mediality." *The Johns Hopkins Guide to Digital Media*. Ed. Marie-Laure Ryan, Lori Emerson, and Benjamin J.

Robertson. Baltimore: Johns Hopkins University Press, 2014. 334–337. Print.

Thon, Jan-Noël. "Narrativity." *The Johns Hopkins Guide to Digital Media.* Ed. Marie-Laure Ryan, Lori Emerson, and Benjamin J. Robertson. Baltimore: Johns Hopkins University Press, 2014. 351–355. Print.

Thon, Jan-Noël. "Subjectivity across Media: On Transmedial Strategies of Subjective Representation in Contemporary Feature Films, Graphic Novels, and Computer Games." *Storyworlds across Media: Toward a Media-Conscious Narratology.* Ed. Marie-Laure Ryan and Jan-Noël Thon. Lincoln: University of Nebraska Press, 2014. 67–102. Print.

Thon, Jan-Noël. "Toward a Transmedial Narratology: On Narrators in Contemporary Graphic Novels, Feature Films, and Computer Games." *Beyond Classical Narration: Transmedial and Unnatural Challenges.* Ed. Jan Alber and Per Krogh Hansen. Berlin: De Gruyter, 2014. 25–56. Print.

Thon, Jan-Noël. "Computer Games, Fictional Worlds, and Transmedial Storytelling: A Narratological Perspective." *Proceedings of the Philosophy of Computer Games Conference 2009.* Ed. John R. Sageng. Oslo: University of Oslo, 2009. 1–6. Web.

Thon, Jan-Noël. "Mind-Bender: Zur Popularisierung komplexer narrativer Strukturen im amerikanischen Kino der 1990er Jahre." *Post-Coca-Colanization: Zurück zur Vielfalt?* Ed. Sophia Komor and Rebekka Rohleder. Frankfurt am Main: Peter Lang, 2009. 175–192. Print.

Thon, Jan-Noël. "Perspective in Contemporary Computer Games." *Point of View, Perspective, and Focalization: Modeling Mediation in Narrative.* Ed. Peter Hühn, Wolf Schmid, and Jörg Schönert. Berlin: De Gruyter, 2009. 279–299. Print.

Thon, Jan-Noël. "Zur Metalepse im Film." *Probleme filmischen Erzählens.* Ed. Hannah Birr, Maike Sarah Reinerth, and Jan-Noël Thon. Münster: LIT, 2009. 85–110. Print.

Thon, Jan-Noël. "Unendliche Weiten? Schauplätze, fiktionale Welten und soziale Räume heutiger Computerspiele." *Computer/Spiel/Räume: Materialien zur Einführung in die Computer Game Studies*. Ed. Klaus Bartels and Jan-Noël Thon. Hamburg: University of Hamburg, 2007. 29–60. Print.

Introduction

Contemporary media culture is shaped by technological innovations and the move of media conglomerates from vertical to horizontal integration, which has led to a highly interconnected media landscape where intellectual property is often spread across a variety of media platforms.[1] Among the effects of this technological and cultural media convergence have been the increased visibility of various kinds of *intermedial adaptations*[2] and the continued rise of what may be described as *transmedial entertainment franchises*—entertainment franchises, that is, that transgress the borders of different "media" and hermetically packaged "works." Influential contemporary examples would include the novel-based franchises *The Lord of the Rings* and *A Song of Ice and Fire*, the film-based franchises *Star Wars* and *The Matrix*, the television-based franchises *Doctor Who* and *Lost*, the comics-based franchises *Batman* and *The Walking Dead*, or the video game-based franchises *Tomb Raider* and *Warcraft*.[3] While the transmedial representation of characters, stories, and their worlds has become particularly ubiquitous in contemporary media culture, then, a brief look at the rich storyworlds of Hinduism or Christianity already demonstrates that it is not an entirely new phenomenon. Yet, during the past decade or so, media studies have increasingly become aware of the sociocultural significance of these kinds of transmedial storyworlds as well as the considerable theoretical and methodological challenges their study presents due to the complex forms of authorship involved, the vast amount of material produced, and the vocal participation of fans in the negotiation of transmedial meaning(s).[4]

In light of a number of rather grand claims regarding the pervasiveness of transmedial entertainment franchises and the transmedial storyworlds they represent, though, it seems helpful to take a step back and look at an even more strikingly ubiquitous phenomenon of which the latter are only a small part: regardless of whether the work in question can be understood as an adaptation of another work and/or contributes to the representation of a more or less consistent transmedial universe, whenever we read a novel or a comic, watch a film in the cinema or an episode of our favorite series on television, or play the singleplayer mode of the latest video game, we are engaging with *narrative representations*. Even though it has become something of a cliché within narratology to assert the commercial, aesthetic, and sociocultural relevance of narrative representations across media, the fact remains that narratives indeed are everywhere.[5] Interestingly, however, while there is a broad consensus that narrativity is a transmedial phenomenon, much of current literary and media studies tends to focus on strategies of narrative representation in specific media, neglecting the question to what extent the strategies that can be found there share an intermedial or, rather, a transmedial dimension. If one acknowledges that a significant part of contemporary media culture is defined by narrative representations, and if one accepts that an examination of their similarities as well as their differences will be able to help explain the kind of intermedial adaptations and transmedial entertainment franchises mentioned above as well as generally contribute to a better understanding of the forms and functions of narrative works across media, it becomes evident that media studies need a *genuinely transmedial narratology*.

While there are different ways to conceptualize such a project, the kind of transmedial narratology that this book develops not only allows for the analysis of *transmedial strategies of narrative representation* and their realization within the specific mediality of contemporary films, comics, and video games (as the three narrative media with which I am primarily concerned) but also provides a welcome opportunity to critically reconsider—and, at least occasionally, revise—some of narratology's more canonized terms and concepts. Accordingly, the book provides a *method for the analysis* of particularly salient transmedial strategies of narrative representation as well as a *theoretical frame* within which medium-specific approaches from literary and film narratology, from comics studies and game studies, and from various other strands of current narratological research may be systematically correlated, modified, and expanded to further illuminate the forms and functions of narrative representation across media. Any study of the convergent developments within contemporary media culture sketched above would arguably profit from this kind of theoretical frame as well as from the method for the analysis of transmedial strategies of narrative representation that is developed in the following chapters. Nevertheless, my primary focus is neither on intermedial adaptations nor on the sprawling storyworlds that are represented in transmedial entertainment franchises. Instead, I concentrate on more general questions that apply to narrative representations across media—whether or not they are intermedial adaptations retelling a story(world) that has already been told, and whether or not they are contributing to the representation of a transmedial storyworld in the context of more or less complex convergent arrangements of narrative works in different media.

While this book is primarily concerned with fairly fundamental questions related to the development of a method for the analysis of transmedial strategies of narrative representation and a theoretical frame that allows for the correlation, modification, and expansion of existing approaches to narratological analysis across media, then, its potential areas of application are considerably broader. First, let me reemphasize that a sound understanding of the strategies of narrative representation that are employed by narrative works across media will provide a valuable basis for better understanding not only how intermedial adaptations such as Peter Jackson's *The Lord of the Rings* or *The Hobbit* trilogies, HBO's *Game of Thrones*, or Lucas Arts' *Indiana Jones* video game series relate to their respective "pre-texts" but also how the various elements of transmedial entertainment franchises such as *Star Wars*, *Batman*, and *Warcraft* (as well as more "adaptation-heavy" franchises such as *The Lord of the Rings*, *A Song of Ice and Fire*, and *The Walking Dead*, of course) contribute to the representation of their respective transmedial storyworld(s). Second, understanding the basic principles that allow for *narrative meaning making* across media will also provide a foundation for studies concerned with larger-scale questions of cultural meanings, their socioeconomic contexts, and the ways both are renegotiated in the inter- and transcultural dynamics of our globalized world—which, in turn, will offer much-needed *contextualization* of the transmedial strategies of narrative representation discussed in the following chapters.

Third, while I am primarily concerned with *contemporary media culture* (broadly conceived as spanning from the late 1980s to the present day), these transmedial strategies of narrative representation (and, perhaps even more importantly, their medium-specific realization) are historically variable at least to a certain extent. Accordingly, the method of analysis and the theoretical frame developed here may provide fruitful starting points for future studies that are concerned with the *historization* of the transmedial strategies of narrative representation on which I will focus. Fourth and finally, while my interest is primarily *method(olog)ical and theoretical*, a thorough examination of the principles that govern narrative meaning making in the context of both comparatively abstract conceptual analyses of transmedial strategies of narrative representation and more concrete narratological analyses of their medium-specific realization in contemporary films, comics, and video games may also have some *practical relevance* with regard to filmmaking, comics artistry, video game design, and the production of intermedial adaptations as well as transmedial entertainment franchises, in particular.

Despite these broad areas of potential applications, though, this book's focus will necessarily have to remain comparatively narrow. After chapter 1 has outlined the aims and scope of the project of a transmedial narratology as it is pursued here in more detail, the book's three main parts focus on the representation of storyworlds, the use of narratorial representation that is attributable to some kind of narrator, and the use of subjective representation to provide "direct access" to characters' consciousnesses as three particularly salient (and fairly general) transmedial strategies of narrative representation. To this end, the opening chapter of each part develops a transmedial conceptualization of the respective strategy of narrative representation (that is, chapter 2 discusses the storyworld as a transmedial concept, chapter 4 discusses the narrator as a transmedial concept, and chapter 6 discusses the representation of subjectivity as a transmedial concept), while each concluding chapter analyzes how the respective strategies are realized across media (that is, chapter 3 examines narrative representation across media, chapter 5 examines narratorial representation across media, and chapter 7 examines subjective representation across media).

Throughout the following chapters, I primarily analyze feature films such as Quentin Tarantino's *Pulp Fiction*, Tom Tykwer's *Run Lola Run*, David Cronenberg's *eXistenZ*, David Fincher's *Fight Club*, Bryan Singer's *The Usual Suspects*, Spike Jonze and Charlie Kaufman's *Adaptation.*, Terry Gilliam's *12 Monkeys* and *Fear and Loathing in Las Vegas*, or Ron Howard's *A Beautiful Mind*; graphic novels such as Art Spiegelman's *Maus*, Chris Ware's *Jimmy Corrigan: The Smartest Kid on Earth*, Neil Gaiman's *The Sandman: Preludes and Nocturnes*, Mike Carey and Peter Gross's *The Unwritten: Leviathan*, Alan Moore and Kevin O'Neill's *The League of Extraordinary Gentlemen*, Craig Thompson's *Habibi*, Shaun Tan's *The Arrival*, Frank Miller's *Sin City: Hell and Back*, or Charles Burns's *Black Hole*; and highly narrative video games such as Bungie's *Halo*, Remedy's *Alan Wake*, Bioware's *Dragon Age: Origins*, Hothead's *DeathSpank*, Ubisoft's *Prince of Persia: The Sands of Time*, Supergiant Games' *Bastion*, Monolith's *F.E.A.R.: First Encounter Assault Recon*, Frictional Games' *Amnesia: The Dark Descent*, or Rocksteady's *Batman: Arkham Asylum* as "single works."[6] Yet most if not all of these narrative works are part of an intramedial series, an intermedial adaptation process, and/or a transmedial entertainment franchise. Hence, after I have developed the foundation of a genuinely transmedial narratology by primarily treating the narrative works that I have chosen as examples as if they were "single works," I conclude by briefly revisiting the broader questions and fields of inquiry sketched above and, once more, underscoring transmedial narratology's potential for being contextualized, historicized, and practicabilized. Before I can begin discussing the relation between narrative representations and the storyworlds they represent, though, quite a few more fundamental problems related to the project of a transmedial narratology need to be tackled.

Transmedial Narratology and Contemporary Media Culture

1 Toward a Transmedial Narratology

From Narrative Theory to a Method of Analysis

Despite the fact that narrative accounts of complex historical developments are problematic in both theory and practice, the story of narratology has been told and retold countless of times in the past five decades.[1] Hence, it seems neither necessary nor desirable to attempt another detailed retelling of the events that led from the publication of the eighth issue of *Communications* in 1966 and the first works of classical narratology within French structuralism[2] to the current situation of various postclassical "new narratologies"[3] differing widely in epistemological and methodological orientation. In order to situate the aims and scope of my approach within the narratological tradition, however, it might still be helpful to discuss some of the more prominent strands of recent research. In a somewhat eclectic account of current postclassical narratology, Ansgar Nünning distinguishes eight kinds of approaches: "contextualist, thematic, and ideological approaches/applications of narratology in literary studies"; "feminist narratology"; "transgeneric and transmedial applications and elaborations of narratology"; "pragmatic and rhetoric kinds of narratology"; "cognitive and reception theory-oriented kinds of ('meta-')narratology"; "postmodern and poststructuralist deconstructions of (classical) narratology"; "linguistic approaches/contributions to narratology"; "philosophical narrative theories"; and "other interdisciplinary narrative theories" (see A. Nünning, "Narratology" 249–251).

It is clearly beyond the scope of this chapter to examine all of the items on Nünning's list, but I would still like to single out the three approaches that, according to Jan Christoph Meister, "have turned out to be the dominant methodological paradigms of contemporary narratology" ("Narratology" 340). First, contextualist narratology "relates the phenomena encountered in narrative to specific cultural, historical, thematic, and ideological contexts" (Meister, "Narratology" 340) (and, accordingly, complies with Nünning's category of "contextualist, thematic, and ideological approaches/applications of narratology in literary studies"). Second, cognitive narratology "focuses on the human intellectual and emotional processing of narrative" (Meister, "Narratology" 340) (and, therefore, is closest to Nünning's category of "cognitive and reception theory-oriented kinds of ['meta-']narratology"). Third, transgeneric and intermedial approaches (that refer to Nünning's "transgeneric and transmedial applications and elaborations of narratology") include not only research on the *trans*medial dimensions of narrative but also a variety of *inter*medial and *intra*medial narratological approaches concerned with a single medium or genre such as poetry, drama, painting, music, film, comics, or video games.[4]

It may be worth stressing at this point that the French structuralists of the 1960s and 1970s already considered narrative to be "international, transhistorical, transcultural," and fundamentally transmedial in that it can occur in an "almost infinite diversity of forms" (Barthes, "Introduction" 79). However, many of these early narratologists focused less on this diversity of narrative media (or the relation between their specific mediality and the transmedial properties of narrative representations) than on "a search for the laws which govern the narrated matter" (Bremond, "The Logic" 387), with these "laws" often being found on a level so abstract as to be of little value for the analysis of actual narrative representations. Overly formalistic and epistemologically naive as their works may appear from the perspective of contemporary narratology (as well as, and perhaps even more so, from the perspective of contemporary literary and media theory), the "high structuralists" (see Scholes 157) have not only introduced or refined a number of influential narratological concepts (such as "actant," "event," or the "story"/ "discourse" distinction),[5] but their search for narrative universals also remains an important point of reference for contemporary narratological practice, including the project of a transmedial narratology.

Even beyond the structuralist heydays of the late 1960s and early 1970s, this kind of "story-oriented" narratology was continued by scholars such as Gerald Prince (*A Grammar*), Lubomír Doležel (*Heterocosmica; Narrative Modes*), or Marie-Laure Ryan (*Possible Worlds*), but the publication of Gérard Genette's *Narrative Discourse* evidently marks an erosion of this emphasis on the "story" side of the "story"/"discourse" distinction, leading to the advent of a "discourse-oriented" narratology interested less in the structure of the story itself than in the way it was narrated. Genette remains one of the best-known narratologists to this day, and the terminology he developed in *Narrative Discourse*—and later refined in *Narrative Discourse Revisited*—can certainly be considered a "lingua franca" (A. Nünning and V. Nünning 6; Onega 276; Ryan and van Alphen 112) for the narratological analysis of literary texts. Still, following his repeated insistence on limiting the object domain of narratology to the "*verbal transmission*" (Genette, *Narrative Discourse Revisited* 16, original emphasis)[6] of stories would obviously pose a serious problem for every attempt at "doing transmedial narratology" (as well as for every intramedial narratological approach that does not restrict itself to exclusively or primarily verbal forms of narrative representation).

Fortunately, while Genette's brand of "low structuralism" proved to be extremely successful (see Scholes 157; as well as Cornils and Schernus), his attempts at limiting the object domain of narratology to literary and/or verbal narrative representations did not. Unfortunately, though, many "codifiers of narratology around 1980" (Darby 843), in aspiring to continue the project of a transmedial narratology begun by the "high structuralists," also adopted the project's primarily programmatic nature. Seymour Chatman, for example, remarks in the preface to *Story and Discourse* that "literary critics tend to think too exclusively of the verbal medium, even though they consume stories daily through films, comic strips, paintings, sculptures, dance movements, and music" (9). On closer inspection, however, Chatman's treatment of narrative structure in fiction and film is not only biased toward "the verbal medium" but also largely ignores narrative media beyond literary texts and films.[7] Much in the same vein, Shlomith Rimmon-Kenan's *Narrative Fiction* is exclusively concerned with literary texts, but still begins its introduction by emphasizing that "newspaper reports, history books, novels, films, comic strips, pantomime, dance, gossip, psychoanalytic sessions are only some of the narratives which permeate our lives" (1). Likewise, in *Narratology*, Mieke Bal reflects on her vision of a "visual narratology" all too briefly, claiming that "the analysis of visual images as narrative in and of themselves can do justice to an aspect of images and their effects that neither iconography nor other art historical practices can quite articulate" (162) without going beyond some very general remarks on what such a "visual narratology"—which she, moreover, envisions as being distinct from film narratology—would look like (see Bal, *Narratology* 66–75, 161–170). While this gap between program and implementation remains a persistent problem, one still needs to acknowledge the impressive diversification and sophistication of narratological practice from the 1980s onward—as well as the fact that the work of pioneering scholars such as Chatman, Rimmon-Kenan, and Bal made this diversification and sophistication possible to begin with.

The approach of the present book clearly belongs to Meister's third dominant paradigm,[8] but it is also important to note that "postclassical narratology . . . contains classical narratology as one of its 'moments'" (D. Herman, "Introduction: Narratologies" 2). Indeed, classical or, rather, neoclassical approaches still play an important role in contemporary narratology, as is demonstrated by a number of introductory textbooks by narratologists such as Matías Martínez and Michael Scheffel (*Einführung*), Jakob Lothe, H. Porter Abbott (*The Cambridge Introduction*), Monika Fludernik (*An Introduction*), Wolf Schmid (*Narratology*), or Silke Lahn and Jan Christoph Meister (all of which follow, at least to a certain extent, the project of codifying narratology begun and continued by scholars such as Seymour Chatman [*Coming to Terms*; *Story*], Mieke Bal [*Narratology*], and Shlomith Rimmon-Kenan [*Narrative Fiction*]). Similarly, my own approach is evidently influenced by some of the more postclassical approaches within contemporary narratology, but it still remains partially rooted in the (neo)classical tradition, whose heuristic potential for the analysis of narrative representations across media should not be carelessly dismissed.[9]

So, what are the defining characteristics of a (neo)classical narratology? Since Tzvetan Todorov's coining of the term (see Todorov, *Grammaire* 10), a large number of narratologists such as Mieke Bal (*Narratology*), David Herman (*Story Logic*), Manfred Jahn (*Narratology*), Monika Fludernik (*An Introduction*), Ansgar and Vera Nünning, Shlomith Rimmon-Kenan (*Narrative Fiction* 136–138), Marie-Laure Ryan (*Possible Worlds*), Wolf Schmid (*Narratology*), or Werner Wolf ("Das Problem") have considered narratology to be a *theory of narrative*. In addition to its status as a theory, however, narratology has always been concerned with the *analysis of narrative(s)*. Since the examination of the formal and aesthetic structure of literary and "media" texts is usually also concerned with the development of conceptual frameworks for this examination, it will come as no surprise that narratology is likewise concerned with the "analysis of the techniques of narrative" (Bremond, "The Logic" 387) as well as with the provision of "instruments for the systematic description of all and only narratives" (Prince, "Narrative Analysis" 183), or even with the development of a full-fledged "method of analysis" (Genette, *Narrative Discourse* 23) that does not entirely coincide with the development of a theory of narrative. While *narratology as a theory* of narrative primarily aims at the universal characteristics of narrative in general or narrative media and narrative genres in particular, *narratology as a method* is concerned with the development of terms and concepts for the analysis of a wide variety of different strategies of narrative representation.

At least in the context of this book, then, I am neither exclusively interested in "doing theory" nor in attempting to resolve the "vexed issues" (Kindt and Müller, "Narrative Theory" 210) that writers of literary and media history have to face. My approach is obviously not limited to verbal or literary narrative but rather focuses on the narrative limitations and affordances that the specific multimodal configurations of contemporary films, comics, and video games provide. Yet I still emphasize the neoclassical task of developing a method for the analysis of transmedial strategies of narrative representation as they are realized across media. As I would, moreover, argue that one of the core tasks of the project of a transmedial narratology is to provide a theoretical frame within which various (more or less) medium-specific terms and concepts can be productively related to each other (see also Sachs-Hombach), a certain amount of terminological and conceptual reflection is necessary, but the book's main offering consists of a "toolbox" for the analysis of prototypical aspects of narrative across media which can be described as transmedial strategies of narrative representation. Not least because the kind of transmedial narratology proposed here is confronted with a dual challenge regarding the relation between its general concepts and their specific application, however, it may be worth elaborating on the relation between abstract theoretical or method(olog)ical considerations,[10] on the one hand, and concrete analyses of narrative representations across media, on the other.

Let me begin, then, with a discussion of what Gérard Genette describes as "the paradox of every poetics, and doubtless of every other activity of knowledge as well: . . . that there are no objects except particular ones and no science except of the general" (*Narrative Discourse* 23). Genette here refers to the problematic relation between the abstract nature of narratological concepts and what Marie-Laure Ryan calls "idiosyncrasies of individual texts" ("Introduction" 33), but Lubomír Doležel's distinction between *particularistic* and *universalistic poetics* may help to state the problem more clearly: Narratological approaches that focus on developing a theory of narrative can be considered universalistic since they are "constituted by statements about, or definitions of, generic universals" (Doležel, *Occidental Poetics* 17). Analyses of actual narrative representations can be considered particularistic in that they aim "to describe the individuality and diversity of particular structure" (Doležel, *Occidental Poetics* 72). But the object domain of a book that focuses on the development of a method for the analysis of narrative representations would have to be located in between the universal and the particular. "Exemplification," Doležel remarks, "is incomplete induction because it is based on a nonrepresentative sample of data; nevertheless, it preserves the role of induction as the bridge between empirical particulars and abstract universal" (*Occidental Poetics* 25). Even though the method of analysis that is developed throughout the following chapters can be considered universal(istic) in the sense that its terms and concepts are meant to be applicable to a wide variety of narrative representations across media, the demonstration of its analytical power will necessarily remain particular(istic), with the actual analyses of transmedial strategies of narrative representation that are realized within the mediality of contemporary films, comics, and video games primarily fulfilling exemplifying functions.

In light of the epistemological and methodological problems that any attempt to describe transmedial strategies of narrative representation via the analysis of their medium-specific realization(s) is ultimately confronted with, however, it would evidently seem problematic to base the method to be developed exclusively on a necessarily small number of case studies. Hence, in order to expand this kind of "bottom-up" or inductive mode of reasoning by its "top-down" or deductive counterpart, I will systematically take into account previous narratological research, adhering—at least to a certain extent—to what Tom Kindt and Hans-Harald Müller describe as a *criterion of continuity*, which states that narratology "as a whole should take its initial orientation from the heuristically valuable concepts of twentieth-century narrative theory" ("Narrative Theory" 212).[11] Particularly in light of the dual aim of providing both a method for the narratological analysis of transmedial strategies of narrative representation and a theoretical frame within which medium-specific narratological concepts can be integrated and productively interrelated, I will also attempt to adhere to Kindt and Müller's *criterion of neutrality*. Accordingly, this book's "conceptual apparatus has to be assembled in such a way that it remains compatible with a broad range of interpretive orientations" (Kindt and Müller, "Narrative Theory" 212). While my interest in transmedial strategies of narrative representation may make it necessary to shift the focus of Kindt and Müller's considerations to a certain extent (especially with regard to the inclusion of insights from cognitive theory, which I will discuss in greater detail below), a similar criterion of neutrality in fact forms the basis of how I would position my own approach with regard to contextualist and historicist approaches: although an examination of both the history of narrative representations across media and the cultural contexts in which their production and reception take place might contribute to a better understanding of their forms and functions, there are still far too many unanswered questions on a basic conceptual level to begin painting this kind of broader picture. Still, I hope that the following chapters will provide at least some useful conceptual foundations for future studies of narrative representation across media with a more decidedly contextualist and/or historicist focus.

Incidentally, it might be helpful to specify how my transmedial approach relates to the two other dominant narratological paradigms of contextualist and cognitive narratology before I go on to address the aims and scope of the former. Despite the fact that Ansgar Nünning and Jan Christoph Meister use these terms rather confidently, it actually does not seem too clear which strands of narratological practice we are referring to when we talk about contextualism, in particular. When he coined the term in 1990, Seymour Chatman ("What Can We Learn") used it for scholars as diverse as the speech act theorist Marie Louise Pratt, the literary theorist Barbara Herrnstein Smith, the film theorist Thomas Leitch, and the narratologist Susan S. Lanser, but a decade later, Nünning characterized contextualist approaches as merely "applications of narratological models and categories to specific texts, genres or periods" which are mainly "concerned with issues that are not really germane to narratology" ("Narratology" 251–252). While one cannot help but wonder what happened to the decidedly more ambitious research programs of the scholars originally identified as contextualists by Chatman, I have already mentioned that my interest is not primarily contextualist in Nünning's (or Meister's) sense, since I do not use (existing) narratological approaches as a conceptual basis to analyze the relation between narrative representations and their various historical and cultural contexts. Even so, it seems inadvisable to fall behind the contextualist notion that narratives should be treated "not only as *structures* but also as *acts*, the features of which—like the features of all other acts—are functions of the variable sets of conditions in response to which they are performed" (Herrnstein Smith 227–228, original emphases). Indeed, even neoclassical approaches primarily interested in "narrative structures" would seem to benefit from some reflection on the historical and cultural context(s) in which the production and reception of the narrative work(s) in question took place.

With this in mind, the use of cognitive theory in what David Herman calls "cognitive narrative analysis" (see, e.g., D. Herman, "Narrative" 452) may arguably be regarded as a specific form of contextualism that can serve as a basis for this kind of conceptual reflection, reminding neoclassical narratology of the fact that narrative representations are always situated. Additionally, whereas "cognitive approaches to narrative at present constitute more a set of loosely confederated heuristic schemes than a systematic framework for research on stories" (D. Herman, "Narrative" 452; see also D. Herman, "Introduction"; *Storytelling*) in the field of literary theory, one should not forget that cognitivism has been the dominant paradigm within film narratology since the late 1980s[12] and that, therefore, quite a few of the questions connected to the development of "models attentive both to the text and to the context of stories" (D. Herman, "Introduction: Narratologies" 8) have already been the subject of more or less extensive discussion "beyond literary criticism" (see the title of Meister, *Narratology*). A particularly persistent problem, however, seems to be the *relative amount of attention* a specific narratological approach should give to "the text" (i.e., the narrative strategies a particular narrative work uses to tell a story or, rather, to represent a storyworld) and "the context" (i.e., the processes that determine how recipients understand that story or, rather, that storyworld).

How, then, can (or should) the relationship between narratology as a method for the analysis of narrative representations and approaches to "cognitive narrative analysis" be defined? In an essay defending the import of cognitive (reception) theories into narratology, Jens Eder distinguishes between seven possible kinds of relations of the former to the latter: "(1) incompatibility, (2) unrelated coexistence, (3) the heuristic use of cognitive theory, (4) the modular addition and utilization of cognitive theory, (5) the partial integration of concepts and models from cognitive theory, (6) a narratology anchored in cognitive theory, and (7) a narratology which is part of cognitive theory" ("Narratology" 284–285, footnote 14). Defining this kind of relationship for narratology in general seems to be a rather problematic endeavor, but Eder's graded scale might indeed prove a valuable starting point for an explication of how the specific narratological method developed in this book relates to cognitive theories.

As has already been mentioned, I will draw on models from cognitive theory to a certain extent, so (1) and (2) can be ruled out from the beginning. Yet the terms and concepts I will propose for the analysis of transmedial strategies of narrative representation are firmly rooted in both (neo)classical and transmedial narratology. Hence, (7) and, if perhaps less clearly, (6) can be ruled out as well. The remaining kinds of relations all seem to apply to a certain extent: even though this book focuses on transmedial strategies of narrative representation and how they are realized across different media, the development of analytically powerful and sufficiently complex narratological terms and concepts often necessitates a characterization of these strategies based on a combination of "structural features with functional, reception-dependent features" (Eder, "Narratology" 292). Drawing on general theories of human cognition in order to hypothesize about particular reception processes is, of course, not entirely unproblematic, since these kinds of hypotheses about ideal readers, spectators, or players tend to be based primarily on the reading, viewing, or playing experience of the scholar who does the hypothesizing. As David Herman remarks in *Basic Elements of Narrative*, "to be addressed adequately, these questions must be explored via empirical methods of investigation," but in the absence of relevant empirical research, which I obviously cannot provide by myself, to draw on one's "own native intuitions about stories and storytelling, coupled with traditions of narrative scholarship" (4) and empirically validated general theories about human cognition seems to be the next best thing.[13]

After all, exclusively "text-centered" approaches construct hypotheses about reception processes, too—the authors of these studies just tend not to explicitly reflect on their "intuitions."[14] While I certainly do not want to claim that "text-centered" approaches (to which this book belongs at least to a certain extent) constantly need to refer to reception processes, it still seems that they can profit from systematically problematizing the relation of the "text features" they aim to describe to the processes of reception that form cognitive narratology's center of attention. A good example for the benefit of grounding a method that aims at the narratological analysis of transmedial strategies of narrative representation in cognitive (reception) theories can be found in the discussion surrounding the presence (or absence) of narrators in narrative representations across media. While the postulation of different kinds of hypothetical instances may prove useful with respect to certain analytical aims, it still holds that "heuristic value alone is a weak argument in favour of using a formal system in the humanities" (Pavel, *The Feud* 103), and cognitive theories may help prevent the unwarranted proliferation of analytical concepts by grounding them in typical reading, viewing, or playing experiences of a more or less strongly idealized reader, spectator, or player.[15]

Mediality, Intermediality, and Transmediality

Having located my approach in relation to (neo)classical, contextual, and cognitive narratology, I would now like to provide some additional remarks on the ways in which this book can be considered part of the project of a transmedial narratology. Building on a general notion of *transmediality* as referring to phenomena that manifest themselves across media (*medienübergreifende Phänomene*), Jens Eder and I have proposed to distinguish between three particularly influential strands of research, each associated with a more specific understanding of the term (see Eder and Thon 140). First, literary theories of intermediality tend to emphasize aesthetic and semiotic aspects, understanding the term "transmediality" as referring to (largely) "medium-free" or at least "medially unspecified" phenomena and usually focusing primarily on representational or, more generally, aesthetic strategies. Second, as has already been mentioned, media studies have recently started to examine the transmedial representation of (usually fictional) characters, worlds, and stories across narrative media, commonly deemphasizing representational strategies in favor of what these strategies represent. Third, nonfictional forms of this kind of transmedial representation of "content" in the context of journalism or advertisement campaigns are also subsumed under the label of "crossmediality" within communication studies, in particular, though this is often reduced to content being distributed in print and online form.[16]

While the discourse surrounding "crossmediality" seems less relevant to the issues at hand, I will occasionally touch upon the phenomenon of transmedial storyworlds that are characteristically represented by transmedial entertainment franchises such as *Star Wars*, *Batman*, or *Warcraft*. The importance of these kinds of transmedial entertainment franchises for contemporary media culture notwithstanding, the concept of *transmedial strategies of narrative representation*, which defines the three core parts of this book, primarily pertains to the first variety of transmediality sketched above. In order to get a slightly more detailed picture of what is meant by the term "transmediality" in the following, it will prove helpful to further examine the corresponding concept's relation to the concepts of *intermediality* and *(intra)mediality*. Drawing on Werner Wolf's earlier works (see W. Wolf, *The Musicalization*; as well as W. Wolf, "'Cross the Border'"; "Intermediality"), Irina O. Rajewsky has repeatedly proposed to define this relation (roughly) as follows: the term "intramediality" refers to phenomena that involve only a single medium; the term "intermediality" refers to a variety of phenomena that transcend medial boundaries and involve at least two media; and the term "transmediality" refers to medially unspecified phenomena that are not connected to a given medium or its mediality and can, hence, be realized using the means of a large number of different media (see Rajewsky, *Intermedialität* 13; as well as Rajewsky, "Border Talks"; "Intermediality").

Since I would argue that a transmedial narratology is not (or should not be) primarily interested in intermedial phenomena,[17] it seems unnecessary to go into the details of the distinctions Rajewsky draws between different kinds of intermediality (see Rajewsky, *Intermedialität* 15–18). Moreover, it is evident that Rajewsky is mainly concerned with intermedial phenomena, and her conceptualization of transmediality therefore remains relatively vague. It should also be noted that transmediality is sometimes understood as a kind of intermediality: Werner Wolf, for example, distinguishes between "intracompositional intermediality" and "'extracompositional' intermediality" ("Intermediality" 13).[18] The former refers to intermediality that manifests itself within a "single work" or "semiotic entity," while the latter "applies to any transgression of boundaries between conventionally distinct media of communication" (W. Wolf, "Intermediality" 17), including the subclasses "intermedial transposition" and, indeed, "transmediality," which he nevertheless understands more or less *sensu* Rajewsky as referring to "phenomena that are not specific to individual media" (W. Wolf, "Intermediality" 18).[19] Wolf's explication of the various subclasses of intermediality is convincing in many other respects, but defining the concept of intermediality so broadly that it entails the concept of transmediality seems terminologically counterintuitive at best.[20] At least with regard to the concept of transmedial strategies of narrative representation, then, I will follow Wolf's and Rajewsky's understanding of the term "transmediality" as referring to "a quality of cultural signification" that tends to privilege representational strategies rather than what these strategies represent, but can, for example, also be observed "on the level of ahistorical formal devices that occur in more than one medium, such as motivic repetition, thematic variation, or . . . even narrativity" (W. Wolf, "Intermediality" 18).

I would still like to emphasize once more, though, that while the realization of transmedial strategies of narrative representation "is in each case necessarily media-specific," they are "nevertheless not bound to a specific medium" (Rajewsky, "Intermediality" 46, footnote 6). Hence, I propose to use the term "transmedial narratology" to refer primarily to "those narratological approaches that may be applied to different media, rather than to a single medium only" (Rajewsky, "Intermediality" 46, footnote 6), and, accordingly, are mainly interested not in narrative media per se but in transmedial phenomena that manifest themselves across a range of narrative media. With these further terminological considerations in mind, it appears possible to more clearly define the aims and scope of a transmedial narratology. Gérard Genette's *Narrative Discourse* or Wolf Schmid's *Narratology*, Edward Branigan's *Narrative Comprehension and Film* or Markus Kuhn's *Filmnarratologie*, Martin Schüwer's *Wie Comics erzählen* or Karin Kukkonen's *Contemporary Comics Storytelling*, and Hans-Joachim Backe's *Strukturen und Funktionen des Erzählens im Computerspiel* or Sebastian Domsch's *Storyplaying* may use similar terms and concepts from time to time, but Genette's and Schmid's books are works of literary narratology, Branigan's and Kuhn's books are works of film narratology,[21] Schüwer's and Kukkonen's books are works of comics narratology,[22] and Backe's and Domsch's books are works of "ludo-narratology."[23] They are all primarily interested in the specific mediality of their respective media and, hence, none of them is overly concerned with the development of a genuinely transmedial perspective. Similarly, works such as François Jost's *L'oeil-caméra*, Matthias Hurst's *Erzählsituationen in Literatur und Film*, Sabine Schlickers's *Verfilmtes Erzählen*, or Jakob Lothe's *Narrative in Fiction and Film* focus on the intermedial relations between literary and audiovisual narrative representations and should be considered as contributions to the project of an *inter*medial narratology rather than that of a genuinely *trans*medial narratology.

It has to be noted, however, that this "restrictive" understanding of what constitutes a genuinely transmedial approach to narrative theory and analysis is not universally acknowledged. Instead, "transmedial narratology" is often used as an umbrella term for narratological practices that focus on media other than literary texts. In his essay "Toward a Transmedial Narratology," for example, David

Herman is primarily concerned with the intermedial relations between conversational and literary narrative(s), and although he emphasizes the need for a "general theory about the links between stories and their media" (67), he does not go into much detail as to why and if transmedial narratology should entail (more than) such a theory. Likewise, in the glossary of *Basic Elements of Narrative*, which deals with a range of narrative media from a transmedial perspective, Herman effectively limits himself to stating that transmedial narratology is concerned with "storytelling practices in different media" (194). Marie-Laure Ryan, who is still one of the most prolific scholars in the field today, uses the term "transmedial narratology" interchangeably with terms such as the "study of narrative across media" ("Introduction" 1), "*narrative* media studies" ("Introduction" 33, original emphasis), "the study of the realization of narrative meaning in various media" ("On the Theoretical Foundations" 1), and/or "the transmedial study of narrative" (*Avatars* 4). Once again, it remains unclear whether the label "transmedial narratology" implies a more distinctly *transmedial* perspective than a label such as "narrative media studies."

Evidently, the broad field of "narrative media studies" has been affected by the boom of what Manfred Jahn and Ansgar Nünning have called the "narratological industry" ("Forum" 300), but I would maintain that a genuinely transmedial narratology is not (or should not be) the same as a collection of medium-specific narratological terms and concepts. Ryan's influential anthology *Narrative across Media* is symptomatic in this respect, as the majority of contributions are concerned with the specific mediality of a single narrative medium (exceptions are the introduction by Ryan and the contributions by David Herman and Liv Hausken). This shortcoming might be explained with the limitations of an essay collection, but the problem of "media expertism"[24]—that is, the fact that most scholars specialize in one or two narrative media—indeed seems to be a major pragmatic problem of the still emerging field of transmedial narratology. Nicole Mahne's *Transmediale Erzähltheorie* may serve to further illustrate this point: the small volume consists of an introductory chapter surprisingly light on theory and five largely independent chapters dedicated to the narrative media "novel," "comic," "film," "radio play," and "hyperfiction." Hence, Mahne's work is a collection of rather short introductory essays on the narratology of novels, comics, films, radio plays, and hyperfiction, respectively, but not particularly relevant to the project of a transmedial narratology as it is pursued in the present book.

Still, I would cite the spatial limitations of a book-length study and my own areas of specialization as the main reasons to focus primarily on the representation of storyworlds, the use of narratorial representation that can be attributed to some kind of narrator, and the use of subjective representation to represent characters' consciousnesses as three particularly salient transmedial strategies of narrative representation as well as on their realization within the specific mediality of contemporary films, comics, and video games. The core concepts aiming at these transmedial strategies will be developed in such a way that they can be fruitfully applied to narrative representations in other narrative media, yet the discussion of more than three of these media would go beyond the scope of a single book-length study. Before I can further examine the relation between transmedial strategies of narrative representation and their realization within the specific mediality of contemporary films, comics, and video games, though, some further remarks on my choice of media are necessary: I would argue that the cultural-aesthetic and socioeconomic influence of films, comics, and video games in contemporary media culture is quite significant, but it would certainly have been possible to focus on other narrative media as well, with literary texts, theatrical performances, and what is sometimes called "quality television"[25] perhaps being the most obvious alternatives.[26]

One way or another, however, even distinguishing between contemporary films (as opposed to, say, television series), comics (as opposed to, say, literary texts), and video games (as opposed to, say, theatrical performances) turns out to be not entirely unproblematic insofar as it may be taken as endorsing a kind of media essentialism from which I want to distance myself explicitly. Obviously, the attempt to develop a method of analysis that aims at salient transmedial strategies of narrative representation and their medium-specific realization in contemporary films, comics, and video games entails the assumption that we can attribute a more or less specific mediality to the latter. In order to avoid an overly essentialist take on the problem of mediality, then, some further remarks are necessary on how the term "mediality"—which is usually used to refer to medium-specific qualities—relates to the term "medium," which—despite or rather because of its central importance for media studies and transmedial narratology—is used to refer to a wide variety of different and often contradictory concepts.[27]

As controversial as the question of what a medium is may seem at first glance, though, one can still find a certain amount of consensus both within media studies and beyond. This consensus holds that the term is best understood as referring to a multidimensional concept, which usually emphasizes the semiotic structure and the communicative function(s) of different media.[28] In an attempt to synthesize the term's various aspects into a coherent model, Siegfried J. Schmidt distinguishes between four dimensions of media, namely, a semiotic dimension, a technological dimension, an institutional dimension, and a dimension of media products (see Schmidt, *Kalte Faszination*; a roughly similar proposal was made earlier by Saxer). While the mediality of many newspaper cartoons and webcomics, for example, will be rather similar with regard to their semiotic dimension—that is, both prototypically use combinations of words and pictures in sequences of panels—there are some striking differences not only with regard to their technological dimension—that is, one is printed and the other is published online—but also, and perhaps more importantly, with regard to their institutional dimension—that is, one is published as part of one or several newspapers and the other is most likely (self-)published on a dedicated website.

In many ways similar to Schmidt's distinction, Marie-Laure Ryan has attempted a multidimensional explication of the concept in a more decidedly narratological context, distinguishing between three perspectives that regard media as semiotic phenomena, as technologies with a particular materiality, and as cultural practices: "As a semiotic category, a medium is characterized by the codes and sensory channels upon which it relies. The semiotic approach tends to distinguish three broad media families: verbal, visual, and aural" ("Narration" 268)—which can be combined in "multichannel media." According to Ryan, however, the semiotic approach is refined and expanded by a technological approach, which asks "about the *materials* and the *technologies* that support the various semiotic types" ("On the Theoretical Foundations" 15, original emphases). Finally, Ryan stresses that the cultural practices surrounding different media are "not entirely predictable from semiotic type and technological support" (*Avatars* 23) but may nevertheless play an important role in any attempt to distinguish media that use the same semiotic channels and technologies.

Werner Wolf has likewise highlighted the notion that "some ways of disseminating information are regarded as distinct media from a cultural point of view, despite their lack of a distinct semiotic or technological identity" (Ryan, *Avatars* 23). Wolf makes this distinction in the context of his proposal to define the term "medium" in a "broad sense as a conventionally distinct means of communication, specified not only by particular channels (or one channel) of communication but also by the use of one or more semiotic systems" (*The Musicalization* 35). Following Schmidt, Ryan, and Wolf, then, I would like to once more emphasize that media (and their respective "medialities") can be distinguished by way of the technological or material base and/or the semiotic system(s) they use as well as by way of the sociocultural fact that they are conventionally treated as distinct media, which also entails specific forms of organization and institutionalization with regard to production and distribution contexts.

Still, drawing on Irina O. Rajewsky's more recent discussion of *conventionally distinct media*, one can identify three more or less significant blind spots in Wolf's otherwise convincing approach. First, what we consider to be a distinct medium rests on what we believe to be the social consensus on the matter, and, hence, it would be more precise to speak of media that are "*conventionally perceived as distinct*" (Rajewsky, "Border Talks" 61, original emphasis). Second, the social consensus on what is to be considered as a conventionally distinct medium changes both over time and in different (media) cultures. Hence, one cannot treat media as transhistorical and/or transcultural collective constructs, since their construction "necessarily depends on the historical and discursive contexts and on the observing subject or system" (Rajewsky, "Border Talks" 61).[29] Third, it needs to be acknowledged that even the manifestations of a well-defined conventionally distinct medium can be very different.[30] Accordingly, it may be helpful to adopt a prototypical understanding of mediality and of what constitutes a conventionally distinct medium.

In order to be able to describe the relation of my approach to universalist and particularist poetics more clearly, I would, moreover, like to distinguish between conventionally distinct *media* such as films, comics, and video games, prototypical *media forms* such as feature films, graphic novels, and narrative video games (that are primarily played in the singleplayer mode),[31] and (at least partially transmedial) *media genres* such as horror, superheroes, fantasy, or science fiction (as well as more medium-specific genres such as the first-person shooter, the real-time strategy game, the action-adventure, or the role-playing game). The concept of genre is not too important for my overall argument,[32] but it is worth noting that the present study largely focuses on feature films from the 1990s and early 2000s, graphic novels from the late 1980s and early 1990s, and narrative video games from the 2000s and early 2010s, even though it still attempts to discuss the mediality of films, comics, and video games from a more general perspective.

While I do not yet want to go into too much detail with regard to the specific mediality of contemporary feature films (as a prototypical form of film and/or audiovisual narrative), graphic novels (as a prototypical form of comics and/or graphic narrative), and the highly narrative video games I will primarily focus on (as a prototypical form of video games and/or interactive narrative),[33] it should already be noted that a prototypical understanding of mediality broadens the *potential object domain* of my approach. Evidently, the notion that the method of analysis the following chapters will develop using contemporary feature films, graphic novels, and narrative video games as examples can more or less readily be transferred to and adopted for other forms of audiovisual narrative such as short films and television series (see, e.g., Mittell, *Complex TV*; "Narrative Complexity"; "Strategies"), other forms of graphic narrative such as comic strips or picture series (see, e.g., W. Wolf, "'Cross the Border'"; "Narrative"; "Das Problem"), and other forms of interactive narrative such as interactive fiction (see, e.g., Aarseth, *Cybertext*; Montfort) or alternate reality games (see, e.g., McGonigal; Meifert-Menhart) becomes tenable not only because the transmedial strategies of narrative representation examined here are fairly universal but also because these media forms all share the technological and semiotic dimension of their respective media to a certain extent. Nonetheless, considering that I am mainly immersed in film studies, comics studies, and game studies at the time of this writing, I will focus on contemporary films, comics, and video games to illustrate my more general discussion of the representation of storyworlds, the use of narratorial representation, and the use of subjective representation across media.

On the Aims and Scope of a Transmedial Narratology

Even when leaving the pragmatic constraints of "media expertism" aside, there may, in fact, be good reasons for the limitation of most contemporary narratological approaches to one or two conventionally distinct media. In the introduction to *Narrative across Media*, Marie-Laure Ryan names three of the methodological challenges a transmedial narratology (in both the broad sense of "narrative media studies" and the narrower sense in which the term is used in this book) has to face. First, there "is the temptation to regard the idiosyncrasies of individual texts as features of the medium" (Ryan, "Introduction" 33). Second, there is the problem of "media blindness: the indiscriminating transfer of concepts designed for the study of the narratives of a particular medium . . . to another medium" (Ryan, "Introduction" 34; see also Hausken). Third, there is the problem of "media relativism"—that is, the assumption that, "because media are distinct, the toolbox of narratology must be rebuilt from scratch for every medium" (Ryan, "Introduction" 34). According to Liv Hausken, research perspectives and "theories that are seemingly independent of the medium are usually implicitly tied to a particular medium" (392). Apart from this kind of "total medium blindness," Hausken also perceives a more "nonchalant" variety "endemic to theories and analyses that are unreflectively based on the theoretical premises of other media" (392–393). As interesting as Hausken's examples are, though, it seems questionable to what extent narratology has actually been affected by these varieties of "media blindness." While it is true that the assumption that "certain aspects of every narrative are medium independent . . . forms one of the basic research hypotheses of structuralist narratology" (D. Herman, "Toward a Transmedial Narratology" 51), what at first glance may appear to be a severe case of "media blindness" will, on closer examination, often turn out to be a matter of emphasis rather than principle. Claude Bremond, for example, remarked that the narrative message "is independent of the techniques that support it" ("Le message" 4, my translation from the French), but he also stressed that "the laws which govern the narrated matter" include the conventions "of a culture, a period, a literary genre, a narrator's style, even of the narration itself" ("The Logic" 387). Similarly, Roland Barthes believed that every narrative "shares with other narratives a common structure" ("Introduction" 80) but was quite aware of the "variety of genres, themselves distributed amongst different substances" ("Introduction" 79).

Accordingly, one of the core tasks of a genuinely transmedial narratology would be to aim at the middle ground between "media blindness" and "media relativism," acknowledging both similarities and differences in how conventionally distinct narrative media narrate. For example, most contemporary narratologists will agree with Fotis Jannidis's statement that "all representation takes place in a medium, and the characteristics of each particular medium dictate key properties of any representation that takes place in that medium" ("Narratology" 39). I certainly do not mean to generally accuse this view of "media relativism," but Jannidis's addendum—"with the result that it is simply not possible to discuss representation in abstract terms" ("Narratology" 39)—still seems to be quite problematic in its apparent absolutism. After all, it is painfully obvious that one cannot *but* "discuss representation in abstract terms": just like the notion of a map using a 1:1 scale, the demand to examine narrative representation without *some* degree of abstraction is plainly paradoxical. What Jannidis aims at, however, is the simple fact that the storytelling possibilities of media are very different. It has become evident, then, that one *can* analyze narrative representation from a transmedial perspective, yet every attempt at a transmedial narratology has to acknowledge that "stories are shaped but not determined by their presentational formats" (D. Herman, "Toward a Transmedial Narratology" 54) in order to evade "media blindness" and remain what Ryan and I have recently called "media-conscious" (see Ryan and Thon; see also Thon, "Narratives," for a more recent survey). Hence, it appears that one—if not *the*—core condition for a transmedial narratology to remain "media-conscious" is an awareness of the granularity of its concepts. On the one hand, it should be obvious that many of the terms and concepts developed for the analysis of literary texts cannot be directly applied to other media. On the other hand, this does not mean that our understanding of films, comics, or video games cannot *at all* benefit from narratological concepts developed with literary texts in mind. A truly *radical* "media relativism" that insists on the general impossibility of transferring or adapting narratological concepts across object domains is incompatible with the project of a transmedial narratology (and quite a few other strands of postclassical narratological practice), but we are evidently not confronted with a simple either/or choice between "media relativism" and "media blindness" here.

More specifically, Ryan may be right in remarking that "the distinction story/discourse, as well as the notions of character, event, and fictional world," are "narratological concepts that apply across media" (*Avatars* 6). But even then, these concepts do not apply *in exactly the same way* to every conventionally distinct medium. Not only are the properties ascribed to the "discourse" side of the "story"/"discourse" distinction generally rather medium-specific, but the storyworlds represented by, for example, contemporary films, comics, and video games also tend to differ in significant ways that cannot be reduced to "idiosyncrasies of individual media texts." However, even apparently more medium-specific terms and concepts such as "narrator," "point of view," "perspective," or "focalization" may point at certain transmedial properties of many, most, or all kinds of narrative representations that are revealed when one discusses the respective concept on a sufficiently abstract level.[34] The question, of course, remains if decreasing the granularity of just about any narratological concept until it can somehow be applied to a sufficiently large number of narrative media is, in fact, a good idea. Since this question seems to be intrinsically connected to the aims and scope of the project of a transmedial narratology as it is pursued here, I will conclude this chapter by detailing the criteria for, as well as the processes involved in, the adaptation of narratological terms and concepts across media.

As I have already stated, the present study attempts to adhere to both a criterion of continuity and a criterion of neutrality. But what kind of narratological research should be considered relevant for its purposes? Contemporary narratology is not exclusively concerned with verbal storytelling, and, therefore, the transfer—or, more precisely, the adaptation—of narratological terms and concepts developed with films, comics, video games, or any number of other narrative media in mind certainly is an option; but Werner Wolf's examination of the "conditions and potentials that enable us to meaningfully employ narratological terminology and concepts for phenomena that can be found in fields other than verbal storytelling" ("Metalepsis" 86) still remains a good starting point for a more in-depth discussion of these processes. Keeping in mind the problems of "media blindness" and "media relativism," it seems clear that "the *export-facilitating potential of the phenomena under consideration*" (W. Wolf, "Metalepsis" 86, original emphasis) may, indeed, be considered the most fundamental of these conditions, as it establishes a focus on concepts aiming at strategies of narrative representation that are not bound to a particular conventionally distinct narrative medium and, hence, will most likely prove relevant even if they were originally developed in the context of a medium-specific narratological approach. Yet, according to Wolf, the transmediality of the "phenomenon under consideration" is not the only condition to be satisfied, as he claims that "a *clear narratological conceptualization* and description of typical features is a precondition of a meaningful export in which the exported concept remains recognizable" ("Metalepsis" 86, original emphasis). Such a demand seems quite problematic in light of narratology's general lack of consensus on the definition of even its most fundamental concepts, and Wolf himself acknowledges that one should not "start from an overly rigid conceptualization" ("Metalepsis" 85). Still, I will at least aim to establish, by way of explication and adherence to the criterion of continuity, "typical features or constituents of the phenomenon as discussed in narratology" (W. Wolf, "Metalepsis" 85) that should form the basis of the respective concepts' transmedial (re)formulation.

The necessity of such an approach is further emphasized by a condition that "refers to the *formal appropriateness* of the narratological concept for the target phenomenon in the import domain" (W. Wolf, "Metalepsis" 87, original emphasis), which appears to be primarily a variation of the condition of the "export-facilitating potential" that focuses not on the phenomenon but on the concept under consideration. Nevertheless, it is indeed very likely that concepts aiming at transmedial aspects of a given phenomenon will generally (if not necessarily) prove to be more appropriate for an explication in the context of a transmedial narratology than concepts that aim at its medium-specific aspects. Finally, what Wolf calls "the *heuristic value of the exported notion for the use in the import field*" ("Metalepsis" 87, original emphasis) may be considered both one of the most important and the most elusive of his conditions, since what constitutes heuristic value depends very much on particular research interests and, hence, cannot be generally defined. Nevertheless, one would expect that the heuristic value of the terms and concepts developed in this book will be mainly constituted through their applicability in the context of analyses of narrative representations across media that aim to highlight both similarities and differences in the ways certain conventionally distinct media realize what can be described as transmedial strategies of narrative representation. Evidently, the extent to which established narratological concepts are relevant from a transmedial perspective is very much a matter of granularity. On the one hand, there are comparatively universal concepts that aim at decidedly transmedial phenomena but whose granularity is too low for them to be very useful with regard to the in-depth analysis of narrative representations across media. On the other hand, there are more particular concepts whose granularity may be comparatively high, but which primarily aim at medium-specific phenomena and whose usefulness for the analysis of narrative representation from a transmedial perspective is, therefore, rather limited once more.

While I would still argue that the object domain of a genuinely transmedial narratology is (or should be) the set of transmedial phenomena specific to narrative representations, every transmedial approach to narratological analysis that is not able to in some way specify its concepts with regard to the question of how these phenomena are realized in different narrative media runs the risk of losing a significant amount of its analytical power. Hence, one of the core tasks of such an approach would not only be to define its concepts in such a way that they apply (or *can* be applied) to various narrative media but also to specify these concepts with regard to the "idiosyncrasies" not of individual narrative works but of conventionally distinct narrative media. This does not necessarily mean that medium-specific concepts have to form an integral part of every attempt at developing a transmedial narratology. More often than not, for example, I will only be able to refer to more extensive medium-specific studies for in-depth discussions of the specific mediality of contemporary films, comics, and video games. However, this approach to the "dual nature" of transmedial phenomena should not be misunderstood as indifference toward the specific mediality of the conventionally distinct media in question, but instead be seen as a necessary limitation of scope.

Moreover, even though I focus on salient transmedial strategies of narrative representation, this does not mean that a narratological analysis based on the method developed here cannot benefit from drawing on both more universal and more particular concepts. In fact, I would argue that the criterion of neutrality mentioned earlier includes the demands that narratological concepts be as "neutral" as possible with regard to a variety of different theories of interpretation and that they be as compatible as possible with regard to a variety of other narratological approaches. Hence, the method of analysis developed in the following chapters is fundamentally "modular" in that it aims to be easily expandable by terms and concepts developed in other research contexts—with film studies, comics studies, and game studies as well as theory of fiction, philosophy of mind, and cognitive psychology being the most obvious but certainly not the only relevant neighboring fields. In fact, it is not least because of the increased complexity that follows from the necessity to consider both the transmedial dimension and, albeit perhaps less extensively, the medium-specific dimension of narrative representations that I will limit myself to an examination of certain prototypical transmedial strategies of narrative representation in only three conventionally distinct media.

Once more, though, some further remarks on what are or are not prototypical strategies of narrative representation seem necessary. In fact, the question of when a cultural artifact can (or should) be considered to be a narrative (or a narrative representation) and/or to have the quality of narrativity has been one of narratology's most stubbornly reoccurring problems.[35] As is so often the case with core concepts in the humanities, the proposed definitions of both *narrative* and *narrativity* vary considerably. While I am not particularly interested in the variety of contributions that make very general assertions about all narratives and even less interested in trying to find necessary and sufficient conditions for what is or is not a part of this set, I find it helpful to make more explicit what kinds of representations will be treated as narrative in the context of this book, because one can expect a certain degree of overlap between the more salient properties of narrative and the transmedial strategies of narrative representation on which I will focus. Hence, I will examine three of the most influential strands of narratological approaches to the issue and relate them to the project of a transmedial narratology in general as well as to the aims and scope of this book in particular—if primarily in the sense that my understanding of what narrative representations are will define the corpus of narrative works to be analyzed in the following chapters.

In his decidedly neoclassical *Narratology*, Wolf Schmid distinguishes between broad definitions of narrative that focus exclusively on the "story" side of the canonical "story"/"discourse" distinction, in that they include all representations that represent a change of state and therefore possess at least a minimal degree of "eventfulness,"[36] and narrow definitions of narrative that emphasize both the verbal nature of storytelling and the presence of a narrator as a necessary condition of narrativity.[37] In the context of a transmedial narratology, however, broad definitions of narrative easily lead one to neglect the striking differences between the storytelling abilities of conventionally distinct narrative media, while narrow definitions appear both unnecessarily restrictive and particularly open to misunderstanding (e.g., with regard to the supposedly obligatory presence of a narrator in narrative representations across media). Despite the importance of events and "eventfulness" as well as narrators and verbal narration for narrative representations across media, then, neither of the positions that Schmid reconstructs seem overly helpful.

Aiming to remedy the caveats of these classical approaches, scholars such as Monika Fludernik (*Towards a 'Natural' Narratology* 15–52), Fotis Jannidis ("Narratology"), Marie-Laure Ryan (*Avatars*; "Toward a Definition"), and Werner Wolf ("'Cross the Border'"; "Das Problem") have recently proposed prototypical definitions of narrative that take the term to refer to a "fuzzy set" of representations and, hence, entail a gradual conceptualization of narrativity. Following the early work of Fludernik, Jannidis proposes "to treat the narration in films, the narration in comic strips, and the narration in computer games as different forms of 'narration,' each of which is located at a greater or lesser distance from the prototype, oral narration" ("Narratology" 40). His choice of narrative media is certainly convenient,[38] and our understanding of narrative may indeed be determined "by markedly typical exemplars rather than clear boundaries consisting of atomic features" (Jannidis, "Narratology" 40), but Jannidis does not go into too much detail with regard to the version of prototype theory on which his account is based. Moreover, the proposal that one can or should identify oral narration as *the* narrative prototype in human history and/or contemporary media culture seems to be problematic (yet the same holds for narration—or, rather, narrative representation—in literature, film, comics, and video games). At least, defining one (and only one) narrative prototype would appear to require stronger empirical evidence than the fairly informal observation that "everyday oral narration is far more widespread than written narration (and was also socialized at an earlier date)" (Jannidis, "Narratology" 40, footnote 18).

A less narrow proposal to understand narrative as a prototypical concept has been made by Werner Wolf, who shifts the emphasis from attempting to establish one (and only one) actual prototype of narrative as the primary reference point of a definition to a more explicit awareness of the fact that "a maximum number of traits constitute the ideal prototype as an abstract notion or schema, while concrete phenomena are assessed according to their greater or lesser resemblance with the prototype" ("'Cross the Border'" 86; see also Rosch; as well as Lakoff, "Cognitive Models"; Laurence and Margolis). Not only Wolf's discussion of "narratemes," which draws heavily on Gerald Prince's work on narrativity ("Narrativehood"; *Narratology*; "Remarks"; "Revisiting Narrativity"), but also his focus on the process of "narrativization"[39] seem convincing. Even though Wolf still assumes that "verbal, fictional narration yields the prototype of narrative" ("'Cross the Border'" 91), he does so in a much less essentialist fashion than, for example, in one of his earlier German-language essays, where his reliance on an actual instead of an ideal prototype of narrative led him to propose a problematic typology of different media's narrative potential that ranks instrumental music, pictures, films/comic strips, and drama on a scale according to their distance from *the* narrative prototype of the fairy tale (see W. Wolf, "Das Problem").

However, my skepticism regarding strong hypotheses about actual prototypes of narrative does in no way condone the assumption of some idealized state of equality between all narrative media. It is indeed necessary to acknowledge that, in Marie-Laure Ryan's words, "when it comes to narrative abilities, media are not equally gifted; some are born storytellers, others suffer from serious handicaps" (*Avatars* 4). Still, particularly because there can be little doubt about "literary narrative's paradigmatic status for the narratological study of narrative representation" (Meister, "Narratology" 343), it is important that transmedial narratology remain aware of the fundamental problems inherent in simple—and usually all too ahistorical—typologies of different media's narrative potential. In fact, one could rephrase Ryan's demand that a definition of narrative "should not privilege literary forms" ("Toward a Definition" 26) to the extent that such a definition should not (or at least not without very good reasons) privilege (or ascribe prototypical status to) *any* particular narrative medium. This view also seems implied by Ryan's proposal to regard "the set of all narratives as fuzzy, and narrativity (or 'storiness') as a scalar property" (*Avatars* 7) that can be defined by eight more or less salient characteristics. By simultaneously marking these characteristics as prototypical features and as optional conditions that "offer a toolkit for do-it-yourself definitions" (Ryan, *Avatars* 9), Ryan emphasizes that what we choose to consider as a narrative (or, rather, as a narrative representation) is very much a matter of perspective, indeed.

In the context of this book, I will focus on the first five of Ryan's conditions—that is, I maintain that prototypical narrative representations "must be about a world populated by individuated existents," that "this world must be situated in time and undergo significant transformations," and that these "transformations must be caused by nonhabitual physical events" (Ryan, *Avatars* 8). Moreover, I assume that "some of the participants in the events must be intelligent agents who have a mental life and react emotionally to the states of the world" and that "some of the events must be purposeful actions by these agents," which in turn must be motivated by at least partially "identifiable goals and plans" (Ryan, *Avatars* 8). However, it should be noted that the examples I will analyze in the following chapters are generally even *more narrative* (or more narratively complex) than this definition requires them to be—that is, they tend to meet the conditions that "the sequence of events must form a unified causal chain and lead to closure," that "the occurrence of at least some of the events must be asserted as fact for the story world," and that "the story must communicate something meaningful to the recipient" (Ryan, *Avatars* 8). In fact, most of the contemporary films, comics, and video games I discuss show a great deal of narrative complexity, and quite a few of them can be located within what Werner Wolf has described as the "metareferential turn" in contemporary media culture (see W. Wolf, "Is There a Metareferential Turn"; "Metareference").[40] At least from a fairly broad and primarily transmedial perspective, though, narratively complex films, comics, and video games may be particularly interesting, narratologically speaking—but they tend not to use representational strategies that are fundamentally different from those used by less complex works.

Just as my focus on films, comics, and video games is motivated by their cultural-aesthetic and socioeconomic influence in contemporary media culture, my decision to primarily examine the relation between narrative representations and the storyworlds they represent (in the first part of this book), the use of strategies of narratorial representation that can be attributed to various kinds of narrators (in the second part of this book), and the use of strategies of subjective representation that provide "direct access" to characters' consciousnesses (in the third part of this book) aims to develop a method for the narratological analysis of core prototypical aspects of narrative representations across media—despite the fact that the examples I will be analyzing tend to be rather more narratively complex than what seems to be the default case with regard to films, comics, and video games in contemporary media culture. One way or another, though, the following chapters further back up the claim that the representation of storyworlds, the use of strategies of narratorial representation, and the use of strategies of subjective representation are particularly salient transmedial strategies of narrative representation that are realized across a wide range of conventionally distinct narrative media.[41]

What this book offers, then, is a modest proposal to further establish a genuinely transmedial perspective in the field of "narrative media studies." In order to remain "media-conscious," such a transmedial narratology should not merely aspire to be a collection of medium-specific narratological terms and concepts but, rather, examine a variety of strategies of narrative representation across a range of conventionally distinct narrative media while at the same time acknowledging both similarities and differences in the ways these media narrate. At least within the confines of a single book-length study, such an approach necessitates what I have called a "modular structure," and it is against this background that I aim to provide not only a method for the analysis of a selection of salient transmedial strategies of narrative representation—with a particular focus on strategies of narratorial representation that can be attributed to some kind of narrator and strategies of subjective representation that provide "direct access" to characters' consciousnesses—but also a theoretical frame within which medium-specific approaches from literary and film narratology, from comics studies and game studies, and from various other strands of current narrative, media, and cultural studies may be critically reconsidered, correlated, modified, and expanded to further illuminate the forms and functions of narrative representations across media.

PART 1   *Storyworlds across Media*

2. The Storyworld as a Transmedial Concept

From Models of Narrative Constitution to Conceptualizations of Represented Worlds

Keeping in mind the broad consensus within both classical and postclassical narratology that we can consider prototypical narratives to be representations of worlds that are populated with characters[1] and situated in space and time, it will come as no surprise that the question of how narrative representations across media project these worlds lies at the core of the present study. With this in mind, I will not devote too much attention to the "terminological thicket" (see Dannenberg 6) of the various and often conflicting definitions of terms such as "fabula," "syuzhet," "histoire," "discours," "plot," and "narration" originating in Russian formalism, French structuralism, and Anglo-American theories of the novel,[2] but it is still necessary to revisit the distinction(s) these terms refer to before discussing the concepts of *storyworld* and *narrative representation* in greater detail. As Seymour Chatman remarks, one can, on a very basic level, assume that "the story is the *what* in a narrative that is depicted, discourse the *how*" (*Story* 19, original emphases). Yet there have been various attempts to further differentiate the basic distinction of "story" as referring to what is being represented and "discourse" as referring to its representation. Another well-known "high structuralist," Gérard Genette, distinguishes "between *story* (the totality of the narrated events), *narrative* (the discourse, oral or written, that narrates them), and *narrating* (the real or fictive act that produces that discourse . . .)" (*Narrative Discourse Revisited* 13, original emphases), emphasizing the process by which the "story" is transformed into "discourse."

More recently, Wolf Schmid has argued for the expansion of the two-tier distinction between "story" and "discourse" or the three-tier distinction between "story," "narrative," and "narrating" into a four-tier distinction between "happenings," "story," "narrative," and the "presentation of the narrative." In the framework of Schmid's "ideal genetic model" (*Narratology* 190)—which, unfortunately, contributes to narratology's terminological confusion by its nonstandard usage of the term "narrative"—"happenings are the amorphous entirety of situations, characters and actions explicitly or implicitly represented, or logically implied, in the narrative work" (*Narratology* 190) and can be distinguished from the story as "the result of a *selection* from the happenings" (*Narratology* 191, original emphasis). While the "story" contains "the selected elements in their *ordo naturalis*," Schmid's "narrative" instead "places the elements in an *ordo artificialis*," resulting in "a sequence of presentation" (*Narratology* 191, original emphases). Finally, "the presentation of the narrative is formed by the phenotypic tier . . . , i.e. it is the only tier accessible to empirical observation" (Schmid, *Narratology* 192).

I do not find Schmid's terminological choices entirely convincing, but his four-tier model of narrative constitution still serves to remind us that the distinction between "story" and "discourse" (or "fabula" and "syuzhet," or "histoire" and "discours," or "plot" and "narration," or any two-tier distinction between a level of what is represented and a level of representation) may be considered insufficiently complex in at least two ways. First, Schmid's distinction between "story" and "narrative" demonstrates that it can occasionally be helpful to distinguish not only between the "story" as a succession of represented events and the "discourse" as the representation of these events but also—as I do in this book—between the *story* as a succession of represented events in their chronological order and the "story-as-discoursed" (Chatman, *Story* 43), which is more commonly called the *plot*, as the succession of represented events in the order in which they are represented. Second, and perhaps more importantly in the context of the present study, Schmid's distinction between "happenings" and "story" illustrates that there usually is more to the world of a narrative representation than can unproblematically be said to be part of its story.³

Accordingly, I will follow David Herman and Marie-Laure Ryan in focusing on storyworlds as "the worlds evoked by narratives" (D. Herman, *Basic Elements* 105), or, more precisely, the worlds represented by narrative representations.⁴ But while Herman in particular has contributed a great deal to popularizing the concept of storyworld in contemporary narratology, he was by no means the first to discuss (narrative) representations in terms of their represented worlds. As he remarks himself, "over the past couple of decades . . . , one of the most basic and abiding concerns of narrative scholars has been how readers of print narratives, interlocutors in face-to-face discourse, and viewers of films use textual cues to build up [mental] representations of the worlds evoked by stories, or *storyworlds*" (D. Herman, *Basic Elements* 106, original emphasis). Despite a common conceptual core, various approaches to represented worlds that are located within different research traditions not only use a variety of terms to refer to them but also conceptualize them rather differently. In the following review of a selection of the relevant research, I will generally assume that all represented worlds that are represented narratively can be considered to be storyworlds, but it will also become clear that the questions how the concept of storyworld is best understood, what phenomena the term "storyworld" should be used to refer to, and in what ways storyworlds can be said to exist are answered in a number of different and sometimes contradictory ways.

Despite Herman's claim that "the classical, structuralist narratology failed to come to terms with the referential or world-creating properties of narrative" (*Basic Elements* 106) and the fact that both classical structuralist and recent neoclassical narratological approaches indeed tend to be primarily concerned with what is "actually contained in the text" (Schmid, *Narratology* 4), one can often find a certain awareness that what is represented by narrative representations may go beyond more or less explicitly represented chains of events that are traditionally described as stories. Let me briefly give three examples of this kind of "implicit narrative content" argument from the works of the influential (neo)classical narratologists mentioned above.[5] First, in *Narrative Discourse Revisited*, Gérard Genette—albeit quite briefly—discusses the term "diegesis (*diégèse*) [as] the spatio-temporal universe designated by the narrative" (17, original emphasis, referring to *Narrative Discourse* 27),[6] emphasizing that such a world encompasses more than just the succession of events that constitute the story: the "*diégèse* is indeed a *universe* rather than a train of events (a story); the *diégèse* is therefore not the story but a universe in which the story takes place" (*Narrative Discourse Revisited* 17, original emphases). Against this background, Genette's well-known distinction between various "narrative" or "diegetic levels"—the extra-, intra-, and metadiegetic level in particular—can be understood as an early attempt to distinguish between what I would call *ontologically disconnected subworlds* within a more encompassing storyworld.[7]

Second, in *Story and Discourse*, Seymour Chatman—who does not systematically distinguish between the story and the world of a narrative—discusses what he takes to be "a logical property of narratives," namely, "that they evoke a world of potential plot details, many of which go unmentioned but can be supplied" (29). More specifically, the recipient "must fill in gaps with essential or likely events, traits and objects which for various reasons have gone unmentioned" (Chatman, *Story* 28). Another important point that Chatman raises in passing concerns the problem of mediality: "There is also a class of indeterminacies . . . that arise from the peculiar nature of the medium. The medium may specialize in certain narrative effects and not others" (*Story* 30). Yet, while his argument entails some interesting nods toward Wolfgang Iser's reception theory and Dan Sperber and Deirdre Wilson's relevance theory,[8] Chatman does not provide an in-depth examination of the question how recipients "fill in the gaps" of narrative representations and/or deal with idiosyncrasies related to the particular narrative potential and representational conventions of different media, either.

Third, Wolf Schmid likewise does not call it a world and does not go into any detail with regard to what kinds of inferences are necessary for a recipient in order to arrive at the "abstraction" of the "level of happenings" already mentioned above, but the latter's similarities to Genette's concept of *diégèse* and Chatman's "world of potential plot details" (*Story* 29) are obvious. Despite the emphasis of idealized production processes within his "ideal genetic model" of narrative constitution, Schmid readily concedes that "the happenings of a novel are, after all, not accessible to the reader as such, but only as a construct or, more accurately, a reconstruction formed on the basis of the narrated story" (*Narratology* 196). Since "filling in the gaps" of a representation (narrative or otherwise) is evidently a process relevant to theories of communication and art appreciation well beyond both classical and postclassical narratology, however, it will come as no surprise that the concept of storyworld has not only been present—if only as an "undercurrent"—in structuralist narratology but has also been influenced a great deal by (analytic) philosophy as well as by cognitive linguistics and psychology (leading to its current formulation within cognitive narratology).

Indeed, one of the most influential theoretical frameworks in which the ontological status and internal structure of storyworlds has been discussed since the 1970s is that of possible worlds semantics, which was subsequently developed into what is usually called the theory of fictional worlds. While it is widely acknowledged that neither storyworlds nor fictional worlds are to be conflated with the possible worlds of modal logic, this acknowledgment does not necessarily mean that the concept of possible worlds "can contribute little to the explanation of fictional worlds" (Zipfel, *Fiktion* 83, my translation from the German), as Frank Zipfel claims in his comprehensive study on literary fiction and fictionality. In fact, neither Nicholas Wolterstorff nor Lubomír Doležel (*Heterocosmica*), neither Umberto Eco nor Thomas Pavel (*Fictional Worlds*), neither Ruth Ronen (*Possible Worlds*) nor Marie-Laure Ryan (*Possible Worlds*)—to name only a few of the more important theorists mainly concerned with the represented worlds of literary narrative texts—*directly* equates possible worlds with (fictional) storyworlds. Rather, all of these authors "are careful to emphasize the differences between the original philosophical model of possible worlds and the new narrative model of storyworlds" (Palmer, *Fictional Minds* 33). Against this background, not only the ontological status of storyworlds but also the question of how they relate to their narrative representation seems particularly important. In order to give at least a glimpse of the range of different positions regarding these questions, let me once more offer a brief examination of three particularly influential studies, Doležel's *Heterocosmica*, Ryan's *Possible Worlds, Artificial Intelligence, and Narrative Theory*, and the philosopher Kendall L. Walton's *Mimesis as Make-Believe*—with the latter being considerably less committed to the notion of fictional world than the former two.

In his attempt to develop "a theory of fictionality which is inspired by possible-worlds semantics but which avoids the indefensible identifying of fictional worlds of literature with possible worlds of logic and philosophy" (Doležel, *Heterocosmica* 16), Lubomír Doležel considers fictional worlds to be "*ensembles of nonactualized possible states of affairs*" (*Heterocosmica* 16, original emphasis), stressing that they are not only "*accessed through semiotic channels*" (*Heterocosmica* 20, original emphasis) but also in themselves "*constructs of textual poiesis*" (*Heterocosmica* 23, original emphasis), and can, therefore, be treated as semiotic objects that "exist objectively" (*Heterocosmica* 24). This "objectivist view of meaning" (Margolin, "Text Worlds" 263), however, does not lead Doležel to ignore the complex relation between storyworlds (what he calls "narrative worlds") and their narrative as well as mental representation (what he calls "text" and "mental image," respectively). Not unlike Schmid in his "ideal genetic model" of narrative composition, Doležel understands "literary communication as interaction: in the act of writing the author produces a text and thereby constructs a fictional world; in the act of reading, the reader processes the text and thereby reconstructs the fictional world" (*Heterocosmica* 203). While he argues that authors (and not readers) bring fictional worlds into existence, then, Doležel also examines how "the fictional text's texture manipulates incompleteness . . . , determining the world's saturation," as well as how "markers of implicit meaning in the explicit texture" (*Heterocosmica* 169) allow readers to "fill in the gaps" by means of inference, utilizing not only their shared general knowledge about the actual world (what Doležel calls the "actual-world encyclopedia") but also a more specific kind of knowledge about the storyworld, which is acquired in the act of reading (what Doležel calls the "fictional encyclopedia").

At least partially in contradistinction to Doležel, Marie-Laure Ryan understands fictional worlds not as semiotic objects but as "constructs of the mind" (*Possible Worlds* 19), emphasizing what she describes as "fictional recentering": "Once we become immersed in a fiction, the characters become real for us, and the world they live in momentarily takes the place of the actual world" (*Possible Worlds* 21).[9] Among other things, the concept of "fictional recentering" leads Ryan to describe "narrative universes" as consisting not only of the "factual domain" of a "textual actual world" (which is the object of the recipient's "fictional recentering") but also of various "private worlds of characters": "knowledge-worlds (K-worlds)," "wish-worlds (W-worlds)," "obligation-worlds (O-worlds)," and, maybe most importantly, "fantasy worlds, or rather, F-universes, since their structure is that of a modal system" (Ryan, *Possible Worlds* 111; see also Doležel, *Heterocosmica* 113–132, on "narrative modalities"). So, what is the relation between the mental representation of this kind of "multilayered" storyworld and its narrative representation? According to Ryan, there is a *principle of minimal departure* at work here that allows the recipients to "project upon these worlds everything [they] know about reality, [making] only the adjustments dictated by the text" (*Possible Worlds* 51). It is worth stressing, though, that recipients do not "fill in the gaps" from the actual world itself but from their actual world knowledge, and that, moreover, "the frame of reference invoked by the principle of minimal departure is not the sole product of unmediated personal experience" but includes various forms of medial and generic knowledge, or even a specific "textual universe as frame of reference" (Ryan, *Possible Worlds* 54).

Both Doležel and Ryan point at the concept's transmedial potential but are mainly concerned with the fictional worlds represented by literary texts.[10] Kendall L. Walton, however, argues for a more genuinely transmedial approach that treats various kinds of representations—such as literature, paintings, comics, and films—as "props in games of make-believe," where their primary function is to mandate the imagining of certain "fictional truths."[11] Moreover, he claims that "there are fictional worlds of games of make-believe, fictional worlds of representational works, and fictional worlds of dreams and daydreams" (Walton 58) and that these worlds are "associated with collections of fictional truths" (Walton 69), but he seems to remain undecided on the status of these worlds as well as on whether "phrases appearing to refer to fictional worlds" (Walton 67) actually refer to them at all.[12] Still, Walton's "long, complex, dense, often technical and difficult and extremely wide ranging" (Margolin, "The Nature" 101) study provides not only a sophistication of Ryan's principle of minimal departure in the form of the "reality principle" and the "mutual belief principle"[13] (as two fundamental "principles of generation" that govern the representation of "fictional truths") but also emphasizes that even though it may be a given (narrative) representation's function to mandate certain imaginings and thereby generate certain "fictional truths" as part of its "work world," recipients may still imagine (story)worlds not mandated by the representation as part of their individual "game worlds." While Walton's distinction between "work worlds" and "game worlds" seems to be a good way of effectively combining Doležel's view on storyworlds as semiotic objects with Ryan's view on storyworlds as mental constructs, narratologists should still take care "not to confuse the worlds of games that appreciators play with representational works with the worlds of the works" (Walton 58) when analyzing the representation of storyworlds across media.

Quite apart from the question of what storyworlds *are* (i.e., if they are best understood as semiotic objects, mental constructs, or something at least slightly different altogether), theorists of fictional worlds by and large tend to agree that recipients somehow need to "fill in the gaps" of a narrative representation in order to imagine the storyworld that this representation represents. Of course, the question of how recipients construct mental representations of storyworlds across media has not only been discussed within the theory of fictional worlds but has also been at the center of what is usually called cognitive narratology, with much of the relevant research focusing on literary narrative texts and films. While there also have been some more recent attempts to trace the processes involved in understanding the storyworlds of comics and video games (see, e.g., D. Herman, "Word-Image"; Horstkotte; Kukkonen, "Navigating Infinite Earths"; as well as Backe; Nitsche; Ryan, "From Narrative Games"), I will once more limit myself to examining three of the more influential cognitive approaches to storyworlds across media: Edward Branigan's *Narrative Comprehension and Film* (which focuses on films), Richard J. Gerrig's *Experiencing Narrative Worlds* (which focuses on literary narrative texts), and David Herman's *Story Logic* and *Basic Elements of Narrative* (the latter of which explicitly aims at a transmedial understanding of the concept of storyworld, but mainly focuses on everyday narratives, literary narrative texts, comics, and films).

According to Edward Branigan, "the spectator ... encounters at least two major frames of reference in film: the space and time of a *screen* as well as (a sample of) the space and time of a *story world*" (*Narrative Comprehension* 33, original emphases). As a cognitively informed narratologist, however, he emphasizes that the question of "how on-screen data is transformed through various spatial, temporal, and causal schemes culminating in a perceived story world" (*Narrative Comprehension* 34) is rather complex and that the process of narrative comprehension, of reconstructing the storyworld from its narrative representation, prominently features the "top-down" construction of hypotheses about the spatial, temporal, and causal relations between what is represented in a "bottom-up" fashion. More specifically, Branigan assumes that "the spectator constructs temporal, spatial, and causal situations by assembling parts two at a time" (*Narrative Comprehension* 40)—that is, that the spectator reconstructs spatial, temporal, and causal relations between what is represented in the various shots of a film in order to solve specific perceptual problems posed by the juxtaposition of these shots. Although Branigan mainly focuses on film, it seems that the construction of hypotheses regarding the spatial, temporal, and causal relations among certain parts of a narrative representation can, indeed, be considered a genuinely transmedial phenomenon.

Branigan remains comparatively vague with regard to their ontological status, but cognitive approaches tend to equate the mental representation of a storyworld with the storyworld itself. Evoking the metaphors of "being transported" and of "performing a narrative" in order to explain how readers experience what he calls "narrative worlds," Gerrig was one of the first to explicitly propose to understand the latter as a particular kind of situation model, mentioning that, "though [he] believe[s] that *narrative world* and *situation model* circumscribe similar theoretical claims, [he] will use the expression *narrative world* because, by calling to mind the metaphor of being transported, it better suggests the complexity of the experience of narratives" (6–7, original emphases).[14] Building mainly on cognitive psychology and reader-response theory, Gerrig also focuses on the inferences that readers will draw in the process of reading, stressing the role that causal relations play in the construction of situation models on the basis of narrative representations: "Several traditions of research on narrative worlds have converged on the single conclusion that the perception of causality is critical: experimentation has shown that comprehension is guided by the search for causal relations and that those causal relations, once recovered, provide much of the global coherence of memory representations" (46).

Branigan discusses not only films but also comics, and Gerrig at least hints at the transmedial potential of the concept of storyworld (or "narrative world") when he expresses the hope that "much of what [he says] would remain true regardless of how the experiencer is prompted to construct a narrative world (for example, as a listener, as a viewer, and so on)" (7), but it is David Herman who must be credited with establishing the storyworld as a genuinely transmedial concept within cognitive narratology and beyond. Blending previous research from cognitive narratology with linguists' findings on everyday narrative and Ryan's works on fictional worlds in particular,[15] Herman conceives of storyworlds as "mental models of who did what to and with whom, when, where, why, and in what fashion in the world to which recipients relocate" (*Story Logic* 9) or as "global mental representations" of "the world[s] evoked implicitly as well as explicitly by a narrative, whether that narrative takes the form of a printed text, film, graphic novel, sign language, everyday conversation, or even a tale that is projected but never actualized as a concrete artifact" (*Basic Elements* 106).[16] Emphasizing the importance of how "textual, visual, auditory or other cues anchor themselves in—evoke—storyworlds" (D. Herman, *Story Logic* 10), Herman—in line with more traditional research on how storyworlds are constructed on the basis of narrative representations[17]—concludes that there is no "simple, transparent link between textual cues and narrative micro- and macrodesigns" (*Story Logic* 12).

Accordingly, Herman's *Story Logic*, which is mainly concerned with verbal narrative representation in the context of literary narrative texts, discusses the "narrative microdesigns" of "states, events, and actions," "action representations," "scripts, sequences, and stories," "participant roles and relations," and "dialogues and styles" as well as the "narrative macrodesigns" of "temporalities," "spatialization," "perspectives," and "contextual anchoring" in considerable detail. Interestingly, however, while Herman's more decidedly transmedial *Basic Elements of Narrative* likewise challenges narratology "to slow down and de-automatize the rapid, apparently effortless interpretive processes involved in experiencing narrative worlds" (105), the ways in which "storytellers use the semiotic cues available in a given narrative medium to design . . . blueprints for creating and updating storyworlds" (107) are examined in significantly less detail with regard to nonliterary forms of narrative representation. This is certainly not to say that Herman's observations regarding the representation of storyworlds in comics and face-to-face storytelling are trivial, but his examination of the medium-specific "arrangement of characters in represented scenes, the shapes of speech balloons, and the representation of the scenes in panels that form part of larger sequences of images and textual elements" (*Basic Elements* 107) in graphic novels such as David Clowes's *Ghost World* still pales in comparison to *Story*

Logic's detailed discussion of the "narrative micro- and macrodesigns" characteristic for (exclusively) verbal narrative representation.

So, where does this brief survey of previous research on represented worlds lead us? Despite the fact that comparatively few existing studies actually use the term "storyworld" to refer to the worlds represented by narrative representations, it has become clear that some elements of the corresponding concept are rather well established by now. First, while narrative representations are necessarily realized within the specific mediality of conventionally distinct media, the concept of storyworld can, at least on a certain level of abstraction, be considered to be a transmedial one. This does not necessarily mean that storyworlds across media are all alike, but most theorists seem to agree that there is a common core to the concept, which makes it equally applicable to a range of conventionally distinct media. Second, both narrative representations of storyworlds and these storyworlds themselves are necessarily incomplete, but recipients use their (actual as well as fictional) world knowledge to "fill in the gaps," to infer aspects of the storyworld that are only implicitly represented. This also leads us, third, to the observation that storyworlds—as worlds populated with characters and situated in space and time—consist not only of existents, events, and characters but also of the spatial, temporal, and causal relations between them, which are essential for understanding the various locally represented situations as part of a more global storyworld.[18]

Local Situations, Global Storyworlds, and the Concept of Narrative Representation

In fact, a broad consensus regarding the "basic elements" of stories or storyworlds seems to be firmly in place, despite the method(olog)ical and theoretical differences between (neo)classical and cognitive approaches to narratology.[19] Summarizing the classical structuralist position, for example, Seymour Chatman states that, for any narrative representation, "signifieds are exactly three—event, character, and detail of setting" (*Story* 25), and while his neoclassical approach primarily focuses on events and "eventfulness," Wolf Schmid also mentions "situations, characters," and "actions" as the defining parts of a "represented world" (*Narratology* 31). Likewise, within cognitive narratology, Patrick C. Hogan discusses how "we must continually form and revise situation models of the story, detailed structures with characters, events, motives, and so on" (*Cognitive Science* 118), and David Herman succinctly describes storyworlds as mental models of "the situations, characters, and occurrences . . . being recounted" (*Basic Elements* 106). Against this background, it also seems helpful to distinguish between *locally represented situations* and the more complex *global storyworld as a whole* into which they are combined.[20] Among other things, this will allow us to better account for the fact that narrative representations—and particularly the kind of complex and occasionally metareferential narrative representations on which the present study focuses—tend to represent a selection of spatially, temporally, and causally disconnected situations, and that a significant part of narrative comprehension—of appropriately imagining storyworlds—can be described as consisting of the reconstruction of spatial, temporal, and causal relations among (as well as within) narratively represented situations.

When it comes to the relation between the narrative representation and what is being represented—that is, various local situations that are located within a global storyworld in some way—we may generally distinguish between the *space of the representation* and the *represented space* as well as between the *time of the representation* and the *represented time*. As Herman remarks, "narratives can also be thought of as systems of verbal or visual cues prompting their readers to *spatialize* storyworlds into evolving configurations of participants, objects, and places" (*Story Logic* 263, original emphasis), and in doing so, they "represent the world being told about as one having a [more or less] specific spatial structure" (*Story Logic* 264). Just as it is part of understanding a narrative representation to locate the represented spaces of a given situation within the spatial structure of the storyworld as a whole, then, it is an equally important part of that process to locate the represented flow of time (or sequences of events) of a given situation within the temporal structure of the storyworld as a whole. It should be noted, however, not only that the spatial and temporal dimensions of both local situations and the global storyworld as a whole are closely interconnected but also that the spatiotemporal location of situations within the storyworld is usually not overly precise and sometimes cannot be accomplished at all. As Herman puts it, "when it involves events being assigned indeterminate temporal positions in a storyworld, fuzzy temporality likewise reconfigures the concepts of 'earlier' and 'later' as special limiting cases in a multivalent system" (*Story Logic* 212). Accordingly, Herman's concept of "polychronic narration entails a three-value system spanning Earlier, Later, and Indeterminate" (*Story Logic* 212), but there seems to be no similarly simple set of spatial relations that would allow us to extend the concept into something like "polychronotopic" narrative representation (see Bakhtin).

One way or another, though, locating the situations and events that segments of a given narrative representation represent within the spatiotemporal structure of the storyworld as a whole is a salient part of understanding narrative representations—but there is more to it than that, of course: Werner Wolf, for example, remarks that "the syntactic narratemes comprise *chronology* as a basic principle of concatenation and above all *teleology*: teleology involves plans and goals of characters but also other, for example structural factors" ("'Cross the Border'" 88, original emphases). The stories that narrative representations represent (as part of their storyworlds) are, in other words, often organized teleologically as well as chronologically: the events that form a story "are going somewhere," even though the motivation can be both internal (as is the case with characters' plans and goals) and external to the story(world) (as is the case if authors "want to tell a good story"). Particularly in connection with the kind of internal motivation of the story via characters' plans and goals, "*causality* ... is a further essential means of meaningfully integrating content elements, as it contributes to the explanation and the understanding of what happens in a narrative" (W. Wolf, "'Cross the Border'" 89, original emphasis).[21] Apart from the observation that recipients tend to distinguish between actions and mere "happenings" when they look for causal explanations of the events that are represented as part of a situation, then, the fact that characters, "in contrast to objects, . . . have mental states, such as perceptions, thoughts, feelings, and aims" (Eder, Jannidis, and R. Schneider, "Characters" 13) also explains why they tend to be involved when narrative representations represent not only causally disconnected but also ontologically disconnected situations.

Within (neo)classical narratology, the representation of ontologically disconnected situations is usually described via reference to Gérard Genette's work on "diegetic levels": Genette "define[s] this difference in level by saying that *any event a narrative recounts is at a diegetic level immediately higher than the level at which the narrating act producing this narrative is placed*" (*Narrative Discourse* 228, original emphasis), but he later concedes that "the second narrative can also be neither oral nor written, and can present itself, openly or not, as an inward narrative . . . or . . . as any kind of recollection that a character has (in a dream or not)" (*Narrative Discourse* 231). Genette's terms for these "diegetic levels" necessitate some further remarks, though: as is well known, Genette posits the existence of an "extradiegetic level" on which a primary extradiegetic narrator is located. This extradiegetic narrator narrates the primary "diegetic level" on which an intradiegetic narrator or another kind of intradiegetic character may be located. The intradiegetic narrator may narrate a secondary "metadiegetic level" on which a metadiegetic narrator may be located, who, in turn, may narrate a tertiary "meta-metadiegetic level" possibly containing a meta-metadiegetic narrator, and so on, ad infinitum. There are some terminological as well as conceptual problems with Genette's discussion of "diegetic levels,"[22] but his terms remain widely used and, hence, allow for a comparatively accessible analysis of complex storyworlds' internal structure.

Still, some terminological modification is necessary: Genette's own attempt at a defense against criticism by Mieke Bal and Shlomith Rimmon-Kenan nicely sums up this necessity when he acknowledges that "the way the prefix ['meta-'] functions here is opposite to the way it functions in logic and linguistics, where a metalanguage is a language in which one speaks of a (second) language; in [his] lexicon, a metanarrative is one recounted within a narrative" (Genette, *Narrative Discourse Revisited* 91). While I concede that it is possible to use the "meta-" prefix in the way proposed by Genette, it seems that this inconsistent usage may easily lead to confusion—even more so in a context where not only the concept of metareference but also the more specific concept of metalepsis are of some importance (see later in this chapter). This is why I will follow Mieke Bal (*Narratology* 43–75; "Notes") and Shlomith Rimmon-Kenan (*Narrative Fiction* 87–106) in speaking of *hypo*diegetic instead of *meta*diegetic narrators and "diegetic levels." Moreover, I propose to combine Genette's (modified) terminology with a more neutral description of the *diegetic hierarchy* of subworlds that is as indebted to Schmid (*Narratology* 32–33, 67–68) as it is to Genette, distinguishing between (intra)diegetic primary storyworlds, hypodiegetic secondary storyworlds, hypo-hypodiegetic tertiary storyworlds, and so on.[23] Usually, narrative representations in some way use characters to "anchor" these kinds of subworlds within the respective "higher-order" storyworld, but it is worth repeating that the use of narrating characters (or artifacts that are narratively representing "lower-order" storyworlds, for that matter) are not the only way in which characters may function as "anchors" for the representation of "lower-order" storyworlds. Instead, these subworlds may encompass the whole range of what Ryan describes as "F-universes"—that is, "dreams, hallucinations, fantasies, and fictional [as well as factual] stories told to or composed by the characters" (*Possible Worlds* 119).

As useful as these distinctions may turn out to be in the context of narratological analyses, however, describing the elements of storyworlds in the way sketched above does not yet say all that much about what storyworlds *are*—just as describing what narrative representations represent does not yet say too much about *how* they represent it. As the previous survey has made sufficiently clear, storyworlds may be understood as "imaginable scenarios or sets of conceivable states of affairs constructed and expressed by means of artefacts (semiotic objects), but . . . not identical with these objects" (Margolin, "The

Constitution" 355), which leads many cognitive approaches to emphasize the situation models or, more generally, mental models of the storyworlds that recipients construct on the basis of a given narrative representation. Despite the importance of reception processes for explaining how narrative representations relate to storyworlds, though, conflating "imaginable scenarios" with their imagination or *mental representation* is just as unsatisfactory as conflating them with their narrative or, rather, *medial representation*.[24] In fact, just as most (neo)classical narratologists and theorists of fictional worlds will acknowledge that represented worlds do not exist independently of the "activities of the human mind," most cognitive narratologists seem not all that interested in the *actual* situation models or mental models that recipients construct on the basis of narrative representations, but, rather, in some *ideal* version of these models. While one can find the occasional hint that "it is possible to generalize about the types of inferences readers will regularly draw" (Gerrig 65), such a focus on what may be described as *intersubjective* mental representations is seldom explicitly acknowledged within cognitive narratology. It remains important, then, "not to confuse the worlds of games that appreciators play with representational works with the worlds of the works" (Walton 58) and to distinguish as clearly as possible between the external medial representation of a storyworld, the internal mental representations of that storyworld, and the storyworld itself. Reception processes evidently play an important role in understanding what storyworlds are, and one should not pretend that "meaning generates itself," but the complex forms of intersubjective meaning making that are involved in the representation of storyworlds cannot be reduced to the individual construction of (more or less) *subjective* mental representations, either. Hence, what we need is a theory of narrative representation that also provides at least a rough account of narrative meaning making.

There are certainly alternative theories of representation available, but I will largely follow narratologists such as Richard Walsh and philosophers such as Gregory Currie in subscribing to a broadly *intentionalist-pragmatic account of representation* and the processes of meaning making involved here. Both Walsh and Currie draw heavily on the theories of communication developed by H. P. Grice as well as by Dan Sperber and Deirdre Wilson, which in turn seem largely compatible with earlier classical models of narrative communication as well as with cognitively informed models of narrative comprehension. While Walsh is primarily interested in a theory of fictional representation in literary texts,[25] Currie's approach to representation is more encompassing, as it includes representations beyond the literary text and explicitly refers to fictional as well as nonfictional representation.[26] Accordingly, Currie defines narratives, rather broadly, as "intentional-communicative artefacts: artefacts that have as their function the communication of a story, which function they have by virtue of their makers' intentions" (*Narratives* 6). It should be noted, however, that Currie refers to a relatively weak form of "hypothetical intentionalism" here, as drawing "pragmatic inference to [narrative representation's] intended meaning" (*Narratives* 16) does, under normal circumstances, not entail "a forensic investigation into a person's motives that involves sifting the evidence of diaries, letters, and the reminiscences of friends" (*Narratives* 25). I would argue, then, that a theory of (narrative) representation that explains narrative meaning-making processes via "reflexive communicative intentions" and their reconstruction by the recipients according to certain communicative rules is not only improbable to commit the (in)famous "intentional fallacy," but will also likely be well suited as a basis for the analysis of transmedial strategies of narrative representation.[27]

Still, neither Walsh nor Currie says all that much about what storyworlds are, and while I will not discuss the notion of "intended meaning" in too much detail here, a slightly more in-depth examination of how narrative representations relate to storyworlds and what the latter are if they are neither mental nor medial representations seems to be in order. Combining a pragmatic theory of cinematic meaning with current findings from cognitive film theory and concepts from philosophical theories of fiction, Jens Eder has recently developed a sophisticated account of characters in films as *intersubjective communicative constructs*.[28] Expanding his discussion of the ontological status of characters to include the (story)worlds in which they are located, Eder further remarks that "every fictional world is a communicative artifact that is constituted through the intersubjective construction of mental representations based on fictional texts" (*Die Figur* 78–79, my translation from the German).[29] In light of the problems that both (neo)structuralism's "objectivist" and cognitivism's "subjectivist" accounts of meaning making generate, it is indeed desirable (if not necessary) to describe storyworlds as neither a form of possible worlds existing independently of reception processes nor as mental models existing exclusively in the imagination of any given individual recipient. Hence, I will loosely follow Eder's argument that storyworlds are best understood as normative abstractions[30] about ideal mental representations based on narrative representations and that, therefore, a reconstruction of narrative meaning making needs to take into account recipients' collective mental dispositions, (medium- as well as genre-specific) communicative rules or representational conventions, and (hypothetical) authorial intentions.

Since some of the intentionalist-pragmatic assumptions regarding intersubjectively plausible processes of meaning making entailed in Walsh's and Currie's as well as in Eder's accounts of representation may appear problematic to some, however, I would like to briefly examine the different levels on which (narrative) meaning making occurs in order to more clearly define the kind of "storyworld meaning" with which I am primarily concerned here. In his cognitively informed study of "meaning and meaningfulness in terms of cinematic reception" (Persson 22), Per Persson, for example, distinguishes between as many as six levels of meaning, leading from the perception of formal patterns and basic forms of object recognition (level 0 and level 1) to processes by which "perceptual meanings become more sophisticated and abstract" (29) (level 2). These processes, in turn, result in "an understanding of the *situation* or the *referential meaning*" that involves "constructing a mental model of the situation" (Persson 30, original emphases) (level 3). On an even more abstract level, "the understanding of situations and the establishment of temporal, causal, and spatial relations [as well as, one would have to add, ontological relations] between situations enable scene and plot summarizations" (Persson 32). Finally, while "some level 4 meanings operate on the border between comprehension and interpretation," the meanings generated on level 5 "are univocally referred to as interpretative" (Persson 33).

So, what kind of meaning do we talk about when we talk about storyworlds? If we accept that storyworlds are best understood as intersubjective communicative constructs based on a given narrative representation, it seems that these constructs primarily consist of what both Persson and, more than a decade earlier, David Bordwell have called "*referential* meaning" (Bordwell, *Making Meaning* 8, original emphasis; see also Persson 29–33), including both a complex understanding of situations and more abstract reconstructions of their spatial, temporal, causal, and ontological relations (i.e., Persson's level 3 and level 4). Accordingly, storyworlds are primarily the result of *comprehension* (which "constructs referential and explicit meanings" [Bordwell, *Making Meaning* 9]) and usually do not include meanings based on *interpretation* (which "constructs implicit and symptomatic meanings" [Bordwell, *Making Meaning* 9]; i.e., Persson's level 5).[31] This is not to say that symbolic or symptomatic meanings plays no role in the reception process or that narratology cannot contribute to their explanation, but I would maintain that understanding storyworlds as intersubjective communicative constructs with a normative component works best if one limits their scope to referential meaning.[32] While recipients' collective mental dispositions, (historically variable, genre-, and medium-specific) communicative rules or representational conventions, and (reflexively and hypothetically reconstructed) authorial intentions certainly play a role in the interpretation of narrative representations as well, I remain skeptical whether the result of complex context-oriented acts of interpretation can quite as happily be conceived as intersubjective communicative constructs as the result of "mere comprehension" can.[33]

Incidentally, the proposed conceptualization of storyworlds as intersubjective communicative constructs does not at all imply that, for every given narrative representation, there is one and only one storyworld to be constructed in an intersubjectively valid manner. Rather, narrative representations across media commonly employ *ambiguity*[34] to such an extent that more than one storyworld can be intersubjectively constructed, and, at least in some cases, there may be no way to decide (in an intersubjectively valid manner) which of these constructs is more plausible, "mandated," or "authorized." Patrick C. Hogan speaks of "the *profile of ambiguity* of the work" in this context, by which he refers to "the range of interpretations [or comprehensions] the work sustains and the different degrees to which it sustains them" (*Narrative Discourse* 13–14, original emphasis). Considering that such "profiles of ambiguity" tend to be comparatively less pronounced with regard to a given work's referential meaning, Marie-Laure Ryan's proposal to distinguish between "one text, one world," "one text, many worlds," and "one world, many texts" as the three basic kinds of relations between storyworlds and narrative representations may turn out to be sufficiently sophisticated in many cases (see Ryan, "Story/Worlds/Media").[35] Keeping in mind that narrative representations' combination of what Lubomír Doležel describes as "explicit, implicit, and zero texture" leads not only to "a determinate domain" and a "domain of gaps" but also to an "indeterminate domain" (*Heterocosmica* 182) in the storyworld, however, it still seems important to acknowledge that in some narrative works "the number of plausible interpretations [or comprehensions] is limited and sharply distinct from surrounding possibilities" (Hogan, *Narrative Discourse* 19), while in others "there is a wider range of plausible interpretation [or comprehension] and a much less sharp distinction between more and less plausible alternatives" (Hogan, *Narrative Discourse* 20). In that sense, understanding storyworlds as intersubjective communicative constructs is certainly not meant to suggest that a given narrative work's "profile of ambiguity" should be ignored in favor of an arbitrarily chosen preferred comprehension—instead, I would argue that, in cases where a narrative representation supports multiple comprehensions with equal degrees of plausibility, acknowledging the range of supported storyworlds is a prerequisite for intersubjectively valid meaning making.

On the (In)Completeness, (Im)Possibility, and (Non)Fictionality of Storyworlds

In this context, it might also be fruitful to examine the ways in which intersubjectively constructed storyworlds across media can be understood as possible or impossible, despite the fact that they are evidently rather different from the possible worlds of formal logic. The importance of "filling in the gaps" of narrative representations notwithstanding, some "gaps" can never be "filled" in an intersubjectively valid manner. The main reason for this is that recipients' world knowledge—whether historical or contemporary, nonfictional or fictional, universal or particular—can provide only comparatively general additional information so that they cannot conclusively infer the answer to specific questions such as "Does character X have a birthmark on his or her back?" if the narrative representation does not more or less explicitly provide it. While recipients' may *pretend* that storyworlds are complete in the process Marie-Laure Ryan calls "fictional recentering," most if not all theorists of fictional worlds agree that these worlds are *actually* incomplete.[36] Accordingly, storyworlds necessarily violate the *law of excluded middle*, which, in a translation that loosely approximates Aristotle's words, states that "there cannot be an intermediate between contradictories, but of one subject we must either affirm or deny any one predicate" (IV, §7), and, hence, have to be understood as *logically impossible* on a fairly fundamental level.[37]

Even though it is seldom recognized that violation of the law of excluded middle already leads to logically impossible storyworlds, the latters' incompleteness is usually not contested. Yet there are a number of other, perhaps more interesting ways in which storyworlds can be conceived as possible or impossible—a question that has recently been put back on the narratological agenda by a group of "unnatural narratologists."[38] I agree that an "unnatural" narratology that focuses on "develop[ing] new narratological tools ... to capture the strangeness and extravagance of unnatural narratives" (Alber and R. Heinze, "Introduction" 16) has its merits, but it still seems that, in furthering their research program, (some of) the "unnatural narratologists" may overstate the alleged impossibility of (some) storyworlds. Jan Alber, for example, operates with two rather different notions of impossibility when he claims that "many narrative texts teem with unnatural, i.e., physically or logically impossible, scenarios and events that take us to the most remote territories of what can be imagined" ("The Diachronic Development" 41). While "physically impossible scenarios and events" are "impossible by the known laws governing the physical world ... , logically impossible ones" are "impossible by accepted principles of logic" (Alber, "Impossible Storyworlds" 80).[39] At least from the perspective of fictional worlds theory, however, Alber's "physically impossible storyworlds" turn out to be decidedly possible[40]—in fact, Lubomír Doležel, from whom Alber has borrowed the distinction, emphasizes that "physically impossible worlds are logically possible" and that "only worlds containing or implying contradictions are logically impossible" (Doležel, *Heterocosmica* 116). As interesting as the question of what Marie-Laure Ryan describes as "accessibility relations" certainly is (see Ryan, *Possible Worlds* 31–47), the more controversial question with regard to storyworlds' (im)possibility is whether (or in what ways) "the projection of mutually incompatible events" (Alber, "Impossible Storyworlds" 80) leads to "logically impossible storyworlds" (see also Ashline for a comparatively early account of various other forms of "impossible fictions"). The most salient principle of logic that is violated in these cases is the *law of noncontradiction*, which, according to Aristotle, states that "contradictory statements are not at the same time true" (IV, §6).

In light of the wealth of current research provided by "unnatural narratology," there is no need for an in-depth examination of how the problem of contradiction has historically been discussed in fictional worlds theory and narratology, but it should still be noted that there is a history to this discussion. One way or another, the question whether or not one chooses to acknowledge the possibility of contradiction seems to be closely interrelated with one's conceptualization of storyworlds. On the one hand, theorists such as Ruth Ronen argue that "the coherence of fictional worlds does not collapse when a world of the fictional type contains inconsistencies or impossibilities" (*Possible Worlds* 93). On the other hand, theorists such as Lubomír Doležel hold that "worlds that include or imply contradictions are impossible, unthinkable, 'empty'" (*Heterocosmica* 19) and, hence, that "the authenticity of fictional existence is denied by the logico-semantic structure of the world itself" ("Possible Worlds" 239) in these cases. It is important to note in this context that narrative works across media may, indeed, possess different degrees of "unnaturalness," with postmodernist literature (with which Alber and many other "unnatural narratologists" are primarily concerned) being particularly prone to representing "empty worlds." Brian Richardson, for example, proposes to "distinguish between mimetic, non-mimetic, and anti-mimetic poetics" ("What Is Unnatural Narrative Theory?" 31). If "mimetic texts" more or less closely adhere to what may be described as "realist conventions," the storyworlds represented by "nonmimetic texts"—common in the science fiction and fantasy genres—are significantly less accessible from/similar to the actual world, but still logically possible from the perspective of fictional worlds theory. In the most pronounced cases of "antimimetic texts," however, "the concept of representation is ambiguous or irrelevant" (B. Richardson, "What Is Unnatural Narrative Theory?" 36). Now, while most of if not all the films, comics, and video games discussed in this book can be said to "violate mimetic expectations, the canons of realism, and the conventions of natural narrative" (B. Richardson, "What Is Unnatural Narrative Theory?" 34) to a certain extent, my focus remains on transmedial strategies of narrative representation—and it seems that truly "anti-mimetic strategies of narration" (B. Richardson, "What Is Unnatural Narrative Theory?" 38) cannot unproblematically be included in the realm of narrative representation as it is usually conceptualized.

Once again, though, some further differentiations appear to be in order. As far as the narrative representation of local situations is concerned, I tend to agree with Lubomír Doležel (and others) that situations represented as contradictory are not imaginable, or at least not imaginable in the ways that situations represented as noncontradictory are. Considering that cueing imaginations seems to be what narrative representation is all about, this also means that situations that contain "strong" logical contradictions of the type that break the law of noncontradiction are actually rather difficult to *represent* as well. Graham Priest has written an interesting short story that aims to illustrate the possibility of representing "logically impossible situations or worlds" ("Sylvan's Box" 580) containing obvious contradictions but, at least to my mind, fails to do so quite impressively: "At first, I thought it must be a trick of the light, but more careful inspection certified that it was no illusion. The box was absolutely empty, but also had something in it. Fixed to its base was a small figurine, carved of wood, Chinese influence, Southeast Asian maybe.... The experience was one of occupied emptiness.... The box was really empty and occupied at the same time. The sense of touch confirmed this" (Priest, "Sylvan's Box" 575–576). It is clear that Priest's short story is intended to represent a logically impossible situation, but does it succeed? To me, it seems that Priest's attempt results in a text that cannot be successfully parsed, in a case of "antimimetic" narration that is not representing a situation in any meaningful way anymore, in a narrative work whose contradictory assertions result in the situation it intends to represent becoming "impossible, unthinkable, 'empty'" (Doležel, *Heterocosmica* 19). So, while some of the "unnatural narratologists" may take Priest's story as exemplifying the possibility of representing impossible situations, I think it primarily serves to remind us that even if, as Umberto Eco argued, "worlds where necessary truths do not hold can be imagined and are intuitively possible," they cannot be "constructed" in a meaningful sense of the word: "Such a world is in fact *quoted*, but it is not *constructed*, or—if you want—extensionally *mentioned*, but not intensionally *analyzed*" (234, original emphases). Following Brian Richardson instead of Jan Alber with regard to the problem of impossible situations, then, I would like to emphasize that the kind of "quoted" situations that actually break the law of noncontradiction cannot be unproblematically understood as being part of the realm of prototypical narrative representation anymore.[41]

Particularly when keeping in mind that the present book focuses not on postmodernist literary texts but rather on narrative representations in contemporary films, comics, and video games,[42] it makes sense to distinguish more systematically between *presentational* and *representational aspects* of a given narrative representation in this context. This kind of distinction can most commonly be found in accounts of pictorial representation, with well-known theorists such as Richard Wollheim arguing that the experience of "seeing-in" is characterized by a "twofoldness" of "configurational" and "recognitional" aspects, since "the surface of any picture can contain elements that, though individually visible, make no contribution to what the picture represents" ("On Pictorial Representation" 222).[43] Despite the particular significance of the distinction between presentation and representation in the context of pictorial representation, then, I would maintain that verbal representation may be understood as having presentational and representational aspects as well, and that the distinction is, in fact, transmedially applicable. There doubtless is an experiential and emotional dimension to the distinction, but I am mainly interested in the intricacies of what Gregory Currie calls *representational correspondence* at this point, aiming to provide a theoretical foundation for the observation that "for a given representational work, only certain features of the representation serve to represent features of the things represented" (*Narratives* 59)—which seems to significantly complicate (some of) the assumptions that (some of) the "unnatural narratologists" make regarding "how representations work."

In other words, my main point here is that when dealing with contemporary films, comics, and video games, recipients not only "fill in the gaps" (as it is described by Ryan's principle of minimal departure) but also routinely "ignore" some aspects of narrative representations in order to intersubjectively construct the represented storyworlds. Particularly in cases where the assumption of representational correspondence becomes problematic, recipients will look for alternative *external explanations* related to authors' intentions or representational conventions before trying to imagine implausible or even impossible situations or storyworlds, which would be made necessary by insisting on *internal explanations*. In fact, I would argue that both "filling in the gaps" and "ignoring" certain aspects of a narrative representation are equally crucial parts of comprehending narrative works across media. As has already been mentioned, Kendall L. Walton pointedly describes this aspect of narrative meaning making in terms of a *principle of charity*: "The generation of fictional truths is sometimes blocked (if not merely deemphasized) just, or primarily, because they make trouble—because they would render the fictional world uncomfortably paradoxical. . . . If there is another ready explanation for the artist's inclusion of a feature that appears to generate a given fictional truth, it may not seem that he [or she] meant especially to have it generated. And *this* may argue against recognizing that it is generated" (183, original emphasis). Without specifying the application of charity across media just yet, I would maintain that recipients will generally try to exhaust every possible alternative explanation before trying to imagine a logically impossible, contradictory local situation or a logically impossible, contradictory global storyworld.

Furthermore, I would also argue that it is significantly more difficult to cue recipients into imagining logically impossible situations than it is to cue them into imagining logically impossible storyworlds. While explicit contradictions certainly pose a problem for our imagination in these more global contexts as well, it still is evident that, in unfolding a story and fleshing out its storyworld, narrative representations sometimes successively represent local situations that do not—or not immediately—"add up" to a logically consistent global storyworld. Accordingly, one of the core problems related to the notion of impossible storyworlds is whether such contradictory representations can appropriately be understood as the representation of *one* storyworld that violates the law of noncontradiction, even though *not* violating the law of noncontradiction may be taken to be a core feature of the concept of a world, whether actual or merely represented.[44] A good solution to this problem might be to treat apparently inconsistent storyworlds as compounds of two (or more) logically consistent storyworlds, combined by what Nicholas Rescher and Robert Brandom call "the procedure of [w]orld-disjunction" (10, original emphasis) in their early study of nonstandard possible worlds. Among other things, this also allows us to treat logical inconsistency as "a *local* and not necessarily *global* anomaly" (Rescher and Brandom 24, original emphases), understanding storyworlds as noncontradictory "by default," with exceptions to this rule—which are comparatively rare at least within the mainstream of narrative representations in contemporary media culture—best described as *compounds of noncontradictory subworlds*.

In this context, I would also once more like to stress the dynamic nature of storyworld construction, which leads to recipients' continually expanding and revising their hypotheses about the situations and storyworlds that are being represented as the plot and the story of the narrative representation unfold. Accordingly, what may initially appear as the representation of a contradictory arrangement of situations will, more often than not, turn out to be the representation of a logically consistent storyworld, after all, with contemporary films, comics, and video games employing various (post-hoc) *strategies of plausibilization*, which, in turn, allow the recipients to "naturalize" or, rather, plausibilize the mental models they have constructed of the initially impossible-seeming storyworld. An already fairly sophisticated account of these "reconciling and integrating measures" (Yacobi 114) was developed by Tamar Yacobi during the 1970s and 1980s. Yacobi distinguishes between the "*genetic principle*," which "resolves fictive oddities and inconsistencies in terms of the causal factors that produced the text" (114, original emphasis); the "*generic principle*," which explains "divergences from what is generally accepted as the principles governing actual reality" (115, original emphasis) by reference to generic conventions; the *"existential principle,"* which explains them by reference to "the peculiar structure of reality the reader attributes to the work" (116–117, original emphasis); the *"functional principle,"* which, in cases where impossibilities are, for example, used to comic effect, offers explanation "in terms of the *ends* requiring that divergence and discontinuity" (117, original emphases); and the *"perspectival principle,* which brings divergent as well as otherwise unrelated elements into pattern by attributing them, in whole or in part, to the peculiarities and circumstances of the observer through whom the world is taken to be refracted" (118, original emphasis).

Despite a certain overlap among her five principles, Yacobi's suggestions not only remain useful today but also, in fact, anticipate quite a few core tenets of Jan Alber's recent work within "unnatural narratology." Alber distinguishes between no less than nine "reading strategies" (*Unnatural Narrative* 47)[45] that readers use when trying to make sense of "unnatural narratives." While there is quite a lot of variety with regard to the external as well as internal explanations that recipients may attempt to seek and the kinds of charity they successively may apply when they notice (apparent) violations of the law of noncontradiction and other kinds of physical or logical impossibility, then, it seems to me that Yacobi's "perspectival principle" (which is echoed by Alber's reading strategy of "subjectification") describes one of the most important strategies of plausibilization to be employed when recipients are confronted not with what appear to be narrative representations of contradictory, logically impossible local situations but rather with what appear to be contradictory, logically impossible arrangements of logically possible local situations within the global storyworld as a whole. However, the principle could also be formulated in a more general way that emphasizes the ontological disconnect at which both Yacobi and Alber seem to aim: when encountering an apparently contradictory, logically impossible arrangement of situations, recipients will usually attempt to find reasons to locate the represented situations within different subworlds or on different "diegetic levels" of the storyworld as a whole instead of immediately accepting the possibility that the narrative representation in question is meant to represent a contradictory, logically impossible storyworld. Keeping in mind what has already been said about Gérard Genette's concept of "diegetic levels," though, one must recognize that locating the problematic situations within the "private domains" of a character's memories, hallucinations, dreams, or fantasies is not the only option—instead, inconsistencies may also be located within ontologically disconnected subworlds that are created by an intradiegetic narrator or an intradiegetic narrative work, and they may even be attributed to an extradiegetic narrator (or even just the narrative representation) telling (or representing, as it were) different versions of a story(world).

All of the above notwithstanding, I readily concede that contemporary films, comics, and video games conventionally, commonly, and comparatively unproblematically represent impossible situations and storyworlds, as there are many forms of impossibility that are not quite violating the law of noncontradiction on which the preceding argument has primarily focused. Apart from mere physical impossibilities, which seem largely uninteresting in the present context, what could, perhaps, be described as *representational impossibilities* appear to have become increasingly common in contemporary media culture. Instead of attempting a comprehensive discussion of logical impossibilities that fall short of actually violating the law of noncontradiction, then, I will limit myself to a brief examination of the concept of *metalepsis* as a by now largely conventionalized strategy of narrative representation—figuring prominently not only in contemporary films such as David Cronenberg's *eXistenZ*, David Fincher's *Fight Club*, or Spike Jonze and Charlie Kaufman's *Adaptation.*, but also in contemporary comics such as Neil Gaiman's *The Sandman* series or Mike Carey and Peter Gross's *The Unwritten* series and contemporary video games such as Double Fine's *Psychonauts* or Remedy's *Alan Wake*—that is characterized by a metareferential play with the ontological boundaries between the "diegetic levels" or subworlds discussed above. Just like various other influential narratological terms, the term "narrative metalepsis" was coined by

Gérard Genette, who defines it as "any intrusion by the extradiegetic narrator or narratee into the diegetic universe (or by diegetic characters into a metadiegetic universe, etc.), or the inverse" (*Narrative Discourse* 234–235).[46] As influential as the term has proved to be, however, Genette's narrator-centric definition of the term "narrative metalepsis" is evidently problematic in the context of a transmedial narratology that treats the use of narrators as an optional strategy of narrative representation. Accordingly, Werner Wolf has proposed to use the term to more generally refer to "a usually intentional paradoxical transgression of, or confusion between, (onto)logically distinct (sub)worlds and/or levels that exist, or are referred to, within representations of possible worlds [in the sense of represented worlds]" ("Metalepsis" 91) in his wide-ranging discussion of metalepsis as a transmedial phenomenon (see also the contributions in Kukkonen and Klimek or Pier and Schaeffer). While the proposed definitions vary, of course, there still seems to be a broad consensus that, just like storyworlds, metaleptic transgressions can be represented in a wide variety of conventionally distinct media. Moreover, there is a growing body of studies that examines the medium-specific realization of metaleptic transgressions in media such as films, comics, and video games.[47]

Since I will only be able to hint at the historical breadth of metalepsis as a particularly metareferential and narratologically interesting strategy of narrative representation across media, a few more systematic remarks on the different forms that the phenomenon may take seem to be in order. On the one hand, it is clear that metaleptic transgressions can appear between any two (or more) ontologically disconnected subworlds of the represented storyworld as well as between the storyworld and the level of narrative representation (see, e.g., Feyersinger; Ryan, *Avatars* 204–230; Thon, "Zur Metalepse"). On the other hand, the paradoxical transgressions that characterize all forms of metalepsis may not only be more or less pronounced but also be more or less encompassing. In fact, just as with other forms of initially impossible-seeming narrative representations, it is quite common that what initially appears as a genuine metalepsis is retroactively plausibilized by reference to an additional "higher-order" storyworld or other plausible explanation of the seemingly paradoxical transgression. Accordingly, one may conceive of metalepsis as both a gradual and a processual phenomenon, with quite a few narrative works generating metaleptic effects that (eventually) turn out not to be genuinely paradoxical transgressions after all. In order to get a better grasp of the kind of paradoxical transgressions most commonly at play here, one can, furthermore, distinguish between three forms of metalepsis according to the strength of their metaleptic effect. First, *epistemic metalepses* occur when characters are represented as possessing "impossible" knowledge of "higher-order" subworlds, the fact that they are "merely represented," or the narrative representation itself (such as in *Fight Club*). Second, *ontological metalepses* occur when characters (or other entities) move between ontologically disconnected subworlds or when other forms of metaleptic contamination lead to a "blending" of the latter (such as in *eXistenZ*). Third, *autopoietic metalepses* occur when characters within a subworld of the storyworld are represented as narrating, writing, or otherwise bringing about that very subworld (such as in *Adaptation.*). If no internal explanation for these transgressions is provided, the kind of impossibilities at play here clearly cannot be reduced to physical impossibilities—and while they do not violate the law of noncontradiction either, it seems clear that narrative representations regularly cue their recipients into intersubjectively constructing metaleptic storyworlds containing what I have proposed to call representational impossibilities (see also Thon, "Zur Metalepse," for a more in-depth discussion of the three forms of metalepsis sketched above).

Having established an understanding of storyworlds as intersubjective communicative constructs that are necessarily incomplete but, apart from that, tend to be constructed as logically possible to the extent for which their representation allows, I would like to conclude the present chapter by examining Jan Alber's claim that "the possibility of representing the impossible is the most crucial difference between the world of fiction and other modes of discourse" ("The Diachronic Development" 62). Physically (let alone logically) impossible storyworlds can, indeed, be considered a strong marker of the respective representation's fictionality, since the actual world is, by definition, physically (as well as logically) possible, but it still appears that Alber is overstating the importance of "unnatural narrative" for the realm of *fictional narrative representations*, since the latter do not necessarily have to represent physically impossible storyworlds—and, intuitively implausible as it may seem, *nonfictional narrative representations* do not necessarily have to represent physically possible storyworlds, either. The latter case admittedly is comparatively rare, but the possibility of nonfictional narrative representations representing physically impossible storyworlds still follows from the observation that they cannot appropriately be described as "directly" representing the actual world.[48] While I certainly acknowledge that fictional storyworlds can be more or less "remote" from the actual world and that representations are marked as fictional or nonfictional by more or less specific markers (which are often paratextual rather than textual or representational, though),[49] I would like to maintain that nonfictional narrative representations represent storyworlds in ways very similar to fictional narrative representations.

Incidentally, the notion that there are no fundamental differences between fictional and nonfictional representation with regard to basic processes of narrative comprehension is well established within cognitive narratology. Richard J. Gerrig, for example, stresses that he "intend[s] *narrative* and *narrative world* to be neutral with respect to the issue of fictionality" (7, original emphases), and Edward Branigan argues that "our ability to *understand* a narrative, or nonnarrative, is distinct from our *beliefs* as to its truth, appropriateness, plausibility, rightness, or realism" (*Narrative Comprehension* 192, original emphases). Accordingly, David Herman indeed appears to summarize the standard position within cognitive narratology when he claims that the concept of "*storyworld* applies both to fictional and nonfictional narratives. All narratives have world-creating power, even though, depending on the kind of narrative involved, interpreters bring to bear on those storyworlds different evaluative criteria" (*Story Logic* 16, original emphasis). However, this should not be taken as a "panfictional" position, which would boil down to arguing that all representation is fictional (see Ryan, "Postmodernism"; and the recent survey by Konrad). Instead, I agree with Lubomír Doležel that there is little use in overemphasizing the fictionality of nonfictional representation (or the social construction of reality),[50] since "if reality is called fiction, a new word for fiction has to be invented" (*Heterocosmica* x). There seems to be a relation between fictional and narrative representation that has, among other things, established a certain degree of proximity between theories of fiction and narratology.[51] Yet I do not argue for equating either fictionality and nonfictionality or fictionality and narrativity—what I do argue is that both fictional and nonfictional narrative representations represent storyworlds using rather similar representational strategies.

While there doubtless are differences between fictional and nonfictional narrative representations, and this book is primarily concerned with the former, it may also be worth noting not only that more recent works within film and media studies increasingly emphasize the "hybrid nature" of contemporary forms of pseudo-documentary, mockumentary, and docudrama, such as Larry Charles and Sacha Baron Cohen's *Borat*, Oren Peli's *Paranormal Activity*, Matt Reeves's *Cloverfield*, Neill Blomkamp's *District 9*, Banksy's *Exit through the Gift Shop*, or David Fincher's *The Social Network*,[52] but also that the supposed nonfictionality of graphic memoirs such as Art Spiegelman's *Maus*, David B.'s *Epileptic*, Marjane Satrapi's *Persepolis*, Craig Thompson's *Blankets*, Alison Bechdel's *Fun Home*, or David Small's *Stitches*[53] and documentary games such as C-level's *Waco Resurrection*, Traffic Games' *JFK Reloaded*, Kuma Reality Games' *Kuma\War*, Afkar Media's *Under Siege*, or Danny Ledonne's *Super Columbine Massacre RPG!* is fairly contested within comics studies and game studies as well.[54] Despite the fact that fictionality is usually understood as a "nongradable" phenomenon in philosophical theories of fiction, it would seem that medium-specific accounts of (non)fictionality across media need to stop limiting themselves to describing the communication of (non)fictional communicative intentions primarily on a global level in order to acknowledge the ways in which films, comics, and video games can (and are intended to) play with and subvert the distinction between fictional and nonfictional representation on a more local level, allowing recipients to construct increasingly complex hypotheses about how the represented local situations and/or the represented global storyworld as a whole relate to (some version of) the actual world.

One way or another, though, it could be argued that what are framed as *problems of (non)fictionality* in the discussion surrounding nonfiction film, graphic memoirs, and documentary games are actually *problems of representationality*. Among the media examined in this book, video games are generally seen as most "resistant" to having the fictionality/nonfictionality distinction applied to them. As William Uricchio has remarked, their interactive and nonlinear nature sets them apart from traditional documentary media such as films, photographs, or audio recordings, and "although they can integrate all of these earlier media, [video games] might seem closest to historical documentation only when emulating them, in the process suppressing games' defining interactive relationship with the gamer" (327). Fictional as well as documentary video games may integrate documentary material, but the ways in which their interactive elements contribute to the representation of their respective storyworlds appear to be considerably more interesting (as well as considerably more problematic). Ian Bogost, Simon Ferrari, and Bobby Schweizer, for example, argue that video games can engage with the actual world "through explorable *spatial reality*, which makes the environments of events navigable; through experiential *operational reality* that recreates the events themselves; and through *procedural reality*, or interactions with the behaviors that drive the systems in which particular events take place" (64, original emphases). It would seem, then, that the discussion surrounding documentary games serves to remind us that the specific mediality of video games establishes a particularly unstable relation between the (at least partially narrative) representations they generate and the (at least partially nonfictional) storyworlds they represent.

And this observation, in turn, leads us back to one of the more general questions that reside at the core of the present study: How do narrative representations across media allow their recipients to intersubjectively construct storyworlds? In order to be able to acknowledge the importance of recipients' "filling in the gaps" of narrative representations when imagining storyworlds while at the same time evading a conflation of these storyworlds with their mental representation, I have proposed to subscribe to an intentionalist-pragmatic account of narrative representation that conceptualizes storyworlds as intersubjective communicative constructs with a normative component. It has also already become clear, however, that recipients not only "fill in the gaps" but also routinely "ignore" elements of narrative representations while intersubjectively constructing storyworlds, applying more or less medium-specific forms of charity when the assumption of representational correspondence becomes problematic. While it remains beyond the scope of this book to discuss the wide variety of representational conventions that define the mediality of contemporary films, comics, and video games in too much detail, then, I would still like to use the following chapter to examine some prototypical characteristics of the latters' multimodal configurations and the storyworlds they represent, focusing on the complex interplay between transmedial and medium-specific aspects of narrative representation across media.

3 : Narrative Representation across Media

Multimodal Configurations and Audiovisual Representation in Contemporary Films

As the previous chapter has established, there is a broad consensus that both the concept of storyworld and the concept of narrative representation are applicable across media, though it is usually also assumed that while storyworlds are comparatively "medium-free," narrative representations are fairly medium-specific. On closer inspection, such a view turns out to be overly reductive, both with regard to narrative representations and with regard to the storyworlds they represent. Yet, as has repeatedly been emphasized, transmedial narratology would still do well to acknowledge not only the similarities but also the differences in the ways in which conventionally distinct media such as films, comics, and video games represent storyworlds. In her influential discussion of different media's narrative affordances and limitations, Marie-Laure Ryan proposes a "list of narrative *can do* and *can't do* for language, static images, and instrumental music" (*Avatars* 18, original emphases), according to which language can easily "represent temporality, change, causality, thought, and dialogue," "make determinate propositions by referring to specific objects and properties," "represent the difference between actuality and virtuality or counterfactuality," or "evaluate what it narrates and pass judgments on characters" (*Avatars* 19), while encountering difficulties when attempting to precisely represent the spatial relations within a storyworld and being incapable of showing what elements of the storyworld look like. In contrast, images or, rather, pictures can easily represent the spatial relations within a storyworld as well as the "visual appearance of characters and setting," but they cannot "make explicit propositions," represent the "flow of time, thought, interiority, dialogue," "make causal relations explicit," "represent possibility, conditionality, or counterfactuality," or "make evaluations and judgements" (Ryan, *Avatars* 19). Finally, music may "create suspense and desire for what comes next" and generally "arouse emotions," but cannot "represent thought, dialogue, causality, virtuality," "single out distinct objects, characters, or events in a storyworld," or even "tell a specific story" at all, "since its stimuli have no fixed meaning" (Ryan, *Avatars* 19).

Evidently, most types of narrative representation belong in more than one of Ryan's "media families," and, accordingly, she not only concedes that "moving pictures without sound track can be considered a fourth semiotic type" (*Avatars* 18–19) but also emphasizes that "the affordances of language, pictures, and music complement each other, and when they are used together in multichannel media, each of them builds a different facet of the total imaginative experience" (*Avatars* 20–21). Instead of thinking about "semiotic channels" that may be combined in "multi-channel media," though, it seems preferable to examine the specific multimodal configurations that define the mediality of conventionally distinct media such as films, comics, and video games. Originally introduced in linguistic discourse analysis and education studies in order to acknowledge that, while "language is widely taken to be the most significant mode of communication" in traditional linguistics and communication theory, "representation and communication always draw on a multiplicity of modes, all of which have the potential to contribute equally to meaning" (Jewitt 14), the concept of *multimodality* has become widespread within literary theory and media studies.[1] In no small part due to the increasing popularity of the notion that communication is necessarily multimodal, the relation of terms such as "medium" and "mediality" to terms such as "mode" and "multimodality" is conceived in various different and sometimes contradictory ways, but—at least in contemporary narratology—there appears to be a common consensus that the concept of multimodality is particularly useful for describing the "semiotic resources" that define the mediality—and, hence, also the narrative limitations and affordances—of conventionally distinct media (see also Kress, *Multimodality*; Kress and van Leeuwen; van Leeuwen).

Yet, even with this somewhat fragile consensus in place, it remains unclear what exactly a *mode* is supposed to be. Gunther Kress, who remains one of the most influential theorists of multimodality, defines the term as "a socially shaped and culturally given resource for making meaning. *Image, writing, layout, music, gesture, speech, moving image, soundtrack* are examples of modes used in representation and communication" ("What Is Mode?" 54, original emphases). However, as Lars Elleström remarks from the perspective of media studies, Kress's (and Theo van Leeuwen's) "approach to multimodality has its pragmatic advantages but it produces a rather indistinct set of modes that are very hard to compare since they overlap in many ways that are in dire need of further theoretical discussion" (14). Obviously, I cannot provide an extensive explication of the notion of multimodality, but Charles Forceville seems to be right when he emphasizes that defining the term "mode" is "no easy task, because what is labelled as a mode here is a complex of various factors" (382), including, but not limited to, "sensory modalities" and "semiotic resources." Accordingly, I would agree with Ruth Page that "what might count as a mode is an open-ended set, ranging across a number of systems" (6), but will still largely follow Forceville, Page, and Alison Gibbons in what the latter describes as "a cognitive-narratological approach" (10) to multimodality, focusing on "semiotic modes (as opposed to other, specialist uses of the term)" (Page 6) and their specific combination in contemporary films, comics, and video games, which at least partially determines the latters' mediality.[2]

Despite the fact that the audiovisual strategies of narrative representation characteristic for contemporary films, the verbal-pictorial strategies of narrative representation characteristic for contemporary comics, and the interactive strategies of narrative representation characteristic for contemporary video games are each defined by specific multimodal configurations that, in turn, lead to specific sets of representational affordances and limitations, however, the two most salient (semiotic) modes of representation—which are used by films, comics, and video games alike—are defined by the "difference crudely characterized as between 'pictorial' and 'verbal' representation" (Walton 292).[3] While (neo)classical narratology has focused on verbal representation as consisting of what Ferdinand de Saussure has famously characterized as "arbitrary signs," developments within film narratology since the 1980s as well as Mieke Bal's programmatic demand for a "visual narratology" (see Bal, *Narratology* 66–75, 161–170) have led to an increased awareness not only of the differences between verbal and pictorial representation but also of the latter's narrative potential.[4] I do not aim to make any strong claims about what the intersubjective meaning of storyworlds precisely consists of (beyond the observation that it is constructed intersubjectively and communicatively, by referring to representational conventions and hypotheses about reflexive authorial intentions), but I would maintain that these two fundamental modes of representation—verbal or language-based representation as being characterized by a largely conventional or "arbitrary" relation between what is represented and its representation versus pictorial and, perhaps, other modes of representation where the representation is comparatively "closer to perception"—will also lead to the various elements of a storyworld potentially exhibiting (partially) different qualities.

At the very least, this will be true for the situation models and mental models that recipients construct on the basis of narrative representations: I cannot provide an in-depth discussion of mental representations, but it seems uncontroversial to distinguish between *conceptual* and *nonconceptual mental representations*, with the former (mentally) representing "in a way analogous to expressions of natural languages" and the latter (mentally) representing "in a way analogous to drawings, paintings, maps, photographs or movies" (Pitt n. pag.). While there already are a number of different answers to the question of how conceptual or "propositional" mental representations are best conceived, the nature of the kind of nonconceptual or quasi-perceptual mental representations that are also called "mental imagery" has been even more hotly debated within cognitive psychology since the 1980s.

Now, I do not aim to resolve the debate, but I would still suggest that—even when one follows Per Persson in distinguishing between perceptual, referential, and interpretive forms of meaning and meaning making—both the local situations and the global storyworlds represented in multimodal media such as films, comics, and video games cannot generally be reduced to "propositional content" (as perhaps the most standard form of referential meaning) but will usually contain at least some elements of the sensory or perceptual quality provided by pictorial and other nonverbal elements of the narrative representation.[5]

Against this background, it appears even more necessary for a transmedial narratology that aims to remain "media-conscious" to take into account the medium-specific strategies of narrative representation characteristic for media such as films, comics, and video games and to acknowledge that the complex multimodal configurations that define these media significantly complicate the rough distinction between verbal and pictorial representation sketched above. Due to spatial limitations, however, I will have to restrict myself to only a few brief remarks, leaving the detailed examination of audiovisual, verbal-pictorial, and interactive representation to more specialized works in the fields of film studies, comics studies, and game studies. Concisely put, films' *audiovisual representation of storyworlds* is characterized by the use of mise-en-scène, cinematography, montage, and sound; comics' *verbal-pictorial representation of storyworlds* is characterized by the interplay of drawn pictures, words, panel frames, and page layouts; and video games' *interactive representation of storyworlds* is characterized by the combination of interactive simulation, scripted events, and cut-scenes (the latter of which in particular can, of course, integrate multimodal configurations from many other representational media), which are sometimes arranged in a nonlinear narrative structure that may result in a number of very different narrative representations, depending on player performance, player decisions, and similar parameters. While some transmedial mechanisms governing the meaning-making process—such as Marie-Laure Ryan's principle of minimal departure or Kendall L. Walton's principle of charity—can be identified here as well, the medium-specific strategies of narrative representation employed by films, comics, and video games appear to be particularly salient with regard to the representation of local situations. In contradistinction, the ways in which these situations are located within the global storyworld as a whole—that is, the ways that the spatial, temporal, causal, and ontological relations are (or are not) established between various represented situations—generally appear to be more transmedial, since recipients commonly take their cues from what is being represented as opposed to specific elements of the representation in this context.[6]

Considering that narratological approaches have been institutionalized to a far greater extent within film studies than within comics studies and game studies, I will treat the audiovisual representation of storyworlds in films as something like the "default case" of multimodal storytelling in contemporary media culture, against which the medium-specific characteristics of comics' verbal-pictorial representation of storyworlds and video games' interactive representation of storyworlds become visible.[7] This is not to say that the medium-specific strategies of narrative representation employed by contemporary films are not worthy of a more detailed examination, but since several sophisticated accounts of audiovisual representation are already available within film narratology and beyond, there seems to be no need of, say, rehashing the technological or perceptual foundations of how films represent movement. Instead, I would like to offer three analyses of contemporary feature films, focusing less on their use of mise-en-scène, cinematography, montage, and sound to represent local situations than on the comparatively transmedial ways in which the spatial, temporal, causal, and ontological relations are (or are not) established among these situations, eventually resulting in the construction of complex global storyworlds entailing multiple substories and/or ontologically disconnected subworlds.

Let me begin, then, by taking a closer look at Quentin Tarantino's surprise hit *Pulp Fiction*, whose commercial as well as critical success paved the way for larger-budgeted "mind-benders" such as *Fight Club*,

The Sixth Sense, or *A Beautiful Mind*. While the narrative representation in *Pulp Fiction* is not particularly metaleptic, the film still represents a fairly complex arrangement of interrelated stories with a large cast of characters and three major courses of action, so that intersubjectively constructing a more or less consistent storyworld in the case of these kinds of "network narratives"[8] already challenges the spectator's cognitive abilities to a greater degree than in cases where the narrative representation represents a single main character and a unified course of action. The main courses of action in *Pulp Fiction* can be summarized as, first, the "Vincent Vega and Marsellus Wallace's Wife" story told "from the perspective" of Vincent Vega; second, the "Gold Watch" story told "from the perspective" of Butch Coolidge; and, third, the "Bonnie Situation" story told "from the perspective" of Jules Winnfield. However, the events that make up these substories are not represented chronologically but rather within seven nonchronologically arranged segments of comparatively chronological audiovisual representation.

Accordingly, *Pulp Fiction*'s story as the chronological sequence of represented events differs significantly from its plot as the sequence of events in the order of their representation. The latter begins with a segment of audiovisual representation in which the characters known only as Honey Bunny and Pumpkin attempt to rob a diner. This is followed by an analepsis to an earlier situation in which Vincent Vega and Jules Winnfield try to reacquire a mysterious briefcase. After that, there is a prolepsis, marked by a change in Vincent's and Jules's clothes, which stretches from Marsellus Wallace's conversation with Butch to Vincent rescuing Mia Wallace from the effects of an overdose of heroin. Another analepsis (or, more precisely, what initially appears to be another analepsis) follows, in which Captain Koons gives a gold watch to the young Butch and which later turns out to have been a memory-based dream of the adult Butch. After he wakes up, the story is brought to its conclusion: Butch meets up with Fabienne, shoots Vincent, saves Marsellus, and uses Zed's chopper to leave the city together with Fabienne. The plot has not yet concluded, though: instead, another analepsis follows in which Winston Wolf helps Vincent and Jules to clean their car, removing the remains of an inadvertently shot snitch before Jimmie's wife Bonnie comes home. Afterward, Vincent and Jules have breakfast in the very diner that Honey Bunny and Pumpkin try to rob, which is represented "from Jules's perspective" this time around.

As is well established within film studies by now, it took until the mid-1990s for this kind of (non)chronological (re)organization of events on the level of the plot that is not—or at least not primarily— motivated by framing narrators or reminiscing characters to enter the mainstream of "Hollywood filmmaking."[9] As, for example, David Bordwell remarks, "more and more . . . , flashbacks aren't motivated by character memory or reconstruction. This is a change from traditional practice, in which a framing situation would present a character recounting or reflecting on the past. . . . Now, it seems, audiences' familiarity with flashback structures allows filmmakers to delete the memory alibi and move straight between present and past" (*The Way* 90). Even if it could be argued, then, that films such as *Pulp Fiction* have led to recipients' film-specific narrative schemata and expectations becoming more complex with regard to the different possibilities of (non)chronological (re)organization on the level of the plot, an extensive reorganization of story events will still confront the spectator with a certain amount of cognitive challenge. On the one hand, the intersubjective construction of the storyworld as a whole may, at times, be "a very difficult and uncertain process" (Hogan, *Cognitive Science* 123). Yet, on the other hand, even contemporary "mind-benders" use their mise-en-scène as well as other, perhaps more medium-specific cues such as intertitles or changes in the quality of the pictures to help the spectator figure out the structure of the storywold.

One way or another, though, the intersubjective construction of *Pulp Fiction*'s storyworld will remain a comparatively straightforward process, with only the occasional intradiegetic narrator and segments of subjective representation adding narrative complexity. But this is, of course, not true for all "mind-benders" that have been published during the 1990s: David Cronenberg's *eXistenZ*, for example, extensively plays with the blurring of ontological boundaries and the resulting metaleptic effects, even though most if not all of the apparently paradoxical transgressions can be plausibilized (or "naturalized") by the spectator. The premise for *eXistenZ*'s metalepses is established in the film's opening sequence, which represents a situation in which a new hyperrealistic digital game called eXistenZ is introduced to an expectant audience. The—fairly accessible—assumption that such games create "virtual worlds" is the film's point of departure for establishing the complex diegetic structure of its storyworld, leading to a fundamental underdetermination regarding the ontological status of the represented spaces, events, and characters. This, in turn, forces the spectator to repeatedly reevaluate and modify his or her hypotheses regarding the spatial, temporal, causal, and ontological relations between the represented situations within the storyworld as a whole. The supposedly diegetic primary storyworld represented in the opening sequence is initially expanded by the supposedly hypodiegetic secondary storyworld of the intradiegetic digital game eXistenZ, which creates a supposedly hypo-hypodiegetic tertiary storyworld by way of another digital game I will refer to as eXistenZ_2. As the film progresses, however, the supposed diegetic primary storyworld of the opening sequence turns out to have been created by yet another digital game, transCendenZ, and, hence, is to be comprehended as a hypodiegetic secondary instead of a diegetic primary storyworld until further notice—and, of course, this also means that the subworld created by the digital game eXistenZ is revealed to be a hypo-hypodiegetic tertiary storyworld, and the subworld created by the hypo-hypodiegetic digital game eXistenZ_2 transpires to be a hypo-hypo-hypodiegetic quaternary storyworld.

The main characters of *eXistenZ*'s complex global storyworld, Allegra Geller and Ted Pikul, move rather freely between the different subworlds: within the hypodiegetic secondary storyworld created by transCendenZ, they "enter" the hypo-hypodiegetic tertiary storyworld of eXistenZ, before moving on to the hypo-hypo-hypodiegetic quaternary storyworld of eXistenZ_2. When Ted disrupts the game(s), they briefly go back to the hypodiegetic secondary storyworld of transCendenZ before continuing the game and returning to the hypo-hypo-hypodiegetic quaternary storyworld of eXistenZ_2. From there, they move back to the hypo-hypodiegetic tertiary storyworld of eXistenZ, which seems to increasingly meld with the hypo-hypo-hypodiegetic quaternary storyworld of eXistenZ_2—a meltdown that produces obvious metaleptic effects. After they have finished playing the game(s), a (supposedly) final transgression between subworlds is represented, as Allegra and Ted—or their respective alter egos—return to the diegetic primary storyworld in which the digital game transCendenZ is located. While this representation of a complex arrangement of subworlds is interesting in itself—and still fairly unusual in mainstream feature films[10]—the metaleptic character of *eXistenZ* is not primarily established by the—usually clearly marked—main characters' oscillation between subworlds—particularly since the film makes it quite clear that the diegetic, hypodiegetic, hypo-hypodiegetic, and hypo-hypo-hypodiegetic versions of Allegra and Ted are actually not the same characters. This, in turn, means that there is no "real" transgression between ontological borders even though these plausibilized transgressions will still generate metaleptic effects for most if not all recipients. Instead, the film increasingly represents metaleptic "contaminations" of the subworlds that are initially represented as being ontologically disconnected: after Allegra and Ted have returned to the game, various characters within the hypo-hypodiegetic tertiary storyworld of eXistenZ are represented as possessing "unnatural" knowledge with regard to elements of the hypo-hypo-hypodiegetic quaternary storyworld of eXistenZ_2. This epistemic contamination of the two initially ontologically disconnected subworlds spreads until it becomes entirely undecidable whether Allegra and Ted are located within the hypo-hypodiegetic tertiary storyworld of eXistenZ or the hypo-hypo-hypodiegetic quaternary storyworld of eXistenZ_2. The spectator will still be able to easily plausibilize this kind of blending by referring to the "fictional fact" that both subworlds are part of the digital game eXistenZ, but the reason that is given for the strange behavior of the latter—namely, that a virus has spread from the hypo-hypodiegetic tertiary storyworld of eXistenZ to the hypodiegetic secondary storyworld of transCendenZ—will appear genuinely paradoxical as long as the spectator does not know about the existence of transCendenZ.

Even before the final revelation regarding the ontological status of the hypodiegetic secondary storyworld, this fairly strong ontological metalepsis is soon plausibilized through an inversion of its defining causal relations, though: while the characters initially cannot come up with an explanation for the strange behavior of eXistenZ, Allegra later explains the "virtual" virus within the hypo-hypodiegetic tertiary storyworld of eXistenZ as an effect of an "actual" virus within the hypodiegetic secondary storyworld of transCendenZ—which, at this point in the film, is still represented as the diegetic primary storyworld. In retrospect—having watched the whole film, that is— these transgressions can, moreover, easily be explained by reference to the "fictional fact" that both the hypodiegetic secondary storyworld (in which eXistenZ is located) and the hypo-hypodiegetic tertiary storyworld (created by eXistenZ) are part of the digital game transCendenZ located within the diegetic primary storyworld. Interestingly, this plausibilizing strategy also applies to events within the diegetic primary storyworld itself: in the end, even the diegetic appearance of animals such as a well-recognizable scruffy dog and objects such as the bone pistol, which were initially represented as part of the various subworlds of transCendenZ, can be plausibilized by reference to the ability of digital games such as transCendenZ to access their player's memories in order to provide a more intense playing experience. Accordingly, it seems clear that the variety of subworlds as well as the various changes between them render problematic not only the ontological status of the diegetic primary storyworld (which could, of course, be imagined as being constructed by yet another digital game located within a "higher-order" subworld) but also the internal structure of *eXistenZ*'s storyworld as a whole. Just as the spectator in *Pulp Fiction* will have to focus on establishing the spatial, temporal, and causal relations between the represented situations, then, the spectator of *eXistenZ* will primarily have to focus on establishing the causal and ontological relations between them. Yet, despite the resulting complexity of the narrative representation, *eXistenZ* still allows its recipients to construct a more or less consistent storyworld, since most if not all of the supposedly metaleptic transgressions can be plausibilized once the recipient has finished watching the film.

While this book's focus is not on films that blatantly prevent the recipient from intersubjectively constructing a more or less consistent storyworld—David Lynch's *Lost Highway* is usually mentioned at this point, but there are quite a few other examples—I would like to conclude my discussion of complex storyworld representation in contemporary feature films with an examination of yet another well-known example of a film that generally seems to aim at the representation of more or less logically consistent situations but leaves open how exactly these situations relate to each other spatially, temporally, causally, and ontologically: Tom Tykwer's *Run Lola Run*, which uses a variety of sequences with different pictorial qualities—including animated pictures, black-and-white pictures, video pictures, still pictures, and two distinctive red filter sequences—to represent three different versions of Lola's attempt to save her boyfriend Manni. What makes the film particularly interesting from a narratological point of view is that most recipients will not immediately be able to come up with a satisfying explanation as to why *Run Lola Run* represents three versions of the events that eventually lead to Lola saving Manni. On the one hand, there initially is an extradiegetic voice-over narrator offering some pseudo-philosophical reflections on the human condition, but the film does not give any further cues that the temporal "rewinds" are exclusively located on the level of the representation, which would mean that *Run Lola Run* represents three ontologically disconnected courses of action. On the other hand, there are only very few cues—such as Lola's affinity to shattering clocks with her high-pitched cries or certain metaleptic moments[11] in which Lola appears to possess knowledge acquired in previous "playthroughs"[12]—suggesting that someone or something—perhaps Lola or, rather, her unconditional love for Manni—actually "turns back time" on the level of what is represented as part of the storyworld. Not entirely dissimilar to *Lost Highway*, *Run Lola Run* offers another explanation that is closely connected to the way in which Tykwer employs different forms of audiovisual representation: just as black-and-white pictures are used when the audiovisual representation is framed by the intradiegetic verbal narration of either Lola or Manni, video pictures are used to represent situations within the storyworld in which neither Lola nor Manni is present, and still pictures (in the form of postcards and Polaroids) are used to represent (possible) future developments, the two distinctive red filter sequences also provide further cues with regard to the storyworld's internal structure. In both cases, these sequences mark the transition between the disconnected courses of action, but it is worth taking a closer look at their differences. After Lola's first attempt to save Manni has failed and the latter has been shot by the police, the camera zooms on Lola's face, and the audiovisual representation then cuts to a sequence that—using the distinctive red filter—represents Lola and Manni lying in bed, talking about their life and relationship. The conversation ends with Lola stating that she has to make a decision, followed by another cut to a shot of Lola's face—without the red filter—whispering that she does not want to go away. Right after Lola says "stop," the time—either the time of the representation or the represented time of the storyworld—is "turned back" to the point where Lola leaves her mother's flat.

The ambiguity of the audiovisual representation in *Run Lola Run* may support sharply divergent hypotheses about the structure of the represented storyworld—or, more precisely, about the spatial, temporal, causal, and ontological relations among the three represented courses of action—but if the various occurrences of what would then have to be considered metaleptic forms of knowledge prevent us from assuming that the time of the representation is "turned back" by whoever is responsible for the narrative representation in the first place, and the principle of minimal departure prevents us from assuming that the represented time is "turned back" by Lola's sheer will to save Manni, the red filter sequences allow for yet another—if perhaps not particularly optimistic—explanation: after the intradiegetic Lola has been shot, the first red filter sequence could be taken to mark a transition to a hypodiegetic secondary storyworld, which would mean that the second version of Lola's attempt to save Manni only happens as a "near death experience" in the intradiegetic Lola's mind. Likewise, the second red filter sequence could be taken as marking yet another change of "diegetic level," with the third version of Lola's attempt to save Manni happening as yet another hypo-hypodiegetic tertiary "near death experience" within the hypodiegetic Manni's mind.[13] Such a construction of the storyworld would explain the "turning back" of the time as well as the fact that Lola seems to learn from her previous attempts at saving Manni and to increasingly develop certain "supernatural" powers such as averting Schuster's heart attack by laying her hand on him or forcing the world to let her win at roulette.

While *Run Lola Run* uses fairly film-specific markers to communicate the different ontological status of what is represented in the red filter sequences, I would still maintain that contemporary films may not only represent quite complex storyworlds but also that the relations between the represented situations are more commonly established on the level of what is being represented (which would include content markers such as the fact that Vincent and Jules wear different clothes from one shot to the next in *Pulp Fiction* as well as contextual markers such as the sequences in which Allegra and Ted are shown literally "plugging into the game") rather than on the level of the representation (which would include film-specific representational markers such as those used in the red filter sequences in *Run Lola Run* or the dream sequences in *12 Monkeys*, which I discuss in more detail in chapter 7). Since using the kind of content markers that will primarily be relevant here can be described as a comparatively transmedial strategy of narrative representation, then, it seems that the observations made with regard to *Pulp Fiction*, *eXistenZ*, and (if perhaps to a lesser extent) *Run Lola Run* similarly apply to other non-chronological, "multileveled," and metaleptic films such as Greg Marcks's *11:14*, Paul Haggis's *Crash*, Christopher Nolan's *Memento*, and Robert Altman's *Short Cuts* or Michel Gondry's *Eternal Sunshine of the Spotless Mind*, David Fincher's *Fight Club*, Nolan's *Inception*, and Spike Jonze and Charlie Kaufman's *Adaptation.*, as well as to nonchronological, "multileveled," and metaleptic comics such as Alan Moore and Eddie Campbell's *From Hell*, Chris Ware's *Jimmy Corrigan: The Smartest Kid on Earth*, Charles Burns's *Black Hole*, and Frank Miller's *Sin City: Hell and Back* or Marc-Antoine Mathieu's *L'origine*, Moore's *Promethea*, Neil Gaiman's *The Sandman* series, and Mike Carey and Peter Gross's *The Unwritten* series,[14] and to nonchronological, "multileveled," and metaleptic video games such as Bungie's *Halo 2*, Infinity Ward's *Call of Duty 2*, Daedalic Entertainment's *Memoria*, and Hideo Kojima's *Metal Gear Solid 4: Guns of the Patriots* or Remedy's *Alan Wake*, Double Fine's *Psychonauts*, Dontnod's *Remember Me*, and Telltale Games' *Sam and Max: The Devil's Playhouse*. But of course, even if the processes that establish the spatial, temporal, causal, and ontological relations between the represented situations are largely (though not exclusively) transmedial, all of these examples still employ at least partially medium-specific strategies of narrative representation to represent the respective local situations.

The Principle of Charity and Verbal-Pictorial Representation in Contemporary Comics

The processes involved in the representation (and comprehension) of local situations may be more medium-specific than those involved in the intersubjective construction of these represented situations' relations within the global storyworld as a whole, but there are quite a few transmedial aspects to the former as well: as I already established in the previous chapter, a large part of these processes can be described using Ryan's principle of minimal departure (which refers not only to real-world knowledge but also to knowledge about genre conventions that is utilized in the process of narrative comprehension) and Walton's principle of charity (which is particularly relevant where it refers to the communicative rules and representational conventions that govern representational correspondence). In light of the evident transmediality of Ryan's principle of minimal departure, however, I would like to limit myself to giving a few examples of how Walton's principle of charity is applied transmedially in the context of verbal and pictorial representation before moving to more medium-specific cases. In fact, Walton discusses what has become a standard example to illustrate that verbal representation (which is evidently employed across media) may suggest fairly complex forms of representational correspondence in some cases:

> Most of us will probably prefer not to allow that fictionally Othello is a great literary talent, and even to affirm that fictionally he is not. But this only shifts the paradox. Is it fictional that Othello lacks special literary talent and yet is capable of improvising superb verse while distraught? Shall we deny that fictionally Othello's words "Had it pleased heaven / To try me with affliction" . . . are a superb verse, even though it is manifestly true that they are? Or shall we go so far as to deny that fictionally those are Othello's words? Perhaps it is fictional, rather, that Othello utters an unspecified vernacular paraphrase of the words Shakespeare's actor enunciates. (181–182)

Of course, the problem is not limited to Shakespeare. While character speech tends to be represented using at least partially medium-specific strategies in contemporary films, comics, and video games, the general principle that "representation is *not* verbatim" (Fludernik, *The Fictions* 356, original emphasis) and that the "gap" between *representing* and *represented character speech* can, indeed, be quite pronounced still applies in a fairly transmedial way. There may be no intersubjectively valid way to construct what these characters are "actually"—or, rather, *fictionally*—saying in the represented storyworld, but it still seems clear, for example, that even though the English language is used for representing character speech, the characters in Louis Leterrier's blockbuster film *Clash of the Titans*, Frank Miller's graphic novel *300*, or SCE's action-adventure *God of War* are not represented as "actually" speaking English, since the settings of all of these narrative works are easily recognizable as more or less strongly fictionalized versions of ancient Greece.

Similarly, in the case of pictorial representation across media, the representational correspondence may be complicated or even collapse entirely due to comparatively transmedial representational conventions. A fairly straightforward example is the use of color: Michel Hazanavicius's *The Artist* uses black-and-white pictures for the most part, but there are no good reasons for spectators to imagine the film's storyworld to be black and white. Instead, spectators will assume that the storyworld of *The Artist* is "like our world" (at least "by default"), and this assumption is further reinforced since none of the characters thematize what would certainly be a striking lack of color in a world otherwise appearing to largely conform to our (historicized) real-world expectations. Likewise, readers do not assume that the storyworld of *Sin City* is sometimes monochromatic and sometimes colorful, even though its verbal-pictorial representation most certainly is. Just as the characters in *The Artist* do not acknowledge the lack of color as part of their storyworld, for example, none of the other characters represented in *Sin City: Hell and Back* comment on Deliah's blue coat, which strongly hints at the "fictional fact" that it does not make her stand out as much within the storyworld as it does on the level of narrative representation. Similarly, in video games: when Cellar Door Games' action role-playing game *Rogue Legacy* uses a sepia filter to represent the initial gameplay sequence, most players will understand that this marks the location of the represented events at an earlier point in storyworld time but does not suggest that the storyworld was sepia-colored back then. This kind of pictorial charity or indirect representational correspondence also applies to representational qualities of pictures more generally. A spectator who, watching *Run Lola Run*, would attempt to construct a storyworld where Lola is miraculously transformed from a flesh-and-blood human being to a cartoon character, Pinocchio-style, would clearly misunderstand the film's audiovisual representation (see figure 1).

What about medium-specific charity, then? Since the question of how the representation relates to the storyworld is particularly complex in the case of video games, I will begin by examining a selection

Fig. 1. Animated picture in *Run Lola Run*

of film- and comics-specific aspects of the principle of charity as it relates to complex cases of representational correspondence, focusing primarily on pictorial elements of the representation in order to keep the discussion brief. Even with the increasing ubiquity of computer-generated imagery (and other kinds of special effects; see, e.g., Flückiger, *Visual Effects*), Currie's distinction between "representation-by-origin" and "representation-by-use" seems particularly fruitful to explain some common cases of film-specific charity (see Currie, *Narratives* 12–21).[15] Perhaps the most salient of these is constituted by the fact that many films use actors to represent characters and that, hence, at least some of the elements of the audiovisual representation of characters—their body and their voice, in particular—appears to be somewhat contingent, allowing for easy external explanations of certain features of the representation (see also Dyer on "star images"). It would, for example, be quite misguided to ask for internal explanations of why both Charlie and Donald Kaufman in *Adaptation.* look like the actual actor Nicolas Cage. Likewise with regard to the represented spaces and places (since the sets that are "represented-by-origin" across film genres are commonly, and sometimes rather obviously, not the fictional settings that are "represented-by-use") as well as to the represented actions and sequences of events (say, related to drugs, sex, and violence, whose "representation-by-origin" would be problematic in various ways). While it seems unlikely that substance abuse in Terry Gilliam's *Fear and Loathing in Las Vegas*, the fistfights in David Fincher's *Fight Club*, and the sexual encounters in Steve McQueen's *Shame* would have been authentically "represented-by-origin," this does not diminish what the shots in question are meant to "represent-by-use." And, of course, the fact that not a single situation in Chris Columbus's *Harry Potter and the Philosopher's Stone* was actually filmed at Hogwarts does not prevent the film from fictionally representing Hogwarts. In all of these cases, though, even when recipients suspect that the audiovisual representation of the storyworld should not be taken to be "verbatim," the inferences they can draw regarding the "actual" elements of the storyworld will be fairly limited, since there usually are no alternative "means of access."[16]

Similar observations hold with regard to comics, where the use of drawn pictures allows for a wide range of representational styles between cartoonesque abstraction and detailed realism, which is further complicated by more or less subtle strategies of the combination of words and pictures as well as the combination of framed pictures into sequences of panels within page layouts of varying regularity, flexibility, and density. For example, it seems uncontroversial to assume that characters represented in contemporary comics (usually) do not consist of lines (as their pictorial representation generally does), that the flow of time represented in those comics (usually) does not behave significantly differently than it does in the storyworlds represented by contemporary films (although the events in question are represented one picture at a time), and that there are, for the most part, quite a few conventionalized devices (such as speech balloons, thought bubbles, narration boxes, sound words, or movement lines) that are not part of the represented situations even though it may appear that way to an uninformed observer at first glance. Likewise, it seems clear that the represented situations are commonly meant to be more detailed than their representation (both with regard to the represented spaces and with regard to the representation of storyworld sounds). While the ways in which the principle of charity can be applied (and the resulting typical forms of representational correspondence) may take at least partially medium-specific forms in films and comics, then, the basic problem sketched by Walton with regard to the question of what Othello "actually" says within the storyworld clearly remains in place.

Just as spectators will usually not speculate about how a character in a film "really looks" or "really sounds" despite the fact that at least some of his or her features will evidently be based on the actor who plays the role, it is often difficult or, indeed, impossible to clearly distinguish between presentational and representational aspects of the pictures in comics due to what Martin Schüwer describes as the latters' "inextricable interrelation of materiality and semiotic content of the pictorial form" (23, my translation from the German). Not entirely dissimilar to Walton, Schüwer goes on to ask: "Should one attribute the caricaturesque style of Charles M. Schulz's *Peanuts* exclusively to the discourse and imagine that Charlie Brown and Lucy look entirely different within the narrated world?" (23, original emphasis, my translation from the German). While Schüwer (as well as Jens Balzer, to whose discussion of George Herriman's *Krazy Kat* the former extensively refers) would most likely answer the question in the negative, I am not so sure. From my point of view, the main reason against imagining characters that are represented in particularly cartoonesque or caricaturesque drawing styles as looking partially or even entirely different on the level of the storyworld would be that readers of comics such as *Peanuts* usually do not have an alternative "means of access" beyond the verbal-pictorial representation.[17] However, just as most spectators will understand that *Run Lola Run* does not claim that the outer appearance of Lola within the storyworld changes in any significant way during the stretches of storyworld time represented by the film, for example, most readers of *The Sandman* will understand that it would be pointless to ask why the outer appearance of the main character, Dream, has "changed so much," when what actually changes are the drawing styles of the various artists with whom Neil Gaiman has collaborated over the course of the comics series. Here as elsewhere, though, readers will need reasons to apply medium-specific charity to the verbal-pictorial representation.

Another interesting (if perhaps once more comparatively transmedial) area where the "gap" between presentation and representation or, more precisely, between the level of representation and the level of what is being represented becomes particularly visible is the use of metaphorical strategies of representation in nonfictional graphic memoirs such as Art Spiegelman's *Maus*, David B.'s *Epileptic*, and Bryan Talbot's *The Tale of One Bad Rat*. In cases of fictional serial representation that feature distinctly different drawing styles such as those to be found in Neil Gaiman's *The Sandman* series, the previous installments of the series provide the background against which the limits of representational correspondence become visible. Yet, in graphic memoirs that combine a metaphorical with a nonfictional mode of representation, it is the readers' actual world knowledge that provides this "standard of comparison." Let me use Spiegelman's well-known (auto)biographical graphic novel to illustrate how complex the question of what is actually being represented can become in the case of *metaphorical representations*.[18] While the metaphorical nature of the representation and the references to the Shoah are obvious in this case as well, in the original three-page version of "Maus" that appeared in *Funny Animals* in 1972, the represented storyworld seems, indeed, to be populated by anthropomorphic mice and cats (see figure 2). This is different, however, in the two-part graphic novel *Maus* that was published in 1986 and 1991, whose storyworld is populated not with anthropomorphic mice, cats, and pigs, but with Jews, non-Jewish Germans, and Poles who are merely represented as mice, cats, and pigs (see figure 3). The established medium- and genre-specific representational conventions of comics in general and the graphic novel in particular certainly made it easier to realize this large-scale metaphor, but there is obviously more than just medium-specific charity involved here.

A reader who tries to understand the verbal-pictorial representation in *Maus* too literally will generate a number of inconsistencies.

Fig. 2. Anthropomorphic cats and mice in "Maus"

Fig. 3. Metaphorically represented Germans and Jews in *Maus*

First, there is the problem that *Maus* is paratextually marked as nonfictional and that the existence of anthropomorphic animals is likely not part of the actual world knowledge of most readers. Second, and more importantly, though, not only are the supposed "animals" consistently identified as Jews, non-Jewish Germans, and Poles instead of as mice, cats, and pigs but one can also find some sequences where Jews that pretend to be Poles are represented as wearing pig masks (see figure 4). Now, if the reader were to take what appears to be represented here at first glance (too) literally, a number of "silly questions"[19] would present themselves: Why is the "Polish pig" not noticing the clearly visible mask that Vladek is wearing? And why does Vladek have such a mask on him while hiding from the "Nazi cats" in the first place? By far the more consistent comprehension seems to be that what is represented here are not anthropomorphic animals but rather quite regular human beings whose affiliation with certain social groups is represented by more or less "visible" but nevertheless exclusively metaphorical "masks." These "masks," in other

Fig. 4. Metaphorical pig masks in *Maus*

words, do not exist within the situations that are represented as part of the storyworld; they are primarily a part of the presentation. So, as I hope my brief discussion of Spiegelman's influential work has served to illustrate, even if it arguably does not (yet) require more context-oriented forms of interpretation, the comprehension and intersubjective construction of referential meaning may occasionally entail complex processes of inference based on our knowledge about more or less medium-specific representational conventions and our hypotheses about authorial intentions that allow us to "ignore" certain aspects of a given narrative representation (or, perhaps more precisely, acknowledge that the representational correspondence may turn out to be more complex than we might have initially assumed).

Leaving the medium-specific aspects of comics' verbal-pictorial representation aside for the moment, I want to emphasize, once again, that comics in general and the graphic novels that have become increasingly successful since the late 1980s in particular can—and in fact often do—represent complex storyworlds with multiple "diegetic levels" and nonchronological plots, commonly combining several stories and generating metaleptic effects both within the represented storyworld and on the level of narrative representation. More specifically, well-known works such as Will Eisner's *A Contract with God*, Art Spiegelman's *Maus*, Alan Moore's *Watchmen* or *The League of Extraordinary Gentlemen*, Neil Gaiman's *The Sandman* series or *Batman: Whatever Happened to the Caped Crusader?*, and Frank Miller's *Sin City* series or *Batman: The Dark Knight Returns* have made an increased level of formal complexity available to American mainstream comics—though there is, perhaps, no author who has done this quite as extensively and successfully as Chris Ware. Accordingly, while the works of Eisner, Spiegelman, Moore, Gaiman, and Miller may have been more influential for the development of what one could call the classical graphic novel,[20] Chris Ware's *Jimmy Corrigan: The Smartest Kid on Earth* provides a particularly impressive example of the ways in which comics may not only play with and subvert the representational conventions that define the medium but also use these conventions to represent spatially, temporally, causally, and ontologically disconnected situations in ways that require quite a bit of attention and complex inferential processes from the reader in order to locate them within a more encompassing storyworld. In fact, *Jimmy Corrigan* is widely acknowledged as a formal masterpiece,[21] but it is its use of nonchronological, subjective, and unreliable narrative representation that makes it particularly interesting in the context of the present book.

On a fundamental level, *Jimmy Corrigan* can be described as representing two interrelated stories, resulting in a decidedly nonchronological plot. On the one hand, the graphic novel represents the adult Jimmy Corrigan's attempts to reconnect with his absent father, James William Corrigan, who had abandoned Jimmy and his mother at a young age and who eventually dies while Jimmy is visiting him. On the other hand, this story is intertwined with the earlier events surrounding Jimmy's grandfather, James Reed Corrigan, being abandoned by Jimmy's great-grandfather, William Corrigan, while the two of them visit Chicago's Columbian Exposition in 1893. Interestingly, even though *Jimmy Corrigan* not only makes extensive use of an extradiegetic narrator but also commonly represents the subjective imaginations, memories, and dreams of Jimmy, the encompassing analepses to James Reed's early childhood experiences are not too explicitly "anchored" by the narrator or the memory of another character (such as Jimmy), often leaving it to the reader to figure out that what is represented cannot be part of the "present" that Jimmy experiences. Just as in *Pulp Fiction*, the nonchronological plot as such does not yet lead to the establishment of additional "diegetic levels" or subworlds, since both Jimmy's attempts to reconnect with his father, James William, and James Reed being abandoned by *his* father, William, are represented as part of the diegetic primary storyworld. As I have already noted, however, *Jimmy Corrigan* also extensively represents the imaginations, memories, and dreams of Jimmy, thereby establishing a variety of hypodiegetic secondary storyworlds.

In fact, it could be argued that Ware's formal inventiveness is focused primarily on the representation of Jimmy's subjective experience of the situations of which he is a part, with the combination of words and pictures, the use of conventional strategies of subjective representation such as thought bubbles (or the lack thereof), and even the size of the panels and their arrangement in occasionally rather intricate page layouts contributing to giving the reader an impression not only of what Jimmy thinks but also of how he feels. While some of these subjective representations are clearly marked, it is *Jimmy Corrigan*'s use of unmarked subjective representation that can be particularly disorienting: Ware commonly employs sequences of panels or even single panels representing situations whose spatial, temporal, causal, and ontological relations to the previously represented situations cannot be easily established. In some cases, these changes of represented situations turn out to have been mere analepses (e.g., when the verbal-pictorial representation starts representing the story of Jimmy's grandfather, James Reed), but it is by far more common that the only way in which situations that are represented as spatially, temporally, and causally disconnected can be integrated into the storyworld as a whole is by treating them as representations of hypodiegetic secondary storyworlds "inside the mind" of Jimmy (i.e., as his ontologically disconnected memories, dreams, and imaginations).

Take, for example, the forty-five pages, located roughly after the first quarter of the plot has unfolded, that represent how Jimmy and his father visit a doctor after the former has been hit by a delivery van. On the first three pages, the verbal-pictorial representation uses words (as well as some pictures) that "overlay" the verbal-pictorial representation within the panels to represent Jimmy's thoughts, allowing the reader to "see" how he attempts to compose a letter to his father (triggered by a sign that warns of deer, which leads Jimmy's train of thought to begin a letter with the homonymous "Dear Dad"), tries to decide whether the real deer he sees shortly thereafter may be dangerous (he decides they are not), and remains largely oblivious of the delivery truck driving toward him (and which, as the reader will easily be able to infer from the following sequences, must have mainly hit the sign that warns of deer, merely brushing Jimmy) (see figure 5). Instead of directly representing the consequences of the crash between Jimmy and the delivery van, though, the next five pages represent

Fig. 5. Jimmy and the delivery van in *Jimmy Corrigan: The Smartest Kid on Earth*

various situations in which the former plays around with his tape recorder (recording birdsong and the conversation of strangers) and his telephone (prank calling his mother with a changed voice), but due to the lack of any conventional representational or content markers, it initially remains unclear whether this sequence of panels is meant to represent the experience of the unconscious Jimmy in some way (i.e., a dream, a memory, or a fantasy that would make the represented situations part of a hypodiegetic secondary storyworld) or is merely an analepsis to an earlier part of the diegetic primary storyworld.

However, this initial ambiguity is resolved on the next pages, which represent Jimmy lying in the street in front of the delivery van, slowly coming to his senses while the driver of the van and his father take a look at him. This time, Jimmy's subjective perception of the situation is represented pictorially instead of verbally, with the first panel using a faded turquoise to represent a combination of elements from

Jimmy's dream/imagination/memory located within a hypodiegetic secondary storyworld and the "actual" situation located within the diegetic primary storyworld, while the sixth panel represents the van driver as a masked superhero instead of as just a guy with a red cap (see figure 6). This is followed by five pages representing a spatially, temporally, and causally entirely disconnected situation which is focused on the experience of a man (who might be Jimmy's great-grandfather, William) during what is, perhaps, the American Civil War. This time, there is no indication that the change in represented situation is anything but an analepsis, connected to Jimmy's "present" only through the fact that both men are in need of medical treatment and that, in both situations, a very similar-looking bird is represented building its nest nearby. After the reader has thus been returned to Jimmy's "present," the remaining pages focus on representing him and his father during their visit to the doctor. Once more, though,

Fig. 6. Faded turquoise color scheme and other markers of subjectivity in *Jimmy Corrigan*

98   *Storyworlds across Media*

several single panels as well as sequences of panels represent Jimmy's hypodiegetic memories and imaginations instead of the diegetic primary storyworld: Some of these panels—his memory of having a bleeding nose in school, his imagination of visiting Disneyland with his father,[22] his memory of being rejected by a co-worker called Peggy, and what is most likely (just) his imagination of sitting with a girl in a park—are representationally marked by the use of the faded turquoise color scheme also employed in the first panel that represented Jimmy's subjective perspective after he was hit by the delivery van. Yet other segments of subjective representation remain largely unmarked, representationally, leaving it to the reader to figure out the relation between the represented situations using content markers: this includes extended sequences in which Jimmy remembers Thanksgiving with his mother (see figure 7), fantasizes about the nurse seducing and subsequently marrying him, and imagines being able

Fig. 7. Jimmy remembering Thanksgiving in *Jimmy Corrigan*

to fly, all of which will generate at least some confusion in the reader, even though these situations can eventually be located (exclusively) within the hypodiegetic secondary storyworld of Jimmy's consciousness as well.

This brief discussion of *Jimmy Corrigan* should have already illustrated not only that comics can use a range of more or less innovative strategies of verbal-pictorial representation to represent storyworlds but that these storyworlds can also be considerably complex, entailing the representation of a variety of spatially, temporally, causally, and ontologically disconnected situations that are represented using nonchronological plots and located on multiple "diegetic levels." While *Jimmy Corrigan* arguably could be considered to be part of the mainstream of contemporary graphic novels by now, I would like to take a closer look at a second, perhaps more uncontroversially classical example, namely, the repeatedly mentioned *The Sandman* series, which further exemplifies how graphic novels may use strategies of verbal-pictorial, narratorial, and subjective representation to represent storyworlds whose internal structures are no less complex than those of the storyworlds represented by contemporary films. *The Sandman* tells the story of Dream, one of the seven Endless and the anthropomorphic personification of dreams, who, in 1916, is captured by the magus Roderick Burgess and held as a prisoner for seventy years until an oversight on the part of Roderick's son Alex allows Dream to escape in 1986, take revenge on his captor (or, rather, his captor's son), and start to rebuild his kingdom, The Dreaming. As has already been mentioned, Gaiman's collaboration with a variety of artists (most if not all of whom are of considerable industry fame themselves) has led to a remarkable variety of drawing styles, including a host of fairly different pictorial representations of the series' main character—but the series' long running time has also generated quite a bit of narrative complexity on the level of the storyworld.

Over the course of the seventy-five magazine issues, collected in ten trade paperback volumes, a variety of different stories located in the series' storyworld are told, but while Dream is not always at the center of events, *The Sandman* arguably remains a series about dreams, even in those parts of the narrative representation that focus on other characters. Thus, *The Sandman* tends to use various kinds of narratorial representation and other more or less explicit markers to establish the spatial, temporal, and causal relations of the represented situations somewhat more clearly than *Jimmy Corrigan* does, yet some of the more independent stories—particularly those collected in *The Sandman: Dream Country*, *The Sandman: Fables and Reflections*, and part of *The Sandman: The Wake*—will not always be easily located within the series' storyworld as a whole. Perhaps more importantly for the purpose of the present chapter, though, the series' focus on dreams and The Dreaming leads to quite a few changes in "diegetic level." Despite the fact that these changes are usually marked clearly, Dream's ability to traverse the boundaries between the storyworld's "factual domain" and the supposedly hypodiegetic secondary storyworlds of characters' dreams tends to complicate matters, leading to a number of metaleptic effects.[23]

The first volume of the series, *Preludes and Nocturnes*, already contains a variety of panels and sequences of panels that represent supposedly hypodiegetic dreams of characters located within the diegetic primary storyworld and repeatedly demonstrates Dream's ability to enter these dreams. While the dreams of characters who are located within the diegetic primary storyworld of a given narrative work would—at least within the framework sketched in the preceding chapter—usually be described as hypodiegetic secondary storyworlds, *The Sandman* destabilizes the ontological boundaries between the "factual domain" of the diegetic primary storyworld and the dreams of the characters located in it, establishing the realm of The Dreaming (which is said to consist of the totality of dreams dreamed in the storyworld) as an ontologically disconnected part of the storyworld that nevertheless does not necessarily (or not exclusively) have to be conceived as being located on a different "diegetic level." Despite the explanation that the series offers, then, the transgressions of the boundaries between the diegetic primary storyworld and The Dreaming—which are not limited to Dream entering the dreams of various characters, but also occur, for example, in the form of the escaped nightmares in *The Sandman: The Doll's House* and several other such transgressions in the course of the series—may nevertheless be described as a mild form of ontological metalepsis.

However, the complex internal structure of *The Sandman*'s storyworld is further complicated by its seriality, which in turn may be considered a defining (though of course not necessary) feature of the medium: loosely based on DC's 1974–1976 *The Sandman* series, the storyworld of *The Sandman*—published under DC's Vertigo imprint—retains a complex and somewhat uneasy relationship to the greater "DC universe" in general and the former "versions" of *The Sandman* in particular. Among the comics-specific "guest appearances" to be found in *Preludes and Nocturnes* are not only a number of well-known characters such as John Constantine (who had first appeared 1985 in issue 37 of *Swamp Thing*) and Doctor Destiny (who had first appeared 1961 in issue 5 of *Justice League of America*) but also various well-recognizable places such as the Arkham Asylum (which had first appeared 1974 in issue 258 of *Batman*) or the Manhattan Embassy of the Justice League International (the latter of which had first appeared 1987 in issue 1 of *Justice League*). This kind of "serial transfictionality,"[24] which defines many of the comics published by both DC and Marvel (see also Kukkonen, "Navigating Infinite Earths"), cannot happily be described as a metaleptic phenomenon, however, despite the fact that it contributes to the complexity of contemporary comics storytelling as well as to the subversion or, at least, problematization of traditional notions of "the single work" that seems particularly characteristic for the comics medium, even though it also occurs in film and video games (as well as in literary texts and television, of course).[25]

Another more recent example that also regularly generates metaleptic effects by allowing for transgressions between supposedly ontologically disconnected "diegetic levels" is Mike Carey and Peter Gross's *The Unwritten* series. While the transgression of borders in *The Sandman* occurs between the "factual domain" of the storyworld and The Dreaming, *The Unwritten* focuses on transgressions between the "factual domain" of the storyworld and the "realm of stories." Yet the similarities are quite striking, as the plot of *Tommy*

Taylor and the Bogus Identity and the volumes following it revolves not only around Wilson Taylor's *Tommy Taylor* novel series (whose stories about a boy wizard and his friends fighting against the evil vampire Count Ambrosius entail a plethora of thinly veiled intertextual references to the *Harry Potter* series), significant parts of whose storyworld are represented using "quoted" verbal narration as well as "illustrating" verbal-pictorial representation, and Wilson's "real" son Tom Taylor, who increasingly seems to resemble Tommy Taylor in a fairly peculiar case of metaleptic contamination of the diegetic primary storyworld, but also around the interconnected "realm of stories," which is manipulated by both Wilson and Tom, on the one hand, and the sinister Pullman and his Order of The Unwritten, who have long recognized the power of stories and use it to manipulate the way of the (story)world, on the other. Of course, the highly nonchronological and "multileveled" plot of *The Unwritten* is considerably more complex and the spatial, temporal, causal, and ontological relations between the represented situations that constitute the series' fiercely metaleptic (albeit, for the most part, transparently plausibilized) storyworld are considerably more convoluted than my previous brief remarks may have suggested.

Yet, instead of going into further detail regarding the storyworld's global structure, I would like to emphasize an aspect of the series that illustrates one of the main points of this chapter rather well: since narrative representations across media usually represent ontologically disconnected situations either by reference to some kind of internal mental representation of a character (such as a dream or a fantasy) or to some kind of external narrative representation within the storyworld (such as those that might be provided by a novel or a video game), metalepses in storyworlds such as those of the comics series of *The Sandman* or *The Unwritten* (as well as those of feature films such as Christopher Nolan's *Inception* or video games such as Remedy's *Alan Wake*, the latter of which I will discuss below) usually offer their recipients fairly conventionalized ways to plausibilize the apparently paradoxical transgressions. Just as many of the metaleptic transgressions between The Dreaming and the "factual domain" of the storyworld in *The Sandman* are plausibilized by reference to the supernatural abilities of Dream of the Endless, *The Unwritten* uses a number of more or less subtle strategies to introduce the notion that the interconnected "realm of stories" can be manipulated by some people, including Tom.

One of the less subtle devices that *The Unwritten* uses to this end is a doorknob that Wilson (who appears to have moved into the "realm of stories" completely) has allowed Tom to find and which enables him to jump into and out of the storyworlds of various well-known narrative works that are all somehow connected in the "realm of stories." The doorknob and the associated ability of "story hopping" play an important role throughout the series, but the latter is perhaps most impressively represented in the series' fourth volume, *Leviathan*, where Tom is "sucked" into the storyworld of Herman Melville's *Moby-Dick* (which contains a version of Captain Ahab that more than a little resembles Wilson) and "breaks" the story by "taking over" the verbal narration before managing to escape to the storyworld of Sindbad by using the doorknob on the ocean—which is explicitly plausibilized by Tom's newfound acquaintance, Frankenstein's Monster, who remarks that "the *ocean* flows through many stories." The decidedly metaleptic and more generally metareferential strategies that *The Unwritten* employs serve to illustrate once more, then, that not only contemporary films but also contemporary comics may represent narratively complex global storyworlds whose local situations are spatially, temporally, causally, and ontologically related in ways that require the reader to pay quite a bit of attention during narrative comprehension in order to construct an intersubjectively plausible version of the respective comic's referential meaning.

Nonlinear Narrative Structures and Interactive Representation in Contemporary Video Games

If there is a broad consensus that narrative feature film is one of the dominant forms within the medium of film and that graphic novels can be considered a particularly complex form within the predominantly narrative medium of comics, the question of video games' narrativity is generally deemed somewhat more problematic, even though most video game theorists will by now agree that the single-player modes of contemporary video games regularly represent spaces, events, and characters, and tend to locate these elements in increasingly complex storyworlds.[26] Still, just as with films and comics, a more in-depth consideration of the specific mediality of video games with regard to the narrative strategies they prototypically employ is necessary—in fact, it is arguably even more important with respect to the medium-specific ways in which video games may represent storyworlds than it is with respect to the medium-specific ways in which films or comics may represent storyworlds, since what could be roughly described as video games' *interactivity* and *nonlinearity* result in a number of specific challenges when it comes to the intersubjective construction of storyworlds.[27]

In his influential examination of the relation between video game rules and video games' fictionality (or, rather, *representationality*), for example, Jesper Juul observes that the worlds that appear to be represented in video games often turn out to be not only incomplete but also incoherent, which leads him to argue that "by *game conventions, the player is aware that it is optional to imagine the fictional world of the game*" (*Half-Real* 141, original emphasis). It is, indeed, important to acknowledge that video games may entail large segments where "the narrative design is not the focus of the player's attention" (Ryan, *Avatars* 196) and that it is a common practice of the players of contemporary narrative video games such as Bungie's first-person shooter *Halo*, Remedy's action-adventure *Alan Wake*, or Bioware's role-playing game *Dragon Age: Origins* to skip cut-scenes and dialogues (if the game allows them to). Despite the fact that these observations might seem to resonate well with Juul's thesis that the construction of a mental representation of a storyworld while playing a narrative video game is sometimes optional (or, more precisely, that the importance of video games' storyworlds for the gameplay experience varies across genres as well as from player to player, since different player types focus on different kinds of experience when playing video games),[28] I would maintain that the problem should not be reduced to the game "inviting" the player to construct such a storyworld and the player being able to "refuse the invitation and still play the game" (Juul, *Half-Real* 139).

Instead, I would stress that incomplete and incoherent representations do not necessarily result in incomplete and incoherent storyworlds. Accordingly, I would argue that the inconsistencies discussed by Juul are mainly connected to the mediality of narrative video games and that at least some of these inconsistencies require the application of medium-specific charity based on knowledge about contemporary video games' representational conventions, allowing players to recognize that some elements of the gameplay are not meant to be represented as part of the respective game's storyworld. Again, this complication and partial subversion of traditional notions of representational correspondence is connected to video games' interactivity and nonlinearity. The representation of simulated gameplay may cue players to construct mental representations of something resembling a storyworld (and many video games may be understood as being intended to cue players to construct these kinds of mental representations), but most players will recognize that the resulting mental representations may differ significantly from player to player and from playing session to playing session (which would suggest that perhaps not all elements of the gameplay are meant to contribute to the representation of the intersubjective communicative construct of the storyworld to the same extent). Put bluntly, it seems somewhat unlikely that a player's decision to let the avatars of *Halo* or *Alan Wake* run in circles for half an hour contributes to the representation of the characters of the Master Chief or Alan Wake in the same way as, for example, the games' cut-scenes do.

Aiming at a better understanding of these complex processes of intersubjective storyworld construction, some additional remarks on how precisely contemporary video games use interactive representations to represent local situations and global storyworlds are in order. Most crucially, video games' interactivity complicates and at least partially subverts our traditional notions of representational correspondence because the representation of spaces, events, and characters in video games is not predetermined to the same extent as it is in films and comics. Contemporary video games commonly use a variety of strategies of prototypically narrative representation such as cut-scenes or scripted sequences of events, and the events thus presented are generally highly determined *before* the game is played, yet the actual gameplay mainly consists of representations of events that are determined *while* the game is played so that the mode in which what may be called ludic events are represented is, perhaps, more precisely characterized as interactive simulation than as narrative representation.[29] The player and his or her actions are doubtless of central importance in most video games, but the range of possible game actions and the resulting gameplay are primarily defined by the rules of the game.

Put succinctly, the interactive simulation of the gameplay in contemporary video games can be described as being determined by four kinds of game rules: the game mechanics, the game goals, the possibilities of interaction that a game affords its players, and the rules of representation that determine how the simulated gameplay is represented.[30] Ludic events emerge through the rule-governed ludic interaction of the player with the game spaces and are represented during this interaction according to certain rules of representation. Even though the game constructs the frame within which the gameplay will be realized, then, ludic events are not determined before the game is played. Nevertheless, it should be stressed that the distinction between *rule-governed interactive simulation* and *predetermined narrative representation* as two fairly different modes of representation does not necessarily imply that only prototypically narrative elements such as cut-scenes and scripted sequences of events are contributing to the representation of a video game's storyworld. In fact, the way in which storyworlds are represented in contemporary video games cannot and should not be reduced to either interactive simulation or narrative representation, since it is constituted precisely by the complex interplay between these two modes of representation.[31]

As far as noninteractive and, hence, more prototypically narrative elements are concerned, cinematographic sequences remain most common, with "pre-rendered" cut-scenes increasingly being replaced by "in-engine" cut-scenes that allow for a greater degree of customization. However, following Hugh Hancock, the term "cut-scene" can be used to refer to any noninteractive element in a video game that is used to either contribute to the unfolding of the story or, more generally, to flesh out the storyworld in which the game is situated (see also Klevjer, "In Defense"). Since contemporary video games are capable of "reproducing" or "remediating" the multimodal configurations characteristic for most of the more established narrative media,[32] one can also find a variety of nonfilmic cut-scenes such as the still pictures that are accompanied by elements of verbal narration in Blizzard's real-time strategy game *Warcraft III: Reign of Chaos* and Bioware's role-playing game *Neverwinter Nights* (see figure 8) or the comics sequences in Ubisoft's first-person shooter *XIII* and Remedy's third-person shooter *Max Payne* (see figure 9). What these different forms of cut-scenes generally have in common is that the player's opportunity for participation usually does not extend beyond the decision to cancel the cut-scene. Hence, these noninteractive elements of video games are generally separated quite clearly from the actual gameplay.

Cut-scenes still are an important strategy of narrative representation for many contemporary video games, but predetermined events

Fig. 8. Pictorial representation and verbal narration in *Neverwinter Nights*

Fig. 9. Verbal-pictorial representation and verbal narration in *Max Payne*

are increasingly represented within the actual game spaces as well, allowing the players to continue to interact with the game while the predetermined events take place. In other words, the representation of these kinds of scripted events or sequences of events can be just as predetermined as the representations of events or sequences of events in cut-scenes, but the former are represented simultaneously to the ludic events of the actual gameplay.[33] In that sense, narrative elements in video games usually not only contribute to the unfolding of a story and the fleshing-out of a storyworld but also are used to convey information about the ludic structure of the game, that is, the game's rules and goals. On a comparatively general level, narrative elements in contemporary video games may, moreover, be used to communicate certain systems of norms and values, an ideological or evaluative perspective that the player may draw on in order to make inferences about the game goals as well as the actions necessary to progress in or win the game.[34]

In the context of the present study, however, I would like to limit myself to illustrating how contemporary video games may use cut-scenes as well as scripted events in order to give their players specific information about particular game mechanics and game goals, using Bungie's first-person shooter *Halo* as my first example. In *Halo*'s singleplayer mode, each of the levels is introduced by a cut-scene that contributes to the unfolding of the story, locates the following game spaces in the game's storyworld, and/or summarizes the currently active game goals, but the game begins with a particularly extensive cinematographic cut-scene that shows what appears to be some area of outer space, with an apparently rather small ring-like structure in the foreground and a comparatively large planet in the background. The "virtual camera" pans from the ring-like structure upward, and a spaceship—the Pillar of Autumn—enters the picture from the right.[35] Considering that all of *Halo*'s game spaces are located either on the Pillar of Autumn or on the ring-like structure (which later turns out to be one of the "halos" referred to by the game's title), *Halo*'s opening sequence nicely illustrates how contemporary video games may use cut-scenes to locate the game spaces within the games' respective storyworlds. Yet this first noninteractive sequence also gives the player a variety of hints with regard to the game's core goals and, hence, conveys information about the ludic structure of the game: when the player takes control of the Master Chief for the first time, he or she already knows that the player-controlled character is located on a spaceship under heavy attack by enemy aliens and that he is an ally of the spaceship's crew.

Perhaps unsurprisingly, one can observe an extensive use of scripted events in *Halo*, too, both as contributing to the representation of the storyworld and as conveying information about the game's ludic structure. A good example of the latter can, once more, be found in the opening sequence of the game, when the Master Chief—who, at this point, is already controlled by the player—has to submit to a number of tests. These tests take the form of a sequence of scripted events within the game space identified as the spaceship's Cryo Chamber. The sequence mainly uses scripted spoken character speech for conveying vital information about certain aspects of the game mechanics and the possibilities of interaction, but when the character of Captain Keyes orders the service personnel to send the Master Chief to the bridge, this simultaneously communicates the next local game goal to the player. Once the Master Chief has reached the bridge, the game employs another filmic cut-scene to have Captain Keyes inform the Master Chief (and, hence, also the player) about a significantly more global game goal of *Halo* (as well as most other first-person shooters) when he orders him to leave the ship in order to protect the artificial intelligence Cortana from the aliens. Since Cortana is shown as being stored in the Master Chief's battle armor, the player will not have any problems inferring the goal "survival of the avatar" from this short dialogue sequence.[36] While it seems clear, then, that the gameplay of *Halo* is defined by the interplay of interactive simulation and more prototypically narrative forms of representation such as cut-scenes and scripted sequences of events, I would like to reemphasize that not all of those elements contribute to the representation of the game's storyworld to the same extent.

The complexity of the question which elements of a game's gameplay contribute to the representation of its storyworld has to do with the different "degrees of stability" of the representations that are generated across playthroughs: the (fairly linear) layout of the game spaces and the rules governing the interactive simulation in *Halo* and many other video games across different genres certainly determine a general course of action that may be comprehended as part of the representation of the game's storyworld, but the particular details of the gameplay do not seem to be intersubjectively stable enough to reliably—or, perhaps, *specifically*—contribute to the representation of that storyworld.[37] This line of "representational reasoning"[38] can also be used to explain inconsistencies between the simulated gameplay and more prototypically narrative strategies of representation such as cut-scenes or scripted events. In Blizzard's real-time strategy game *Warcraft III: Reign of Chaos*, for example, some parts of the single-player campaign allow for the player-controlled hero Prince Arthas to die during the gameplay, only to be alive again in the next cut-scene. This kind of contradiction, which appears to imply logical inconsistency at first glance, necessitates the application of medium-specific charity: most players will understand that the rule-governed death of Arthas during the gameplay was not represented with a particularly high degree of stability. Moreover, the external explanation for Arthas's oscillation between life and death provided by the rule-governed nature of the simulated gameplay makes asking for an internal explanation that might involve some kind of magical resurrection, a long-lost twin brother, or the like rather "silly" (admittedly, though, the possibility of building an Altar of Kings where fallen heroes can be resurrected as part of the gameplay at least hints at a potential internal explanation).[39]

Now, these kinds of "unstable" elements of the gameplay and the game spaces might be distinguished from more "stable" elements, whose representation can be explained externally by reference to their primarily ludic functions. Take, for example, the "save points" or "save crystals" in Square's *Final Fantasy* series. While these are represented as part of the series' various game spaces, there arguably are no spheres or crystals within the games' storyworlds that allow characters to "turn back time" when they choose to. Instead, the "save points" and "save crystals" are best comprehended as manifestations of a game mechanism that allows the players to "turn back time" by loading a save game, which, again, provides an external explanation for their apparent representation that makes asking for an internal explanation appear "silly." Another example would be the inventory system commonly found in role-playing games, which often places plausible restrictions on the weight of equipment a character can carry but not on its volume. Once more, it seems clear that games such as *Final Fantasy VII*, *Diablo*, or *Dragon Age: Origins* are not, in fact, intended to represent their characters as being able to arrange several full sets of plate armor in such a way that they can be crammed in their backpacks (see figure 10). Asking what kind of magical or technological assistance is used to accomplish this feat would be "silly" because the fact that several full sets of plate armor seem to appear in a character's backpack is easily explained externally by reference to the game rules that govern the use of the inventory.

Having established that many details of the game spaces and the simulated gameplay of contemporary video games do not necessarily contribute to the representation of these games' storyworlds (similarly to the observation made earlier that certain aspects of actors' bodies

Fig. 10. A backpack full of plate armor in *Dragon Age: Origins*

and voices in contemporary film or idiosyncrasies of individual drawing styles in contemporary comics do not necessarily contribute to the representation of the storyworlds of these narrative works), I would like to underscore that the partial subversion of conventional notions of representational correspondence to be observed here primarily refers to the relation between the narrative representation and the local situations that are represented by it, not to the construction of the spatial, temporal, causal, and ontological relations between the latter as part of the global storyworld as a whole. However, just like contemporary films and comics, at least some contemporary video games cue their recipients into constructing complex storyworlds that may contain multiple substories or subworlds and employ nonchronological plots or metaleptic strategies of narrative representation in the process. As my second sample analysis, then, I would like to offer a brief look at *Alan Wake*'s highly metaleptic representation of a storyworld defined by the conventions of the horror genre, with the player controlling the best-selling writer Alan Wake, who has suffered from writer's block for the past two years.[40] Remedy's action-adventure begins with a filmic cut-scene introducing the voice of the extradiegetic narrator telling his own story and, moreover, framing the following sequences as a dream of the protagonist—that is, a supposedly hypodiegetic secondary storyworld located within the game's as-of-yet largely unrepresented diegetic primary storyworld. This initial nightmare sequence fulfills salient ludic functions not only by conveying information about the game mechanics (including the game's rather interesting light-based combat mechanic) but also by generally establishing the threat of an ominous Dark Presence as the conflict motivating most of the following gameplay.

After Alan has (apparently) awoken from the hypodiegetic secondary storyworld of his dream, the game uses a succession of cut-scenes and heavily scripted gameplay sequences to represent the diegetic Alan and his wife Alice standing on a ferry that just arrives in Bright Falls, a small mountain town in which they plan to take a short vacation. Yet, when Alan goes into a diner to get the key and instructions on how to get to the cabin Alice has rented from a man called Carl Stucky on the level of the (supposedly) diegetic primary storyworld, the game increasingly starts fulfilling the expectations evoked by the horror genre. Instead of meeting up with Carl Stucky, Alan is approached by a veiled woman dressed wholly in black who later turns out to have been an avatar of the Dark Presence but for the time being just mentions that "Stucky could not make it" and gives Alan a key and a map leading him and his wife to a cabin on an island in the middle of nearby Cauldron Lake. After Alan and Alice have arrived at the cabin, they get in an argument over Alice's attempt to help Alan with his writer's block by not only bringing a typewriter into the cabin but also arranging appointments with the psychologist Dr. Hartman, who specializes in helping artists overcome creative crises. Taking a walk in the dark to escape the situation (since Alice, who suffers from nyctophobia, will not follow him there), Alan soon runs back to the cabin when he hears Alice crying for help. He arrives too late to save her, though, as a cut-scene represents her being dragged into the lake by some unseen force, causing Alan to jump in right after her.

From this point in the plot, the represented events increasingly depart from the expectations connected to the initially "realistic" setting of Bright Falls: Alan awakes a week later, after what seems to have been a car accident about which he cannot remember anything, finding himself confronted with the task of getting back to Bright Falls, evading further attacks of the Taken (some of which turn out to be shadowy versions of Carl Stucky), and coming across scattered pages of a manuscript entitled *Departure*, which identifies Alan as its author and describes situations that the diegetic Alan has already experienced or will be experiencing in the course of the game, establishing what increasingly turns out to be a peculiar case of autopoietic metalepsis. While it initially seems difficult to make sense of these strange events, Alan continues to piece together information from various sources—including dialogues with other characters, the manuscript pages, radios that broadcast the program of the local radio station, television sets that play the fictional television show *Night Falls* as well as scenes in which a supposedly hypodiegetic version of Alan is shown writing and heard reflecting about his situation, and even an old heavy metal record by a (fictional) band called The Old Gods of Asgard—before he eventually remembers what happened during the week that has passed between Alice's disappearance and the car crash.

Even then, the game does not entirely resolve the ambiguity surrounding the ontological status of the represented situations and their precise location in the storyworld as a whole. Right until the end of the game, Alan's resurfacing memories of the seven days following Alice's disappearance (which are represented by filmic cut-scenes, for the most part), combined with the other sources of information sketched above (some of which trigger Alan's memories), indicate roughly the following version of the storyworld: There is a Dark Presence trapped under Cauldron Lake that is trying to escape using its ability to "turn fiction into reality." After its initial attempt to use the writer Thomas Zane was thwarted by his resistance and eventual death when he drowned in Cauldron Lake, the Dark Presence forced Alan Wake to write *Departure* during the week between Alice's disappearance and the car crash. However, Thomas Zane's somehow still present consciousness taught Alan Wake to resist the will of the Dark Presence while writing the manuscript, allowing him to escape and (assisted by his agent, Barry, the local sheriff, Sarah Breaker, and a hermit called Cynthia Weaver) to eventually use The Clicker (an old light switch he originally employed to help Alice deal with her nyctophobia) to banish the Dark Presence. When Alan finds another version of himself instead of Alice at the bottom of the lake, he decides to continue working on the manuscript of *Departure*, sacrificing his own freedom in order to free Alice from the lingering grasp of the Dark Presence. Now, even in this brief summary, *Alan Wake*'s tendency toward "plot holes" may already shine through, but, interestingly, the game ends with Alice's voice saying "Alan, wake up" over a black screen, hinting at the possibility that "it was all just a dream," which would, of course, plausibilize all of the previously encountered representational impossibilities and narrative improbabilities just as readily as—and, perhaps, more convincingly than—the uncanny powers of the Dark Presence.[41]

Having established that contemporary video games—just like contemporary films and contemporary comics—may represent complex storyworlds with multiple "diegetic levels," employing not only nonchronological plots but also metaleptic strategies of narrative representation, I would like to stress once again that there is a narratologically significant distinction to be drawn between the different playthroughs resulting from what can be roughly described as video games' interactivity and the different playthroughs resulting from what can be abbreviated as their nonlinearity. When it comes to the questions of how video games represent storyworlds and how players comprehend these representations, too much emphasis on the differences resulting from interactivity can lead to an overly simplistic conception of video game-specific narrative comprehension that, for example, may not be able to sufficiently distinguish between Alan Wake or the Master Chief running in circles for half an hour (say, because the player's attention is occupied with something else or because he or she is trying to prove a point) and the same characters fighting the threat of the Dark Presence or The Flood, respectively (both of which are very clearly part of the games' respective storyworlds). In this context, Jesper Juul distinguishes between "games of emergence," in which the gameplay is determined by a comparatively small number of game rules, and "games of progression," in which the player actualizes a predetermined sequence of events (see Juul, *Half-Real* 67–83). Genre conventions are obviously important here: the narrative structure of first-person shooters such as *Halo* or action-adventures such as *Alan Wake* tends to progress in a fairly linear fashion—yet at least some of the ludic events are evidently "emergent" in these cases as well, leading Juul to describe these games as *"progression games with emergent components"* in which "the player has to traverse a number of areas each of which can be negotiated in a number of ways" (*Half-Real* 71–72, original emphasis).

There are less linear forms of "progression," though, when the quest structure that is characteristic for role-playing games such as Bioware's *Baldur's Gate*, *Neverwinter Nights*, and *Dragon Age: Origins* leads to a more decidedly nonlinear arrangement of predetermined narrative representations of events. Video games with this kind of nonlinear narrative structure allow players to actualize significantly different representations during subsequent playthroughs. Accordingly, these games are arguably meant to represent (or, rather, meant to be able to represent) several different stories and storyworlds, depending on player decisions, gameplay performance, and comparable parameters. In Bioware's role-playing game *Dragon Age: Origins*, for example, the use of cut-scenes, scripted events, and interactive simulation is combined with a variety of genre-typical quests into a highly nonlinear narrative structure.[42] For starters, the player can choose his or her avatar from three conventional classes (warrior, mage, or rogue) and races (elves, humans, or dwarves), which—together with a variety of further options for customization including male and female gender, facial features, hair color, and so forth—not only results in considerable differences in the character(s)[43] that the players of *Dragon Age: Origins* may control but also influences the ways in which the beginning of the game's story may be represented: while the respective experiences of elven or human mages (who have to prove their worth as prospective members of the Circle of Magi) as well as those of human warriors and rogues (who have to survive an attack on their noble family's fortress) are relatively similar, an elven warrior or rogue will make considerably different experiences depending on whether he or she is a member of the Dalish elves (who live a largely independent life in the woods) or a city elf (who lives a life full of oppression by the human majority), and a dwarfen warrior or rogue will make at least partially different experiences in the dwarfen city of Orzammar depending on whether he or she is part of a noble family or a mere commoner.

Despite these differences across playthroughs that result from the highly nonlinear narrative structure of *Dragon Age: Origins*, there are considerable similarities as well: in every one of the six background-specific "origin stories," the player-controlled character will eventually make the acquaintance of Duncan, the captain of the Order of the Grey Wardens in the Kingdom of Ferelden, which protects the land from the demonic threat of the Darkspawn. Having been selected to join the Grey Wardens, the player-controlled character and Duncan will travel to the fortress of Ostagar to assist King Cailan and his general Loghain, the father of Queen Anora, in fighting an upcoming crucial battle against the Darkspawn, who have risen again after a period of relative peace and quiet. Once he or she has arrived at Ostagar, the player-controlled character formally joins the Grey Wardens, which entails drinking some Darkspawn blood—a practice that allows the Grey Wardens to sense the Darkspawn and, ultimately, to defeat their leader, the Archdemon. After the player-controlled character has survived the dangerous Ritual of Joining, he or she and another Grey Warden called Alistair are tasked with lighting a beacon to signal Loghain's men to flank the Darkspawn horde. However, when the signal is lit, the general instead abandons the battle, causing Ostagar to be overrun and King Cailan to be killed.

The player-controlled character and Alistair would have been killed in the battle as well had it not been for the help of the witch Flemeth and her daughter (and apprentice) Morrigan. After the player has chosen the appropriate dialogue option,[44] the player-controlled character, Alistair, and Morrigan eventually decide that in order to stop the Darkspawn from overrunning the Kingdom of Ferelden, they have to gather an army and kill the Archdemon leading the Darkspawn hordes. Accordingly, the player-controlled character (as well as, of course, the player) is tasked with securing the help of four influential factions: the Dalish Elves, the Dwarves of Orzammar, the Circle of Magi, and the (human) Soldiers of Redcliffe. While the order in which the player-controlled character establishes alliances with the four factions is up to the player and, hence, the developing plot may vary considerably not only with regard to the interactive simulation of the gameplay but also in terms of the arrangement of scripted events and cut-scenes, there are still considerable similarities with regard to the core elements of the game's storyworlds. Independently of the player's choices, for example, the traitorous general Loghain returns to the capital of Ferelden, Denerim, blames the betrayal at Ostagar on the Grey Wardens, and declares himself the queen's regent.

Hence, after the player-controlled character has secured the support of the Dalish Elves, the Dwarves of Orzammar, the Circle of Magi, and the Soldiers of Redcliffe (in any order that the player chooses), a meeting among the warring nobles of Ferelden is called during which the player-controlled character confronts Loghain. Here, the player can choose to have the player-controlled character kill Loghain or spare his life, the latter of which results in Alistair leaving the party and Loghain joining the Grey Wardens in order to take Alistair's place, and either have Anora crowned queen, have Alistair crowned king, or have Anora and Alistair marry each other and reign Ferelden together. With the forces of Ferelden united, the player-controlled character (and, once more, the player) has to make another choice that heavily influences the storyworld whose representation the respective player actualizes: the reason the Archdemon can only be killed by a Grey Warden is that, after the host body is killed, its "demonic essence" will move into the next available Darkspawn body. Since the Grey Wardens have ingested Darkspawn blood, they can kill the Archdemon's host body and then sacrifice themselves in order to permanently banish the "demonic essence." The night before the final battle, however, Morrigan reveals her long-hatched plan to conceive a child of one of the Grey Wardens (either a male player-controlled character, Alistair, or Loghain) and guide the "demonic essence" into the unborn child's body, which would then be born a demigod. The player can either make the player-controlled character accept Morrigan's offer or decline it, the latter of which results in her leaving the party.

After the Archdemon and its army are defeated, and if Morrigan's offer has been rejected, the player can finally choose to either have the player-controlled character kill the Archdemon (which, of course, also results in his or her self-inflicted death) or let Alistair or Loghain make the necessary sacrifice. One way or another, the Archdemon is killed, and the game ends with a cut-scene representing a ceremony in which the player-controlled character and his or her allies are honored for saving the Kingdom of Ferelden and, perhaps, the world—followed by an "epilogue" that summarizes the effects that the player's various choices have on the further development of the storyworld. As this analysis of *Dragon Age: Origins*' nonlinear narrative structure has hopefully made clear, then, the interactive simulation of the gameplay is not the only way in which the representation of existents, events, and characters in video games differs from the representation of existents, events, and characters in films and comics. Instead, video games with a nonlinear narrative structure may represent not just one but several different courses of action and, hence, different storyworlds depending on the player's performance, the player's choices, and similar parameters. Accordingly, in the case of video games such as *Dragon Age: Origins* that employ a nonlinear narrative structure (and in contradistinction to video games such as *Halo* or *Alan Wake* that, despite their interactivity, sport a largely linear narrative structure), it seems best to describe the video game-specific realization of the transmedial strategy of representing storyworlds in terms of an arrangement of "virtual storyworlds," only one of which can be actualized in any given playthrough.[45]

Even though both the concept of narrative representation and the concept of storyworld are genuinely transmedial and not only literary texts but also contemporary films, comics, and video games can represent complex storyworlds that may contain multiple stories arranged in nonchronological plots and multiple "diegetic levels" whose ontological borders are sometimes metaleptically transgressed, I hope to have made sufficiently plausible that comprehending and intersubjectively constructing these storyworlds requires at least some knowledge about medium-specific representational conventions. However, the application of medium-specific charity that allows recipients to cope with some of the more complex and indirect forms of representational correspondence to be found in verbal and pictorial as well as in audiovisual, verbal-pictorial, and interactive modes of representation has turned out to be particularly salient with regard to the representation of local situations, while the ways in which these situations are located within the global storyworld as a whole by establishing spatial, temporal, causal, and ontological relations between them appears to be generally more transmedial, as recipients here primarily take their cues from what is being represented as opposed to medium-specific elements of the representation.

Indeed, it has become evident not only that the level of narrative representation is not as medium-specific as is commonly assumed, since, for example, verbal and pictorial modes of representation are widely employed across media, and recipients generally need to "fill in the gaps" adhering to some version of the principle of minimal departure, but also that the level of the storyworld is not as "medium-free" as one might think, with contemporary films' storyworlds appearing particularly prone to narrative complexity, contemporary comics' storyworlds being commonly defined by their seriality,[46] and contemporary video games often representing not a single storyworld but rather a nonlinear arrangement of multiple "virtual storyworlds."[47] Finally, my various sample analyses have also repeatedly touched upon the ways in which narrative works across media employ strategies of narratorial representation that are attributable to some kind of narrator and strategies of subjective representation to provide "direct access" to characters' consciousnesses, thereby adding narrative complexity to their respective narrative representations and the storyworlds they represent. While not quite as fundamental as the representation of storyworlds, these are still fairly salient strategies of narrative representation, which motivates the more in-depth discussion provided in the second part and the third part of this book, respectively.

PART 2 | *Narrators across Media*

4 : The Narrator as a Transmedial Concept

Narrative Communication, Narrative Comprehension, and the Problem of Authorship

In literary narratology, the concept of the narrator is defined by the notion that literary narrative texts should be treated not merely as communication, but as "communicated communication," not merely as representation, but as "represented representation" (see Janik; Walsh, "Who Is the Narrator?").[1] Or, as Wolf Schmid remarks, "a narrative work does [not] just narrate, but represents an act of narration. The art of narrative is structurally characterized by the doubling of the communication system: the *narrator's communication* in which the narrated world is created is part of the fictive represented world, which is the object of the real *author's communication*" (*Narratology* 33, original emphases, my typo correction). Accordingly, Schmid distinguishes between the "concrete author," who creates the literary narrative work for the "concrete reader(s)," the "abstract author" (more commonly called the "implied author"), who creates the "represented world" for the "abstract reader(s)," the "fictive narrator," who creates the "narrated world" for the "fictive reader(s)," and the characters in the "narrated world," who can communicate narratively as well, creating merely "quoted worlds" (see Schmid, *Narratology* 34–88). While Schmid may use somewhat unusual terms to refer to some of the concepts he introduces as part of his model of literary narrative communication, the resulting conceptual distinctions are still highly conventionalized within literary narratology.

Let me mention a few additional canonical examples: following Wayne C. Booth's distinction between the "real author" and the "implied author" of a literary work in *The Rhetoric of Fiction*, Seymour

Chatman prominently distinguishes between the "real author," the "implied author," and the "narrator" as well as between the "real reader," the "implied reader," and the "narratee" (see *Story* 147–151; see also Chatman, *Coming to Terms* 74–138, for a more detailed discussion of the "implied author" and its relation to the narrator). Replicating Gérard Genette's exclusive focus on fictional narrators (see Genette, *Narrative Discourse* 212–262; *Narrative Discourse Revisited* 79–129), Shlomith Rimmon-Kenan distinguishes only between the "real author," the "real reader," the "(fictional) narrator," and the "(fictional) narratee"—albeit her argument that the "implied author" should not be treated as a participant in the communication process does not deny the concept's general usefulness (see Rimmon-Kenan, *Narrative Fiction* 88–90). Similarly, Mieke Bal limits herself to the well-established distinction between the "(biographical) author" and the "narrator," emphasizing that "the notion of an implied author is . . . not limited to narrative texts, but can be applied to any text" (*Narratology* 18). At least within classical literary narratology, then, a number of influential narratologists postulate a multitier model of narrative communication that includes slots for a "biographical" or "actual author," a "fictional" or "represented narrator," and the narrated characters, sometimes including an additional slot for the "abstract" or "implied author"—with the latter term in particular commonly being used to refer either to a kind of "unified textual meaning" that "includes not only the extractable meanings but also the moral and emotional content of each bit of action and suffering of all of the characters" (Booth, *The Rhetoric* 73) or to "the *image he* [or she—the biographical author, that is] *creates of himself* [or herself]" (Booth, *The Rhetoric* 395, original emphasis)—in between the "biographical" or "actual author" and the "fictional" or "represented narrator."

However, while a position that describes literary narrative representation as "communicated communication" seems to imply that even in cases where there are next to no markers of a narrator's presence apart from the fact that "we hear a voice speaking of events, characters, and setting" (Chatman, *Story* 197), we can (and, in fact, often do) assume his or her (fictional or represented) "existence," there has been some controversy over the status of these kinds of highly "covert" narrators, with a host of "optional-narrator theories" providing arguments against the assumption of "pan-narrator theories" that fictional literary narrative texts always represent a fictional narrator that is distinct from the author (see, e.g., Banfield, *Unspeakable Sentences*; Kania; Lanser, *The Narrative Act*; as well as the survey by Patron). Most recently, Tilmann Köppe and Jan Stühring have summarized the discussion, showing that common arguments in favor of "pan-narrator theories"—what they call the "analytic argument," the "ontological gap argument," the "blocked inference argument," the "argument from creation," and the "argument from mediation"—are, in fact, not sufficient to assume the "existence" of a narrator in every fictional narrative text.[2] At the very least, it seems clear that conceptualizing the narrator as a logical necessity (in fictional narrative texts) while insisting that the ("implied") author has "no voice, no direct means of communicating" (Chatman, *Story* 148), makes it rather hard to appropriately account for those cases where readers imagine an *authorial* as opposed to (only) a *narratorial voice*.[3]

A comparatively early attempt to remedy classical narratology's overly exclusive focus on narratorial voices has been made by Susan S. Lanser, who distinguishes the "historical author" and the "authorial" or "extrafictional voice" of a narrative text from its "public" or "private narrator(s)," emphasizing that, "in every text . . . , even a fictional text, an authorial voice does communicate historical information. This authorial voice is an *extrafictional* entity whose presence accounts, for example, for organizing, titling, and introducing the fictional work" (*The Narrative Act* 122, original emphasis). Admittedly, even proponents of a "voiceless implied author" would perhaps not attribute the title and other extrafictional epitexts of a fictional work to its narrator (on epitexts and peritexts as different forms of paratexts, see, e.g., Genette, *Paratexts*). Lanser goes further than that, however, when she stresses that "total separation between authorial and narrating voices is only one of many textual possibilities" (*The Narrative Act* 150) and that, ultimately, "the unmarked case of narration for public narrators is that the narrating voice is equated with the textual author (the extrafictional voice or 'implied author') unless a different case is marked—signaled—by the text" (*The Narrative Act* 151). Following Lanser, then, the authorial voice of a fictional narrative text would, "in the absence of direct markings" (*The Narrative Act* 151) separating it from the narratorial voice, be perceived to speak extrafictionally as well as fictionally. This is a wide-reaching claim, of course, and whether one is prepared to follow Lanser's line of argument will depend not only on one's conceptualization of the narrator but also on one's conceptualization of authorship, "implied" or otherwise.

Yet, before I can provide additional remarks on the question of authorship, I would like to mention a highly influential alternative approach to narrators and narration that has primarily been developed within the cognitively informed film narratology of the late 1980s to early 1990s, and whose fundamental assumptions about how "film narration" works are markedly different from those prevalent in (neo)classical literary narratology, in particular. The focus of inquiry of this kind of cognitive approach to "film narration" tends to be on the functions of narrative representation and, more importantly, on the process of narrative comprehension, rather than on the authors, narrators, or other "communicating instances" that (neo)classical narratology would postulate as the "source" of at least the former. Perhaps most saliently, David Bordwell defines (fictional) "film narration" as *"the process whereby the film's syuzhet and style interact in the course of cueing and channeling the spectator's construction of the fabula"* (*Narration* 53, original emphasis). While Bordwell tends to anthropomorphize his concept of "film narration" to a certain degree when he attributes qualities such as "knowledgeability" (which encompasses a film narration's "range of knowledge" and "depth of knowledge"), "self-consciousness," and "(un)communicativeness" to it, he also famously insists that the concept of "film narration" obliterates the need for the concept of a necessarily present narrator that is distinct from the authors or, perhaps, merely the "makers" of a film. Hence, it would seem that Bordwell's concept of "film narration" does not have all that much to contribute to a transmedial conceptualization of the narrator—but, of course, there are other cognitively informed film narratologists who have tackled this problem.

Building on Bordwell as well as Lanser, Edward Branigan has proposed what remains one of the most sophisticated accounts of "film narration" in current film studies, distinguishing between the "historical author," the "extrafictional narrator," the "nondiegetic narrator," the "diegetic narrator," the characters in "nonfocalized narration," "external focalization," "internal focalization" that remains on the "surface" of a character's consciousness, and "internal focalization" that goes into greater "depth" (see Branigan, *Narrative Comprehension* 86–124). Despite the indisputable relevance of Branigan's approach to "film narration" (which also briefly touches on comics) for the project of a transmedial narratology, there are quite a few problems inherent in his model that prevent it from being particularly well suited for providing the basis of a transmedial conceptualization of the narrator: On the one hand, Branigan may be correct in observing that, "although there is a firm distinction among narration, (nonfocalized) action, and (external and internal) focalization, it is often convenient in analyzing narrative to use the terms 'narration' and 'narrator' in a general sense to refer to all three types of agency in order to concentrate on the overall regulation and distribution of knowledge throughout a text that determines how and when a reader acquires knowledge" (*Narrative Comprehension* 106). Yet, as important as the "distribution of knowledge" and the resulting "knowledge hierarchies" (see Branigan, *Narrative Comprehension* 72–76) among spectators, narrators, and characters are for narrative representations across media (which Bordwell's conceptualization of "film narration" stresses as well), it seems terminologically unsatisfying to equate "narration" with what Branigan calls "focalization," even if it may appear to be more "convenient" in the context of his cognitively oriented theory of narrative comprehension. On the other hand, and more importantly, however, Branigan's willingness to draw that equation is rooted in his conceptualization of "narration," which, in turn, makes even his conceptualization of the "historical author," the "extrafictional narrator," the "nondiegetic narrator," and the "diegetic narrator" turn out to be less compatible with traditional conceptualizations of similar terms from literary narratology than one would expect at first glance.

More specifically, Branigan's argument that "a narration may be *implicit* in a text" (*Narrative Comprehension* 90, original emphasis) is contingent on his primary interest not in authors and/or narrators as ("implied" or hypothetical, fictional or represented) "sources" to which various aspects of narrative representations can be attributed but rather in "perceptual 'contexts' . . . or *levels*, within which specific mental operations will be successful in organizing aural and visual data into a narrative pattern of events" (*Narrative Comprehension* 86, original emphasis). While Branigan draws on Lanser's discussion of what he calls "a hierarchy of roles," he primarily appears to distinguish between the "levels" of the "historical author," the "extrafictional narrator," the "nondiegetic narrator," and the "diegetic narrator" (as well as between the four additional levels of "focalization") to "explain how data is systematically recast by the spectator from one perceptual context to another" (Branigan, *Narrative Comprehension* 86)—which, once more, is certainly laudable but does not contribute too much to a transmedial conceptualization of the narrator that attempts to adhere to both the criterion of continuity and the criterion of neutrality sketched in chapter 1. I agree with cognitive film narratology's insistence on the importance of processes of narrative comprehension and the related notion that any narrator we might want to describe as a representational strategy of narrative works across media (not just film) will have to be "perceivable" by or, rather, "comprehensible" to, the recipients of that work (not just certain critics who may be heavily invested in "perceiving" it due to their previous theoretical commitments). Likewise, I have no qualm with cognitive film narratology's emphasis of the importance of a narrative representation's "knowledgeability" and the resulting "hierarchies of knowledge" among recipients, narrators, and characters, some aspects of which I will further remark on in the third part of this book. Yet it would still seem that Bordwell's as well as, albeit to a lesser degree, Branigan's focus on the recipient's activity deemphasizes questions connected to authorship, intended meaning, and the real or represented "sources" of narrative representation too strongly to be able to (exclusively) serve as the basis for the explication of the transmedial concept of the narrator that this chapter aims to provide.

Accordingly, I would like to continue my attempt at such an explication with a more detailed examination not of narrators but rather of authors, focusing on the question of how conceptualizations of authorship are related to positions sometimes described as "actual," "hypothetical," and "anti-intentionalism," as well as on the question of how the forms of cooperative, collaborative, and collective authorship that define the production not only of contemporary films but also (if perhaps to a slightly lesser extent) of contemporary comics and (to an even greater extent) of contemporary video games complicate such matters. As Derek Johnson and Jonathan Gray remark, "to see press or marketing for almost any item of media today without seeing the invocation of at least one author figure is rare" (2).[4] Authors (or, perhaps, *author figures*) evidently remain important in contemporary media culture, then, and it seems also quite uncontroversial to say that narrative works across media are generally authored (as opposed to merely produced) to some extent, but there is evidently some reluctance (particularly) among narratologists to discuss the author (or, more commonly, authors) of these narrative works in any detail. This reluctance cannot be fully explained by either classical or postclassical narratology's focus on narrative representations as products as opposed to the contexts of their cultural production. Accordingly, Jens Eder may be right in stressing that "even if one assumes that spectators understand films [as well as, presumably, that readers understand comics and players understand video games] as intentionally designed communication devices . . . , one does not have to attribute their design to narrators or implied authors, but can also trace them back to the real filmmakers [or comics writers and artists, or game designers and developers] as authors or author collectives" (*Die Figur* 616, my translation from the German). Still, it would seem that any such attempt will have to address at least two interconnected problems related to the notion of authorship in narrative works across media: the *problem of intentionalism* and the *problem of collective authorship*.

Let me start with the former: Following the banishment of the biographical author from the realm of interpretation out of fear of the "intentional fallacy,"[5] the "implied author" has commonly been used as a kind of "catch all term" that allowed for the attribution of the overall design of a literary text to a single unified "source" without having to subscribe to "actual intentionalist" theories of meaning.[6] Seymour Chatman, for example, sees the "implied author" as "a way of naming and analyzing the textual intent of narrative fictions under a single term but without recourse to biographism" (*Coming to Terms* 75), and Gregory Currie defines it as "the imagined agent whose intentions coincide with those which ordinary pragmatic inference suggests were productive of" (*Narratives* 65) a given narrative work. At least in the context of a transmedial narratology, the core question to be asked here seems to be how we go about attributing the design of narrative works across media to their authors or author collectives: while it may be considered fairly uncontroversial that the construction of hypotheses about communicative intentions is important for various forms of narrative comprehension and meaning making, the relevant hypotheses about these communicative intentions are usually constructed primarily (if not exclusively) on the basis of the narrative work in question (as opposed to, say, the diary of its author). Against this background, "actual intentionalism" may be seen as problematic both because of its basic epistemological assumptions regarding the external "accessibility" of authorial intentions and because of the complex decision-making processes involved in the creation of contemporary films, comics, and video games (to which I will return below).[7]

Nevertheless, I would generally agree with a variety of proponents of the "implied author" (as well as various more "moderate" intentionalists) that the notion of a "hypothetical or postulated author in the conceptual context of hypothetical intentionalism" (Kindt and Müller, *The Implied Author* 181) remains useful, even though—in light of the by now quite complex conceptual history of the term and despite the fact that some aspects of the (ongoing) debate surrounding it[8] will still be relevant for an examination of authors and narrators across media—such a construct does not necessarily have to be called "implied author." Due to the focus of the present study, however, I am in fact less interested in the occasionally quite thorny problems of intentionalist interpretation that are commonly addressed by reference to a hypothetical or postulated author than in the general idea or mental construct of an author that recipients form while reading a literary text—and, perhaps, also while viewing a film, reading a comic, or playing a video game. Indeed, "the idea that the implied author stands for images that authors produce of themselves in their works" (Kindt and Müller, *The Implied Author* 180) has long been part of the term's conceptual history, but it is important to note here not only that authors do not necessarily need to "have the [actual] intention of creating an image of themselves in their works" (Schmid, "Implied Author" 161) but also that, at least from the perspective of cognitive narratology, it does not matter much whether they have these intentions or not, as long as the narrative work in question supports the intersubjective communicative construction of some kind of hypothetical author by the recipients of that work.

Still, since the author of a given narrative work "exists not only as a biographical person ... who has created a text, but also as a cultural *legend* created by texts" (Branigan, *Narrative Comprehension* 87, original emphasis), the "images of the author" that readers (as well as, perhaps, spectators and players) construct while reading (or viewing, or playing) can evidently be more or less "fleshed out." Without going into too much detail here, I propose to distinguish three prototypical cases (asking my readers to keep in mind that questions of authorship are not at the core of either this chapter or the book of which it is a part). First, I would maintain that not only critics (whether intentionalists or not) but also recipients in general may postulate a fairly abstract *hypothetical author* to whom the overall design of the narrative work in question can be attributed (though, as will become clear in the following, this kind of attribution tends to be more complicated in contemporary films, comics, and video games than it is in most literary texts, since the former are usually more obviously authored collectively than the latter). Second, one can distinguish these kinds of abstract hypothetical authors from more concrete *author figures* that are represented (with varying degrees of detail and "accuracy") in a work's paratexts (i.e., its peritexts as well as, and perhaps more importantly, its epitexts). Third, some narrative works may represent certain characters as if they were the authors of the work in question, and these (occasionally, but not necessarily, "fictionalized"[9]) *authoring characters* often also function as the works' narrators. Of course, the notion that recipients may construct hypothetical authors, author figures, and authoring characters does not at all deny the importance of the actual authors that produce narrative works across media—although I will follow the majority of other narratologists in focusing more on the former than on the latter, as questions of "actual intentionalism" or production culture studies may be interesting in themselves but tend to be somewhat less relevant for understanding the kind of meaning-making processes with which I am primarily concerned here.[10]

Some further remarks are necessary with regard to the second problem mentioned above, however, since the question whether one can appropriately speak of a single "implied" or, rather, hypothetical author with regard to multimodal media such as films, comics, and video games is significantly complicated by the complex forms not only of production and distribution but also of cooperative, collaborative, and collective authorship that are characteristic for these media. A novel usually is the result of several people's work as well, but most other narrative media are commonly more visibly created by a group of people with different roles and degrees of authority: there are graphic novels such as Art Spiegelman's *Maus*, Frank Miller's *Sin City* series, and Craig Thompson's *Habibi* that have a single author responsible for most if not all the decisions involved in their creation, but it already becomes considerably harder to come up with convincing examples of narratively complex fictional feature films or narrative video games that are created by a single author in this sense, and at least with regard to contemporary media culture, it would seem that the distribution of production roles and artistic responsibility tends to be significantly more complex and often changes as a project develops. Hence, while there may be cases where one person is identified as the single author of a given film, comic, or video game (even though he or she will still commonly not actually be the only person who has contributed to the work in some way), the situation is usually not as clear-cut, and some version of collective authorship—which, more often than not, is situated within and determined by complex and powerful institutionalized frameworks of cultural production—appears to be the default case.

It may seem obvious that not only films and video games but also comics and even literary texts are commonly produced by a group of people rather than by a single individual, yet the question to what extent—or, perhaps, under which conditions—we can speak of an *author collective* appears to be comparatively more controversial. As actual authors tend to be excluded from narratological approaches that primarily focus on the narrative work as a product instead of on its production, however, I will limit myself to a very brief sketch of the range of positions (within film studies in particular) regarding the question of who does and does not qualify as an *author* (as opposed to a mere *contributor*) of a given narrative work. "From the defense of *la politique des auteurs* by figures such as François Truffaut to Andrew Sarris' articulation of the auteur theory, a wide range of critics and theorists have explicitly treated many of the major directors of mainstream and 'art' cinema as authors" (Meskin 12, original emphasis),[11] but more recent accounts of film authorship generally tend to emphasize at least the possibility of cooperatively, collaboratively, collectively, or simply "multiply authored films" (Meskin 21). Berys Gaut, for example, reconstructs existing theories of film authorship in some detail, refuting "actual auteurism" and some of the more salient strategies its proponents commonly employ to attribute film authorship to a single author (usually the director) as well as what could be described as "implied single authorship," concluding that "there are multiple actual and constructed [i.e., hypothetical or 'implied'] authors of mainstream films" ("Film Authorship" 167–168).

Nevertheless, most other influential accounts of film authorship that underscore its cooperative, collaborative, and/or collective aspects seem to argue against the kinds of authorial constructs that Gaut explicitly allows for, focusing on the actual authors (or filmmakers), instead.

Perhaps most well known among these, Paisley Livingston defines the author rather broadly as "the agent (or agents) who intentionally make(s) an utterance, where 'utterance' refers to any action, an intended function of which is expression or communication" (134). Yet he emphatically argues against what he considers an "anti-realist notion of authorship" that would result in the construction of a "make-believe persona ... referred to variously as the 'real,' 'fictional,' 'implied,' or 'postulated' author," emphasizing that, instead, "the interpreter [or recipient] must decide, on a case-by-case basis, whether a film [or other narrative work] has or has not been made in a way that involves individual or collective authorship or some other sort of process" (145). Paul Sellors, another influential theorist of film authorship who also claims some degree of transmedial applicability when he aims to provide a foundation for his argument by "looking at authorship across various media" (263), builds on Livingston's account of film authorship,[12] but stresses the contribution of "stars, cinematographers, scriptwriters, composers, choreographers, producers, directors, and so forth" more strongly, resulting in what "may seem like an unacceptable escalation of authors" (Sellors 270). Finally, in an even more explicitly transmedial account of "artistic collaborations" (which, however, also draws on the accounts of film authorship developed by Gaut, Livingston, and Sellors, respectively), Sondra Bacharach and Deborah Tollefsen "develop a theory of coauthorship that appeals to the notion of a joint commitment" (23). Building on Margaret Gilbert's "plural subject theory" instead of John R. Searle's more widely referenced account of "we-intentions,"[13] Bacharach and Tollefsen argue that "viewing artistic groups as plural subjects helps distinguish mere contributors from coauthors, because individuals must be jointly committed to creating a work of art as a body in order to count as part of the plural subject or social group" (31).

While I tend toward a fairly permissive conceptualization of authorship as being easily attributed to even the most minor "jointly committed" contributors to a narrative work, it seems unnecessary to choose a single one of the above-mentioned accounts. It should, however, have become clear that a core problem that transmedial narratology has to address in some way lies in the observation that one not only has "to think of global [collective] authorship . . . as a matter of degree" (Livingston 143) but also that one has to acknowledge that the distribution of production roles, decision power, and artistic responsibility is complex to begin with and often changes as a project develops. As has already been mentioned, tracing these dynamic production processes and the resulting "*intentional flux*" (Burnett 112, original emphasis) would go beyond the scope of this book (and, at least traditionally, tends to be beyond the scope of narratology, whether neoclassical, cognitive, or transmedial), but it still seems clear that the fact that many if not most narrative works in multimodal media are collectively authored does affect narrative comprehension: in the process of forming hypotheses about the storyworlds represented by a given narrative work, recipients also tend to make certain assumptions of a comparatively general nature about the processes involved in its creation, and these assumptions are (usually) based on the knowledge they have about the *prototypical* distribution of work, decision making, and authority according to historically specific, highly conventionalized production roles.[14] It is against this background that recipients will process available information regarding *unusual* distributions of work (which tends to be conveyed via paratexts, particularly but not exclusively via peritexts such as titles and credits), decision making, and authority in cases of collective authorship. Hence, general historical knowledge about prototypical authorial constellation plays an important role in how recipients imagine a film's, comic's, or video game's *hypothetical author collective*.

Even though I do propose to distinguish between the "flesh-and-blood" author(s) of a narrative work and the intersubjective communicative constructs as which the work's hypothetical author or hypothetical author collective can be described, then, I will not use the term "implied author"—both because of its complex conceptual history and, more importantly, because it suggests a unity and homogeneity of the authorial construct in question that seems inappropriate at least in the context of a transmedial narratology that is primarily concerned with (often) collectively authored multimodal narrative works. As has already been mentioned, however, narratological communication models tend to postulate the existence not only of the actual author(s) and (some version of) the "implied author" of a work (the latter of which I propose to substitute with the concept of a hypothetical author or hypothetical author collective) but also of a "narratorial" or, more commonly, "narrating instance" as distinct from both of these "authorial" or "authoring instances."[15] Accordingly, I will now proceed to examine various conceptualizations of "narrating instances" from literary narratology, film narratology, comics studies, and game studies—which, in turn, will allow me to further explicate the narrator as a transmedial concept and to provide a more sophisticated answer to the question under which conditions we can speak of narrators in literary texts as well as in contemporary films, comics, and video games.

Narrating Characters, "Narrating Instances," and the Problem of Attribution

So, what *is* a narrator? What do we mean when we say that a narrator "tells the story" of a literary text, a comic, a film, or a video game? Considering that the narrator's forms and functions are among the most central problems within classical as well as postclassical narratology, the present chapter cannot reconstruct the development of the concept in literary narratology in anything resembling its entirety. Still, I would like to begin by sketching two major lines of argument. On the one hand, narratologists such as Richard Walsh ("Who Is the Narrator?") emphasize the (self-)representation of a *narrating character* that is distinct from the author (who is usually still thought of as a single author within literary narratology, even though literary texts are more commonly also produced by a group of people, of course) as a necessary condition for speaking of a narrator. On the other hand, narratologists such as Richard Aczel propose an understanding of the term "narrator" as referring to a bundle of *narratorial functions* ranging from the selection, organization, and (re)presentation of elements of the storyworld to evaluative comments and self-characterizations of a narrating character.

Walsh's position boils down to understanding the concept of the narrator as exclusively referring to (narrating) characters: "There is nothing about the internal logic of fictional representation that demands a qualitative distinction between narrators and characters. Such narrators, being represented, *are* characters" ("Who Is the Narrator?" 498, original emphasis). While Walsh's insistence that we attribute the verbal narration in literary narrative texts either to a narrating character or to the author seems plausible at first glance,[16] he might be overstating his case when he claims that extradiegetic heterodiegetic narrators "cannot be represented without thereby being rendered homodiegetic or intradiegetic" and that, therefore, actual extradiegetic heterodiegetic narrators "are in no way distinguishable from authors" ("Who Is the Narrator?" 510–511). Walsh certainly has a point regarding the somewhat problematic in-between status of the "extradiegetic level," but extradiegetic narrators can, at least in literary narrative texts, *by definition* be represented through their own narration without necessarily being homodiegetic or becoming intradiegetic narrators (see also my remarks on Gérard Genette's distinctions between extradiegetic and intradiegetic as well as heterodiegetic and homodiegetic narrators in multimodal media below). Still, there seem to be some narrators that are, indeed, "indistinguishable" from the author, and one might follow Walsh (as well as an increasing number of other narratologists, ranging from Susan S. Lanser via Fotis Jannidis to Tilmann Köppe and Jan Stühring) in arguing against describing the "source" of the verbal representation as a narrator in these cases.

The core question emerging here, then, is what we mean when we say that narrators are more or less explicitly represented by a narrative work, literary or otherwise: What are the cues that allow us to assume the presence of a narrator to whom we can attribute the (verbal) narration? Despite having become increasingly contested within literary narratology as well, the common view that (fictional) verbal narration in literary narrative texts "always contains symptoms, no matter how weak they may be" (Schmid, *Narratology* 64), that allow the reader to construct a (fictional) speaker as distinct from the author might remain defensible. But when transferred to multimodal media such as films, comics, or video games, such a view becomes even less plausible, since the multimodal configurations characteristic for these media are not limited to verbal narration and, hence, do not as self-evidently activate the cognitive schema underlying what Ansgar Nünning calls the "mimesis of narration" (see A. Nünning, "Mimesis," as well as Bareis)—that is, the impression that (fictional) verbal narration is, indeed, the representation of an act of representation. Before I return to this question, though, let me sketch the second line of argument regarding the ontological status of the narrator mentioned above.

In contrast to Walsh, Aczel argues for a distinction between the concepts of narrator and voice: "A text either has a narrator or it hasn't, but voice is a relative category: it can be more or less strongly detectable. If narrative voice is the (effective) *means* of identifying a narrator function as such, the two must necessarily be held as discrete" (490, original emphasis). Yet, if one follows Walsh's argument that authors can choose either "to narrate a representation or to represent a narration" ("Who Is the Narrator?" 505), it remains unclear to what extent "style necessarily evokes a subjective center" (Aczel 472) different from the author and to what extent further characteristics of literary narrative texts indicate the presence of a narrator. As Aczel remarks, "the issue here is at least partly terminological. If one chooses to restrict the term 'narrator' to an identifiable teller persona, then there ostensibly are narratorless narratives. This does not, however, address the problem of to whom one attributes functions of (nonpersonified) selection, organization, and comment" (492). Against this background, Aczel "prefer[s] to see the 'narrator' as an umbrella term for a cluster of possible functions, of which some are necessary (the selection, organization, and presentation of narrative elements) and others optional (such as self-personification as teller, comment, and direct reader/narratee address)" (492).

If the narratorial functions Aczel identifies are evidently important for contemporary films, comics, and video games as well, the proposal to use "narrator" as an umbrella term for a bundle of narratorial functions is unsatisfactory both from a conceptual and a terminological perspective, as it prevents a clear distinction between the (obligatory) presence of (the results or traces of) processes of selection, organization, and (re)presentation of storyworld elements, on the one hand, and the (facultative) presence of a (verbally realized) narratorial voice that is distinct from that of the author(s), on the other. Perhaps not surprisingly, then, I propose to follow Walsh, Jannidis, and others in generally treating narrators as constructs "organized in the form of characters" (Jannidis, "Wer sagt das?" 159, my translation from the German), while at the same time acknowledging that these narrating characters do not always have to be fully realized. Accordingly, I would argue that readers of literary texts and comics as well as film spectators and video game players can construct some kind of narrating character even if there are only very few, or conflicting, or problematic cues given by the narration. Yet one of the very basic cues that seems necessary (albeit perhaps not sufficient) in most cases—and that literary narratologists, for obvious reasons, tend to take for granted—is precisely the presence of verbal narration that we can attribute to some kind of "speaker."[17]

Despite the fact that the limitation of the concept of voice to verbal narration may seem commonsensical to some, there have been various attempts—for example by French narratologists such as André Gaudreault and François Jost as well as by American narratologists, of whom Seymour Chatman is probably the most influential—to identify a more or less intangible "image-maker," "grand imagier," "enunciator," "implied," "cinematic," or otherwise "elusive" narrator "behind" the audiovisual representation in films.[18] As Katherine Thomson-Jones has argued somewhat more extensively in "The Literary Origins of the Cinematic Narrator," one of the main reasons for the insistence on postulating a "narrating instance" that is not represented but still can be deemed responsible for the audiovisual representation seems to be the fact that the respective theorists tend—in one way or another—to take literary narrative texts as their starting point. Accordingly, the notion of an "elusive narrator" or nonrepresented "narrating instance" to whom (or which) we can attribute the audiovisual narration in the feature film is seldom found in narratological approaches developed within film studies itself—but even the proponents of "enunciation theory" (e.g., Gaudreault and Jost) or the "cinematic narrator" (e.g., Chatman) usually implicitly acknowledge or even explicitly emphasize that such a "narrating instance" is not similar to a narrating character at all. In fact, one of the various problems of these approaches seems to be that the kind of nonrepresented "narrating instance" they postulate is not sufficiently distinguished from "implied authors" (or hypothetical authors and hypothetical author collectives, for that matter). In light of the ubiquity of these comparatively broad and relatively vague conceptualizations of "narrating instances," it seems helpful to examine some of the more influential proposals not only from film narratology but also from comics studies and game studies.

Gaudreault and Jost, two key proponents of "enunciation theory" in the francophone tradition, sum up their position as follows. First, "there are no stories without a storytelling instance" ("Enunciation" 45). Second, in film, "events seem to tell their own stories. Yet this is misleading, because without any mediation there would have been no recording and we would not have seen the events at all" (Gaudreault and Jost, "Enunciation" 45). From this follows, third, that "in such cases where the soundtrack allows us to hear the words of a narrator, film calls on two narrative instances. But while one tells one story in an overt manner, as in a living voice, the grand image-maker does [not] show himself [or herself]" (Gaudreault and Jost, "Enunciation" 46, my typo correction).[19] Gaudreault and Jost further discuss the cues that the audiovisual representation supposedly provides for the spectator to construct some kind of "narrating instance" responsible for the selection, organization, and (re)presentation of storyworld elements, but their claim that "it matters little what name has been given to these instances (shower of images, grand image-maker, narrator, filmic narrator, enunciator, etc.)" ("Enunciation" 61) is quite counterintuitive, particularly since they also mention the conceptually rather different possibility of attributing these decisions to "the authorial instance, the manifest empirical author, the concrete author" ("Enunciation" 62) without going into any detail on why assuming the existence of the kind of nonrepresented "narrating instance" they call the "grand image-maker" would be preferable to begin with.

Let me briefly compare Gaudreault and Jost's approach with Chatman's no less influential attempts to transfer the classical model of narrative communication from literary narrative texts to narrative films. While the argument in Chatman's *Story and Discourse* amounts to assuming an "implied author" responsible for both the verbal narration and the audiovisual representation and, therefore, makes the presence of a narrator optional, an expanded—and, at least from my point of view, considerably more problematic—version of this argument is put forward in *Coming to Terms*. Once more referring to the notion that there can be no narration without a narrator, Chatman forcefully argues in favor of assuming a "cinematic narrator" responsible for the audiovisual representation in the feature film to be distinguished from both "voice-over narrators" responsible for verbal narration and the "implied author" who controls both kinds of representation and/or their respective narrators. According to Chatman, though, the "cinematic narrator" is not a narrating character but "the composite of a large and complex variety of communicating devices" (*Coming to Terms* 134), including, but not limited to, "noise," "voice," and "music" on the "auditory channel" as well as "nature of image," "cinematography," and "editing" on the "visual channel." It should be noted that Chatman's observations regarding the means that feature films typically employ in order to represent stories or storyworlds (and which could be described as nonpersonified narratorial functions as defined by Aczel) are quite valuable in themselves. Yet the question remains why we should call a meaningful composition of these representational means "(cinematic) narrator."

If the "cinematic narrator" really was just a composition of representational means or a bundle of narratorial function, the problem with it would be primarily terminological, but even then I would not agree with Gaudreault and Jost that how we name these "instances" matters little: speaking of a "cinematic narrator" (or "enunciator") when we refer to a composition of representational means (or, more simply, the film) would confuse the narration with the narrator, the "enunciation" with the "enunciator," the act with the actor. More importantly, however, it remains wholly unclear how exactly such a "narrating instance" responsible for the audiovisual representation of the storyworld should be distinguished from narrating characters, on the one hand, and "the authorial instance, the manifest empirical author, the concrete author" (Gaudreault and Jost, "Enunciation" 62), on the other. The problematic relation between supposedly de-anthropomorphized, nonpersonified, and, most importantly, nonrepresented "narrating instances" and "authoring instances" surfaces, once more, if one keeps in mind that Chatman mainly developed his concept of a "cinematic narrator" responsible for the audiovisual representation of storyworld elements[20] and sometimes complemented by narrating characters responsible for the (optional) verbal representation of storyworld elements (as "one of the cinematic narrator's devices" [*Coming to Terms* 134], no less) after his original proposal in *Story and Discourse* to attribute the audiovisual representation of storyworld elements directly to the "implied author" was heavily criticized by David Bordwell and others.[21]

The "narrating instances" postulated by Gaudreault and Jost, Chatman, and others, are not, in fact, anything like the narrators-as-narrating-characters on which this book will primarily focus. Even though it may be "tempting to ask why anyone still thinks that narrative fiction films must always have narrators" (Thomson-Jones, "The Literary Origins" 76), the debate surrounding the concept of a nonrepresented "narrating instance" in the sense sketched above is not only far from settled in film studies but seems to have only just begun in comics studies and game studies. Following Chatman rather than Gaudreault and Jost, a number of more recent works in German film narratology (whose authors usually have a background in literary theory as well) have defended some version of the "cinematic narrator." Let me briefly examine two of these works. In her 1997 book *Verfilmtes Erzählen*, Sabine Schlickers attempts to transfer Wolf Schmid's model of narrative communication to film, equating the "implied author" with an "implied director" and the narrator with the "camera" (see Schlickers, *Verfilmtes Erzählen* 68–73).[22] Interestingly, Schlickers acknowledges that Jost's (as well as Gaudreault and Jost's) concept of the "grand image-maker" or "enunciator" is closer to literary narratology's concept of the "implied author" than it is to the concept of the narrator (see Schlickers, *Verfilmtes Erzählen* 76–77; as well as Gaudreault, *From Plato*; Gaudreault and Jost, "Enunciation"; Jost, *L'oeil-caméra*), but she nevertheless goes on to construct a "narrating instance" in the absence of anything actually resembling a narrator: arguing that the production of the audiovisual representation is attributed to "the camera," she proposes to use the latter term to refer to the "filmic narrating instance," noting that "'camera' in this sense is always to be understood as a fictional instance or a metaphor" (Schlickers, *Verfilmtes Erzählen* 77, my translation from the German), but leaving open why one would want to use the camera as a metaphor for the "source" of the audiovisual representation as well as how exactly the latter becomes a "fictional instance" without being represented as such (see also Branigan, *Projecting a Camera*, for a thorough examination of film studies' tendency to use the camera as a metaphor).

While Schlickers focuses on film adaptations, Markus Kuhn is concerned more exclusively with the medium specificity of audiovisual representation in his 2011 book *Filmnarratologie*, even though he mainly (and programmatically) refers to Gérard Genette's work in developing his argument. Kuhn's observations and (occasionally all too) brief analyses are often illuminating, yet his insistence not only on speaking of "verbal narrating instances" but also on generally assuming the presence of a "visual narrating instance" responsible for the audiovisual narration (in addition to both the actual filmmakers and an "implied director") again seems to be largely motivated by the attempt to apply the communication model established with regard to literary narrative texts to the narratological analysis of films (see Kuhn 72–80, 81–118). In fact, it might be argued that Kuhn—not unlike Chatman, to whom he explicitly refers and whose concept of the "cinematic narrator" he claims to refine—uses the term "visual narrating instance" more or less interchangeably with "(audio)visual representation," mainly referring to the representation itself rather than to its "source."[23] Apart from the fact that storyworld representation in films usually includes auditory as well as visual elements, and, hence, Kuhn's "visual narrating instance" would be more appropriately described as an "audiovisual narrating instance,"[24] it remains wholly unclear why one would need to attribute a film's audiovisual representation to a nonrepresented "narrating instance" different from some kind of "authoring instance" in the first place.[25] It is certainly helpful to distinguish between narratorial and what may provisionally be called nonnarratorial elements of the overall representation in multimodal media, but such a distinction in no way necessitates the attribution of the audiovisual representation to a nonrepresented "(audio)visual narrating instance."

Perhaps not as rampant as it is in certain areas of film narratology, the assumption of what one could call a nonrepresented "verbal-pictorial narrating instance" has, likewise, gained some traction in comics studies over the past few decades. Influenced by "filmic enunciation theory" and psychoanalysis (instead of Chatman's line of argument in favor of the concept of a "cinematic narrator"), Philippe Marion in particular has developed a theory of "graphic enunciation" that distinguishes not only between the processes of "narration," where the events of the story are presented by means of a narrator (in the sense of a narrating character), and "monstration," where the events of the story are performed by the characters themselves, but also between the processes of "monstration" and "graphiation," each of which leaves "traces" that can be read as symptoms of the "monstrator" and the "graphiator," respectively (see also the concise

English-language summary in Baetens). It might be worth stressing here that "monstration" and "graphiation" both leave their "traces" in the verbal-pictorial representation of storyworld elements, with "graphiation" creating "a kind of persisting opacity and prevent[ing] the act of monstration from being fully transparent and transitive" (Marion 36; translation in Baetens 149). While Marion's notion of "graphiation" as "a set of graphic markers evoking the presence of a drawing instance" (Surdiacourt 174) may, indeed, help us get a clearer idea of the medium-specific ways in which comics narrate by emphasizing that its pictures are (usually) drawn, graphic enunciation theories, once more, tend to blur the lines between biographical authors, hypothetical authors or hypothetical author collectives, nonrepresented "verbal-pictorial narrating instances," and narrators-as-narrating-characters. This is further reinforced by the fact that—not unlike the film narratologists discussed above—the various "enunciative" models of narrative communication developed within comics studies tend to distinguish between "narrating" and "authoring instances" in rather different ways.[26]

Let me give another brief example: claiming that Marion's distinction between the "monstrator" and the "graphiator" is redundant, Thierry Groensteen has recently proposed to distinguish between the "monstrator" as "the instance responsible for the *putting into drawing* . . . of the story" ("The Monstrator" 4, original emphasis; see also Groensteen, *Comics* 79–119) and the "recitant" as the "authority responsible for [the verbal] enunciation" ("The Monstrator" 7), which is supposedly primarily realized "in the form of *voice-over*" ("The Monstrator" 6, original emphasis). His argument in favor of assuming a "monstrator" behind the graphic representation of storyworld elements, however, does not seem to break new ground. According to Groensteen, "the term *monstration* underlines the fact that what is *seen* is the result of something being shown and thus of a decision regarding enunciation" ("The Monstrator" 4, original emphases). Yet, while it is certainly true that "when faced with a *comic*, the reader, whether or not he or she discerns the presence of an agent of narration, of someone speaking to him or her, cannot, in any case, fail to be aware of the fact that the images that he or she sees *have been drawn*, that they are artefacts" (Groensteen, "The Monstrator" 4, original emphases), this does not necessitate the assumption of a "monstrator." Incidentally, Groensteen's terminological choices seem particularly unfortunate, as he further postulates a "narrator" as "the ultimate authority that is responsible for the selection and organisation of all the information that makes up the storytelling" ("The Monstrator" 14), only allowing it to delegate some of its "powers" to the "monstrator" (i.e., a "verbal-pictorial narrating instance") and the "recitant" (i.e., a "verbal narrator").

Despite the fact that I do agree with Groensteen (and, quite probably, the majority of other comics scholars) that the relation between verbal and pictorial elements is of central importance for the way in which comics represent storyworlds, I find his terminological decisions rather unconvincing—and, just as with "filmic enunciation theories" or notions of a "cinematic narrator," terminological problems easily lead to conceptual ones in this context. In fact, Groensteen explicitly acknowledges the metaphorical nature of the way he uses terms such as "enunciator," "narrator," or "monstrator," noting that they "have the same suffix, one that suggests a person that acts," and acknowledging that "this vocabulary can be awkward or even lead to confusion. It is of course understood that it is the author alone who is a physical person, an individual, and [Groensteen is] not suggesting that phantomesque little men are acting in his place or at his side" (Groensteen, "The Monstrator" 14, footnote 21). However, he seems to give no reason why we would want to use terminology that is awkward or confusing and suggests "phantomesque little men" when all that is meant really are representational means or narratorial functions. This is not to say that we should generally refrain from attributing the verbal-pictorial representation to anyone, as comics are, of course, no less authored than literary texts (or films, or video games), but it is quite redundant to attribute the verbal-pictorial representation to a "monstrator" (i.e., a variation of the nonrepresented "verbal-pictorial narrating instance"), who, in turn, is attributed to a "narrator" (i.e., an inappropriately named version of what the Chatman of *Story and Discourse* would call an "implied author"). Moreover, such an attribution is not at all required to be able to precisely distinguish between verbal-pictorial representation and verbal narration.

Having reconstructed the discourse surrounding nonrepresented "narrating instances" in film studies and comics studies in some detail, the question remains whether similar observations can be made with regard to game studies. Despite the fact that what I have characterized as the interactive and nonlinear nature of video games leads to striking differences between their specific narrative limitations and affordances and those of literary narrative texts, films, and comics, a few attempts exist to transfer the classical model of narrative communication to video games as well.[27] Once more, let me briefly examine two examples. Espen Aarseth's *Cybertext*, a work that has significantly contributed to the emergence of game studies as an independent field of academic study, programmatically emphasizes the differences between "cybertexts" and literary texts. Nevertheless, Aarseth proposes a model of the "intrigue communication structure" in adventure games that not only includes a "real creator" and an "implied creator" but also distinguishes between the "voice" as the "source" to which we can attribute the verbal narration in such games and the "intrigant" as "neither implied author nor narrator but an immanent adversary who inhabits rather than trancends the game" (*Cybertext* 127) (as well as their respective counterparts on the "user's side," i.e., the "puppet," the "intriguee," the "implied user," and the "real user"). While Aarseth is aware that "the danger of this model lies in its resemblance to the communication models of narratology, which may lead to attempts at on[e]-to-one mapping between the two" (*Cybertext* 126–127, my typo correction), he is doing exactly that—or, at least, his distinctions seem strikingly similar to those discussed in literary narratology, film narratology, and comics studies. The aspects of a video game's design that Aarseth proposes to attribute to the "intrigant" are evidently different from the aspects of a film's design that Kuhn proposes to attribute to the "visual narrating instance" or the aspects of a comic's design that Groensteen proposes to attribute to the "monstrator," but it seems as doubtful to me that there is (or that it is helpful to postulate) a nonrepresented "intrigant" who "inhabits" the video game as that there is (or that it is helpful to postulate) a nonrepresented "narrating instance" to be distinguished from the hypothetical author or hypothetical author collective in films or comics.

Building on Aarseth's work (as well as on the classical models of communication in literary narrative texts and drama developed by Ansgar Nünning, *Grundzüge*, and Manfred Pfister, respectively), Kirsten Zierold has recently presented a similar attempt to transfer the classical model of narrative communication to video games. One of the more interesting aspects of Zierold's model is that she—in explicit opposition to Britta Neitzel's notion of the player as an "implied author"[28]—emphasizes the control that the authors of video games exert over the way the game's story unfolds while it is being played. Following a somewhat superficial critique of the notion of the "implied author,"[29] Zierold insists that "the narrator of narrative texts as well as Aarseth's intrigant of digital games fulfills a different function in the reception process than the implied author. The latter embodies structural and procedural principles, thereby determining the reception process, while the narrator and the intrigant are manifested on the level of the diegesis and the interface, respectively, allowing them to introduce an additional perspectivation of the events" (151, my translation from the German). Concluding that the notion of an "implied author" is not capable of describing these "structural and procedural principles" due to inconsistencies in the term's conceptual history as well as the specific characteristics of authorship in the context of video games, and also claiming that there are no (verbal) narrators to be found either (which is, of course, plain wrong),[30] Zierold still chooses to retain Aarseth's notion of an "intrigant" (and the corresponding "intriguee" or "player|avatar"). Again, it seems to me that Zierold has discarded two potentially useful if perhaps not entirely unproblematic notions (i.e., that of verbal narration attributed to a narrator-as-narrating-character and that of the "implied author" as referring to the "traces" of authorship manifesting themselves in what is being authored) in favor of a significantly less useful and conceptually problematic notion (i.e., the "intrigant," whose relation to notions of "implied" or, rather, hypothetical authorship remains characteristically ill-defined).[31]

So, where does my review of attempts to transfer the classical model of narrative communication from literary narrative texts to films, comics, and video games lead us? If we understand narrators as narrating characters that do not have to be conceptualized as being *necessarily* present in narrative works across media but, instead, are best described as an *optional* strategy of narrative—or, more precisely, narratorial—representation, it seems that we are primarily left with an *attribution problem*. As David Bordwell has famously put it: "Even if no voice or body gets identified as a locus of narration, can we still speak of a narrator as being present in a film? In other words, must we go beyond the process of narration to locate an entity which is its source?" (*Narration* 61–62). At this point, it is important to stress that distinguishing between different representational means is not the same as attributing them to some kind of "source" and, moreover, the former is not contingent on the latter. But of course, the claim that the various semiotic elements of multimodal media such as film (which combines auditive and visual modes of representation), comics (which combine verbal and pictorial modes of representation), and video games (which add interactivity to the mix) can fulfill different representational functions and that it hence may be important to distinguish among them in narratological analyses is entirely uncontested. What I would like to contest, however, is the claim that we need to attribute the representation of storyworlds to a "narrating instance"—as distinct not only from more or less explicitly represented narrators-as-narrating-characters but also from both actual and hypothetical authors or author collectives—even in cases where there are next to no cues that would allow the recipients to comprehend the "narrating instance" in question as being (self-)represented in some way.

While I do not believe that there is much to be gained from calling a bundle of representational means narrator ("cinematic" or otherwise) and, furthermore, would argue that postulating the existence of a narrator (or "narrating instance") whose presence is not in any way "made fictional" (or, more generally, represented) quite clearly overextends the concept,[32] I would not agree with Bordwell that "to give every film [or other multimodal narrative work] a narrator or implied author is to indulge in an anthropomorphic fiction" (*Narration* 62). As we have seen, the kind of "narrating instances" that are proposed by the likes of Seymour Chatman, Sabine Schlickers, and Markus Kuhn may be a lot of things but are generally not anthropomorphic, and the "implied author" of a narrative work is not appropriately characterized as fictional. On the one hand, then, Bordwell is certainly right in stressing that "on the principle that we ought not to proliferate theoretical entities without need, there is no point in positing communication as the fundamental process of all narration, only to grant that most films 'efface' or 'conceal' this process" (*Narration* 62). On the other hand, generally insisting that the nonnarratorial representation "narrates itself" (as Bordwell does) seems highly counterintuitive to me, since both recipients in general and critics in particular (including Bordwell) regularly attribute the design of narrative works across media to their authors (which, for reasons primarily connected to the complexity of collective authorship as well as the epistemological pitfalls of "actual intentionalism," may be best conceptualized as hypothetical in the context of a transmedial narratology that does not focus on the kind of dynamic production processes that are more appropriately pursued within production culture studies).

(Non)Narratorial Representation and Some Aspects of Narrators across Media

Keeping in mind that hypothetical author collectives do not necessarily have to be "fleshed out" with regard to their individual members, I would like to reemphasize that both the authorial and the narratorial configurations of a given narrative work can be rather complex: perhaps most importantly, contemporary films, comics, and video games may, on the one hand, attribute not only narratorial but also *authorial functions* to their narrators (a question to which I will return below) and, on the other hand, more or less explicitly represent their authors or certain members of their respective author collective as narrators. I tentatively agree with Branigan that "establishing exact categories for the narrations is usually less important than recognizing pertinent relationships and gradations" (*Narrative Comprehension* 100), but one can still observe a prototypical "division of labor" between (hypothetical) author(s) and (fictional or, perhaps, merely represented) narrators in most contemporary films, comics, and video games (as well as other multimodal media): at least in the context of fictional narrative representations, recipients will usually attempt to attribute verbal narration to some kind of (fictional) narrator (even if there are only a few cues to such a narrator's presence apart from the presence of the verbal narration itself), while attributing the audiovisual, verbal-pictorial, or interactive representation to the work's hypothetical author collective in a majority of cases. As should have already become clear during the previous discussion, I will speak of *narratorial representation* with regard to the former and of *nonnarratorial representation* with regard to the latter—though I would also like to acknowledge that there are cases of "verbal narration" so "covert" as to be more appropriately described as part of the *nonnarratorial* representation and, albeit perhaps less commonly, cases where a "narrating" character is represented as the "source" of parts of the multimodal representation, which may then be described as audiovisual, verbal-pictorial, or interactive *narratorial* representation.

Leaving these comparatively specific cases aside for the moment, what kind of narrators-as-narrating-characters to whom recipients can attribute the kind of narratorial representation that prototypically takes the form of verbal narration can be distinguished not only in literary narrative texts but also in films, comics, and video games? Most generally, this question aims at what Uri Margolin, discussing literary narrative texts, calls the "textually projected role" of a narrator: "Is the narrator presented as a reporter . . . who vouches for the truth of his [or her] assertions regarding the narrated? Or as an editor or publisher transmitting and vouching for the prior existence and/

or authenticity of the documents . . . he [or she] is presenting . . . ? Or as an author-fabricator, a storyteller engaged in the invention of stories . . . ? Or maybe as an oral teller . . . , presenting a story to a live audience with a focus on the performative or transmissive aspects" ("Narrator" 362)? What Margolin's enumeration of possible *narratorial roles* makes clear is that narrative works across media may not only use characters as narrators that are more or less explicitly represented as being the authors of the work in question (what I have proposed to call authoring characters as opposed to primarily paratextually represented author figures) but also generally attribute authorial as well as narratorial functions to the narrators-as-narrating-characters they employ.

From this observation, Gregory Currie draws perhaps the most radical conclusion when he admits that "it is tempting to think that we can separate two activities: narrative-making and narrative-telling," but ultimately maintains that "for virtually all cases of narrative we are likely to come across, there is no distinction that should or can be made between authors and narrators" (*Narratives* 65). At least as far as the authors/narrators of narrative representations across media are concerned, I find Currie's argument rather convincing—as long as one keeps in mind that refraining from distinguishing between the authors and the narrators of narrative representations does not entail any claims regarding the distinction between represented and actual authors/narrators (or the distinction between fictional and nonfictional authors/narrators, for that matter). It would seem, then, that not just the actual authors of a given narrative work may be considered to be its "narrators" in a certain sense but also that most if not all represented narrators across media can be considered to be not just the "tellers" but also the "makers" of the narratorial representation that is attributed to them, not just its narrators but also its authors. However, even if one subscribes to a fairly permissive conceptualization of authorship (as I do), it still seems evident that there are differences in the degree to which narrators across media are perceived as authors, with what Marie-Laure Ryan describes as the narrator's "*creative* (or self-expressive)" function that "resides in the activity of shaping and encoding the story, of forming discourse in the mind," being perhaps more important to the *authorial role* of narrators than what she calls the narrator's "*testimonial* (or assertive)" function, which "consists of presenting the story as true of its reference world," and the narrator's "*transmissive* (or performative)" function, which "can take the form of either oral performance or written inscription" ("The Narratorial Functions" 147, original emphases).

Leaving the problem of narrators' authority over the narratorial representation that can be attributed to them aside for the moment, the question of how narrating characters are represented in films, comics, and video games leads us back to what Seymour Chatman calls the narrator's "degree[ ] of audibility" or the "sense of a narrator's presence" (*Story* 196), which is mainly connected to the optional narratorial functions also discussed by Richard Aczel. In the absence of these markers, the "source" of a given verbal narration may barely be (self-)represented as a narrating character, becoming so "covert" that it may seem more appropriate to describe the verbal elements as part of the nonnarratorial representation. Still, many (if not most) cases of narratorial representation across media will be attributable to comparatively more "overt" narrators. But of course, there is more to a narratological analysis of narrators across media than the cues that are provided for their "presence." Let me start with the narrator's position within the *narratorial hierarchy*. As has already been mentioned, Gérard Genette identifies an "extradiegetic level" on which a primary extradiegetic narrator is located. That extradiegetic narrator narrates the diegetic primary storyworld, on which a secondary intradiegetic narrator, who narrates a meta- or, rather, hypodiegetic secondary storyworld, may be located (see Genette, *Narrative Discourse* 227–234; *Narrative Discourse Revisited* 84–95). However, the distinction between extradiegetic and intradiegetic narrators does not apply in the same way to multimodal narrative representations as it does to exclusively verbal narrative representations. One of the consequences of limiting the term "narrator" to refer to narrating characters in the sense sketched earlier is that, in multimodal media such as films, comics, and video games, we can encounter intradiegetic narrators without having previously encountered an extradiegetic narrator (as "covert" as such a narrator may be). Hence, it will be helpful to say a few more words about the distinction between extradiegetic and intradiegetic narrators as it applies to the narrative media examined in this book.

Since intradiegetic narrators cannot be defined as being narrated by extradiegetic narrators in films, comics, and video games, the core question becomes: Is the narrator located within the diegetic primary storyworld or "outside" of it? And this question, in turn, is connected to a second question: Does the film, comic, or video game provide any information about the specific situation in which a given narrator narrates that can be attributed to a "source" different from the narrator? The additional criterion proposed here is necessary since "overt" extradiegetic narrators may, of course, very well provide at least some information about the situation in which they narrate through the strategies mentioned above without thereby locating themselves in the diegetic primary storyworld at all. If there is another source that provides information about the situation in which a given narrator narrates—be it another narratorial voice or some other, nonnarratorial element of the representation—one can usually assume that this very information locates the narrator in question in "a storyworld of his or her own." While one can generally distinguish extradiegetic from intradiegetic narrators in films such as Tom Tykwer's *Run Lola Run*, comics such as Neil Gaiman's *The Sandman: Preludes and Nocturnes*, and video games such as Bioware's *Dragon Age: Origins*, then, I would also like to consider the common special case of narrators that are initially (self-)represented as if they were extradiegetic but later turn out to have been intradiegetic all along, which also serves to remind us that narratorial roles in general may change over time. This kind of "narratorial twist," which may render the narrating situation fairly paradoxical—as is the case with the narrating cowboy in Joel and Ethan Coen's *The Big Lebowski* or the narrator of *Bastion*, who is analyzed in the next chapter—or be easily plausibilized—as is the case when the voice-over narrator turns out to have been an intradiegetic version of Dilios, telling the story of

King Leonidas to his fellow Spartans at the end of Zack Snyder's film adaptation of *300*, or when the verbal narration in Alan Moore and Dave Gibbons's *Watchmen* turns out to be part of Rorschach's intradiegetic diary—sometimes also relocates much or even all of the previously represented situations within a hypodiegetic secondary instead of the initially constructed diegetic primary storyworld.[33]

While the distinction between extradiegetic and intradiegetic narrators refers to the *absolute* ontological position of a narrator within the narratorial hierarchy defined by the system of "diegetic levels" or subworlds that make up the storyworld as a whole, Genette discusses the *relative* ontological position of narrators with regard to the story they narrate as well: heterodiegetic narrators are not part of the story(world) they narrate; homodiegetic narrators are part of that story(world) (see Genette, *Narrative Discourse* 243–252; *Narrative Discourse Revisited* 96–113). Now, there are obvious problems with that distinction, in that it accounts neither for the rather subtle differences of involvement that homodiegetic narrators may exhibit nor for the difference between a narrator who is not part of the *story* he or she narrates and a narrator who is not part of the *storyworld* he or she narrates.[34] Moreover, there are quite a few films such as Mel Gibson's *Braveheart*, comics such as Peter Milligan's *Enigma*, and video games such as Hothead's *DeathSpank* whose narrators are initially represented as being heterodiegetic but eventually turn out to have been homodiegetic—a change of narratorial role that may be less decisive than when a narrator who is initially represented as extradiegetic turns out to have been intradiegetic all along, but still often forces the recipient to reassess his or her initial hypotheses about the represented storyworld. Yet, despite these lacunae, Genette's terms are well established and can, at least in principle, be retained in order to describe the *degree of involvement* of narrators in films, comics, and video games—even though they may occasionally be in need of further differentiation, which could, among other things, also include a closer examination of the relation between the *narrating I* and the *experiencing I*.[35] Refining Genette's distinction, Susan S. Lanser distinguishes between a "narrator who has no place in the story world," an "uninvolved eyewitness," a "witness-participant," a "minor character," a "co-protagonist," and the "sole protagonist" (*The Narrative Act* 160; the latter is sometimes also called "autodiegetic"). Yet this attempt at differentiation primarily refers to the experiencing I's involvement in the story the narrating I tells, which leaves unaddressed the question to what extent the narrating I is (cognitively, emotionally, or otherwise) involved in the story it tells—a question that may turn out to be relevant since a high degree of involvement tends to render the narrator unreliable.

Before discussing the functions of narratorial representation across media in slightly more detail, though, I would like to add a few more remarks on its various forms: since the distinction between extradiegetic and intradiegetic narrators hinges on the question to what extent the narrating situation is represented as part of the diegetic primary storyworld, which, in turn, usually boils down to the question of whether the narrating situation is represented by the nonnarratorial representation of multimodal media such as films, comics, and video games, it will come as no surprise that the consideration of a narrator's "textually projected role" may also be used to further illuminate the definition of narratorial representation as "communicated communication," emphasizing that the mode used to represent verbal narration does not have to be the same mode that verbal narration is represented as employing. In other words, the *represented mode of the verbal narration* may (and in fact often does) differ from the *verbal narration's mode of representation*. While the verbal narration is usually represented using spoken voice in contemporary films, using written text in contemporary comics, and using either spoken voice, written text, or both in contemporary video games, one can, on a transmedial level, distinguish between verbal narration represented as spoken, represented as written, and represented as thought.

Yet the represented mode of the verbal narration is not necessarily specified by a given narrative work: the default represented mode of verbal narration may arguably be conceived of as spoken (see, e.g.,

Aczel; A. Nünning, "Mimesis"; Walsh, "Who Is the Narrator?"), but extradiegetic narrators whose verbal narration's mode of representation is written commonly do not provide sufficient markers to allow recipients to intersubjectively construct the represented mode of the verbal narration as either spoken, written, or thought, resulting in the represented mode of the narratorial representation remaining unspecified. Similar indeterminacies are common with regard to intradiegetic narrators as well. On the one hand, it may, for example, be difficult to distinguish between an extradiegetic narrator who tells a story in which he or she plays a part and an intradiegetic thinking narrator. However, while the former kind of narrator is very common within contemporary films, comics, and video games, the use of intradiegetic characters' internal voices for verbal narration is rather rare in comparison.[36] On the other hand, it also often remains unspecified whether a given segment of intradiegetic verbal narration is meant to represent the written words of, for example, a letter (such as, albeit with very different effects, in Jim Abrahams's *Hot Shots! Part Deux*, David Small's *Stitches*, or Konami's *Silent Hill 2*), the thoughts of the character reading it, or even the thoughts of the character having written it (or being represented as writing it).

Another partially connected question is how nonnarratorial representation relates to narratorial representation. Sarah Kozloff claims (with some justification) that we usually "find it easiest to accept voice-over narrators as primary, framing storytellers when the voice-over is simultaneous with the film's opening shots, when one has seen as little as possible of the story world" (50). But while the narratorial representation of extradiegetic narrators frames the nonnarratorial representation at least to some extent, contemporary films, comics, and video games commonly use intradiegetic *nonframing narrators* whose hypodiegetic secondary storyworlds are exclusively represented by their verbal narration. Still, even in the case of intradiegetic narrators, the more interesting instances are usually constituted by *framing narrators*, whose narratorial representation is represented in such a way that the nonnarratorial representation can be understood as contributing to—or commenting on, or correcting—the representation of the storyworld the narrator in question tells about in some way, without the film, comic, or video game necessarily identifying that narrator as somehow being in control of the nonnarratorial representation.

An early in-depth discussion of this has been provided by David Black, who describes what he calls the "conventional voiceover structure" as follows: "A verbal narrating act on the part of a revealed or invisible, named or anonymous character, accompanies, triggers, or leads into an enacted sequence, which overlaps temporally with the voice and which is at least initially posited as a concrete, illustrative version of the story which the voice has been or is relating" (20). In fact, the relation between narratorial and nonnarratorial representation that Black describes here seems to be fairly generalizable with regard to framing narrators across media (which he calls "'invoking' narrators" [20]). Despite the fact that there is no consensus regarding the question of *representational hierarchy* in the case of extradiegetic narrators, in particular, I would maintain that whether recipients comprehend the "source" of a given strand of narratorial representation as extra- or intradiegetic, hetero- or homodiegetic, and framing or nonframing does not yet say anything (or at least not very much) about the degree of *narratorial control* that the respective narrator may or may not be represented as exerting on the audiovisual representation of the storyworld. As Black goes on to note, "the enacted sequence . . . is of course not literally the result of the verbal narration. Indeed, it appears to be presented directly by the same primary authorial agency which constructed the narrating character in the first place" (20), which would be the hypothetical author collective or, if one prefers to follow the early Chatman, an "implied author." Accordingly, "the problematic resides within this enacted sequence itself, in the innate tension between a story which is ostensibly—diegetically—attributed to a talking human narrator, and a discourse which is manifestly not consubstantial with any verbal narration, taped in its entirety or implied" (D. A. Black 20). Indeed, the "tension" between (facultative) narratorial and (obligatory) nonnarratorial strategies of representation increasingly turns out to be at the center of the ways in which multimodal media employ narrators—yet Black seems to hint at two rather different questions here.

On the one hand, Black's observations remind us that the answer to the question which "diegetic level" is represented by the nonnarratorial representation commonly appears as unspecified as the verbal narration's represented mode of representation: while an intradiegetic narrator's nonfictional[37] verbal narration is adequately described as representing a hypodiegetic secondary storyworld, the situation is usually not as clear-cut with regard to the nonnarratorial representation that he or she may frame. Particularly if the narrator's account of the diegetic primary storyworld's past is represented as being "accurate," there is no reason to comprehend the narrator in question as unreliable, and there are no contradictions between what the narrator narrates and what the audiovisual, verbal-pictorial, or interactive representation represents, it commonly remains unspecified (or becomes increasingly undecidable) whether what is represented by the nonnarratorial representation should be comprehended as being the diegetic primary storyworld (in which the narrator is located), the hypodiegetic secondary storyworld (which the narrator's verbal narration represents), or both (which may be a valid option in cases where one cannot discern any significant differences between the diegetic primary and the hypodiegetic secondary storyworld). Incidentally, this tendency of the nonnarratorial representation to "slide" from contributing to the representation of a hypodiegetic secondary storyworld to contributing to the representation of the diegetic primary storyworld in which the former is "anchored" also applies to cases where the framing is not narratorial but rather "subjective," marking the hypodiegetic secondary storyworld as a memory or memory-based dream (for further discussion of this, see the third part of this book). Moreover, it often also remains unspecified whether a segment of the nonnarratorial representation that is framed by an intradiegetic homodiegetic narrator's verbal narration contributes to the representation of the hypodiegetic secondary storyworld of his or her verbal narration or to the hypodiegetic secondary storyworld of the memory that his or her narration actualizes (or to both).

On the other hand, Black's characterization of the "tension" that defines the use of narrators in films (as well as other multimodal media such as comics and video games) also aims at the question of whether there is an intrinsic and more or less stable representational hierarchy between the narratorial and the nonnarratorial representation. While Black argues that nonnarratorial representation is, indeed, always "primary," such a claim is not entirely uncontested within film narratology. Markus Kuhn, for example, "assumes that there is no necessarily fixed hierarchical relation between the *visual narrating instance* and the *verbal narrating instance*, as long as the latter can be located on the extradiegetic level" (86, original emphases, my translation from the German). Interestingly, though, Kuhn goes on to mainly discuss what I would call the *quantitative* and *qualitative relations* between narratorial and nonnarratorial representation (focusing on how the latter may lead to various forms of unreliability), which does not define the kind of representational hierarchy that Black describes in any significant way. Still, if one accepts that films, comics, and video games can use extradiegetic narrators at all,[38] the observation that narrators across media may (and, in fact, often do) fulfill not only narratorial but also a variety of authorial functions makes it appear more appropriate to argue that recipients will need comparatively strong markers—such as those provided in Spike Jonze and Charlie Kaufman's *Adaptation.* and Art Spiegelman's *Maus* or, perhaps, in Shane Black's *Kiss Kiss Bang Bang* and Alan Moore and Kevin O'Neill's *The League of Extraordinary Gentlemen*—to intersubjectively construct an extradiegetic or intradiegetic narrator as being in control of both the narratorial and the nonnarratorial representation, instead of generally assuming that the narratorial representation can be "subsumed" under the nonnarratorial representation in all films, comics, and video games.

Even in films, comics, and video games that do use a narrator, the narratorial representation is usually not uniformly present throughout all parts of the narrative work in question. Instead, it would seem that Britta Hartmann's observation that the narratorial voice tends to be most salient in the opening sequences and toward the end of many feature films can tentatively be generalized as applying to comics and video games as well (though, admittedly, the comparatively complex films, comics, and video games that are mainly analyzed in this book are *not* particularly suitable to substantiate that claim, as they tend to either employ narratorial representation extensively or use no narrator at all). Let me conclude, then, by saying a few more words on the range of qualitative relations between narratorial and nonnarratorial representation in the context of what is usually described as *narratorial* or, more generally, *narrative unreliability*.[39] Similarly starting from the observation that voice-over narrators in the feature film tend to "speak only intermittently and do not mediate every moment of the story" (Kozloff 74), Sarah Kozloff emphasizes that there are quite a few cases where "the viewer notes a certain overlap between the information provided visually and that provided by the narration" (20). Hence, she distinguishes between "overlapping," "complementary," and "disparate" combinations of narratorial and nonnarratorial representation in the feature film.[40]

While this is a good starting point, I want to use slightly different terms and—modifying one of the even more sophisticated differentiations proposed by Kuhn—add a fourth type of relation, distinguishing between *unrelated, redundant, complementary,* and *contradictory combinations* of narratorial and nonnarratorial representation. Since Kozloff and Kuhn agree that we should speak of a "degree of correspondence between narration and images" (see Kozloff 103) and that it is "impossible to formulate general rules for the identification of these relations" (Kuhn 99, my translation from the German), however, I would also like to stress the heuristic character of these distinctions. Generally, I would argue—and will illustrate that argument in the following chapter—that it is neither the mode of representation that is used to represent the narratorial representation (or its represented mode) nor the question which narratorial role its narrator fulfills (i.e., whether that narrator is extra- or intradiegetic, hetero- or homodiegetic, reliable or unreliable) but rather the combination of narratorial and nonnarratorial representation that primarily defines the medium-specific forms and functions of narrators across media. More specifically, the relation between narratorial and nonnarratorial representation will be important in multimodal media that employ some form of narratorial or narrative unreliability.

As I have repeatedly hinted at on the previous pages, there is a "kind of partial unreliability . . . unique to two-track media such as the cinema" (Chatman, *Coming to Terms* 136) that also tends to underscore the sometimes quite complex interplay between narratorial and nonnarratorial representation. It would go beyond the scope of this chapter to extensively discuss the existing research, yet it is still worth noting that the term "unreliability" has, in the past few years, become quite popular not only within literary but also within film narratology and that the label is currently attached to a large number of sometimes only loosely interrelated phenomena, not all of which seem overly relevant to the purpose of this book.[41] Still, it will be helpful to at least distinguish between *representational unreliability*, where the "fictional facts" of the storyworld are represented (or, perhaps, comprehended) unreliably, and *evaluative unreliability*, where the "fictional facts" are evaluated (or, perhaps, interpreted) unreliably.[42] Again, this is a rough distinction that might turn out to be in need of further differentiation,[43] but it still captures the difference between the *unreliable representation* of storyworlds in films such as David Fincher's *Fight Club*, comics such as Neil Gaiman's *Batman: Whatever Happened to the Caped Crusader?*, or video games such as Supergiant Games' *Bastion* and the *unreliable evaluation* of these elements by their respective narrators.

Now, it would be overly reductive to say that the unreliable evaluation of storyworld elements can only be realized through verbal narration, but it nevertheless seems that evaluative unreliability is not as easily realized in nonnarratorial representation as is representational unreliability.[44] However, since the combination of narratorial and nonnarratorial representation characteristic for multimodal media considerably complicates the supposedly simple problem of representational unreliability, and since there is still no consensus within literary narratology about how evaluative unreliability is best conceptualized—a debate epitomized in Ansgar Nünning's well-known question, "Unreliable, compared to what?" (see A. Nünning, "Unreliable")—the present study will focus on the former.[45] Indeed, representational unreliability in films, comics, and video games arguably serves to highlight not only the range of different functions that the use of narratorial representation in multimodal media may fulfill (with narrators being used to orient or disorient the recipients of narrative works across media with regard to the intersubjective construction of the represented storyworld in a variety of ways)[46] but also stresses the importance of the relation between narratorial and nonnarratorial representation.

Before I can further examine this relation and the resulting medium-specific realization of the use of narrators in contemporary films, comics, and video games, let me briefly summarize some of the core aspects of the narrator as a transmedial concept: on a fundamental level, I have proposed to understand narrators as narrating characters to whom recipients may attribute the kind of narratorial representation that prototypically takes the form of verbal narration. This narratorial representation can be distinguished from nonnarratorial representation that prototypically takes the form of audiovisual representation in films, verbal-pictorial representation in comics, or interactive representation in video games, and that will usually not be attributed to narrators but rather to hypothetical authors or hypothetical author collectives. The narrative complexities introduced by framing (as opposed to nonframing) narrators, the relation between narratorial and nonnarratorial representation, and the relation between the verbal narration's mode of representation and its represented mode are of central importance for the analysis of narrators across media. However, the latter can also be described using various perhaps more conventionalized narratological categories: according to their position within the narratorial hierarchy, their degree of involvement in the stories they tell, and their representational as well as evaluative (un)reliability. Having established that, even when limited to narrators-as-narrating-characters, the narrator remains a decidedly transmedial concept, I will now take a closer look at how contemporary films, comics, and video games realize strategies of narratorial representation in more or less medium-specific ways.

5 Narratorial Representation across Media

Strategies of Narratorial Representation in Contemporary Films

One does not have to look very hard to find a variety of different examples of contemporary films employing fairly "overt" extradiegetic narrators who are either heterodiegetic—such as the voice-over narrators at the beginning of Tom Tykwer's *Run Lola Run* and *Perfume: The Story of a Murderer*—or homodiegetic—such as the unnamed narrator in David Fincher's *Fight Club* and the dead narrator in Sam Mendes's *American Beauty*. Likewise, these films use a variety of intradiegetic narrators that may be either heterodiegetic or homodiegetic—both when the narratorial representation frames the audiovisual representation, as in Bryan Singer's *The Usual Suspects* (where Verbal Kint acts as a largely homodiegetic framing narrator and his antagonist David Kujan acts as a heterodiegetic framing narrator), and when it does not, as in the Burger King or foot massage dialogue sequences from Quentin Tarantino's *Pulp Fiction*. In all of these cases, the specific mediality of the feature film at least partially determines the ways in which narrators can be realized: with the exception of subtitles, early silent film's intertitles, and written inserts which are sometimes used to specify the temporal and spatial location of the represented situations within the storyworld as a whole, verbal narration in feature films tends to be represented through spoken language, independently of whether it is meant to be understood as spoken, written, or thought. Accordingly, even when a voice-over narrator more or less directly adapts the words of a literary narrator, as is the case in *Perfume* as well as in *Fight Club*,[1] the medium-specific mode of representation of the verbal narration adds various characterizing paraverbal cues such as voice quality, pitch, and speaking style to its represented mode. While it seems uncontroversial to attribute film's spoken voice-over narration to a narrator-as-narrating-character, then, these narrators are usually not represented as being in control of the audiovisual representation, even though the audiovisual representation commonly contributes to the representation of the storyworld about which they tell their narratees.

It is clearly beyond the scope of this chapter to catalogue the diversity of forms in which narrators may be realized within contemporary feature films,[2] but *Run Lola Run* once again provides a good example of how films that do not emphatically organize their global strategy of narrative representation around the use of a narrator (as is the case in *The Usual Suspects*, *Fight Club*, or Spike Jonze and Charlie Kaufman's *Adaptation.*, among others) may still "casually" use extradiegetic as well as intradiegetic narrators to add some narrative—or, more precisely, narratorial—complexity to the representation of their storyworld(s). In the opening sequence preceding the titles, *Run Lola Run* not only presents the spectator with written intertitles that quote the poet T. S. Eliot and the soccer player/manager Sepp Herberger[3] but also uses an extradiegetic heterodiegetic voice-over narrator to offer some pseudo-philosophical reflections on the human condition and the nature of time. The distinctive voice of Hans Paetsch certainly provides sufficient cues to allow the spectators to intersubjectively construct a narrating character, but the relation between his brief musings and the following sequences seems underspecified, at best—it could even be argued that these musings barely qualify as narration. Likewise, the ontological status of what is represented by the audiovisual representation—which shows some of the film's main actors as part of a larger crowd, using overlit and out-of-focus pictures as well as some additional color changes to mark the questionable ontological status of the represented situations (see figure 11)—remains unspecified, but is perhaps best comprehended as being external to the film's storyworld.

However, *Run Lola Run* repeatedly employs additional forms of narratorial representation, using intradiegetic narrators to provide details about the storyworld, contribute to the unfolding of the story,

Fig. 11. Introductory sequence in *Run Lola Run*

and balance the "hierarchy of knowledge" between the main characters: when Lola and Manni use the phone to tell each other what has gone wrong during their previous criminal activities, they function as intradiegetic narrators whose verbal narration represents a hypodiegetic secondary storywold. Using black-and-white pictures to mark the different ontological status of the represented situations, the audiovisual representation also contributes to the representation of these hypodiegetic secondary storyworlds, although—due to the nonfictional nature of Lola's and Manni's verbal narrations—the initial change in "diegetic level" gradually morphs into what might also be comprehended as a mere analepsis, representing not the hypodiegetic secondary storyworlds of Lola's and Manni's verbal narration but rather the earlier point in the diegetic primary storyworld time to which they refer. Besides these instances of intradiegetic framing narrators,[4] *Run Lola Run* also repeatedly uses nonframing narrators when representing situations in which Lola, in particular, tells other characters about the events that have recently happened to her or Manni without the audiovisual representation contributing to the representation of the verbal narration's hypodiegetic secondary storyworld.

Apart from these clear cases of an "introductory" extradiegetic heterodiegetic and several framing as well as nonframing intradiegetic homodiegetic narrators, *Run Lola Run* also uses a more subtle form of written intertitles to temporally locate certain situations represented by the audiovisual representation in the storyworld's "future." During the three "versions" of Lola's attempt to save Manni, the audiovisual representation repeatedly employs a series of still pictures to represent—or, rather, summarize—different courses of the future life of various characters that Lola meets: a woman with a buggy, a man on a bicycle, and a clerk in the bank where Lola's father works (different courses of the future lives of the latter two of which are only summarized in the first two "versions," since the development of events during the third "version" prevents Lola from meeting them a "third time"). In all of these cases, though, the still pictures are initialized by a brief intertitle that reads "UND DANN" ("subsequently"; see figure 12), marking the following sequence as a strongly compressed but otherwise quite extensive prolepsis. It would be possible to describe these brief intertitles as a rudimentary form of highly "covert" narration attributable to an extradiegetic heterodiegetic narrator, but in light of the near absence of any cues that would allow the spectator to construct such a narrator-as-narrating-character, it actually seems more appropriate to treat this kind of verbal element as a

Fig. 12. Intertitle "UND DANN" ("subsequently") in *Run Lola Run*

part of the nonnarratorial audiovisual representation instead (and, hence, attribute it to the hypothetical author collective of which the film's director, Tom Tykwer, is perhaps the most recognizable author figure).[5]

As this brief analysis of *Run Lola Run* has served to illustrate, then, forms of narratorial representation (as well as other verbal elements more appropriately described as part of the nonnarratorial representation) are commonly used in contemporary films to provide the spectator with spatiotemporal orientation in the face of narrative complexity. But, of course, narrators do not necessarily have to further narrative comprehension: indeed, it seems that contemporary films quite often—and perhaps more so than contemporary comics and video games[6]—make use of unreliable narrators that tend to disorient rather than orient the spectators. Accordingly, the following discussion will focus on contemporary feature films that use narratorial representation to unreliable (and metaleptic) effect: as has already been mentioned in the previous chapter, representationally unreliable nonnarratorial representation is usually attributed to characters in some way, either to the (often "misreporting") unreliable narration of a narrator or to the (often "underreported") unreliable perception of a "regular" character. Incidentally, two of the examples mentioned above—*The Usual Suspects* and *Fight Club*—realize what may be considered as the two prototypical forms of representational unreliability in contemporary feature films.

In *The Usual Suspects*, large parts of the audiovisual representation are framed by Verbal Kint's highly unreliable verbal narration, thereby quite likely "misreporting" a number of key elements of the diegetic primary storyworld. In contradistinction to *Run Lola Run*, neither the nonfictional verbal representation attributed to Verbal nor the parts of the audiovisual representation that it frames are representing the diegetic primary storyworld, emphasizing the importance of distinguishing between mere analepses and the representation of (nonfictional) hypodiegetic secondary storyworlds. Interestingly, though, the reliable parts of the audiovisual representation (which represent the diegetic primary storyworld in which Verbal acts as a largely homodiegetic intradiegetic narrator) are also framed by a form of highly "covert" and fairly rudimentary verbal narration—which, once more, might be more appropriately described as part of the non-narratorial representation (attributable to the film's hypothetical author collective, of which the author figures of the director Bryan Singer and the script writer Christopher McQuarrie are perhaps the most salient members) than attributed to a separate extradiegetic heterodiegetic narrator-as-narrating-character, however "covert" he or she may be. More specifically, there are three points in the film where written inserts are used to spatially as well as temporally locate the situations represented in the following sequences within the diegetic primary storyworld. The very first sequence that follows the titles is framed by a written insert that reads "San Pedro, California—last night." In the sequence that follows, Verbal is first represented as testifying to the District Attorney, introducing the storyworld's "present" (in relation to the events that took place "last night").

While Verbal's verbal narration appears to frame the following audiovisual representation of how the "usual suspects" are arrested and put into the same holding cell at first glance, the second written insert—"New York City—6 weeks ago"—as well as the pronounced discrepancy between what Verbal could know and what the spectator is shown ultimately indicates that the audiovisual representation does not contribute to the representation of the hypodiegetic secondary storyworld of Verbal's verbal narration but, instead, reliably represents an earlier point in the diegetic primary storyworld's time. However, the audiovisual representation of the arrests, which is not simultaneously accompanied by Verbal's voice-over, needs to be distinguished from the audiovisual representation of the lineup and the following interaction of the "usual suspects" in the holding cell, which is more clearly framed by Verbal's unreliable verbal narration and emulates its representational unreliability, since it does not show him as the criminal mastermind he later turns out to have been.[7] This first segment of unreliable audiovisual representation is followed by another segment of reliable audiovisual representation that is, once more, framed by the third and final written insert—"San Pedro, California—present day." The remainder of the film uses the audiovisual representation to either represent the diegetic primary storyworld reliably or to contribute to the representation of the hypodiegetic secondary storyworld created by the intradiegetic Verbal's unreliable verbal narration (as well as, occasionally, the hypo-hypodiegetic tertiary storyworlds of hypodiegetic narrators' verbal acts of narration occurring within Verbal's version of events).

As interesting as the results of Verbal's "web of lies" are from a narratological point of view, the "misreporting" or lying unreliable narrators in films such as Akira Kurosawa's *Rashomon*, Alfred Hitchcock's *Stage Fright*, or *The Usual Suspects* constitute only one of two prototypical cases: while *The Usual Suspects* largely attributes the representational unreliability of the audiovisual narration to the representational unreliability of Verbal's verbal narration, the representational unreliability in films such as David Fincher's *Fight Club*, M. Night Shyamalan's *The Sixth Sense*, or Ron Howard's *A Beautiful Mind* is not motivated by a lying narrator but by the "underreported" representation of the unnamed experiencing I's subjective worldview. Yet, in contrast to *The Sixth Sense* and *A Beautiful Mind*, *Fight Club* uses an extradiegetic homodiegetic narrator, who remains unnamed and unshown but can be identified through the highly recognizable paraverbal characteristics of Edward Norton's voice. *Fight Club*, too, uses an unreliable narrator, then, but the narrating I seems not so much to lie as to represent the experiencing I's specific worldview without sufficiently marking it. Since, moreover, the audiovisual representation "illustrates" the narrating I's verbal narration for the first two-thirds of the film, the interaction between the representation of a character's subjective version of the storyworld and an intersubjective or, perhaps, even objective version of it forms a key element of this kind of representational unreliability. This becomes particularly apparent during the central "twist" of *Fight Club*, when the experiencing I finally understands that Tyler Durden is a hallucination of his, while the audiovisual representation repeatedly—albeit rather briefly—switches to an intersubjective mode of representation, revealing the nonexistence of Tyler in the diegetic primary storyworld.

For the time being, however, I would like to focus on *Fight Club*'s characteristic use of an unreliable narrator whose unreliable verbal narration still at least partially motivates the representational unreliability of the audiovisual representation, even though both cases of unreliability are eventually motivated by the unreliable perception of the narrator's experiencing I. The opening sequence that follows the titles provides a good example of the difficulties in locating a given narrator within the narratorial hierarchy that may arise from the potential incongruity between the represented mode of the verbal narration and its mode of representation—which, in turn, is due to the fact that not only spoken but also written and, albeit to a lesser extent, thought narration is conventionally represented in the form of spoken voice-over in contemporary films. While this is occasionally contested,[8] the film arguably provides a number of cues that mark the voice-over narrator as extradiegetic, including the rather clear marker that the speech of the experiencing I is impaired by the gun barrel in his mouth, while the verbal narration that reflects on this state of affairs—"With a gun barrel between your teeth, you speak only in vowels"—is enunciated clearly, as well as the use of deictic and other linguistic markers indicating both a temporal and an emotional distance between the narrating I and the experiencing I that makes comprehending the voice-over as merely the internal voice of the latter comparatively implausible.

Moreover, *Fight Club* provides a good opportunity to (re)examine the question of representational hierarchy between narratorial and nonnarratorial modes of representation. On the one hand, the unnamed narrating I's verbal voice-over narration is clearly represented as "triggering" the various analepses of the audiovisual representation, even though the unnamed extradiegetic narrator is not represented as having the ability to evoke the respective sounds and moving pictures himself. On the other hand, *Fight Club* uses a number of metaleptic strategies to destabilize the supposedly clear-cut

Fig. 13. Metaleptically hesitant expression of the experiencing I in *Fight Club*

distinctions between extradiegetic and intradiegetic narratorial positions, narrating I and experiencing I, or narratorial and nonnarratorial representation. While the hesitant expression on the face of the diegetic experiencing I during the opening sequence, shortly before the second analepsis (see figure 13), could already be described as a mild form of epistemic metalepsis subverting the distinction between an extradiegetic narrating I and an intradiegetic experiencing I, most of *Fight Club*'s metaleptic transgressions are marked more clearly. A particularly strong example of a transgression that combines elements of epistemic and ontological metalepsis can be found in the sequence of the film that is framed by the unnamed narrating I with the words "Let me tell you a little bit about Tyler Durden . . ." (see figure 14). Here, the extradiegetic narrating I appears to paradoxically enter the diegetic primary storyworld, the very world to whose representation his verbal narration contributes at least partially.

Tyler initially seems unaware of the presence of the unnamed narrating I, but they both address the same extradiegetic narratee. Interestingly, though, the implausible knowledge of Tyler is not limited to the domain of the extradiegetic narrating I but includes the audiovisual representation as well: when the narrating I explains how films that are shown in the cinema use cue marks—or "cigarette burns," as Tyler calls them—to signal the projectionists when a reel needs to be changed and just such a cue mark briefly appears in the

Fig. 14. The narrating I telling an extradiegetic narratee "a little bit about Tyler Durden" in *Fight Club*

Fig. 15. Tyler Durden pointing at the "cigarette burn" on the film picture in *Fight Club*

upper-right corner of the picture, Tyler points his finger at it (see figure 15). For one, this testifies to a kind of implausible knowledge that both Tyler and the experiencing I (who, of course, eventually turn out to be the same person, in a way) possess regarding their status as characters in a film: when the initial representation of the situation in which Tyler has put a gun in the mouth of the experiencing I is completed (with some overlap) at the end of the film, both the experiencing I—"I *still* can't think of anything"—and Tyler—"flashback humor"—seem aware of the "extrafictional fact" that they are characters within the film's diegetic primary storyworld. In addition, however, Tyler's increased awareness of the audiovisual representation, in combination with the "fictional fact" that he uses his job as a projectionist as an opportunity to insert pornographic pictures into family films, prepares the ground for an additional metaleptic "twist" that seems to subvert the conventional notion that voice-over narrators usually do not control the audiovisual representation.

The picture of a semi-erect penis—a "nice big cock," in Tyler's words—that is briefly inserted into the audiovisual representation at the end of *Fight Club* hints at the existence of an extradiegetic counterpart to the intradiegetic Tyler, since it was this very picture that the latter was previously shown to have inserted into family films (see figure 16). Of course, there is a perfectly plausible explanation for the (re)appearance of the pornographic picture: the filmmakers put it there. (Or, if one prefers to remain careful and technical: the presence of the pornographic picture can be attributed to the film's hypothetical author collective, of which the author figure of the director David Fincher is perhaps the most visible member.) Accordingly, to say that the film represents an extradiegetic version of Tyler responsible for the audiovisual representation would, perhaps, be a somewhat overenthusiastic "reading" of the pornographic picture's second appearance, but *Fight Club* gestures at the potential of metaleptic narratorial arrangements to subvert the distinction between narratorial representation (which prototypically takes the form of spoken verbal narration in the medium of film) and nonnarratorial representation

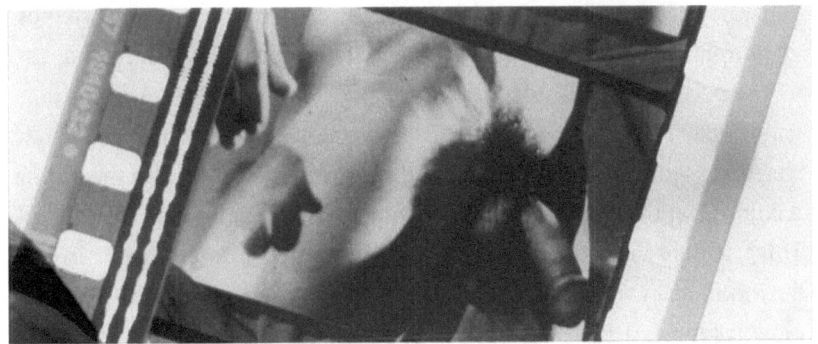

Fig. 16. Tyler Durden inserting a pornographic picture into a family film in *Fight Club*

(which prototypically takes the form of audiovisual representation in the medium of film). As should also have become clear during the preceding analyses, though, neither the extradiegetic homodiegetic narrator voiced by Edward Norton in *Fight Club* nor the intradiegetic homodiegetic narrator Verbal Kint in *The Usual Suspects* directly controls the audiovisual narration, and the representation of these kinds of in-control narrators (who are usually represented as authoring characters in some way) remains fairly rare, at least in contemporary mainstream film.[9]

Where they are represented as being in control not only of their verbal narration but also of the audiovisual representation, narrators in contemporary feature films usually get some kind of more encompassing authorship ascribed to them (beyond having "authored" the verbal narration that is still attributed to them, that is). To take another well-known (and highly metaleptic) example: Spike Jonze and Charlie Kaufman's *Adaptation.* tells the story of the scriptwriter Charlie Kaufman, who is hired to adapt Susan Orlean's novel *The Orchid Thief* for the screen. As opposed to the narratorial representation in *Fight Club*, the voice-over in *Adaptation.* is consistently attributable to Charlie's experiencing I (making him one of the comparatively rare cases of intradiegetic thinking narrators who actually have an entirely plausible reason to "think stories to themselves," although he also acts as an intradiegetic speaking and an intradiegetic writing narrator in some situations). But even without an additional extradiegetic narrating I, it is one of the central narrative strategies of *Adaptation.* to prevent the spectator from locating certain characters precisely on a single "diegetic level." For starters, *Adaptation.* extensively refers to actual persons: Susan Orlean is not just a fictional character (played by Meryl Streep) within the fictional storyworld of *Adaptation.* but also the actual author of the actual novel *The Orchid Thief*, which—just like the corresponding novel and character in the fictional storyworld of *Adaptation.*—tells a story about the actual person John LaRoche (who is played by Chris Cooper in *Adaptation.*). Likewise, Charlie Kaufman (who is played by Nicolas Cage) is not just a fictional scriptwriter in the diegetic primary storyworld of

Adaptation., but also an actual scriptwriter the production of whom's actual film *Being John Malkovich* is likewise "fictionalized" as part of the diegetic primary storyworld of *Adaptation.* Moreover, the scriptwriting guru Robert McKee (who is played by Brian Cox) to whom Charlie's fictional twin brother Donald (also played by Nicolas Cage) as well as Charlie himself goes looking for advice, is, of course, once more not only a fictional character within the fictional diegetic primary storyworld of *Adaptation.* but also an actual scriptwriting guru, who has authored actual scriptwriting manuals (the best known of which is probably *Story*, which also appears in *Adaptation.*'s storyworld).

Yet it does not stop here: Charlie and Donald Kaufman, the latter of whom has no actual counterpart of which I would be aware, are both listed as the actual scriptwriters of *Adaptation.*, which is an adaptation of the actual novel *The Orchid Thief* that the actual Susan Orlean has authored and the fictional counterpart of which the fictional Charlie is hired to adapt for the screen within the diegetic primary storyworld of *Adaptation.* It seems clear, then, that *Adaptation.* employs a fairly complex form of "mirroring strategies" between reality and fiction, but that does not necessarily make the represented storyworld and/or its representation metaleptic. In fact, the film also uses a highly complex arrangement of narratorial voices and nonnarratorial written inserts to frame the audiovisual representation as representing various points in the storyworld's time as well as various "diegetic levels" without thereby generating particularly metaleptic effects: the written inserts that mark the points in storyworld time that the respective sequences represent range from "Hollywood, CA Four Billion and Forty Years Earlier" (at the beginning of the film, the idea of which Charlie is later represented as developing) via "New Yorker Magazine, Three Years Earlier" (when Susan is represented as writing her *New Yorker* article that later scores her the book contract) and "State Road 29, Florida, Two Years Earlier" (when John is represented as "hunting orchids") to "North Miami, Nine Years Earlier" (when the car crash is represented in which John's mother and uncle died and his subsequently divorced wife was heavily injured). All of these, as well as several other written inserts, could be comprehended as part of the nonnarratorial representation, spatiotemporally locating the represented situations within the storyworld as a whole and, hence, primarily marking more or less simple analepses. However, all of the above-mentioned sequences are framed narratorially as well: the first by Charlie's verbal narration, the second by his work on the script for the adaptation of *The Orchid Thief*, the third by Susan's written narration that is part of her article for the *New Yorker*, and the fourth by John telling the story of the car crash to Susan via the phone. Without a doubt, then, *Adaptation.* is narratively complex and extensively plays with the kind of "ontological indeterminacy" that commonly occurs when multimodal media use framing narrators. However, the film only becomes genuinely metaleptic when the decisions of the diegetic Charlie (and his twin brother) within the diegetic primary storyworld are increasingly represented as influencing the level of narrative representation, which ultimately allows the film to pretend that the diegetic Kaufman brothers work on the actual script of *Adaptation.*, and, hence, create the storyworld of which they are a part.

In the course of the highly nonchronological and "multileveled" plot, it is not only the actual film *Adaptation.* that cues the spectator to oscillate between Charlie's working process and its result. Rather, this process is also commented on by the fictional Charlie himself: somewhat similarly to *Fight Club*, *Adaptation.* employs a key sequence in which its paradoxical narratorial-authorial configuration becomes particularly apparent. More specifically, this sequence represents the at least mildly metaleptic situation of the fictional Charlie dictating a rough version of the script for another sequence that has already been represented as well as experienced by Charlie, and the latter even explicitly states that he is writing himself into his script (see figure 17 and figure 18).[10] If doubts remain that *Adaptation.* presents a case of particularly metareferential metaleptic representation in which diegetic—and, despite the reference to actual persons and artworks, fictional—characters work on the script of the film that represents just the storyworld in which they are located, these doubts are further

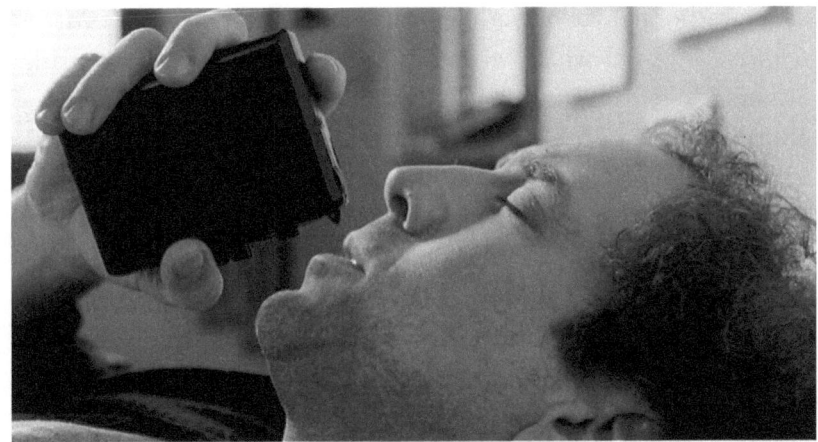

Fig. 17. The diegetic Charlie Kaufman dictating parts of his script in *Adaptation*.

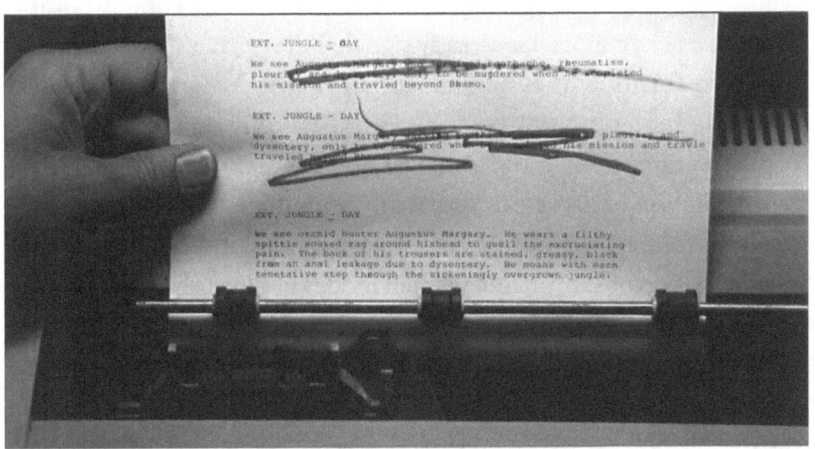

Fig. 18. The diegetic Charlie Kaufman typing parts of his script in *Adaptation*.

resolved during the last third of the film. The relevant turning point in both the story and the plot is marked by a situation in which Charlie asks Donald for help with the script for the *Orchid Thief* adaptation. After this situation has been represented, the film morphs from a "character study" that mainly consists of Charlie's voice-over reflections on life and writing into what Jan Christoph Meister describes as a "traditional shoot-out-plus-car-chase narrative" ("The *Metalepticon*" n. pag.) which leads to Charlie and Donald uncovering Susan's and John's criminal activities, both Donald and John dying—Donald is shot, John is killed by an alligator—and Susan going to jail. That the film ends not only with a largely metareferential thinking voice-over by Charlie—in which he plans to conclude the script with a sequence in which Charlie plans to conclude the script with a sequence, in which . . .[11]—but also with the song "Happy Together," which Donald had previously used in his own script "The Three" and which he, moreover, has hummed shortly before finally succumbing to his wounds, further stresses the particular kind of autopoietic metalepsis that permeates *Adaptation*.

While narratorial representation is necessarily realized within the specific mediality of conventionally distinct media such as films, comics, or video games, my brief examination of contemporary films' use of narrators has already signaled the possibility of considering both forms and functions of this rather salient strategy of narrative representation as transmedial, if only on a certain level of abstraction: comics and video games may use different modes of representation of narrator's verbal narration than film (or, more precisely, put different emphasis on written modes of representation or a combination of spoken and written modes of representation, respectively), and verbal-pictorial as well as interactive modes of representation may offer different limitations and affordances to representing intradiegetic narrators than audiovisual modes of representation, but the established distinctions between extradiegetic and intradiegetic or heterodiegetic and homodiegetic narrators as well as the range of possibilities between using reliable narrators to orient and unreliable narrators to disorient the recipients apply to films, comics, and video games alike. Still, some differences remain regarding the prototypical forms and functions of narrators and narratorial representation that go beyond the question of whether intradiegetic narrators are represented via a sequence of shots, an arrangement of panels on the page, or even a segment of simulated gameplay. Accordingly, I will focus on these medium-specific aspects in the following, emphasizing the relation between the verbal narration's mode of representation and its represented mode as well as the question of narratorial control over what would usually be expected to be nonnarratorial elements of the overall representation in contemporary comics, on the one hand, and the relation between narratorial and nonnarratorial representation in video games as well as the question how video games' narrators fulfill not only narrative but also ludic functions in the context of the medium's (obligatory) interactivity and (facultative) nonlinearity, on the other.

Strategies of Narratorial Representation in Contemporary Comics

Let me stress again, then, that while there are a number of medium-specific particularities in the ways in which narratorial representation is conventionally realized in comics, the variety of narrators and the prototypical relations between narratorial and nonnarratorial representation to be found in contemporary graphic novels still seem, at least in certain respects, rather similar to the use of narrators and narratorial representation in contemporary feature films. Since (printed, nondigital) comics cannot make use of an auditive channel, the verbal narration's default mode of representation is usually written,[12] even though its represented mode may, once again, be spoken, written, or—albeit somewhat less commonly—thought. As has already been mentioned in chapter 3, the most strongly conventionalized medium-specific strategies of verbal representation in comics are narration boxes, speech balloons, and thought bubbles. The latter two are regularly used to represent (spoken or thought) verbal narration attributable to intradiegetic (or "lower-order") narrators; but the potential uses of narration boxes are significantly broader, with the same form—which is usually constituted by spaces separated from the remaining contents of the panel, as in Frank Miller's *Batman: The Dark Knight Returns* (see figure 19), but also includes words being written directly into the panel, as in Chris Ware's *Jimmy Corrigan: The Smartest Kid on Earth* (see figure 20)—commonly being employed to represent either the characteristically unspecified narration of an

Fig. 19. Subjective narration boxes in *Batman: The Dark Knight Returns*

extradiegetic narrator, the spoken voice of an intradiegetic speaking narrator, the written narration of an intradiegetic writing narrator, or the internal voices of characters, which may, in some cases, function as intradiegetic thinking narrators as well.[13]

Just as in contemporary feature films, however, heterodiegetic narrators in comics tend to be extradiegetic and are often limited to giving spatiotemporal coordinates, as in the beginning of Alan Moore and Kevin O'Neill's *The League of Extraordinary Gentlemen* series (see figure 21), but there are also extradiegetic heterodiegetic narrators that (subsequently) make more extensive use of their narratorial voice, as in Neil Gaiman's *The Sandman* series (see figure 22). While it might be argued that the default represented mode of comics' characteristically unspecified extradiegetic verbal narration should be taken to be spoken rather than written or thought (as "hearing voices" seems more strongly conventionalized than reading texts in the case of verbal narration), this general tendency is undermined in both *The*

Fig. 20. Subjective frameless narration boxes in *Jimmy Corrigan: The Smartest Kid on Earth*

League of Extraordinary Gentlemen and *The Sandman*. On the one hand, the latter represents the verbal narration attributable to its "covert" extradiegetic narrator using narration boxes that—through their color and shape—seem to emulate the look of writing paper.[14] On the other hand, the former's peritexts introduce a variety of fictional characters that are, perhaps, closer to authoring characters than to mere author figures—including "fictionalized" versions of the writer Alan Moore and the artist Kevin O'Neill as well as the wholly fictional editor Scotty Smiles[15]—which arguably emphasizes the verbal narration's mode of representation over its represented mode. Since *The Sandman* does not provide additional cues beyond the verbal narration itself that would point toward the presence of a fictional narrator-as-narrating-character and the relation between the "fictionalized" author figures/authoring characters represented in *The League of Extraordinary Gentlemen*'s fictional paratexts and the highly

Fig. 21. Extradiegetic heterodiegetic narrator in *The League of Extraordinary Gentlemen*

Fig. 22. Extradiegetic heterodiegetic narrator in *The Sandman: Preludes and Nocturnes*

"covert" verbal narration that provides the reader with spatiotemporal orientation likewise remains unspecified during most of the series, one could argue that the verbal narration may be more appropriately described as part of the nonnarratorial representation—attributable to the hypothetical author collective, of which the author figures of the writers Alan Moore and Neil Gaiman, respectively, are perhaps the most salient members—than as a separate strand of narratorial representation, once more. Yet *The Sandman*, in particular, renders such a description problematic, as the series employs the verbal narration in question quite extensively, which makes it appear less "covert," even though it could still be either attributed to (some member of) the hypothetical author collective (such as Neil Gaiman) or, alternatively, to a highly "covert" extradiegetic heterodiegetic narrator.

Homodiegetic narrators, on the other hand, are more easily realized in the extradiegetic and the intradiegetic variety, but deciding which is which may occasionally prove difficult in the case of (potentially) intradiegetic thinking narrators due to the characteristically unspecified represented mode of extradiegetic verbal narration. A prototypical example of a particularly "overt" extradiegetic homodiegetic narrator can be found in Craig Thompson's controversial graphic novel *Habibi*, the verbal narration of which clearly locates Dodola's narrating I outside of the diegetic primary storyworld in which her experiencing I is located via deictic markers such as the use of the past tense, while simultaneously giving the reader next to no information about the situation in which the act of narration takes place (see figure 23).[16] Despite the fact that Dodola's narrating I is initially marked as extradiegetic, then, there is some fluctuation regarding her degree of involvement in the story—or, rather, stories—she tells that is also connected to her multiple positions within the narratorial hierarchy: the main part of the overall narrative consists of her and her ward/friend/lover Zam's life story, leading to a high degree of involvement that makes her narratorial role in these segments homodiegetic. *Habibi* includes various smaller mythical and religious stories from within the diegetic primary storyworld, however, and the narration of some of these can be attributed to Dodola's

Fig. 23. Dodola functioning as an extradiegetic homodiegetic narrator in *Habibi*

experiencing I (which in turn becomes an intradiegetic narrating I), causing her to oscillate between an extradiegetic, (largely) homodiegetic and an intradiegetic, (largely) heterodiegetic narratorial role throughout the graphic novel.

While there are some situations in *Habibi* where Dodola's intradiegetic I tells stories without the verbal-pictorial representation contributing to the respective storyworlds' construction, her appearances as an intradiegetic framing narrator telling mythical and religious stories to Zam are rather more interesting from a formalist point of view. The whole graphic novel uses a wide variety of complex page layouts, and the pages that represent Dodola as an intradiegetic framing narrator are no exception: when Dodola tells Zam the story of the "huge flood," for example, her extradiegetic homodiegetic narrating I introduces the situation via a narration box that is superimposed on the first panel representing the flood ("Zam loved stories") before the verbal-pictorial representation represents Dodola sitting at Zam's bedside, where she starts telling the story via a speech balloon ("In ancient times, there was a huge flood - -") (see figure 24). When the verbal-pictorial representation starts using pictures of the story's "defining moments" that contribute to the representation of the hypodiegetic secondary storyworld evoked by the diegetic Dodola's verbal narration, the latter's representation is continued by using narration boxes as well. Interestingly, *Habibi* also uses the frame of the page (instead of the frame of the individual panels) to mark the different ontological status of the represented situations: only the panel that represents the narrating situation located within the diegetic primary storyworld is largely framed by white space, while the other panels contributing to the representation of the hypodiegetic secondary storyworld about which Dodola tells Zam are surrounded by a broad, ornate frame that is drawn around the page margins.[17] The significance not only of what is represented in the panels but also of how they are framed becomes even more apparent when one of the comparatively rare situations in which Dodola acts as an intradiegetic homodiegetic narrator is represented later in the course of the graphic novel's developing plot: when she starts telling the story of how she first met Zam in the camp of the slave traders that held both of them captive to Nadidah (her handmaiden in the palace where she is kept as a slave in the Sultan's harem later on), the verbal-pictorial representation that "illustrates" Dodola's verbal narration is surrounded by a solid black frame (see figure 25).

In this context, it is also worth noting that *Habibi* not only extensively uses calligraphic elements to explore the importance of writing in Islam and beyond but that Dodola's experiencing I is also shown as having been taught reading and writing by her husband at an early age and that she subsequently develops a sustained interest in precisely those relations between writing and religious experience that are explored by the graphic novel. Hence, while the verbal-pictorial

Fig. 24. Dodola functioning as an intradiegetic heterodiegetic narrator in *Habibi*

Fig. 25. Black frames marking the "mood" of the story in *Habibi*

representation may not be attributable to Dodola in the same way that the verbal narration is, there are several points in *Habibi* where the latter is metareferentially intertwined with both an examination of its own status as written speech and the pictorial representation of symbols to such an extent that the distinction between narratorial and nonnarratorial representation becomes less clear-cut than it usually is in fictional comics (or films, or video games, for that matter) (see figure 26 and figure 27).

The way in which Dodola is represented as being in control of the verbal-pictorial representation in *Habibi* does not seem much more explicit than the way in which Tyler Durden is hinted at as being in control of the audiovisual representation in *Fight Club*, but, as has

Fig. 26. The representation of writing blurring the lines of authorship in *Habibi*

Fig. 27. The representation of maps blurring the lines of authorship in *Habibi*

already been mentioned in the previous chapter, comics' specific mediality makes it comparatively easy to represent not only elements of verbal narration but also the verbal-pictorial representation as being attributable to a narrator fulfilling at least some authorial functions. This has to do with the forms of authorship to be found in the medium: while there may be some films and video games with a single author as well—and the majority of comics do not have a single author, of course—it is much easier to represent a narrator as simultaneously being a "personified graphiator" responsible for the verbal-pictorial representation in comics than it is to represent a narrator as being simultaneously responsible for the verbal narration and the audiovisual representation in a film or the interactive representation in a video game.[18] However, this usually entails representing the narrator in question as some kind of authoring character, and the occurrence of these author-narrators tends to be limited to nonfictional comics, with fictional comics such as *Habibi* usually just exploring the borders of narratorial control.[19]

Despite the complex narratorial structure of *Habibi* and the occasional gesture toward the authorship of its narrator, it is usually easy to figure out who is narrating what in which mode at any given point in the graphic novel. Yet this is not always the case, and the question of whether we should understand a given verbal narration as spoken, written, or thought is closely connected to the question of whether we should understand a given narrator as extradiegetic or intradiegetic.[20] With its variety of narratorial voices (marked through differently colored narration boxes), Gaiman's *The Sandman* series provides a good example of this kind of indeterminacy. In addition to the apparently written verbal narration that we can attribute to a comparatively "covert" extradiegetic and heterodiegetic narrator (or, alternatively, understand as part of the nonnarratorial representation attributable to the hypothetical author collective),[21] the series' first volume, *Preludes and Nocturnes*, already introduces a second, more uncontroversially narratorial brand of narration that can be attributed to the story's main character, Dream of the Endless, who initially comments on the unfolding story in the present tense (see figure 28). It seems clear that the verbal-pictorial representation does not represent Dream's experiencing I as actually speaking in these situations, which would, at a first glance, imply an extradiegetic homodiegetic

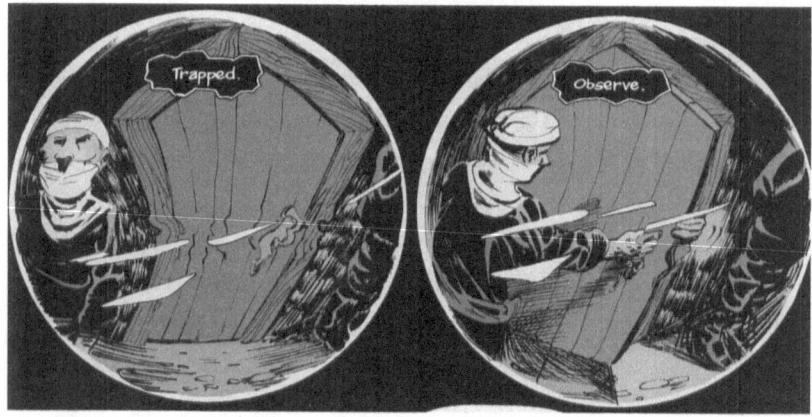

Fig. 28. Initial representation of Dream's internal voice in *The Sandman: Preludes and Nocturnes*

narrator whose verbal narration's represented mode remains characteristically unspecified. But the reader can imagine him thinking the initial part of the verbal narration in question and, hence, also imagine him to be an intradiegetic thinking narrator. Indeed, several of the later segments of the verbal narration that is attributable to Dream could still be interpreted in a way that would make him an intradiegetic thinking narrator (e.g., "It feels so good to be back . . . I left a monarch. Yet I return naked, alone . . . Hungry."; see figure 29), but the narration boxes increasingly use deictic markers (including a rather interesting switch to the past tense later on; see figure 30) that locate Dream's narrating I outside of the diegetic primary storyworld in which his experiencing I is located.[22] While there is still some amount of indeterminacy regarding the location of the narrating I at several points in his verbal narration at least on a local level, then, on a global level it seems more plausible to understand Dream as a second extradiegetic—albeit homodiegetic—narrator, whose verbal narration complements the rather more "covert" verbal narration either attributable to an extradiegetic heterodiegetic narrator or comprehensible as part of the nonnarratorial representation attributable to the hypothetical author collective.[23]

Not only do all three graphic novels discussed so far use extradiegetic narrators—a fairly "covert" heterodiegetic narrator on the verge of nonnarratorial representation in *The League of Extraordinary Gentlemen*, a very "overt" homodiegetic narrator in *Habibi*, and both a heterodiegetic and a homodiegetic narrator in *The Sandman*—but they also all use intradiegetic narrators, both heterodiegetic and homodiegetic. At times, it may be difficult to distinguish between Dream as an extradiegetic unspecified narrator and Dream as an intradiegetic thinking narrator in *The Sandman*, since Gaiman and his various collaborators use formally similar speech balloons/ thought bubbles/narration boxes for any verbal representation attributable to Dream, but there are also various instances of spoken narration that are clearly attributable to Dream as an intradiegetic—or, perhaps, hypodiegetic[24]—homodiegetic narrator, where the narrative situation in question is explicitly represented by the

Fig. 29. Indeterminacy of the narrator's diegetic status in *The Sandman: Preludes and Nocturnes*

Fig. 30. The narratorial representation's switch to the past tense in *The Sandman: Preludes and Nocturnes*

verbal-pictorial representation (see figure 31). Similarly, *The League of Extraordinary Gentlemen* and *Habibi* represent intradiegetic narrators explicitly several times, and using different represented modes of narration, including the letters written by Ms. Murray in the former (rendering her an intradiegetic homodiegetic writing narrator; see figure 32) and the stories told to Habibi by Dodola's experiencing I in

Fig. 31. Intradiegetic homodiegetic narrator in *The Sandman: Preludes and Nocturnes*

the latter (rendering her an intradiegetic heterodiegetic speaking narrator). While more extensive narratological analyses of these cases could, for example, focus on the narrative functions of these narrators[25] or reconstruct the fluctuating quantitative and qualitative relations between the verbal narratorial representation and the verbal-pictorial nonnarratorial representation,[26] I would, instead, like to revisit another transmedial problem that becomes particularly visible in comics: To what extent can narrators be considered to be authors of the stories they tell?

As has already been mentioned in the previous chapter, most if not all narrators across media can be considered to be not just the "tellers"

Fig. 32. Narration in an intradiegetic letter in *The League of Extraordinary Gentlemen*

but also the "makers" of the narratorial representation that is attributed to them. However, even if one subscribes to a fairly permissive conceptualization of authorship (as I do), it seems clear that there are differences in the saliency with which narrators across media are perceived as authors. The fact that we tend to think of authored narrative works not only as "artfully expressed" in a (semi)permanent material form but also as "made up" or fictional makes it rather awkward to speak of Ms. Murray and Dodola as authors, yet they both clearly are narrators and also do exert at least some authority over the "creation" and "transmission" of the respective stories they tell. While these brief remarks may be sufficient to come to terms with the (low) "degree of authorship" of intradiegetic narrators such as Ms. Murray in *The League of Extraordinary Gentlemen* or Dodola in *Habibi*, the fact that extradiegetic homodiegetic narrators (or framing intradiegetic narrators, for that matter) in multimodal media are usually not represented as being in control of the narrative representation as a whole further complicates the issue. Hence, I would like to conclude my examination of comics' use of narrators by offering a brief analysis of the complex interplay of authorship and narration to be found in Art Spiegelman's *Maus*.

In contrast to the fictional and "fictionalized" author figures/authoring characters of *The League of Extraordinary Gentlemen*, the author figures and authoring characters represented in so-called graphic memoirs tend to be largely nonfictional, with *Maus* providing one of the most famous as well as one of the still more interesting examples of a highly metareferential and self-reflexive authoring character. As I have argued in the first part of the present study, *Maus*'s metaphorical representation of Jews as mice, Germans as cats, Poles as pigs, and so on, does not make it necessary to comprehend the self-representation of the autobiographical narrator's experiencing I as a mouse (see figure 33) and his narrating I/authoring I as a human wearing a mouse mask as "fictionalized" (see figure 34), since what is represented here is the "nonfictional truth" of Spiegelman being Jewish. But of course, the self-representation of Spiegelman still differs quite a bit from more realistic (or simply less metaphorical)

Fig. 33. Art Spiegelman's self-representation in *Maus*

Fig. 34. Art Spiegelman's "authoring I" wearing a metaphorical mask in *Maus*

self-representations in other graphic memoirs such as David Small's *Stitches* or works of graphic journalism such as Joe Sacco's *Palestine*. In all of these cases, though, one can attribute not only the verbal narration but also the verbal-pictorial representation to the authoring characters Art, David, and Joe, respectively, which is contingent on both graphic memoirs and graphic journalism characteristically being realized as single-author works. Perhaps more importantly for the purpose of this book, however, *Maus* also provides a particularly striking example of a complex narratorial arrangement: it begins with the extradiegetic homodiegetic narrator Art telling a story and the accompanying sequence of panels contributing to the representation of the respective diegetic primary storyworld (see, once more, figure 33). Thus far, this is nothing out of the ordinary, but *Maus* also uses a framing as well as a nonframing intradiegetic narrator (see figure 35 and figure 36), since the representation of the graphic novel's diegetic primary storyworld focuses on Art talking with his father Vladek about the latter's survival of the Holocaust, and taping the latter's verbal narration in order to make a comic out of it (see figure 37)—which, incidentally, the actual Spiegelman has also done (with his actual father) while working on *Maus* (see the extensive contextualizing material collected in Spiegelman, *MetaMaus*).

Thus, authorship is negotiated in complex ways in Spiegelman's graphic memoir. On the one hand, the extradiegetic homodiegetic

Fig. 35. Intradiegetic homodiegetic framing narrator in *Maus*

Fig. 36. Intradiegetic homodiegetic nonframing narrator in *Maus*

Fig. 37. Art taping Vladek's verbal narration in *Maus*

narrator Art is represented as authoring not only the verbal narration representing the diegetic primary storyworld but also the overall verbal-pictorial representation of the graphic novel: this entails the (for the most part) very "overt" verbal narration and the fact that most of what is represented of the diegetic primary storyworld focuses on Art working on what the reader has reason to believe will later become *Maus* as well as more explicit peritextual forms of authorial self-representation such as those to be found at the beginning of *Maus*'s second part, when Spiegelman draws himself at his desk, wearing a mouse mask (which is not entirely dissimilar to the pig masks discussed in chapter 3) and reflecting on his newfound fame and the inappropriateness of "marketing strategies" in light of the graphic novel's representation of the (auto)biography of a Holocaust survivor (see, once more, figure 34).[27] On the other hand, the intradiegetic homodiegetic narrator Vladek is evidently represented as authoring the verbal narration that evokes the hypodiegetic secondary storyworld, if only to a somewhat smaller extent: despite the fact that Vladek is represented as telling his story to Art in order to allow the latter to create *Maus*, it seems clear that the former retains at least some degree of authorship over the representation of the hypodiegetic secondary storyworld via the "testimonial function" of his verbal narration, in particular.

However, the fact that the "creative" and "transmissive functions" are primarily fulfilled by Art complicates the narrating/authoring situation: even apart from the question how "verbatim" Art (both the represented authoring character and the actual author of *Maus*, Art Spiegelman) can represent the verbal narration of Vladek (which is not only a standard problem of the theory of autobiography but also touches on issues of representational correspondence that have already been discussed in chapter 3), the fact that Art's verbal-pictorial representation contributes more extensively to the representation of the hypodiegetic secondary storyworld than Vladek's verbal narration while at the same time marking the latter as the "source" that fulfills crucial "testimonial functions," in particular, once more emphasizes the tension between Art's and Vladek's authorship. This "authorial tension" becomes particularly visible when the verbal-pictorial representation attributable to Art is marked as being unreliable to the extent that it is (primarily)[28] based on the verbal narration attributable to Vladek, even though it will (at least appear to) give additional information about the hypodiegetic secondary storyworld. On the one hand, the "hierarchy of knowledge" between Art and Vladek is thematized explicitly: at the beginning of the first chapter of the second part, "Mauschwitz" in "And Here My Troubles Began (From Mauschwitz to the Catskills and Beyond)," the diegetic Art is represented as mentioning his doubts about the project to his girlfriend Françoise during a long car drive to visit Vladek in his bungalow in the Catskills: "There's so much I'll never be able to understand or visualize," Art says, "I mean, reality is too *complex* for comics. . . . So much has to be left out or distorted." After Françoise has tried to calm him—"Just keep it honest, honey"—the graphic novel changes the focus of Art's reflections, making it even more overtly metareferential: "See what I mean. . . . In real life you'd *never* have let me talk this *long* without interrupting." At the beginning of the second chapter of the second part, "Auschwitz (Time Flies)," what is perhaps best described as Art's extradiegetic narrating I (even though it is explicitly represented in these seven and a half pages) likewise discusses the medium-specific representational limitations that he faces with his "shrink," Pavel.

Apart from these explicit appearances, the resulting unreliability is also, on the other hand, negotiated more subtly, when, for example, the verbal-pictorial representation "illustrates" parts of Vladek's story about another prisoner who claimed to be a non-Jewish German that Vladek is represented as telling Art on the patio of a hotel close to his bungalow (located within the diegetic primary storyworld) and the initial pictorial representation of the prisoner as a Jew/mouse is changed into the pictorial representation of the prisoner as a German/cat, whose unreliable status is marked by a distinct shading after Art has been represented as having asked Vladek, "Was he *really*

Fig. 38. Oscillation between different "historical truths" in *Maus*

a German?" and Vladek concedes, "Who knows—it *was* German prisoners also . . . But for the Germans this guy *was Jewish*!" (see figure 38).

Having focused on the use of narratorial representation to unreliable and metaleptic effects in contemporary feature films such as *Fight Club*, *The Usual Suspects*, and *Adaptation.* (with the narrators in *Run Lola Run* functioning as a largely reliable and nonmetaleptic foil against which the unreliability and "metalepticity" of the former becomes visible) and on questions of authorship and narratorial control in contemporary graphic novels such as *The Sandman*, *The League of Extraordinary Gentlemen*, *Habibi*, or *Maus*, I will now examine narrators and narratorial representation in contemporary narrative video games, particularly emphasizing the kind of ludic functions that are connected to the medium's interactivity and nonlinearity.

Strategies of Narratorial Representation in Contemporary Video Games

Since computers are currently capable of emulating various kinds of semiotic systems, including audiovisual and verbal-pictorial sequences, the range of narrators in contemporary narrative video games is at least as broad as it is in feature films and graphic novels. Accordingly, the main difference between narrators in films or comics and narrators in video games lies not in the latters' common combination of written and spoken modes of representation to represent verbal narration. Instead, it is constituted by the fact that the verbal narration in video games relates to the noninteractive nonnarratorial representation in cinematographic or other kinds of cut-scenes as well as to the interactive parts of the game, to the simulated gameplay. As has already been mentioned in the general discussion of video game-specific forms of narrative representation in chapter 3, this also leads to a more diverse range of possible functions, as narrators in video games not only contribute to the unfolding of the story and the "fleshing out" of the storyworld but also, and perhaps more importantly, help the player to locate the various game spaces within the storyworld as a whole and convey information about game mechanics and game goals. The use of narratorial representation to fulfill both narrative and ludic functions has become quite widespread in contemporary video games, and narrators of various kinds can be found across a number of different genres: the two most common forms seem to be the use of extradiegetic narrators, both hetero- and homodiegetic, that introduce the game's storyworld as well as the basic conflict(s) motivating the gameplay and intradiegetic, usually homodiegetic narrators who give the player-controlled character (and, thereby, the player) directions regarding game mechanics or comparatively local game goals. Intradiegetic homodiegetic narrators can be found across genres but are particularly common in role-playing games such as Bioware's *Baldur's Gate* or *Neverwinter Nights*, yet while the extradiegetic heterodiegetic variety is realized even more broadly, with early "covert" examples including first-person shooters such as LucasArts' *Star Wars: Dark Forces* and, once more, role-playing games such as *Baldur's Gate* or *Neverwinter Nights*, the extradiegetic homodiegetic variety seems particularly characteristic for third-person shooters such as those in Remedy's *Max Payne* series or action-adventures such as those in its *Alan Wake* series.

However, quite a few more complex examples are available as well. On the one hand, this includes a heightened complexity in the forms of verbal narration that is illustrated, for example, by games such as 10 Interactive's *Hitman: Blood Money*, CD Projekt RED's *The Witcher 2: Assassins of Kings*, or Bioware's *Dragon Age II*, all of which use interview or interrogation situations to arrange the gameplay in rather interesting ways by framing it via the interviewed/interrogated intradiegetic narrators, thereby marking it as contributing to the representation of the hypodiegetic secondary storyworlds that the latter narrate. On the other hand, there has been a notable increase in intradiegetic unreliable narrators—such as "Guilty Spark" in Bungie's *Halo* and Harlan Doyle in Crytek's *Far Cry*, Sandy Bravitor in Hothead's *DeathSpank* and Atlas in Irrational Games' *Bioshock*, or GlaDOS in Valve's *Portal* and Fletcher in Hidden Path Entertainment's *Defense Grid: The Awakening*—that are usually somehow involved in the stories they tell and tend to mislead the player-controlled character as well as the player in some way. Instead of providing in-depth analyses of these comparatively specific cases, though, I want to briefly examine four more generally relevant examples, focusing on the formal complexities that can be found in contemporary action-adventures and role-playing games, in particular, in order to explore the medium-specific influence of video games' interactivity and nonlinearity on their use of narrators and narratorial representation, specifically focusing on the latters' ludic functions.

Let me begin, then, by revisiting Bioware's *Dragon Age: Origins*, a role-playing game that serves to illustrate rather well the formal complexity of narratorial representation without putting its use of narrators front and center: The game's introductory cut-scene already uses a voice-over whose extradiegetic narrator changes from being heterodiegetic (when he speaks about the distant past of the game's storyworld) to being homodiegetic (when his narration arrives in the present) and eventually turns out to be a major character in the game's narrative framework. That character, a Captain of the Grey Wardens named Duncan, later also acts as an intradiegetic narrator, both homo- and heterodiegetic as well as both framing and nonframing—though it should be noted that the verbal narration in *Dragon Age: Origins* (and many other contemporary video games) is generally not used to simultaneously frame the interactive simulation of events that constitute the main part of the gameplay, but is primarily employed during cut-scenes or dialogue sequences. Particularly where it is attributed not to the extradiegetic but to the intradiegetic version of Duncan (i.e., to his diegetic experiencing I which temporally acts as a speaking narrating I in these cases), the functions of his verbal narration cannot be reduced to contributing to the unfolding of the story or to spatio-temporally locating the game spaces within the storyworld, but also entail conveying information about game mechanics and game goals.

Duncan is not the only narrator that *Dragon Age: Origins* employs, though. On the one hand, there are various other intradiegetic and usually homodiegetic narrators whose functions range from primarily narrative, when other characters fill the player-controlled character in on recent (or not so recent) events, to primarily ludic, when other characters act as "quest-givers" who may also tell the player-controlled character what happened subsequently, but do so primarily in order to ask him or her for help. When the player-controlled character and Alistair first meet Morrigan, for example, she acts as an intradiegetic narrator with a primarily narrative function, telling them about how her mother saved them after the Battle of Ostagar. In fact, the members of the player-controlled character's party provide a whole range of (more or less) optional verbal narration, acting as intradiegetic narrators with a primarily narrative function (when they tell the player-controlled character about their respective "background stories") that is sometimes complemented by a secondary ludic function (since making the player-controlled character listen to their stories may influence his or her "affiliation rating" positively). Yet the party members' verbal narrations occasionally develop a more

Narratorial Representation across Media   209

pronounced ludic function, when past events lead them to more or less directly ask the player-controlled character for help. Examples of this would include assisting Alistair in his attempt to reunite with his sister, Goldanna, which utterly fails independently of the player's choices; helping Leliana by finding and defeating the assassins that Marjolaine sent to kill her; or helping Oghren to get back together with his "old flame" Felsi. Since the reward for those quests once more tends to be limited to an increase in "affiliation rating," though, the ludic functions of party members acting as intradiegetic narrators still remain comparatively limited. However, there are also quite a few other characters whose primary function is that of a "quest-giver" and who mainly act as intradiegetic homodiegetic narrators in order to get the player-controlled character to help them, thereby significantly propelling the plot forward.[29]

On the other hand, an extradiegetic heterodiegetic narrator takes over the narratorial reins immediately after the initial cut-scene, providing additional verbal narration represented in both spoken and written form, depending on the player-controlled character's "background," among other things, and fulfilling comparatively important narrative functions closely connected to the game's nonlinear narrative structure during the final cinematographic cut-scene, which represents the events following the defeat of the Archdemon, in particular. Interestingly, though, the verbal narration itself is changed only very slightly by the player decisions preceding that final cut-scene, as the narrator refers to Ferelden's "new king" or "queen" depending on whether the player-controlled character has helped Alistair or Anora claim the throne. The effects of some of the other player choices—whether the player-controlled character has sacrificed him- or herself to slay the Archdemon, has allowed Alistair or Loghain to make the sacrifice, or has entered into the dark pact with Morrigan—are primarily represented by the "in-engine" audiovisual representation that accompanies the verbal narration attributable to the unnamed extradiegetic heterodiegetic narrator as well as by an additional intradiegetic narrator: either King Alistair honoring the sacrifice of the player-controlled character or Queen Anora honoring the sacrifice of the player-controlled character, Alistair, or Loghain. While the nonlinear narrative structure and the resulting player choices are already reflected in the combination of narratorial and nonnarratorial representation during the game's final cinematographic cut-scene, then, this is not yet the game's ending: instead, the cut-scene is followed by an "epilogue" combining still pictures with additional verbal narration that is exclusively represented in written form this time and briefly summarizes core developments within the storyworld that have been influenced by player choices preceding the defeat of the Archdemon.

Apart from the observation that extradiegetic verbal narration whose mode of representation is exclusively written appears to be less readily attributable to a narrator-as-narrating-character than extradiegetic verbal narration that is also spoken (which adds various paraverbal qualities to the narratorial voice, making it easier to construct a narrating character as its source) and, hence, the verbal narration during *Dragon Age: Origins*' "epilogue" might be more appropriately described as part of the nonnarratorial representation to be attributed to the hypothetical author collective, once more, the interrelation of the resulting narratorial representation and the preceding events not only emphasizes the game's nonlinear narrative structure (and the resulting impression of narratively significant player agency) yet again, but also provides a fair amount of (narrative) closure independently of which storyworld representation the player's performance and the player's choices have ultimately actualized. As *Dragon Age: Origins* illustrates, then, a nonlinear narrative structure does not prevent contemporary video games from using a wide variety of extra- and intradiegetic, hetero- and homodiegetic, framing and non-framing, or reliable and unreliable narrators, since different versions of a given narrator's verbal narration (or, as is the case in *Dragon Age: Origins*, different narrators' verbal narrations) can be actualized by the player's actions (just as it is generally the case with other narrative strategies in contemporary video games, such as cut-scenes or scripted sequences of events). In fact, the use of a nonlinear narrative structure is so well established in the role-playing game genre that one can increasingly find genre parodies that self-reflexively use narrators to comment on their medium-specific limitations and affordances in general as well as on their nonlinear narrative structure in particular.[30]

Against this background, let me sketch what I would consider a fairly successful example of such a self-reflexive use of narratorial representation that focuses at least partially on the limitations and affordances that arise from nonlinear narrative structures before I go on to discuss the question how verbal narratorial representation may relate to the interactive nonnarratorial representation that constitutes the main part of most contemporary video games' gameplay. Just like the extradiegetic version of Duncan in *Dragon Age: Origins*, the decidedly old and only "barely intradiegetic"[31] narrator that appears in the introductory cut-scene of the first part of Hothead's *DeathSpank* series turns out to have been more involved in the story she tells than most players will have initially expected.[32] At the end of *DeathSpank: Thongs of Virtue*, the second part of the action role-playing game series, the narrator reveals herself to be Sandy Bravitor, the mentor of the player-controlled character, DeathSpank (see figure 39). This

Fig. 39. The narrator is revealed to be Sandy Bravitor in *DeathSpank: Thongs of Virtue*

final "twist" seems particularly relevant for the issue at hand, since both installments of the series repeatedly use Sandy's "barely hypodiegetic" experiencing I—instead of what turns out to have been her "barely intradiegetic" narrating I in one version of the nonlinear narrative structure—to convey game goals to both DeathSpank and the player.[33] This is only one of two possible endings the game offers, though: just before the final cut-scene, Sandy asks DeathSpank to sacrifice himself in order to save the world from the supposedly corrupted Thongs of Virtue, but the game gives the player a choice here, and he or she can choose to let DeathSpank fight Sandy. Hence, in this case, DeathSpank can kill the character who, if she is not killed, turns out to have become the "barely intradiegetic" narrator from whom DeathSpank otherwise takes the narratorial reins, acting as a new homodiegetic narrator (whose location within the storyworld as a whole is not specified), and going on to narrate his own story (see figure 40).[34] Strictly speaking, this development does not cause logical inconsistencies within the storyworld(s) of *DeathSpank: Thongs of Virtue* since the initially introduced narrator does not too explicitly reveal herself to be Sandy if DeathSpank kills her (although even then, there certainly are hints such as the similarities in their respective voices), but the *DeathSpank* series still makes visible some of the medium's specific affordances and limitations with regard to the use of narrators.

While the use of narratorial representation in *Dragon Age: Origins* and the *DeathSpank* series is not only influenced by player decisions taken in the context of the simulated gameplay and helps the player to spatiotemporally locate the game spaces in the storyworld as a whole but also fulfills more straightforward ludic functions, its occurrence is largely limited to cut-scenes (or, in the case of intradiegetic narrators, to dialogue sequences that allow only for comparatively rudimentary forms of interactivity as well). However, video games are not in themselves limited to using narratorial representation in combination with noninteractive forms of nonnarratorial representation. A comparatively early example of a video game that uses a particularly "overt" narrator who also contributes to the interactive

Fig. 40. DeathSpank takes up the narratorial duties in *DeathSpank: Thongs of Virtue*

representation of the gameplay is Ubisoft's *Prince of Persia: The Sands of Time*. Here, the Prince himself acts as a homodiegetic narrator who might, again, be comprehended as being rendered "barely intradiegetic" via a rather ambiguous introductory cut-scene and, more importantly, various remarks on the narrating situation that he himself provides—"You may wonder who I am or why I say this. Sit down, and I will tell you a tale like none that you have ever heard." As such, he is perhaps more appropriately described as an extradiegetic homodiegetic narrator, after all. Whatever the case may be, the narratorial representation is represented in the form of a spoken voice-over, accompanying both the cut-scenes and the interactive simulation of ludic events that make up the main part of the gameplay. *Prince of Persia: The Sands of Time*'s use of narratorial representation may occasionally seem forced, but it still illustrates a medium-specific aspect of the use of narrators in video games that is defined by their (obligatory) interactivity rather than by their (facultative) nonlinearity. Put into a nutshell, one can observe a fundamental tension between the mode of representation and the represented mode of the verbal narration: *actually*, the player of *Prince of Persia: The Sands of Time* interacts with the game spaces according to specific game rules, and some of the resulting ludic events "trigger" certain prerecorded "pieces" of verbal narration—in other words, the gameplay causes the narratorial representation. Fictionally or, more precisely, *representationally*, though, the Prince's narrating I tells a story to a narratee (who remains unnamed) within the diegetic primary storyworld, and while the Prince himself is not represented as causing the nonnarratorial representation that accompanies his verbal narration, the gameplay as well as the regularly appearing cut-scenes are clearly marked as contributing to the representation of the latter's "barely hypodiegetic" secondary storyworld, which allows the player to pretend that the gameplay has already happened—at least as far as it can be comprehended as contributing to the representation of the storyworld that the verbal narration attributable to the Prince's narrating evokes. This mildly paradoxical situation is metareferentially emphasized when the player is unable to meet the various challenges that the gameplay provides, leading to the death of the Prince's experiencing I, as the Prince's narrating I regularly corrects himself or, rather, the interactive representation of the death of his experiencing I, with remarks such as "That's not how it happened" before the game resets to the most recent savepoint.

A more recent example that makes even more extensive use of narratorial representation to frame the predetermined representation of storyworld elements via cut-scenes as well as the interactive simulation that constitutes the main part of the actual gameplay is Supergiant Games' action role-playing game *Bastion*, whose narrator—an old man named Rucks—extensively comments on predetermined as well as ludic events (see figure 41). Once again, the basic principle at work here is not particularly complex: *Bastion* uses about three thousand predetermined "pieces" of verbal narration, represented in spoken as well as written form, that are triggered by a variety of player actions (or, more precisely, by a variety of actions of the player-controlled

Fig. 41. Interactive narrator in *Bastion*

character).³⁵ The comparatively high number of prerecorded "narration pieces" notwithstanding, the variation regarding the selection and organization of these pieces turns out to be lower than some critics may have initially expected, but *Bastion* remains one of still rather few video games in the tradition of *Prince of Persia: The Sands of Time* whose gameplay can, with some justification, be described as narratorially dominated. Despite the considerably higher overall presence of narratorial representation in *Bastion*, then, the relevant processes remain similar to *Prince of Persia: The Sands of Time*: from the perspective of the *actual* game mechanics, player actions lead to ludic events that, under certain conditions, trigger various pieces of the narratorial representation.³⁶ However, within the game's *representational* logic, the gameplay contributes to the representation of the storyworld evoked by the verbal narration—that is, it is initially represented as being caused (if only indirectly) by the narratorial representation instead of the other way around. Unsurprisingly, the narrator of *Bastion* also exhibits the particular kind of *ludic unreliability* related to the possibility of the player failing the challenges presented by the interactive gameplay: when the player lets the player-controlled character fall from the edge of what remains of the world after the man-made catastrophe referred to as the Calamity, only to have him

Fig. 42. Ludic unreliability of the narrator in *Bastion*

reappear from above (which is an integral part of the game mechanics and merely sanctioned by a small loss of health), for example, the narrator sometimes comments on this in a fashion similar to the narrator in *Prince of Persia: The Sands of Time* (e.g., "And then he falls to his death . . . I'm just fooling!"; see figure 42). Yet, despite these similarities between the interactive narrators of *Prince of Persia: The Sands of Time* and *Bastion*, the latter not only makes more extensive use of its narrator's narratorial voice—which, incidentally, entails more conventional forms of representational unreliability as well—but also represents a considerably more complex narrating situation.

Initially, the player could attribute *Bastion*'s verbal narration to an extradiegetic heterodiegetic narrator who may be fairly "overt" due to the combination of a written and spoken mode of representation and the paraverbal cues of Merle Cunningham's characteristic voice, but is neither represented in the narrating situation nor seems to be a part of the story he tells, as his verbal narration is largely focused on the player-controlled character that is referred to only as the Kid. Yet, when the Kid reaches the Bastion (a complex village-like structure that can later be used to "turn back time" or, alternatively, to evacuate the remaining survivors of the Calamity),[37] he meets the experiencing I of the narrator, Rucks, who thereby turns out to be homo- rather than heterodiegetic. Since much of the game as well as much of the verbal narration attributable to Rucks's narrating I focuses on the adventures of the Kid, however, the former's degree of involvement is still relatively small. In fact, the narratorial representation does not always follow the events experienced by the Kid as closely as the interactive representation that constitutes the main part of the gameplay—and Rucks mentions that the Kid has told him about his adventure, hinting at some kind of technological or magical connection between the two, which stops working when the distance between them gets too large, leading Rucks to admit that he cannot "hear him anymore." Despite these caveats, though, the narrator seems to possess a fairly implausible and largely unexplained knowledge of the Kid's adventures that is more commonly found in extradiegetic heterodiegetic than in extradiegetic homodiegetic narrators.

Yet Rucks is not only represented as being more involved in the story he tells than most players will have initially expected (which, as the discussion of *Dragon Age: Origins* and the *DeathSpank* series has already shown, has become a common strategy in contemporary video games). He also subsequently turns out to be an intra- instead of an extradiegetic narrator, when it is revealed that he tells the story not to some unspecified extradiegetic narratee, but rather to Zia, an Ura refugee who has also survived the Calamity, while they both wait for the Kid to return with the final shard that is needed to repair the Bastion (and which Ulf, yet another Ura survivor, has stolen). This "narratorial twist" could be comprehended as retroactively locating the situations that have been represented before the Kid's return to the Bastion within a hypodiegetic secondary storyworld narrated by Rucks—to which the representation of the interactive gameplay would then be understood as contributing. However, it is more appropriate to describe Rucks's verbal narration and the interactive gameplay as rather loosely connected, since the former is clearly marked as nonfictional, but Rucks keeps on narrating even after having admitted that he does not know what the Kid experiences anymore. Under such a description, the nonnarratorial representation would appear to be primarily contributing to the representation of the diegetic primary storyworld in which Rucks's narrating I is located, with the former narrating a hypodiegetic secondary storyworld that, being nonfictional, could still be taken to be largely similar to the diegetic primary storyworld represented by the gameplay. Further emphasizing the independence of the narratorial and the nonnarratorial representation, the game also uses a number of written inserts, which cannot be attributed to Rucks and are perhaps best described as part of the nonnarratorial representation, to temporally locate the various segments of the gameplay during which the Kid is represented as reacquiring the final shard (and, at least in one of the actualizable versions of the nonlinear narrative structure, as bringing Ulf back to the Bastion) within the storyworld as a whole.[38]

Let me conclude, then, by reemphasizing that contemporary video games serve to remind us rather forcefully that even clearly transmedial strategies of narrative or, more precisely, narratorial representation such as the use of narrators are necessarily realized within the specific mediality of conventionally distinct media and that medium-specific representational conventions lead to different narrative limitations and affordances. However, as the analyses presented in this chapter have also illustrated, contemporary films, comics, and video games may all use narrators and narratorial representation in complex ways. With regard to the forms that this transmedial strategy of narrative representation may take, the previous pages have shown that films such as *Run Lola Run*, *The Usual Suspects*, *Fight Club*, or *Adaptation.*, comics such as *The League of Extraordinary Gentlemen*, *The Sandman*, *Habibi*, or *Maus*, and video games such as *Dragon Age: Origins*, *DeathSpank*, *Prince of Persia: The Sands of Time*, or *Bastion* can, indeed, use the full range of narrators—extradiegetic and intradiegetic, heterodiegetic and homodiegetic, framing and nonframing, and being represented as speaking, writing, or thinking.

With regard to the functions that this use of narrators and narratorial representation across media fulfills, my necessarily cursory analyses have shown how the narratorial representation of unreliable narrators may be combined with both reliable and equally unreliable nonnarratorial representation in a variety of ways to disorient the recipients with regard to the intersubjective construction of storyworlds; how narrators may fulfill not only narratorial but also authorial functions up to the point where they are represented as being in control of the narratorial as well as of the nonnarratorial representation; and how narrators and narratorial representation may fulfill not only primarily narrative functions in contributing to the unfolding of the story and the "fleshing out" of the storyworld but also, in the case of contemporary video games, primarily ludic functions such as conveying information about the game mechanics and game goals. While my analyses should have served to reemphasize the saliency of the use of narrators as a transmedial strategy of narrative or, rather, narratorial representation, then, it has also become clear at more than one point that asking "Who narrates?" simply does not suffice. Instead, even a comparatively simple narratological analysis regularly has to ask "Who perceives?" or, to rephrase the second of Gérard Genette's famous pair of questions, who is represented as experiencing the local situations that make up the global storyworld as a whole and to what extent can the narrative representation be said to be subjective. I will focus on these questions in the third, and final, part of this book.

PART 3 *Subjectivity across Media*

6 : Subjectivity as a Transmedial Concept

Perspective, Point of View, and Focalization

Narrative representations are, qua definition, about worlds populated with characters that get some kind of "mental life" ascribed to them, experience the represented situations, and function as agents in a more or less complex network of goals, plans, and motivations.[1] It comes as no surprise, then, that the problem of subjectivity—or, more precisely, the wealth of strategies that narrative representations may employ in order to represent the subjective consciousnesses of their characters—has been at the center of narratological interest for the past five decades, with the discussion having been primarily defined by the three terms "perspective," "point of view," and "focalization."[2] As is often the case in contemporary narratology, though, there is no common consensus regarding the question to which concepts these terms should refer.[3]

Indeed, at least in a narratological context, particularly the first two terms, "perspective" and "point of view," are commonly understood as referring to roughly the same concepts: Burkhard Niederhoff, for example, states that "perspective in narrative may be defined as the way the representation of the story is influenced by the position, personality and values of the narrator, the characters and, possibly, other, more hypothetical entities in the storyworld," but adds that "the more common term in Anglo-American criticism, which will be treated as equivalent here, is 'point of view'" ("Perspective" 384).[4] Similarly, Wolf Schmid remarks that "*point of view* and *perspective*—terms which will be used synonymously—are, as a rule, taken to denote the *narrative*—or the *narrator's*—point of view or perspective" (*Narratology* 89, footnote 1, original emphases). While "perspective" and "point of view" are sometimes seen as interchangeable, then, even individually the terms may be used to refer to rather different concepts.

In fact, Schmid soon runs into a fundamental terminological problem that tends to occur when narratologists discuss "perspective" or "point of view." There seems to be a widespread consensus in classical as well as contemporary narratology that, "unlike such textual elements as character, plot, or imagery, point of view is essentially a *relationship* rather than a concrete entity" (Lanser, *The Narrative Act* 13, original emphasis), but there are at least two kinds of "relationships" to which terms such as "perspective" or "point of view" may refer. Schmid defines "perspective" quite inclusively as "*the complex, formed by internal and external factors, of conditions for the comprehension and representation of happenings*" (*Narratology* 99, original emphasis), but he primarily treats it as a function of narrative representation, using the term to refer to the way in which a representation of "happenings" relates to their comprehension. If one concedes that "every represented fictive entity in a narrative work potentially has a point of view or perspective of his or her own" (Schmid, *Narratology* 89, footnote 1), however, the two terms may also refer to how a represented character's consciousness relates to the storyworld in which that character is located. In fact, Schmid uses the terms in this sense himself when he distinguishes between "narratorial" and "figural perspective/point of view" and defines the latter as allowing the narrator to "narrate from the perspective of one or more of the narrated characters" (*Narratology* 105).[5]

In an attempt to disentangle the "terminological thicket" surrounding terms such as "perspective" and "point of view," Jens Eder distinguishes yet another type of concept commonly associated with the former. First, the term "perspective" may be defined as referring to a "(primarily) mental system of conditions of characters or narrating instances on whose basis they experience or represent the fictional world" (Eder, *Die Figur* 580, my translation from the German). These kinds of "mental perspectives" refer to how a character's consciousness relates to the storyworld in which it is located. Second, the term "medial perspective" may be used to refer to "the way in which media texts employ visual or narrative modes of representation or convey information" (Eder, *Die Figur* 580, my translation from the German). Third, one can also speak of "an overarching textual or receptional perspective consisting of the relations between individual character and narrator perspectives" (Eder, *Die Figur* 580, my translation from the German). Even if Eder were right in claiming that "the variety of meanings attributed to the term 'perspective' can be traced back to the common core" (*Die Figur* 582, my translation from the German) of "mental perspective," then, this would not change the fact that both "perspective" and "point of view" are terms regularly used to refer not only to what amounts to the relation between characters' consciousnesses and the storyworld in which these characters are located but also to the relation between characters' consciousnesses and the narrative representation that is used to represent them—and that, moreover, both of these forms of "perspective" may be examined on a local as well as a global level, the latter of which then leads one to describe narrative representations' "mental" as well as "medial perspective structures."[6]

It should be obvious by now that one can seldom generalize the use of narratological terms, yet the particular conceptual history associated with "point of view" seems to have turned it into an even more encompassing and problematic term than "perspective." Despite Seymour Chatman's early insistence that "point of view does *not* mean expression; it only means the perspective in terms of which the expression is made" (*Story* 153, original emphasis), the confusion between comprehension and representation often found in protonarratological discussions of "literary point of view"[7] also occasionally (re)appears within film studies: Bruce Kawin, for example, tends to equate the character whose subjectivity is represented with the narrator of the audiovisual representation in question, emphasizing that "it is unnecessary . . . to present a character in a conventional 'storytelling' pose in order to identify him [or her] to the audience as a narrator" (14). Similarly, Edward Branigan claims that the use of point-of-view shots generates a situation where "the activity of narration has been

Subjectivity as a Transmedial Concept 225

transferred to a character within the narrative" (*Point of View* 57). Yet, even apart from these rather specific terminological inaccuracies,[8] the more fundamental problem remains that "point of view" cannot only be "understood as the optical perspective of a character whose gaze or look dominates a sequence, or, in its broader meaning, the overall perspective of the narrator toward the characters and the events of the fictional world" (Stam, Burgoyne, and Flitterman-Lewis 83), but is also commonly used to refer to strategies of representation as different as the local conceptualization of a point-of-view shot as a specific form of "subjectivizing editing" and its global conceptualization as the "range and/or depth of knowledge which the narration supplies" (Bordwell, *Narration* 60).

Considering that the broader meaning of what Chatman describes as "one of the most troublesome of critical terms" (*Story* 151) is unlikely to ever become "as sharply delimited as one might wish" (G. Wilson, *Narration* 3), it comes as no surprise that Gérard Genette's proposal to use the (then) freshly minted term "focalization" instead of terms such as "perspective" and "point of view" is often considered a major breakthrough among literary narratologists, even though there seem to be surprisingly few who are actually satisfied with his account of "focalization." As is well known, Genette systematically distinguishes "the question *who sees?* and the question *who speaks?*" (*Narrative Discourse* 186, original emphases) (or "*who perceives?*" [*Narrative Discourse Revisited* 64, original emphasis] and "who speaks?"), emphasizing that the latter should be asked (and answered) separately from the former.[9] However, Genette goes on to distinguish three "types of focalization" that are defined not by the acts of seeing or perceiving that inform the narrative, but rather by different degrees of knowledge: "zero focalization" is described "by the formula *Narrator > Character* (where the narrator knows more than the character, or more exactly, *says* more than any of the characters knows [sic!]"; "internal focalization" is described by the formula "*Narrator = Character* (the narrator says only what a given character knows)"; "external focalization" is described by the formula "*Narrator < Character* (the narrator says less than the character knows)" (*Narrative Discourse* 189, original emphases). These mild inconsistencies ultimately suggest, then, that Genette's concept of "focalization" can, indeed, be seen as "an amalgamation of two wholly independent elements," namely, "the perception of the world invented by the author through narrators and other agents also invented by the author," on the one hand, and "the regulation of narrative information within the communication between author and reader" (Jesch and M. Stein 59), on the other.

Even if one leaves the problem that there "is no direct link" (Schmid, *Narratology* 93) between perception and knowledge aside, though, Genette's typology seems flawed at best. As one of his most influential critics, Mieke Bal, has pointed out, "in the second type, the 'focalized' character *sees*; in the third type, he [or she] does not see, he [or she] is *seen*. The difference this time is not between the 'seeing' agents, but between the objects of that seeing" ("The Narrating" 241, original emphases). Moreover, it is notoriously difficult to distinguish the first "focalization type," "zero focalization" (or "nonfocalization"), from "multiple internal focalization," which has led various early critics such as Bal ("The Narrating"), Berendsen, Chatman ("Characters"), Edminston, Kablitz, or Nelles ("Getting Focalization") to question the former's validity. In fact, the questionable status of "zero focalization" points at a third problem inherent in Genette's discussion of "focalization" in general and his triad of "focalization types" in particular, namely, the underdetermined granularity of his concepts. On the one hand, Genette's focus on "focalization types" and deviations from these types—"*alterations*" such as "*paralipsis*," which consists of the narrator "giving less information than is necessary in principle," and "*paralepsis*," which consists of the narrator "giving more [information] than is authorized in principle in the code of focalization governing the whole" (*Narrative Discourse* 195, original emphases)— seems to imply an analytical movement from global to local structure, yet one cannot help but wonder how we are supposed to establish a global "focalization type" in the first place, if not through local analysis. On the other hand, the fact that Genette explicitly allows for "changes in focalization" (*Narrative Discourse* 194) and even appears to understand "zero focalization" as referring to both a global and a local structure[10] leave open the possibility to conceptualize "focalization" as referring to the local relation between a given segment of the narrative representation and a represented character's consciousness (or the represented characters' consciousnesses).

As has already been mentioned, an influential reconceptualization of "focalization" that attempts to operationalize the term for this kind of more local analysis has been developed by Bal. After a number of critiques and modifications of Genette's original proposal(s), she arrives at a conceptualization of "focalization" that strongly differs from Genette's in various respects but suffers from a number of problems of its own, in particular with regard to the contested concept of the "focalizer" (or "focalizor"). What is particularly relevant for the purpose of the present study, however, is the fact that Bal's conceptualization of "focalization" is the first to explicitly and systematically distinguish between a "focalizing subject" and a "focalized object." In both cases, she proposes to use a rather simple internal/external distinction: "internal focalization" exclusively "lies with one character which participates in the fabula," while "external focalization" means that "an anonymous agent, situated outside the fabula, is functioning as focalizor" (Bal, *Narratology* 148). Interestingly, though, Bal emphasizes that the internal/external distinction also applies to the "focalized object," which "can be perceptible [= external] or imperceptible [= internal]" ("The Narrating" 250). While it may often be difficult to distinguish between the "focalizing subject" and the "focalized object," particularly in cases where a character's consciousness constitutes both the subject and the object of "focalization" (and the present book will largely focus on strategies of subjective representation that subjectively represent what Bal calls the "focalized object"), Bal's distinction certainly serves to sharpen our awareness for local strategies of subjective representation. Yet, despite a certain "visual bias" and more programmatic demands for a "visual narratology" (Bal, *Narratology* 162), Bal's conceptualization of "focalization" remains firmly rooted within literary narratology.

Among the countless attempts to apply either Genette's or Bal's conceptualization of "focalization" to narrative representations beyond the literary text, Edward Branigan's modification of the term in the context of a considerably more extensive examination of audiovisual subjectivity (and objectivity) seems to be the most relevant for the purpose of this chapter.[11] Among other things, this is due to Branigan's emphasis on the analysis of local segments of narrative representation with regard to their relation to characters' consciousnesses. Branigan distinguishes between "nonfocalized" representation, where the "way we learn about characters is through their actions and speech in much the same way that characters learn from each other" (*Narrative Comprehension* 100); "external focalization" that "represents a measure of character awareness but from outside the character"; and "internal focalization" that "is more fully private and subjective than external focalization," ranging "from [the representation of] simple perception (e.g., the point-of-view shot), to impressions (e.g., the out-of-focus point-of-view shot depicting a character who is drunk, dizzy, or drugged), to 'deeper thoughts' (e.g., dreams, hallucinations, and memories)" (*Narrative Comprehension* 103). My attempt to sharpen Branigan's definition of "nonfocalized" representation in order to distinguish it more clearly from "external focalization" will lead me to propose a somewhat different distinction between objective, intersubjective, and subjective modes of representation, but my examination of transmedial strategies of subjective representation remains highly indebted to Branigan's discussion of "focalization" in *Narrative Comprehension and Film* as well as to his earlier study, *Point of View in the Cinema*. Before I can develop further my own conceptualization of the representation of subjectivity and of strategies of subjective representation, though, it will be helpful to mention a few additional attempts to transfer either Genette's or Bal's conceptualization of "focalization" to films, comics, and video games, which tend to be as conceptually interesting as they are terminologically problematic.

Another influential attempt to transfer Genette's concept of "focalization" to film has been made by François Jost, who—not entirely dissimilar to the postulation of various nonrepresented "narrating instances" responsible for different aspects of film's audiovisual representation already tackled in chapter 4—uses the observation that terms such as "point of view" and "focalization" tend to refer to, "on the one hand, perceiving, and on the other hand, thinking and knowing" ("The Look" 72) as a starting point to distinguish between "focalization," "ocularization," and "auricularization." While "*focalization* designates the cognitive point of view adopted by the narrative, with the equalities or inequalities of knowledge expressed at their full strength" (Jost, "The Look" 74, original emphasis), "ocularization" and "auricularization" describe the relation between what the film makes visible or audible and what its characters see or hear, respectively. Jost further distinguishes between "primary internal ocularization/auricularization," where changes in the quality of the film's picture or sound mark that it represents the visual or auditive perception of a character, "secondary internal ocularization/auricularization," where such a representation is marked by the context of the picture or sound in question, and "zero ocularization/auricularization," where the picture or sound are not attributed to the visual or auditive perception of any specific character. Jost's terminological choices may not be entirely convincing, yet his emphasis on the "disconnect" between how film's audiovisual representation relates to the represented characters' perceptions and how it relates to their knowledge is certainly helpful—though, once more, not all film narratologists would agree.[12] Primarily building on Bal's rather than Genette's concept of "focalization," Celestino Deleyto, for example, argues that Jost's "focalization" and "ocularization" actually "designate much the same thing" (Deleyto 222), before he insists that "in film . . . , there can appear, simultaneously, several focalisers, external and internal, on different points of the frame (and outside)" (Deleyto 223). While Deleyto's approach to "focalization" has been fairly influential as well, its reductionist foundation leads him to postulate, rather unconvincingly, "the almost permanent existence of an external focaliser in a film narrative" that allegedly "accounts for the general tendency of the medium towards narrative objectivity" (222). Whether one calls it "ocularization/auricularization" or not, what Deleyto refers to here is not the whole range of meanings commonly associated with "focalization."

Now, while the representation of subjectivity is perhaps most extensively discussed in literary and film narratology, there have been quite a few attempts to transfer the terms "perspective" and "point of view" as well as the term "focalization" to comics and to video games—albeit with varying results. Even though they are not adding too many genuinely new aspects to the discussion, some of the attempts to apply the term "focalization" to comics at least serve to emphasize the importance of distinguishing between narratorial and nonnarratorial forms of "focalization" and/or strategies of subjective representation, a distinction that tends to be less pronounced in the more influential accounts of "focalization" within film narratology: Martin Schüwer, for example, may use somewhat problematic terms when he proposes to distinguish between the "verbal parts" and the "visual parts" of a comic, but his insistence that an analysis of comics' "focalization" needs to ask not only "from whose perspective are perceptions/thoughts/feelings *shown*" but also "from whose perspective are perceptions/thoughts/feelings *told*" (392, my emphases, my translation from the German) seems laudable. Despite the admirable detail in which Schüwer's study examines some of comics' medium-specific strategies of narrative representation, though, his discussion of "internal" and "external focalization" ultimately remains fairly brief and refrains from engaging the question of how narratorial forms of "focalization" are realized in comics. Instead, he focuses primarily on the ways in which nonnarratorial point-of-view panels and thought bubbles may or may not be used to subjectively represent a character's consciousness and how, even in the absence of these "strong" forms of "internal focalization," other strategies may also more indirectly contribute to the representation of characters' consciousnesses. Indeed, the way that the term "focalization" is used may become even less technical in some areas of comics studies, when, for example, Karin Kukkonen claims that the "oriental architecture" in some of the page margins in Bill Willingham's *Fables: Arabian Nights (and Days)* "tells us that this part of the story is told from the Oriental fairy tale characters' perspective" and, thus, "visually represents an act or process of focalization" ("Comics" 48).

More recently, though, Silke Horstkotte and Nancy Pedri have proposed a comics-specific approach to "focalization" that emphasizes precisely those parts of the term's conceptual history that aim at the function(s) of the narrator: building on Mieke Bal and Shlomith Rimmon-Kenan rather than on Gérard Genette, they stress that "optical perspectivation is only one dimension within a broader category of focalization that also includes aspects of cognition, ideological orientation, and judgment" (Horstkotte and Pedri 331), all of which have "to be signaled by distinctly subjective discourse markers in all texts, including visual and multimodal ones" (Horstkotte and Pedri 334). Perhaps even more important than their insistence on the multidimensional or "multiaspectual" nature of "focalization" is Horstkotte and Pedri's proposal to "operate with a binary typology of focalization that sets off the subjective inflection of *character-bound focalization* against a more neutral *narratorial* one" (335, original emphases). It should be noted, however, that their argument "for preserving focalization as a central category of narratological analysis, rather than erasing it in favor of a broader consideration of consciousness presentation in fiction" (Horstkotte and Pedri 335), results in a conceptualization of "focalization" that is strikingly different from, say, the conceptualization developed by Schüwer in that it focuses on Bal's "focalizing subject" as opposed to her "focalized object," defining the term with regard to the "filter function" of represented consciousnesses instead of the question to what extent a narrative representation represents those consciousnesses as its "content." That this is only one of many potential conceptualizations of "focalization" may be further illustrated by a brief look at the recent work of yet another prolific comics narratologist, Kai Mikkonen, who, in "operating with a consciously limited notion of focalisation, restricted to questions of access to perception in strict sensory bounds," not only confines the concept to "the information the narrative conveys about the spatial and physical point of observation, and the sensory range of that position" ("Focalization" 72), but also largely ignores the distinction between "focalizing subject" and "focalized object" as well as the distinction between narratorial and nonnarratorial forms of "focalization" (even though Mikkonen explicitly mentions Genette's and Bal's accounts of "focalization" and, moreover, also provides a brief nod to Horstkotte and Pedri's conceptualization of the term).

It might be worth noting at this point that my remarks on previous conceptualizations of "focalization" are not meant as an overly harsh critique of any specific approach. Instead, I intend the examples of film- and comics-specific accounts of "focalization" given so far to illustrate that there is no common understanding of the term in film studies and comics studies any more than in literary narratology—although most if not all of the existing approaches to "focalization" in literary texts, films, and comics will have something relevant to say about transmedial aspects of strategies that aim at the representation of subjectivity, their medium-specific realization, or both.[13] Still, despite the fact that the specifically narratological term "focalization" seems to suggest a certain technical quality rather more strongly than the comparatively general terms "perspective" and "point of view," the lack of consensus regarding the concepts that the term in question should be used to refer to is similarly glaring in all three cases. While the various attempts to transfer terms such as "point of view," "perspective," or "focalization" to films and comics may help us to better understand some of the medium-specific as well as transmedial aspects of strategies of subjective representation, then, they also illustrate the terminological dilemma into which contemporary narratology has maneuvered itself, and which might ultimately indicate a comparatively radical terminological solution. Incidentally, both of these observations are even more relevant with regard to studies that examine "point of view," "perspective," and/or "focalization" in video games: at least some of these studies may propose fruitful modifications and expansions of established approaches to the representation of subjectivity from literary and film narratology, in particular, but even in those cases, a keen awareness of video games' medium-specific limitations and affordances tends to be combined with a certain terminological "sloppiness" that further adds to the already existing confusion surrounding terms such as "perspective," "point of view," and "focalization."

A comparatively early but still paradigmatic example is Britta Neitzel's influential discussion of three types of representational rules that are commonly used in contemporary video games: the "objective point of view," which is sometimes also called a "god's eye perspective," can be found in games where the spatial position from which the game spaces are represented is not connected to the spatial position of a character or other entity within these game spaces; the "semi-subjective point of view," which is also called "third-person perspective," can be found in games where the spatial position from which the game spaces are represented is connected to the spatial position of a character or other entity within these game spaces, but does not coincide with that position; and the "subjective point of view," which is also called "first-person perspective," can be found in games where the spatial position from which the game spaces are represented coincides with the spatial position of a character or other entity within these game spaces.[14] However, Neitzel not only uses the terms "perspective" and "point of view," somewhat interchangeably, but also relates the three types of "point of view" she distinguishes to Gérard Genette's three types of "focalization," arguing that an "objective point of view" can be understood as a form of "zero focalization," a "semi-subjective point of view" can be understood as a form of "internal focalization," and a "subjective point of view" can be understood as a form of "external focalization" (since the latter does not, or at least not fully, represent the body of the player-controlled character). At the very least, the connections that Neitzel draws here are highly unconventional, with related approaches from film and comics studies usually conceptualizing the medium-specific counterparts of the "semi-subjective point of view" as a form of "external focalization" and those of the "subjective point of view" as a form of "internal focalization" (or "external ocularization" and "internal ocularization," respectively, in those approaches that follow François Jost).

While I do not agree with what I consider an inappropriate short circuit of the terms "perspective," "point of view," and "focalization," then, it should be emphasized that the three forms of "point of view" that Neitzel distinguishes are, indeed, well suited for the analysis of most if not all contemporary video games. Yet, more importantly, what allows Neitzel's approach to remain relevant to the present day is her insistence that the interactivity of video games necessitates distinguishing not only between different forms of "point of view" as the spatial position from which the game spaces are represented but also between different forms of "point of action" as the actional position from which the player may interact with these game spaces. Accordingly, Neitzel's approach to "point of view/point of action" has modified and expanded rather significantly any concept of "point of view" (or "perspective," or "focalization") that could have been developed with literary texts, films, or comics in mind. I will not further discuss Neitzel's conceptualization of video games' "point of action" here,[15] but I would still like to stress that this kind of medium-specific modification and expansion of existing conceptualizations of "perspective," "point of view," and "focalization" is still surprisingly uncommon in the field of game studies. In *Video Game Spaces*, for example, Michael Nitsche largely limits himself to illustrating the fairly general claim that the complexity of contemporary video games allows them to use and combine "the character-bound focalizer and the external focalizer" (146), which he seems to model largely following Mieke Bal. Another example of terminological "sloppiness" would be Jonne Arjoranta's more recent account of "focalization" in video games, which manages to nonchalantly claim (without much explanation) that "games have the usual focalizations (zero, external, internal)" (1), yet also mentions that Genette supposedly "calls these perspective" and "classifies perspective into three categories: zero focalization, external focalization and internal focalization," even though "focalization is the point of view things are seen from" (5).

Instead of discussing those or other similarly problematic attempts to conceptualize "focalization" in video games as largely similar to "focalization" in literary texts and films, let me conclude this interlude on (more or less) medium-specific conceptualizations of "focalization" by mentioning a more recent study of the representation of subjectivity in films and video games by Benjamin Beil. Despite the title of his book, *First Person Perspectives*, Beil proposes to use none of the three "popular" narratological terms "perspective," "point of view," or "focalization," instead building on Edward Branigan and Seymour Chatman in his examination of "character-centered filters," "distributed filters," "the subjective," and the "interest focus" as prototypical "strategies of subjectivization." Once more, neither Beil's terminological decisions nor his conceptual considerations appear particularly convincing (at least not if one takes it to be one of his aims to provide a systematically sound taxonomy of strategies of subjective representation in contemporary video games), but his work is nevertheless worth singling out (in a positive sense) for two reasons. On the one hand, while it may not result in the development of terminologically and conceptually convincing alternatives, Beil's decision to abandon the well-established terms "perspective," "point of view," and "focalization" remains preferable to conceptualizing these terms in the ways in which, for example, Neitzel or Nitsche conceptualize them. On the other hand, and perhaps more importantly, Beil's focus on a wide variety of different examples may occasionally appear arbitrary, but it nevertheless demonstrates rather impressively that films and video games (as well as comics, for that matter) may represent characters' subjectivity using very different strategies, whose heterogeneity tends to resist any attempt at systematization. Before I further examine this relation between the universal and the particular using my previously outlined approach to describe salient prototypical strategies of narrative representation on a transmedial level as well as their medium-specific realization in contemporary films, comics, and video games, however, some further remarks on the terminological and conceptual foundation of my account of subjectivity across media appear to be in order.

From the Representation of Subjectivity to Subjective Representation

As my survey of some of the more influential accounts of "perspective," "point of view," and "focalization" in literary narratology, film studies, and beyond has shown, the conceptual histories associated with these terms have become so complex and convoluted that using them will very likely lead to various kinds of misunderstandings.[16] Just as one could argue, for example, that "point of view" should "*not mean expression*" (Chatman, *Story* 153, original emphasis) or that the "the variety of meanings attributed to the term 'perspective' can be traced back to the common core" (Eder, *Die Figur* 582, my translation from the German) of "mental perspective," one could demand that the term "focalization" should only refer to an activity exclusively attributable to "the narrator, or . . . the *author* himself [or herself]" (Genette, *Narrative Discourse Revisited* 73, original emphasis). Such demands, however, would not change the fact that the term "point of view" is also used to refer to the "range and/or depth of knowledge which the narration supplies" (Bordwell, *Narration* 60), that the term "perspective" is often understood more inclusively as "*the complex, formed by internal and external factors, of conditions for the comprehension and representation of happenings*" (Schmid, *Narratology* 99, original emphasis), and that the term "focalization" is also commonly used to refer to the nonrepresentational activity of "a character within the represented world" (Rimmon-Kenan, *Narrative Fiction* 75)—an activity that Genette, somewhat ironically, calls "*prefocalization*" (*Narrative Discourse Revisited* 78, original emphasis).

Despite the fact that the works of Edward Branigan (on "point of view" and "focalization") and Jens Eder (on "perspective"), in particular, will turn out to be quite valuable for my discussion of transmedial strategies of subjective representation, it is necessary to confront the fundamental question of "whether the narratological properties that we wish to identify are well captured by this term [the term 'point of view,' in this case]—or indeed by *any* single term—or whether its complexities render it imprecise and confusing" (Chatman, *Coming to Terms* 141, original emphasis). Of course, Seymour Chatman was mainly concerned with the question "whether the *same* name (whether 'point of view' or 'perspective' or 'vision' or 'focalization') should cover the mental acts of different narrative agents" (Chatman, *Coming to Terms* 141, original emphasis),[17] but I would argue that both the question and his (negative) answer can, at least to a certain extent, be generalized, since the "terminological thicket" that surrounds the three terms most commonly associated with narratological discussions of the representation of subjectivity makes using them appear increasingly undesirable.

Hence, instead of contributing to the prolonged use of terms that seem to have outlived their usefulness for quite some time now, I propose to employ more neutral (and, arguably, more precise) expressions such as *the representation of subjectivity* or, more specifically, *the subjective representation of a character's consciousness or mind* during my examination of transmedial strategies of subjective representation in this and the following chapter.[18] Although it seems preferable to using "charged" terms such as "point of view," "perspective," and "focalization," then, speaking of the representation of subjectivity and (strategies of) subjective representation without further explanation may still invite a number of misunderstandings. What I propose to call the representation of subjectivity is usually considered to be a prototypical feature of narrative, but this includes comparatively indirect modes of representation that allow recipients to infer certain aspects of the represented characters' consciousnesses or minds without providing anything amounting to what may roughly be described as "direct access."[19] It is precisely this kind of "direct access" to a represented character's consciousness or mind that what I propose to call subjective representation provides. In order to develop a better grasp of the distinction between the representation of subjectivity as a fundamental prototypical feature of narrative representations across media and specific strategies of subjective representation that provide "direct access" to a character's consciousness or mind, then, let me say a few more words on the question of how subjective representation relates to *non*subjective representation in the context of a "bottom-up" approach to transmedial narratological analysis.

As Edward Branigan's examination of "focalization" makes clear, what is represented by narrative representations across media can often be understood as "diegetically intersubjective, or 'objective,' in the sense that it is reported independently by a narrator, or else appears seemingly without any mediation as a 'fact' of some kind" (*Narrative Comprehension* 161). But of course, this does not mean that the recipients cannot infer, at least to a certain extent, how the characters that are intersubjectively represented in this way experience the situation, how they perceive the represented storyworld elements, what "is on their minds." While much of classical narratological research focused on what Alan Palmer calls "speech category accounts" of the representation of characters' consciousnesses in literary texts, the past decade has seen an increasing interest in *inter*subjective representations of subjectivity, in "the whole minds of fictional characters in action" ("The Construction" 28). What Lisa Zunshine describes as our "mind-reading skills"—that is, "our ability to explain people's behavior in terms of their thoughts, feelings, beliefs, and desires" (6)—is no longer seen as being limited to the actual world, but "constructions of fictional minds" appear to be "inextricably bound up with presentations of action. Direct access to inner speech and states of mind is only a small part of the process of building up the sense of a mind in action" (Palmer, *Fictional Minds* 210–211; see also Palmer, *Social Minds*). In a similar trajectory, Per Persson examines the role of folk psychology with regard to the construction of characters' minds in the feature film, underscoring that "mental attribution of fictional characters is not solely a question of face and body-cue ability," since these are always "placed within a context of mental states" (183).

As important as Palmer's and Zunshine's as well as Branigan's and Persson's emphasis on the functions of intersubjective segments of representation for the recipient's comprehension of characters' consciousnesses certainly is, though, it should not lead to any kind of simple equation of intersubjective with objective modes of representation. Even if we leave the more philosophical implications of objectivity, intersubjectivity, and subjectivity aside,[20] it seems clear that narrative representations may not only, first, represent storyworld elements as they are (subjectively) represented in the consciousness of a particular character and, second, represent storyworld elements as they are (intersubjectively) perceived or experienced by a group of characters, but also, third, represent storyworld elements that are not perceived or experienced by any character in the storyworld at all.[21] Particularly if one keeps in mind that some nonsubjective modes of representation contribute significantly to the recipients' construction of hypotheses about what the represented characters' "have on their minds," then, a further heuristic distinction between objective and intersubjective modes of representation appears to be quite useful for any "bottom-up" attempt to analyze a narrative representation's global *structure of subjectivity* as the specific combination of local strategies of subjective as well as intersubjective representation.[22]

Incidentally, my insistence on drawing such a distinction should not be misunderstood as a claim that subjectivity, intersubjectivity, and objectivity are always clearly delineated: just as our "mental perspective" on something can be "more or less subjective or objective" (Eder, *Die Figur* 587, my translation from the German), so can the intersubjective representation of storyworld elements, since "objectivity and subjectivity interact in a narrative film [or other narrative works across media] by being alternated, overlapped, or otherwise mixed, producing complex descriptions of space, time, and causality" (Branigan, *Narrative Comprehension* 161). Yet the observation that we are confronted with a scalar rather than a binary distinction between subjectivity and objectivity does not prevent us from identifying certain "points" on that scale that appear to be particularly salient for narrative representations across media. At least in contemporary films, comics, and video games, *intersubjective representation* may be considered the unmarked case, while *objective representation* and *subjective representation* may both be considered marked cases, albeit on opposing ends of a continuum that measures the extent to which a given segment of a narrative representation represents characters' consciousnesses. While objective representation suggests that the storyworld elements in question are not perceived or imagined by any characters at all, subjective representation suggests that the storyworld elements in question are perceived or imagined by only one character (and often in a way that is not compatible with an intersubjective version of the storyworld).[23] Having established the primarily narratological distinction between strategies of subjective, intersubjective, and objective representation, I would like to add a few more general remarks on the concept of subjectivity and its relation to concepts such as perception, experience, and consciousness as they are discussed in the philosophy of mind (as well as, albeit less controversially, in cognitive psychology).

Perhaps unsurprisingly, the discussion surrounding these terms is fairly complex, and a comprehensive reconstruction appears well beyond the scope of this chapter.[24] Instead, let me briefly examine three influential takes on the issue, beginning with Thomas Nagel's famous essay "What Is It Like to Be a Bat?," which establishes most if not all of the crucial relations between the concepts mentioned above. In essence, Nagel is concerned with the "subjective character of experience," which he takes to be a defining element of consciousness, since "an organism has conscious mental states if and only if there is something that it is like to *be* that organism—something it is like *for* the organism" ("What Is It Like" 436, original emphases). In other words, what could also be called "perceptual or 'primary' consciousness" (M. Smith, "Consciousness" 42)—as opposed to "self-consciousness" (M. Smith, "Consciousness" 42)—is already highly subjective, because our perceptions, our experience of the world around us,[25] are closely interrelated to "how it is like to be us," to perceive, to experience the world around us the way we do (and not, say, the way a bat does). From this, Nagel concludes that "our own experience provides the basic material for our imaginations, whose range is therefore limited" ("What Is It Like" 439), but this observation should not be mistaken to mean that our imaginations—particularly those "evoked" by narrative representations—cannot attempt to "simulate" the subjective experiences that are alien to us.[26] Instead, it would seem that the "experiential makeup" (as well as, perhaps, what Marco Caracciolo calls the "*experiential background*" [232, original emphasis]) of the latter can be more or less close or remote from ours, so that we may have fairly accurate imaginations of how it is to be another human being but not how it is to be a bat—or, rather, how it is "for a *bat* to be a bat" (Nagel, "What Is It Like" 439, original emphasis). However, the fact that the subjective experience of a bat remains fundamentally "inaccessible" to humans does not prevent narrative representations across media to try and represent these as well as other alien forms of subjective experience: indeed, while perception, experience, and consciousness are highly subjective, narrative representations may still try to represent them, generating what Maike Sarah Reinerth calls "intersubjective subjectivity" ("Intersubjective Subjectivity?" n. pag.).

Nagel's essay already gives us a solid idea of the ways in which perception, experience, and consciousness are subjective not only by way of being internal to the person "having" them but also by way of being connected to his or her specific "outlook on the world." Still, some further remarks on how these concepts relate to each other as well as to the more encompassing concept of the mind as entailing conscious and unconscious mental states are necessary. I will derive these remarks from yet another influential philosophical account of consciousness that was developed by John R. Searle in *Mind, Language, and Society*. Like Nagel, Searle emphasizes consciousness's "inner, qualitative, and subjective nature" (*Mind* 41), allowing for a more precise description not only of the relations among but also of the fundamental subjectivity of perception, experience, and consciousness: according to Searle, "conscious states and processes are *inner* in a very ordinary spatial sense in that they go on inside my body, and specifically inside my brain" (*Mind* 41, original emphasis), but also "in a second sense, and that is that any one of our conscious states exists only as an element in a sequence of such states" (*Mind* 42). Moreover, "conscious states are *qualitative* in the sense that for each conscious state there is a certain way that it feels, there is a certain qualitative character to it" (Searle, *Mind* 42, original emphasis). And, finally, "conscious states are *subjective* in the sense that they are always experienced by a human or animal subject. Conscious states, therefore, have what we might call a 'first-person ontology'" (Searle, *Mind* 42, original emphasis).

It would seem, then, that describing *consciousness* (as well as, perhaps, *experience* and, albeit to a lesser extent, *perceptions*[27]) as being defined by its *internality*, its *qualitative character*,[28] and its *subjectivity* is not only comparatively uncontroversial but also helpful as a conceptual and terminological foundation of the following. I would like to further emphasize two other well-established and closely interrelated distinctions that will also turn out to be relevant in the context of this chapter and that Searle discusses in some detail, namely, *intentional* versus *nonintentional mental states*[29] and *conscious* versus *unconscious mental states*. On the one hand, while conceding that "not all conscious states are intentional, and not all intentional states are conscious" (Searle, *Mind* 65), Searle underscores that "most . . . conscious phenomena . . . represent objects, events, and states of affairs in the world" (*Mind* 64). Still, it is important to note that our minds allow us to have at least some conscious states such as a general sense of anxiety or elation that are not "intentional" (in the specific sense in which the term is used in the philosophy of mind), making them *conscious nonintentional mental states*, as well as to "have beliefs and desires, hopes and fears, even when [we are] sound asleep [if our sleep is 'dreamless,' that is]" (Searle, *Mind* 65), which are, therefore, *unconscious intentional mental states*. Yet, according to Searle, "we only understand intentionality in terms of consciousness," and while "there are many intentional states that are not conscious, . . . they are the sort of thing that could potentially be conscious" (*Mind* 65).[30] Perhaps unsurprisingly, then, the representation of subjectivity across media (and the argument presented in this chapter) tends to focus on *conscious intentional states*.

Obviously, more could be said about all of these aspects as well as about an even greater number of more "thorny" issues such as the relation between the mind and the brain,[31] the "hard problem" of the existence of consciousness,[32] or the contested concept of self-consciousness. But considering that I aim at the representation of subjectivity across media rather than at a comprehensive discussion of subjectivity as it relates to perception, experience, and consciousness, it seems sufficient to sketch some of the more salient types of conscious intentional states that are at the center of the ways in which characters' subjective consciousnesses are represented in contemporary media culture. While *what* is internally represented (i.e., the "content" of intentional states) will doubtless be relevant for the comprehension of a given narrative representation as well, I would argue that the question of *how* it is internally represented (i.e., the "mode" of intentional states) is even more important in the context of this chapter. In order to further differentiate the "modes" of conscious intentional states as internal mental representations of the world while at the same time emphasizing their external narrative representation (or at least the possibility that these internal mental representations are represented externally as part of narrative representations), it will be helpful to return to Jens Eder's above-mentioned account of "mental perspective" as "*the specific way in which intentional objects are mentally represented in a consciousness*" (*Die Figur* 584, original emphasis, my translation from the German), which leads him to distinguish between five modes of intentional mental states.

First, "perceptual perspective" describes the way in which a narrator or character perceives a given object (or imagines it in a way close to perception); second, "epistemic perspective" refers to what a narrator or character knows or believes about a given object; third, "evaluative perspective" describes the way in which a narrator or character evaluates a given object with regard to aesthetic, moral, or other criteria; fourth, "motivational perspective" refers to what a narrator or character wants or wishes with regard to a given object; and fifth, "emotional perspective" describes the emotions, feelings, or moods that a narrator or character (or person) experiences with regard to a given object. Both the representation of unconscious intentional states (such as certain forms of "nonactualized" knowledge or beliefs) and the representation of conscious nonintentional states (such as general feelings of anxiety or elation) play a role with regard to the ways in which contemporary films, comics, and video games may represent their characters' subjectivity, but the kinds of conscious intentional states that Eder's discussion of "mental perspective" helps to further distinguish still seem to be more important, at least for the purposes of the present study.

Particularly as far as the kind of nonnarratorial strategies of representation that primarily employ "signs close to perception" (Sachs-Hombach 73, my translation from the German) are concerned, I would argue that contemporary films, comics, and video games—in providing what one could describe as "direct access" to characters' minds—tend to stress not only the representation of conscious intentional states but also a specific kind of these states, namely, perceptual or quasi-perceptual ones. Hence, this chapter will likewise focus on representations that provide "direct access" to perceptual or quasi-perceptual aspects of characters' consciousnesses, allowing me to discuss the representation of various kinds of "mental imagery" that occur in the context of (perceptual) hallucinations, (retrieved) memories, (lucid) dreams, and fantasies, while at the same time deemphasizing the—usually less "direct"—representation of other aspects of characters' minds, such as knowledge, beliefs,[33] norms, values, wishes, motivations, emotions, and moods.[34] This is certainly not to say that the representation of these other aspects of characters' minds is not important, though: the representation of (quasi-)perceptual aspects of a character's consciousness may not only be "colored" by the recipient's hypotheses about the knowledge, beliefs, norms, values, wishes, motivations, emotions, and moods of that character, but some representations of (quasi-)perceptual aspects of a character's consciousness are arguably also representations of that character's knowledge, beliefs, norms, values, wishes, motivations, emotions, or moods—either because these other aspects of the character's consciousness take (quasi-)perceptual forms (which seems to regularly apply to wishes and emotions, in particular) or because the film, comic, or video game in question uses what only *appears to be* the

Subjectivity as a Transmedial Concept 245

representation of nonconceptual aspects of the character's consciousness to *metaphorically represent* conceptual aspects of it (a strategy that is also sometimes used to represent unconscious or even nonconscious mental states).[35]

Against this background, it might also be worth repeating that it is quite common to conceptualize "point of view," "perspective," and "focalization" as multidimensional or, perhaps, "multiaspectual" concepts in both classical and contemporary narratology. Following the "dual nature" of Gérard Genette's concept of "focalization," however, much of the previous research has focused on either the representation of characters' (quasi-)perceptions or the representation of characters' knowledge.[36] Yet, quite independently of the challenges that the transfer of Genette's term from literary narrative texts to other narrative media poses, his discussion of "focalization" as a relation between the narrator and a single character tends to reduce the complexity of what one could call "epistemic perspective structures" beyond an acceptable level. As Edward Branigan has convincingly shown, it may be useful to "measure relative knowledge" by evaluating locally "whether the spectator knows more than (>), the same as (=), or less than (<) a particular character at a particular time" (*Narrative Comprehension* 74–75), but the resulting global structures are usually *not* focused on a single character. Instead, Branigan argues that "the organization of a group of disparities whereby some perceivers are represented as acquiring more accurate knowledge about certain events relative to other perceivers" (*Narrative Comprehension* 74) is more appropriately described as a "hierarchy of knowledge," and such "hierarchies of knowledge" (or "epistemic perspective structures") may not only include the knowledge of characters and narrators, but also continuously evolve over the course of the narrative representation's developing plot.

One of the reasons why Genette's concept of "internal focalization" can be so misleading is that local strategies of *subjective* representation tend to play a minor role in the global development of "epistemic perspective structures." Instead, *intersubjective* modes of representation seem to be considerably more relevant (at least from a quantitative point of view), as they allow recipients to draw inferences about characters' knowledge on the basis of what kind of storyworld elements these characters are represented as perceiving. Incidentally, this is one of the main reasons why, in the context of a "bottom-up" analysis of the strategies of subjective representation that a given narrative work employs, it is important not only to examine segments of subjective as well as of intersubjective and objective representation but also to distinguish between different segments of intersubjective representation according to the characters or groups of characters that are represented as "being conscious about" or experiencing the represented events. While it is obvious, then, that "if one perceives something, one usually also acquires knowledge about it" (Eder, *Die Figur* 586, my translation from the German), there still is "no *direct* link" (Schmid, *Narratology* 93, my emphasis) between perception and knowledge. Nevertheless, just as a character's perception may lead him or her to acquire knowledge, thereby changing his or her position in the narrative representation's "hierarchy of knowledge," the latter may also provide important context for segments of subjective representation that provide "direct access" to (quasi-)perceptual aspects of that character's consciousness.

These general observations on "hierarchies of knowledge" also seem to apply to other aspects of characters' consciousnesses: just as the recipient's knowledge in relation to the knowledge he or she can attribute to a storyworld's characters and narrators constitutes a more or less complex "epistemic perspective structure," the norms and values that the recipient can attribute to a storyworld's characters and narrators constitute a more or less complex "evaluative perspective structure." As Murray Smith notes, in understanding a film, we need "to consider, first, how such 'systems of value' are constructed; secondly, the range of possible types of moral structure; and thirdly, the different ways in which a narration may unfurl these moral structures through time" (*Engaging Characters* 189). Particularly if one subscribes to a broad understanding of "evaluation," however, a given narrative representation's "evaluative perspective structure" may well entail aspects of the "motivational perspectives" and "emotional perspectives" of characters, since the wishes, motivations, emotions, and moods that characters experience with regard to a given object will necessarily also be based on and in turn influence their evaluation of that object.[37] Unfortunately, it would go well beyond the scope of the present study to examine the (at least partially medium-specific) realization of these aspects of what one could then describe as "evaluative," "motivational," and "emotional perspective structures" in contemporary films, comics, or video games in any detail,[38] but it is worth stressing, yet again, that the subjective representation of (quasi-)perceptual aspects of a character's consciousness is often intricately interrelated with the representation of the knowledge, beliefs, norms, values, wishes, motivations, emotions, or moods of that character—and, of course, all of these aspects of characters' consciousnesses may be represented using narratorial as well as nonnarratorial and subjective as well as intersubjective strategies of representation.

On the one hand, then, contemporary films, comics, and video games can use both narratorial and nonnarratorial strategies of narrative representation in order to represent storyworld elements subjectively, intersubjectively, or objectively. On the other hand, segments of both subjective and intersubjective representation—whether they are realized through narratorial or nonnarratorial strategies of representation—may contribute to the representation of characters' minds in general and (quasi-)perceptual aspects of characters' consciousnesses in particular. As far as the subjective representation of (quasi-)perceptual aspects of characters' consciousnesses is concerned, a narratological analysis would have to ask at least the following questions: Does a given segment of the narrative representation use narratorial or nonnarratorial strategies of subjective representation, or both? If a given segment of the narrative representation uses strategies of subjective representation, the (quasi-)perceptual aspects of the consciousness of which character(s) are being represented? What are the functions, narrative or otherwise, of the strategies of subjective representation thus employed? Despite the importance of intersubjective as well as objective strategies of representation for what I have proposed to call the structure of subjectivity of a narrative work and the fact that both the representation of subjectivity and the more specific strategies of subjective representation will usually include not only perceptions and quasi-perceptions (such as hallucinations, memories, dreams, and fantasies) but also other aspects of characters' consciousnesses (such as their knowledge, beliefs, norms, values, wishes, motivations, emotions, and moods), I will use the remainder of this chapter and the analyses presented in the following chapter to focus on narratorial and nonnarratorial strategies of subjective representation that provide "direct access" to characters' (quasi-)perceptions as well as on these strategies' combination in occasionally rather complex structures of subjectivity.

Narratorial and Nonnarratorial Strategies of Subjective Representation

Let me start, then, with a few more remarks on narratorial strategies of subjective representation or, in other words, with the ways in which contemporary films, comics, and video games may use narrators to provide "direct access" to (quasi-)perceptual and other aspects of characters' consciousnesses or characters' minds. Even if one takes into account that narratorial strategies of subjective representation (as well as narratorial strategies of intersubjective and objective representation, for that matter) tend to be not quite as complex in contemporary films, comics, and video games as they are in certain kinds of literary texts that have traditionally informed literary narratology's discussion of the representation of characters' consciousnesses, the low extent to which specific kinds of narratorial strategies of subjective representation are attended to in film studies, comics studies, and game studies is still surprising. This is not to say that film narratology in particular fails to regularly point out the fact that narrators can be used to realize strategies of objective and intersubjective as well as of subjective representation. However, there still exist only very few accounts of the latter that go beyond this fairly obvious observation in systematically distinguishing, or providing in-depth examinations of, different forms of these strategies.[39] Apart from the mistaken assumption that the distinction between heterodiegetic and homodiegetic narrators corresponds to the distinction between objective or intersubjective and subjective representation (which, despite its obvious conflation of two very different questions, is still more common than one would expect), studies that focus on subjectivity in film appear to largely ignore narratorial strategies of subjective representation, while studies that focus on narrators in film appear to primarily examine narratorial strategies of subjective representation *ex negativo*—by more or less explicitly excluding subjective voice-over from their respective object domains, that is.

Sarah Kozloff, for example, argues that, "in talking about voice-over *narration*, we can and should bracket out other types of speech by invisible speakers. . . . As for fiction films, they often use asynchronous speech to signal eavesdropping on a character's private reveries. In 'interior monologue,' we hear the rush of a character's thoughts or feelings in his or her own voice . . . ; in 'subjective' or 'delusional' sound, we hear what the character 'hears' echoing in his or her mind" (4–5, original emphasis). I certainly agree that forms of voice-over and narration boxes in films, comics, and video games may indeed represent not only the narratorial voice of a narrator but also what Kozloff calls the "interior monologue" of a nonnarrating character. Accordingly, voice-over will occasionally be more appropriately comprehended as part of the nonnarratorial representation rather than as a form of narratorial representation, although these kinds of internal voices may also function as a form of narration in the admittedly rare cases where they can be attributed to an intradiegetic thinking narrator. Yet it would seem that films as well as comics and video games commonly use more clearly narratorial strategies of subjective representation as well, at least some of which will actually appear to be very similar to the nonnarratorial representation of characters' internal voices and none of which Kozloff discusses in any detail, let alone with anything resembling a systematizing intention. This is even more surprising as Kozloff herself remarks that "interior monologue may be so interlaced with narration that the blend is undefinable" (6), which leads her to explicitly include these and other "impure" forms of voice-over in the object domain of her study.

Avrom Fleishman also examines "interior monologue" (as well as "interior dialogue" and "interior soliloquy," all three of which he understands as subforms of what he calls "mindscreen narration") in a more recent study. "An arrangement of the dubbed voices in films," Fleishman writes, "could be made in a fourfold schema based on two characteristics: whether or not the voice is heard by other characters, and whether or not the human source of the voice is seen by them at or about the time it speaks" (75). When using these two criteria to identify different types of voices, "the resulting four classes would include *voice-off* (heard and seen), *interior monologue* (not heard by others even when the character is on-screen with them), the *acousmêtre* (heard but not seen), and *voice-over* (neither heard nor seen by [other] characters)" (Fleishman 75, original emphases, original square brackets). Compared to Kozloff's study, however, Fleishman's examination of "voice-over narration" turns out to be even less relevant to the question of which narratorial strategies of subjective representation films (and comics, and video games) may use, as it lacks not only a systematic approach to different forms of the latter (which Kozloff does not provide, either) but also a systematic distinction between narratorial and nonnarratorial strategies of subjective representation (which Kozloff at least implies).

Indeed, the confusion regarding the status of narratorial strategies of subjective representation within film narratology in particular seems to prevail to the present day: Markus Kuhn, for example, mentions that homodiegetic voice-over may either represent the "inner voice of the character" (271, my translation from the German) whose voice is used in the voice-over, or not. While Kuhn's suggestion to use the frequency of a voice-over as a criterion to distinguish between a character's internal voice and an extradiegetic homodiegetic narrator's narratorial voice is already unconvincing, his insistence on attributing all kinds of homodiegetic voice-over, including a character's internal voice, to an extradiegetic homodiegetic narrator (or, rather, a "verbal narrating instance") is particularly problematic. Claiming that the nonnarratorial representation (i.e., the audiovisual representation in films as well as, presumably, the verbal-pictorial representation in comics and the interactive representation in video games) can unproblematically represent character speech but cannot, under any circumstances, represent character thought seems highly counterintuitive—and since Kuhn does not give any reasons for this surprisingly strong claim, I would maintain that one should allow for narratorial as well as nonnarratorial strategies of subjective representation that may represent characters' internal voices. In further discussing the different strategies that films, comics, and video games may employ to this end, I would like to revisit one of the core sources on which Kozloff, Fleishman, and Kuhn more or less explicitly build,[40] namely, the typology of narratorial strategies of subjective representation proposed by the literary narratologist Dorrit Cohn in her groundbreaking study of characters' interiority, *Transparent Minds*.

Even though Cohn is exclusively concerned with literary texts and, hence, her concepts will have to be modified to allow for their transmedial application, her distinction between "psycho-narration," "narrated interior monologue," "quoted interior monologue," and "autonomous interior monologue" still seems considerably more sophisticated than most of the conceptual and terminological distinctions developed within film studies, comics studies, and game studies so far.[41] "Psycho-narration" is the most complex of Cohn's categories, encompassing all varieties of "the narrator's discourse about a character's consciousness" that relies entirely on his or her "own words" and, therefore, can be distinguished from "narrated interior monologue" as "a character's mental discourse in the guise of the narrator's discourse" as well as from the two forms of "interior monologue" that Cohn proposes to distinguish as being defined by different ways to provide "direct access" to "a character's mental discourse" (*Transparent Minds* 14). The first of these forms, "quoted interior monologue," is still "mediated (quoted explicitly or implicitly) by a narrating voice that refers to the monologist by third-person pronoun [or first-person pronoun, in the case of 'self-quoted interior monologue'] in the surrogating text; the second, unmediated, and apparently self-generated, constitutes an autonomous first-person form [i.e., 'autonomous interior monologue'], which it would be best to regard as a variant—or better, a limit-case—of first-person narration" (Cohn, *Transparent Minds* 15).[42] It seems that contemporary films, comics, and video games tend to privilege "psycho-narration" (or, rather, "self-narration") over "narrated interior monologue" and a specific form of "quoted interior monologue" over entirely "autonomous interior monologue," but Cohn's typology of literary strategies of subjective representation still provides a good starting point to come to terms with some of the more complex forms of narratorial strategies of subjective representation across media.

The extradiegetic heterodiegetic narrators in films such as Tom Tykwer's *Perfume: Story of a Murderer*, comics such as Neil Gaiman's *The Sandman: Preludes and Nocturnes*, and video games such as Bioware's *Baldur's Gate* may occasionally provide "direct access" to the represented characters' minds and (quasi-)perceptions, yet highly subjective heterodiegetic narrators appear to be comparatively rare in multimodal media.[43] As has already become clear in the previous chapters, however, contemporary films, comics, and video games commonly attribute narratorial strategies of subjective representation to extradiegetic homodiegetic narrators such as those in David Fincher's *Fight Club*, Gaiman's *The Sandman: Preludes and Nocturnes* (which employs both a homo- and a heterodiegetic narrator), or Remedy's *Alan Wake*. Still, it would seem that the specific limitations and affordances of multimodal media in general as well as the fact that their narrative representation always consists of combinations of narratorial and nonnarratorial representation (if the narrative work in question employs a narrator at all, that is) further complicate the analysis of narratorial strategies of subjective representation. Most fundamentally, this refers to the by now well-established fact that, whether they are attributable to extra- or intradiegetic and hetero- or homodiegetic narrators, the use of narratorial strategies of subjective representation in contemporary films, comics, and video games may be combined with nonnarratorial strategies of subjective as well as intersubjective and objective representation, and the resulting range of potential relations—which may be described as unrelated, complementary, redundant, or contradictory—warrants at least some focused attention in the context of narratological analyses that aim at reconstructing what I have proposed to call a narrative work's structure of subjectivity.

Perhaps more importantly, though, while the ways in which films, comics, and video games employ "psycho-narration" (which is used commonly) and "narrated interior monologue" (which is used only very rarely) appear to be rather similar to the ways these narratorial strategies of subjective representation are used in contemporary (or not so contemporary) novels, some further remarks on the form of "quoted interior monologue" and "autonomous interior monologue" in multimodal media are in order: since films, comics, and video games always also employ nonnarratorial representation to represent their respective storyworlds, genuinely "autonomous interior monologue" is realized with comparative ease in these media, but it may be used considerably more locally than in the kind of "first-person novels" that Cohn had in mind when developing the concept. "Quoted interior monologue," by contrast, may appear to be very rare in contemporary films, comics, and video games at first glance but turns out to be perhaps even more common than "autonomous interior monologue" if one takes into account that its status as quotation remains unmarked in many cases. It is, in other words, not unusual that a segment of what was introduced as the narratorial voice of an extradiegetic homodiegetic narrator's narrating I abruptly quotes the "interior monologue" of his or her intradiegetic experiencing I without making the fact that there is "quotation going on" particularly transparent. Since my earlier remarks on speech representation (as well as all other forms of representation)[44] never being "verbatim" also apply to the representation of "interior monologue," deciding whether a given segment of what was introduced as narratorial representation attributable to the narrating I of an extradiegetic homodiegetic narrator is or is not best comprehended as quoting the "interior monologue" of its experiencing I may often be quite difficult, if not downright impossible. Indeed, precisely because the representation of both character speech and "interior monologue" is never "verbatim," I would argue that if a narratorial voice has previously been introduced, a subsequent quotation of a character's "interior monologue" (whether it is or is not explicitly marked) can usually be understood as being both a representation of the latter and a representation of how the former represents it—a narratorial strategy of subjective representation, that is, which more or less transparently quotes a character's "interior monologue" on a local level, but in so doing still remains a part of the global narratorial representation.

In order to mark the differences between a transmedial and a novel-specific conceptualization of narratorial strategies of subjective representation, then, I will use slightly different terms to refer to what are still concepts very similar to those developed by Cohn, albeit being based on distinctions that are drawn slightly differently. First, the *narratorial representation of a character's mind* entails the variety of strategies Cohn subsumes under the labels "psycho-narration" and "self-narration," yet this rather broad concept may be specified with regard to the aspect(s) of the character's mind that are represented, such as the narratorial representation of memories, dreams, fantasies, and hallucinations, knowledge and beliefs, norms and values, wishes and motivations, emotions and moods, or combinations thereof.[45] Again, more detailed analyses will follow, but it might already be noted that *Fight Club*, *The Sandman*, and *Alan Wake* all make extensive use of this strategy. Second, I propose to further distinguish this still relatively broad category from a less "encompassing" form of the *narratorial representation of a character's (quasi-)perceptions*, where the subjective representation in question still refers, at least partially, to the "factual domain" of the storyworld in which the (quasi-)perceiving character is located.[46] Examples of this can be found in films such as Terry Gilliam's *Fear and Loathing in Las Vegas*, comics such as Frank Miller's *Sin City: Hell and Back*, and video games such as— once more—*Alan Wake*, all of which I will also examine in the following chapter.

Now, the realization of what Cohn calls "(self-)narrated interior monologue" is certainly possible in multimodal media as well, but it seems that the form is found very rarely if ever—or, perhaps, is just very difficult to notice—in contemporary films, comics, and video games, due to their tendency to employ "non-omnipresent" homodiegetic narrators when it comes to narratorial strategies of subjective representation.[47] Hence, I will focus, third, on the *narratorially framed representation of a character's internal voice* as being comparable to what Cohn describes as "(self-)quoted interior monologue," while at the same time emphasizing that contemporary films, comics, and video games commonly do not mark the internal voice in question as being quoted (which makes speaking of it as being framed by the narratorial representation seem more appropriate). Once more, interesting variations of this narratorial strategy of subjective representation can, for example, be found in *Fear and Loathing in Las Vegas*, *Sin City: Hell and Back*, and Charles Burns's *Black Hole*. Fourth and finally, the narratorially framed representation of internal voices can still be considered a part of the narratorial representation that constitutes its context, yet the *nonnarratorial representation of a character's internal voice*, which refers to multimodal media's usually more local realization of what Cohn calls "autonomous interior monologue," also appears in films such as Ron Howard's *A Beautiful Mind*, comics such as Frank Miller's *Batman: The Dark Knight Returns*, and video games such as Rocksteady's *Batman: Arkham Asylum*—and the observation that this form of the representation of internal voices is not, by default, a part of the narratorial representation anymore (even though it does, in fact, sometimes constitute narratorial representation in its own right, which is to be attributed to an intradiegetic or "lower-order" thinking narrator) leads me to the question which (other) nonnarratorial strategies of subjective representation contemporary films, comics, and video games may employ.

As I have already noted, film theory in general and film narratology in particular have given both the representation of subjectivity and audiovisual—or, more specifically, pictorial[48]—strategies of subjective representation considerable attention. Among the early works of classical film theory that discuss subjectivity are, for example, Hugo Münsterberg's *The Photoplay*, Bela Balázs's *Iskusstvo Kino*, and André Bazin's essays on the cinema, but the most influential of these (comparatively) early works seems to be Jean Mitry's *The Aesthetics and Psychology of the Cinema*, particularly with regard to the distinction Mitry proposes between an "objective," a "personal," a "semi-subjective," and a "subjective image."[49] Despite the fact that it remains influential, then, Mitry's account of the "subjective image" suffers from an overly pronounced focus on visual/pictorial features of the single shot, which deemphasizes the role of both sound and editing for the audiovisual representation of subjectivity. Accordingly, early film narratology has proposed various further differentiations of audiovisual/pictorial strategies of subjective representation, primarily (but not exclusively) aimed at what Christian Metz calls "a purely *mental* image" ("Current Problems" 46, original emphasis). Bruce Kawin, for example, distinguishes between the "subjective camera" (Mitry's "subjective image"), the "point of view" (Mitry's "semi-subjective image"), and the "mindscreen" (Metz's "purely mental image").[50] Despite the importance of the works of Mitry, Metz, and Kawin (as well as Münsterberg, Balász, and Bazin), though, their "proto-narratological" orientation leads to a number of conceptual and terminological problems that make any attempt to develop a transmedial heuristic for the analysis of nonnarratorial strategies of subjective representation based on their terms and concepts appear problematic.[51]

In *Point of View in the Cinema*, Edward Branigan provides a terminologically more convincing description of the point-of-view shot that remains a major benchmark for much of contemporary film narratology and, moreover, locates it in the broader field of audiovisual/pictorial strategies of subjective representation, distinguishing between "six major forms of subjectivity: reflection, POV, perception, projection, flashback, and mental process" (79). While "reflection" mainly seems to refer to the use of what Mitry described as a "semi-subjective image" (which is why I will not include it in my discussion of nonnarratorial strategies of subjective representation), and "flashback" may be used to refer to the representation of a specific kind of "mental process" as well as to intersubjective or objective modes of representation, the remaining four categories of "POV," "perception," "projection," and "mental process" cover a large part of what may be considered the most salient audiovisual/pictorial strategies of subjective representation in feature films and beyond. More importantly, Branigan not only analyzes the narrative functions of these (as well as other) strategies in considerable detail but also examines the manifold, more or less strongly conventionalized, and at least partially medium-specific *markers of subjectivity* that communicate the "subjective nature" of the respective segments of the nonnarratorial representation, characteristically taking the form of "superimpositions, titles, slow motion, spinning images, intercuts, lighting, or color" (*Point of View* 90) in film.

Building on his earlier *Narration in Light: Studies in Cinematic Point of View* as well as on Branigan's work, George Wilson has elaborated on four rather similar audiovisual/pictorial strategies of subjective representation in his essay "Transparency and Twist in Narrative Fiction Film," calling them "point-of-view shots," "subjectively inflected point-of-view shots" (which roughly correspond to Branigan's "perception shots"), "subjectively inflected impersonal shots" (which roughly correspond to Branigan's "projection"), and "subjectively saturated shots" (which include Branigan's categories of "flashback" and "mental process"). In fact, it seems as if Wilson's general discussion of these four particularly salient audiovisual/pictorial strategies of subjective representation—which can usually be correlated to "a reasonably clear marking of the fact that they are, in one of several different ways, 'subjective'" even though "the nature and functioning of the factors that contextually mark the epistemic status of a movie segment . . . can be surprisingly elusive" ("Transparency" 81)—captures an emerging consensus (within film studies, at least).[52] The question remains, however, how these audiovisual/pictorial strategies of subjective representation can be appropriately conceptualized in the context of a transmedial narratology.

First, what is usually called a point-of-view shot in film theory may be transmedially defined as referring to segments of a narrative representation where the storyworld is pictorially represented from the spatial position of a particular character. It is obvious that the spatial position of a character heavily influences his or her perception, but this (primarily) pictorial strategy of subjective representation usually still represents an intersubjectively valid version of the storyworld, albeit from the specific spatial position and resulting "visual perspective" of a particular character. Hence, the merely *spatial point-of-view sequence* may be considered the "least subjective" of the pictorial strategies of subjective representation examined in the following. This is different, second, in the special case of the *(quasi-)perceptual point-of-view sequence* alternatively described as "perception shot" (Branigan) and "subjectively inflected point-of-view shot" (Wilson), where the pictorial representation not only approximates the spatial position of a character but also represents more clearly subjective (quasi-)perceptual aspects of his or her consciousness, resulting in a representation of storyworld elements that can often not be considered to be intersubjectively valid anymore.

While the point-of-view shot tends to be mainly marked contextually (through the highly conventionalized point-of-view structure that shows a character, then shows what that character perceives from his or her spatial position, and finally shows the character again), the "perception shot" often uses additional *representational markers* such as filters, blurred lines, or unusual coloring in order to communicate the subjective quality of what is being shown (in addition to the point-of-view-structure). Yet, considering that "perception shots" are usually treated as a special case of point-of-view shots and that the markers of subjectivity that define the former can be rather subtle, it might be best to think of these two (primarily) pictorial strategies of subjective representation as opposed points on a continuum of representations that always approximate the spatial position of a particular character but add additional aspects of his or her subjective (quasi-)perception to varying degrees. Moreover, even though I will occasionally use the term "point of view" in the comparatively narrow and technical sense in which it is often used in film studies, since coining entirely new terms would seem like a textbook case of "radical media relativism," I will generally speak of spatial point-of-view sequences and (quasi-)perceptual point-of-view sequences when discussing these strategies on a transmedial level, since referring to their realization in comics and video games as "shots" would render any transmedial concept unnecessarily metaphorical.[53]

As important as the pictorial aspects of these strategies of subjective representation are in the context of a transmedial narratology that focuses on films, comics, and video games, I want to emphasize that even nonnarratorial strategies of subjective representation in multimodal media cannot be reduced to their pictorial aspects. More specifically, just as the representation of *storyworld space* can be more or less strongly "subjectivized" in the spatial point-of-view sequence or the (quasi-)perceptual point-of-view sequence, so can the representation of *storyworld sound* be more or less strongly "subjectivized" as well.[54] Accordingly, one could follow Michel Chion in (cautiously) speaking of a (spatial) *point of audition*[55] from which storyworld sound is represented. As opposed to the representation of storyworld space in the spatial point-of-view sequence, however, representing storyworld sound roughly from the represented characters' spatial position is very much the default case in films as well as in comics and video games, which is why spatial point-of-audition sequences may be considered even less subjective than spatial point-of-view sequences. Moreover, (quasi-)perceptual point-of-view sequences may also be combined with more genuinely subjective representations of "aural object[s]" (Metz, "Aural Objects" 24)—such as the nonnarratorial representation of internal voices—and these kinds of "auditory subjectivity" (Schlickers, "Focalization" 250) are not limited to audiovisual modes of representation, either.[56]

Yet, as is well established within film studies and begins to be acknowledged within comics studies and game studies, too, the subjective representation of storyworld sound tends to require representing the spatial point of audition of the character in question at least to some extent, whereas the representation of (quasi-)perceptual aspects of a character's consciousness beyond his or her spatial position does not necessitate the pictorial representation's approximation of that character's spatial position at all. In what I propose to call, third, *(quasi-)perceptual overlay* (and which more or less corresponds to Branigan's "projection" and Wilson's "subjectively inflected impersonal shots"),[57] this is precisely what happens: the pictorial representation in films such as *Fight Club* or *A Beautiful Mind*, comics such as *Sin City: Hell and Back* or Chris Ware's *Jimmy Corrigan: The Smartest Kid on Earth*, and video games such as Rocksteady's *Batman: Arkham Asylum* or Yager Development's *Spec Ops: The Line* commonly does not approximate the spatial position of a character but still represents other (quasi-)perceptual aspects of a character's consciousness to such an extent that the resulting representation of storyworld elements cannot be considered intersubjectively valid anymore. Just as in the (quasi-)perceptual point-of-view sequence, then, what is represented in segments of (quasi-)perceptual overlay seems often closer to a character's "private domain" than to the "factual domain" of the storyworld, which is commonly marked via *content markers* on the level of what is being represented as well as via representational markers on the level of the representation—but, at the same time, it is represented as (at least partially) being that character's perception of the "factual domain." Once more, though, I would argue not only that (quasi-)perceptual overlay is commonly combined with the subjective representation of storyworld sound but also that the subjective representation of storyworld sound in a certain segment of the narrative representation may suffice to describe the latter as a form of (quasi-)perceptual overlay—if it is not a form of (quasi-)perceptual point-of-view sequence, that is, since both of these forms are defined by the representation of what seems closer to a character's "private domain" than to the "factual domain" of the storyworld, while still being best comprehended as the character's (quasi-)perception of that "factual domain."

It is this latter criterion that allows us to distinguish (quasi-)perceptual overlay from, fourth, the *nonnarratorial representation of internal worlds*, where what is represented is intended to be comprehended as being neither the "factual domain" of the storyworld nor a character's (quasi-)perception of it, but rather a character's memories, dreams, or fantasies that may still take the form of quasi-perceptions, yet are not represented as a "subjectivized" version of the "diegetic level" on which the remembering, dreaming, or fantasizing character is located anymore.[58] These kinds of subjective representation—called "mental processes" by Branigan and "subjectively saturated shots" by Wilson—are defined, in other words, by a change of "diegetic level" within the storyworld as a whole: if the character to whom we can ascribe the "private domain" is located in the diegetic primary storyworld, what is represented in the case of a nonnarratorial representation of internal worlds would be a hypodiegetic secondary storyworld (and the same would be true for at least some forms of the narratorial representation of a character's mind briefly mentioned above).[59] While (quasi-)perceptual overlay, once more, tends not to be marked by transparent markers of subjectivity and, therefore, can require relatively complex processes of inference in order to be recognized, the nonnarratorial representation of internal worlds in films such as Terry Gilliam's *12 Monkeys* or Michel Gondry's *Eternal Sunshine of the Spotless Mind*, comics such as *The Sandman: Preludes and Nocturnes* or *Black Hole*, and video games such as Remedy's *Max Payne* or *Alan Wake* seems somewhat more strongly conventionalized and often uses both the kind of *contextual markers* typical for spatial point-of-view sequences and the more *simultaneous markers* typical for (quasi-)perceptual point-of-view sequences, even though there is no stable 1:1 relationship between these (at least partially medium-specific) markers of subjectivity and the ontological status of the represented storyworld elements.[60]

Furthermore, the nonnarratorial representation of internal worlds does not necessarily have to be marked using a priori contextual markers (where the nonnarratorial representation represents a character lost in memory, dreaming, or daydreaming before the respective memory, dream, or fantasy is represented) but may also rely exclusively on a posteriori contextual markers (the most strongly conventionalized of these being the representation of a dreaming character waking up, which makes the preceding segment of the nonnarratorial representation recognizable as having been the representation of a dream). I would also stress that not only simultaneous but also both kinds of contextual markers may take different forms: as I have already established, contextual content markers, where what is represented rather than how it is represented communicates the different ontological status of the following or the preceding segment(s) of the representation, may be more common (or at least more easily recognizable) than contextual representational markers such as zooms on characters' faces or white fades that are sometimes used to mark the ontological transition, but both forms also often appear simultaneously with the representation of the situations that are intended to be comprehended as subjective. And, of course, contemporary films such as *Fear and Loathing in Las Vegas*, comics such as *Sin City: Hell and Back*, and video games such as *Alan Wake* may also use contextual as well as simultaneous *narratorial markers*, where the narratorial rather than the nonnarratorial representation marks a specific segment as subjective, either before, after, or during the respective situations' nonnarratorial representation.

Before examining the use of these markers of subjectivity in contemporary films, comics, and video games, on the one hand, and the strategies of subjective representation that they are used to make transparent (or leave intransparent), on the other, let me conclude this chapter by summarizing the key elements of the method of analysis that was offered on the previous pages: In the context of a "bottom-up" approach to the analysis of subjectivity across media, it is useful to distinguish between local strategies of subjective, intersubjective, and objective representation, whose specific combination leads to a global arrangement of these strategies within a narrative work's structure of subjectivity. Despite the importance of intersubjective modes for the representation of characters' consciousnesses or characters' minds, however, the focus of the present study remains on the subjective representation of (quasi-)perceptual aspects of characters' consciousnesses—representations, that is, which provide the recipient with "direct access" to the conscious intentional states that "are on a character's mind" at a given point in storyworld time, including his or her perception of the storyworld as well as quasi-perceptual hallucinations, memories, dreams, and fantasies.

Despite the importance of strategies of subjective representation for narrative works across media, though, I would also like to stress again that these strategies can be realized in various ways: while the narratorial and nonnarratorial strategies of subjective representation as well as the markers of subjectivity sketched above can be described from a transmedial perspective as well, the next chapter will examine their medium-specific realization and combination in contemporary films, comics, and video games. However, the wide variety and "context-dependency" of both narratorial and nonnarratorial strategies of subjective representation necessitates a more dedicated focus on case studies that differ at least slightly from the more systematic analyses presented in chapter 3 and chapter 5. Accordingly, the salient prototypical forms of narratorial and nonnarratorial strategies of subjective representation that I have proposed to distinguish are, perhaps even more so than the strategies of narrative representation and the strategies of narratorial representation discussed in the first and second parts of this book, meant to be taken primarily as a tentative transmedial heuristic that is still in need of being differentiated further with regard not only to the medium-specific but also to the work-specific realization of strategies of subjective representation in contemporary films, comics, and video games.

7 Subjective Representation across Media

Strategies of Subjective Representation in Contemporary Films

Except for David Cronenberg's *eXistenZ*,[1] all of the main film examples from the previous parts of this book employ some form of subjective representation, with the nonnarratorial representation of internal worlds being particularly common: In Quentin Tarantino's *Pulp Fiction*, the most noticeable example of the latter would be the sequence in which Butch's dream of how he got his father's gold watch is represented, with the film using a highly conventionalized a posteriori contextual content marker that represents the dreamer waking up after the dream. In Tom Tykwer's *Run Lola Run*, the red filter sequences constitute another salient and narratively significant case of the nonnarratorial representation of internal worlds that is marked representationally both before and during the sequence itself, using a zoom on the face of the character whose internal world is represented as a conventional a priori contextual marker and the distinctive red filter already mentioned in chapter 3.

Bryan Singer's *The Usual Suspects* likewise makes narratively relevant use of the nonnarratorial representation of internal worlds—in combination with spatial point-of-view sequences as part of the pictorial representation and (quasi-)perceptual overlay as part of the auditive representation—when, for example, David Kujan finally "pieces together" the information available to him and realizes that Verbal Kint is not who he pretended to be. While perhaps even more narratorially dominated than *The Usual Suspects*, Spike Jonze and Charlie Kaufman's *Adaptation.* also employs nonnarratorial representations of internal worlds in combination with (quasi-)perceptual overlay to intransparently represent the sexual fantasies of Charlie's experiencing I using only an a posteriori contextual marker and more subtle simultaneous content markers.² Finally, as I will show in more detail below, David Fincher's *Fight Club* uses not only a highly subjective extradiegetic homodiegetic narrator but also a particularly intransparent form of (quasi-)perceptual overlay and the nonnarratorial representation of internal worlds extensively and repeatedly. Before I discuss *Fight Club*'s use of strategies of subjective representation any further, though, let me begin by examining an example that nicely illustrates how recipients' understanding of what it is, precisely, that is represented by nonnarratorial representations of internal worlds may change as a film's plot develops and its story unfolds.

Terry Gilliam's *12 Monkeys* opens with a sequence that represents a man being shot at an airport with a boy watching the shooting (although the extent to which spectators will realize that this is what is represented during their first viewing of the film may vary, as the events are not represented in a particularly explicit way).³ There are striking simultaneous representational markers (including the use of overlit pictures and slow motion)⁴ as well, but it becomes clear that what is represented here is a dream only when the dreamer, who appears to have slept in some kind of prison, is shown waking up in what has become a highly conventionalized form of an a posteriori contextual content marker (see figure 43 and figure 44). As it turns out, the dreamer, James Cole, is a prisoner located in a postapocalyptic future where a virus has killed 99 percent of the human population (as opposed to the previously represented airport located in the hypodiegetic secondary storyworld of his dream, which appears to be quite contemporary). In order to reduce his sentence, James "volunteers" to scout the earth's surface, catching animals that may help the remaining humans to better understand the nature of the virus. Since he seems to be good at this task, James is eventually asked to participate in a high-risk time travel operation to find out more about the virus in "the past." He agrees, and the time travel appears to have indeed been successful, as a written insert identifies the next segment of the audiovisual representation as representing "Baltimore • April

Fig. 43. First "full-fledged" nonnarratorial representation of James Cole's dream in *12 Monkeys*

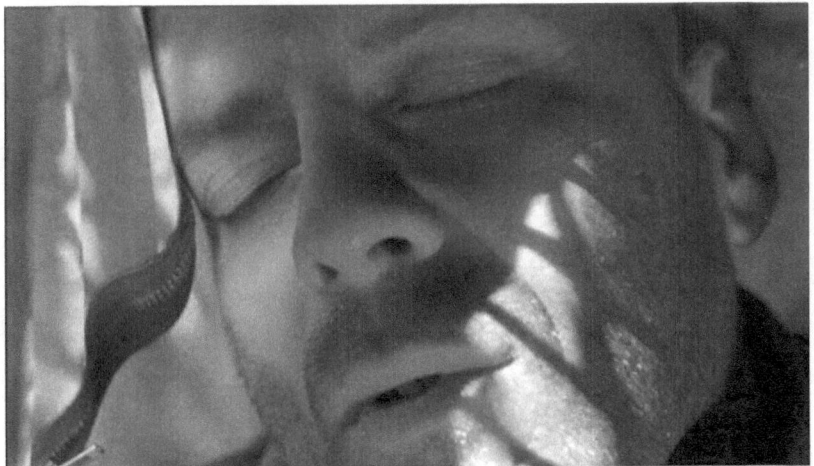

Fig. 44. A highly conventionalized a posteriori contextual content marker in *12 Monkeys*

1990." However, things are not quite as simple, for James—who, moreover, should have been sent to 1996 rather than 1990—has been arrested by the Baltimore police and is treated by the psychiatrist Kathryn Railly for what appears—at least from the perspective of the inhabitants of 1990s Baltimore as well as, perhaps, from the perspective of a first-time spectator at this point in the film—to be a psychotic episode.

It seems clear, then, that the subworld where James "volunteered" for the time travel operation and the subworld where he is treated for a presumed psychotic episode are spatially and temporally disconnected, yet it is the nature of their causal and ontological relation that is puzzling and in no small part determines *12 Monkey*'s structure of subjectivity: Is the James of 1990s Baltimore a time traveler who *remembers* a distant future, or is he (just) a mental patient who *hallucinates* that future? James's dream about the airport shooting plays an important role in how *12 Monkeys* pits these two mutually exclusive comprehensions of what is being represented against each other. As it turns out, it is a recurring dream, the changing contextualization of which ultimately contributes to privileging a comprehension of *12 Monkeys* as representing the experience of a time traveler rather than that of (just) a mental patient. The second time that James is represented as dreaming of the airport shooting, *12 Monkeys* again uses simultaneous representational markers in combination with an a posteriori contextual content marker to communicate the different ontological status of the represented situations. But this time around, James wakes up in his bed in a mental institution in 1990s Baltimore instead of in his bed in the prison in "the future." After James has unsuccessfully tried to escape from the mental institution, he is restrained and sedated—but somehow still escapes from his cell. This is followed by the third iteration of the dream sequence, which uses the by then well-established combination of simultaneous representational markers and an a posteriori contextual content marker, with James waking up in "the future" once again, providing a ready plausibilization for his otherwise highly unlikely escape from the mental institution located in 1990s Baltimore. The fourth time that James is represented as dreaming of the airport shooting uses both a priori and a posteriori content markers (as well as simultaneous representational markers)—more importantly, though, the dream "reveals" that the woman running toward the man who has been shot looks like Kathryn, albeit the former is blond instead of brunette.[5]

After the fifth, and most extensive, iteration of the dream sequence that once more uses only simultaneous representational and an a posteriori contextual content marker, James recognizes Kathryn, who has dyed her hair blond, as the woman from his dream. Indeed, the film ends with James and Kathryn trying to prevent Dr. Peters, who plans to spread the virus across the world, from boarding the plane, James drawing a gun and being shot by policemen while a younger version of himself watches. What 12 Monkeys illustrates quite impressively, then, is not only how the nonnarratorial representation of internal worlds tends to heavily rely on contextual content markers (which, in contradistinction to simultaneous representational markers, tend to be fairly transmedial) but also how the hypotheses that recipients form about the kinds of internal worlds that are represented may have to be reconsidered and revised as the plot of a narrative work progresses. In the case of James's dream in 12 Monkeys, the fact that it increasingly turns out to be a *memory-based* dream further reinforces a number of interesting shifts in the "hierarchy of knowledge" between James and Kathryn, who interact on a comparatively local level, as well as more globally between the people of "the future" (including the various other time travelers that are sent to the past) and the people of 1990s Baltimore (including both Dr. Peters and Jeffrey Goines, the latter of whom James and Kathryn mistake for the source of the virus). And, of course, the resulting "hierarchy of knowledge" includes not only all of the characters mentioned above but also the spectator, who will most likely have lost any remaining doubts about the global structure of the storyworld by the fifth iteration of the dream sequence, even though James and Kathryn lose their respective doubts only when James is represented as knowing the exact wording of the voicemail that Kathryn leaves to "the future" in advance, because he has "heard it already."

As the recurring memory-based dream sequence in 12 Monkeys also reminds us, then, it may be difficult (if not impossible) to distinguish between the representation of characters' hallucinations, memories, dreams, and fantasies (or "mere" analepses, for that matter), but most films still do not leave their spectators in doubt regarding the subjectivity of the represented situations for too long. As has previously been mentioned, however, David Fincher's *Fight Club* provides a particularly interesting—and certainly influential—example of a film that uses intransparent strategies of subjective representation to unreliable effect, combining an at times fairly subjective extradiegetic homodiegetic narrator (who repeatedly provides "direct access" to the experiencing I's thoughts and, perhaps more importantly, to his emotional states, in what I have proposed to call the narratorial representation of a character's mind) with extensive segments of (quasi-)perceptual overlay and an interesting "corrective" use of the nonnarratorial representation of the experiencing I's memories. Considering that I have already examined the form and function of the narratorial representation that is attributable to the highly unreliable and metaleptic narrator of *Fight Club* in chapter 5, I will focus on the film's nonnarratorial strategies of subjective representation in the following. Yet I would maintain that the narrator's verbal narration is, indeed, occasionally quite subjective in the sense(s) sketched in the previous chapter.[6]

Obviously, the way in which *Fight Club* uses (audiovisual) nonnarratorial strategies of subjective representation is considerably more complex than the way in which it uses (verbal) narratorial strategies of subjective representation, and the film's structure of subjectivity is defined, most saliently, by an extended form of intransparent (quasi-)perceptual overlay that represents Tyler Durden as if he were a character within the "factual domain" of the storyworld, even though it eventually turns out that he is only a hallucination of the experiencing I (who does what he attributes to Tyler himself). Again, the way in which the narrating I emphasizes the experiencing I's insomnia—while the audiovisual representation "prepares" this (quasi-)perceptual overlay using four brief "subliminal pictures" of Tyler and represents him passing the experiencing I in one of the many airports the latter visits as part of his job as a "recall coordinator" for a big car manufacturer before finally representing their first "dialogue" on board a plane—certainly provides a variety of cues that spectators already "in the know" will be able to recognize, but these cues arguably do not suffice to give away *Fight Club*'s essential "twist" to first-time spectators. Instead, it would seem that these spectators are meant to have their lingering suspicions regarding Tyler's ontological status confirmed only during the key sequence that represents the experiencing I as likewise realizing that he himself *is* Tyler.

This key sequence also illustrates *Fight Club*'s complex use of nonnarratorial strategies of subjective representation: after the experiencing I, during his attempt to follow Tyler's trail around the world, has been greeted as Tyler Durden by one of the barkeepers of the newly founded international fight clubs and has returned to his hotel room to phone Marla Singer, who also addresses him as Tyler, the latter suddenly appears in the hotel room, making the experiencing I finally realize that they are, indeed, the same person. On the one hand, the audiovisual representation switches between using the by then well-established (quasi-)perceptual overlay to represent Tyler talking to the experiencing I and an intersubjective mode of representation that represents the latter alone in his hotel room, talking to himself (see figure 45 and figure 46). On the other hand, the representation of the diegetic primary storyworld in which the experiencing I talks to Tyler and/or to himself is repeatedly interrupted by the "full-fledged" nonnarratorial representation of the resurfacing memories of the experiencing I,[7] which—albeit still being describable as hypodiegetic secondary storyworlds—successively "correct" the previous representation of key points in the story. These "corrections" culminate in the realization that the experiencing I beat himself up and drank a bottle of beer by himself instead of having his initial fistfight with Tyler and sharing a bottle of beer with the latter afterward, founded the first fight club on his own, and is the one who was regularly "fucking" Marla.[8]

Once the central premise of the film is established, *Fight Club* takes that premise and runs with it: when the experiencing I tries to prevent the members of Project Mayhem from blowing up the buildings of several credit card companies, Tyler reappears, but he behaves less and less like an actual human being, abruptly appearing and disappearing in physically impossible ways. Tyler evidently still has some

Fig. 45. Tyler Durden talking to the unnamed experiencing I in *Fight Club*

Fig. 46. The unnamed experiencing I talking to himself in *Fight Club*

hold over the experiencing I's mind, though, which is demonstrated in yet another sequence that combines (quasi-)perceptual overlay representing the two of them fighting with an intersubjective (or, perhaps, even objective) mode of representation via a surveillance camera that shows how the experiencing I beats himself up, drags himself across the underground garage, and throws himself down a flight of stairs (see figure 47 and figure 48). The film concludes with the highly metaleptic variation of the opening sequence, after which the experiencing I convinces himself that Tyler's gun is in his hands, shoots himself in the face, thereby "killing" Tyler, and is joined by a kidnapped Marla to watch the "theater of mass destruction" caused by Project Mayhem. Significantly, this final segment of *Fight Club* is not accompanied by

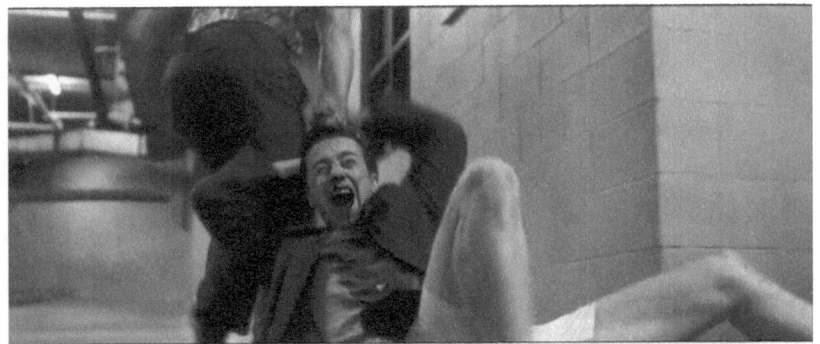

Fig. 47. Tyler Durden dragging the experiencing I around in *Fight Club*

Fig. 48. The experiencing I dragging himself around in *Fight Club*

narratorial representation anymore—which arguably highlights once again that despite the indisputable presence of the extradiegetic homodiegetic narrator during large segments of the film, *Fight Club*'s overall structure of subjectivity does not rely too much on narratorial representation.[9]

Before examining a film whose structure of subjectivity relies more heavily on narratorial representation, I would like to offer a brief analysis of a third example, Ron Howard's *A Beautiful Mind*, in order to illustrate how (quasi-)perceptual overlay can be used to represent the highly subjective worldview of a paranoid schizophrenic without any additional framing by some form of narratorial representation—and also how strongly *Fight Club*'s (eventual) success[10] has contributed to moving the initially intransparent use of (quasi-)perceptual overlay into the mainstream. The core "twist" of *A Beautiful Mind* is achieved via the intransparent use of (quasi-)perceptual overlay, but the film actually employs a broader variety of—for the most part highly conventionalized—nonnarratorial strategies of subjective representation than *Fight Club*,[11] including (quasi-)perceptual overlay and the nonnarratorial representation of internal worlds as well as spatial point-of-view sequences and (quasi-)perceptual point-of-view sequences. Indeed, during the opening sequence that represents a welcome address at Princeton, the film uses a still comparatively intersubjective spatial point-of-view sequence to establish the relation between John Nash and his friend/rival Martin Hansen. In the sequence immediately following the opening sequence, however, the use of point-of-view sequences becomes more subjective, when a brief spatial point-of-view sequence of John looking at a colleague's unusual tie pattern is followed by an only slightly longer (quasi-)perceptual point-of-view sequence in which the pictorial representation simulates how John perceives that tie in a rather unusual way, as he compares its geometric pattern to that of rays of light and slices of lemon (see figure 49 and figure 50).

While this striking visualization of John's mathematical prowess is alluded to repeatedly during the remainder of the film,[12] the latter's structure of subjectivity is still defined by the intransparent use of (quasi-)perceptual overlay that first occurs in the sequence immediately following the two sequences already discussed,[13] when John's imaginary roommate Charles Herman is introduced. When John subsequently begins imagining himself as working for the pentagon as a code breaker (though in fact he is stuck in a boring office job), Charles is joined by William Parcher, who functions as John's "contact" in the increasingly sophisticated cold war scenario in which he imagines himself as participating, eventually taking over part of the role of Charles in functioning as an easily recognizable symptom of John's paranoid schizophrenia, and Charles's niece Marcee, who ultimately leads John to realize his mental condition (or at least acts as a catalyzer for that realization). Prima facie, the intransparent use

Fig. 49. John Nash's (quasi-)perception of rays of light in *A Beautiful Mind*

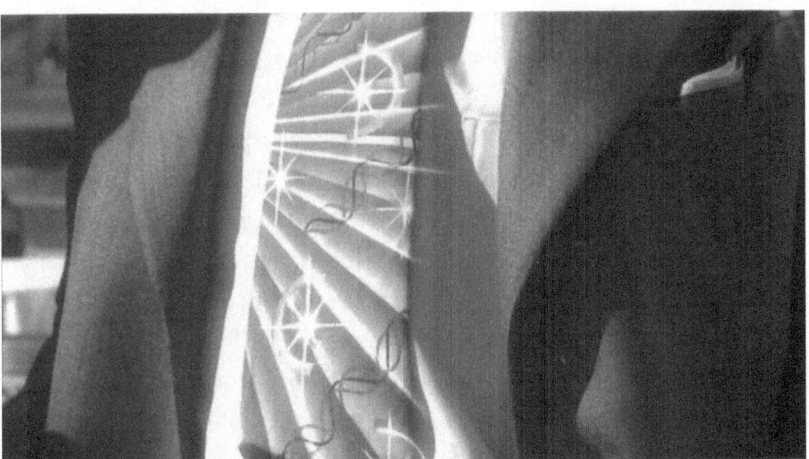

Fig. 50. John Nash's (quasi-)perception of his colleague's tie in *A Beautiful Mind*

of (quasi-)perceptual overlay may make *A Beautiful Mind* appear strikingly similar to *Fight Club*: the imagined friend(s)/foe(s) (Tyler Durden and Charles/Marcee/William, respectively), the female "love interest" suffering from the male protagonist's mental condition (Marla Singer and John's wife Alicia, respectively), and the key sequence in which the spectator comes to realize the existence of that very condition and the nonexistence of the imagined friend(s)/foe(s). On closer inspection, however, the differences in the ways in which the two films prepare and execute their respective "twists" turn out to be significant. Concisely put, *Fight Club* uses the "Tyler Durden twist" to *not* represent large parts of what the experiencing I does, while *A Beautiful Mind* uses more varied forms of (quasi-)perceptual point-of-view sequences and (quasi-)perceptual overlay to extensively represent events that later turn out to have existed only in John's mind.

Perhaps even more importantly, the key sequence is realized differently in *A Beautiful Mind*: the psychiatrist Dr. Rosen has John (who, naturally, thinks Dr. Rosen is a Russian spy) committed to a psychiatric hospital, which leads to the spectator, John's wife Alicia, and finally John himself realizing that the latter is a paranoid schizophrenic and that neither William nor Charles and Marcee are real.[14] Since Dr. Rosen's diagnosis takes place almost exactly in the middle of *A Beautiful Mind*, a further complication follows, whose need for a solution eventually triggers a second key sequence: at some point after his wife has given birth to their son, John stops taking his medication because it makes him unable to think mathematically, preventing him from working, and diminishes his sex drive, which increasingly puts a strain on his marriage. Unsurprisingly, his hallucinations return and he starts reimagining the by-now familiar cold war code-breaking scenario. When his wife discovers his newly constructed "base of operations" in the garden shed, and when he endangers her and their newborn child in an attempt to protect them from the hallucinated William, Alicia leaves the house and gets in the car, ready to drive away from her marriage for good. After Alicia has left the house, Charles and Marcee suddenly appear, and John realizes that the latter has not aged a day during the years that have passed since he first "met" her and that, hence, not only Marcee but also Charles and William are mere hallucinations of his. Not unlike *Fight Club*'s "corrective" use of the nonnarratorial representation of the experiencing I's memories, the audiovisual representation of *A Beautiful Mind* uses a cacophony of nonnarratorially represented internal voices (or, more precisely, John's auditive memories of other characters' voices) accompanying a montage sequence of short shots representing John's various memories, until he finally runs out of the house, stops his wife's car, and shouts out the simple truth: "She never gets old. Marcee can't be real. She never gets old."

If *Fight Club*'s experiencing I eventually solves his mental problems by shooting himself in the face, thereby "killing" the personification of his hallucinations, Tyler Durden, John's solution in *A Beautiful Mind* is to "apply his mind" in order to learn—supported by the love and trust of his wife and the help of his old friend/rival Martin, who allows him to return to Princeton—to ignore and, eventually, live with his hallucinations. Accordingly, the two films' endings are quite different as well: while the experiencing I and Marla watch the "theater of mass destruction" caused by Project Mayhem at the end of *Fight Club*, *A Beautiful Mind* ends with John accepting the Nobel Prize in Economics, being applauded by his loving wife, his son, and his colleagues—but also still seeing the imaginary Charles, Marcee, and William, who wait for him after the ceremony. Having provided a rough impression of the complex ways in which "mind-benders" may combine mostly nonnarratorial strategies of subjective representation to rather different effect, then, I want to conclude my discussion of contemporary films by examining a fourth example that illustrates more clearly than *Fight Club* (and, of course, *12 Monkeys* and *A Beautiful Mind*) how narratorial and nonnarratorial strategies of subjective representation can be combined to form a particularly complex structure of subjectivity—which, however, remains largely transparent despite its extensive representation of drug-induced hallucinations.

Terry Gilliam's *Fear and Loathing in Las Vegas*, an adaptation of Hunter S. Thompson's novel of the same title that Gilliam directed after finishing work on *12 Monkeys*, opens with the narratorial voice of the protagonist, Raoul Duke, using the exact same words with which Thompson's novel begins. The way in which the film has its narrator speak these words pointedly subverts the conventional distinction between what would presumably be an extradiegetic homodiegetic narrating I and its diegetic counterpart, the experiencing

I, as well as between extradiegetic speaking and intradiegetic thinking narrators: after the voice-over, which can, at least initially, be attributed to an extradiegetic homodiegetic narrator, has introduced the narrated situation and the general theme of the film's story—"We were somewhere around Barstow on the edge of the desert when the drugs began to take hold"—the narrator goes on to quote direct speech that is clearly attributable to his experiencing I—"I remember saying something like"—but instead of letting the voice of the narrating I speak the quotation, the nonnarratorial audiovisual representation represents the experiencing I speaking it himself: "I feel a bit lightheaded, maybe you should drive." Continuing to reproduce the exact words of Thompson's novel, the film goes on to narratorially represent the hallucinatory quasi-perceptions of the experiencing I, which still largely refer to the "factual domain" of the storyworld: "Suddenly there was a terrible roar all around us and the sky was full of what looked like huge bats, all swooping and screeching and diving around the car."

Further emphasizing both the subjectivity of the narratorial representation and the film's play with the borders between the narrating I and the experiencing I, the former once more quotes the latter—"And a voice was screaming"—but has the narrating I and the experiencing I scream the (quoted) character speech in unison (with only a slight temporal shift that makes the doubling of the voices easily perceivable): "Holy Jesus! What are these goddamn animals?" Interestingly, while *Fear and Loathing in Las Vegas*'s audiovisual representation goes on to make extensive use of both (quasi-)perceptual point-of-view sequences and (quasi-)perceptual overlay, the initial audiovisual representation of the experiencing I's hallucinations is limited to a (quasi-)perceptual point of audition and the representation of reflections of what indeed appear to be bats in the experiencing I's sunglasses (see figure 51). After this subtle form of what might still be described as (quasi-)perceptual overlay, the film's opening sequence concludes with yet another interesting blurring of the borders between the narrating I and the experiencing I, when the latter begins to mumble more and more audibly while the former contemplates whether

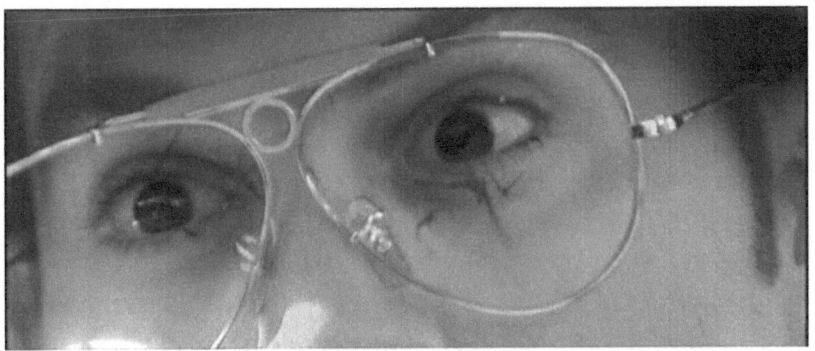

Fig. 51. (Quasi-)perceptual overlay of bats in *Fear and Loathing in Las Vegas*

or not to kill a hitchhiker that Raoul and Dr. Gonzo have picked up, until the experiencing I's mumbling eventually gets audible enough to suggest that the previous parts of the voice-over would actually have to be attributed to the experiencing I as an intradiegetic thinking narrator, making it appear as an intransparent form of the narratorially framed representation of the latter's internal voice, which is marked as such only a posteriori: "Hmm? Jesus, did I say that? Or just think it? Was I talking? Did they hear me?"

This collapse of the voice of the extradiegetic homodiegetic narrator's narrating I with that of his experiencing I temporarily acting as an intradiegetic thinking narrator remains largely confined to the film's opening sequence,[15] but the latter still effectively serves to introduce the core elements of *Fear and Loathing in Las Vegas*: an extradiegetic homodiegetic narrator who is highly subjective in that he regularly provides "direct access" to the mind, (quasi-)perceptions, and internal voice of his experiencing I, and an audiovisual representation that likewise employs a variety of strategies of subjective representation to represent the experiencing I's drug-induced hallucinations (the representation of which tends to be fairly transparent, though, as the experiencing I's drug use is explicitly represented and the narratorial representation also tends to explicitly comment on the former's drug-related hallucinatory experiences, providing both simultaneous and contextual narratorial markers of subjectivity).

After Raoul has "dropped acid," he and Dr. Gonzo are represented as arriving at a hotel in Las Vegas, with not only the strength of the former's drug-induced hallucinations but also the extent of their representation gradually increasing: the acid's initial effects are represented via a spatial point-of-view sequence that morphs into a (quasi-)perceptual point-of-view sequence, when Raoul perceives the face of the parking attendant in an increasingly distorted way (see figure 52). In the following, *Fear and Loathing in Las Vegas* uses a variety of (quasi-)perceptual point-of-view sequences to represent the intensifying effects of the acid, including the pattern of the carpet creeping up a man's leg, the receptionist's head suddenly taking the form of a moray eel, and the other patrons in the hotel bar appearing as anthropomorphic reptiles (see figure 53). It is at this point that the film also starts representing Raoul's hallucinations through more encompassing forms of (quasi-)perceptual overlay (see figure 54), even though it may be worth stressing once again that—in contradistinction to *Fight Club* and *A Beautiful Mind*—most if not all the forms of subjective representation in *Fear and Loathing in Las Vegas* are marked quite clearly using a priori contextual as well as simultaneous narratorial, representational, and content markers, with the narrating I's regular comments on the experiencing I's state(s) of mind and "status updates" on the effects of the drugs that the latter takes being particularly salient.

Fig. 52. Distorted face of the parking attendant in *Fear and Loathing in Las Vegas*

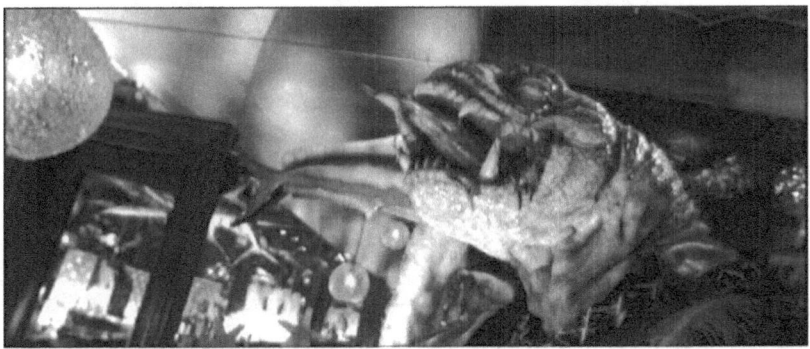

Fig. 53. Anthropomorphic reptiles in a bar in *Fear and Loathing in Las Vegas*

Fig. 54. Switch to (quasi-)perceptual overlay in *Fear and Loathing in Las Vegas*

The density of subjective representations in *Fear and Loathing in Las Vegas* diminishes after Raoul's and Dr. Gonzo's arrival at the hotel, but there are other extended representations of the experiencing I's drug-induced hallucinations that combine both narratorial and nonnarratorial strategies of subjective representation, with the most extensive of these being contextually marked by a representation of Raoul taking a generous overdose of Dr. Gonzo's adrenochrome in yet another hotel room: after the subjectivity of the following sequence has been further marked by the narratorial representation of the experiencing I's (quasi-)perceptions and a rare case of narratorially framed

Subjective Representation across Media

representation of the experiencing I's internal voice that even uses an *inquit* formula—"I could already feel the stuff working on me. The first wave felt like a combination of mescaline and methedrine. Maybe I should take a swim, I thought"—the nonnarratorial representation once more employs an extensive combination of (quasi-)perceptual point-of-view sequences and (quasi-)perceptual overlay to represent the drug's rather harrowing effects before Raoul loses consciousness. Once he has regained consciousness, a number of what may be either "mere" analepses or comparatively subtle nonnarratorial representations of the experiencing I's memories (triggered by Raoul listening to his tape recorder, among other things)[16] allow the spectator to "follow" Raoul while he pieces together a rough version of what happened the other night: a succession of ever more depraved actions and unlikely events that did, however, ultimately result in Dr. Gonzo boarding his plane and Raoul returning to the typewriter in his hotel room to finish the article he is supposed to write, before he drives back to California.[17] Despite the fact that there certainly is more to be said about every one of the handful of films discussed so far, the previous case studies should already have served to illustrate the range of the ways in which contemporary feature films may realize both narratorial and nonnarratorial strategies of subjective representation. Having once more taken their film-specific realization as the "default case" of multimodal narrative representation in contemporary media culture, I will now examine some of the medium-specific aspects of these strategies in contemporary comics and video games.

Strategies of Subjective Representation in Contemporary Comics

While perhaps not quite as ubiquitous as they are in contemporary films, strategies of subjective representation[18] are commonly employed in contemporary comics as well: Art Spiegelman's *Maus* and Mike Carey and Peter Gross's *The Unwritten* are primarily concerned with narratorial framing, but Alan Moore and Kevin O'Neill's *The League of Extraordinary Gentlemen* and Craig Thompson's *Habibi* already use various strategies of subjective representation, even though these strategies do not dominate the overall narrative representation.[19] This is increasingly the case in both Chris Ware's *Jimmy Corrigan* and Neil Gaiman's *The Sandman*, however, where strategies of subjective representation are featured prominently. Let us begin with a closer look at how *The Sandman* represents dreams, then: as has previously been mentioned, the first volume, *Preludes and Nocturnes*, already underscores the series' preoccupation with dreams as well as with the blurring of the boundaries between dream (or The Dreaming) and reality (or the "factual domain" of the storyworld), when it demonstrates Dream's ability to enter the dreams of other characters. This is how he escapes his prison in 1988, when the circle that binds him is inadvertently damaged by Alex Burgess's wheelchair, allowing Dream to take sand from the dream of one of his guards, which he later uses to force his captors into sleep, taking food and clothes from the dreams of other characters, and eventually appearing in the dream of Alex, his original captor's son. After a brief interrogation as to the whereabouts of his "tools" (a ruby, a mask, and a pouch that contain a significant part of Dream's power and whose reacquisition will motivate many of the stories represented by the first few volumes of the series), Dream punishes Alex with the "gift of eternal waking," transforming his dream into a sequence of situations in which Alex seems to wake up from the dream but never actually does. Accordingly, even though there are no strong representational markers, *The Sandman* here uses a succession of a posteriori contextual content markers (taking the form of the highly conventionalized representation of a dreamer waking up) in combination with striking simultaneous content markers (making it increasingly clear that what is represented here is part of a "neverending nightmare") to communicate that the previously represented situations are still part of Alex's dream. As interesting as the eternal waking sequence from *The Sandman: Preludes and Nocturnes* is, then, it mainly illustrates how contemporary comics may use comparatively transmedial forms of the nonnarratorial representation of internal worlds.

Another form of the nonnarratorial representation of internal worlds from the series' fourth volume, *Season of Mists*, illustrates

Fig. 55. A priori contextual content marker in *The Sandman: Season of Mists*

more clearly how *The Sandman* uses not only comparatively transmedial but also more medium-specific markers of subjectivity. The dream sequence in question is contextually marked, though both a priori and a posteriori contextual content markers are used this time: the character in question, Hob Gadling, is shown sleeping next to his lover before the verbal-pictorial representation starts representing his dream (see figure 55) and then, again, when he awakes after the dream sequence (see figure 56). The nonnarratorial representation of the dream itself is also marked as subjective by what is represented: the strange combination of elements from very different times in history—including a dream version of Queen Elizabeth I interacting with a computer—cannot readily be plausibilized as part of the diegetic primary storyworld's "factual domain," but is, of course, easily explained as part of Hob's dream, since Hob is more or less immortal. Finally, *The Sandman* uses subtle but still rather effective (and, once more, comparatively medium-specific) simultaneous representational markers to communicate the different ontological status

Fig. 56. A posteriori contextual content marker in *The Sandman: Season of Mists*

of the represented situations. On the one hand, this refers to the faded colors and diffuse lines used to represent Hob's dream, which emphasizes the "drawn" quality of the pictures as well as the different ontological status of its "content." On the other hand, and perhaps more importantly, the frames of the panels representing the dream have a slightly "fuzzy" or "wavy" quality to them, which is, indeed, a highly conventionalized comics-specific marker of subjectivity in the context of the nonnarratorial representation of internal worlds.

As the nonnarratorial representation of internal worlds seems particularly widespread in contemporary comics, I would like to briefly mention yet another example that further illustrates the medium specificity of this strategy of subjective representation, even though—or perhaps particularly because—it does not represent a prototypical form of the medium: Shaun Tan's *The Arrival* uses sepia-colored pictures without any recognizable words or conventionalized representational strategies such as speech balloons or thought bubbles to represent the story of a man who has to leave his family and make a new home in a strange country before he is eventually reunited with what recipients will likely assume is his daughter and her mother. The plot largely follows the chronology of the story, but *The Arrival* manages quite successfully to introduce not only characters that tell *their* refugee stories to the unnamed man, functioning as intradiegetic homodiegetic framing narrators, but also one character—an old man at a bar—who arguably frames the representation not of a narrated but, rather, of a remembered hypodiegetic secondary storyworld, resulting in a fairly subtle form of the nonnarratorial representation of internal worlds. This change of "diegetic level" is represented via the pictorial representation of the remembering character, which functions as an a priori contextual content marker (see figure 57), as well as by a marked change in the panel borders and page layout—including the addition of a "represented page" framing the panels, making them appear to have been ripped out of a photo album or magazine (see figure 58).[20]

Having illuminated some of the ways in which comics may realize the nonnarratorial representation of internal worlds, I would now like

Fig. 57. A priori contextual content marker of the memory sequence in *The Arrival*

Fig. 58. Nonnarratorial representation of the old man's memories in *The Arrival*

to focus on the ways in which they may use spatial point-of-view sequences, (quasi-)perceptual point-of-view sequences, and (quasi-)perceptual overlay. In order to do so, I will return to Alan Moore and Kevin O'Neill's *The League of Extraordinary Gentlemen*. The first volume of the series initially uses various segments of intersubjective representation focusing primarily, albeit not exclusively, on Ms. Murray and the ways in which she makes the acquaintance of Mr. Quatermain, Captain Nemo, Dr. Jekyll/Mr. Hyde, and Mr. Griffin.[21] While *The League of Extraordinary Gentlemen* does not use strategies of subjective representation extensively, then, the few points at which it does appear particularly interesting. On the one hand, this refers to a page whose panels show the invisible Mr. Griffin applying white makeup to his face in front of a mirror, illustrating that spatial point-of-view sequences do not necessarily have to be marked contextually (as is conventionally the case not only in films but also in comics), but can also just use simultaneous content markers located on the level of what is represented, instead, requiring the reader to draw inferences on the basis of what is being shown—in this case mainly

Subjective Representation across Media

the painted face in the mirror and the pot of makeup hovering before it (see figure 59).

The spatial point-of-view sequence representing Mr. Griffin is unusual both because of the absence of contextual markers and because of the presence of largely unrelated, yet not contradictory, narratorial representation,[22] but the only other clearly marked segment during which the first volume of *The League of Extraordinary Gentlemen* uses nonnarratorial strategies of subjective representation contains a highly conventional form of a (quasi-)perceptual point-of-view sequence through which the reader learns that Mr. Hyde has a peculiar way of perceiving the world in that he can literally "see" temperature. The arrangement of panels on the page corresponds closely to the classical point-of-view structure that is well established within both film theory and film history: in the second panel on the page in question, the perceiving character, Mr. Hyde, is shown; in the third panel what he perceives is shown; and in the fourth panel, Mr. Hyde is shown again (see figure 60). Accordingly, the verbal-pictorial representation uses a combination of (a priori as well as a posteriori) contextual content and simultaneous representational markers to communicate that what is represented in the third panel is not an intersubjective representation of the "factual domain" of the storyworld but rather a representation of Mr. Hyde's subjective perception of it. Just as it was the case in the spatial point-of-view sequence representing Mr. Griffin looking at himself in the mirror, though, this applies only to the pictorial aspects of the verbal-pictorial representation, since the character speech of both Mr. Hyde and Mr. Griffin is represented intersubjectively through the conventionalized form of the speech balloon.

Particularly in light of the comparatively complex arrangement of segments of intersubjective representation that characterizes *The League of Extraordinary Gentlemen*, it should also be mentioned that this (quasi-)perceptual point-of-view sequence helps to prepare an interesting "hierarchy of knowledge" between Mr. Griffin, Mr. Hyde, and the reader, which will become relevant in the series' second volume: after Mr. Griffin has betrayed the League to the invading

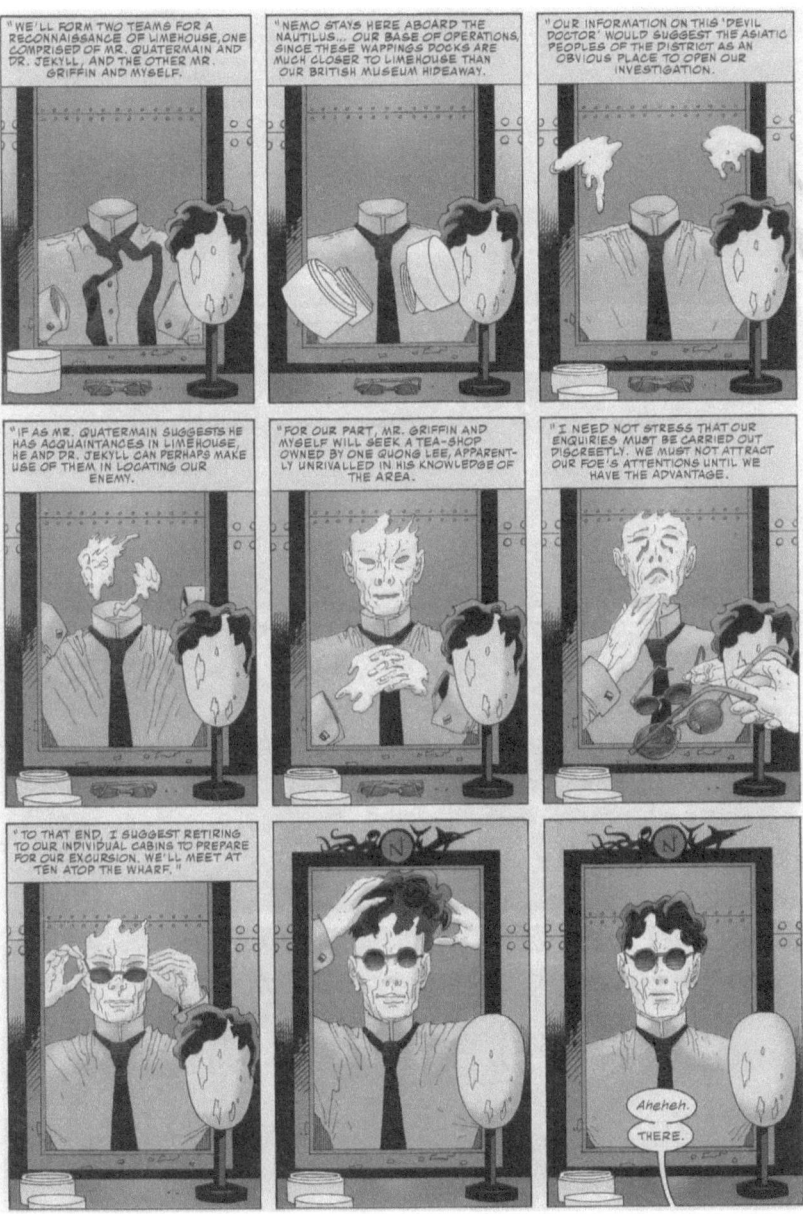

Fig. 59. Mr. Griffin applying makeup in *The League of Extraordinary Gentlemen*

Fig. 60. Mr. Hyde "seeing" temperature in *The League of Extraordinary Gentlemen*

Martian Molluscs, Mr. Hyde uses his enhanced sense of smell to track down the invisible traitor in the British Museum, locking the door to the room in which Mr. Griffin is hiding and mocking him for thinking he is truly invisible. At this point, the reader (as well as, of course, Mr. Hyde) already knows what Mr. Griffin does not, namely, that Mr. Hyde can "see" Mr. Griffin's body heat perfectly well—which is also briefly represented subjectively by what may be described either as a subtle single-panel (quasi-)perceptual point-of-view sequence or as a single-panel (quasi-)perceptual overlay, before Mr. Hyde uses his enhanced visual perception to brutally rape and murder the supposedly invisible Mr. Griffin in what is certainly one of the most gruesome parts of *The League of Extraordinary Gentlemen*'s first two volumes. Yet, despite the important narrative functions that strategies of subjective representation fulfill in *The League of Extraordinary Gentlemen*, the resulting structure of subjectivity is still fairly simple. In order to show that contemporary comics may also use more complex combinations of narratorial and nonnarratorial strategies of subjective representation, then, I would like to examine two additional examples, both of which make extensive use of (at times) highly subjective narratorial representation and a variety of nonnarratorial strategies of subjective representation.

Let me begin with Frank Miller's *Sin City*, the seventh volume of which, *Hell and Back*, uses not only a wealth of subjective narration boxes attributable to the extradiegetic homodiegetic narrating I of Wallace, a former elite soldier turned short-order cook, but also nonnarratorial strategies of subjective representation in at times quite interesting ways, with a sequence that uses (quasi-)perceptual overlay to represent the diegetic Wallace's drug-induced hallucinations once more being particularly salient. Before I analyze this sequence in more detail, though, I would like to say a few more words about *Sin City: Hell and Back*'s use of narratorial representation. The graphic novel opens with the verbal-pictorial (or, rather, exclusively pictorial) representation representing Wallace driving in his car and a succession of narration boxes providing the reader with a fairly "direct access" to the experiencing I's perceptions and thought processes. The verbal narration uses the present tense and, hence, does not explicitly mark a temporal difference between the narrating situation and the narrated situations. Yet any attempt to directly attribute the narratorial representation to the diegetic Wallace as an intradiegetic thinking narrator will ultimately remain unconvincing, as it seems highly unlikely that anybody would think this kind of extensive verbal narration to him- or herself. While the narration boxes in the opening sequence of *Sin City: Hell and Back* arguably contain narratorial representations of the mind and (quasi-)perceptions of Wallace's experiencing I that are attributable to his extradiegetic narrating I rather than narratorially framed or nonnarratorial representations of the former's internal voice, then, the way in which the narration boxes are used varies considerably during the following segments of the graphic novel. Before I discuss these variations, however, I want to take a brief look at some of *Sin City: Hell and Back*'s nonnarratorial strategies of subjective representation.

One of the more subtle examples of these can likewise be found in the opening sequence of the graphic novel, when the experiencing I is represented as remembering what happened previously, with the narration boxes switching to the past tense and the nonnarratorial representation using the kind of "fuzzy" or "wavy" panel borders that have already been discussed with regard to *The Sandman* functioning as simultaneous representational markers of the nonnarratorial representation of the experiencing I's memories.[23] The primary narrative function of these memory sequences is to provide the reader with information about events that have taken place at an earlier point in storyworld time, but *Sin City: Hell and Back* also makes more subjective use of the nonnarratorial representation of internal worlds, when Wallace's experiencing I is represented as meditating in order to remember what has happened after he was shot with a tranquilizer during his attempt to save Esther from killing herself: the representation of his initial efforts to remember is quite interesting in itself, as it combines the nonnarratorial representation of Wallace's memories with narration boxes that seem considerably closer, at times, to nonnarratorially representing the experiencing I's internal voice than the previous narratorial representation was, making the sequence in question most appropriately describable as employing a form of narratorially framed representations of the internal voice of Wallace's experiencing I. Yet this strategy of subjective representation is further expanded in what follows: after Wallace is represented as being arrested and sitting in a holding cell, the nonnarratorial representation metaphorically represents the "contents" of Wallace's mind (see figure 61), which also functions as a rather unusual a priori contextual marker for the subsequent nonnarratorial representation of Wallace's visualization of himself sitting in his "private place" that is not marked via simultaneous representational markers. However, the representation of Wallace imagining himself sitting in his "private place" is followed by the nonnarratorial representation of his resurfacing memories that, once more, uses the established simultaneous representational marker of the "fuzzy" panel borders—as well as, of course, the rather striking narratorially framed representations of the internal voice of Wallace's experiencing I, which function as an additional narratorial marker of subjectivity throughout the sequence.

Apart from these comparatively complex combinations of the narratorial representation of Wallace's mind, the narratorial representation of Wallace's (quasi-)perceptions, and the narratorially framed representation of Wallace's internal voice with the nonnarratorial representation of Wallace's internal worlds and some instances of spatial and/or (quasi-)perceptual point-of-view sequences,[24] *Sin City: Hell and Back* is also noteworthy for a particularly extensive form of (quasi-)perceptual overlay that is used to represent Wallace's hallucinations after he is shot with a tranquilizer for the second time and subsequently drugged: the representation of Deliah, Gordo, and Maxine administering the drug acts as a conventional a priori contextual content marker, but the different ontological status of at least some elements of the following sequences is also communicated by salient simultaneous content markers, as the represented events quite clearly fail to follow the rules of the previously established diegetic primary storyworld, and no less salient simultaneous representational markers, as the verbal-pictorial representation

Fig. 61. Nonnarratorial representation of the "contents" of Wallace's mind in *Sin City: Hell and Back*

is uncharacteristically colorful as well (see figure 62). Yet I would argue that the sequence in question is still more appropriately described as a form of (quasi-)perceptual overlay than as a "full-fledged" nonnarratorial representation of the internal world of Wallace's drug-induced hallucination, as it becomes increasingly clear that what is represented is still at least partially the latter's perception of the diegetic primary storyworld's "factual domain," albeit a heavily distorted one. This becomes particularly apparent once the drug's effects—as well as the colors used in its representation—"cool off" and Wallace is starting to recognize the car he crashed in, even though he is still hallucinating heavily (see figure 63). Moreover, *Sin City: Hell and Back* once again combines this eye-catching nonnarratorial strategy of subjective representation with narration boxes providing narratorially framed representations of the diegetic experiencing I's internal voice rather than a narratorial voice exclusively attributable to Wallace's extradiegetic narrating I. However, the latter's narratorial voice reasserts itself when the experiencing I forces

Fig. 62. Onset of Wallace's hallucinations in *Sin City: Hell and Back*

Subjective Representation across Media 295

Fig. 63. Wallace's hallucinations "cooling off" in *Sin City: Hell and Back*

Maxine to administer an antidote and subsequently shoots her before losing consciousness, allowing the narrating I to narratorially represent the former's quasi-perceptions once again (see figure 64).

Having illustrated some of the ways in which contemporary comics may combine narratorial strategies of subjective representation[25] with nonnarratorial strategies of subjective representation to create occasionally quite complex structures of subjectivity, I would like to conclude my discussion of subjective representation in contemporary comics by examining another graphic novel exemplifying this kind of narrative complexity rather well: Charles Burns's *Black Hole* not only uses narratorial representation attributable to two different (largely) extradiegetic homodiegetic narrators but also employs a

Fig. 64. Narratorial representation of (quasi-)perceptions in *Sin City: Hell and Back*

number of formally inventive forms of nonnarratorial strategies of subjective representation, which, though mostly describable as nonnarratorial representations of internal worlds, make interesting use of comics' medium-specific limitations and affordances.

Despite the fact that one can find instances of spatial point-of-view sequences, (quasi-)perceptual point-of-view sequences, and (quasi-)perceptual overlay as well,[26] I would like to begin by focusing on two recurring forms of nonnarratorial strategies of subjective representation, both of which involve the "full-fledged" representation of internal worlds. On the one hand, *Black Hole* regularly makes use of a conventional form of the nonnarratorial representation of internal worlds that uses contextual content markers (either a priori, a posteriori, or both), simultaneous representational markers (taking the form of the "fuzzy" or, rather, "wavy" panel borders already mentioned in my analysis of *The Sandman* above), and both contextual and simultaneous narratorial markers to communicate the different ontological status of the represented situations (which tend to be either dreams or memories) (see figure 65). On the other hand, and perhaps more interesting at least from a formalist perspective, *Black Hole* also repeatedly uses panels combining narration boxes that contain at times highly subjective narratorial representation with the pictorial representation of a character's internal world in one part of the panel (whose subjectivity is likewise marked by the well-established "wavy" panel borders) and the intersubjective representation of the character whose internal world is represented in another (see figure 66 and figure 67).

While *Black Hole* uses nonnarratorial strategies of subjective representation in interesting ways, then, its structure of subjectivity is more saliently defined by its use of narratorial strategies of subjective representation as well as by the interplay between nonnarratorial and narratorial strategies of subjective representation. *Black Hole* employs narratorial representation extensively, using it to represent the respective narrating I's "mental perspective" on the represented events and to contribute to the representation of the diegetic primary storyworld's "factual domain" as well as to provide "direct access" to the respective experiencing I's mind and (quasi-)perceptions both with and without the nonnarratorial representation providing that kind of "direct access" via what is usually some variety of the nonnarratorial representation of internal worlds at the same time. In addition, *Black Hole*—even more so than *Fear and Loathing in Las Vegas* and *Sin City: Hell and Back*—extensively plays with the possibilities not only of using narration boxes to represent verbal narration attributable to the extradiegetic homodiegetic narrating Is of Keith and Chris (and, in at least one instance, the experiencing I of Keith briefly functioning as an intradiegetic speaking narrator) but also of using them to "move closer" to the narrators' respective experiencing

Fig. 65. Nonnarratorial representation of Chris's dream in *Black Hole*

Fig. 66. Vertical (inter)subjective representation in *Black Hole*

Fig. 67. Horizontal (inter)subjective representation in *Black Hole*

Is, resulting in several instances of narratorially framed and, perhaps, even nonnarratorial representations of the internal voices of the latter.

Initially, the narratorial representation attributable to Keith tends to be marked quite clearly as extradiegetic by the use of past tense and other deictic markers. However, following the nonnarratorial representation of a dream of Keith that uses the "wavy" panel borders mentioned above as a simultaneous representational marker and a conventional a posteriori contextual content marker representing how Keith is waking up, chapter 16 ("A Dream Girl") introduces narration boxes whose verbal narration is still clearly attributable to Keith, but employs the present tense and, hence, seems closer to his experiencing

I's internal voice than his previous past tense narration, with some of the respective narration boxes being perhaps best described as cases of the narratorially framed representation of the internal voice of Keith's experiencing I. Nevertheless, any attempt to comprehend the narration boxes in question as a representation of Keith's internal voice making him function as an intradiegetic thinking narrator in either one of these segments remains problematic, as it appears quite implausible that a character would use such an extended internal voice to comment on the situations he experiences or remembers *while he experiences or remembers them*—and, hence, such a comprehension would need stronger markers than the mere use of the present tense, which neither the narratorial nor the nonnarratorial representation provides.

This is different in the case of the narration boxes attributable to Chris, which are commonly employed in combination with the nonnarratorial representation of her internal worlds and, moreover, also introduced by using the present tense and other deictic markers that make them appear closer to the experiencing I's internal voice than the narratorial representation attributable to Keith ever becomes. When the narration boxes attributable to Chris are introduced in chapter 3 ("Sssssssss"), the accompanying nonnarratorial representation of Chris's dream, which uses an a priori contextual content marker (as well as the first occurrence of the "wavy" panel borders already mentioned above), provides some initial cues regarding the question of whether or not the narration boxes are meant to represent the experiencing I's internal voice. The diegetic Chris is represented as "hissing" in her sleep, and when the verbal-pictorial representation starts representing her dream, the accompanying narration boxes start with a similar "hissing sound" (see figure 65). In the following chapter ("Racing towards Something"), additional cues are offered when the verbal-pictorial representation uses speech balloons to represent how Chris's diegetic experiencing I finishes a sentence whose representation was begun using narration boxes (see figure 68) and, even more clearly, when the verbal-pictorial representation uses thought bubbles to represent how her diegetic experiencing I thinks the beginning of a verbal

Fig. 68. Chris's experiencing I finishing her narrating I's sentence in *Black Hole*

narration whose representation is later continued using narration boxes (see figure 69). While the narratorial representation in the chapters that focus on Chris later starts using the past tense and other deictic markers that make it more appropriately attributable to an extradiegetic homodiegetic narrator once again, Chris's initial verbal narration may be one of only comparatively few cases where one could arguably speak not so much of the nonnarratorial representation of a character's internal voice (or, alternatively, of the narratorially framed representation of the experiencing I's internal voice that is marked as such only a posteriori) but, rather, of a "full-fledged" intradiegetic thinking narrator with some justification. Having sketched some of the ways in which contemporary comics may employ narratorial as well as nonnarratorial strategies of subjective representation, then, I will conclude the present chapter by analyzing the realization and interrelation of these strategies in contemporary video games, particularly focusing on interactive forms of subjective representation as well as on their ludic functions.

Fig. 69. Chris functioning as an intradiegetic thinking narrator in *Black Hole*

Strategies of Subjective Representation in Contemporary Video Games

Once more perhaps not quite as well established as it is in contemporary films, the use of both narratorial and nonnarratorial strategies of subjective representation is by now at least as common in video games as it is in comics. Bungie's first-person shooter *Halo* does not use much in the way of subjective representation apart from the genre-specific form of the spatial point-of-view sequence, and Hothead's *DeathSpank* series likewise does not saliently employ any of the subjective strategies sketched in the previous chapter, but the other examples that I have discussed in the first and second part of this book all realize at least one of the more pronounced forms of narratorial or nonnarratorial strategies of subjective representation. As I have previously noted, the opening sequence of Remedy's *Alan Wake* extensively represents a dream of the main protagonist by using a complex combination of cut-scenes, scripted sequences of events, and interactive gameplay; Bioware's *Dragon Age: Origins* likewise not only uses cut-scenes to represent the player-controlled character's clairvoyant dreams but also, on several occasions, allows him or her to enter the dreams of other characters in The Fade; Ubisoft's *Prince of Persia: The Sands of Time* uses cut-scenes to represent the internal worlds of the experiencing I, as well as a combination of cut-scenes and an extended interactive gameplay sequence to represent what is narratorially marked as a "shared dream" by the player-controlled Prince and Princess Farah; finally, the intradiegetic homodiegetic narrator Rucks of Supergiant Games' *Bastion* uses "heterosubjective"[27] narratorial representation of the Kid's mind and (quasi-)perceptions, and the game also employs extensive forms of (quasi-)perceptual overlay with a primarily ludic function when the player-controlled character comes into contact with hallucinogenic parts of the flora and fauna populating the game's storyworld, as well as what could be described as a nonnarratorial interactive representation of the internal world of the Kid, when his passing out after taking a drag from a pipe he found is followed by a profoundly weird gameplay sequence that appears to be intended to represent the Kid's hallucinatory dream.

As this brief look at the ways in which the previously analyzed video games use strategies of subjective representation already indicates, the medium-specific realization of the latter is primarily defined by what one could abbreviate as video games' interactivity. In fact, even what may be described as spatial point-of-view sequences on a transmedial level is already realized in particularly medium-specific ways in video games, since the spatial position from which the game spaces are represented is both more static and more flexible than it is in comics and films. It is more static because most games use roughly the same kind of "spatial perspective" in their gameplay sequences, and it is more flexible because the "virtual camera" adapts to the gameplay, and players are often given the opportunity to change its angle and distance. Still, one can draw some distinctions: real-time strategy games such as those in Blizzard's *Warcraft* or Westwood's *Command & Conquer* series typically use what can be described as an "objective point of view" or "god's eye perspective," where the position from which the game space is represented is not determined by the position of a character in that space. Action-adventure games such as those in SCE's *God of War* or Remedy's *Alan Wake* series typically use what can be described as a "semi-subjective point of view" or "third-person perspective," where the position from which the game space is represented is determined by the position of the player-controlled character but does not coincide with that position. Finally, first-person shooter games such as those in id Software's *Doom* or Bungie's *Halo* series typically use what can be described as a "subjective point of view" or "first-person perspective," where the position from which the game spaces are represented coincides with the position of the player-controlled character. Accordingly, I would like to begin my discussion of subjective representation in contemporary video games by examining a first-person shooter, though one that makes extensive use not only of spatial but also of (quasi-)perceptual point-of-view sequences, constructing a somewhat more complex structure of subjectivity than, for example, *Doom 3* or *Halo* do.

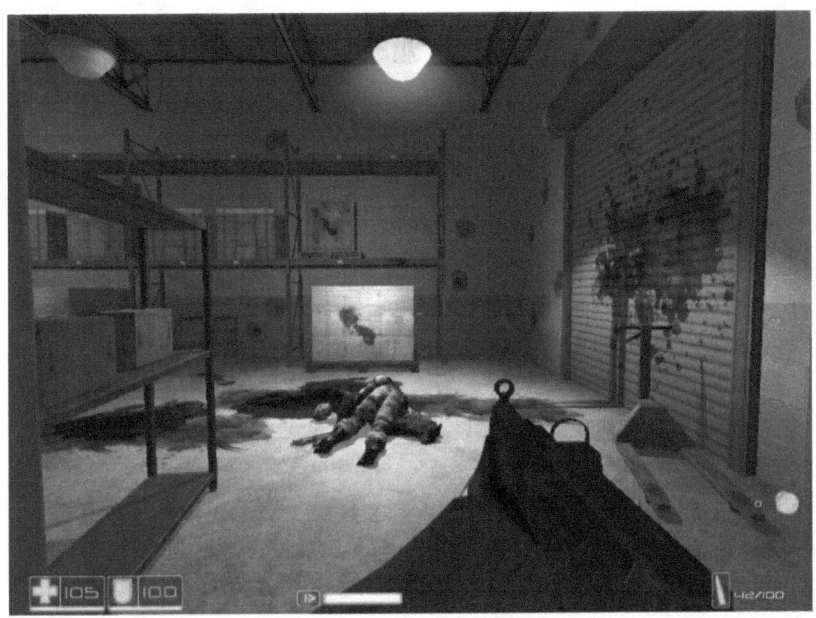

Fig. 70. Spatial point-of-view sequence in *F.E.A.R.*

In Monolith's *F.E.A.R.: First Encounter Assault Recon*, the player controls an unnamed soldier who is introduced as a member of a task force that takes on paranormal threats. As is typical for first-person shooters, *F.E.A.R.* represents events, existents, and characters using the medium-specific form of a spatial point-of-view sequence rather extensively (see figure 70), even maintaining this still comparatively intersubjective form of subjective representation in most of its cutscenes.[28] Yet the extent to which *F.E.A.R.* employs not only spatial but also (quasi-)perceptual point-of-view sequences is unusual. On the one hand, this refers to by now highly conventionalized ways of using a simultaneous representational marker that commonly takes the form of a (partial) red filter to represent the player-controlled character's pain when he is being hurt. The ludic function of this medium-specific kind of (quasi-)perceptual point-of-view sequence is evident: since preventing the player-controlled character from dying is the primary game goal of *F.E.A.R.* (and most if not all other first-person shooters), it is important for the player to know whether the player-controlled character gets hurt.²⁹ In fact, the use of these kinds of representational markers in the context of (quasi-)perceptual point-of-view sequences or (quasi-)perceptual overlay that primarily represent the player-controlled character being hurt has become something of the "default case" in contemporary video games, with first-person shooters such as those in the *Halo* series, action-adventures such as those in the *Alan Wake* series, and role-playing games such as Bioware's *Dragon Age: Origins* or Supergiant Games' *Bastion* providing some particularly well-known examples.³⁰

On the other hand, however, *F.E.A.R.* also allows the player to use a medium-specific form of "slow motion," which slows down the simulated gameplay while allowing the player-controlled character to act at full speed, thereby representing the latter's superhuman reflexes. As noted, employing slow motion in general and employing it to represent the superhuman reflexes of a character in particular may have originally been film-specific strategies of subjective representation, with the use of "bullet time" in the Wachowski siblings' *The Matrix* being one of the more influential examples (though it is also commonly found in contemporary comic adaptations such as Zack Snyder's *300* and *Watchmen*, or Timur Bekmambetov's *Wanted*). Yet *F.E.A.R.*—not unlike other games using similar mechanisms, including People Can Fly's *Painkiller,* Saber Interactive's *Time Shift,* and, unsurprisingly, Shiny Entertainment's *Enter the Matrix*—adapts the strategy to video games' specific limitations and affordances. Perhaps most importantly, *F.E.A.R.*'s use of "slow motion" in what is a particularly interesting form of (quasi-)perceptual point-of-view sequence (which uses a simultaneous representational marker as well) fulfills a primarily ludic function in that it allows the player, who will most likely not have superhuman reflexes, to appropriately control a character who has—and who can, therefore, conquer challenges that would lead to his inevitable defeat if reacting with superhuman reflexes were a task entirely left to the player.

Apart from these two rather different examples of (quasi-)perceptual point-of-view sequences with a primarily ludic function, *F.E.A.R.* uses other forms of (quasi-)perceptual point-of-view sequences representing the player-controlled character's hallucinations as well as some "full-fledged" nonnarratorial representations of the player-controlled character's memories or memory-based hallucinations that seem to fulfill primarily narrative functions: *F.E.A.R.* extensively employs elements of the horror genre, but does so in a way that lets its story unfold gradually, resulting in a plot that withholds quite a lot of (narratively) crucial information from both the player-controlled character and the player. Even during *F.E.A.R.*'s opening sequences, which task the F.E.A.R. team with eliminating a man named Paxton Fettel, (quasi-)perceptual point-of-view sequences are used to represent what most likely are mere hallucinations of the player-controlled character and ultimately lead to "full-fledged" nonnarratorial representations of what is perhaps best comprehended as memory-based hallucinations—though it is not quite clear on whose memories these hallucinations are based, precisely. Yet the game's plot takes an even stranger turn when much of the F.E.A.R. team is killed by what appears to be a little girl in a red dress, who eventually turns out to be the psychic ghost of Alma Wade, a girl with extraordinary paranormal powers and mother to both Paxton and the player-controlled character.

The hallucinatory (quasi-)perceptual point-of-view sequences—which are also commonly combined with a (quasi-)perceptual point of audition that is used to nonnarratorially represent how the player-controlled character hears Alma's voice "inside his mind"—become more intense when Alma appears, forcing the player-controlled character to either back away (in the early stages of the game; see figure 71) or to shoot her before she reaches him, making her disappear again (during the later encounters). While these sequences contain rather obvious representations of the player-controlled character's hallucinations, then, they are still best described as (quasi-)perceptual point-of-view sequences, since what is represented is usually still comprehensible as being based on the "factual domain" of the game's storyworld. Just as it does during the opening sequences, though, *F.E.A.R.* also continues to combine these segments of interactive (quasi-)perceptual point-of-view sequences (which are primarily used

Fig. 71. The player-controlled character's first encounter with Alma in *F.E.A.R.*

to generate *F.E.A.R.*'s genre-specific atmosphere and to represent the considerable threat that Alma poses) with the noninteractive nonnarratorial representation of the player-controlled character's memories or memory-based hallucinations (which are primarily used to represent *F.E.A.R.*'s "backstory," including, but not limited to, the fact that both Paxton and the player-controlled character are Alma's sons). It is certainly just as important to distinguish whether a given strategy of subjective representation is realized merely as part of the noninteractive elements of a video game or also as part of its interactive gameplay as it is to distinguish between narratorial and nonnarratorial strategies of subjective representation. Yet *F.E.A.R.* also illustrates the necessity of more detailed examinations of how contemporary video games combine a variety of strategies of subjective representation to generate considerably complex structures of subjectivity.

As should have become clear, then, video games realize transmedial strategies of subjective representation in decidedly medium-specific ways, but an appropriate analysis of these strategies' realization is contingent on taking into account not only their use of narratorial and nonnarratorial as well as interactive and noninteractive forms of representation but also their narrative and ludic functions. In order to expand on these questions a little more, let me offer a second example that illustrates how "subjective gameplay" may be used to impair the player's abilities in order to represent certain unusual mental conditions of the player-controlled character, rather than to enhance the player's ability to interact with the game spaces, as is the case in F.E.A.R.'s use of "slow motion" to represent the player-controlled character's superhuman reflexes: Frictional Games' *Amnesia: The Dark Descent* is one of the more recent of an increasing number of games that use what is sometimes called a "sanity meter" to implement the player-controlled character's mental condition into the game mechanics[31]—other influential examples being Headfirst's *Call of Cthulhu: Dark Corners of the Earth*, Silicon Knights' *Eternal Darkness: Sanity's Requiem*, Rogue Entertainment's *American McGee's Alice*, and Quantic Dream's *Indigo Prophecy*. Self-identifying as a "first-person survival game," *Amnesia: The Dark Descent* may appear similar to first-person shooters such as F.E.A.R. at first glance, but it is actually very different, at least with regard to its game mechanics.

Exclusively representing its game spaces using the kind of spatial point-of-view sequences that also defines the first-person shooter genre (without using cut-scenes or significantly changing the "spatial perspective" in other ways), *Amnesia: The Dark Descent* is not making the survival of the player-controlled character, Daniel, contingent on "shooting the bad guys." Daniel wakes up in a castle, unable to remember who he is or why he is where he is, but he soon finds out that the castle is full of monsters hunting him. Without going into too many specifics about *Amnesia: The Dark Descent*'s fairly convoluted plot—which culminates in Daniel, who gradually regains his memories throughout the game, preventing the game's villain, Alexander, from using a mysterious orb and the dimensional travel it allows for some kind of sinister goal or other—I want to point out how well strategies of subjective representation are implemented into the game mechanics: trying to escape the monsters that hunt him, Daniel may attempt to hide in the darkness, but doing so decreases his "sanity meter." This decrease in "sanity," which is also accelerated when Daniel looks at a monster directly, is remedied when he stays in well-lit places, but unfortunately doing so also means that he is highly visible to any nearby monsters. Apart from that, only progress in the game's story (or self-medication with laudanum, which can occasionally be found in the castle) increases Daniel's "sanity," so that the game produces an intense need for the player to let Daniel explore the castle even further before he "loses his sanity" completely.

When the monsters reach Daniel or he is hurt in other ways, *Amnesia: The Dark Descent* uses a conventional version of the simultaneous representational marker already mentioned, with red claw marks and splashes of blood representing that Daniel is being wounded. More importantly yet, a decrease in "sanity" leads to (quasi-)perceptual rather than spatial point-of-view sequences representing Daniel's disturbed perceptions of his surroundings, both in the form of scripted sequences of events and as a part of the core game mechanics. Significantly, this is not limited to the audiovisual representation, but also includes the player's possibilities of interaction: a decrease of "sanity" leads to the picture becoming blurry, which of course makes interacting with the game spaces significantly harder. However, it also influences the speed and precision of Daniel's movements—which is a conventionalized aspect of the video game-specific use of subjective representation by now and can also be found in more mainstream video games such as Rockstar's *Grand Theft Auto IV* or Blizzard's *World of Warcraft*, where it is used to represent the player-controlled character's intoxication, among other things. Still, the way that *Amnesia: The Dark Descent* integrates this kind of (quasi-)perceptual point-of-view sequences into its overall game mechanics is certainly noteworthy and helps to create an "atmosphere of fear" that only very few other contemporary video games (such as *F.E.A.R.* or other horror video games) will be able to achieve to a similar extent.

Let me conclude my discussion of *Amnesia: The Dark Descent* by mentioning that while the implementation of the "sanity meter" serves primarily ludic functions, the game also extensively uses both nonnarratorial representations of Daniel's internal voice and an interesting form of (quasi-)perceptual point-of-audition sequences that likewise fulfill primarily narrative functions: modifying a strategy of intradiegetic narratorial representation that is well established within the first-person shooter genre, in particular,[32] *Amnesia: The Dark Descent* employs a succession of scripted sequences of events that represent Daniel's resurfacing memories but exclusively use the auditive channel in combination with written subtitles in order to do so (although these sequences are also marked by white fades functioning as reasonably conventionalized a priori and a posteriori contextual representational markers). Not only does this strategy of subjective representation quite successfully allow the game to gradually represent its "backstory" without having to interrupt the interactive gameplay, it also serves to further illustrate that strategies of subjective representation may be realized using a variety of "semiotic resources" and are certainly not limited to pictorial representation. Nevertheless, the focus of *Amnesia: The Dark Descent*'s use of nonnarratorial strategies of subjective representation clearly remains on Daniel's (quasi-)perception of the storyworld's "factual domain."

Before I return to the initial dream sequence in Remedy's *Alan Wake* to illustrate how contemporary video games may combine narratorial strategies of subjective representation with comparatively complex forms of the "full-fledged" nonnarratorial representation of internal worlds, however, I would like to offer yet another example that illustrates how strategies similar to those discussed in the context of *F.E.A.R.* and *Amnesia: The Dark Descent* may be realized in video games that do not (or at least not primarily) represent their game spaces using spatial point-of-view sequences.[33] Comparable to *F.E.A.R.*'s use of "slow motion," Rocksteady's *Batman: Arkham Asylum* allows the player to switch between an intersubjective mode of representation and what is called the "detective mode": a kind of (quasi-)perceptual overlay that activates a number of enhancements in Batman's cowl, all of which are necessary to solve the game's various puzzles (see figure 72 and figure 73). Moreover, while these

Fig. 72. Intersubjective representation in *Batman: Arkham Asylum*

Fig. 73. "Detective mode" in *Batman: Arkham Asylum*

enhancements include some kind of radio device that Batman uses to talk to Oracle (the superhero identity of Barbara Gordon, Commissioner Jim Gordon's daughter), he also "talks to himself" in sequences that may be comprehended as nonnarratorial representations of Batman's internal voice. In a game set in an asylum for the criminally insane that has been taken over by Batman's archenemy the Joker, though, it will come as no surprise that this kind of still fairly intersubjective (quasi-)perceptual overlay[34] is not all there is to it.

Instead, at several points in *Batman: Arkham Asylum*, strategies of subjective representations are used to decidedly more unreliable effect, most strikingly in those segments of the game where Batman is affected by a hallucinogenic gas that is the trademark weapon of yet another one of his enemies, the Scarecrow. Accordingly, several passages of the game simulate Batman's increasingly hallucinatory (quasi-)perceptual experience by sliding from intensifying forms of (quasi-)perceptual overlay to the "full-fledged" nonnarratorial representation of internal worlds, during which a hypodiegetic version of the Caped Crusader has to face his various fears or relives the traumatic childhood experience of witnessing his parents being murdered.[35] While Batman is searching for the kidnapped Jim, he encounters the Scarecrow for the first time, which is followed by what later turns out to already have been (quasi-)perceptual overlay representing Batman finding what he thinks is Jim's body. A sequence with "reduced interactivity"[36] ensues, during which the player can only let Batman walk down yet another corridor and talk to what turns out to be the hallucination of a "phone operator" temporarily replacing the Oracle. During this "internal dialogue," the representation becomes increasingly surreal and, hence, recognizable as being subjective, which is further stressed by the menacing music functioning as a simultaneous representational—or, perhaps, *presentational*—marker.[37]

Once Batman has arrived in the morgue, the game also makes more recognizable use of a (quasi-)perceptual point of audition to represent whispering ghostly voices that quite clearly only Batman can hear. The (quasi-)perceptual overlay is intensified when the inventory of the morgue is starting to "act on its own," culminating in a cut-scene in which Batman is represented as opening two of the three body bags that are laid out there, only to find his dead parents (with his father blaming Batman for their deaths and his mother begging for help). This cut-scene can still be described as combining forms of (quasi-)perceptual overlay and (quasi-)perceptual point-of-view sequences, since what is represented is still referring to the storyworld's

Fig. 74. The first Scarecrow sequence in *Batman: Arkham Asylum*

"factual domain" to some extent, but the whole sequence ultimately functions as an a priori contextual content marker for the nonnarratorial interactive representation of Batman's hallucinations that follows: when Batman opens the third body bag, the Scarecrow's head jumps out at him, the picture becomes blurry (which functions as a highly conventionalized a priori contextual representational marker), and Batman falls to the floor. When Batman stands up again, he finds himself in the first of three distinctive Scarecrow sequences, all of which are meant to represent the hallucinations that Batman experiences due to the former's trademark weapon (see figure 74). In contrast to the sequences that use (quasi-)perceptual overlay as a transition between the intersubjective representation of the "factual domain" of the game's storyworld and the nonnarratorial representation of the internal world of Batman's hallucinations, which employ an unchallenging form of interactive representation, the Scarecrow sequences use an unusual mode of gameplay that focuses not so much on Batman's combat abilities but rather on a "hide and seek" game against the unrelenting gaze of a huge imaginary Scarecrow, which Batman (who also imagines himself *as* the Scarecrow; see figure 75) defeats using the light of an equally imaginary bat signal.

Fig. 75. Batman imagining himself as the Scarecrow in *Batman: Arkham Asylum*

Batman's second confrontation with the Scarecrow follows a similar pattern: the sequence begins with a very subtle representation of gas being routed into the corridors through which Batman is moving (which, however, is likely to be recognized as the a priori contextual content marker that it is by most first-time players when Batman briefly coughs, since the hallucinogenic effect of the Scarecrow's trademark weapon has already been established). During a steadily intensifying form of (quasi-)perceptual overlay in what is, once more, less an interactive gameplay sequence than a sequence of scripted "environmental" events during which the game's interactivity is heavily reduced, one of Arkham Mansion's long halls is gradually transformed into the back alley where the (most likely) eight-year-old Bruce Wayne witnessed his parents being murdered (see figure 76). Again, the game also uses a (quasi-)perceptual point of audition to represent Batman's memory-based hallucinations (much in the same way that the device is used in *Amnesia: The Dark Descent*), until the sequence culminates in a cut-scene representing Batman imagining himself as the eight-year-old Bruce, kneeling in front of his parents (see figure 77). Another "barely interactive" sequence combines (quasi-)perceptual overlay representing Batman/Bruce walking further down

Subjective Representation across Media   317

Fig. 76. A hall transforming into a back alley in *Batman: Arkham Asylum*

Fig. 77. Batman imagining himself as the young Bruce in *Batman: Arkham Asylum*

the hall with a (quasi-)perceptual point-of-audition sequence representing how Jim gently interrogates the now orphaned young Bruce, before the second Scarecrow sequence follows, which lets Batman battle against a bunch of skeletons but, apart from that, employs game mechanics similar to those in the first Scarecrow sequence—including Batman using the bat signal to defeat the Scarecrow.

However, the representation of Batman's third and final encounter with the Scarecrow deviates from the established pattern in ways that further serve to illustrate how films, comics, and video games may use strategies of subjective representation to generate metaleptic effects: while Batman moves through Arkham Asylum's intensive treatment area, what initially appears to be an error in the game software lets the interactive representation grind to a halt (see figure 78). This mild metalepsis is followed by a modified version of *Batman: Arkham Asylum*'s opening sequence, with the (player-controlled) Joker now fulfilling the role of Batman and vice versa. After the Joker has shot Batman, a standard "game over" screen appears (see figure 79), but if the player chooses the "retry" option, another segment of the nonnarratorial representation of Batman's Scarecrow-related hallucinations follows, with the hypodiegetic Batman escaping from his grave and battling the hallucinated giant Scarecrow one last time. Despite the fact that this segment is longer than the previous Scarecrow sequences—and, moreover, briefly interrupted by a cut-scene that represents the diegetic version of the Scarecrow administering an extra dose of the hallucinogenic drug to the diegetic Batman—the game mechanics of the battle remain largely unmodified, eventually

Fig. 78. "Fake crash" before the third Scarecrow sequence in *Batman: Arkham Asylum*

Fig. 79. "Game over" before the third Scarecrow sequence in *Batman: Arkham Asylum*

resulting in Batman using the bat signal to defeat the Scarecrow yet again. Interestingly, though, once the hallucinatory Scarecrow is defeated, Batman is represented as stepping over the bodies of various thugs that roughly match the body types of the skeletons he had to fight during the hallucinatory sequence. This implies quite forcefully that Batman's drug-induced hallucinations are ultimately still based on the storyworld's "factual domain," which would arguably make at least the third Scarecrow sequence a border case between the "full-fledged" nonnarratorial representation of Batman's internal world and a "mere" (quasi-)perceptual overlay.

While *Batman: Arkham Asylum* once more illustrates that video games can use strategies of subjective representation to rather different effect as well as focus either on their narrative or ludic functions (or a combination of both), the range of these strategies extends well beyond the still comparatively local use of (quasi-)perceptual point-of-view sequences, (quasi-)perceptual overlay, and the nonnarratorial representation of internal worlds in *F.E.A.R.*, *Amnesia: The Dark Descent*, and *Batman: Arkham Asylum*—with some games framing considerably larger segments of their interactive gameplay as contributing to the nonnarratorial representation of internal worlds, in particular. As the ludic nature of the sequences in question usually also leads to a foregrounding of the ludic functions of video games' strategies of subjective representation, these games furthermore tend to highlight the fact that both the nonnarratorial representation of (quasi-)perceptual aspects of a character's consciousness and the nonnarratorial representation of a character's internal worlds is necessarily connected to the player's actions in some way. More specifically, at least the "full-fledged" nonnarratorial representation of a character's internal world through interactive gameplay usually presupposes that the player-controlled character (or, more precisely, the player controlling the character) is, to a certain extent, capable of acting not only in the storyworld as it is perceived by that character but also in (or, rather, on) the more clearly subjective internal worlds of that character's memories, dreams, or fantasies. By now, quite a few video games such as Analgesic Productions' *Anodyne* or HyperSloth's *Dream* frame large parts of or even their entire gameplay as the nonnarratorial representation of the player-controlled character's internal world(s), but one can also find an increasing number of video games such as Double Fine's *Psychonauts* or Dontnod's *Remember Me* (as well as, incidentally, Bioware's *Dragon Age: Origins* and, perhaps, Ubisoft's *Prince of Persia: The Sands of Time*) that represent the player-controlled character as acting in (or on) *other* characters' internal worlds—which is, of course, a fairly transmedial strategy of subjective representation that also appears in films such as Christopher Nolan's *Inception* or comics such as Neil Gaiman's *The Sandman*.

Against this background, I would like to conclude my discussion of subjective representation in contemporary video games by returning to an example that illustrates the ways in which larger segments of interactive gameplay may be narratorially as well as nonnarratorially marked as representing the player-controlled character's internal world, without the game in question necessarily putting strategies of subjective representation front and center: since Remedy's *Alan Wake*'s complex story has already been summarized in chapter 3, I will now mainly focus on the way in which the game initially uses a combination of cut-scenes, scripted events, and interactive simulation to represent a nightmare that the player-controlled hypodiegetic experiencing I of *Alan Wake* experiences before it increasingly "invades" the diegetic primary storyworld as well. As I have previously noted, the game begins with a cinematographic cut-scene introducing the narratorial voice of the extradiegetic homodiegetic narrator, which is used to frame the following sequences as a dream of the protagonist quite explicitly: "I've always had a vivid imagination, but this dream unsettled me. It was wild, and dark, and weird, even by my standards. So yes, it began with a dream." The game does not provide "direct access" to Alan's experiencing I via the kind of voice-over that I have proposed to call either the narratorially framed or the nonnarratorial representation of a character's internal voice, but the ever-present narratorial voice of the narrating I continues to contribute quite a bit of (rather heavy-handed) narratorial representation of the experiencing I's mind and (quasi-)perceptions during much of the following gameplay as well.

Let me get back to the dream sequence, though: the remainder of the initial cut-scene shows how the hypodiegetic Alan, who is desperately trying to reach his destination in a place called Night Springs, runs his car into a hitchhiker, who is apparently killed by the impact. A moment later, though, the hitchhiker's body has disappeared, and it is at this point that the player gains control of Alan. The player is then required to have Alan run a little way down the road before a short cut-scene represents a lighthouse, the reaching of which the narrator immediately identifies as the main goal of the dream sequence: "I had to go to the lighthouse. I knew there was something important waiting for me there." Using the additional guidance provided by a kind of "compass" in the top-left corner of the screen, which always shows the current goal to be reached—and which, just like the other elements of the graphic user interface and the extrafictional directions addressed directly to the player, is best understood as external to the fictional representation—the player is supposed to let Alan jog down a path that leads away from the road toward the lighthouse (see figure 80). After the first few steps, however, the interactive gameplay is interrupted, once more, by another cinematographic cut-scene showing a

Fig. 80. Extrafictional directions and other elements of the interface in *Alan Wake*

shadowy figure with an axe appearing next to the car, vanishing, and immediately reappearing in front of Alan. During the gameplay sequence that follows, Alan is chased down the path leading away from the road by the shadowy figure, which, in a series of scripted events, threatens Alan and eventually starts attacking him: "You don't even recognize me, do you, writer? You think you're God? You think you can just make up stuff? Play with people's lives and kill them when you think it adds to the drama?"

While it seems clear that the main ludic function of *Alan Wake*'s opening sequence is to allow the player to become acquainted with the game's core mechanics and possibilities of interaction via extrafictional instructions and the necessity to follow them in order to let Alan survive the attacks of the shadowy figure (in rapid succession, the player learns about how he or she can let Alan jump, evade attacks, and sprint),[38] this sequence further introduces a number of thematic elements that remain central to the unfolding story—the autopoietic metalepsis that the hypodiegetic Alan also increasingly begins to become aware of being the most important of these—when the ever-present narrator states that his experiencing "I realized that the hitchhiker was a character in the story I'd been working on" and the shadowy figure asks, right on cue: "How does it feel to die by the hands of your own creation?" After some more running, Alan meets a character called Clay Steward, who leads him to a small log cabin. Another cinematographic cut-scene represents the door of the cabin being slammed shut and the shadowy figure brutally murdering Clay, leaving Alan trapped in the cabin (which the narrator emphasizes as well, in case the player was not paying attention). With the nightmare becoming increasingly nightmarish, a series of scripted events represents a mysterious voice that seems to originate from the light surrounding the lighthouse, prompting Alan to escape the cabin, and subsequently explains to him (as well as to the player) additional details of the game's interesting light-based combat mechanics.

Apart from conveying information about the game's core mechanics, the nightmare sequence also gives the player quite a few pointers regarding the game goals, both on a specific level that refers to the way in which to deal with the so-called Taken and on a more general level that refers to the threat of the Dark Presence taking over the world. In fact, it is a core ludic function of the nightmare sequence to establish the threat of the Dark Presence as the conflict motivating most of the following gameplay, before Alan reaches the lighthouse and the sequence concludes with a final cut-scene in which Alan is represented as waking up and which, therefore, functions as a conventionalized a posteriori contextual content marker (which is also further reinforced by the ever-present narratorial representation) that appears to communicate the end of the dream sequence—"appears," because *Alan Wake*'s ending implies that all of the events that are represented after this point are still part of that or some other dream. Now, it may occasionally be more effective to exclusively use cut-scenes for shorter forms of the nonnarratorial representation of internal worlds (and this is, in fact, repeatedly done in the further course of the game), but the opening sequence of *Alan Wake* still illustrates that, while video games may use the full range of strategies of subjective representation, including the narratorial representation of a character's mind and the "full-fledged" nonnarratorial representation of a character's internal worlds, it is important not only to differentiate between specific kinds of narratorial and nonnarratorial representation and ask how they are combined to generate a video game's structure of subjectivity but also to distinguish between interactive gameplay, scripted sequences of events, and noninteractive cut-scenes, all the while acknowledging the ludic as well as the narrative functions of the various forms of subjective representation that are thus realized.

I want to conclude, then, by underscoring once more that one can describe certain narratorial and nonnarratorial strategies of subjective representation on a transmedial level, yet that it is still necessary to pay close attention to the medium- and work-specific realization of these strategies when analyzing the structure of subjectivity of films such as *12 Monkeys*, *Fight Club*, *A Beautiful Mind*, or *Fear and Loathing in Las Vegas*, comics such as *The Sandman: Season of Mists*, *The Arrival*, *The League of Extraordinary Gentlemen*, *Sin City: Hell and Back*, or *Black Hole*, and video games such as *F.E.A.R.: First Encounter Assault Recon*, *Amnesia: The Dark Descent*, *Batman: Arkham Asylum*, or *Alan Wake*. As I have established in this and the previous chapter, the structures of subjectivity of these films, comics, and video games are constructed by using, for example, narratorial representations of characters' minds, narratorial representations of characters' (quasi-)perceptions, narratorially framed representations of characters' internal voices, nonnarratorial representations of characters' internal voices, spatial point-of-view sequences, (quasi-)perceptual point-of-view sequences, (quasi-)perceptual overlay, or the "full-fledged" nonnarratorial representation of internal worlds.

While perhaps not quite as pronounced as the analyses presented in the second part of this book, the previous pages have also shown how contemporary films, comics, and video games may employ a variety of transmedial and medium-specific markers of subjectivity—including simultaneous as well as contextual content, representational, and narratorial markers—in order to render the different ontological status of the situations that are represented by subjective representations transparent or to leave it intransparent, at least initially, the latter of which may generate complex forms of representational unreliability. Finally, my focus on the medium- and work-specific realization of strategies of subjective representation as well as on their functions has served to further illuminate video games' somewhat exceptional status among the narrative media the present study has examined, since their interactivity, in particular, leads to the strategies of subjective representation in contemporary video games commonly fulfilling not only narrative but also ludic functions.

Conclusion
Roads Not (Yet) Taken

This book's point of departure was the observation that the ubiquity of narrative representations in contemporary media culture necessitates a genuinely transmedial narratology that provides not only a method for the analysis of transmedial strategies of narrative representation and their realization within the specific mediality of films, comics, and video games but also a theoretical frame within which medium-specific approaches from literary or film narratology, from comics studies or game studies, and from other relevant fields of research can be critically examined as well as systematically correlated, modified, and expanded to further illuminate the forms and functions of narrative representation across media. In pursuing this project, I have attempted to adhere to a criterion of continuity that emphasizes the relevance of previous research as well as to a criterion of neutrality that underscores the importance of remaining compatible with a broad range of theories and methods. In other words, the method of analysis I have developed throughout the previous chapters has, from the outset, been intended to be readily expandable by approaches from other research contexts. I would like to use the final few pages of this book, then, not to summarize my findings but, rather, to briefly sketch some areas of potential expansion and application, some "roads not (yet) taken."

Maybe most obviously, these entail the possibility of examining the realization of transmedial strategies of narrative representation in media other than contemporary films, comics, and video games. A particularly fruitful expansion of this kind would aim at the realization of these strategies in contemporary "quality television," focusing, for example, on narratively complex television series such as *Breaking Bad*, *Game of Thrones*, *Lost*, *Sherlock*, *The Walking Dead*, or *The Wire*. Other, perhaps less obvious potentials for *medial expansion* would include theatrical performances and literary texts. Moreover, there is also quite a bit of potential left for *conceptual expansion*. This would entail not only the further critical examination, correlation, and modification of medium-specific terms and concepts from film narratology, comics studies, and game studies (or literary narratology, performance studies, and television studies, for that matter) but also the discussion of certain transmedial aspects of narrative representation to which I have not paid as much attention as they doubtlessly deserve. Examples of the latter would include strategies of "plot design" or taxonomies aiming at the "inventory" of storyworlds, the complex problem of authorial voices or the forms and functions of evaluative unreliability, and the representation of characters' emotions as well as their relation to recipients' emotions.

Another way to expand the scope of the method of analysis that this book has developed would be to apply it to corpora "beyond the single work." Evidently, this observation is not limited to the fact that most of the comics and video games that I have analyzed in the previous chapters are part of a more encompassing intramedial series.[1] Rather, quite a few of my main examples could also be analyzed as intermedial adaptations or, alternatively, as narrative works that form the basis of such adaptations.[2] Accordingly, it might prove interesting to compare the strategies of narrative, narratorial, and subjective representation that, say, Chuck Palahniuk's novel *Fight Club*, Alan Moore and Kevin O'Neill's comics series *The League of Extraordinary Gentlemen*, or Ubisoft's video game *Prince of Persia: The Sands of Time* and their respective film adaptations by David Fincher, Stephen Norrington, and Mike Newell employ. More specifically, while current adaptation studies have increasingly, and for good reasons, moved away from the issue of "fidelity," a narratologically informed comparison of adaptations could still provide interesting perspectives on questions such as how Frank Miller's comics series *Sin City* relates to his and Robert Rodriguez's film adaptation (which not only combines several of the original story lines but also employs a rather distinct visual style that is evidently influenced by the comics), how Alan Moore and Dave Gibbons's *Watchmen* relates to Zack Snyder's film adaptation (which tells roughly the same story but is much less successful in emulating the strategies of narratorial representation that all but define the comic), or how Terry Gilliam's *Fear and Loathing in Las Vegas* manages to "adapt" the strategies of subjective representation of the Hunter S. Thompson novel on which it is based.[3]

Furthermore, my observations on which elements of the gameplay of contemporary video games are meant to contribute to the representation of these games' storyworlds as well as my focus on the ludic functions of the video game-specific realization of strategies of narrative, narratorial, and subjective representation might also help explain why a film adaptation such as Simon West's *Lara Croft: Tomb Raider* opens with a sequence that self-reflexively represents Lara Croft (who is played by Angelina Jolie) doing things that appear very similar to what the video game version of her character does during the gameplay of the action-adventure series, only to successively mark the sequences as having merely represented a training simulation—or why a film adaptation such as Andrzej Bartkowiak's *Doom* struggles to captivate what makes *Doom 3* a compelling first-person shooter. In addition, the method of analysis developed in the previous chapters might also prove helpful in considering why, for example, Traveller's Tales' *Lego The Lord of the Rings* succeeds not only as an adaptation of Peter Jackson's *The Lord of the Rings* trilogy but also as the action-adventure that it primarily is, or why Rocksteady's *Batman: Arkham Asylum* manages to capture the "look and feel" of the current iteration of the franchise without being an actual adaptation of Christopher Nolan's *Batman* film trilogy (and, arguably, does so more convincingly than straightforward adaptations such as Eurocom's *Batman Begins*).

Indeed, the way in which *Batman: Arkham Asylum* relates not only to Nolan's *Batman Begins*, *The Dark Knight*, and *The Dark Knight Rises* but also to the larger *Batman* franchise might serve to emphasize that an examination of intermedial adaptations is not sufficient for coming to terms with the complex ways in which contemporary films, comics, and video games (as well as television series, literary texts, and even theatrical performances) transgress the notion of the "single work." While most transmedial entertainment franchises entail various forms of what may be described as "retellings" or, perhaps less restrictively, as adaptations, they are more saliently defined by the expansion and modification of initially *work-specific storyworlds* that are thus "compounded" into *transmedial storyworlds* and *transmedial universes*.[4] Take, for example, the video games in the particularly complex *Star Wars* franchise: it is clear that the (as of the time of this writing)[5] six feature films represent the "canonical core" of the *Star Wars* universe, yet there are not only games such as *Lego Star Wars* and *Lego Star Wars II: The Original Trilogy* that, despite their striking "lego-ization,"[6] primarily aim to "retell" the films' stories and, hence, can be described as adaptations (just like the *Lego The Lord of the Rings* game mentioned above), but also games such as those in the *Star Wars: Knights of the Old Republic* series that aim not at a "retelling" of the films' stories but, rather, at a logically consistent expansion of the storyworld that the latter are representing. This is not to say that there are no minor inconsistencies in both series, but most of the more recent *Star Wars* games—as opposed to the early *Star Wars* comics, for example—do not aim at a modification of the transmedial storyworld that is at the core of *Star Wars*' transmedial universe.

In order to provide some scope, let me briefly contrast this state of affairs with the dominant relation between the work-specific as well as transmedial storyworlds in the less encompassing comics-based franchise of *The Walking Dead*, which has recently received much attention: at first glance, AMC's television series may appear to be an adaptation of Robert Kirkman's comics series, and the first season of Telltale's adventure game series may, in turn, appear to be an adaptation of the television series, but the differences in the stories these series tell turn out to be quite striking and do, in fact, seem to make a description of the television series' work-specific storyworld as a modification of the comics series' work-specific storyworld appear more appropriate. In contrast, the adventure game series takes even more liberties—including a change in the main protagonist—but does so in a way that makes it appear as a largely consistent expansion of the comics series' work-specific storyworld rather than as either a "faithful" retelling or a comparatively less "faithful" modification. And, finally, Terminal Reality's first-person shooter *The Walking Dead: Survival Instinct* is intended to expand the work-specific storyworld of the television series rather than that of the comics series. While it would seem that a more detailed analysis of these kinds of transmedial storyworlds and transmedial universes could benefit from the method developed in the previous chapters in general and my transmedial conceptualization of storyworlds in particular, then, any narratologically informed approach to transmedial entertainment franchises would also have to tackle considerably more complex problems related, for example, to questions of collective authorship and fan participation during the making of transmedial meaning(s).

Incidentally, the necessity of examining questions of collective authorship and audience participation in the negotiation of meaning not only but particularly when analyzing transmedial entertainment franchises brings me back to the three more general areas of conceptual expansion that have already briefly been mentioned in the introduction. First, my detailed reconstruction of the basic principles that allow for narrative meaning making across media could serve as a foundation for attempts at a further *contextualization* of the method of analysis developed in the previous chapters. Starting from the striking observation that a large majority of both the authors having authored and the characters being represented in my main examples are "straight white males" (which appears to be typical of the mainstream of contemporary media culture), one could, for example, critically reconstruct the interrelation between "identity politics" and narrative production, representation, or comprehension—as well as, perhaps, develop accounts of narrative production, representation, and comprehension that try to make these hegemonial actors' Other(s) more visible.[7] Second, the obvious observation that transmedial strategies of narrative representation are, at least to a certain extent, historically variable makes the *historization* of the project of a transmedial narratology appear particularly desirable. The two examples that most readily come to mind are studies concerned with the historical development of narratorial representation across media or studies concerned with the historical development of subjective representation across media. However, it would appear just as promising to attempt to provide a historically oriented account of intermedial adaptations or transmedial entertainment franchises. Third, and finally, my thorough examination of the principles that govern narrative meaning making in contemporary films, comics, and video games may also have some practical relevance with regard to filmmaking, comics artistry, and video game design—or the production of intermedial adaptations and transmedial entertainment franchises, for that matter. Indeed, the method of analysis that this book has developed might, in turn, be enriched and further sophisticated by "best practice" studies that aim not only at analyzing but also at optimizing transmedial strategies of narrative representation.[8]

However, let me conclude by emphasizing once more that this wealth of opportunities for medial as well as conceptual expansion and areas of intermedial as well as transmedial application depends on the theoretical and methodological foundation that the previous chapters have developed. My comparatively narrow focus on particularly salient strategies of narrative representation that are used to represent storyworlds, strategies of narratorial representation that can be attributed to narrators, and strategies of subjective representation that provide "direct access" to characters' consciousnesses as well as on their realization within the specific mediality of contemporary films, comics, and video games was necessary to provide this theoretical and methodological foundation. With such a foundation arguably provided by the present study, though, I am very much looking forward to seeing which additional building blocks will be added to the project of a genuinely transmedial narratology in the hopefully not too distant future.

Notes

Introduction

1. See, for example, Gray, who remarks that "a common first line for books on contemporary media, and for many a student essay on the subject, notes the saturation of everyday life with media" (*Show* 1). Evidently, Gray's remark is nothing but a subtle way to note just that. But so is quoting Gray, of course. For accounts of the kind of technological, cultural, and socioeconomic dynamics at play here, see, e.g., Brookey; Deuze; Evans; Gardner, *Projections*; Jenkins, *Convergence Culture*; Jenkins, Ford, and Green; D. Johnson.
2. While adaptation studies has grown into a rather well-tended field of its own by now, its focus still largely appears to be on the intersection of literary criticism and film studies, with comics studies and game studies only just beginning to become interested in practices of intermedial adaptation. See, e.g., Corrigan; Hutcheon; McFarlane; as well as the contributions in Albrecht-Crane and Cutchins; MacCabe, K. Murray, and Warner; Naremore.
3. For further discussion of these franchises, see, e.g., Mikos et al.; or K. Thompson, *The Frodo Franchise*, on *The Lord of the Rings*; Klastrup and Tosca, "Game of Thrones," on *A Song of Ice and Fire*; Brooker, *Using the Force*, on *Star Wars*; Jenkins, *Convergence Culture*, on *The Matrix*; Harvey; or Hills, *Triumph*, on *Doctor Who*; Mittell, "Strategies"; or the contributions in Pearson on *Lost*; Brooker, *Batman*; *Hunting the Dark Knight*; or the contributions in Pearson and Uricchio on *Batman*; Jenkins, "*The Walking Dead*," on *The Walking Dead*; Deuber-Mankowsky on *Tomb Raider*; Thon, "Computer Games"; or the contributions in Corneliussen and Walker Rettberg on *Warcraft*.
4. For further discussion of these questions, see the early groundbreaking works by Jenkins, *Textual Poachers*; Kinder; Lévy; the studies of specific franchises mentioned above; as well as, e.g., Dena; Eder, "Transmediale Imagination"; Evans; Gray, *Show*; Hills, *Fan Cultures*; Jenkins, "Transmedia 202"; "Transmedia Storytelling"; Klastrup and Tosca,

"Transmedial Worlds"; Mittell, *Complex TV*; Parody; Ryan, "Story/Worlds/Media"; "Transmedial Storytelling"; Scolari; Thon, "Converging Worlds"; M. J. P. Wolf. See also the recent contributions in Boni; Kinder and McPherson; Pearson and A. N. Smith.

5. Barthes has famously claimed that "the narratives of the world are numberless" and that "narrative is international, transhistorical, transcultural" ("Introduction" 79). Indeed, the generalization that "narrative is everywhere" (B. Richardson, "Recent Concepts" 168) seems only slightly exaggerated, though it is a core concern of the present book to not leave it at that. Rather, it would seem that B. Richardson's general observation is in dire need of more specific analyses, allowing us to understand how different kinds of narrative representation can be realized across media.

6. It might be worth noting that many of these works have secured largely uncontested places in the canon of contemporary media culture and, unsurprisingly, have received quite a bit of academic attention during the past few decades. However, as the specific focus of the present book is comparatively unusual within media studies, and as the analyses presented in the following chapters are my own, I will refer to existing research on the films, comics, and video games that I have chosen as examples rather sparingly.

1. Toward a Transmedial Narratology

1. See, e.g., the more recent research surveys by Brooke-Rose; Fludernik, "Beyond Structuralism"; "Histories"; Fludernik and Margolin; D. Herman, "Histories"; "Introduction"; "Introduction: Narratologies"; Jahn and A. Nünning, "Briefings"; "Forum"; Meister, "Narratology"; A. Nünning, "Narratology"; "Surveying Contextualist and Cultural Narratologies"; A. Nünning and V. Nünning; Onega and García Landa; Prince, "Narratology"; "Surveying Narratology"; B. Richardson, "Recent Concepts"; Ryan and van Alphen. See also the emerging trend to publish companions, dictionaries, and/or handbooks of narratology, e.g., D. Herman, *The Cambridge Companion*; D. Herman, Jahn, and Ryan; L. Herman and Vervaeck, *Handbook*; Hühn et al.; Martínez, *Handbuch*; Phelan and Rabinowitz; Prince, *A Dictionary*; *A Dictionary*, rev. ed. Daniel Stein and I have recently made similar remarks in the context of a discussion of the state of comics narratology (see D. Stein and Thon, "Introduction").

2. See Barthes, "Introduction"; Bremond, "Le message"; Genette, "Frontières"; Greimas, "Eléments"; Todorov, "Les catégories." Here, as in the

following, I will provide my own English translations of French and German sources only where translated editions are not available. One way or another, I will not include the original texts of translated quotations or references to the original editions in the Works Cited (except for the rare cases where I refer to the English translations of films or comics that were originally released/published in other languages), so as to not unnecessarily inflate the page count.

3. According to Fludernik, "Histories," the term "classical narratology" was first used by Hoesterey. The terms "postclassical narratology" and "new narratologies" were introduced by D. Herman, "Introduction: Narratologies"; "Scripts."

4. See, e.g., Bernhart; Hühn, "Transgeneric Narratology"; Hühn and Schönert; Hühn and Sommer; McHale, "Beginning to Think"; "Narrative"; Müller-Zettelmann; Semino; as well as the contributions in Hühn and Kiefer; Schönert, Hühn, and M. Stein on poetry; Breger; Fludernik, "Narrative"; Hühn and Sommer; Jahn, "Narrative Voice"; Korthals; A. Nünning and Sommer, "Diegetic and Mimetic Narrativity"; "Drama"; Rajewsky, "Von Erzählern"; B. Richardson, "Drama"; "Voice"; Sommer, "Drama"; Weidle on drama and theatrical performances; Bal, *Reading Rembrandt*; Pochat; as well as the contributions in Bogen, Brassat, and Ganz; Kemp, *Der Betrachter*; *Der Text*, on painting; and W. Wolf, "Music"; as well as the contributions in Bernhart, Scher, and W. Wolf; Bernhart and W. Wolf on (instrumental) music. On the relation among the terms "(intra)mediality," "intermediality," and "transmediality," see, e.g., Rajewsky, "Border Talks"; Thon, "Mediality"; W. Wolf, "Intermediality"; as well as the brief discussion later in this chapter.

5. The distinction between "fabula" and "syuzhet" (see, e.g., Shklovsky), "histoire" and "discours" (see, e.g., Todorov, "Les catégories"), or "story" and "discourse" (see, e.g., Chatman, *Story*) remains one of the core distinctions of narratology to the present day, although the meaning attributed to the terms varies considerably (see, e.g., Martínez and Scheffel, *Einführung* 20–26). On the concepts related to the term "actant," see, e.g., Greimas, *Structural Semantics*; as well as the earlier account by Propp and the later by Bal, *Narratology* 195–208. On the concepts related to terms such as "event" and "eventfulness," see, e.g., Prince, *A Grammar*; as well as Hühn, "Event"; "Functions"; Meister, *Computing Action*; "The Temporality Effect"; Schmid, "Narrativity"; *Narratology* 8–21.

6. It should be noted, however, that Genette has not been consistent in his usage of this verbally biased definition of narrativity: in *Métalepse*, for

example, he treats feature films as narrative representations without voicing doubts about their narrativity.
7. As will become clear in the following, though, there may be good reasons for this kind of limitation and, one way or another, Chatman's groundbreaking work—which has done much to establish narratological perspectives in the United States, providing the foundations of a modern transmedial narratology in the process—remains influential within literary as well as film narratology.
8. This is not to say, however, that it exclusively belongs there, since Meister's three dominant paradigms should not be misconstrued as being mutually exclusive, when in fact the three approaches can be described as pursuing at least partially complementary goals.
9. The view that "throwing the conceptual baby out with the formalist bathwater" (A. Nünning, "Surveying Contextualist and Cultural Narratologies" 61) might be rather undesirable seems to have become consensus even among proponents of the more postclassical strands of contemporary narratology. See, e.g., Fludernik, *Towards a 'Natural' Narratology*; D. Herman, *Story Logic*; Lanser, *The Narrative Act*.
10. Interestingly, while there is much talk about methods and methodology within both classical and postclassical narratology, the two terms are seldom distinguished explicitly. In the context of this book, *method* will be understood as referring to a way of systematically engaging with the world (using narratological terms and concepts to analyze the narrative strategies employed by contemporary films, comics, and video games, for example), while *methodology* will be used to refer to discussions of the appropriateness of certain methods for certain tasks (when trying to decide whether we should generally postulate the presence of a narrator as distinct from the author in narrative representations across media, for example).
11. While laudable, the even stronger demand that "narrative theory must take sufficient account of those models and concepts for the description of narrative texts which have been developed since the nineteenth century in the fields of poetics, rhetoric and the professional analysis of literary texts" (Kindt and Müller, "Narrative Theory" 214) seems to go beyond the scope of the present book. See Kindt and Müller, *The Implied Author*, for an implementation of the principle with regard to the "implied author."
12. See, e.g., Bordwell, *Narration*; Branigan, *Narrative Comprehension*; *Point of View*; N. Carroll, *Engaging the Moving Image*; Currie, *Image*; Eder, *Die Figur*; Grodal, *Embodied Visions*; *Moving Pictures*; Ohler;

Persson; Plantinga, *Moving Viewers*; G. M. Smith, *Film Structure*; E. Tan; Wuss.

13. See, e.g., Bortolussi and Dixon; Emmott; Fludernik, *Towards a 'Natural' Narratology*; Gerrig; D. Herman, *Story Logic*; Zunshine, for studies of literary narrative in the context of cognitive psychology; as well as the works from cognitive film narratology mentioned above. Another area of cognitive theory that seems relevant is constituted by the theories of metaphor and embodied cognition that have been developed by scholars such as Fauconnier and Turner; M. Johnson, *The Body*; *The Meaning*; Lakoff, *Women*; Lakoff and M. Johnson, *Metaphors*; *Philosophy*; Marks, Hammeal, and Bornstein; Turner.

14. It might also be worth mentioning reader-response theory (*Rezeptionsästhetik*) as a second influential strand of reception theories that largely ignores actual reception processes. See, e.g., Fish; Iser, *The Implied Reader*; Jauss; and the contributions in Tompkins. While the terminology evidently differs, cognitively informed approaches and reader response-oriented approaches within media studies often come to partially similar conclusions. Compare, e.g., Fahlenbrach; Mikos on film and television; or Fahlenbrach and F. Schröter; Thon, "Immersion," on the immersive effects of video games.

15. See, e.g., Eco 7–11; Eder, *Die Figur* 80–106; Jannidis, *Figur* 28–33 on the notion of an ideal or model recipient. In fact, cognitive theories of character such as those developed in Eder, *Die Figur*, or Jannidis, *Figur*, provide a good example of how cognitive reception theories may help in getting a clearer picture of narrative phenomena. See also D. Herman's distinction between "'etic' and 'emic' approaches to narrative study" (*Basic Elements* 3).

16. See, e.g., Davidson; J. B. Singer et al. For the related discussion of "mediatization" within communication studies, see, e.g., Hepp; Hjarvard; Krotz; and the contributions in Hepp and Krotz; Lundby. See also Jenkins, *Convergence Culture*; Sigismondi on "media convergence."

17. However, see also Thon, "Narratives," for a more detailed discussion of the interplay among medium-specific, intermedial, and transmedial perspectives within a "media-conscious" narratology. The notion of a media-conscious narratology was initially developed in Ryan and Thon.

18. Among W. Wolf's earlier work on the concept of intermediality, *The Musicalization* is particularly noteworthy. See also the contributions in Helbig, *Intermedialität*; Paech; Paech and J. Schröter for a sample of alternative approaches to intermediality that more clearly originate in the field of media studies.

19. It should be noted, however, that while the term "transmediality" is primarily used to refer to representational strategies that can be observed across media, both Rajewsky and W. Wolf also explicitly refer to transmedial "content phenomena" such as "motifs" or "default situations."

20. W. Wolf's notion that a concept referring to phenomena *between* conventionally distinct media should somehow entail a concept referring to phenomena *beyond* (or above) them might even be considered a symptom of the fact that there is an impressive body of research on intermediality but that the term "transmediality" is used decidedly less often. Unfortunately, this does not mean that the use of the latter term is free of major contradictions. See, e.g., the alternative definitions by U. Meyer; as well as the contributions in U. Meyer, Simanowski, and Zeller or Gernalzick and Pisarz-Ramírez.

21. If any medium-specific narratology "beyond the literary text" can be said to rival literary narratology's level of institutionalization within literary studies, it will doubtless be film narratology, which has been increasingly institutionalized within film studies (as well as film philosophy) since the 1980s. For a selection of influential book-length studies, some of which also discuss literary narrative texts and not all of which may be happily characterized as focusing primarily on narratological issues, see, e.g., Bordwell, *Narration*; *The Way*; Branigan, *Narrative Comprehension*; *Point of View*; Buckland, *The Cognitive Semiotics*; Chatman, *Coming to Terms*; *Story*; Currie, *Image*; *The Nature*; Eder, *Die Figur*; Gaudreault, *From Plato*; Gaudreault and Jost, *Le récit*; Grodal, *Embodied Visions*; *Moving Pictures*; Hurst; Jost, *L'oeil-caméra*; Kawin; Kozloff; Kuhn; Lothe; Metz, *L'énonciation*; *Film Language*; *Language and Cinema*; Persson; Schlickers, *Verfilmtes Erzählen*; G. M. Smith, *Film Structure*; M. Smith, *Engaging Characters*; E. Tan; K. Thompson, *Breaking the Glass Armor*; *Storytelling*; G. Wilson, *Narration*; Wulff.

22. While film narratology was established in the 1980s within film studies, one cannot yet speak of a comics narratology to the same extent. As D. Stein and I have reconstructed in more detail (see D. Stein and Thon, "Introduction"), there is an increasing interest in narratological approaches within the broader field of comics studies, and a number of scholars such as Kukkonen ("Comics"; "Space") or Mikkonen ("Graphic Narratives"; "Subjectivity") follow D. Herman (*Basic Elements*; "Word-Image") in considering graphic narrative to provide an important "test case" for a transmedial narratology. Perhaps even more importantly, the past decade has seen a significant rise in studies concerned with the medium-specific strategies of narrative representation that comics

employ, focusing not only on fairly basic features of their mediality such as the combination of words and ("drawn") pictures, the interplay of panels and panel borders, and the arrangement of sequences of panels in various forms of page layouts but also on the medium-specific realization of salient narrative phenomena and/or narratological concepts referred to by terms such as "storyworld," "narrator," and "focalization." See, e.g., L. L. Abbott; Carrier; Groensteen, *Comics*; *The System*; Hatfield; Horstkotte and Pedri; Lefèvre; Packard; Peeters; Postema; H. J. Pratt; Round; Schüwer; and the contributions in Gardner and D. Herman, *Graphic Narratives*; D. Stein and Thon, *From Comic Strips*. See also the considerably earlier attempts within German *Erzählforschung* to come to (narratological) terms with comics by, e.g., Brednich; Hünig; Schnackertz. Moreover, there has been an increased narratological interest in various kinds of generic, cultural, and historical specificities of graphic narrative that the present study can do nothing but point out (see, e.g., Aldama; Nama; Schmitz-Emans). Although Gardner and D. Herman's belief that "of all the alliances forged with related fields in recent years, the most profitable for comics studies will be that with narrative theory" ("Graphic Narratives" 6) may still seem somewhat overenthusiastic, since "anyone trying to map the burgeoning field of comics studies will quickly realize that there is no dearth of theories and methods on which scholars may draw" (D. Stein and Thon, "Introduction" 2), the development of a dedicated comics narratology or "graphic narrative theory" is certainly well on its way.

23. Even though there now is a broad consensus that it was less about the question whether (or to what extent, or in what way) video games are (or can be, or should be) narrative than it was about establishing an "independent academic structure" (Aarseth, "Computer Game Studies" n. pag.), narratological approaches within game studies still seem obliged to mention the so-called ludology vs. narratology debate as something of a "founding myth" of the field. So am I. Fortunately, this "founding myth" is well documented, so that I will keep the reconstruction comparatively brief. For a rough impression of the polemical tone that dominated much of the debate, see, e.g., Eskelinen, "Towards Computer Game Studies," and Jenkins, "Game Design." See also Aarseth, "Computer Game Studies"; Frasca, "Ludologists"; "Simulation"; J. H. Murray, *Hamlet*; Neitzel, "Narrativity"; as well as the surveys by Ryan, *Avatars* 181–203; Thon, "Game Studies." As early as 1999, Gonzalo Frasca proposed to use the (already existing) term "*ludology* (from *ludus*, the Latin word for 'game'), to refer to the yet non-existent

'discipline that studies game and play activities'" ("Ludology" n. pag., original emphases), and while Frasca explicitly intended "not to replace the narratologic [sic!] approach, but to complement it" ("Ludology" n. pag.), not all of the self-identified "ludologists" shared his position. Commenting on the supposed inappropriateness of looking for narrative elements in video games, Markku Eskelinen remarked that "luckily, outside theory, people are usually excellent at distinguishing between narrative situations and gaming situations: if I throw a ball at you, I don't expect you to drop it and wait until it starts telling stories" ("Towards Computer Game Studies" 36). While obviously inappropriate with regard to both form and content, Eskelinen's simile is an especially (in)famous example of the "vehement and often polemic body of criticism . . . directed at studies that see the computer game as one possible form of future storytelling, or simply treat the computer game as a narrative medium at all" (Neitzel, "Narrativity" 227). By now, the debate seems to be largely passé, with key "ludologists" such as Aarseth ("A Narrative Theory"), Juul (*Half-Real*), and even Eskelinen (*Cybertext Poetics*) acknowledging that (some) video games may be narrative (in some way), and that examining this aspect of the medium may actually turn out to be fruitful, after all. Moreover, there is also a slow but steady increase in explicitly narratological studies dedicated more or less exclusively to video games' narrativity. See, e.g., the book-length studies by Backe; Domsch; Engelns; Neitzel, "Gespielte Geschichten"; as well as Thon, "Immersion"; "Perspective"; "Unendliche Weiten?," for a selection of my own work in this area, on which much of the discussion of video games' narrativity in the following chapters draws. See also, once more, the survey in Thon, "Game Studies."

24. As W. Wolf has remarked, "interdisciplinarity presupposes multidisciplinary competence, and this requirement imposes obvious limits on each scholar" ("Metalepsis" 105; see also W. Wolf, "Narratology," on the transmedial expansion of narratology).

25. For further discussion of "quality television," see, e.g., Swanson; and the contributions in Jancovich and Lyons; McCabe and Akass; Spigel and Olsson. More importantly, if only partially related, see Mittell, "Narrative Complexity," for an influential discussion of narrative complexity in contemporary television series. On the latter, see also Mittell, *Complex TV*; and the contributions in Allrath and Gymnich; Blanchet et al.; Hammond and Mazdon. On the related question to what extent recent technological innovations in the context of media convergence have changed television as a medium, see, e.g., Evans; Gillan; Lotz.

26. While my decision against focusing on literary texts primarily has to do with the fact that much of contemporary narratology still exhibits a "literature bias" and my decision against discussing theatrical performance is based on their comparatively low "impact" in current popular culture, my decision to not examine the increasingly complex series that can be found in contemporary television was primarily motivated by pragmatic considerations: since film narratology is already highly institutionalized and much of the (supposedly) film-specific strategies of narrative representation that I will discuss are also employed in television series, focusing on television series instead of films would have unnecessarily complicated my argument. However, see Mittell, *Complex TV*, for some brief introductory remarks on the relation between film and television series with regard to transmedial narratological analysis.
27. For a selection of recent approaches to the concept of medium, see, e.g., Bolter and Grusin; Luhmann, *The Reality*; Manovich; Mock; J. H. Murray, *Inventing the Medium*; Ryan, *Avatars*; Sachs-Hombach; Schmidt, *Kalte Faszination*; Vogel; as well as the contributions in Münker and Roesler. See also the survey in Thon, "Mediality," on which much of the following builds.
28. As Mock demonstrates in his concise explication of the concept in the context of media and communication studies, the term "medium" is usually understood as referring to means of communication, which can, however, be conceptualized rather differently. According to Mock, the three most influential strands of such conceptualizations are media as "means of perception," media as "means of understanding," and media as "means of distribution" (focusing on physical or, perhaps, material aspects, semiotic aspects, and technical aspects of the various media, respectively).
29. It should be noted, however, that neither Rajewsky nor I argue in favor of a "radical anti-essentialism" that would insist that "media do not exist" because they cannot easily be defined using necessary and sufficient conditions and, moreover, do not remain transhistorically and transculturally stable.
30. See also Vogel's impressive attempt at a "theory of rationality" that takes the form of a theory of media, in which he distinguishes between "media elements" (162), "medial constellations" (164), and the "scope of possibilities of a medium" (165), emphasizing that the possible—or *permissible*—number of combinations of "media elements" into "medial constellations" that a given medium provides is often approaching infinity.

31. See also Mock, who—following Holly—identifies a fourth basic conceptualization of media as "forms of communication" (in contradistinction to "means of perception," "means of understanding," and "means of distribution"). It should be noted, though, that I use the term "media form" in a more specific way than Mock, since I am referring to conventionalized forms *within* a medium, while Mock describes "forms of communication" such as letters, telephone, email, newspaper, radio, or television *as media* in the context of institutional media theories.

32. Not unlike the concepts of medium and narrative, the concept of genre has been both highly influential and notoriously contested. The term originates in literary studies (see, e.g., Frye; Hernadi; Todorov, *The Fantastic*), but it was made popular within film studies, particularly with regard to what Bordwell, Staiger, and K. Thompson describe as classical Hollywood cinema (see also the standard works on Hollywood genres by Rick Altman; Neale; Schatz). By now, however, the concept of genre has become similarly well established in television studies, comics studies, and game studies (see, e.g., Feuer; Mittell, *Genre*, on television genres; Duncan and M. J. Smith 196–245; Gravett on comics genres; Egenfeldt-Nielsen, J. H. Smith, and Tosca 45–96; Rauscher on video game genres). Not unlike the notion of medium specificity (or mediality), the notion of genre specificity is confronted with the problematic relation between universalist and particularist poetics, which can, once more, be adequately addressed by understanding genre as a prototypical concept.

33. Even if one subscribes to a comparatively broad conceptualization of narrativity that primarily entails the representation of storyworlds (as worlds situated in time and space that are prototypically populated with characters of some kind), quite a few video game genres such as the abstract puzzle game or simple casual games cannot happily be characterized as narrative or can only be characterized as narrative in a most rudimentary way. However, there are some genres, such as the real-time strategy game, the first-person shooter, the (action-)adventure game, and the role-playing game, whose singleplayer modes have traditionally been organized around stories and whose narrative complexity has increased significantly over the past decade or so. More generally, the 2000s and 2010s have not only seen the rise of massively multiplayer online role-playing games and other forms of primarily "social" games as well as an increasing hybridization of the genres and genre conventions that were established during the 1990s but also generated a tendency toward narrative complexity, metareferentiality, and a

generally higher sophistication of the narrative strategies employed by the genres defining the media form of narrative video games. While the question of video games' narrativity has been the subject of much debate during the early formative stage of the interdisciplinary field of game studies, most if not all video game theorists will by now agree that the singleplayer modes of at least some contemporary video games are narrative in some way. (Incidentally, the question whether one should speak of "video games," "computer games," or "digital games" seems comparatively uninteresting, as despite their somewhat different connotations, all three terms now tend to be used largely interchangeably in the interdisciplinary field of game studies.)

34. See also the distinction between "medium-free concepts," "transmedially valid concepts," and "medium-specific concepts" discussed in Ryan and Thon.
35. See, e.g., H. P. Abbott, "Narrativity," and the contributions in Pier and García Landa as well as the distinction between "being a narrative" and "having narrativity" in Ryan, *Avatars* 11; "Introduction" 9; "On the Theoretical Foundations" 6. See also the discussion of digital media's narrativity in Thon, "Narrativity," on which much of the following builds.
36. See, e.g., Prince, *Narratology* 4; as well as Hühn, "Event," or Schmid, "Narrativity"; see also Dannenberg; Kafalenos; B. Richardson, *Unlikely Stories*, on the condition of causality.
37. See, e.g., Genette, *Narrative Discourse Revisited*; as well as Chatman, *Story*, or Prince, *Narratology*; see also the discussion of the "speech-act approach to narrative" in Ryan, *Avatars* 4–6, and the discussion of narrators in the second part of this book.
38. Convenient in the sense that it corresponds to the range of narrative media covered in the present study, which, as has already been mentioned, is not the result of an arbitrary decision but is, instead, based on their sociocultural relevance and economic success in the media landscape of the past three decades.
39. See W. Wolf, "'Cross the Border'" 86, who refers to Fludernik, *Towards a 'Natural' Narratology* 315, as having originally coined the term. See also Culler, *Structuralist Poetics* 153–157, on the more general process of "naturalization."
40. My choice of examples is also at least partially based on the observation that narrative complexity has become increasingly commercially successful within contemporary media culture. This is particularly well established with regard to film (with the rise of the "mind-bender" since

roughly the mid-1990s leading to a steady number of commercially successful films that deviate from the chronological and causal linearity characteristic for what is known as classical Hollywood cinema) and television (where the sheer amount of available screen time allows for highly complex plot developments), but it also applies to comics (where narratively complex graphic novels have begun entering the mainstream since the late 1980s) and video games (which have begun to tell ever more complex stories since around the mid-2000s). See, e.g., Bordwell, *The Way*; Buckland, "Introduction"; Eig; Elsaesser; S. Johnson; Thon, "Mind-Bender," on narratively complex films. See also, e.g., Mittell, "Narrative Complexity," on narrative complexity in contemporary (American) television series.

41. It might be worth noting, however, that while it could be argued that allowing recipients to intersubjectively construct a storyworld is *the* most salient prototypical function of narrative representations, both the use of strategies of narratorial representation and the use of strategies of subjective representation should be conceived as being more optional (though both of these strategies can still be found not only in films, comics, and video games but also in literary texts, theatrical performances, and television series). Moreover, there is quite a bit of historical variation with regard to the use of narrators and the representation of characters' consciousnesses, the more detailed reconstruction of which would doubtless be a fascinating endeavor—albeit one which will have to be postponed to a potential follow-up study.

2. The Storyworld as a Transmedial Concept

1. "The term 'character' is used to refer to participants in storyworlds created by various media" (Jannidis, "Character" 14). While I will not discuss characters in too much detail, they are evidently salient elements of most if not all narrative representations (or, rather, the storyworlds that these representations represent). Accordingly, theories that have been developed to describe the forms, functions, and ontological status of characters tend to be relevant for a transmedial conceptualization of storyworlds as well. See, e.g., Eder, *Die Figur*; Eder, Jannidis, and R. Schneider, "Characters"; Eder and Thon; Jannidis, *Figur*; Klevjer, "What Is the Avatar?"; Margolin, "Characters"; "Individuals"; "The What"; R. Schneider; F. Schröter and Thon, "Simulierte Spielfiguren"; "Video Game Characters"; and the contributions in Eder, Jannidis, and R. Schneider, *Characters*; Leschke and Heidbrink for various accounts of characters across media; as well as

the remarks on the ontological status and the "inventory" of storyworlds below.

2. For a more detailed discussion of the relation between various terms and concepts within this terminological field, see, e.g., Dannenberg 19–132; L. Herman and Vervaeck, *Handbook* 41–102; Martínez and Scheffel, *Einführung* 20–26; Meister, *Computing Action* 3–27; Ronen, "Paradigm Shifts"; Schmid, *Narratology* 175–190. See also the particularly influential classical accounts of narrative order put forth by, e.g., Bal, *Narratology* 80–99; Chatman, *Story* 62–79; Genette, *Narrative Discourse* 33–85; *Narrative Discourse Revisited* 21–32; Rimmon-Kenan, *Narrative Fiction* 42–58; Schmid, *Narratology* 190–215; Sternberg, *Expositional Modes*. It may be worth noting at this point that while I would argue that phenomena such as *analepsis* (or "flashback") and *prolepsis* (or "flash-forward")—as well as various other strategies of reordering the chronology of the story(world) on the level of plot—are genuinely transmedial, I will not give them too much attention, as their transmediality is fairly evident and largely uncontested. See, for example, Jannidis, who emphasizes that "analepsis ultimately depends on a structural prerequisite which is practically the smallest common denominator of all narration: the sequentiality of the representation. Effects such as analepsis and prolepsis are created when the represented order deviates from the underlying order of the actions. The number of such basic phenomena is considerably limited because in most cases ... additional, medium-specific factors come into play" ("Narratology" 38). However, where I use the above terms in order to accessibly describe forms of temporal reordering (or "anachronies"), I will roughly follow Genette, who defines "as *prolepsis* any narrative maneuver that consists of narrating or evoking in advance an event that will take place later, ... as *analepsis* any evocation after the fact of an event that took place earlier than the point in the story where we are at any given moment" (Genette, *Narrative Discourse* 40, original emphases).

3. Incidentally, Schmid himself briefly mentions "characters in a storyworld" (*Narratology* 14), but this should certainly not be mistaken as a theoretical commitment to the concept. Like so much else in both classical and postclassical narratology, the details of the distinction between story and storyworld remain a matter of considerable debate, but there seems to be a solid consensus that recipients usually infer quite a lot about events and existents that cannot happily be considered to be part of a given narrative representation's story anymore. See the brief discussion of Ryan's principle of minimal departure and Walton's

"principles of generation" as well as D. Herman's take on storyworlds as global mental representations below.
4. D. Herman, on the one hand, has developed the concept of storyworld in a number of publications, of which *Story Logic* and *Basic Elements of Narrative* are the most important. Ryan, on the other hand, has only recently started using the term "storyworld" (see Ryan, "Story/Worlds/Media") but has published widely on narratively represented fictional worlds (see, e.g., Ryan, *Avatars*; *Narrative*; *Possible Worlds*; as well as the brief discussion of Ryan's approach to fictional worlds within the framework of possible worlds theory below).
5. Of course, the distinction between *explicit* and *implicit representation* is far from unproblematic: as, for example, Currie remarks, contrasting "the explicit content of a narrative with its implicit or inferred content . . . suggests a division between content that is unambiguous—written into the text, visible on the stage or screen, etc.—and content which is a matter of interpretation. In fact, it is all a matter of interpretation [or, rather, comprehension]" (*Narratives* 12–13). In one way or another, though, it seems widely accepted that storyworlds entail a larger amount of "represented facts" than the stories that are located within them.
6. Genette here explicitly refers to the proto-narratological concept of *diégèse* developed around 1950 by Anna and Etienne Souriau as part of what they called "filmology," referring to "everything which happens according to the filmic representation and everything that is part of the reality which the film presupposes as part of its meaning" (Souriau 237, my translation from the French). While its explanatory power may appear limited when compared to more recent notions of represented worlds, this early concept of a represented world in film has not only inspired Genette's thinking on the matter but also exerted some influence in French film theory and experienced a bit of a renaissance in recent German film studies. See, e.g., Metz, "A Profile"; Gaudreault, "Mimèsis"; as well as Fuxjäger; Kessler.
7. See Genette, *Narrative Discourse* 227–243; *Narrative Discourse Revisited* 84–95. As usual, Genette's terms remain immensely influential, even though the lack of a clear distinction between "narrative" and "diegetic levels" can lead to a number of problems. See also Bal, *Narratology* 43–75; "Notes"; Rimmon-Kenan, *Narrative Fiction* 87–106; Schmid, *Narratology* 34–88, for terminological alternatives; as well as the further discussion of "diegetic levels" below.
8. See, e.g., Iser, *The Act of Reading*; *The Implied Reader*; "Indeterminacy"; Sperber and D. Wilson. Most of the theories of (narrative)

representation or comprehension discussed in the following emphasize the role of inference in meaning making. See also Grice for an earlier canonical work on pragmatic inferences as well as Currie, *Narratives* 12–21, for a more recent, concise, and at least broadly narratological discussion, to which I will briefly return below.

9. In *Narrative as Virtual Reality*, Ryan has developed her understanding of "fictional recentering" as a form of immersion in considerably more detail, and the concept of immersion has turned out to be particularly influential in game studies. See already J. H. Murray, *Hamlet*; as well as Calleja; Ermi and Mäyrä; McMahan; Neitzel, "Medienrezeption"; Thon, "Immersion"; see also Grau on immersion while appreciating art; as well as Schweinitz, "Totale Immersion," on immersion during film viewing. Moreover, see below for a brief discussion of Gerrig's use of the metaphor of "being transported" (to which Ryan explicitly refers) and the narratological take on "deictic shift theory" developed in D. Herman, *Basic Elements*; *Story Logic*.

10. While Doležel only hints at the transmedial applicability of the concept of fictional worlds by way of emphasizing the semiotic mode of their representation (i.e., verbal representation in the case of literary narrative texts), Ryan more explicitly proposes "to explore fictionality and narrativity as distinct properties, and to address both issues from an interdisciplinary perspective—a perspective which may be called semiotic, since [her] approach is largely formalist, and [her] concern is signification in all kinds of texts, not just in literary ones" (*Possible Worlds* 2–3). Even though Ryan still discusses nonliterary representations only very briefly in *Possible Worlds, Artificial Intelligence, and Narrative Theory*, she has later focused on the representation of fictional worlds and/or storyworlds in a variety of conventionally distinct media "beyond the literary text." See, e.g., Ryan, *Avatars*; *Narrative*; "Story/Worlds/Media."

11. Walton's theory of make-believe has not only been very influential within the theory of fiction (see, e.g., Currie, *The Nature*; Lamarque and Olsen; Ryan, *Possible Worlds*) but has also been applied to media not discussed by Walton (see the various contributions in Bareis and Nordrum; as well as, e.g., Tavinor; Thon, "Computer Games"; Walker Rettberg on make-believe and video games).

12. Despite endorsing neither the notion of fictional world nor the framework of possible worlds theory, then, Walton still appears to be less skeptical in this regard than certain other philosophers from the analytic tradition. Currie, for example, emphasizes that "fictional

worlds, if there are any, cannot be assimilated to possible worlds" (*The Nature* 54), which, among other things, leads him to conclude that "the appeal to fictional worlds seems merely to inflate our ontology without producing growth or understanding" (*The Nature* 56).

13. While Ryan developed her principle of minimal departure considerably earlier than *Possible Worlds, Artificial Intelligence, and Narrative Theory* was published (see Ryan, "Fiction"), Walton is certainly right in noting that the "reality principle," which describes the "strategy . . . of making fictional worlds as much like the real one as the core of primary fictional truths permits" (144–145), and the "mutual belief principle," which refers to "the real world not as it actually is but as it is or was mutually believed to be in the artist's society" (152), both "have been proposed (in various formulations) and discussed fairly extensively, especially in connection with literary representations" (144). See, e.g., Lewis; Rabinowitz; Wolterstorff. Still, Ryan's and Walton's takes on the issue appear most influential within a narratological context.

14. See also Johnson-Laird on mental models as well as, e.g., Hogan, *Cognitive Science,* on situation models. Gerrig prefers "the term *situation model* because . . . the term *mental model* is used ambiguously in the psychological literature" (6, original emphases), but both terms are commonly used interchangeably. See also van Dijk and Kintsch as well as, e.g., Werth on discourse models.

15. This includes connecting Ryan's notion of "fictional recentering" and Gerrig's metaphor of "being transported" with Segal's account of "deictic shift theory," Emmott's concept of "contextual frames," and Werth's "text world theory." Werth in particular is concerned with how "we build up mental constructs called *text worlds* . . . as conceptual scenarios containing just enough information to make sense of the particular utterance they correspond to" (7, original emphasis). In fact, there are quite a few similarities between Werth's discussion of sub-worlds and Ryan's examination of the "modal structure" of storyworlds, but—due to Werth's emphasis on verbal representation—I will refrain from discussing "text world theory" in any detail.

16. The distinction between *local* and *global mental representations* is well established within cognitive theory. Basically, it aims at what van Dijk calls "microstructures" and "macrostructures." As van Dijk notes in the foreword to *Macrostructures,* "in cognitive psychology and artificial intelligence, it has appeared that processing of discourse and interaction . . . cannot properly be accounted for without the global organization of complex information. . . . These various global structures

are accounted for in terms of *macrostructures*. Macrostructures are higher-level semantic or conceptual structures that organize the 'local' microstructures of discourse, interaction, and their cognitive processing" (v, original emphasis).

17. See, for example, Walton's work on "principles of generation," in the course of which he sets out to ask whether there is "a relatively simple and systematic way of understanding how fictional truths are generated, a limited number of very general principles that implicitly govern the practice of artists and critics" (139), and concludes that "for purposes of divining fictional truths there is no substitute for a good nose: a combination of imagination and common sense, leavened within limits by charity and informed by familiarity with the medium, genre, and representational tradition to which the work in question belongs as well as by knowledge of the outside world—all of this combined, of course, with sensitivity to the most subtle features of the work itself" (184). Despite a large amount of (medium- as well as genre-specific) variation, though, there may still be a number of general principles governing narrative representation—with some version of Ryan's principle of minimal departure and Walton's principle of charity (which is discussed in slightly more detail below) evidently being strong candidates, albeit perhaps not the only ones.

18. While my own approach is, perhaps, best located within a post-Genettean "discourse-oriented" narratology primarily interested in *how* narrative representations represent storyworlds, some of the approaches to storyworlds mentioned above focus more intensely on the question of *what* narrative representations represent. In *Heterocosmica*, for example, Doležel provides an in-depth discussion of different types of fictional worlds as well as a fairly complex taxonomy that allows for a meticulous description of their "inventory," in the context of which he also offers a rather influential discussion of the "modal constraints" governing the internal structure of these worlds. Ryan has, likewise, developed detailed taxonomies of the "inventory" of fictional worlds and, more recently, storyworlds (see Ryan, "Story/Worlds/Media"). While I will not attempt to develop a typology of storyworlds and will also not discuss their "inventory" in any detail, my examination of the transmedial concept of storyworld certainly aims to remain compatible with approaches such as those developed by Doležel and Ryan—even more so, since both of them also provide extensive discussion of questions that are closer to the present study's focus.

19. While I have not discussed this in much detail in the previous survey, there is comparatively little controversy within (neo)structuralist narratology that what is represented by a narrative representation generally consists of existents, events, and characters. See, e.g., Bal, *Narratology* 175–227; Chatman, *Story* 43–145; Rimmon-Kenan, *Narrative Fiction* 6–42. Contemporary narratology's approaches to the analysis of narratively represented objects and spaces, events and "eventfulness," or characters and their actions have become more sophisticated than those developed by the early structuralists, but a strong focus on space, time, and causality remains. See, e.g., Dennerlein; D. Herman, *Story Logic* 263–299; Ryan, "Space," for more extensive discussions of "narrative space"; Hühn, "Event"; Meister, *Computing Action*; Schmid, "Narrativity," for influential conceptualizations of events and "eventfulness"; and, once more, the various accounts of the representation and narrative functions of characters across media mentioned above. On temporality and causality, see also Ricoeur.

20. As I have already stated, storyworlds are commonly conceptualized as a complex kind of mental representation usually described as either a mental model or a situation model within cognitive narratology. See, e.g., Gerrig; D. Herman, *Basic Elements*; *Story Logic*; Hogan, *Cognitive Science*; as well as the foundational works by Johnson-Laird; Garnham; van Dijk and Kintsch. Johnson-Laird, for example, "argue[s] that there are at least three major kinds of representation—mental models, propositional representations, and images," with the latter being "treated as a special class of models" (146), since both the former and the latter are "analogous to the structure of the corresponding state of affairs in the world—as we perceive or conceive it" (156). While it is true that "the term *mental model* is used ambiguously in the psychological literature" (Gerrig 6, original emphasis, referring to Garnham), in the context of cognitive narratology both terms are usually understood broadly as referring to "mental representations of the people, objects, locations, events, and actions described in a text" (Zwaan 15) or other kind of narrative representation. At least if we define a *situation* roughly as "a particular kind of state of affairs, in which the place and time are held constant" (Werth 68), though, it is arguably more helpful to conceive of *situation models* as a specific kind of *mental models*—i.e., as comparatively simple local mental representations of narratively represented situations that are combined into a usually more complex global mental model of the storyworld as a whole. However, as I argue below, these mental representations of narratively represented situations

and/or storyworlds should not be conflated with the narratively represented situations and/or storyworlds themselves.
21. A significant part of understanding a storyworld consists in constructing the causal relations between the represented events—and "even the construction of causal connections between basic events can turn out to be dependent on specific pieces of contextual knowledge" (Meister, *Computing Action* 24), thereby necessitating rather complex processes of inference. In his analysis of the representation of events and action in literary texts, Meister also discusses different kinds of motivation and causality as well as the relation between "the model of *causa finalis* and the model of *causa efficiens*, that is, between the principles of finality and causality" (*Computing Action* 126, original emphases) in considerably more detail. For additional narratological discussion of causality, see also Dannenberg; Doležel, *Heterocosmica*; Kafalenos; Pier, "After This"; B. Richardson, *Unlikely Stories*.
22. Emphasizing that "diegetic levels" are not "narrative levels" is important, since not all "kind[s] of recollection that a character has (in a dream or not)" (Genette, *Narrative Discourse* 231) are narrative representations as they are conceptualized in the present study.
23. Elsewhere, I have proposed to use the distinction between first-order, second-order, and third-order storyworlds in combination with an unmodified version of Genette's terminology (see Thon, "Toward a Transmedial Narratology"; "Who's Telling the Tale?"), but the implications this entails regarding "higher-order" storyworlds as being "further down the rabbit hole" of embedded "diegetic levels" seem increasingly awkward to me. On the one hand, the terminology here is simply inconsistent with Bal's and Rimmon-Kenan's argument that we should call a secondary subworld "hypodiegetic" instead of "metadiegetic." On the other hand, when I speak of "higher-order" or "lower-order" subworlds, I refer to their position within the "diegetic hierarchy" of the global storyworld as a whole. Accordingly, I would like to be able to describe a primary diegetic storyworld as being "higher-order" than a secondary hypodiegetic storyworld, even though this may be different from how the "higher-order"/"lower-order" distinction is commonly employed in mathematical logic (see, e.g., Enderton) or neuroscience (see, e.g., Edelman).
24. The term "representation" can refer to *internal* mental representation as well as to *external* medial representation. For influential works on external medial representation see, e.g., the discussion of the classical accounts by Ferdinand de Saussure in Culler, *Ferdinand de Saussure*, or

of Charles S. Peirce in Atkin; as well as the transmedial accounts of external representation from analytic philosophy by Goodman, *Languages*; Walton. Since the present book is mainly concerned with fictional narrative representations, the term "representation" will evidently not be limited to representations of the actual world or social reality (see, e.g., Hall; Mitchell). Likewise, I am obviously not concerned with political representation (see, e.g., Birch). Moreover, as important as internal mental representations that recipients form on the basis of external medial representations are for an understanding of the meaning-making processes that play a role in how storyworlds are constructed, I will use the term "narrative representation" exclusively to refer to the external medial representation of storyworlds. This is not to say that I disagree with scholars who have suggested that the way we organize our experiences is inherently narrative (see, e.g., Bruner), but I would still insist that the differences between this kind of internal narrative representation and external narrative representations justify a terminological distinction.

25. However, Walsh also acknowledges that the concept of fictional narrative representation is a part of the more general concept of narrative representation, and that the comprehension of narrative representation is at least partially to be conceived as "panfictional" when he argues that "relevant information, in fiction, is supplied by assumptions with the capacity to inform a cognitive environment that includes the assumption of fictionality itself, as well as a set of general assumptions that might be collectively labelled 'narrative understanding' . . . , and more specific assumptions relating to, for instance, generic expectations of the text in hand and the particulars of its subject matter" (*The Rhetoric* 31).

26. While Grice as well as Sperber and D. Wilson are primarily concerned with verbal communication, both Walsh—who, perhaps overly confident, claims that "it goes without saying that relevance theory's inclusive model of communication as ostensive behaviour provides a way to embrace fictions in nonlinguistic media without difficulties" (*The Rhetoric* 32)—and Currie maintain that a pragmatic theory of meaning that focuses on "reflexive intentions" and pragmatic inferences can be applied to narrative representation across media.

27. Wimsatt and Beardsley's "intentional fallacy" is commonly invoked in methodological discussions concerned with intentionalist interpretations of literary texts, in particular. While such an invocation does not necessarily suggest a firm grasp on the intricacies of the debate

surrounding various forms of intentionalist theories of literary interpretation, it might still be worth stressing that the kind of "hypothetical intentionalism" pursued in the present study can be considered comparatively uncontroversial. See also the more detailed discussion of "hypothetical intentionalism" in chapter 4.

28. See Eder, *Die Figur* 61–130; *Was sind Figuren?* 8–55, who draws on cognitive reception theories mainly developed within film studies and philosophical theories that understand fictional objects as abstract entities. Considering that Eder also proposes to locate characters in the "third world" of Popper's "three world theory," it might be worth stressing, once more, that I do not conceptualize storyworlds as existing independently of actual meaning-making processes. Popper distinguishes between "first, the world of physical objects or of physical states; secondly, the world of states of consciousness, or of mental states, or perhaps of behavioural dispositions to act; and thirdly, the world of *objective contents of thought*, especially of scientific and poetic thoughts and of works of art" (106, original emphasis). I certainly agree with Popper (and Eder) that the "content" of narrative works cannot be exclusively located in the "second world" of mental representations, but when Popper discusses "the (more or less) *independent existence of the third world*" (107, original emphasis), it is important to emphasize that there is no complete "independence" to be observed in these cases—at least not as far as my conceptualization of storyworlds and the characters located in them is concerned. Put simply, storyworlds are what recipients *should* imagine based on narrative representations, but they do not exist independently of these imaginations, and recipients are, of course, quite free to imagine something entirely different.

29. As will be discussed in slightly more detail below, I do not limit the concept of storyworld to fictional narrative representations. Accordingly, I would also allow for *non*fictional characters, which leads to a more precise distinction between the intersubjective communicative constructs of persons represented nonfictionally and the actual persons these intersubjective communicative constructs are meant to refer to. Eder goes halfway toward acknowledging the need for such a distinction when he emphasizes that not even the mental model of George W. Bush constructed by an ideal recipient is George W. Bush himself. However, from the observation that "mental models of real persons must not be confused with these persons themselves," Eder merely concludes that "the model of a character cannot be the character itself" (*Was sind Figuren?* 30, my translation from the German), but continues to conflate

actual persons with (nonfictionally) represented persons (i.e., nonfictional characters).

30. According to Eder, characters (as well as storyworlds) are best understood as *normative* intersubjective constructs "based on normative abstractions about ideal character models" (*Die Figur* 78, my translation from the German). See also Eder, *Die Figur* 61–130; *Was sind Figuren?* 8–55, for a more detailed discussion of the normativity of characters (and storyworlds) as intersubjective communicative constructs as well as an examination of the distinction between "empirical reception," "intended reception," and "ideal reception."

31. This kind of distinction between comprehension and interpretation is well established within film studies. See, e.g., Bordwell, *Making Meaning* 1–18; Branigan, *Narrative Comprehension*; Eder, *Die Figur* 95–106; Persson 1–45; Staiger; G. Wilson, "On Film Narrative." It is, perhaps, comparable to the distinction between description and interpretation sometimes—albeit rather differently—drawn within (neo)classical narratology. Kindt and Müller, for example, have examined "(a) whether contributing, in whatever way, to the interpretation of literary texts is regarded as a task proper to narratology, and (b) how the relationship, if any, of narratology to interpretation has been defined" ("Narrative Theory" 206; see also Kindt and Müller, *The Implied Author*; "Narratology"). One way or another, though, a description (or analysis) of the transmedial strategies of narrative representation that this book focuses on would arguably also need to refer to processes of comprehension, for the most part.

32. To some cognitive film theorists, my focus on referential meaning might smack of "cognitivist bias." I readily concede the importance of perceptual, emotional, and other experiential aspects of the reception process for the "entertainment experience" that most if not all contemporary feature films, graphic novels, and narratively complex video games offer. However, I still maintain that these aspects of film viewing, comic reading, and video game playing are not too salient with regard to the question how storyworlds are represented in the narrative works that generate the respective experiences. Accordingly, what motivates the present study's focus on referential meaning is perhaps less a "cognitivist bias" than an informed choice to focus on questions of narrative representation and, hence, narrative comprehension as opposed to other aspects of the (at least partially medium-specific) experience that films, comics, video games, and various other narrative media afford their recipients.

33. This is even more clearly the case since I do not examine the differences in meaning-making processes that occur in different "interpretive communities" (see Fish). As has already been mentioned, I believe that the historization and contextualization of narratology is a worthwhile endeavor, but at least with regard to the project of a transmedial narratology developed in this book, the amount of fundamental conceptual and theoretical problems left to tackle prevents me from pursuing this path. Yet it seems fairly uncontroversial to say that referential meaning is less dependent on (though certainly not independent of) historical or sociocultural contextualization than more clearly interpretive meaning and, hence, that there is, perhaps, not all that much variation with regard to how different contemporary "interpretive communities" understand storyworlds *as storyworlds* (which still does not say anything much about other "modes of understanding"), after all.
34. Of course, the importance of ambiguity for communication in general and literary communication in particular is well established within linguistics and literary theory alike. See, e.g., Brown and S. C. Levinson; Grice; Sperber and D. Wilson; as well as, e.g., Bode; Martínez, *Doppelte Welten*; Rimmon-Kenan, *The Concept*.
35. Considering that video games with a nonlinear narrative structure generate markedly different narrative representations during different playthroughs, one might have to add a "many texts, many worlds" relation to Ryan's three basic texts/worlds relations, though. See chapter 3 for a more detailed discussion of the specific kind of "compounding" to which the nonlinearity of video games may lead.
36. Rather freely combining elements of possible worlds theory with Walton's theory of representation-as-make-believe, Ryan argues that "we know that the textual universe, as a whole, is an imaginary alternative to our system of reality; but for the duration of the game, as we step into it, we behave as if the actual world of the textual universe were *the* actual world. . . . Contemplated from without, the textual universe is populated by characters whose properties are those and only those specified by the text; contemplated from within, it is populated by ontologically complete human beings" (*Possible Worlds* 23, original emphasis). However, the incompleteness of fictional worlds has been fairly uncontested relatively early in fictional worlds theory. See, e.g., Castañeda; Doležel, *Heterocosmica*; Heintz; Howell; Lewis; Margolin, "Individuals"; Parsons; Pavel, *Fictional Worlds*; Ronen, "Completing the Incompleteness"; Routley; Wolterstorff.

37. If one takes nonviolation of the law of excluded middle as a necessary condition for logical possibility, that is. While I cannot examine the relation of modern logic and possible worlds theory in any detail, it is worth noting that there have been various attempts at developing theories of nonstandard possible worlds, sometimes also, if slightly misleadingly, called *im*possible worlds. See, e.g., Beall and van Fraassen; Lycan, *Modality*; Priest, *An Introduction*; Proudfoot; Rescher and Brandom; Restall; Salmon; Woods; Yagisawa. See also the surveys by Berto; Ryan, "Impossible Worlds."
38. See, e.g., Alber, "The Diachronic Development"; "Impossible Storyworlds"; *Unnatural Narrative*; Alber and Bell; Alber et al., "Unnatural Narratives"; Nielsen, "Fictional Voices?"; "Natural Authors"; B. Richardson "Beyond Story"; *Unnatural Voices*; "What Is Unnatural Narrative Theory?"; Tammi; as well as the contributions in Alber and R. Heinze, *Unnatural Narratives*; Alber, Nielsen, and B. Richardson; Hansen et al. See also the earlier but still influential work of McHale, *Postmodernist Fiction*; Fludernik, "How Natural Is 'Unnatural Narratology,'" on how "unnatural" narratology relates to the "natural" narratology developed in Fludernik, *Towards a 'Natural' Narratology*, to which some of the "unnatural narratologists" have responded in Alber et al., "What Is Unnatural about Unnatural Narratology?"; and the fierce critique of the group's terminological and conceptual basis in Klauk and Köppe, "Reassessing Unnatural Narratology," to which some of the "unnatural narratologists" have responded in Alber et al., "What Really Is Unnatural Narratology?"
39. More recently, Alber distinguishes further between "physically" and "humanly impossible scenarios and events" (Alber, *Unnatural Narrative*, 25). I have no qualm with that distinction as such, yet the fact remains that both "physically" and "humanly impossible" storyworlds may have what Ryan would call "low accessibility" but are not logically impossible in the strong sense of the term sketched above.
40. Logically possible, that is, at least if one leaves aside the fact that they are necessarily incomplete and, hence, always already violate the law of excluded middle.
41. It would seem, then, that the approach to transmedial narratology developed in this book will be well equipped to deal with (the medium-specific equivalent of) what B. Richardson calls "mimetic" and "nonmimetic" texts, but not with what he calls "antimimetic" texts. The main reason for this limitation, however, is that I am mainly concerned with transmedial strategies of narrative representation, while B.

Richardson's "antimimetic" texts cannot be described as representing a storyworld anymore, instead "destabilizing the ontology of this projected world and simultaneously laying bare the process of world construction" (McHale, *Postmodernist Fiction* 101). "Nonmimetic" texts—particularly those from the science fiction and fantasy genres—on the other hand, may very well "play around with the physically or logically impossible" (Alber, "The Diachronic Development" 59), but the kind of logical impossibility at stake here is usually not pronounced enough to prevent recipients from intersubjectively constructing a logically consistent storyworld (or at least a storyworld which they can easily pretend is logically consistent): "In the case of the former [i.e., the fantasy genre], the unnatural can be explained in terms of the supernatural, while in the case of the latter [i.e., the science fiction genre], the impossible can be explained through potential technological progress or simply the setting in the future" (Alber, "The Diachronic Development" 59).

42. Whether one wants to accept Priest's short story as a representation of a logically impossible situation that violates the law of noncontradiction is evidently contingent on one's conceptualization of representation. Moreover and perhaps more importantly, representations intended to represent logically impossible situations that violate the law of noncontradiction are even more difficult to realize using nonverbal or multimodal modes of representation than they are using verbal modes of representation whose "propositional form" may make it comparatively less problematic to combine two contradictory propositions (although it certainly remains problematic). Accordingly, there are very few (if any) films, comics, and video games representing logically impossible situations that violate the law of noncontradiction in ways comparable to Priest's short story, though there may well be other ways in which narrative works across media attempt to represent logically impossible storyworlds.

43. Wollheim's account of the "twofoldness" characteristic for the experience of "seeing-in" (which can be understood as a reaction to the "illusionistic" account of pictorial representation developed by Gombrich, *Art*; *The Image*, as well as, perhaps, to the more general semiotic approach of Goodman, *Languages*) has changed considerably over the years. See, e.g., Wollheim, *Art*; "On Pictorial Representation"; *Painting*.

44. It might be worth noting, if only in passing, that even phenomena such as quantum superposition do not have to be construed as violating the law of noncontradiction. From a phenomenological perspective, this

should be fairly obvious, as quantum superposition is evidently located on a "scale" that is largely irrelevant with regard to the apparent or actual contradictions that tend to occur in narrative representations or, rather, during narrative comprehension. At least for someone who has not received extensive training in theoretical physics and formal logic, the issue admittedly becomes difficult to pursue beyond the realm of storyworlds, yet it appears that, even within the actual world, quantum superposition does not have to be described as contradictory (see, e.g., Becker Arenhart and Krause).

45. In the account of these "naturalizing," "diegetizing," or, rather, plausibilizing reading strategies that he provides in *Unnatural Narrative*, Alber distinguishes between "the blending of frames" (48), "generification (evoking generic conventions from literary history)" (49), "subjectification (reading as internal states)," "foregrounding the thematic" (51), "reading allegorically," "satirization and parody" (52), "positing a transcendental realm," "do it yourself" (53), and "the Zen way of reading" (54). See also the earlier account in Alber, "Impossible Storyworlds"; as well as the emphasis on conventionalization in Alber, "The Diachronic Development."

46. For post-Genettean accounts of metalepsis within literary narratology, see, e.g., Alber and Bell; Fludernik, "Scene Shift"; Häsner; D. Herman, "Toward a Formal Description"; Klimek; Malina; McHale, *Postmodernist Fiction*; Meister, "The *Metalepticon*"; Nelles, *Frameworks* 121–162; Pier, "Métalepse"; Roussin; Ryan, *Avatars* 204–230.

47. For further discussion, see, e.g., Campora; Feyersinger; Genette, *Métalepse*; Kuhn 357–366; Limoges; Thoss, *When Storyworlds*; Thon, "Zur Metalepse," on metalepsis in films; Kukkonen, "Metalepsis"; Nöth; Schuldiner; Thoss, *When Storyworlds*, on metalepsis in comics; and Harpold; Neitzel, "Metacommunication"; Nöth, Bishara, and Neitzel 119–196; Rapp on metalepsis in video games. Incidentally, Thoss's recently published study of metalepsis in literary fiction, comics (including *The League of Extraordinary Gentlemen* and *The Unwritten*), and films (including *Adaptation.* and *Fight Club*) can be considered a successful contribution to the project of a transmedial narratology, albeit one with a very specific focus and, hence, a comparatively limited scope.

48. As, for example, David Gorman puts it, "fictional statements need not actually be untrue because it would not make any difference to a work's fictional status whether any of the statements made in it turned out to be true by coincidence. . . . Likewise factual discourse is intended to be

true, although it may not be: mistaken statements are still factual ones" (163). Evidently, whether one finds this statement convincing depends, once more, on one's conceptualization of fictionality. Perhaps unsurprisingly, given the intentionalist-pragmatic account of (narrative) representation that informs the present study, I subscribe to what could be described as an intentionalist-pragmatic (or, perhaps, "institutional") account of fictionality as well (see, e.g., Searle, "The Logical Status"; Currie, *The Nature*; Lamarque and Olsen; as well as the further narratological discussion by Punday, *Five Strands*; and the various recent surveys collected in Klauk and Köppe, *Fiktionalität*).

49. See the discussions of literary "markers of fictionality" by Cohn, "Signposts"; Genette, *Fiction*; Hamburger; Jacquenod; Riffaterre; Zipfel, *Fiktion*. See also the recent survey in Zipfel, "Fiction"; as well as the recent discussion between Nielsen, Phelan, and Walsh, on the one hand, and Dawson, on the other.

50. See, e.g., Schmidt, "The Fiction," for this kind of radical constructivist position. This is not to deny the epistemological appropriateness of more moderate forms of constructivism (see, e.g., Bateson; Luhmann, *Social Systems*; Piaget), but there still seems to be a fairly significant difference between arguing for "the social construction of reality" (see Berger and Luckmann) and examining "the construction of social reality" (see Searle, *The Construction*). See also, e.g., Goodman, *Ways*, on processes of plural world construction or Bruner on the narrative construction of reality.

51. See, e.g., Cohn, *The Distinction*; "Signposts"; Genette, *Fiction*; Martínez and Scheffel, "Narratology"; Punday, *Five Strands*; Ryan, *Possible Worlds*; Schaeffer; Walsh, *The Rhetoric*; Zipfel, *Fiktion*. See also Thon, "Fiktionalität," on which much of the following builds.

52. See, e.g., Hight; Paget; Roscoe and Hight; as well as the contributions in C. J. Miller; Nash, Hight, and Summerhayes; Rhodes and Springer. Of course, all of these build more or less extensively on rather sophisticated theories of documentary and nonfiction film. For a sample of works on documentary film from the 1990s, see, e.g., Nichols, *Blurred Boundaries*; *Representing Reality*; Winston; and the contributions in Renov. For recent works on nonfiction film, see, e.g., N. Carroll, "Fiction"; "Nonfiction Film"; Plantinga, "Defining Documentary"; *Rhetoric*; Ponech, "What Is Non-fiction Cinema?"; *What Is Non-fiction Cinema?* See also Odin for a pragmatic account of (non)fiction film that emphasizes spectators' ability to oscillate between different "stances" regarding the (non)fictionality of certain aspects of a film; as well as Currie, *Image*;

The Nature, for additional discussions of nonfiction film. The term "documentary film" is usually understood in a more narrow sense than the term "nonfiction film," as the "indexicality" of the photographic image supposedly fulfills an "evidence generating function" in the former but not (necessarily) the latter.

53. For a sample of recent research on graphic memoirs, see, e.g., Chute; Gardner, "Autography's Biography"; A. Miller; Pedri; Whitlock; or the contributions in Chaney; Grünewald; Tolmie. See also Adams 121–160; Gadassik and Henstra; Woo on Sacco's brand of graphic journalism in works such as *Palestine* and *Safe Area Goražde*.
54. See, e.g., Aarseth, "Doors"; Atkins; Walker Rettberg on video games' fictionality; C. Heinze; Uricchio; Schwarz on "historical" video games; Bogost, Ferrari, and Schweizer; Bogost and Poremba; Fullerton; Galloway, McAlpine, and Harris; Poremba; Raessens on documentary games.

3. Narrative Representation across Media

1. See A. Gibbons for an excellent survey of previous research from the perspective of cognitive literary theory; Bateman for a survey from the perspective of linguistics; Elleström for a survey from the perspective of media studies; Page for a survey from the perspective of narratology.
2. According to this approach, "modes are fluid, and determining what counts as a mode must be based on their context of use. In addition to this, it may be helpful to consider the ways in which different signifying systems are perceived, cognised, and interpreted" (A. Gibbons 10). Despite the common emphasis of semiotic modes and reception processes that can be observed in the works of Forceville, Page, and A. Gibbons, it might also be worth noting that the latter eventually proposes the development of a more specific theoretical and methodical program. This program, which she calls "*multimodal cognitive poetics*," is still "driven by the cognitive approach but is crucially supported by tools from visual communication and multimodality studies" (A. Gibbons 24, original emphasis).
3. It should be noted that Walton proposes a slightly different distinction between "sensory depictions," referring to "a notion of *depiction* which comprises more than pictures and more than *visual* representations," and "verbal representations," among which "*narrated* representations are perhaps most distinctive" (292, original emphases). While Walton's discussion of "depiction" as including not only pictorial representations but also other kinds of "signs close to perception" (Sachs-Hombach 73, my translation from the German) provides an interesting opportunity

to expand the traditional notion of pictorial representation beyond the realm of the visual, then, his account of "narrated representation" seems fairly standard in comparison and does not appear to be particularly relevant for the purpose of the present study.

4. See, e.g., W. Wolf, "Description"; "Narrative"; "Das Problem." Perhaps unsurprisingly, issues of pictorial representation also play a particularly crucial role in the emerging field of comics narratology (see the surveys in Gardner and D. Herman, "Graphic Narratives"; D. Stein and Thon, "Introduction"). At least with regard to the multimodal configurations characteristic for contemporary films, comics, and video games, I would argue that distinguishing between verbal and *pictorial* representation is more helpful than distinguishing between verbal and *visual* representation—as Ryan does when she proposes "three broad media families: verbal, visual, and aural" (*Avatars* 18)—since a substantial part of verbal representation in multimodal media is presented visually (i.e., in the form of written verbal representation, with films and video games moreover being able to use sound for realizing spoken verbal representation). While I tend to focus on verbal and pictorial representation, then, I will still refer to the combination of modes that define film's mediality by using the established term "audiovisual representation" as opposed to, say, "aural-pictorial representation" or even "verbal-aural-pictorial representation."

5. This might be a somewhat controversial claim in the context of the theory of fictional worlds, as analytic philosophers tend to think of fictional worlds as consisting of propositions, and, indeed, it seems that whenever metafictional or, rather, metarepresentational communication about what is or is not the case in a given storyworld takes place, the object of this metarepresentational communication will usually be a given narrative representation's propositional content. As, for example, Walton notes, we may be tempted to "identify fictional worlds with classes of propositions, provided only that we allow that the classes constituting fictional worlds, unlike those constituting possible worlds, need not be either consistent or complete" (66), or we could identify "fictional worlds not with sets of propositions but with sets of *propositions-as-indicated-by-a-given-work*" (66–67, original emphasis). However, since understanding storyworlds as intersubjective communicative constructs is not contingent on these constructs having (exclusively) "propositional form," I would like to keep open the possibility that at least some "nonpropositional content" will be part of some intersubjectively constructed storyworlds.

6. Incidentally, I do not make any strong claims regarding the extent to which sensory data from the narrative representation of local situations will be part of the mental models that recipients construct of the global storyworld as a whole. When comparing the ways in which recipients intersubjectively construct the referential meaning of local situations with the ways in which they intersubjectively construct the spatial, temporal, causal, and ontological relations between these situations, however, it seems that the former tends to be considerably more medium-specific than the latter.

7. Despite the problematic nature of claims about the "origins" of conventionally distinct media such as films, comics, and video games, it seems reasonably clear that verbal-pictorial narrative representation is significantly older than audiovisual narrative representation, and that audiovisual narrative representation is yet again reasonably older than the kind of interactive narrative representation to be found in video games. However, the histories of comics and film are closely intertwined through much of the twentieth century (see, e.g., Gardner, *Projections*), just as the histories of comics, film, and video games have become increasingly intertwined since the beginning of the twenty-first century (see, e.g., Brookey). While I acknowledge the crucial differences among strategies of audiovisual representation in contemporary films, strategies of verbal-pictorial representation in contemporary comics, and strategies of interactive representation in contemporary video games, then, one can still observe a certain amount of convergence not only with regard to what films, comics, and video games represent but also with regard to how they represent it. All things considered, then, media specificity is no less a construct than transmediality. For further discussion, see, e.g., N. Carroll, "The Specificity"; Doane; Thon, "Mediality."

8. See Bordwell, *The Way*. For additional discussion of plural character constellations in contemporary films, see also Tröhler. Further critically and commercially successful examples of these kinds of films would include Robert Altman's *Short Cuts*, Marcks's *11:14*, and Haggis's *Crash* as well as, if perhaps with a slightly different emphasis, Gilliam's *12 Monkeys* or Nolan's *Memento*. See also Thon, "Mind-Bender," on which much of the following builds.

9. What is meant here is not "films made in the outskirts of Los Angeles" but rather a certain commercial aesthetics primarily developed within the Hollywood studio system of the twentieth century and still very influential in the twenty-first. See, e.g., Bordwell, *The Way*; Bordwell, Staiger, and K. Thompson; K. Thompson, *Storytelling*.

10. Other examples would include Gondry's *Eternal Sunshine of the Spotless Mind*, Gilliam's *12 Monkeys*, Jonze and Kaufman's *Adaptation.*, Mangold's *Identity*, B. Singer's *The Usual Suspects*, or Nolan's *Inception*. However, in all of these cases, the respective subworlds are framed narratorially or via the subjectivity of a character, both of which will be discussed in more detail in the following chapters. The Wachowski siblings' *The Matrix* series provides a significantly more mainstream example that employs a "multilevel" structure similar to (albeit ultimately less complex than) that of *eXistenZ*, with The Matrix being an artificial or "virtual world" in which the machines that rule the storyworld's "factual domain" keep humans as slaves who do not know they are slaves.
11. There are also some more pronounced occurrences of metaleptic transgressions in those parts of the film that use animated pictures (see figure 1), particularly when Lola's mother watches an animated representation of Lola running down some stairs on her TV moments before the film shows an animated version of Lola running down the stairs of her mother's house. However, these mild forms of local ontological metalepsis do not seem to contribute anything to explaining the structure of the storyworld as a whole.
12. Incidentally, interpretations of *Run Lola Run* as being somehow influenced by video game aesthetics are quite common (see, e.g., Wedel), but they do not explain much with regard to the question of how the three courses of action relate to each other causally and/or ontologically.
13. Or, alternatively, still in the diegetic Lola's mind. Whatever the case may be, the hypodiegetic Manni and everything he experiences would be imagined by the diegetic Lola.
14. As is commonly the case, these comics, which have initially been published in single magazine form, were then collected in series of trade paperbacks. I will, however, only include works to which I specifically refer during my analyses in the Works Cited, rather than listing the countless installments of the numerous intramedial series and transmedial entertainment franchises that I mention throughout this book.
15. Currie argues that "photography depends on representation-by-origin, because the process that goes into making a photograph involves the leaving of a visible trace on a surface by exposure of that surface to light emitted or reflected from the source; the source is then what the photograph represents-by-origin. . . . We make progress when we see that a photograph, or movie, or video image can represent in more ways than one, representing one thing by origin and something else by use.

We regularly press things into representational service by using them to represent.... And, something which is a representation-by-origin of one thing may also be a representation-by-use of something else.... So a photograph or film image may represent one thing by origin—Cary Grant for instance—while representing something else because of the use of that image in a project of narrative communication" (*Narratives* 19–20).

16. The audiovisual representation characteristic for contemporary feature films is, indeed, *audio*visual. Just as the absence of "diegetic" sound in large parts of the audiovisual representation of *The Artist* does not imply that the represented storyworld is largely devoid of sound, though, the presence of "diegetic" sounds does not imply a conflation of "representation-by-use" and "representation-by-origin" any more readily than it does in the case of the pictorial representation of storyworld space. See, e.g., Branigan, *Narrative Comprehension*; Chion, *Audio-Vision*; *Film*; Flückiger, *Sound Design*, on various forms and functions of sound in film, including discussions of the distinction between "diegetic" and "nondiegetic" sound. While I cannot discuss strategies of auditive representation in any detail here, it should at least be noted that, since film's auditive representation is not necessarily more "verbatim" than its pictorial representation, I am generally skeptical of film studies' distinction between "diegetic" and "nondiegetic" elements of the auditive as well as the pictorial representation. To put it bluntly, there generally cannot be any "diegetic" elements of the narrative representation, although it is of course possible for different elements of the narrative representation to contribute to the representation of "diegetic" storyworld elements more or less directly.

17. This is also true with regard to the representational correspondence between verbal elements of the representation and the storyworld sounds they are used to represent. An interesting example can be found at the beginning of the second volume of Moore and O'Neill's *The League of Extraordinary Gentlemen*, which uses various unparsable symbols to represent an alien language spoken on (a "fictionalized" version of) Mars. Evidently, the readers of *The League of Extraordinary Gentlemen* will not be able to intersubjectively construct how this language sounds—but then again, that is at least partially true for speech balloons that use written English to represent spoken English as well. See also the discussion of comics' sound representation in Khordoc; Petersen as well as the discussion of pictorial representations of storyworld sounds in wordless comics such as Kuper's *The System*, de

Crécy's *Prosopopus*, and S. Tan's *The Arrival* in Beronä; Kunzle. See also Hague for a recently published study of comics' sensory affordances.

18. *Maus* has raised a lot of critical attention, and I do not claim that I can say anything genuinely new about it at this point, but it remains a masterpiece well suited to illustrate not only the processes characteristic for metaphoric comprehension and interpretation but also the limitations and affordances of narratorial representation within comics' specific mediality. For selected further discussions of various aspects of *Maus*, see, e.g., Berlatsky 145–186 or Hirsch (focusing on autobiography) as well as Ewert or McGlothlin (focusing on strategies of narrative and/ or narratorial representation). See also the wealth of additional material collected in Spiegelman, *MetaMaus*.

19. According to Walton, "silly questions . . . are pointless, inappropriate, out of order. To pursue or dwell on them would be not only irrelevant to appreciation and criticism but also distracting and destructive. The paradoxes, anomalies, apparent contradictions they point to seem artificial, contrived, not to be taken seriously. We don't take them seriously. Ordinarily we don't even notice them" (176). However, he also notes that "declaring a question to be silly does not answer it; it is an excuse, however legitimate, for not answering it. Perhaps our silly questions should not arise in the course of ordinary interaction with the work, but they are fair game for the theorist, standing as he [or she] does somewhat apart from appreciation and criticism and observing them from without" (Walton 180). See also, e.g., Currie, *Narratives* 58–65.

20. It could be argued that the increased narrative complexity of comics in the late 1980s and early 1990s has defined what one might consider the classical graphic novel. For roughly similar arguments, see, e.g., Gravett; C. Meyer; Weiner.

21. To give only a few examples: Drucker describes a "tension between the presentational and the representational" that "pushes back on the ideas of linguistic transparency as well as on the idea of self-evident visuality that traditionally separated realms of word and image as sign systems" (45); Kuhlman and Ball emphasize how Ware's work "exposes and manipulates the language of comics in ways that demand a great deal of the reader and test the representational possibilities of the medium" (x); and Groensteen claims that "layout is quite evidently one of the foundations of [Ware's] poetics and one of the areas in which he has been particularly innovative" (*Comics* 47–48).

22. The fact that *Jimmy Corrigan* tends to pictorially represent the hypodiegetic young Jimmy just like the diegetic old one (without doing that

consistently, either) also adds to the difficulty of figuring out which panels and sequences of panels represent hypodiegetic dreams, memories, and imaginations, and which represent the diegetic primary storyworld.

23. Just as in *eXistenZ*, these transgressions are no full-fledged metalepses, as Dream's powers provide a ready explanation for them. Still, in light of the principle of minimal departure, the effect of these transgressions might best be described as metaleptic, even though the metalepses in question are usually not in need of further plausibilization.

24. See Ryan, "Transfictionality." It might be worth mentioning, at this point, that the concept of storyworld developed in the previous chapter may also prove useful to refine our understanding of what it is, precisely, that transmedial entertainment franchises such as *The Lord of the Rings*, *Star Wars*, *Doctor Who*, *Batman*, or *Tomb Raider* represent. More specifically, my proposal to understand storyworlds as noncontradictory "by default" and to describe contradictory storyworlds as compounds of noncontradictory subworlds seems to be well suited to be applied to transmedial entertainment franchises, albeit with some minor modifications. I will provide some further remarks on what such a research program would entail in the conclusion of the present study. For more in-depth discussion, see Thon, "Converging Worlds."

25. Actually, these kinds of "serial contaminations" of storyworlds represented in comics are comparatively common even beyond the sprawling "universes" of DC and Marvel (see, once more, Kukkonen, "Navigating Infinite Earths"). Another example already mentioned is Moore and O'Neill's *The League of Extraordinary Gentlemen*, the first two volumes of which bring together characters from a range of different preestablished storyworlds in a vaguely Victorian steam-punk setting.

26. See, e.g., Jenkins, "Game Design"; Juul, *Half-Real*; Ryan, *Avatars* 181–203; or Backe; Domsch; Engelns; as well as Thon, "Computer Games"; "Game Studies"; "Unendliche Weiten?," on which much of the following builds.

27. Interactivity in particular is commonly thought of as a "silly and abused term" (Aarseth, "Genre Trouble" 52) or an unhappily "entrenched notion in studies of digital media" (Bogost 40), but still appropriately captures the fact that video games are, at their prototypical core, interactive cultural artifacts. See also Aarseth, *Cybertext*, on video games' "ergodicity" as well as Bogost on their "procedurality." Likewise, some theorists may prefer adjectives such as "branching" or "cascading" to describe what I call the nonlinear narrative structure of video games,

yet the concepts to which these terms are referring remain rather similar.

28. See Bartle for a still influential discussion of "player types." On the different kinds of experience that contemporary video games may (or may not) afford their players, see, e.g., Calleja; Fahlenbrach and F. Schröter; Klimmt; McMahan; J. H. Murray, *Hamlet*; Ryan, *Narrative*; Thon, "Immersion."

29. See, e.g., Aarseth, "Genre Trouble"; Frasca, "Simulation"; Ryan, *Avatars* 181–203; Thon, "Unendliche Weiten?" For Frasca, video games are "a particular way of structuring simulation, just like narrative is a form of structuring representation" ("Simulation" 224). I would not draw the distinction between simulation and narrative representation quite as sharply, yet I would still maintain that the concept of simulation remains rather useful when one attempts to describe the medium-specific ways in which video games may represent storyworlds. While I furthermore tend to agree with Jannidis that "if we want to talk of a narration in computer games at all . . . it is mainly the organization of event-sequences that we have to be concerned with" ("Event-Sequences" 293), I find his critique of the term "simulation" as not sufficiently taking into account the "organizing intelligence" video game players may perceive behind the gameplay quite unconvincing, since the "intelligence" of the "simauthor" that manifests itself in the rules of the game is an essential component of Frasca's conceptualization of simulation. See also the further discussion in chapter 4.

30. See, e.g., Thon, "Unendliche Weiten?," which builds on Frasca, "Simulation"; Järvinen, "Making and Breaking Games"; Neitzel, "Point of View," among others. I would like to emphasize, at this point, that there were good reasons for early ludology to refer to classical works on nondigital games and play such as Avedon; Caillois; Huizinga; and Sutton-Smith. While I have become increasingly less interested in the question of whether or not video games are/can be/should be narrative (as opposed to the question *how* they are narrative), I would certainly not contest that video games are like other kinds of games in some ways. See also the "classical game model" developed in Juul, *Half-Real*.

31. On the one hand, this kind of combination of interactive simulation and narrative representation will arguably be perceived as a more or less homogenous story by some players. On the other hand, it seems rather problematic to generally talk about "emergent narratives" (see Jenkins, "Game Design"), since the events that make up the event sequence are, in most cases, not entirely emergent. While Juul's critique of the often

unreflected use of terms like "emergent narrative" is certainly justified (see Juul, *Half-Real* 159), Richard Rouse's proposal to distinguish between the "designer's story" and the "player's story" (203–206) still seems to retain at least some heuristic value in this context.

32. Contemporary video games do not only emulate audiovisual and verbal-pictorial strategies of narrative representation in their cut-scenes but also more generally use a form of computer-generated animation that is combined with an auditive channel to represent the more interactive segments of their gameplay. See, e.g., Collins, *Game Sound*; *Playing with Sound*; Jørgensen, *A Comprehensive Study*, for a discussion of various forms and functions of game sound.

33. The heuristic distinction between cut-scenes and scripted events primarily aims at the difference between noninteractive segments of the narrative representation and predetermined representations of events that occur during the interactive simulation of the actual gameplay—one could, without a doubt, draw considerably more detailed distinctions with regard to the strategies of narrative representation that contemporary video games employ, particularly since technological advances increasingly allow for the "real-time" generation of cut-scenes as well as for the "cinematic" design of the gameplay's interactive simulation (see also the more detailed discussion in Thon, "Game Studies"). Examples of games with particularly "cinematic" gameplay would include Midway's *Stranglehold*, Naughty Dog's *Uncharted: Drake's Fortune*, or the 2013 reboot of the *Tomb Raider* franchise. Moreover, role-playing games such as *Dragon Age: Origins* increasingly use "in-engine" cut-scenes to represent the player-controlled characters according to the choices that the player has made with regard to their equipment and other aspects of their outer appearance, and there is also a tendency—recently realized rather impressively by Ubisoft's *Assassin's Creed* and its successors—to allow players to change the angle of the "virtual camera" during otherwise largely noninteractive cut-scenes.

34. While I would argue that orienting him- or herself with regard to the game mechanics and game goals may be considered *the* core task of the player in many contemporary video games, a detailed discussion of this question is not possible in the context of the present book. For further discussion of "evaluative point of view" and "ideological perspective structure" in video games, see Thon, "Perspective." See also the discussion surrounding "persuasive games" and "procedural rhetoric" in, e.g., Bogost; Schrape; Sicart.

35. As I have noted elsewhere (see Thon, "Perspective"), terms such as "virtual camera" are evidently metaphorical when used to describe the computer-generated imagery of contemporary video games, but considering that these games tend to use quite a few film-specific representational conventions in at least their filmic cut-scenes, speaking of a "virtual camera" in these cases still seems appropriate.
36. One can also find quite a bit of verbal narration in many if not most of *Halo*'s generally rather dialogue-heavy cut-scenes. In the cut-scene prefacing the first level of the singleplayer mode, Captain Keyes and Cortana talk about events that have occurred immediately beforehand. Here, Captain Keyes and Cortana function not just as characters in the diegetic primary storyworld of the game but also as intradiegetic and homodiegetic verbal narrators. However, this kind of intradiegetic representation of hypodiegetic secondary storyworlds is not limited to the verbal mode of representation but may also take nonverbal or, rather, multimodal forms when, for example, the player-controlled Master Chief finds a video in the helmet of a marine called Private Jenkins, who has been killed by aliens. The video shows the events that led to Jenkins's death, and as the Master Chief watches it, *Halo* uses a cut-scene to show the (intradiegetic) film sequence depicting these (hypodiegetic) events (located in a secondary storyworld) to the player as well. See also chapter 5 for a more detailed discussion of narrators in contemporary video games, albeit one that uses different examples.
37. This may also apply to the design of the game spaces, when it appears to be primarily motivated by ludic considerations. A case in point would be the randomly generated dungeons of Blizzard's *Diablo* series: asking for an internal explanation as to why the space of the storyworld occasionally rearranges itself would evidently lead to "silly questions," as these rearrangements are more plausibly explained externally—i.e., with reference to the game spaces' ludic functions. Video games may, of course, also provide internal explanations for this. In Easy Game Station's action role-playing game *Recettear: An Item Shop's Tale*, for example, the player controls a shopkeeper who hires heroes to get her new items to sell in her shop from various dungeons and, at one point, the shopkeeper's fairy companion/debt collector remarks that these (randomly generated) dungeons "rearrange" themselves overnight.
38. Of course, the issue of representational correspondence is also further complicated by various elements of the graphic user interface of contemporary video games. As, for example, Punday notes, the elements of the graphic user interface "essentially introduce different kinds of

spaces," and "these UI spaces" are, "to various degrees, diagrammatic in nature" ("Seeing into the Worlds" 59). Mistaking elements of the graphic user interface for elements of the game spaces and/or for elements of the game's storyworld(s) would doubtless lead to "silly questions," then. Yet, as the IKEA sequence in Fincher's *Fight Club* or the excessive use of diagrams in Ware's *Jimmy Corrigan* illustrate, the integration of diagrammatic elements is not only reasonably conventionalized but also a comparatively transmedial form of "hybrid" representational correspondence. For further discussion of the graphic user interfaces of contemporary video games, see, e.g., Jørgensen, *Gameworld Interfaces*. For further discussion of diagrammatic forms of communication and representation in general, see, e.g., Bender and Marrinan; or the contributions in Pombo and Gerner.

39. Here and in the following, the term "silly" is used to refer to the kinds of "silly questions" discussed by philosophical theories of representation such as those developed by Currie, *Narratives*, or Walton. See also F. Schröter and Thon, "Simulierte Spielfiguren," for additional discussion of *Warcraft III: Reign of Chaos* in the context of a video game-specific theory of character, which has been further developed in F. Schröter and Thon, "Video Game Characters."

40. While *Alan Wake* self-identifies as "A Psychological Action Thriller," its use of a "semi-subjective point of view" and "direct point of action" (see Neitzel, "Point of View"; Thon, "Perspective") to represent action-oriented gameplay that combines a rather interesting light-based combat mechanic with more conventional forms of weapon-based combat, as well as its heavy use of strategies of narrative representation such as cut-scenes and scripted events to represent a largely linear story, make it easily identifiable as an action-adventure. However, *Alan Wake* and its sequel *Alan Wake's American Nightmare* as well as Remedy's earlier influential action-adventures/third-person shooters *Max Payne* and *Max Payne 2: The Fall of Max Payne* represent comparatively complex storyworlds, making extensive use of an extradiegetic narrator telling his own story as well as representing the experiencing I's dreams, fantasies, memories, and hallucinations.

41. *Alan Wake* employs an episodic form in itself, with each of the six episodes being introduced by a brief "Previously on Alan Wake . . ." segment that recapitulates the most important plot developments. Furthermore, Remedy has published serial expansions in the form of two downloadable episodes ("The Writer" and "The Signal") and a stand-alone sequel, *Alan Wake's American Nightmare*, further unfolding

the story and fleshing out the storyworld beyond what I have sketched above.

42. Bioware is a game developer that has proven particularly influential for the role-playing game genre, with games such as those in the *Baldur's Gate*, *Neverwinter Nights*, *Star Wars: Knights of the Old Republic*, *Mass Effect*, and *Dragon Age* series enjoying both commercial and critical success and defining to an increasingly large extent what players expect from role-playing games with nonlinear narrative structures.

43. See Eder and Thon; F. Schröter and Thon, "Simulierte Spielfiguren"; "Video Game Characters," for more detailed discussions of the medium-specific characteristics of video game characters. Perhaps most importantly, video game characters are, in a vast majority of cases, both fictional—or, more generally, *represented*—entities and ludic objects that fulfill certain usually rather salient functions in the context of the respective game's simulated gameplay.

44. The genre-typical way in which dialogue is handled in *Dragon Age: Origins* combines a nonlinear arrangement of dialogue options from which the player can choose with the audiovisual representation of the resulting conversations via simple cut-scenes.

45. I would like to stress, yet again, the narratologically significant distinction between the different playthroughs resulting from interactivity and the different playthroughs resulting from nonlinearity. As will have become clear, only the latter should be taken as leading to the representation of different storyworlds, each of which can be described as the playthrough-specific realization of an arrangement of "virtual storyworlds." Accordingly, video games with a nonlinear narrative structure add the possibility of an entirely different kind of "compounding" to the conceptualization of storyworlds as being noncontradictory "by default" that was developed in the previous chapter. However, see also Thon, "Game Studies," for a discussion of local forms of meaning making in the context of highly configurable and/or massively multiplayer online role-playing games that are not primarily concerned with the intersubjective construction of the respective game's storyworld(s).

46. While I have not discussed this question in any detail, one could even argue that the seriality of many early comics was an important prerequisite for the development of graphic novels' narrative complexity, as, even apart from the sprawling and increasingly transmedial "universes" of DC and Marvel, comics tend to be serialized in a variety of ways, with some of the best-known graphic novels—such as Spiegelman's *Maus*, Gaiman's *The Sandman* series, Moore and D. Gibbons's *Watchmen*,

Moore and O'Neill's *The League of Extraordinary Gentlemen*, F. Miller's *Sin City* series, or Ware's *Jimmy Corrigan*—having originally been published in a series of single magazine issues before being collected in one or several trade paperback volumes (or other more durable and "culturally prestigious" material forms).

47. These tendencies are not exclusively medium-specific and may, perhaps, be more appropriately described in terms of genre-specific conventions, as the storyworlds of comics and video games may also contain significant degrees of narrative complexity (while some films do not exhibit such complexity); serial expansions and modifications play an important role with regard to films and video games as well (while some comics are not part of a series); and there are at least some cases—such as the "choose your own plot development" segment in the third volume of Carey and Gross's *The Unwritten: Dead Man's Knock*, as opposed to the decidedly linear audiovisual representation in Tykwer's *Run Lola Run*—where nonlinear narrative structures can be found in noninteractive media (while some interactive media do not employ a nonlinear narrative structure).

4. The Narrator as a Transmedial Concept

1. An earlier and considerably shorter version of the argument developed in this and the following chapter has been published in Thon, "Toward a Transmedial Narratology." See also Thon, "Who's Telling the Tale?," for a discussion of authors and narrators in comics; as well as Thon, "Game Studies," for a discussion of narrators in video games.

2. For earlier surveys of the discussion surrounding the "cinematic narrator," which refer to rather similar arguments, see Thomson-Jones, *Aesthetics and Film* 72–86; "Cinematic Narrators"; "The Literary Origins." At least in the context of a transmedial narratology, the two most commonly encountered of these arguments seem to be, on the one hand, the "a priori argument" (Thomson-Jones, "The Literary Origins" 82, referring to Gaut, "The Philosophy") or the "analytic argument," which "claims that the concept of narrative analytically entails the concept of a narrator" but "does not give us any information regarding the ontological status of the narrators of fictional narratives" and, hence, "only establishes that there is a narrator and not that there is a fictional narrator" (Köppe and Stühring 63), and, on the other hand, the "argument from means of access" (Thomson-Jones, "The Literary Origins" 83) or the "ontological gap argument," which "claims that only fictional narrators can have access to fictional worlds" (Köppe and Stühring 64)

but does not address that, if "only fictional persons [were to] have access to fictional worlds . . . , only fictional persons [would] have access to the utterances of a fictional narrator" (Köppe and Stühring 65).

3. While some narratologists would deny the "implied author" the ability to "speak," Booth himself has been fairly explicit about the question of the "implied author's voice" when he notes that "in so far as a novel does not refer directly to this author [the 'implied author'] there will be no distinction between him [or her] and the implied, undramatized narrator" (*The Rhetoric* 151). In discussing the various voices that narrative representations across media may or may not construct, one should keep in mind that all of us persistently and conventionally "play roles" in everyday interaction and that, hence, authors (as opposed to the represented narrators that may also be part of a given narrative work) may very well be capable of using different "registers," of disorienting their readers with regard to the intersubjective construction of the represented storyworld, and of pretending to evaluate the represented events in certain ways that are different from the ways they would evaluate them in other contexts or "frames"—with at least the latter sometimes (though inappropriately or, rather, unconvincingly) being used to make what Köppe and Stühring call the "blocked inference argument," according to which "the illocutions . . . of a fictional narrative have to be attributed to a fictional narrator simply because it would be false or absurd to attribute them to the author" (65). See Goffman for an influential early account of the "role-play" activities we partake in during everyday interaction.

4. Interestingly enough, D. Johnson and Gray go on to emphasize that "each and every item carries with it the ghosts of authors not mentioned" (2), and not only our perception of authorship but also its discussion in much of current media studies tends to reduce the often complex processes of co-creation and the negotiation of authority to author figures that are particularly visible "in the press and in the popular imagination" (4), ignoring what Caldwell, "Authorship," describes as authorship "below the line." Given the narratological focus of this book, I cannot examine the complexity of *actual* collective authorship (in the broadest sense of the term, which will be further explicated below) in any detail, either, but the essays collected in Gray and D. Johnson certainly demonstrate that current production culture studies have interesting things to say about these issues—even though these things are, perhaps, not necessarily narratologically relevant in all cases. See in particular the essays by Caldwell, "Authorship," on film

authorship; I. Gordon on comics authorship; and Consalvo on video games authorship; as well as the more general studies by Caldwell, *Production Culture*; Hesmondhalgh and Baker; D. Johnson; and the contributions in Hartley; D. Johnson, Kompare, and Santo; Mayer, Banks, and Caldwell.

5. See, once more, Wimsatt and Beardsley as well as Barthes, "The Death," on the "death of the author" and Foucault on the author as "author function" (which he imagines as eventually vanishing, too). It may be worth noting, though, that there has also been a significant increase in attempts to "resurrect" the author (or to argue that "reports of its death were greatly exaggerated") within literary theory during the past two decades. See, e.g., the various contributions (including some rather extensive surveys) in Detering; Donovan, Fjellestad, and Lundén; Dorleijn, Grüttemeier, and Korthals Altes; Irwin; Jannidis et al.; Schaffrick and Willand.

6. As Kindt and Müller have reconstructed in impressive detail, Booth's concept of the "implied author" allowed him to combine two positions that, prima facie, were very much at odds with each other: "On the one hand, he wanted to bring author and recipient back into focus in the academic study of literature; on the other hand, he wanted to avoid stepping outside the work itself and thus committing one of the fallacies that the New Criticism had established as heresies of interpretation theory" (Kind and Müller, *The Implied Author* 49–50).

7. As, for example, Peter Lamarque has noted, "the debate between anti-intentionalists, like Wimsatt and Beardsley, and intentionalists has grown ever more subtle and complex, pursued by critics and philosophers alike, but shows no signs of abating" (177). If one follows Kindt and Müller (as well as many other participants in the debate) in distinguishing between "hypothetical intentionalism and actual intentionalism" as "the two basic lines currently being pursued in the context of intentionalistic interpretation" (*The Implied Author* 170), however, it would seem that, at least as far as problems of comprehension (as opposed to problems of interpretation) are concerned, adhering to some version of "hypothetical intentionalism" as the basis for a theory of (narrative) representation is both sufficient (since the kind of questions that might tempt "actual intentionalists" to start looking for authorial intentions beyond the work under examination will usually be questions of interpretation, not of comprehension) and comparatively uncontroversial (since it is widely, if not generally, accepted that the comprehension of narrative representations requires the construction of

hypotheses about intentions that manifest themselves in the former). Moreover, "hypothetical intentionalism" also appears fairly compatible with the concept of the "implied author": according to J. Levinson, for example, "instead of speaking of beliefs or attitudes that would be *reasonably attributed* to the actual author on the basis of the work, contextually grasped, we can speak of the beliefs or attitudes that just straightforwardly *belong* to the implied author—he or she being a construction tailor-made to bear them" (229, original emphases). However, see also the more critical survey by Spoerhase.

8. See, for example, the special issue of *Style* from 2011 (45.1), edited by B. Richardson, in which a number of well-known narratologists have revisited the concept of the "implied author" (see B. Richardson, *The Implied Author*).

9. It might be misleading to speak of "fictionalized" authoring characters, as most theories of fiction do not allow for degrees of fictionality. What is meant here is that both author figures in general and authoring characters in particular can be represented more or less accurately with respect to the actual world, but their representation can also be marked more or less openly as being fictional. The discussion of theories of (non)fictionality in film and media studies in Thon, "Fiktionalität," at least briefly touches on this question. Of course, research on autobiography has long recognized that authoring characters functioning as narrators may be more or less strongly "fictionalized." See, e.g., Cohn, *The Distinction*; "Signposts"; Genette, *Fiction*; Löschnigg, "Narratological Perspectives"; "Postclassical Narratology," for narratological discussions.

10. Nevertheless, *some* account of collective authorship is necessary in the context of a transmedial narratology—and, moreover, such an account may also enrich our understanding of reception processes. As, for example, Gray notes, "while by no means a quick fix to all concerns with theories of the singular authorial genius, theories of authorial multiplication have significantly refined and sophisticated how we think of audiences. These theories are perhaps most easily illustrated with a profoundly collaborative medium such as film, television, or videogames" ("When Is the Author?" 92). Gray even goes as far as claiming, albeit in a rather polemical fashion quite obviously overextending the concept, that "nothing has a single author" ("When Is the Author?" 93). While my own conceptualization of authorship is fairly permissive, already, I would still allow for narrative works that have single authors—but quite apart from the question who the author of a given

narrative work is (or, more commonly with regard to films, comics, and video games, who its authors are), it seems important to note that the latter—that is, the narrative work in question—is indeed not unproblematically given. As Gray claims, "any text is always open, never concluded or complete, and thus any notion of authorship based on the assumption that the text has already been created is a problematic one. Instead, the text will continue to happen, requiring us to ask when it happens and who are the individuals, teams, and/or communities who are active in its creation at those moments" ("When Is the Author?" 107–108). While I would be more ready than Gray to accept the notion of a "finished work," it is certainly the case that films, comics, and video games (as well as television series and other works of popular culture) are continuously revised, rewritten, and reappropriated. See also Fiske as well as Gray, *Show*; Hills, *Fan Cultures*; Mittell, *Complex TV*, for influential recent discussions of the complex negotiation of meaning between authors/producers and recipients/fans.

11. See also, e.g., Truffaut or Bazin; and Sarris or Wollen. As, for example, Buscombe has noted in an early critical survey of the so-called auteur theory, "not only was the original *politique [des auteurs]* of *Cahiers [du Cinéma]* somewhat less than a theory; it was itself only loosely based upon a theoretical approach to the cinema which was never to be made fully explicit. The *politique*, as the choice of term indicates, was polemical in intent and was meant to define an attitude to the cinema and a course of action. In the pursuit of this course *Cahiers* did inevitably reveal some of the theory on which the *politique* was based; but usually this appeared incidentally, and at times incoherently" (22, original emphases). Since contemporary film (or at least contemporary Hollywood cinema) does not seem in dire need of a *politique* aiming at its nobilitation and, moreover, since the present study is not overly concerned with questions of artistic evaluation, I will not discuss the aims and scope of the *politique des auteurs* in greater depth.

12. While closer to Gaut than to Livingston with regard to the "permissiveness" of an appropriate definition of authorship, Sellors still notes that "what is missing from Gaut's account is a detailed analysis of how action and intention function in *collectives*," which leads him to develop further Livingston's account of collective authorship as being defined by "shared intentions," focusing on the question whether "collective intentions [are] aggregates of individual intentions, or . . . primitive and therefore not analyzable in terms of individual intentions," before eventually concluding that the latter holds and "we-intentions"

sufficiently explain "an individual's action in a group action" (Sellors 268, original emphasis).

13. For various versions of Gilbert's "plural subject theory," see Gilbert, *Joint Commitment*; *On Social Facts*; *A Theory*. See also Searle, "Collective Intentions," as well as, e.g., Bratman; Tomasello; Tuomela on "shared intentions" and forms of cooperation.

14. For one of the most influential "historicizing" discussions of film authorship in the "classical studio system," see Bordwell, Staiger, and K. Thompson. See also, e.g., Dyer for a discussion of the contributions of stars to filmmaking (as opposed to auteur theory's focus on directors); D. Stein; Uidhir; and the contributions in Williams and Lyons for more in-depth discussions of the historical development of prototypical authoring practices in comics; as well as Aarseth, "The Game"; Consalvo for some additional discussions of authorship in video games. While the notion that at least some films and comics have authors (of some kind) appears to be uncontroversial, research on video game authorship is still quite scarce. Against this background, I would like to stress, once more, that I do not propose to limit authorship in video games to what Aarseth describes as "game auteurs" ("The Game" 261). Instead, I explicitly acknowledge that "the great majority of videogames currently being created are the products of many hands" (Consalvo 325)—and, as far as these hands belong to members of a "jointly committed group," many authors.

15. See the previous discussion of some of the models of narrative communication proposed by Bal, Chatman, Genette, Rimmon-Kenan, and Schmid. From a broader historical perspective, it may also be worth mentioning Kayser's proto-narratological insistence that, "in all narrative art, the narrator is never the known or still unknown author, but a role that the author invents and fulfills" (125, my translation from the German). Other influential proto-narratological approaches to the problem of the narrator have been developed by Friedemann; Hamburger. For further discussion of early and "unusual" accounts of the narrator in literary texts, particularly that of Hamburger and of Banfield, *Unspeakable Sentences*, see, once more, Patron.

16. However, see, once more, the work of Lanser on how we may often actually attribute the narration in literary narrative texts to both a narrating character and the author (at the same time). As has already been mentioned, Lanser's elegant discussion of the "both/and logic" of attributing authorial and narratorial voices (see Lanser, *The Narrative Act*) is also taken up in Branigan's influential work on "film narration,"

which arguably provides one of the most sophisticated accounts of "implied narration" in film (and other multimodal media) available today, even though it does so in a way that is not too helpful in getting a better grasp of the transmedial concept of the narrator, as such (see Branigan, *Narrative Comprehension*; as well as Branigan, *Point of View*, for an earlier version of the argument that "focalization" is similar to "narration," to which I will return in the third part of this book).

17. There are, of course, cases where intradiegetic characters are, more or (usually) less explicitly, represented as the authors of a multimodal narrative representation that is, likewise, located within the diegetic primary storyworld. Another border case that is no less interesting can be found in the form of characters who are represented as verbally narrating a story, but whose story is exclusively represented nonverbally, or, rather, by way of the audiovisual, verbal-pictorial, or interactive representation characteristic for comics, films, and video games, respectively. See, e.g., S. Tan's *The Arrival*, which is discussed in more detail in chapter 7.

18. See, e.g., D. A. Black; Branigan, *Narrative Comprehension* 62–100; Burgoyne; Chatman, *Coming to Terms* 124–138; Gaudreault, *From Plato*; Gaudreault and Jost, "Enunciation"; *Le récit*; Kozloff 43–49; Metz *L'ènonciation*; "The Impersonal Enunciation"; G. Wilson, *Narration*; "On Film Narrative"; as well as the more recent surveys and discussions by Currie, *Narratives* 65–85; Gaut, "The Philosophy"; Grodal, "Film Narrative"; Thomson-Jones, *Aesthetics* 72–86; "Cinematic Narrators"; "The Literary Origins"; G. Wilson, "Elusive Narrators."

19. The typo, "does *now* show itself," may be significant, however, as it indeed appears to be quite problematic to talk about "anthropomorphized constructs" that "do not show themselves."

20. While Chatman's conceptualization of the "cinematic narrator" as a bundle of representational means seems to be at odds with conceptualizing it as the "source" of the audiovisual representation, his insistence on postulating "a *presenter* of the story" (*Coming to Terms* 133, original emphasis) as distinct from the "implied author" suggests otherwise.

21. Bordwell famously claimed that "to give every film a narrator or implied author is to indulge in an anthropomorphic fiction" (*Narration* 62). Even in explicitly reacting to this criticism of his earlier approach, Chatman still develops his "cinematic narrator" based on "the need for the concept of cinematic implied authorship" (*Coming to Terms* 130), and consistently argues for using the term "implied author" to denote

"the principle within the text to which we assign the inventional tasks" of creating "both the story and the discourse (including the narrator)" (*Coming to Terms* 133).

22. Schlickers modifies her original account in a more recent essay (see Schlickers, "Focalization"), but the fundamental problems sketched below persist, and, hence, the proposed communication model remains ultimately unconvincing.

23. Of course, Chatman's concept of the "cinematic narrator" is rather more sophisticated (or, at least, more extensive) than Kuhn's concept of the "visual narrating instance," as it not only more emphatically includes the "auditory channel" as part of its "communicating devices" (Chatman, *Coming to Terms* 134) but also seems to offer a generally more convincing account of the latter. See also Chion, *Audio-Vision*; *Film*; *The Voice* for further discussion of the forms and functions of film's auditive elements (as well as their relation to its visual or, more precisely, pictorial elements).

24. A fact that Kuhn himself explicitly acknowledges—though that acknowledgment does not lead him to adopt a different terminology due to his "focus on the visual aspects of the extralinguistic narration in the film and the simplicity of the wording" (86, my translation from the German). While Kuhn's focus on visual (or, rather, pictorial) aspects of the audiovisual representation seems common enough within film narratology (and, in fact, is echoed in the present study as well), adopting reductive terminology because the "wording is simpler" appears to be a rather surprising move in a study that elsewhere puts such strong emphasis on terminological accuracy.

25. While there are reasons to prefer constructing a nonrepresented "authoring instance" to constructing a nonrepresented "narrating instance," my main criticism of attempts to transfer the classical model of narrative communication from literary texts to multimodal media such as films, comics, and video games is not merely terminological (i.e., along the lines of "nonrepresented 'narrating instances' are not at all like narrators-as-narrating-characters and hence we should not use similar terms to refer to these concepts"), but primarily aims at the multiplication of nonrepresented "communicating instances" that can be observed in most if not all of these attempts. Quite apart from the question whether it is more plausible to postulate some version of the "implied author" or a nonrepresented "narrating instance," then, it seems rather clear to me that we certainly do not need to postulate *two* (or even more) nonrepresented "communicating instances" of this kind.

See also the further discussion of what I consider to primarily be an attribution problem below.

26. Incidentally, Marion as well as Baetens and Surdiacourt seem to understand the "graphiator" (as well as the "monstrator") of a comic as being closer to some kind of hypothetical author (or "implied author") than to a narrator-as-narrating-character, which at least Marion explicitly distinguishes from the former. Against the background sketched above, I want to clarify that I do not argue against postulating a hypothetical "authoring instance" to which the design of a comic can be attributed, though calling such an instance "graphiator" (or "monstrator") seems unnecessarily reductive.

27. See, e.g., Aarseth, *Cybertext* 97–128; Eskelinen, *Cybertext Poetics* 181–207; Jannidis, "Event-Sequences"; Neitzel, "Narrativity"; Thon, "Perspective"; Zierold 141–169.

28. While Neitzel has revised her original proposal to treat the avatar as the narrator (see Neitzel, "Gespielte Geschichten" 135) in her more recent essay "Point of View und Point of Action," she still seems to subscribe to a "concept of shared authorship" ("Levels of Play" 60) that has led her to propose "borrowing the term 'implied author' from literary theory in order to describe the function of the player as an author implied by the game," distinguishing the latter from the function of "the implied creator," who "makes the initial selection from the mass of conceivable possibilities by making a subset of them available as choices in the program" (Neitzel, "Levels of Play" 61). I do not find Neitzel's terminological choices particularly convincing and, moreover, remain skeptical with regard to her claim that the player of a video game exerts some kind of authorship *just by playing it*.

29. Which, in turn, largely follows the critique of the concept in A. Nünning, "Renaissance," even though Zierold also briefly refers to the considerably more detailed and thorough critical reconstruction by Kindt and Müller, *The Implied Author*. As already mentioned earlier, I do not find the term "implied author" particularly helpful myself, but Zierold's decision to focus on the ill-defined concept of the "intrigant" because the term "implied author" has a troubled conceptual history remains rather inexplicable—or, rather, unexplicated.

30. Zierold claims that "such a narrator is not to be found in digital games" (152, my translation from the German). Admittedly, Zierold's remark could be read as referring to the kind of nonrepresented "narrating instance" that I would, likewise, refrain from postulating for video games. One way or another, though, she does not draw an explicit

distinction between nonrepresented and represented narrators, of which there is, in fact, quite an overabundance in contemporary video games, nor does she discuss the latter as part of her attempt at systematization.

31. More specifically, I agree with Jannidis that "the player's awareness of an intelligence that invents the events and their sequence and presents them to him [or her]" ("Event-Sequences" 293) should be taken seriously and with Frasca that such a *"simauthor"* ("Simulation" 228, original emphasis) is, indeed, best comprehended as an "authoring instance," albeit a hypothetical one. In other words, my critique of Aarseth's "intrigant" and Zierold's appropriation of it once more primarily aims at the concept's redundancy with regard to a conceptualization of some kind of a hypothetical author collective (which is commonly, albeit not convincingly, reduced to some version of the "implied author" within literary and film narratology as well as within comics and game studies). At least when it comes to the question to whom or what players can attribute the design of the interactive representation, there seems to be no need to postulate both an "intrigant" and a hypothetical author collective—but while the latter may be thought of as entailing the core functions of the former, only referring to the former is inappropriately reductive.

32. See also the discussion of literature- and film-specific "optional-narrator theories" as well as, e.g., Schüwer on comics and Neitzel, "Point of View," on video games. Schüwer insists that "Genette's concept of narration can be transferred to the verbal elements of comics—particularly to the narration boxes—without reservation, but not to the pictorial elements.... The visual component of comics as well as films does not have a counterpart in everyday communication. There are no 'picture projectionists' in the way that there are human narrating voices. Accordingly, comics cannot activate the cognitive schema of a personalized narrating voice via the graphic channel" (389, my translation from the German). Neitzel flatly claims that "neither the player nor the avatar can be the narrator of a video game, because neither the player nor the avatar narrate [except, one would have to add, in cases where the latter *does* narrate]" ("Point of View" 28n13, my translation from the German).

33. Evidently, this "narratorial twist" and the resulting ontological relocation of the previously represented situations within the storyworld as a whole can also aim at "lower-order" subworlds. If, for example, a narrator who was initially represented as if he or she were intradiegetic successively turns out to have been hypodiegetic, what was initially marked as situations belonging to a hypodiegetic secondary storyworld

Notes to pages 151–157 381

may turn out to actually belong to a hypo-hypodiegetic tertiary storyworld. Incidentally, applying these kinds of fairly technical labels to the various represented (narrating) situations seems less interesting and perhaps also less important than precisely describing their ontological (inter)relation.

34. Genette's discussion of this question in *Narrative Discourse* (243–252) and *Narrative Discourse Revisited* (96–113) is rather nuanced and cannot be reduced to a simple distinction between heterodiegetic and homodiegetic narrators. In fact, it seems that there are not very many intradiegetic heterodiegetic narrators who are neither part of the story nor the storyworld they tell, which likely has to do with the fact that the narration attributed to these kinds of narrators is usually fictional and that there are comparatively few everyday situations in which fictional verbal narration regularly takes place (at least not in the form of spoken everyday communication, that is). An interesting example of a film that plays with these expectations is Burton's *Big Fish*, where the presumedly fictional "tall tales" of the intradiegetic narrator eventually turn out to have been only slightly exaggerated "life stories."

35. The term "narrating I" refers to the version of the homodiegetic narrator that *narrates* what an ontologically distinct version of him- or herself, referred to by the term "experiencing I," *experiences* or, rather, has experienced. The interplay of narratorial and nonnarratorial representation characteristic for multimodal media such as films, comics, and video games complicates the distinction between the narrating I and the experiencing I at least slightly, since both the narratorial and the nonnarratorial representation may contribute to the representation of both the narrating I and the experiencing I.

36. One of the reasons for this might be that, while the use of writing to communicate narratively is still comparatively common in everyday situations, the narrating situation that intradiegetic thinking narrators establish is not: silently telling stories to oneself seems, indeed, to be as far removed from the prototypical narrating situation as it gets (and might indicate a certain amount of mental instability, such as in the highly paranoid thinking narrator in Gilliam's *Fear and Loathing in Las Vegas*, who is further examined in chapter 7).

37. Of course, the fact that the narratorial representation attributable to an intradiegetic (or "lower-order") narrator may, in some cases, be considered nonfictional in the context of the narrating situation in which it is produced does not say anything about whether the narrative work of which this situation is a part is fictional or nonfictional. If the

intradiegetic (or "lower-order") narrator in question is part of a fictional narrative work, his or her narratorial representation remains fictional in the context of the actual world even if it is represented as being nonfictional in the context of the narrating situation in which it is (fictionally) produced.

38. D. A. Black suggests otherwise, but it seems that his argument against extradiegetic narrators in film is mainly due to a reductionist conceptualization of the extradiegetic narrator, which ultimately appears rather void, as it does not accept *any* meaningful definition of an extradiegetic narrator in film, to begin with: "Even voiceover narrations that imitate the language and enjoy the spatio-temporal abstraction of the novelistic extradiegetic narrator are, nonetheless, entities of a secondary fictional order, included within an enveloping discourse. They are contingent on the prior narrating act of the actual filmic text itself—prior in necessity, whether or not in time. . . . They are not extradiegetic because the persistence of the text does not hinge on their activity. They do not instigate or cause the film" (21). As has already been mentioned, I would allow for an extradiegetic narrator in cases where the narratorial voice is not located within "a storyworld of its own," even though I tend to agree with D. A. Black that the "source" of extradiegetic verbal narration is usually not represented as being in control of the audiovisual representation.

39. Regarding the quantitative relations between narratorial and nonnarratorial representation, one could, for example, distinguish between *purely narratorial, narratorially dominated, nonnarratorially dominated,* and *purely nonnarratorial* segments of narrative representations across media (see also Thon, "Who's Telling the Tale?"). Since prototypical films, comics, and video games necessarily employ audiovisual, verbal-pictorial, and interactive representation but only make optional use of verbal narration, it would furthermore seem helpful to begin by examining these quantitative relations on a local level, focusing on the presence (or absence) of narratorial representation in particular segments of the dynamically developing narrative representation, before eventually arriving at a description of the dominant quantitative relations between narratorial and nonnarratorial representation in a given narrative work on a global level. However, since this kind of analysis seems to be relatively straightforward, I will not discuss it in too much detail here.

40. Kozloff does not explicitly distinguish between narratorial and nonnarratorial representation, but rather between "narration" and "images."

Still, her overall argument makes it quite clear that the two distinctions are meant to be taken as fairly similar.

41. For a first impression, see, e.g., Cohn, "Discordant Narration"; Olson; Zerweck on unreliability in literary texts; Brütsch; Currie, "Unreliability"; as well as the discussion in Chatman, *Story* 228–237; *Coming to Terms* 74–160; and Lothe 25–27 on unreliability in literature and film; Anderson; Helbig, "'Follow the White Rabbit!'"; Thon, "Mind-Bender"; as well as the book-length studies by Ferenz and, more convincingly, Laass on unreliability in film. See also the contributions in D'hoker and Martens; Helbig, *"Camera"*; Kindt and Köppe; Liptay and Y. Wolf; A. Nünning, *Unreliable Narration*.

42. Booth, who coined the term "unreliable narrator," focuses on what I describe as evaluative unreliability, "call[ing] a narrator *reliable* when he [or she] speaks for or acts in accordance with the norms of the work (which is to say, the implied author's norms), *unreliable* when he [or she] does not" (*The Rhetoric* 158–159, original emphases). In the narratological works on unreliability that follow Booth, however, the distinction between what I describe as representational unreliability and evaluative unreliability is well established. See, e.g., "factual inaccuracy" versus "ideological unreliability" in Fludernik, "Defining (In)Sanity"; "unreliable narration" versus "discordant narration" in Cohn, "Discordant Narration"; and "mimetic unreliability" versus "axiological unreliability" in Kindt; or, focused on unreliability in film, "factual-mimetic unreliability" versus "normative-ideological unreliability" in Helbig, "'Follow the White Rabbit!'"; "descriptive unreliability" versus "normative unreliability" in Ferenz; "factual unreliability" versus "normative unreliability" in Laass.

43. Phelan, for example, distinguishes between "misreporting," "misinterpreting," "misevaluating," "underreporting," "underinterpreting," and "underevaluating" as six forms of narratorial unreliability, allowing for a more nuanced analysis that takes into account not only the differences between "reporting, interpreting, and evaluating" (*Living to Tell* 50) as three core activities commonly attributed to the narrator but also the differences between narratorial unreliability that is defined by what Olson describes as "untrustworthy" as opposed to merely "fallible" narration, respectively. More recently, Hansen has proposed to distinguish between "intranarratorial," "internarratorial," "intertextual," and "extratextual unreliability," leading to a more precise description of the frame that allows the reader (or, more generally, the recipient) to comprehend a narrator as unreliable. See also Phelan, "Estranging

Unreliability," for further differentiation with regard to "estranging" versus "bonding unreliability."

44. I do not contest that multimodal media can make use of evaluative unreliability, but they tend to do so primarily via narratorial representation, as realizing evaluative unreliability without a narrator is much harder than realizing representational unreliability. As Currie insisted comparatively early, though, "narrative unreliability is a concept separable from the concept of an unreliable *narrator*" ("Unreliability" 19, original emphasis). I remain skeptical with regard to Currie's extensive reference to the "implied author" as being "epistemically dominant over the narrator in this sense: that the intentions of the implied author *determine* what is true in the story, while the mental economy of the narrator is thought of simply as a part of the story itself and not as authoritative" ("Unreliability" 20, original emphasis), but as has already been discussed, this skepticism is largely terminological, since I prefer to understand the nonnarratorial representation as being attributable to the hypothetical author collective of a film rather than as being "attributable to the film's implied maker" ("Unreliability" 27). All in all, though, I tend to agree that "there is something awkward—indeed, something close to incoherence—about the idea of a controlling narrator in film" (Currie, "Unreliability" 21) and that it is "better to say simply that in such a case we have unreliable narrative without a narrator" (Currie, "Unreliability" 22).

45. Even nonnarratorial representational unreliability is usually related to characters in some way—either to the (commonly "misreporting") unreliable verbal narration of a narrator or to the (commonly "underreported") unreliable perception of a "regular" character. While the characters whose unreliable perception is represented by the nonnarratorial representation cannot be said to "narrate" in any meaningful sense of the word and, accordingly, I would argue against describing the character whose perception is somehow emulated or, rather, simulated by the nonnarratorial representation as a kind of "character narrator" (as some have suggested), it would seem that the second kind of motivation of nonnarratorial representational unreliability is, in fact, more common and, perhaps, also more interesting. See the further discussion of strategies of subjective representation in the third part of this book.

46. In the case of video games, where narrative functions are generally intertwined with ludic functions, narrators also provide orientation or generate disorientation with regard to the ludic structure of the game.

See the more detailed discussion in the context of the sample analyses provided in the following chapter.

5. Narratorial Representation across Media

1. Both of these films are adaptations of well-known contemporary novels, namely, Patrick Süskind's *Das Parfum* and Chuck Palahniuk's *Fight Club*.
2. See, e.g., Kozloff or Chion, *The Voice*, for a general discussion of voice-over narration, Ferenz or Laass for a discussion of unreliable narrators in films ranging from the classical examples of *Rashomon* and *Stage Fright* to the more recent standard examples of *Fight Club* and *The Usual Suspects*, as well as Thon, "Mind-Bender"; "Zur Metalepse," for a discussion of self-reflexive and metaleptic narrators in films such as *Adaptation.* and *Fight Club*.
3. While the quotes themselves are evidently attributable to (some version of) T. S. Eliot and Sepp Herberger, then, the *quoting* would arguably be more of an authorial than a narratorial activity.
4. As well as hypodiegetic and hypo-hypodiegetic narrators, if one chooses to comprehend the relation between the represented situations the way I tentatively proposed in chapter 3.
5. Of course, my argument that these kinds of highly "covert" and rather rudimentary forms of "verbal narration" are not unproblematically described as narratorial representation does not imply that one cannot distinguish between pictorial, auditive, verbal, and other elements of the audiovisual representation.
6. Particularly if one takes into account the increase in narrative complexity that can be observed in contemporary comics and video games, it seems quite unlikely that films are intrinsically more capable of realizing narratorial or, rather, narrative unreliability in general and representational unreliability in particular, however. Rather, it seems that their cultural influence and certain developments that have moved the "mind-bender" into the mainstream during the 1990s allowed them to popularize complex strategies of representational unreliability sooner (which, incidentally, does not imply that such strategies were entirely absent in the films of previous decades).
7. *The Usual Suspects* does not allow the spectator to intersubjectively construct the story(world) "how it really was," but limits itself to marking Verbal's version of the story as highly unreliable. While it becomes increasingly clear that the hypodiegetic secondary storyworld that Verbal tells Kujan about does not have much in common with the

diegetic primary storyworld in which he does so, the recipient only gets very limited "access" to the latter.

8. Or just not made very clear, as when Ferenz claims that "Jack [the name that is given to the unnamed narrator in the film's script], who is established as the film's character-narrator within a matter of seconds during the film's opening shot, is trying to come to terms with his troubled situation in the upper floor of a skyscraper" and draws a somewhat skewed "distinction between the narrating-I (the remembering narrator) and the experiencing-I (the remembered experiences)" (106).

9. There are quite a few examples such as *Fight Club*, *Adaptation.*, or S. Black's *Kiss Kiss Bang Bang* where the audiovisual representation follows the verbal narration of a more or less explicitly represented narrator rather closely, which may create the impression that the narrator "triggers" certain aspects of the audiovisual representation, sometimes also implying at least some degree of authorship in the process. However, while comics can easily realize the kind of "authorial" narrators represented as being in control not only of the verbal narratorial representation but also of the verbal-pictorial representation that prototypically cannot be attributed to a narrator, the specific mediality of films and video games makes representing this kind of narratorial configuration significantly more difficult, with video games such as *Ultima Underworld* (featuring Warren Spector), *Metal Gear Solid: Peace Walker* (featuring Hideo Kojima), *The Return of Ishtar* (featuring Masanobu Endo), *Half-Life* (featuring Gabe Newell), *Spore* (featuring Will Wright), or the games in the *DeathSpank* series (featuring a range of strongly "fictionalized" members of Hothead Games in the "Hot Cave" and on the "Hot Island")) usually limiting the "intratextual" representation of authoring characters to (more or less strongly "fictionalized") cameo appearances.

10. While the fictional Charlie is clearly represented as one of the authors of *Adaptation.* (i.e., as the film's scriptwriter), he is not represented as being fully in control of the audiovisual representation. The extent to which this is possible in feature films is perhaps more clearly illustrated by the narrator in *Kiss Kiss Bang Bang*, Harry Lockhart, who is not only highly metareferential (making various self-reflexive remarks such as "Okay, I was a bad narrator, again" or direct spectator addresses such as "And you? How about it, film-goer?") but is also represented as being capable of stopping the audiovisual representation and of directly adding diagrammatic markers to the picture. In fact, *Kiss Kiss Bang*

Bang provides a plausibilizing explanation of the narrator's unusual abilities: while Harry's narrating I is initially represented as extradiegetic (and homodiegetic), the film ends with a sequence that represents Harry as having spoken the previous verbal narration in front of a computer that supposedly contains a film that was produced after the previously represented events took place and, hence, can be comprehended as allowing Harry's narrating I to not only provide but also control the audiovisual representation that has accompanied his verbal narration. Among other things, the ending of *Kiss Kiss Bang Bang* also illustrates the limitations inherent in using static distinctions between extradiegetic and intradiegetic narrators or diegetic primary and hypodiegetic secondary storyworlds for describing the dynamic unfolding of the plot not only of contemporary films but also of comics, video games, and other multimodal media. Technically, the fact that *Kiss Kiss Bang Bang* represents the narrating situation in which its narratorial representation is generated would indicate that the narrator, who is initially represented as extradiegetic, could be described as eventually turning out to be intradiegetic, leading to a relocation of the previously represented situations within a hypodiegetic secondary storyworld instead of a diegetic primary storyworld. Considering that the representation of the narrating situation seems to be primarily meant as an entertaining "twist ending" and, moreover, the narrating I of Harry Lockhart (as well as his friend and boss Perry van Shrike) is represented as having authored at least parts of the film, arguably allows for an alternative description that (perhaps somewhat paradoxically but nevertheless closer to the film's overall representational logic) suggests a comprehension of the ending as a brief representation of *Kiss Kiss Bang Bang*'s "extradiegetic level," acknowledging that the final revelation that what the spectator has seen is a fictional film within the film does not fundamentally alter how any of the previously represented situations will be comprehended.

11. The sequence could also be described as a fairly pronounced case of *mise en abyme*—a term that, according to W. Wolf, refers to "a discrete lower-level element or structure 'mirror[ing]' an analogous element or structure on the framing higher level" ("Framing Borders" 198). Moreover, mise en abyme is closely related to metalepsis. As, for example, Meister remarks, "one of the consequences of looking at metalepsis's formal properties is the realization that the distinction between *mise en abyme* and *metalepsis* concerns mainly the level of apparentness and unavoidability which the aporia

assumes in a particular work" ("The *Metalepticon*" n. pag., original emphases).

12. More specifically, comics can use either verbal or pictorial modes of representation, and while the verbal narration's mode of representation is written in a large majority of cases, there are some examples of comics using pictures to represent verbal narration too. This is comparatively common in wordless comics such as S. Tan's *The Arrival*, where, for obvious reasons, intradiegetic narrators' narration is not presented verbally at all. I will also discuss the ways in which *The Arrival* employs strategies of subjective representation in more detail in chapter 7.

13. Arguably, the potential narrative functions of narration boxes are similar, then, to what is commonly described as "voice-over narration" in film (which, incidentally, can also be found in many contemporary video games). While it is often helpful to distinguish between verbal narration attributable to an extradiegetic narrator (whose represented mode is usually not specified), verbal narration attributable to an intradiegetic thinking narrator, and representations of a character's internal voice that are not happily characterized as verbal narration anymore, I certainly acknowledge that these distinctions are not always easily drawn and that some narrative works (or, rather, their authors) may actively try to subvert them. One way or another, it seems that there are only very few thinking intradiegetic narrators, as actually using a character's internal voice to narrate (i.e., represent the character in question as "thinking thoughts" that can be understood as a narrative representation in possessing at least a minimal degree of narrativity) generates highly implausible narrating situations. I further discuss this question in the third part of the present study.

14. This effect is significantly more pronounced in *The Sandman*, though it can also be observed in *The League of Extraordinary Gentlemen*.

15. While the parts of *The League of Extraordinary Gentlemen* that represent the "fictionalized" author figures/authoring characters of Alan Moore and Kevin O'Neill are more clearly marked as peritexts than the segments of *Kiss Kiss Bang Bang* that represent the authoring character of Harry Lockhart and Perry van Shrike, my decision to describe the formers' representation as external to the comic's storyworld and, hence, to argue that the extraordinary Ms. Murray and the equally extraordinary gentlemen who accompany her are best comprehended as being located within a diegetic primary storyworld is just that: a decision to draw the ontological borders between the represented situations in a certain way that does not prevent me from acknowledging that these

borders could also be drawn differently—resulting, for example, in a description of the fictional Alan Moore, Kevin O'Neill, and Scotty Smiles as being located within a diegetic primary storyworld and the fictional Mr. Bond, Ms. Murray, and Mr. Quatermain as being located within a hypodiegetic secondary storyworld instead.

16. However, the way in which the narrator narrates and the use of the past tense throughout her whole narration makes it clear that the narration takes place sometime *after* the narrated events. This is, of course, the prototypical narrating situation.

17. While not a general rule, *Habibi* often uses these kinds of ornate margins when the verbal-pictorial representation illustrates Dodola's intradiegetic heterodiegetic verbal narration.

18. Of course, this also has to do with the technological dimension of comics, films, and video games: while the latter two require quite an extensive technological apparatus to be produced (as well as watched and played), the former can, at least in principle, be made not only by a single author but also with comparatively simple technological means.

19. A special case is constituted by intradiegetic (or "lower-order") authoring characters that are not represented as authoring (some aspect of) the narrative work of which they are a part (such as Charlie Kaufman in *Adaptation.*, Art Spiegelman in *Maus*, or, perhaps, the inhabitants of the "Hot Island" or the "Hot Cave" in Hothead's *DeathSpank* series), but rather as authoring an intradiegetic narrative work of some kind (such as Wilson Taylor as the author of the *Tommy Taylor* series in Carey and Gross's *The Unwritten* series or Art Spiegelman as the author of "Prisoner on the Hell Planet" in *Maus*, Harvey Pekar in Springer Berman and Pulcini's film adaptation of *American Splendor* or Nick Reve and his team shooting a low-budget film in DiCillo's *Living in Oblivion*, and Alan Wake writing *Departure* in Remedy's *Alan Wake* or, albeit not entirely to the point, Stan Lee appearing as a "fictionalized" superhero in Beenox's video game adaptation of *The Amazing Spider-Man*).

20. Additional cases illustrating the difficulties that may arise when readers try to decide whether a given homodiegetic verbal narration should be attributed to an extradiegetic speaking or an intradiegetic thinking narrator can be found in F. Miller's *Sin City* series. In *Sin City: The Hard Goodbye*, for example, what may initially appear like an intradiegetic thinking narrator increasingly seems to turn out to be an extradiegetic speaking narrator via the kind of deictic markers also found in *Fight Club*, only to lead to a somewhat paradoxical conclusion that suggests that the verbal narration is attributable to an intradiegetic thinking

narrator after all, when the narrator's experiencing I dies on the electric chair. I will further discuss the narratorial uses of characters' internal voices in the third part of this book.

21. Let me reemphasize that while one cannot draw a clearly demarcated line between "covert" verbal narration still qualifying as narratorial representation and verbal elements more appropriately being understood as part of the nonnarratorial representation attributable to the hypothetical author collective, I would argue that the initial verbal narration in *The Sandman* series is best described as the former.

22. This would make the initial use of the narration boxes that are attributed to Dream describable as a narratorially framed representation of the internal voice of Dream's experiencing I that is only marked as such a posteriori. See the third part of this book for further discussion of this strategy of subjective representation.

23. The written narration in Rorschach's diary that frames much of the overall narrative representation in Moore and D. Gibbons's *Watchmen* may be considered an example of an apparent narratorial indeterminacy that works the other way around. Introduced as being attributable to an apparently extradiegetic narrator, it later becomes clear that the diary in question is located within the diegetic primary storyworld, rendering the narrator clearly intradiegetic (or, rather, rendering the narrative representation attributable to Rorschach intradiegetic, which makes it a standard case of how fictional as well as nonfictional intradiegetic or "lower-order" narrators commonly act not only as narrators but also as a kind of author).

24. As I have previously noted, Dream's supernatural abilities occasionally make locating him within the storyworld as a whole rather tricky: for example, Dream enters the dream of Alex Burgess, which arguably can be described as a hypodiegetic secondary storyworld, but Dream himself may still be thought of as diegetic, since the ability to transgress the ontological boundaries between the storyworld's "factual domain" and The Dreaming is part of what defines him as one of the seven Endless and the anthropomorphization of dreams.

25. While there are quite a few examples of unreliable narration in the medium of comics as well, it seems that the primary function of comics' narratorial representation is orientation, not disorientation. While this is certainly not intrinsic to the "semiotic dimension" of the medium (and, hence, might be more appropriately explained by reference to genre-specific than by reference to medium-specific representational conventions), narrative works that employ representational unreliability

as their core strategy of narrative representation seem significantly more common among contemporary (mainstream) feature films than they are among contemporary (mainstream) graphic novels.

26. There are, of course, graphic novels such as J. Smith's *Bone* that use a largely verbal-pictorial (or nonnarratorial) mode of representation and at least some special cases such as Moore and D. Gibbons's *Watchmen*, certain segments of which could be described as exclusively verbal (or narratorial). Nonetheless, even in more clearly narratorially dominated works such as *The Sandman: Preludes and Nocturnes* or *Habibi*, the combination of narratorial and nonnarratorial representation is in constant flux. While both the quantitative and the qualitative relations between narratorial and nonnarratorial representation can be examined with regard to the global structure of a given narrative work, then, it often seems more useful to describe these relations on a local level first—i.e., with regard to the stories told by particular narrators. For further discussion of the relations between narratorial and nonnarratorial representation as well as between words and pictures in comics, see also, e.g., McCloud; Rippl and Etter; Schüwer 445–458.

27. The second chapter of the second part of *Maus*, "Auschwitz (Time Flies)" in "And Here My Troubles Began (From Mauschwitz to the Catskills and Beyond)," starts with a representation of Art Spiegelman wearing a mouse mask and speaking with a distinctly authorial voice: "Vladek died of congestive heart failure on August 18, 1982 . . . Françoise and I stayed with him in the Catskills back in August 1979 [which was represented in the first chapter of the second part, "Mauschwitz"]. Vladek started working as a tinman in Auschwitz in the spring of 1944 . . . I started working on this page at the very end of February 1987. In May 1987 Françoise and I are expecting a baby. . . . Between May 16, 1944, and May 24, 1944 over 100,000 Hungarian Jews were gassed in Auschwitz. . . . In September 1986, after 8 years of work, the first part of MAUS was published. It was a critical and commercial success." He goes on to link the commercial success of *Maus* to his feelings of depression, followed by representations of absurd interactions with journalists and people who want to turn *Maus* into a "franchise," which leads him to (once more, metaphorically) regress into childhood before the sequence is concluded by his visit to Pavel, his "shrink," who is "a Czech Jew, a survivor of Terezin and Auschwitz," and Art's return to the tape recorder, where hearing his dead father's voice makes him experience the "regress to childhood" once again. Not only the masks but also the subject matter clearly mark this highly metareferential sequence as

representing situations that are not only temporally, spatially, and causally but also ontologically disconnected from those represented in the previous chapters (and in the first part of the graphic novel in particular), yet it remains somewhat unclear how one should describe this ontological disconnect. What does seem clear is that the "masked" Art represented here can be comprehended as being the "source" of the supposedly extradiegetic narratorial representation of the previous chapters. One way of describing the sequence, then, would be to say that *Maus* establishes a new "diegetic level" that renders the previously established diegetic primary storyworld (told by Art) hypodiegetic and the previously established hypodiegetic secondary storyworld (told by Vladek) hypo-hypodiegetic. Due to the sequences' focus on Art's authorship, the pronounced use of "animal masks" instead of "animal heads" to mark membership in certain social groups, and the metareferential use of the tape recorder with Vladek's voice, though, I prefer to treat these seven and a half pages as a particular kind of peritext that does not establish a new "diegetic level," but, rather, can be comprehended as representing parts of the "extradiegetic level" on which the narrating I of the author-narrator Art is located. See also my previous remarks on *Kiss Kiss Bang Bang* and *The League of Extraordinary Gentlemen*.

28. Of course, both the real A. Spiegelman and the represented Art have done extensive research to complement V. Spiegelman's/Vladek's narration, but the focus of the graphic novel is still on the latter.
29. I would also like to at least mention that ascribing a primary ludic function to a given element of verbal narration is usually contingent on the respective game goals being reinforced via interface elements such as the extrafictional player directions I will briefly return to below or other forms such as the "questlog" that can commonly be found in contemporary role-playing games in particular. In this context, it might also be worth noting that "questlogs" and similar devices commonly contain verbal narration, in turn—just as many contemporary video games commonly allow the player-controlled character(s) to find artifacts that contain "optional" intradiegetic verbal narration. For a more extensive discussion of video game interfaces, see, once more, Jørgensen, *Gameworld Interfaces*.
30. Contemporary media culture's tendency toward self-reflexivity and metareference has also led to quite a few metaleptic narrators being found in video games. Examples include the narrators addressing the player in Telltale Games' point-and-click adventure *Sam and Max: The*

Devil's Playhouse and Hothead's role-playing game *On the Rain-Slick Precipice of Darkness: Episode One*. See also the interactively unreliable narrators in *Prince of Persia: The Sands of Time* and *Bastion*, which are analyzed further below. A very recent example that combines a narratorially dominated gameplay with an explicit reflection not only on video games' obligatory interactivity but also on their facultative nonlinearity is Davey Wreden's *Source* mod *The Stanley Parable*, which features an extradiegetic heterodiegetic narrator who tells the story of the player-controlled character Stanley but whose narratorial representation is combined with nonnarratorial interactive gameplay that continuously allows the player to make choices that blatantly contradict the verbal narration. While *The Stanley Parable* was published after the main work on the present study had already concluded, I would expect that it will draw some attention from the narratologically inclined parts of game studies in the not too distant future. For additional discussion, see Thon, "Game Studies."

31. While the narrating situation in which the verbal narration originates is explicitly represented, in a way, the player is given so little detail (apart from the rather distinctive qualities of the narrator's voice) that it may seem somewhat problematic to speak of an intradiegetic narrator without additional qualification here. More specifically, while it may be technically true that the "intradiegetic" narrator's verbal narration frames the entire gameplay, which, therefore, would have to be described as contributing to a hypodiegetic secondary storyworld, such a description is fairly uninteresting due to the rather simple nature of this narratorial framing. Moreover, it could also be argued that the initial change of "diegetic level" soon morphs into a mere analepsis, since the verbal narration is clearly marked as nonfictional even though the narrator may turn out to be not entirely reliable (in that, at least in one actualizable version of the game's nonlinear narrative structure, her narrating I withholds a rather crucial piece of information regarding the part she plays in the story she tells, just as her generally rather manipulative experiencing I refrains from telling DeathSpank about the relation between the Thongs of Virtue and her family history). Under this description, the gameplay would then morph from being a representation of a nonfictional hypodiegetic secondary storyworld to the representation of an earlier point in the diegetic primary storyworld's time.

32. The narrator is rather clearly—albeit somewhat ambiguously—marked as homodiegetic, though, when she introduces her narration by

mentioning that she has to tell the narrated events before she becomes "too old to remember."

33. The verbal narration of the narrator, who in one actualizable version of the nonlinear narrative structure turns out to have been Sandy Bravitor's ("barely intradiegetic") narrating I, is limited to a few cut-scenes, but the somewhat naive player-controlled character DeathSpank repeatedly encounters and is manipulated by the narrator's significantly younger experiencing I within the "barely hypodiegetic" secondary storyworld (who, incidentally, also functions as a "barely hypodiegetic" narrator during the "final revelation").

34. In fact, he continues to do so in the third installment of the series, *The Baconing*.

35. Or, as Greg Kasavin of Supergiant Games explained to me in a personal email correspondence on July 29, 2013: "Virtually all of the narration (and all the content in *Bastion* in general) is scripted by hand for each level. We ensured some lines [of the narratorial representation] played conditionally and some lines would not play depending on how quickly the player[-controlled character] was moving. We also ensured that no lines repeated during play, unless the player re-played an entire scenario (though even then we tended to have alternate lines that would play). We recorded more than 3,000 lines of narration in all." It might be worth noting that Supergiant Games has further developed their take on narratorially dominated gameplay in the recently published *Transistor*.

36. Incidentally, this may also lead to inconsistencies that necessitate the application of medium-specific charity when, for example, a player plays through a level very fast, thereby skipping certain "pieces" of the verbal narration that subsequently appear to be missing.

37. The game's nonlinear narrative structure is reflected in the narratorial representation as well: after the first playthrough, the player-controlled character can choose whether he wants to use the Bastion to "turn back time" or to evacuate the (up to) four survivors. If the player chooses to start a "New Game+" afterwards, the narrator sometimes uses different "narration pieces" that make him seem on the brink of remembering that he has told the tale of the Kid before—which, through the Bastion's ability to "turn back time," may, indeed, be true not only on the level of representation but also on the level of the storyworld.

38. It might be worth noting here that *Bastion* also uses yet another nonnarratorial verbal strategy of representation that seems to play an increasingly important, albeit ultimately auxiliary, role in contemporary narrative video games: the various loading screens in *Bastion* contain

"pieces" of highly "covert" verbal narration that may contribute to the representation of comparatively specific situations, give more general information about the game's "backstory," or even employ an extrafictional voice that gives hints regarding the game mechanics. In fact, this use of *nonnarratorial narrative* and *extrafictional ludic communication* in the context of loading screens is fairly common in contemporary video games (and can be traced back to early text adventures such as Crowther's *Adventure*, in addition to having commonly been employed by classical role-playing games such as *Baldur's Gate*), with the previously mentioned *Dragon Age: Origins* providing another good example of the device's range of forms and functions: the loading screens in *Dragon Age: Origins* may contain "descriptive" details about the game's storyworld and highly condensed pieces of the game's "backstory" as well as clearly extrafictional direct player addresses and a particularly interesting form of a metaleptic extrafictional voice that addresses the player as if he or she was the player-controlled character. Incidentally, contemporary video games' use of both "fictionalized" and "nonfictionalized" forms of extrafictional directions addressed to the player is certainly not limited to loading screens, with *Prince of Persia: The Sands of Time* and *DeathSpank* providing additional examples of how extrafictional directions may be realized using written inserts instead of the medium-specific form of intertitles that loading screens arguably constitute.

6. Subjectivity as a Transmedial Concept

1. See, e.g., Eder, *Die Figur* 565–646; Fludernik, *Towards a 'Natural' Narratology* 20–43; D. Herman, *Basic Elements* 137–160; Palmer, *Fictional Minds* 1–27; Ryan, *Avatars* 6–12; W. Wolf, "Narrative." See also the detailed discussion of the prototypical features of narrativity in chapter 1. An earlier and considerably shorter version of the argument developed in this and the following chapter has been published in Thon, "Subjectivity." See also Thon, "Perspective," for a discussion of different dimensions of "perspective" in contemporary video games.
2. Readers interested in more extensive surveys of previous research on "perspective," "point of view," and "focalization" in literary narratology may, for example, consult Alber and Fludernik; Broman; D. Herman, "Hypothetical Focalization"; L. Herman and Vervaeck, "Focalization"; Jahn, "Focalization"; "More Aspects"; "Windows"; Kablitz; Niederhoff, "Focalization"; "Perspective"; Nieragden; Prince, "A Point of View"; Schmid, *Narratology* 89–99; Surkamp, "Perspective"; and the

contributions in Hühn, Schmid, and Schönert. In the following, I will also examine selected accounts from literary and film narratology as well as from comics studies and game studies, emphasizing, albeit not exclusively, medium-specific conceptualizations of the genuinely narratological term "focalization" (as opposed to the more widely used terms "perspective" and "point of view").

3. To complicate matters even further, both the term "perspective" and the term "point of view" are commonly used in areas outside of classical as well as postclassical narratology such as art history and theories of pictorial representation. See, e.g., the discussion of "visual" or "pictorial perspective" in pictures by Damisch; Sachs-Hombach; as well as, e.g., Schüwer on comics; and Günzel on video games.

4. Niederhoff generally argues for the "peaceful coexistence" of terms such as "perspective," "point of view," and "focalization." See also Niederhoff, "Focalization"; "Fokalisation."

5. Not unlike Eder, to whose distinction of five types of "mental perspective" I will return below, though of course employing a rather different conceptualization of "perspective" and/or "point of view," Schmid further argues that there are at least five "parameters, aspects, and facets, in each of which the phenomenon of point of view manifests itself in a distinct way" (*Narratology* 100). First, "spatial perspective/point of view" is defined as being "constituted by the location from which the happenings are perceived, with the restrictions of the field of vision that result from the standpoint" (Schmid, *Narratology* 101). Note that Schmid describes "spatial perspective/point of view" as the most literal variety of the term(s): "The concept of spatial point of view is the only one of the terms that express a reference of comprehension and representation to a subject that fulfills the intension of *point of view* or *perspective* in the actual, original sense of the word. All other uses of the term *point of view* are more or less metaphorical" (*Narratology* 101, original emphases). Second, "ideological perspective/point of view" is defined as "encompass[ing] various factors that determine the subjective relationship of the observer to an occurrence: knowledge, way of thinking, evaluative position and intellectual horizons" (Schmid, *Narratology* 101). Third, "temporal perspective/point of view" is defined as "denot[ing] the interval between the original comprehension and the later acts of comprehension and representation" (Schmid, *Narratology* 102). Fourth, the "highly metaphorical" "linguistic perspective/point of view" is defined as referring to the way in which a narrator can "decide whether to narrate in his or her own language or with the terms and

style of an involved third person" (Schmid, *Narratology* 103). There are good reasons not to treat "language" as constituting an independent dimension of "point of view/perspective/focalization" and instead understand the respective phenomena as "verbal indicators" (Rimmon-Kenan, *Narrative Fiction* 84) of subjective representation. Since the purely verbal forms of representation that both Uspensky (17–56) and Schmid (*Narratology* 103–104) seem to be aiming at in this respect are not a particularly salient part of the object domain of this book, though, I will refrain from discussing this question in any detail here. Fifth, "perceptual perspective/point of view," which "is often actually identified with point of view or perspective," is defined as referring to "the prism through which the occurrence is perceived" (Schmid, *Narratology* 104). Without going into any detail here, it should be noted that multidimensional or "multiaspectual" conceptualizations of "perspective," "point of view," and/or "focalization" are not entirely uncommon.

6. Originally coined by Pfister in *The Theory and Analysis of Drama* (57–68), the term "perspective structure" is now often applied to the analysis of literary narrative texts as well. See A. Nünning, *Grundzüge* 64–83; "Mimesis"; Surkamp, *Die Perspektivenstruktur*. While I am generally not convinced that distinguishing between "mental" and "medial perspective" will help solve contemporary narratology's "terminological confusion" in this area, I will briefly discuss particularly salient forms of "perspective structures" in the following.

7. See, e.g., Friedman; Lubbock; as well as the more recent studies by Klepper; Lintvelt; Rabatel, *La construction*; *Une histoire*; and the survey by Niederhoff, "Perspective." See also the influential discussion of "narrative situations" by Stanzel, *Narrative Situations*; *A Theory*, as well as the critique and modification of Stanzel's continuously evolving account by, e.g., Cohn, "The Encirclement"; Diengott and the (problematic) attempts by Hurst; Stanzel, *A Theory* 85–87, to apply the model to film.

8. In cases of "narration which is oriented to the point of view of a character" (Currie, *Narratives* 138), calling this character a "narrator" can only be considered terminologically inaccurate if one presupposes a certain conceptualization of the term. While I do not consider it particularly helpful to speak of "implied narrators" in the context of a transmedial narratology (see chapter 4), the notion of "first-person narration" may still lead to occasionally rather illuminating analyses of nonverbal and multimodal representations in the feature film and beyond.

9. More specifically, Genette intends to end the "confusion between the question *who is the character whose point of view orients the narrative perspective?* and the very different question *who is the narrator?*" (*Narrative Discourse* 186, original emphases). Interestingly, Genette mentions that it would have been better to define "focalization" with regard to questions such as *"who perceives?"* or *"where is the focus of perception?"* (*Narrative Discourse Revisited* 64, original emphases) in a chapter entitled "Perspective," reserving the following chapter entitled "Focalizations" for a discussion (and rather stern refusal) of Bal's criticism.

10. As rhetorically refined as terminologically unconvincing, Genette claims that "the right formula would be: *zero focalization = variable, and sometimes zero, focalization.* Here as elsewhere, the choice is purely operational. This looseness will undoubtedly shock some people, but I see no reason for requiring narratology to become a catechism with a yes-or-no answer to check off for each question, when often the proper answer would be that it depends on the day, the context, and the way the wind is blowing" (*Narrative Discourse Revisited* 74, original emphasis). Still, as, for example, Branigan remarks, "zero focalization" as "'multi-focalization' . . . is not a necessary component of omniscience nor is it useful in examining local effects of character action and awareness" (*Narrative Comprehension* 107). For a more detailed discussion of "omniscience" in literary texts, see, e.g., Culler, "Omniscience"; Morreall; Sternberg, "Omniscience."

11. See Branigan, *Narrative Comprehension* 100–107. Other contributions on "focalization" in film include, e.g., Deleyto; Jost, "The Look"; *L'oeil-caméra*; "Le regard romanesque"; Kuhn 119–194; Schlickers, *Verfilmtes Erzählen* 127–167; "Focalization"; Schweinitz, "Die Ambivalenz"; "Multiple Logik." See also, e.g., Horstkotte and Pedri; Kukkonen, "Comics"; Mikkonen, "Focalization"; "Graphic Narratives"; "Subjectivity"; Round; Schüwer 392–404 on "focalization" in comics and, e.g., Arjoranta; Beil 37–39; Eskelinen, *Cybertext Poetics* 170–179; Neitzel, "Point of View"; Nitsche 145–155 on "focalization" in video games.

12. Jost's distinction between "ocularization," "auricularization," and "focalization" has become a rather common point of reference in recent German film narratology, at least. See, e.g., Kuhn 119–194; Orth; Schlickers, *Verfilmtes Erzählen* 127–167; "Focalization"; Schweinitz, "Die Ambivalenz"; "Multiple Logik."

13. See also the recently published study by Ciccoricco for a transmedial approach to the representation of minds in narrative media that focuses

on novels, interactive fiction, and video games. For further discussions of interactive fiction, see also Aarseth, *Cybertext*; Bell; Montfort.
14. See Neitzel, "Point of View"; as well as Neitzel, "Gespielte Geschichten"; "Narrativity." See also Thon, "Perspective," where I expand on the notion of "spatial point of view/perspective" by also examining "actional point of view/perspective" and "ideological point of view/perspective."
15. Once more, see also the detailed discussion of different forms of "point of action" in Thon, "Perspective," where I propose to distinguish not only between "subjective," "semi-subjective," and "objective points of view" but also between "subjective," "semi-subjective," and "objective points of action."
16. This is a common complaint both within literary narratology and beyond, even though it seldom leads to an abandonment of the terms "perspective," "point of view," and "focalization," in particular. See, e.g., Fludernik, *Towards a 'Natural' Narratology* 343–347; Palmer, *Fictional Minds* 48–52; Schmid, *Narratology* 89–99; as well as Chatman, "Characters"; Eder, *Die Figur* 579–628, on films; Horstkotte and Pedri; Mikkonen, "Focalization," on comics; Beil 29–42; Thon, "Perspective," on video games.
17. See also Chatman, "Characters." I will not use the distinction between "filter," "center," "slant," and "interest-focus" that Chatman proposes (as, for example, Beil does) and will, moreover, focus on strategies that provide "direct access" to nonnarrating characters or the experiencing Is of narrating characters, but the representation of (fictional) subjectivity can, of course, refer to both narrating and nonnarrating characters' minds, and the question how the consciousness of the narrating I "colors" the narratorial representation without the latter providing "direct access" to the former as such is, indeed, rather interesting. See, e.g., Eder, *Die Figur* 613–623; Horstkotte and Pedri; Schmid, *Narratology* 99–174.
18. It might be worth stressing, however, that my decision to refrain from using the *terms* "perspective," "point of view," and "focalization" should in no way be construed as an argument against the heuristic value of the various *concepts* that are associated with them. Indeed, while I would maintain that the terms themselves are largely "beyond saving," the present chapter is still very clearly committed to the criterion of continuity sketched in the introduction of this book. Incidentally, it should also be noted that I will, in fact, occasionally refer to "perspective" and "point of view" in their more technical senses in the context of art history and film studies—i.e., as describing the "spatial perspective"

used in pictorial representations and film's highly conventionalized use of point-of-view shots rather than more complex and encompassing forms of "medial," "narrative" and/or "mental perspective/point of view."

19. Speaking of "direct access" to characters' consciousnesses does not question the mediated nature of narrative representation (see, e.g., Palmer, *Fictional Minds* 131–136). Rather, I use the term as a convenient shorthand to describe forms of representation that are marked as not representing an intersubjective version of the "factual domain" of a storyworld but rather some aspect of the perceptions, quasi-perceptions, consciousness, and/or mind of a character that is located in that very storyworld.

20. See also Nagel, *The View*; as well as, e.g., Popper; Rescher; Rorty. As will have already become clear during my discussion of storyworlds as intersubjective communicative constructs in chapter 2, I would not overemphasize the relevance of the notion of objectivity with regard to questions of epistemology and meaning making in the actual world, where the interplay between subjectivity and intersubjectivity appears to be more pertinent to the issues at hand. Since narrative representations provide "privileged access" to the storyworlds they represent, however, they can offer an objective version of what is or is not the case in these worlds, providing what Nagel calls "the view from nowhere." (At least in principle, this holds for both fictional and nonfictional narrative representations, insofar as both the former and the latter represent storyworlds rather than the actual world. Yet the extent to which an "objectively represented" nonfictional storyworld corresponds to the actual world is, of course, an entirely different matter.)

21. This distinction does not coincide with Schmid's "simple, binary opposition" (*Narratology* 105) between "narratorial" and "figural point of view/perspective"—even more so since there are countless films, comics, and video games where large parts of the representation are not explicitly based on an act of comprehension by either a narrator or a character. However, Schmid seems to be aware of the possibility of a third mode of more or less "neutral" or "objective" representation when he discusses Cohn's proposal to distinguish between "authorial" and "figural" modes of representation (see Cohn, "The Encirclement" 179–180; *Transparent Minds* 145–161). Schmid remarks that, in his "book, the concept *authorial* refers not to the narrator but to the author," and proposes to distinguish between "*authorial, narratorial* and *figural*" (Schmid, *Narratology* 105, footnote 15, original emphases) modes of

representation, but does not go into any detail regarding the implications of an "authorial" mode of representation. See chapter 4 for some additional discussion of authorial and narratorial modes of representation. See also Thon, "Who's Telling the Tale?," for a more detailed examination of what may be described as comics' strategies of *authorial representation*.

22. I had the fortunate opportunity to test the analytical usefulness of this distinction in the context of various undergraduate courses in media analysis that I taught at the University of Hamburg, the University of Mainz, and the University of Tübingen, and would like to express my gratitude to the participants for their kind criticism and challenging questions, both of which led me to eventually draw the distinction the way it is presented here.

23. On this kind of "objective" representation in literary texts see, e.g., Banfield, "Describing the Unobserved"; Broich. The borders between modes of representation can, of course, be drawn differently, but Genette's distinction between "internal focalization," "external focalization," and "nonfocalization" (see Genette, *Narrative Discourse* 189–194; *Narrative Discourse Revisited* 64–71) as well as Mitry's distinction between the "subjective," "semisubjective," and "objective image" (see Mitry 206–219) remain common points of reference despite a tendency toward twofold distinctions. Moreover, various approaches that seem to adhere to the subjective/objective distinction at first glance often allow for further subdivisions of these categories. See, e.g., Branigan, *Narrative Comprehension* 125–191; Deleuze 73–88; Deleyto.

24. For recent general discussions of the problem of consciousness, see, e.g., Carruthers; Chalmers; Damasio; Dennett; Lycan, *Consciousness*; Metzinger; Searle, *Mind*. For influential approaches to the representation of characters' consciousnesses within literary narratology and film studies, see, e.g., Cohn, *Transparent Minds*; Fludernik, *Towards a 'Natural' Narratology*; Grodal, *Embodied Visions*; *Moving Pictures*; D. Herman, *Basic Elements*; *Storytelling*; Palmer, *Fictional Minds*; *Social Minds*; Persson; Zunshine. Unsurprisingly, the questions of how characters' consciousnesses and characters' minds are represented and comprehended are also examined in some detail in the theories of character already briefly discussed in chapter 2.

25. While certainly not the only theory of (quasi-)perception available, I will follow Searle and others in generally treating perception and perceptual experience as a form of intentional mental state or internal mental representation. For further discussion, see the studies of

consciousness mentioned above as well as the ecological account developed by J. J. Gibson. See also the more general recent studies by, e.g., Crane; Foster; Noë. Without going into too much detail with regard to the debates surrounding conceptual and nonconceptual "content" that chapter 3 has already touched upon, it seems fairly uncontroversial that *perceptions* and *quasi-perceptions*—i.e., mental states that are *like* perceptions without actually being perceptions, one of the most well-researched forms of which is "mental imagery"—have at least some irreducible sensory, phenomenal, or nonconceptual qualities (sometimes called "qualia"). For further discussion of the relation between perception and quasi-perception (or "mental imagery" or "imagined perception"), see also the survey by Thomas; as well as, e.g., Currie and Ravenscroft, which provides an in-depth discussion of "recreative imagination"; and McGinn; A. Richardson; Rollins on "mental imagery."

26. In the context of a considerably more detailed examination of "the dependence of imaginings on other kinds of mental states" (Currie and Ravenscroft 19) such as beliefs, desires, and perceptions, Currie and Ravenscroft also mention the relevance of "theories of mental simulation" which roughly argue "that to understand and predict the behaviour of others we need not depend on the possession of an apparently rather complex psychological theory; instead we can draw on our capacity to simulate other people's reasoning and decision-making" (50). See, e.g., Goldman, "Interpretation"; *Simulating Minds*; R. M. Gordon, "Folk Psychology"; "The Simulation Theory"; and the (other) contributions in Davies and Stone, *Folk Psychology*; *Mental Simulation*.

27. In fact, Searle explicitly includes "visual perception" (*Mind* 99) among the conscious intentional states, and it seems evident that the qualitative character of conscious mental states is closely related to experience.

28. Or, as Metzinger puts it in what remains one of the most extensive studies of "consciousness, the phenomenal self, and the first-person perspective" (1), "in conscious experience there is a world, there is a self, and there is a relation between both—because in an interesting sense this world appears *to* the experiencing self" (5, original emphasis), which leads him to describe "subjective experience" as "the dynamics of exclusively *phenomenal* representational processes" (20, original emphasis).

29. Somewhat unhappily, the way that the terms "intentional" and "intentionality" are used in the philosophy of mind is rather different from the way the terms "intentional" and "intentions" are used in the context of

literary theory's "(hypothetical) intentionalism." As Searle remarks, "intentionality," in the context of the philosophy of mind, "is the general term for all the various forms by which the mind can be directed at, or be about, or of, objects and states of affairs in the world," but it "is an unfortunate word" in that it "suggests that intentionality, in the sense of directedness, must always have some connection with 'intending' in the sense in which, for example, I intend to go to the movies tonight" (*Mind* 85–86).

30. Searle later specifies this argument using another well-established distinction between the mind and the brain, emphasizing yet again that "if a state is a genuine unconscious *mental* state, then it must be at least the sort of state that could be conscious. We need, therefore, to distinguish *nonconscious* states of the brain . . . from *unconscious* mental states that are realized in the brain" (*Mind* 86–87, original emphases). As the present book is primarily concerned with *conscious mental states*, occasionally touches on *unconscious mental states*, and does not discuss *nonconscious brain states* at all, I will leave it at that.

31. See, e.g., M. Smith's proposal to triangulate "the phenomenological level . . . , the psychological level . . . , and the neurological level" ("Triangulating Aesthetic Experience" 83) of aesthetic experience.

32. See, once more, M. Smith, who notes that "the question of the function(s) of the conscious mind has come to be known as one of the 'easy problems' in debates around consciousness. The hard problem arises from the very fact that consciousness exists" ("Consciousness" 41).

33. Just like consciousness and (quasi-)perception, knowledge is a rather complex and contested concept that has been extensively examined within cognitive psychology and the philosophy of mind. For general discussions of knowledge and epistemic justification, see, e.g., Alston; Chisholm; Williamson. Large parts of the narratological discussion have—at least implicitly—focused on knowledge that takes "propositional form," but in any case, it seems that nonverbal narrative representations cannot as easily provide "direct access" to either "propositional knowledge" ("knowing that") or "processual knowledge" ("knowing how") as they can provide "direct access" to (quasi-)perceptual aspects of a represented character's consciousness. A similar observation applies to norms and values, which also tend to take "propositional form."

34. Perhaps no less than the field of research on consciousness, the field of research on emotions is characterized by a terminological and

conceptual heterogeneity of approaches from philosophy of mind, cognitive psychology, phenomenology, and psychoanalysis, leading to a situation where the use of terms such as "emotion," "feeling," "affect," or "mood" requires at least some additional explanation. For the purpose of this chapter, though, it seems sufficient to follow G. M. Smith in roughly distinguishing between *emotions* as being determined by "an action tendency, an orientation toward objects, and a goal orientation" ("Local Emotions" 104) and *moods* as being "less clearly object-, goal-, and action-oriented" ("Local Emotions" 105). However, considerably more could be said on this and related questions. For general studies from the philosophy of mind, see, e.g., Goldie; Nussbaum; Voss. Moreover, the questions of how characters' emotions can be represented by narrative works across media and how these works can "evoke" emotions in their recipients have recently moved to the center of cognitively oriented film studies and film philosophy. See, e.g., N. Carroll, *The Philosophy*; *Theorizing the Moving Image*; Fahlenbrach; Grodal, *Embodied Visions*; *Moving Pictures*; Hogan, *Cognitive Science*; Plantinga, *Moving Viewers*; G. M. Smith, *Film Structure*; M. Smith, *Engaging Characters*; E. Tan; and the contributions in Plantinga and G. M. Smith; as well as Bartsch, Eder, and Fahlenbrach; Brütsch et al.; Grau and Keil. See also, e.g., Hanich; Sobchack on film phenomenological approaches; Hogan, *What Literature*; Winko on emotions and literature; Keen; C. W. Schneider on emotions and comics; Perron, "A Cognitive Psychological Approach"; *Silent Hill*; as well as Frome; Järvinen, "Understanding Video Games"; Juul, *The Art*; and the contributions in Perron, *Horror Video Games*, on emotions and video games.

35. Moreover, even though my focus will primarily be on how both narratorial and nonnarratorial strategies of subjective representation provide "direct access" to represented characters' (quasi-)perceptions, the question how the subjectivity not only of narrating and nonnarrating characters but also of authors and, perhaps, even recipients can systematically be taken into account would certainly be worthy of future consideration. As has already been mentioned, the question of how the norms and values that a narrative work represents relate to the norms and values of the work's authors, as well as the question of how the emotions and moods that a narrative work represents relate to the emotions of the work's recipients, has been particularly productive within literary and film narratology. For further discussion of the norms and values of narrating and nonnarrating characters as well as of authors and recipients, see, e.g., Booth, *The Company*; Korthals Altes;

Phelan, *Reading People*, on literary texts; Eder, *Die Figur*; M. Smith, *Engaging Characters*, on films; F. Schröter and Thon, "Simulierte Spielfiguren"; "Video Game Characters"; Thon, "Perspective"; Zierold on video games.

36. While many narratologists who use Genette's model as a primary point of departure focus on the representation of perception and knowledge, one can also find several attempts to examine the narrative representation of other aspects of characters' minds. The earliest explicitly multidimensional conceptualization of "point of view" that I know of was proposed by Uspensky, who emphasizes that "we may consider point of view as an ideological and evaluative position" or "as a spatial and temporal position," that "we may study it with respect to perceptual characteristics" or "in a purely linguistic sense" (6), in order to arrive at a conceptualization of "point of view" that distinguishes between an "ideological plane," a "phraseological plane," a "spatial and temporal plane," and a "plane of psychology" (see also the critical discussion in Schmid, *Narratology* 95–99). Another early multidimensional model of "point of view" has been developed by Chatman, who distinguishes between a "perceptual," a "conceptual," and an "interest" dimension of the concept, emphasizing that "texts, any kind of text, even ordinary conversation, may entail one or any combination of these senses" (*Story* 152). Chatman does not openly acknowledge Uspensky's work in *Story and Discourse*, but it seems that he was aware of it, since the translators of the English edition of Uspensky's *A Poetics of Composition* "wish to thank Seymour Chatman for first bringing to our attention the necessity for this translation" (xvii). In yet another early multidimensional model, Rimmon-Kenan similarly emphasizes that the "purely visual sense of 'focalization' is too narrow," instead proposing to distinguish between not only a "perceptual facet" of focalization that includes "sight, hearing, smell, etc." (*Narrative Fiction* 78) and primarily manifests itself within spatiotemporal coordinates but also a "psychological facet" that consists of "the cognitive and the emotive orientation of the focalizer towards the focalized" (*Narrative Fiction* 80) as well as an "ideological facet" that consists of "'the norms of the text' . . . in accordance with which the events and characters of the story are evaluated" (*Narrative Fiction* 82–83). While the notion that a narrative representation (both narratorial and nonnarratorial) may be "colored" not only by characters' spatiotemporal positions and (quasi-)perceptions but also by their emotions or systems of norms and values is rather widespread in both classical and contemporary narratology, then, there

are still comparatively few studies that systematically discuss these aspects of subjective representation in any detail. See also the criticism of multidimensional models of focalization presented in L. Herman and Vervaeck, "Focalization"; Lorente; Margolin, "Focalization"; the early film-oriented consideration of "point of view" in Aumont; and, once more, the discussion of "mental perspective" in Eder, *Die Figur*, as well as of "medial perspective" in Schmid, *Narratology*.

37. Persson, for example, emphasizes that it is not only "necessary for the spectator to understand the specific and often short-term goals that fluctuate to the same extent that emotions and other mental states do" (186) but also that "goals and actions are often motivated by emotions" (192) and that "perceptions imprint beliefs in the mind, which in turn frame and specify goals and actions" (193).

38. However, see Thon, "Perspective," for a more detailed discussion of the medium-specific functions of "points of evaluation" and the resulting "evaluative perspective structures" in contemporary video games that puts particular emphasis on the relation between the players' and the player-controlled characters' norms and values as well as on the players' evaluation of in-game actions with regard to the game goals.

39. This is rather surprising, in fact, as the nonnarratorial representation of subjectivity figures prominently not only within film narratology but also within the more general fields of film theory and film philosophy. Still, landmark studies such as Branigan, *Point of View*; Kawin; and G. Wilson, *Narration* (to all three of which I will return below) discuss narratorial strategies of subjective representation only in passing and often only as an optional addition to nonnarratorial strategies of subjective representation. Even Chion, whose comprehensive work on sound in film also entails a thorough examination of the concept of voice, largely limits himself to noting that recipients understand some voices as existing only "in the mind" of a character "because they conform to audio conventions that establish a sound as subjective, making it unrealistic" (*The Voice* 52).

40. Only Fleishman directly quotes Cohn in this context, but Kozloff uses the term "interior monologue," which features prominently in Cohn's work, and Kuhn lists her *Transparent Minds* in his bibliography.

41. Cohn differentiates the first three of these forms further, depending on whether they occur in "third-person novels" or "first-person novels," while at the same time emphasizing their similarities as well: "In some respects a first-person narrator's relationship to his [or her] past parallels a narrator's relationship to his [or her] protagonist in a

third-person novel. The kind and extent of the distance between subject and object, between the narrating and the experiencing self, here also determines a whole range of possible styles and techniques, analogous to those [characteristic for] psycho-narration in third-person novels" (Cohn, *Transparent Minds* 143). While I will not distinguish between "third-person" and "first-person" narratorial strategies of subjective representation on a terminological level, I would still like to acknowledge that Cohn's discussion of the latter is perhaps even more relevant to the purpose of the present chapter than her discussion of the former.

42. While this may, indeed, be a border case in literary texts, without the presence of a (fictional) narrator, "autonomous interior monologue" may become fully "nonnarratorial" in multimodal narrative works such as films, comics, and video games (or, alternatively, constitute thought verbal narration).

43. Kozloff even goes as far as claiming that at least one "aspect of literary omniscience, privileged access to a character's consciousness (focalization 'from within'), does not apply to film. All the painstaking work in narrative theory measuring the distance between the narrative discourse and the character's consciousness in terms of syntax... is largely irrelevant to narrative cinema. A film narrator is perfectly capable of telling us what characters are thinking, yet such 'inside views' seldom occur. Traditionally, since film is not exclusively mediated through such a narrator, it has employed other means to reveal characters' thoughts and emotions, including nuances of performance, close-ups, expressionistic lighting, or music. When verbalization of inner states is desirable or necessary, films are more likely to allow characters to express themselves directly through interior monologue than to have the narrator articulate their feelings" (81). If one leaves aside the lack of a distinction between extradiegetic homodiegetic narratorial strategies of subjective representation and "interior monologue," Kozloff's remarks seem to generally apply to multimodal media.

44. Just as nonnarratorial representations of consciousness cannot be *reproductions* of that consciousness (see, e.g., Metz, "Current Problems" 45–49, on Mitry), so is the narratorial representation of consciousness still a representation—with all the caveats this implies. Fludernik's insistence that "representation is *not* verbatim" (*The Fictions* 356, original emphasis) may also serve to remind us, once more, of films', comics', and video games' tendency to use narratorial as well as nonnarratorial forms of metaphorical representations of subjectivity.

45. Without particularly endorsing Bal's conceptualization of "focalization," we may still note that all of the following strategies of subjective representation provide "direct access" to the internal worlds of what Bal would describe as the "focalized object." However, it should also be stressed, once more, that the resulting representations may also contain "traces" of what she would describe as "focalizing subjects" and that my focus on the former certainly does not prevent me from acknowledging the latter.
46. I will further discuss this question during my examination of nonnarratorial strategies of subjective representation below, which can be described according to whether they constitute a "full-fledged" nonnarratorial representation of internal worlds or, rather, some other form of subjective representation that is less "encompassing" in its "subjectivization."
47. My focus on *salient* narratorial strategies of subjective representation does not in any way preclude the possibility of *other* narratorial strategies of subjective representation—such as what might, perhaps, be called the *narratorially filtered representation of a character's internal voice*—being realized in contemporary films, comics, and video games.
48. Not unlike the present study, film theory and film narratology tend to foreground the pictorial aspects of audiovisual representation, even though other, particularly auditive, aspects are evidently also important. However, see the brief discussion of the representation of storyworld sound below.
49. Mitry distinguishes between, first, the "descriptive" or "objective image," in which "the camera records the drama, movement, or action from an angle capable of giving the best possible description of the events being filmed" (218); second, the "personal image," where "the subjectivity comes from the filmmaker, the showman or storyteller" (206); third, the "associated" or "semisubjective image," which "*adopts the viewpoint of a particular character*" (219, original emphasis) without coinciding with that viewpoint; and, fourth, the "analytic" or "subjective image," where "the camera sees . . . what the characters in the drama see" (207). Moreover, Mitry emphasizes that the latter "is not the objectification of a subjective viewpoint but, quite the opposite, the 'subjectification' of a certain objective representation" (209), but this mainly serves to illustrate, once more, that the subjective image is (only) intended to *represent* a character's (quasi-)perceptions as opposed to *reproducing* these (quasi-)perceptions exactly "the way they are."
50. "Point of view" does *not* refer to a point-of-view shot here.

51. Kawin's examination of "mindscreen" as the audiovisual representation of "the field of the mind's eye" (10), for example, is very perceptive at times, but his terminological choices appear idiosyncratic, at best. Moreover, Kawin tends not only to equal experiencing characters with narrating characters in cases "where a character appears to present his [or her] own view of himself [or herself] and his [or her] world" (18), but also conflates the subjective representation of the represented characters' minds with the subjective representation of the filmmakers' minds, thereby rendering the concept of "mindscreen" unnecessarily all-inclusive.

52. Naturally, different terms are used by different authors, but I would still maintain that the four strategies of nonnarratorial representation examined in the following cover at least a very large part of the ways in which contemporary films, comics, and video games may use their audiovisual, verbal-pictorial, and interactive representation to represent (quasi-)perceptual aspects of characters' consciousnesses. See also, for example, Eder's distinction between "POV shots," "subjectivized POV shots," "partially imagined shots," and "fully imagined shots" (see Eder, *Die Figur* 610–613) or Kuhn's distinction between "mindscreen," "mental metadiegesis," "mental projection," "mental inserts," and "mental metalepsis" (see Kuhn 119–194).

53. Then again, one might argue that speaking of "shots" with regard to digital film is not significantly less metaphorical than it is with regard to contemporary comics and video games—or simply note that speaking of "shots" in nondigital film has always been metaphorical.

54. Note also the distinction between "subjectivization" and "the subjective" that has been proposed by Brinkmann in a comparatively early account of the use of subjective voice-over in film noir. According to Brinkmann, "subjectivization" should only refer to cases where "either an objective correlation of the subjective view is offered or it is made clear in other ways that the perception of reality is subjectively defined" (102, my translation from the German). In contradistinction to this conceptualization of "subjectivization," Brinkman argues that "the representation of dreams or thoughts that have no objective counterpart" should be described as an independent "level of inner reality, of the subjective as such" (102, my translation from the German).

55. See Chion, *Le son*; and the brief (self-)critical remarks in Chion, *Audio-Vision* 89–94, where he also likens the subjective point of audition to an internal "auricularization" *sensu* Jost. See also Flückiger, who emphatically argues against the notion of a "clear positioning of the

recipient through the sound track" (*Sound Design* 370, my translation from the German).

56. Indeed, the mode of representation of storyworld sound differs across media, with (sound) films primarily employing auditive modes of representation, comics using both written and pictorial modes of representation, and video games focusing on auditive modes of representation, but commonly also using writing to represent character speech (as well as, on occasion, characters' internal voices). Flückiger, *Sound Design* 362–411, provides a comprehensive discussion of subjective film sound. See also Khordoc; Kunzle; Petersen on "sound" in comics and Collins, *Game Sound*; *Playing with Sound*; Jørgensen, *A Comprehensive Study*, on sound in video games.

57. Describing this strategy as a form of "overlay" not only allows me to emphasize its representational aspects but also prevents me from having to use somewhat more problematic terms such as "shot" or "projection." While the former seems primarily connected to the mediality of nondigital film (see also the discussion of digital film images in Flückiger, *Visual Effects*), the latter is used quite differently in the context of psychoanalysis (see, e.g., Klein).

58. While recipients will not always be able to easily distinguish between these different types of internal worlds, it may be worth noting that memories, dreams, and fantasies can, in fact, fulfill quite different narrative functions with regard to the overall narrative representation. For further discussion of the narrative functions of memories and dreams, in particular, see, e.g., Branigan, *Narrative Comprehension* 100–107; *Point of View* 73–102; Eder, *Die Figur* 610–623; Grodal, *Moving Pictures* 129–156; Kawin 3–22, 65–87; Kuhn 152–156; Reinerth, "Spulen"; Walsh, *The Rhetoric* 103–129; G. Wilson, *Narration* 82–144; "Transparency."

59. At least in principle, this also applies to representations of accurate memories, although in practice, it is often difficult to clearly distinguish between the subjective representation of accurate memories (if there is such a thing) and mere "flashbacks" that are "triggered" by the representation of accurate memories (or, rather, are triggered by characters being represented as remembering them). See, e.g., Bordwell, *The Way*; Branigan, *Point of View*; Eder, *Die Figur*; Kawin; Kuhn; G. Wilson, "Transparency," on this particular problem in the context of feature films; as well as the discussion of nonfictional narratorial representation in chapter 4 and chapter 5. In addition, the change of "diegetic level" that defines the nonnarratorial representation of internal worlds allows for the "lower-order use" of strategies of subjective representation with

regard to the consciousnesses of the characters that are located within the internal world that is being represented. Unfortunately, it is beyond the scope of this chapter to discuss the resulting forms of "multiplied subjectivity" in greater detail.

60. The "indeterminacy" of markers of subjectivity is also emphasized by, e.g., Branigan, *Point of View*; Eder, *Die Figur*; Grodal, *Moving Pictures*; Kawin; Reinerth, "Spulen"; G. Wilson, "Transparency."

7. Subjective Representation across Media

1. In *eXistenZ*, one cannot find a clear example of the nonnarratorial representation of internal worlds, but what the film represents is arguably not so much a succession of different "diegetic levels" constructed via various digital games but rather the players' gameplay experience of these different "diegetic levels." However, there are quite a few problems with such a comprehension of the film's narrative representation, as no part of the film is strongly marked as either Allegra Geller's or Ted Pikul's subjective experience.

2. This specific strategy of intransparent subjective representation has clearly arrived in the mainstream, with films as diverse as Avary's *The Rules of Attraction* and Frears's *The Queen* using it, albeit with different "content." Other mainstream films that use extended forms of intransparent (quasi-)perceptual overlay would be Amenábar's *The Others* and Shyamalan's *The Sixth Sense*. However, the "full-fledged" representation of internal worlds remains even more common in films ranging from Gilliam's *Brazil* to Zemeckis's *Forrest Gump* and from Jeunet's *Amélie* to Stiller's recent remake of *The Secret Life of Walter Mitty*. Interesting variations can be found in Singh's *The Fall*, which employs a combination of reasonably reliable (fictional) narratorial representation attributable to Roy and considerably more unreliable ("factualized") nonnarratorial representations of the accompanying imaginations of Alexandria; Gondry's *The Science of Sleep*, which makes it increasingly hard to figure out whether what is represented is the "factual domain" of the storyworld or, rather, the (day)dreams of Stéphane; Gondry's *Eternal Sunshine of the Spotless Mind*, which represents a hypodiegetic version of Joel as "entering" the "landscapes" of his own memories while they are being "erased"; and Nolan's *Inception*, which represents Cobb and his team as being able to "enter" the subconsciousnesses of *other* characters. For some additional discussion of the distinction between *transparent* and *intransparent* strategies of narrative representation, see, e.g., G. Wilson, "Transparency."

3. Gilliam's later films in particular tend to extensively use strategies of subjective representation to narratively ambitious effect, so that it comes as no surprise that both his oeuvre in general and *12 Monkeys* (which may not be a straightforward adaptation of a novel or another narrative work but was nevertheless inspired by Marker's *La jetée*) in particular have received quite a bit of attention within current film studies.
4. Reinerth, "Spulen," provides further discussion of the representational markers of subjectivity that *12 Monkeys* employs. While slow motion in particular might appear to be one of the comparatively few genuinely film- or, at least, audiovisual representation-specific representational markers of subjectivity at first glance, it is also increasingly used in video games to the point where recent first- or third-person shooters appear to use slow motion even more commonly than contemporary feature films. See also the discussion of an interesting form of video game-specific "slow motion" below.
5. The sequence is still the representation of a hypodiegetic dream of the diegetic James and, therefore, does not "reveal" anything in a strong sense. Indeed, Kathryn explains her occurrence in James's dream as being caused by his recent experiences, but James disagrees: "No, I think it was always you. Very strange."
6. Most of these instances of subjective narratorial representation remain fairly conventional, ranging from the narratorial representation of the experiencing I's mind and (quasi-)perceptions to what may be comprehended as the narratorially framed representation of his internal voice, but one can also find a more interesting variation of these general strategies of subjective narratorial representation: after he has started living with Tyler in an abandoned house, the experiencing I finds a stack of old medical magazines, within which anthropomorphized inner organs function as narrators, telling stories about themselves (e.g., "I am Jack's medulla oblongata."). In the following, the narrator repeatedly uses this strategy to represent the emotional states of the experiencing I (e.g., "I am Jack's inflamed sense of rejection" or "I am Jack's broken heart"), illustrating rather nicely that while verbal narration is more easily used to provide "direct access" to the knowledge and emotions of characters (among other aspects of their minds) than nonnarratorial forms of representation, films (and other multimodal media) may still use rather complex (and at least partially metaphorical) strategies to reach that goal.
7. *Fight Club* also uses quite a few conventional nonnarratorial representations of internal worlds representing the experiencing I's memories,

dreams, and imaginations both in sequences that use a posteriori contextual content markers and in sequences that use a priori as well as a posteriori contextual content markers or, at least sometimes, employ what I have called the narratorial representation of the experiencing I's mind. See, for example, the sequence that represents the experiencing I fantasizing about a plane crash (which is, however, still rather clearly marked as subjective by a thinly veiled a priori contextual narratorial marker), the sequence in which the experiencing I dreams of Marla Singer having sex with an unidentified person (which also heavily uses representational markers that already strongly suggest that what is represented is not part of the storyworld's "factual domain"), or the series of sequences where the experiencing I visits (or tries to visit) his "mental cave," using a technique he learned about during a "guided meditation session."

8. Interestingly, then, while the intransparent use of (quasi-)perceptual overlay leads to large segments of what most recipients will initially comprehend as intersubjective representation turning out to actually have been highly subjective, the "full-fledged" representation of the experiencing I's memories during the film's key sequence may be subjective by definition but still paints a more accurate picture of the storyworld's "factual domain" as it is or would have been intersubjectively perceived by the other characters (though what is represented here is still the secondary hypodiegetic storyworld of the experiencing I's memories, instead of the primary diegetic storyworld that they refer to).

9. Alternatively, it might also be argued that the absence of narratorial representation after the conclusion of the opening sequence suggests that the former can be attributed to the experiencing I functioning as a diegetic thinking narrator while he is hallucinating that Tyler shoves a gun barrel in his mouth. However, I would maintain that such a comprehension is comparatively implausible due to the "distance" between the narrating I and the experiencing I that is communicated via deictic markers and other elements within the verbal narration as well as the sheer extent of the latter.

10. *Fight Club*'s initial performance at the box office did not fulfill the studio's expectations, but its DVD release has been very successful, turning it into a so-called cult classic. See, e.g., Bing.

11. While *A Beautiful Mind* is an adaptation of Sylvia Nasar's unauthorized biography of John Forbes Nash Jr. as well, the former's lack of an extradiegetic narrator—as opposed to the extradiegetic narrator in *Fight Club* who at least partially reuses the words of the extradiegetic narrator

in Chuck Palahniuk's novel of the same name—seems rather appropriate if one keeps in mind that Nasar's biography uses a comparatively "covert" narratorial voice. This is not to say that *A Beautiful Mind* uses no narrators at all, though. There even is an interesting case of the audiovisual representation "illustrating" John's hypothesizing about how he and his colleagues could maximize their chances of "getting laid," which leads to him developing the theory that eventually earns him the Nobel Prize. One way to comprehend this sequence would lead to its description as a form of nonnarratorial representation of the internal world of John's hypothesizing. As has been previously discussed, however, it might be more appropriate to argue that what the audiovisual representation represents here are not John's thinking processes as such but rather the "hypothetical events" that he tells his colleagues about as an intradiegetic homodiegetic framing narrator. Whatever the case may be, quite a few instances of intradiegetic narration appear in *A Beautiful Mind*, but the film clearly does not use an extradiegetic narrator the way *Fight Club* does.

12. More specifically, *A Beautiful Mind* repeatedly uses (quasi-)perceptual point-of-view sequences to represent John's thought processes while he imagines himself as a code breaker, with some of the (quasi-)perceptual point-of-view sequences—as well as some of the (quasi-)perceptual overlays—using the auditive channel to nonnarratorially represent John's internal voice mumbling numbers, while he is thinking about the supposedly hidden codes.

13. Not unlike *Fight Club*, *A Beautiful Mind* also provides at least some cues that will be recognizable as hinting at its core "twist" during a second (or third, or fourth) viewing. When John and Charles are represented as playing billiards, for example, Martin greets John by saying, "Hey Nash, who's winning? You or you?"—which would most likely just be taken as a comment on John's fiercely competitive relation to Martin during a first viewing, but could of course also be comprehended as a comment on Nash playing billiards by himself by a spectator who is already "in the know."

14. While the setting of the key sequence is markedly different from *Fight Club*, there are also some structural similarities: in *A Beautiful Mind*, it is John's wife who, after the initial revelation by Dr. Rosen, "follows the trail" of her husband and gradually discovers "material evidence" of his mental condition when she enters his office, finding its walls covered with papers and handwritten lines "connecting the dots," and also subsequently finds the letter box of an abandoned house still containing

all the "reports" that John thought he was delivering to the Pentagon. Naturally, John is taking a little longer to realize his predicament, but when Alicia confronts him with his still-sealed "reports" and he subsequently cannot find the code-generating radium diode he hallucinated the government implanting in his arm, he finally agrees to accept treatment from Dr. Rosen.

15. The experiencing I is repeatedly represented as moving his lips in a way that might be comprehended as suggesting that he still functions as an intradiegetic thinking narrator, but the verbal narration's use of past tense and other deictic markers ultimately suggest that most of *Fear and Loathing in Las Vegas* is, indeed, narrated by an extradiegetic homodiegetic narrator whose narrating I remains more or less clearly distinguishable from his experiencing I. What the film's opening sequence nicely illustrates, then, is that attributing narratorial representation to an intradiegetic thinking narrator in an intersubjectively plausible way is contingent on comparatively strong markers, while attributing it to an extradiegetic speaking (or unspecified) narrator does not need these markers, as extradiegetic narrators constitute the unmarked case—much in the same way that comprehending part of a narrative representation as subjective needs comparatively strong markers of subjectivity, whereas comprehending it as intersubjective does not.

16. This is, arguably, the only clearly marked case of a nonnarratorial representation of internal worlds in *Fear and Loathing in Las Vegas*, as well as the only case where nonnarratorial subjective representation is used to represent not merely the experiencing I's hallucinations but also a fairly interesting—and highly metaphorical—form of hypothetical imagination: shortly before the adrenochrome starts taking effect, the experiencing I imagines what might happen to him and Dr. Gonzo if Lucy, an underage girl whom the latter picked up, gave drugs to, and at least tried to seduce, went to the police. The sequence uses a combination of a priori contextual and simultaneous content markers, when the audiovisual representation represents the face of Raoul and the sound of a cell slamming shut before a rather different situation is represented, in which some version of Lucy (looking suspiciously like how one could imagine Alice from some version of Lewis Carroll's *Alice's Adventures in Wonderland*) testifies against Raoul and Dr. Gonzo in a rather theatrical court, and whose spatial, temporal, causal, and ontological relation is most appropriately comprehended as being defined by the latter situation's location "in the mind" of Raoul.

17. The narratorial arrangement of *Fear and Loathing in Las Vegas* is further complicated by the fact that Raoul not only functions as an extradiegetic homodiegetic and, at least at some points, an intradiegetic thinking narrator but also as an intradiegetic speaking and an intradiegetic writing narrator. As the focus of the present chapter is on subjective representation rather than on narratorial representation across media, though, I will not further pursue the relation between these various narratorial roles.
18. As has already been mentioned, there are quite a few highly conventionalized medium-specific strategies of subjective representation that contemporary comics may employ. Of these, the use of thought bubbles and narration boxes is a particularly simple way of providing the readers with "direct access" to a character's thoughts and/or other aspects of a character's mind via verbal representation. But, of course, comics can also represent characters' minds within thought bubbles, narration boxes, or even the panels themselves in exclusively pictorial ways, as in Mazzucchelli's *Asterios Polyp* or Ware's *Jimmy Corrigan: The Smartest Kid on Earth*.
19. However, *Habibi* actually uses nonnarratorial representations of internal worlds quite a lot, repeatedly representing the memories, dreams, and fantasies of both Zam's and Dodola's experiencing Is.
20. Still, the rather similar ways in which *The Arrival* introduces its "framing characters" also serves to remind us that it may be difficult to distinguish not only between different kinds of internal worlds such as memories, dreams, and fantasies but also between the nonnarratorial representation contributing to the representation of a hypodiegetic secondary storyworld that is evoked by an intradiegetic narrator and the nonnarratorial representation of a hypodiegetic secondary storyworld that is marked as "merely" the internal world of a diegetic character.
21. Interestingly enough, the intersubjective status of these segments of the representation is further emphasized by the lack of a translation of character speech that is represented in Arabic, French, and Chinese. As has briefly been mentioned in chapter 3, this principle is expanded in the second volume of *The League of Extraordinary Gentlemen*, when some form of Martian character speech is represented without a "translation."
22. The narration boxes accompanying the spatial point-of-view sequence are attributable not to Mr. Griffin but to Ms. Murray, who is located in another room, describing the League's plan of attack in what may be understood as a hypothetical form of anterior verbal narration. Accordingly, Ms. Murray functions as a secondary homodiegetic narrator,

though not a subjective one: *The League of Extraordinary Gentlemen* here combines a narratorial strategy of intersubjective representation and a nonnarratorial strategy of subjective representation, with the narratorial voice telling one part of the story, the sequence of panels another. In other words, in comics as well as in films and video games, the subjectivity, intersubjectivity, or objectivity of the narratorial and the nonnarratorial representation are not contingent on each other.

23. As is usually the case, there remains at least some ambiguity regarding the question whether what is represented here is actually meant to be the hypodiegetic secondary memories of the experiencing I, a "mere" analepsis representing an earlier point in the diegetic primary storyworld's time, or both—the latter of which seems to be the most likely answer, though, if one considers the comparatively salient and highly conventionalized use of simultaneous representational markers of subjectivity and the fact that the reader is given no reason to doubt the reliability of Wallace's memory.

24. *Sin City: Hell and Back* also uses some spatial or, perhaps, even (quasi-)perceptual point-of-view sequences connected to characters aiming various firearms at or using binoculars to survey Wallace. While certainly close to the subjective perception of the character in question, I would still argue that these kinds of "device-oriented" point-of-view sequences are best described as "merely spatial," since they not only represent the "factual domain" of the storyworld in a comparatively intersubjective mode of representation but also arguably represent it only from the specific spatial position from which the character in question perceives it, including the effects of the device but not representing other aspects of the character's perception.

25. While the comics I have chosen as case studies in this chapter all employ strategies of narratorial representation and, hence, do not use nonnarratorial representations of characters' internal voices (although they could, of course), it should be noted that the latter can still commonly be found in contemporary comics such as Moore and D. Gibbons's *Watchmen* or F. Miller's *Batman: The Dark Knight Returns*, both of which would be worthy of further consideration, as they use differently colored narration boxes to allow their readers to attribute the respective voices to different characters, which illustrates rather well that contemporary comics (as well as contemporary films and video games) can use both narratorial strategies of subjective representation and the nonnarratorial representation of internal voices,

though this becomes apparent mainly if the former and the latter are marked as having different "sources" (see figure 19 in chapter 5).

26. The first chapter, "Biology 101," already combines a (quasi-)perceptual point-of-view sequence morphing into the nonnarratorial representation of the internal world of Keith's imagination (until he passes out) with a (quasi-)perceptual point-of-view sequence morphing into a spatial point-of-view sequence (when he regains consciousness). See also the comparatively subtle use of (quasi-)perceptual overlay representing Keith's acid-induced hallucinations (subtle when compared to *Fear and Loathing in Las Vegas*, that is).

27. An extradiegetic homodiegetic narrator that provides "direct access" to the mind and/or (quasi-)perceptions of a character that is not his or her experiencing I, that is.

28. *F.E.A.R.* still does use cut-scenes rather extensively, though, as opposed to highly narrative first-person shooters in the tradition of Valve's *Half-Life* and *Half-Life 2*, who, despite their high narrativity, limit themselves to using scripted events.

29. Both spatial and (quasi-)perceptual point-of-view sequences tend to represent storyworld sounds accordingly—i.e., by using a spatial or (quasi-)perceptual point of audition, when, for example, grenade explosions result in a temporary tinnitus in *Call of Duty*. See also, once more, Thon, "Subjectivity."

30. Of course, this strategy of subjective representation is not particularly stable and, hence, makes only comparatively unspecific assertions about the "inner life" of the player-controlled character in question—namely, that he or she can feel (some sort of) pain. Similar observations hold with regard to the other primarily ludic forms of (quasi-)perceptual point-of-view sequences and (quasi-)perceptual overlay discussed in the following. *F.E.A.R.*, for example, certainly represents *that* the player-controlled character has superhuman reflexes, but does not determine *where* (i.e., at which position in storyworld space) or *when* (i.e., at which point in storyworld time) he makes use of these. In a certain sense, then, strategies of subjective representation that fulfill primarily ludic functions can be considered to be a part of the graphic user interface at least as much as they can be considered a part of the representation of the respective game's storyworld.

31. While *Amnesia: The Dark Descent* does not represent the "sanity meter" explicitly, contemporary video games may use various forms of head-up displays or other elements of the graphic user interface to explicitly represent "health," "magical power," "sanity," or various other traits of

their respective characters. While I will not discuss these strategies in any detail in the present study, I see no reason not to consider at least some of these "ludic statistics" as highly medium-specific forms of subjective representation. See also, once more, Jørgensen, *Gameworld Interfaces*.

32. See the representation of Paxton Fettel's and Alma Wade's "telepathic voices" in *F.E.A.R.* as well as, for example, the use of (intradiegetic) voice recordings and similar strategies in id Software's *Doom 3*, Crytek's *Far Cry*, or Bungie's *Halo*.

33. Indeed, not only contemporary first-person shooters such as Bungie's *Halo*, Infinity Ward's *Call of Duty*, Crytek's *Far Cry*, id Software's *Doom 3*, and Monolith's *F.E.A.R.* but also action-adventures such as Remedy's *Alan Wake*, SCE's *God of War*, or Crystal Dynamics' current "reboot" of *Tomb Raider*, third-person shooters such as Remedy's *Max Payne*, Epic Games' *Gears of War*, or Yager Development's *Spec Ops: The Line*, and role-playing games such as Bioware's *Dragon Age: Origins*, Bethesda's *Fallout 3*, or Supergiant Games' *Bastion* employ more or less pronounced versions of the red filter effect to communicate that the player-controlled character is being hurt.

34. It might even be argued that *Batman: Arkham Asylum*'s "detective mode" is more appropriately described as a specific form of "device-based" spatial point-of-view sequence, comparable to the spatial point-of-view sequences representing the use of binoculars or sniper rifles in F. Miller's *Sin City: Hell and Back* and closer to the spatial point-of-view sequence than to the (quasi-)perceptual point-of-view sequence in the first volume of Moore and O'Neill's *The League of Extraordinary Gentlemen*. I ultimately find such a line of reasoning unconvincing, though, since Batman's cowl enhances his perceptual powers quite considerably and, moreover, is represented as a "near-organic" part of the one superhero who is mainly defined by his "technological prowess." See also the use of (quasi-)perceptual point-of-view sequences and (quasi-)perceptual overlay to represent the player-controlled character's neuro-enhanced superior abilities in Eidos's *Deus Ex: Human Revolution* and Bethesda's *Fallout 3*.

35. Just as with opponents such as the Joker or the Scarecrow, this traumatic event that defines Batman as a superhero is well established by the comics and other elements of the particularly complex *Batman* franchise. For further discussion of the franchise, see, e.g., Brooker, *Batman*; *Hunting the Dark Knight*; or the contributions in Pearson and Uricchio.

36. Again, video games that use sequences with "reduced interactivity" instead of cut-scenes to represent narratively important elements of the storyworld have become quite common recently, with the first two installments of Remedy's *Max Payne* series—*Max Payne* and *Max Payne 2: The Fall of Max Payne*—providing particularly salient examples of the nonnarratorial interactive representation of internal worlds.
37. Considerably more could be said on the narrative functions of music not only in video games but also in films. See, e.g., Bullerjahn; Chion, *Film*; Kalinak on film music; Cheng; Collins, *Game Sound*; *Playing with Sound*; Stingel-Voigt on music in video games.
38. Other games that make prominent use of introductory dream sequences that effectively function as "gameplay tutorials" are Starbreeze's *The Chronicles of Riddick: Escape from Butcher Bay* and *The Chronicles of Riddick: Assault on Dark Athena* as well as Silicon Knights' *Eternal Darkness: Sanity's Requiem*. Another interesting early example of interactive dream sequences can be found in Bioware's *Baldur's Gate II: Shadows of Amn*, when the player-controlled character increasingly comes to terms (in one way or another) with the fact that he or she supposedly is a child of the dark god Bhaal.

Conclusion

1. Indeed, the fundamental seriality of a significant segment of contemporary cultural production is noteworthy not only from a narratological point of view but also from the more general perspectives of media studies and production culture studies. At first glance, a transmedial narratology may appear to be mainly interested in the ways in which the various installments of a series use similar or different strategies of narrative representation or in the question to what extent these installments can be said to represent a consistent storyworld. However, see, e.g., Kelleter; I. Gordon; Denson and Jahn-Sudmann for broader examinations of television's, comics', and video games' seriality.
2. As has already been mentioned in the introduction, adaptation studies still primarily focus on the intersection of literature and film, but comics studies and game studies are increasingly beginning to become interested in practices of intermedial adaptations as well. See, e.g., Constandinides; Cutting; Keller; Kuhlman; Schmitz-Emans; Thoss, "Tell It." Incidentally, even if what I would call the *expansion* and *modification* of storyworlds (following Doležel, *Heterocosmica*, and Ryan, "Transfictionality") are perhaps the more interesting operations in the context of transmedial entertainment franchises, it should be

stressed that most of these franchises also entail salient cases of what may be described as *redundancy*. For further discussion, see Thon, "Converging Worlds."

3. Of course, such comparative narratological analyses would have to go considerably beyond the overly reductive descriptions provided above. Take, for example, the *Watchmen* comic and its film adaptation. On the one hand, the film makes quite a few noticeable changes to specific details of the story told by the comic, even though the major "plot points" of both the former and the latter tend to remain functionally equivalent. On the other hand, the film tries to emulate the comic's complex narratorial structure, repeatedly employing voice-over narration meant to represent Rorschach's diary entries and the silent reflections of Dr. Manhattan, respectively. Still, these segments of narratorial representation not only appear rather heavy-handed, they also leave out several of the more interesting strategies to be found in the comic—including the written verbal narration from the diegetic comic book *The Black Freighter* and the various "excerpts" from diegetic texts that frame all but the last of the comic's twelve chapters.

4. As has briefly been hinted at in chapter 3, my proposal to understand storyworlds as noncontradictory "by default" and to describe contradictory storyworlds as compounds of noncontradictory subworlds seems to be well suited to be applied to transmedial entertainment franchises, resulting in a heuristic distinction between the *work-specific storyworlds* of "single narrative works," the noncontradictory *transmedial storyworlds* that may be constructed out of work-specific storyworlds, and the often quite contradictory *transmedial universes* that may be constructed out of transmedial storyworlds, in turn. See Thon, "Converging Worlds," for a more in-depth discussion of this distinction and the resulting research program.

5. In 2012, Disney acquired Lucasfilm and, hence, is now the owner of the *Star Wars* franchise. This has not only led to the production of a third trilogy of *Star Wars* films (the first of which, *Star Wars Episode VII: The Force Awakens*, was not yet available at the time of this writing, though it had already been scheduled for release on December 18, 2015), but has also sparked quite a bit of speculation regarding the fate of the "canon system." Shortly after the acquisition, however, Disney made it clear that, while the first six feature film episodes (*The Phantom Menace*, *Attack of the Clones*, *Revenge of the Sith*, *A New Hope*, *The Empire Strikes Back*, and *Return of the Jedi*) as well as the CGI feature film pilot and television series *Star Wars: The Clone Wars* will continue to form at least

part of the franchise's "canonical core," the former "expanded universe" will not retain its canonical status. See, once more, Thon, "Converging Worlds," for a more detailed discussion of this development.

6. Of course, the release and impressive critical as well as commercial success of *The Lego Movie* in 2014 forcefully reminded us that the *Lego* franchise itself has become profoundly transmedial. However, while the gameplay of the *Lego Star Wars* video games certainly takes more than a few cues from the *Lego* rather than the *Star Wars* franchise, with Lego blocks and the affordances they provide for the (re)construction of the game spaces offering an important part of the game mechanics, these games still appear to primarily aim at a "retelling" of the stories originally told by the *Star Wars* feature films. However, see also Buerkle for a more detailed discussion of some of the questions that the "legoization" of *Star Wars* raises.

7. Clearly, such a program—which could, perhaps, be briefly described as being primarily interested in the relation between narrative and ideology—is already considerably more established within literary narratology than it is within transmedial narratology (or film narratology, comics narratology, and the narratologically inclined parts of game studies, for that matter). See, e.g., Lanser, *Fictions*; Warhol; or the various contributions in Warhol and Lanser on the intersection between narratology and gender/queer studies; as well as, e.g., Prince, "On a Postcolonial Narratology"; Sommer, "'Contextualism'"; or the contributions in Dwivedi, Nielsen, and Walsh on the intersection between narratology and postcolonial studies.

8. While this has evidently not been the focus of the present book, it might also be worth noting that several practitioner guides to filmmaking, comics artistry, video game design, and transmedial productions have turned out to be quite influential within film studies, comics studies, game studies, and (trans)media studies. See, e.g., McKee; Vogler on film; Eisner, *Comics*; McCloud on comics; Salen and Zimmerman; Schell on video games; and Bernardo; Weaver on transmedial entertainment franchises. In fact, the line between "practitioners" and "academics" is occasionally quite difficult to draw in the latter case, with academics such as Dena or Jenkins rather explicitly pursuing normative questions and integrating "how-to" elements into their scholarly works.

Works Cited

11:14. Dir. Greg Marcks. New Line Cinema, 2003. Film.
12 Monkeys. Dir. Terry Gilliam. Universal Pictures, 1995. Film.
300. Dir. Zack Snyder. Warner Bros. Pictures, 2006. Film.
Aarseth, Espen. "Computer Game Studies, Year One." *Game Studies* 1.1 (2001): n. pag. Web. December 1, 2013.
———. *Cybertext: Perspectives on Ergodic Literature*. Baltimore: Johns Hopkins University Press, 1997. Print.
———. "Doors and Perception: Fiction vs. Simulation in Games." *Intermédialités* 9 (2007): 35–44. Print.
———. "The Game and Its Name: What Is a Game Auteur?" *Visual Authorship: Creativity and Intentionality in Media*. Ed. Torben Grodal. Copenhagen: Museum Tusculanum Press, 2004. 261–269. Print.
———. "Genre Trouble: Narrativism and the Art of Simulation." *FirstPerson: New Media as Story, Performance, and Game*. Ed. Noah Wardrip-Fruin and Pat Harrigan. Cambridge MA: MIT Press, 2004. 45–55. Print.
———. "A Narrative Theory of Games." *Proceedings of the International Conference on the Foundations of Digital Games 2012*. 129–133. Web. December 1, 2013.
Abbott, H. Porter. *The Cambridge Introduction to Narrative*. Cambridge: Cambridge University Press, 2002. Print.
———. "Narrativity." *Handbook of Narratology*. Ed. Peter Hühn, John Pier, Wolf Schmid, and Jörg Schönert. Berlin: De Gruyter, 2009. 309–328. Print.
Abbott, Lawrence L. "Comic Art: Characteristics and Potentialities of a Narrative Medium." *Journal of Popular Culture* 19.4 (1986): 155–176. Print.
Aczel, Richard. "Hearing Voices in Narrative Texts." *New Literary History* 29.3 (1998): 467–500. Print.
Adams, Jeff. *Documentary Graphic Novels and Social Realism*. Bern: Peter Lang, 2008. Print.

Adaptation. Dir. Spike Jonze. Columbia Pictures, 2002. Film.
Adventure. Will Crowther, 1976. PDP-10.
Alan Wake. Remedy Entertainment/Microsoft, 2012. PC. [Originally published as *Alan Wake*. Remedy Entertainment/Microsoft, 2010. Xbox.]
Alan Wake's American Nightmare. Remedy Entertainment, 2012. PC.
Alber, Jan. "The Diachronic Development of Unnaturalness: A New View on Genre." *Unnatural Narratives—Unnatural Narratology*. Ed. Jan Alber and Rüdiger Heinze. Berlin: De Gruyter, 2011. 41–67. Print.
———. "Impossible Storyworlds—and What to Do with Them." *Storyworlds: A Journal of Narrative Studies* 1 (2009): 79–96. Print.
———. *Unnatural Narrative: Impossible Worlds in Fiction and Drama*. Lincoln: University of Nebraska Press, 2016. Print.
Alber, Jan, and Alice Bell. "Ontological Metalepsis and Unnatural Narratology." *Journal of Narrative Theory* 42.2 (2012): 166–192. Print.
Alber, Jan, and Monika Fludernik. "Mediacy and Narrative Mediation." *Handbook of Narratology*. Ed. Peter Hühn, John Pier, Wolf Schmid, and Jörg Schönert. Berlin: De Gruyter, 2009. 174–189. Print.
Alber, Jan, and Rüdiger Heinze. "Introduction." *Unnatural Narratives—Unnatural Narratology*. Ed. Jan Alber and Rüdiger Heinze. Berlin: De Gruyter, 2011. 1–19. Print.
———, eds. *Unnatural Narratives—Unnatural Narratology*. Berlin: De Gruyter, 2011. Print.
Alber Jan, Stefan Iversen, Henrik Skov Nielsen, and Brian Richardson. "Unnatural Narratives, Unnatural Narratology: Beyond Mimetic Models." *Narrative* 18.2 (2010): 113–136. Print.
———. "What Is Unnatural about Unnatural Narratology? A Response to Monika Fludernik." *Narrative* 20.3 (2012): 371–382. Print.
———. "What Really Is Unnatural Narratology?" *Storyworlds: A Journal of Narrative Studies* 5 (2013): 101–118. Print.
Alber, Jan, Henrik Skov Nielsen, and Brian Richardson, eds. *A Poetics of Unnatural Narrative*. Columbus: Ohio State University Press, 2013. Print.
Albrecht-Crane, Christa, and Dennis Cutchins, eds. *Adaptation Studies: New Approaches*. Madison: Fairleigh Dickinson University Press, 2010. Print.
Aldama, Frederick Luis. *Your Brain on Latino Comics: From Gus Arriola to Los Bros Hernandez*. Austin: University of Texas Press, 2009. Print.
Allrath, Gaby, and Marion Gymnich, eds. *Narrative Strategies in Television Series*. Basingstoke: Palgrave Macmillan, 2005. Print.
Alston, William P. *Epistemic Justification: Essays in the Theory of Knowledge*. Ithaca NY: Cornell University Press, 1989. Print.
Altman, Rick. *Film/Genre*. London: British Film Institute, 1999. Print.

The Amazing Spider-Man. Beenox/Activision, 2012. Xbox 360.
Amélie. Dir. Jean-Pierre Jeunet. Miramax Films, 2001. Film. [Originally released in French as *Le fabuleux destin d'Amélie Poulain*. 20th Century Fox, 2001. Film.]
American Beauty. Dir. Sam Mendes. DreamWorks Pictures, 1999. Film.
American McGee's Alice. Rogue Entertainment/Electronic Arts, 2000. PC.
American Splendor. Dir. Shari Springer Berman and Robert Pulcini. Fine Line Features, 2003. Film.
Amnesia: The Dark Descent. Frictional Games, 2010. PC.
Anderson, Emily R. "Telling Stories: Unreliable Discourse, *Fight Club*, and the Cinematic Narrator." *Journal of Narrative Theory* 40.1 (2010): 80–107. Print.
Anodyne. Analgesic Productions, 2013. PC.
Aristotle. *Metaphysics*. Trans. W. D. Ross. HTML by Steve Thomas. Adelaide: eBooks@Adelaide, 2013. Web. December 1, 2013.
Arjoranta, Jonne. "Meaning Effects in Video Games: Focalization, Granularity and Mode of Narration in Games." *Proceedings of the Games and Literary Theory Conference 2013*. 1–20. Web. December 1, 2013.
The Artist. Dir. Michel Hazanavicius. The Weinstein Company, 2011. Film.
Ashline, William L. "The Problem of Impossible Fictions." *Style* 29.2 (1995): 215–234. Print.
Assassin's Creed. Ubisoft, 2007. PlayStation 3.
Atkin, Albert. "Peirce's Theory of Signs." *The Stanford Encyclopedia of Philosophy*. Ed. Edward N. Zalta. Stanford: Stanford University, 2010. Web. December 1, 2013.
Atkins, Barry. *More than a Game: The Computer Game as Fictional Form*. Manchester: Manchester University Press, 2003. Print.
Aumont, Jacques. "Le point de vue." *Communications* 38 (1983): 3–29. Print.
Avedon, Elliott M. "The Structural Elements of Games." *The Study of Games*. Ed. Elliott M. Avedon and Brian Sutton-Smith. New York: Wiley, 1971. 419–426. Print.
B., David. *Epileptic*. Trans. Kim Thompson. London: Jonathan Cape, 2005. Print. [Originally published in French as *L'ascension du Haut-Mal*. Vols. 1–6. Paris: L'Association, 1996–2003. Print.]
Bacharach, Sondra, and Deborah Tollefsen. "We Did It: From Mere Contributors to Coauthors." *Journal of Aesthetics and Art Criticism* 68.1 (2010): 23–32. Print.
Backe, Hans-Joachim. *Strukturen und Funktionen des Erzählens im Computerspiel: Eine typologische Einführung*. Würzburg: Königshausen und Neumann, 2008. Print.

The Baconing. Hothead Games, 2011. PC.

Baetens, Jan. "Revealing Traces: A New Theory of Graphic Enunciation." *The Language of Comics: Word and Image.* Ed. Robin Varnum and Christina T. Gibbons. Jackson: University Press of Mississippi, 2001. 145–155. Print.

Bakhtin, Mikhail M. "Forms of Time and of the Chronotope in the Novel: Notes toward a Historical Poetics." *The Dialogic Imagination: Four Essays.* Ed. Michael Holquist. Trans. Caryl Emerson and Michael Holquist. Austin: University of Texas Press, 1981. 84–258. Print.

Bal, Mieke. "The Narrating and the Focalising: A Theory of the Agents in Narrative." *Style* 17.2 (1983): 243–269. Print.

———. *Narratology: Introduction to the Theory of Narrative.* 2nd ed. Toronto: University of Toronto Press, 1997. Print.

———. "Notes on Narrative Embedding." *Poetics Today* 2.2 (1981): 41–59. Print.

———. *Reading Rembrandt: Beyond the Word-Image Opposition.* New York: Cambridge University Press, 1991. Print.

Balázs, Bela. *Iskusstvo Kino.* Moskau: Goskinoizdat, 1945. Print.

Baldur's Gate. Bioware/Black Isle Studios, 1998. PC.

Baldur's Gate II: Shadows of Amn. Bioware/Black Isle Studios, 2000. PC.

Balzer, Jens. "Der Horizont bei Herriman: Zeit und Zeichen zwischen Zeitzeichen und Zeichenzeit." *Ästhetik des Comics.* Ed. Michael Hein, Michael Hüners, and Torsten Michaelsen. Berlin: Erich Schmidt, 2002. 143–152. Print.

Banfield, Ann. "Describing the Unobserved: Events Grouped around an Empty Centre." *The Linguistics of Writing: Arguments between Language and Literature.* Ed. Nigel Fabb, Dereck Attridge, Alan Durant, and Colin MacCabe. Manchester: Manchester University Press, 1987. 265–285. Print.

———. *Unspeakable Sentences: Narration and Representation in the Language of Fiction.* Boston: Routledge, 1982. Print.

Bareis, J. Alexander. "Mimesis der Stimme: Fiktionstheoretische Aspekte einer narratologischen Kategorie." *Stimme(n) im Text: Narratologische Positionsbestimmungen.* Ed. Andreas Blödorn, Daniela Langer, and Michael Scheffel. Berlin: De Gruyter, 2006. 101–122. Print.

Bareis, J. Alexander, and Lene Nordrum, eds. *How to Make Believe: The Fictional Truths of the Representational Arts.* Berlin: De Gruyter, 2015. Print.

Barthes, Roland. "The Death of the Author." *Image Music Text.* Ed. and trans. Stephen Heath. New York: Hill and Wang, 1977. 142–148. Print.

———. "Introduction to the Structural Analysis of Narratives." *Image Music Text*. Ed. and trans. Stephen Heath. New York: Hill and Wang, 1977. 79–124. Print.
Bartle, Richard. "Hearts, Clubs, Diamonds, Spades: Players Who Suit MUDS." 1996. Web. December 1, 2013.
Bartsch, Anne, Jens Eder, and Kathrin Fahlenbrach, eds. *Audiovisuelle Emotionen: Emotionsdarstellung und Emotionsvermittlung durch audiovisuelle Medienangebote*. Cologne: Herbert von Halem, 2007. Print.
Bastion. Supergiant Games/Warner Bros. Interactive, 2011. PC.
Bateman, John A. *Multimodality and Genre: A Foundation for the Systematic Analysis of Multimodal Documents*. Basingstoke: Palgrave Macmillan, 2008. Print.
Bateson, Gregory. "A Theory of Play and Fantasy." *Steps to an Ecology of Mind*. Chicago: University of Chicago Press, 1972. 177–193. Print.
Batman: Arkham Asylum. Rocksteady/Eidos Interactive, 2009. PC.
Batman Begins. Dir. Christopher Nolan. Warner Bros. Pictures, 2005. Film.
Batman Begins. Eurocom/Electronic Arts, 2005. PlayStation 2.
Bazin, André. *Ontologie et langage*. Vol. 1 of *Qu'est-ce que le cinéma*. Paris: Éditions du Cerf, 1958. Print.
Beall, J. C., and Bas C. van Fraassen. *Possibilities and Paradox: An Introduction to Modal and Many-Valued Logic*. Oxford: Oxford University Press, 2003. Print.
A Beautiful Mind. Dir. Ron Howard. Universal Pictures/DreamWorks Pictures, 2001. Film.
Bechdel, Alison. *Fun Home: A Family Tragicomic*. Boston: Houghton Mifflin, 2006. Print.
Becker Arenhart, Jonas R., and Décio Krause. "Contradiction, Quantum Mechanics, and the Square of Opposition." 2014. Web. December 1, 2014.
Beil, Benjamin. *First Person Perspectives: Point of View und figurenzentrierte Erzählformen im Film und im Computerspiel*. Münster: LIT, 2010. Print.
Being John Malkovich. Dir. Spike Jonze. USA Films, 1999. Film.
Bell, Alice. *The Possible Worlds of Hypertext Fiction*. Basingstoke: Palgrave Macmillan, 2010. Print.
Bender, John, and Michael Marrinan. *The Culture of Diagram*. Stanford: Stanford University Press, 2010. Print.
Berendsen, Mariet. "The Teller and the Observer: Narration and Focalization in Narrative Texts." *Style* 18.2 (1984): 140–158. Print.
Berger, Peter L., and Thomas Luckmann. *The Social Construction of Reality: A Treatise in the Sociology of Knowledge*. New York: Anchor Books, 1966. Print.

Berlatsky, Eric L. *The Real, the True, and the Told: Postmodern Historical Narrative and the Ethics of Representation*. Columbus: Ohio State University Press, 2011. Print.

Bernardo, Nuno. *The Producer's Guide to Transmedia: How to Develop, Fund, Produce and Distribute Compelling Stories across Multiple Platforms*. London: beActive Books, 2011. Print.

Bernhart, Walter. "Überlegungen zur Lyriktheorie aus erzähltheoretischer Sicht." *Tales and "their telling difference": Zur Theorie und Geschichte der Narrativik: Festschrift zum 70. Geburtstag von Franz K. Stanzel*. Ed. Herbert Foltinek, Wolfgang Riehle, and Waldemar Zacharasiewicz. Heidelberg: Winter, 1993. 359–375. Print.

Bernhart, Wolfgang, Steven Paul Scher, and Werner Wolf, eds. *Word and Music Studies: Defining the Field; Proceedings of the First International Conference on Word and Music Studies at Graz, 1997*. Amsterdam: Rodopi, 1999. Print.

Bernhart, Wolfgang, and Werner Wolf, eds. *Word and Music Studies: Essays on the Song Cycle and on Defining the Field; Proceedings of the Second International Conference on Word and Music Studies at Ann Arbor, MI, 1999*. Amsterdam: Rodopi, 2001. Print.

Beronä, David A. "Wordless Comics: The Imaginative Appeal of Peter Kuper's *The System*." *Critical Approaches to Comics: Theories and Methods*. Ed. Matthew J. Smith and Randy Duncan. New York: Routledge, 2011. 17–26. Print.

Berto, Francesco. "Impossible Worlds." *The Stanford Encyclopedia of Philosophy*. Ed. Edward N. Zalta. Stanford: Stanford University, 2013. Web. December 1, 2013.

Big Fish. Dir. Tim Burton. Columbia Pictures, 2003. Film.

The Big Lebowski. Dir. Joel Coen and Ethan Coen. Gramercy Pictures, 1998. Film.

Bing, Jonathan. "'Fight Club' Author Books Pair of Deals." *Variety* April 11, 2001. Web. December 1, 2013.

Bioshock. Irrational Games/2K Games, 2007. PC.

Birch, A. H. *Representation*. London: Pall Mall Press, 1971. Print.

Black, David A. "Genette and Film: Narrative Level in the Fiction Cinema." *Wide Angle* 8.3–4 (1986): 19–26. Print.

Blanchet, Robert, Kristina Köhler, Tereza Smid, and Julia Zutavern, eds. *Serielle Formen: Von den frühen Film-Serials zu aktuellen Quality-TV- und Onlineserien*. Marburg: Schüren, 2010. Print.

Bode, Christoph. *Ästhetik der Ambiguität: Zu Funktion und Bedeutung von Mehrdeutigkeit in der Literatur der Moderne*. Tübingen: Niemeyer, 1988. Print.

Bogen, Steffen, Wolfgang Brassat, and David Ganz, eds. *Bilder, Räume, Betrachter: Festschrift für Wolfgang Kemp zum 60. Geburtstag.* Berlin: Dietrich Reimer, 2006. Print.

Bogost, Ian. *Persuasive Games: The Expressive Power of Videogames.* Cambridge MA: MIT Press, 2007. Print.

Bogost, Ian, Simon Ferrari, and Bobby Schweizer. *Newsgames: Journalism at Play.* Cambridge MA: MIT Press, 2010. Print.

Bogost, Ian, and Cindy Poremba. "Can Games Get Real? A Closer Look at 'Documentary' Digital Games." *Computer Games as a Sociocultural Phenomenon: Games without Frontiers—War without Tears.* Ed. Andreas Jahn-Sudmann and Ralf Stockman. Basingstoke: Palgrave Macmillan, 2008. 12–21. Print.

Bolter, Jay David, and Richard Grusin. *Remediation: Understanding New Media.* Cambridge MA: MIT Press, 1998. Print.

Boni, Marta, ed. *World Building: Transmedia, Fans, Industries.* Amsterdam: Amsterdam University Press, 2017. Print.

Booth, Wayne C. *The Company We Keep: An Ethics of Fiction.* Berkeley: University of California Press, 1988. Print.

———. *The Rhetoric of Fiction.* Chicago: University of Chicago Press, 1961. Print.

Borat: Cultural Learnings of America for Make Benefit Glorious Nation of Kazakhstan. Dir. Larry Charles. 20th Century Fox, 2006. Film.

Bordwell, David. *Making Meaning: Inference and Rhetoric in the Interpretation of Cinema.* Cambridge MA: Harvard University Press, 1989. Print.

———. *Narration in the Fiction Film.* Madison: University of Wisconsin Press, 1985. Print.

———. *The Way Hollywood Tells It: Story and Style in Modern Movies.* Berkeley: University of California Press, 2006. Print.

Bordwell, David, Janet Staiger, and Kristin Thompson. *The Classical Hollywood Cinema: Film Style and Mode of Production to 1960.* New York: Columbia University Press, 1985. Print.

Bortolussi, Marisa, and Peter Dixon. *Psychonarratology: Foundations for the Empirical Study of Literary Response.* Cambridge: Cambridge University Press, 2003. Print.

Branigan, Edward. *Narrative Comprehension and Film.* Abingdon: Routledge, 1992. Print.

———. *Point of View in the Cinema: A Theory of Narration and Subjectivity in Classical Film.* Berlin: De Gruyter, 1984. Print.

———. *Projecting a Camera: Language-Games in Film Theory.* New York: Routledge, 2006. Print.

Bratman, Michael E. *Faces of Intention: Selected Essays on Intention and Agency*. Cambridge: Cambridge University Press, 1999. Print.

Braveheart. Dir. Mel Gibson. Paramount Pictures, 1995. Film.

Brazil. Dir. Terry Gilliam. Universal Pictures, 1985. Film.

Breaking Bad. AMC, 2008–2013. Television.

Brednich, Rolf W. "Die Comic Strips als Gegenstand der Erzählforschung." *Studia Fennica* 20 (1976): 230–240. Print.

Breger, Claudia. *An Aesthetics of Narrative Performance: Transnational Theater, Literature, and Film in Contemporary Germany*. Columbus: Ohio State University Press, 2012. Print.

Bremond, Claude. "The Logic of Narrative Possibilities." Trans. Elaine D. Cancalon. *New Literary History* 11.3 (1980): 387–411. Print.

———. "Le message narratif." *Communications* 4 (1964): 4–32. Print.

Brinkmann, Christine N. "Der voice-over als subjektivierende Erzählstruktur des Film Noir." *Narrativität in den Medien*. Ed. Rolf Kloepfer and Karl-Dietmar Möller. Münster: MAkS, 1986. 101–118. Print.

Broich, Ulrich. "Gibt es eine 'neutrale' Erzählsituation?" *Germanisch-Romanische Monatsschrift* 33 (1983): 129–145. Print.

Broman, Eva. "Narratological Focalization Models: A Critical Survey." *Essays on Fiction and Perspective*. Ed. Göran Rossholm. Bern: Peter Lang, 2004. 57–89. Print.

Brooker, Will. *Batman Unmasked: Analyzing a Cultural Icon*. London: Continuum, 2001. Print.

———. *Hunting the Dark Knight: Twenty-First Century Batman*. London: I. B. Tauris, 2012. Print.

———. *Using the Force: Creativity, Community and* Star Wars *Fans*. London: Continuum, 2002. Print.

Brooke-Rose, Christine. "Whatever Happened to Narratology?" *Poetics Today* 11.2 (1990): 283–293. Print.

Brookey, Robert A. *Hollywood Gamers: Digital Convergence in the Film and Video Game Industries*. Bloomington: Indiana University Press, 2010. Print.

Brown, Penelope, and Stephen C. Levinson. *Politeness: Some Universals in Language Usage*. Cambridge: Cambridge University Press, 1987. Print.

Bruner, Jerome S. "The Narrative Construction of Reality." *Critical Inquiry* 18 (1991): 1–21. Print.

Brütsch, Matthias. "From Ironic Distance to Unexpected Plot Twists: Unreliable Narration in Literature and Film." *Beyond Classical Narration: Transmedial and Unnatural Challenges*. Ed. Jan Alber and Per Krogh Hansen. Berlin: De Gruyter, 2014. 57–79. Print.

Brütsch, Matthias, Vinzenz Hediger, Ursula von Keitz, Alexandra Schneider, and Margrit Tröhler, eds. *Kinogefühle: Emotionalität und Film.* Marburg: Schüren, 2005. Print.

Buckland, Warren. *The Cognitive Semiotics of Film.* Cambridge: Cambridge University Press, 2000. Print.

———. "Introduction: Puzzle Plots." *Puzzle Films: Complex Storytelling in Contemporary Cinema.* Ed. Warren Buckland. Chichester: Wiley-Blackwell, 2009. 1–12. Print.

Buerkle, Robert. "Playset Nostalgia: *Lego Star Wars: The Video Game* and the Transgenerational Appeal of the Lego Video Game Franchise." *Lego Studies: Examining the Building Blocks of a Transmedial Phenomenon.* Ed. Mark J. P. Wolf. New York: Routledge, 2014. 118–152. Print.

Bullerjahn, Claudia. *Grundlagen der Wirkung von Filmmusik.* Augsburg: Wißner, 2001. Print.

Burgoyne, Robert. "The Cinematic Narrator: The Logic and Pragmatics of Impersonal Narration." *Journal of Film and Video* 42.1 (1990): 3–16. Print.

Burnett, Colin. "Hidden Hands at Work: Authorship, the Intentional Flux, and the Dynamics of Collaboration." *A Companion to Media Authorship.* Ed. Jonathan Gray and Derek Johnson. Chichester: Wiley-Blackwell, 2013. 112–132. Print.

Burns, Charles. *Black Hole.* Originally published as twelve separate comic books, 1995–2004. New York: Pantheon, 2005. Print.

Buscombe, Edward. "Ideas of Authorship." *Theories of Authorship.* Ed. John Caughie. London: Routledge, 1981. 22–34. Print.

Caillois, Roger. *Man, Play, and Games.* Trans. Meyer Barash. New York: Free Press, 1961. Print.

Caldwell, John T. "Authorship Below-the-Line." *A Companion to Media Authorship.* Ed. Jonathan Gray and Derek Johnson. Chichester: Wiley-Blackwell, 2013. 349–369. Print.

———. *Production Culture: Industrial Reflexivity and Critical Practice in Film and Television.* Durham: Duke University Press, 2008. Print.

Calleja, Gordon. *In-Game: From Immersion to Incorporation.* Cambridge MA: MIT Press, 2011. Print.

Call of Cthulhu: Dark Corners of the Earth. Headfirst/Bethesda, 2005. Xbox.

Call of Duty. Infinity Ward/Activision, 2003. PC.

Call of Duty 2. Infinity Ward/Activision, 2005. PC.

Campora, Matthew. "Art Cinema and New Hollywood: Multiform Narrative and Sonic Metalepsis in *Eternal Sunshine of the Spotless Mind.*" *New Review of Film and Television Studies* 7.2 (2009): 119–131. Print.

Caracciolo, Marco. "Those Insane Dream Sequences: Experientiality and Distorted Experience in Literature and Video Games." *Storyworlds across Media: Toward a Media-Conscious Narratology.* Ed. Marie-Laure Ryan and Jan-Noël Thon. Lincoln: University of Nebraska Press, 2014. 230–249. Print.

Carey, Mike, and Peter Gross. *The Unwritten: Dead Man's Knock.* Vol. 3 of *The Unwritten* series. Finishes by Ryan Kelly, colors by Chris Chuckry and Jeanne McGee, lettered by Todd Klein, covers by Yuko Shimizu. Originally published in single magazine form as *The Unwritten* #13–18, 2011. New York: DC Comics/Vertigo, 2011. Print.

———. *The Unwritten: Leviathan.* Vol. 4 of *The Unwritten* series. Finishes by Vince Locke and Al Davison, colors by Chris Chuckry, lettered by Todd Klein, covers by Yuko Shimizu. Originally published in single magazine form as *The Unwritten* #19–24, 2011. New York: DC Comics/Vertigo, 2011. Print.

———. *The Unwritten: Tommy Taylor and the Bogus Identity.* Vol. 1 of *The Unwritten* series. Colors by Chris Chuckry and Jeanne McGee, lettered by Todd Klein, original series covers by Yuko Shimizu. Originally published in single magazine form as *The Unwritten* #1–5, 2009. New York: DC Comics/Vertigo, 2010. Print.

Carrier, David. *The Aesthetics of Comics.* University Park: Pennsylvania State University Press, 2000. Print.

Carroll, Lewis. *Alice's Adventures in Wonderland.* London: Macmillan, 1865. Print.

Carroll, Noël. *Engaging the Moving Image.* New Haven: Yale University Press, 2003. Print.

———. "Fiction, Non-fiction, and the Film of Presumptive Assertion: A Conceptual Analysis." *Film Theory and Philosophy.* Ed. Richard Allen and Murray Smith. Oxford: Oxford University Press, 1999. 173–202. Print.

———. "Nonfiction Film and Postmodernist Skepticism." *Post-Theory: Reconstructing Film Studies.* Ed. David Bordwell and Noël Carroll. Madison: University of Wisconsin Press, 1996. 283–306. Print.

———. *The Philosophy of Horror or Paradoxes of the Heart.* New York: Routledge, 1990. Print.

———. "The Specificity of Media in the Arts." *Journal of Aesthetic Education* 19.4 (1985): 5–20. Print.

———. *Theorizing the Moving Image.* Cambridge: Cambridge University Press, 1996. Print.

Carruthers, Peter. *Phenomenal Consciousness: A Naturalistic Theory.* Cambridge: Cambridge University Press, 2000. Print.

Castañeda, Hector-Neri. "Fiction and Reality: Their Fundamental Connections: An Essay on the Ontology of Total Experience." *Poetics* 8.1–2 (1979): 31–62. Print.

Chalmers, David J. *The Conscious Mind: In Search for a Fundamental Theory.* Oxford: Oxford University Press, 1996. Print.

Chaney, Michael, ed. *Graphic Subjects: Critical Essays on Autobiography and Graphic Novels.* Madison: University of Wisconsin Press, 2011. Print.

Chatman, Seymour. "Characters and Narrators: Filter, Center, Slant, and Interest-Focus." *Poetics Today* 7.2 (1986): 189–204. Print.

———. *Coming to Terms: The Rhetoric of Narrative in Fiction and Film.* Ithaca NY: Cornell University Press, 1990. Print.

———. *Story and Discourse: Narrative Structure in Fiction and Film.* Ithaca NY: Cornell University Press, 1978. Print.

———. "What Can We Learn from Contextualist Narratology?" *Poetics Today* 11.2 (1990): 309–328. Print.

Cheng, William. *Sound Play: Video Games and the Musical Imagination.* Oxford: Oxford University Press, 2014. Print.

Chion, Michel. *Audio-Vision: Sound on Screen.* Ed. and trans. Claudia Gorbman. New York: Columbia University Press, 1994. Print.

———. *Film, a Sound Art.* Trans. Claudia Gorbman. New York: Columbia University Press, 2009. Print.

———. *Le son au cinéma.* Paris: Cahiers du Cinéma, 1985. Print.

———. *The Voice in Cinema.* Trans. Claudia Gorbman. New York: Columbia University Press, 1999. Print.

Chisholm, Roderick. *Theory of Knowledge.* 3rd ed. Englewood Cliffs: Prentice Hall, 1989. Print.

The Chronicles of Riddick: Assault on Dark Athena. Starbreeze/Tigon/Atari, 2009. PC.

The Chronicles of Riddick: Escape from Butcher Bay. Starbreeze/Tigon/Vivendi, 2004. PC.

Chute, Hillary L. *Graphic Women: Life Narrative and Contemporary Comics.* New York: Columbia University Press, 2010. Print.

Ciccoricco, David. *Refiguring Minds in Narrative Media.* Lincoln: University of Nebraska Press, 2015. Print.

Clash of the Titans. Dir. Louis Leterrier. Warner Bros. Pictures, 2010. Film.

Cloverfield. Dir. Matt Reeves. Paramount Pictures, 2008. Film.

Clowes, Daniel. *Ghost World.* Originally published in *Eightball* #11–18, 1993–1997. Seattle: Fantagraphics, 1997. Print.

Cohn, Dorrit. "Discordant Narration." *Style* 34.2 (2000): 307–316. Print.

———. *The Distinction of Fiction*. Baltimore: Johns Hopkins University Press, 1999. Print.

———. "The Encirclement of Narrative: On Franz Stanzel's *Theorie des Erzählens*." *Poetics Today* 2.2 (1981): 157–182. Print.

———. "Signposts of Fictionality: A Narratological Perspective." *Poetics Today* 11.4 (1990): 775–804. Print.

———. *Transparent Minds: Narrative Modes for Presenting Consciousness in Fiction*. Princeton: Princeton University Press, 1978. Print.

Collins, Karen. *Game Sound: An Introduction to the History, Theory, and Practice of Video Game Music and Sound Design*. Cambridge MA: MIT Press, 2008. Print.

———. *Playing with Sound: A Theory of Interacting with Sound and Music in Video Games*. Cambridge MA: MIT Press, 2013. Print.

Consalvo, Mia. "Dubbing the Noise: Square Enix and Corporate Creation of Videogames." *A Companion to Media Authorship*. Ed. Jonathan Gray and Derek Johnson. Chichester: Wiley-Blackwell, 2013. 324–345. Print.

Constandinides, Costas. *From Film Adaptation to Post-Celluloid Adaptation: Rethinking the Transition of Popular Narratives and Characters across Old and New Media*. New York: Continuum, 2010. Print.

Corneliussen, Hilde G., and Jill Walker Rettberg, eds. *Digital Culture, Play, and Identity: A* World of Warcraft *Reader*. Cambridge MA: MIT Press, 2008. Print.

Cornils, Anja, and Wilhelm Schernus. "On the Relationship between the Theory of the Novel, Narrative Theory, and Narratology." *What Is Narratology? Questions and Answers regarding the Status of a Theory*. Ed. Tom Kindt and Hans-Harald Müller. Berlin: De Gruyter, 2003. 137–174. Print.

Corrigan, Timothy, ed. *Film and Literature: An Introduction and Reader*. 2nd ed. New York: Routledge, 2012. Print.

Crane, Tim. *Elements of Mind: An Introduction to the Philosophy of Mind*. Oxford: Oxford University Press, 2001. Print.

Crash. Dir. Paul Haggis. Lionsgate, 2004. Film.

Culler, Jonathan. *Ferdinand de Saussure*. Rev. ed. Ithaca NY: Cornell University Press, 1986. Print.

———. "Omniscience." *Narrative* 12.1 (2004): 22–34. Print.

———. *Structuralist Poetics: Structuralism, Linguistics, and the Study of Literature*. Ithaca NY: Cornell University Press, 1975. Print.

Currie, Gregory. *Image and Mind: Film, Philosophy, and Cognitive Science*. Cambridge: Cambridge University Press, 1995. Print.

———. *Narratives and Narrators: A Philosophy of Stories.* Oxford: Oxford University Press, 2010. Print.

———. *The Nature of Fiction.* Cambridge: Cambridge University Press, 1990. Print.

———. "Unreliability Refigured: Narrative in Literature and Film." *Journal of Aesthetics and Art Criticism* 53.1 (1995): 19–29. Print.

Currie, Gregory, and Ian Ravenscroft. *Recreative Minds: Imagination in Philosophy and Psychology.* Oxford: Oxford University Press, 2002. Print.

Cutting, Andrew. "Interiority, Affordances, and the Possibility of Adapting Henry James's *The Turn of the Screw* as a Video Game." *Adaptation* 5.2 (2012): 169–184. Print.

Damasio, Antonio. *The Feeling of What Happens: Body and Emotions in the Making of Consciousness.* New York: Harcourt, 1999. Print.

Damisch, Hubert. *The Origin of Perspective.* Trans. John Goodman. Cambridge MA: MIT Press, 1994. Print.

Dannenberg, Hilary P. *Coincidence and Counterfactuality: Plotting Time and Space in Narrative Fiction.* Lincoln: University of Nebraska Press, 2008. Print.

Darby, David. "Form and Context: An Essay in the History of Narratology." *Poetics Today* 22.4 (2001): 829–852. Print.

The Dark Knight. Dir. Christopher Nolan. Warner Bros. Pictures, 2008. Film.

The Dark Knight Rises. Dir. Christopher Nolan. Warner Bros. Pictures, 2012. Film.

Davidson, Drew. *Cross-Media Communications: An Introduction to the Art of Creating Integrated Media Experiences.* Pittsburgh: ECT Press, 2010. Print.

Davies, Martin, and Tony Stone, eds. *Folk Psychology: The Theory of Mind Debate.* Oxford: Blackwell, 1995. Print.

———, eds. *Mental Simulation: Evaluations and Applications.* Oxford: Blackwell, 1995. Print.

Dawson, Paul. "Ten Theses against Fictionality." *Narrative* 23.1 (2015): 74–100. Print.

DeathSpank. Hothead Games/Electronic Arts, 2010. PC.

DeathSpank: Thongs of Virtue. Hothead Games/Electronic Arts, 2010. PC.

de Crécy, Nicolas. *Prosopopus.* Charleroi: Dupuis, 2003. Print.

Defense Grid: The Awakening. Hidden Path Entertainment, 2008. PC.

Deleuze, Gilles. *Cinema 1: The Movement-Image.* Trans. Hugh Tomlinson and Barbara Habberjam. London: Athlone Press, 1986. Print.

Deleyto, Celestino. "Focalisation in Film Narrative." *Narratology: An Introduction*. Ed. Susana Onega and José Á. García Landa. London: Longman, 1996. 217–233. Print.

Dena, Christy. "Transmedia Practice: Theorising the Practice of Expressing a Fictional World across Distinct Media and Environments." PhD thesis University of Sidney, 2009. Web. December 1, 2013.

Dennerlein, Kathrin. *Narratologie des Raumes*. Berlin: De Gruyter, 2009. Print.

Dennett, Daniel C. *Consciousness Explained*. Boston: Little, Brown, and Company, 1991. Print.

Denson, Shane, and Andreas Jahn-Sudmann. "Digital Seriality: On the Serial Aesthetics and Practice of Digital Games." *Eludamos: Journal for Computer Game Culture* 7.1 (2013): 1–32. Web. January 1, 2014.

Detering, Heinrich, ed. *Autorschaft: Positionen und Revisionen*. Stuttgart: Metzler, 2002. Print.

Deuber-Mankowsky, Astrid. *Lara Croft: Cyber Heroine*. Trans. Dominic J. Bonfiglio. Minneapolis: University of Minnesota Press, 2005. Print.

Deus Ex: Human Revolution. Eidos/Square Enix, 2011. PC.

Deuze, Mark. "Convergence Culture in the Creative Industries." *International Journal of Cultural Studies* 10.2 (2007): 243–263. Print.

D'hoker, Elke, and Gunther Martens, eds. *Narrative Unreliability in the Twentieth-Century First-Person Novel*. Berlin: De Gruyter, 2008. Print.

Diablo. Blizzard, 1996. PC.

Diengott, Nilli. "Reflections on Narrative Poetics: Aspects of Franz K. Stanzel's Typology Viewed through a Genettian Perspective." *Canadian Review of Comparative Literature/Revue Canadienne de Littérature Comparée* 17.1–2 (1990): 45–56. Print.

District 9. Dir. Neill Blomkamp. TriStar Pictures, 2009. Film.

Doane, Marie Ann. "The Indexical and the Concept of Medium Specificity." *differences* 18.1 (2007): 128–152. Print.

Doležel, Lubomír. *Heterocosmica: Fiction and Possible Worlds*. Baltimore: Johns Hopkins University Press, 1998. Print.

———. *Narrative Modes in Czech Literature*. Toronto: University of Toronto Press, 1973. Print.

———. *Occidental Poetics: Tradition and Progress*. Lincoln: University of Nebraska Press, 1990. Print.

———. "Possible Worlds and Literary Fictions." *Possible Worlds in Humanities, Arts and Sciences*. Ed. Allén Sture. Berlin: De Gruyter, 1989. 221–242. Print.

Domsch, Sebastian. *Storyplaying: Agency and Narrative in Video Games*. Berlin: De Gruyter, 2013. Print.

Donovan, Stephen, Danuta Fjellestad, and Rolf Lundén, eds. *Authority Matters: Rethinking the Theory and Practice of Authorship*. Amsterdam: Rodopi, 2008. Print.
Doom. Dir. Andrzej Bartkowiak. Universal Pictures, 2005. Film.
Doom 3. id Software/Activision, 2004. PC.
Dorleijn, Gillis J., Ralf Grüttemeier, and Liesbeth Korthals Altes. *Authorship Revisited: Conceptions of Authorship around 1900 and 2000*. Leuven: Peeters, 2010. Print.
Dragon Age: Origins. Bioware/Electronic Arts, 2009. PC.
Dragon Age II. Bioware/Electronic Arts, 2011. PC.
Dream. HyperSloth/Mastertronic, 2015. PC.
Drucker, Johanna. "What Is Graphic about Graphic Novels?" *English Language Notes* 46.2 (2008): 39–55. Print.
Duncan, Randy, and Matthew J. Smith. *The Power of Comics: History, Form and Culture*. New York: Continuum, 2009. Print.
Dwivedi, Divya, Henrik Skov Nielsen, and Richard Walsh, eds. *Narratology and Ideology: Negotiating Context, Form, and Theory in Postcolonial Narratives*. Columbus: Ohio State University Press, 2018. Print.
Dyer, Richard. *Heavenly Bodies: Film Stars and Society*. 2nd ed. New York: Routledge, 2004. Print.
Eco, Umberto. *The Role of the Reader: Explorations in the Semiotics of Text*. Bloomington: Indiana University Press, 1979. Print.
Edelman, Gerald M. "Naturalizing Consciousness: A Theoretical Framework." PNAS 100.9 (2003): 5520–5524. Web. December 1, 2013.
Eder, Jens. *Die Figur im Film: Grundlagen der Figurenanalyse*. Marburg: Schüren, 2008. Print.
———. "Narratology and Cognitive Reception Theories." *What Is Narratology? Questions and Answers regarding the Status of a Theory*. Ed. Tom Kindt and Hans-Harald Müller. Berlin: De Gruyter, 2003. 277–301. Print.
———. "Transmediale Imagination." *Auslassen, Andeuten, Auffüllen: Der Film und die Imagination des Zuschauers*. Ed. Julian Hanich and Hans Jürgen Wulff. München: Fink, 2012. 207–238. Print.
———. *Was sind Figuren? Ein Beitrag zur interdisziplinären Fiktionstheorie*. Paderborn: mentis, 2008. Print.
Eder, Jens, Fotis Jannidis, and Ralf Schneider. "Characters in Fictional Worlds: An Introduction." *Characters in Fictional Worlds: Understanding Imaginary Beings in Literature, Film, and Other Media*. Ed. Jens Eder, Fotis Jannidis, and Ralf Schneider. Berlin: De Gruyter, 2010. 3–64. Print.

———, eds. *Characters in Fictional Worlds: Understanding Imaginary Beings in Literature, Film, and Other Media*. Berlin: De Gruyter, 2010. Print.

Eder, Jens, and Jan-Noël Thon. "Digitale Figuren in Kinofilm und Computerspiel." *Film im Zeitalter neuer Medien II: Digitalisierung und Kino*. Ed. Harro Segeberg. München: Fink, 2012. 139–181. Print.

Edminston, William F. "Focalization and the First-Person Narrator: A Revision of the Theory." *Poetics Today* 10.4 (1989): 729–744. Print.

Egenfeldt-Nielsen, Simon, Jonas H. Smith, and Susana P. Tosca. *Understanding Video Games: The Essential Introduction*. 2nd ed. New York: Routledge, 2013. Print.

Eig, Jonathan. "A Beautiful Mind(fuck): Hollywood Structures of Identity." *Jump Cut: A Review of Contemporary Media* 46 (2003): n. pag. Web. December 1, 2013.

Eisner, Will. *Comics and Sequential Art*. Tamarac: Poorhouse, 1985. Print.

———. *A Contract with God and Other Tenement Stories*. New York: Baronet Books, 1978. Print.

Elleström, Lars. "The Modalitites of Media: A Model for Understanding Intermedial Relations." *Media Borders, Multimodality and Intermediality*. Ed. Lars Elleström. Basingstoke: Palgrave Macmillan, 2010. 11–50. Print.

Elsaesser, Thomas. "The Mind Game Film." *Puzzle Films: Complex Storytelling in Contemporary Cinema*. Ed. Warren Buckland. Chichester: Wiley-Blackwell, 2009. 13–41. Print.

Emmott, Catherine. *Narrative Comprehension: A Discourse Perspective*. Oxford: Oxford University Press, 1997. Print.

Enderton, Herbert B. "Second-Order and Higher-Order Logic." *The Stanford Encyclopedia of Philosophy*. Ed. Edward N. Zalta. Stanford: Stanford University, 2009. Web. December 1, 2013.

Engelns, Markus. *Spielen und Erzählen: Computerspiele und die Ebenen ihrer Realisierung*. Heidelberg: Synchron, 2014. Print.

Enter the Matrix. Shiny Entertainment/Atari, 2003. PC.

Ermi, Laura, and Frans Mäyrä. "Fundamental Components of the Gameplay Experience: Analysing Immersion." *Changing Views—Worlds in Play*: DiGRA Conference Proceedings 2005. Web. December 1, 2013.

Eskelinen, Markku. *Cybertext Poetics: The Critical Landscape of New Media Literary Theory*. London: Continuum, 2012. Print.

———. "Towards Computer Game Studies." *FirstPerson: New Media as Story, Performance, and Game*. Ed. Noah Wardrip-Fruin and Pat Harrigan. Cambridge MA: MIT Press, 2004. 36–44. Print.

Eternal Darkness: Sanity's Requiem. Silicon Knights/Nintendo, 2002. GameCube.

Eternal Sunshine of the Spotless Mind. Dir. Michel Gondry. Focus Features, 2004. Film.

Evans, Elizabeth. *Transmedia Television: Audiences, New Media and Daily Life*. New York: Routledge, 2011. Print.

Ewert, Jeanne "Reading Visual Narrative: Art Spiegelman's *Maus*." *Narrative* 8.1 (2000): 87–103. Print.

eXistenZ. Dir. David Cronenberg. Miramax Films, 1999. Film.

Exit through the Gift Shop. Dir. Banksy. Producers Distribution Agency, 2010. Film.

Fahlenbrach, Kathrin. *Audiovisuelle Metaphern: Zur Körper- und Affektästhetik in Film und Fernsehen*. Marburg: Schüren, 2010. Print.

Fahlenbrach, Kathrin, and Felix Schröter. "Game Studies und Rezeptionsästhetik." *Game Studies: Aktuelle Ansätze der Computerspielforschung*. Ed. Klaus Sachs-Hombach and Jan-Noël Thon. Cologne: Herbert von Halem, 2015. 165–208. Print.

The Fall. Dir. Tarsem Singh. Roadside Attractions, 2006. Film.

Fallout 3. Bethesda, 2008. PC.

Far Cry. Crytek/Ubisoft, 2004. PC.

Fauconnier, Gilles, and Mark Turner. *The Way We Think: Conceptual Blending and the Mind's Hidden Complexities*. New York: Basic Books, 2002. Print.

Fear and Loathing in Las Vegas. Dir. Terry Gilliam. Universal Pictures, 1998. Film.

F.E.A.R.: First Encounter Assault Recon. Monolith Productions/Vivendi, 2005. PC.

Ferenz, Volker. *Don't Believe His Lies: The Unreliable Narrator in Contemporary American Cinema*. Trier: Wissenschaftlicher Verlag Trier, 2008. Print.

Feuer, Jane. "Genre Study and Television." *Channels of Discourse, Reassembled: Television and Contemporary Criticism*. 2nd ed. Ed. Robert C. Allen. Chapel Hill: University of North Carolina Press, 1992. 138–160. Print.

Feyersinger, Erwin. *Metalepsis in Animation: Paradoxical Transgressions of Ontological Levels*. Heidelberg: Winter, 2016. Print.

Fight Club. Dir. David Fincher. 20th Century Fox, 1999. Film.

Final Fantasy VII. Square, 1997. PlayStation.

Fish, Stanley. *Is There a Text in This Class? The Authority of Interpretive Communities*. Cambridge MA: Harvard University Press, 1980. Print.

Fiske, John. *Reading the Popular*. 2nd ed. Abingdon: Routledge, 2010. Print.

Fleishman, Avrom. *Narrated Films: Storytelling Situations in Cinema History*. Baltimore: Johns Hopkins University Press, 1992. Print.

Flückiger, Barbara. *Sound Design: Die virtuelle Klangwelt des Films*. Marburg: Schüren, 2001. Print.

———. *Visual Effects: Filmbilder aus dem Computer*. Marburg: Schüren, 2008. Print.

Fludernik, Monika. "Beyond Structuralism in Narratology: Recent Developments and New Horizons in Narrative Theory." *Anglistik* 11.1 (2000): 83–96. Print.

———. "Defining (In)Sanity: The Narrator of *The Yellow Wallpaper* and the Question of Unreliability." *Grenzüberschreitungen: Narratologie im Kontext/Transcending Boundaries: Narratology in Context*. Ed. Walter Grünzweig and Andreas Solbach. Tübingen: Narr, 1999. 75–95. Print.

———. *The Fictions of Language and the Languages of Fiction: The Linguistic Representation of Speech and Consciousness*. London: Routledge, 1993. Print.

———. "Histories of Narrative Theory (II): From Structuralism to the Present." *A Companion to Narrative Theory*. Ed. James Phelan and Peter J. Rabinowitz. Malden: Blackwell, 2005. 36–59. Print.

———. "How Natural Is 'Unnatural Narratology'; or, What Is Unnatural about Unnatural Narratology?" *Narrative* 20.3 (2012): 357–370. Print.

———. *An Introduction to Narratology*. Trans. Patricia Häusler-Greenfield and Monika Fludernik. Abingdon: Routledge, 2009. Print.

———. "Narrative and Drama." *Theorizing Narrativity*. Ed. John Pier and José Á. García Landa. Berlin: De Gruyter, 2008. 355–383. Print.

———. "Scene Shift, Metalepsis, and the Metaleptic Mode." *Style* 37.4 (2003): 382–400. Print.

———. *Towards a 'Natural' Narratology*. London: Routledge, 1996. Print.

Fludernik, Monika, and Uri Margolin. "Introduction." *Style* 38.2 (2004): 148–187. Print.

Forceville, Charles. "Non-verbal and Multimodal Metaphor in a Cognitivist Framework: Agendas for Research." *Cognitive Linguistics: Current Applications and Future Perspectives*. Ed. Gitte Kristiansen, Michel Achard, René Dirven, and Francisco J. Ruiz de Mendoza Ibáñez. Berlin: De Gruyter, 2006. 379–402. Print.

Forrest Gump. Dir. Robert Zemeckis. Paramount Pictures, 1994. Film.

Foster, John. *The Nature of Perception*. Oxford: Oxford University Press, 2000. Print.

Foucault, Michel. "What Is an Author?" *Modern Criticism and Theory: A Reader*. 2nd ed. Ed. David Lodge and Nigel Wood. Harlow: Longman, 2000. 174–187. Print.

Frasca, Gonzalo. "Ludologists Love Stories, Too: Notes from a Debate That Never Took Place." *Level Up: DiGRA Conference Proceedings 2003*. 92–99. Web. December 1, 2013.

———. "Ludology Meets Narratology: Similitude and Differences between (Video)Games and Narrative." *Ludology.org* 1999. Web. December 1, 2013.

———. "Simulation versus Narrative: Introduction to Ludology." *The Video Game Theory Reader*. Ed. Mark J. P. Wolf and Bernard Perron. Abingdon: Routledge, 2003. 221–235. Print.

Friedemann, Käthe. *Die Rolle des Erzählers in der Epik*. Darmstadt: Wissenschaftliche Buchgesellschaft, 1965. Print.

Friedman, Norman. "Point of View in Fiction: The Development of a Critical Concept." *PMLA* 70.5 (1955): 1160–1184. Print.

Frome, Jonathan. "Representation, Reality, and Emotions across Media." *Film Studies* 8 (2006): 12–25. Print.

Frye, Northrop. *Anatomy of Criticism: Four Essays*. Princeton: Princeton University Press, 1957. Print.

Fullerton, Tracy. "Documentary Games: Putting the Player in the Path of History." *Playing the Past: History and Nostalgia in Video Games*. Ed. Zach Whalen and Laurie N. Taylor. Nashville: Vanderbilt University Press, 2008. 215–238. Print.

Fuxjäger, Anton. "Diegese, Diegesis, diegetisch: Versuch einer Begriffsentwirrung." *montage AV* 16.2 (2007): 17–37. Print.

Gadassik, Alla, and Sarah Henstra. "Comics (as) Journalism: Teaching Joe Sacco's *Palestine* to Media Students." *Teaching Comics and Graphic Narratives: Essays on Theory, Strategy and Practice*. Ed. Lan Dong. Jefferson: McFarland, 2012. 243–260. Print.

Gaiman, Neil. *Batman: Whatever Happened to the Caped Crusader?* Art by Andy Kubert and Scott Williams, colors by Alex Sinclair, lettered by Jared K. Fletcher. Originally published in *Secret Origins* #36, *Secret Origins Special* 1, *Batman Black and White* #2, *Batman* #868, *Detective Comics* #853, 1989–2009. New York: DC Comics/Vertigo, 2009. Print.

———. *The Sandman: The Doll's House*. Vol. 2 of *The Sandman* series. Art by Mike Dringenberg, Malcolm Jones III, Chris Bachalo, Michael Zulli, and Steve Parkhouse, colors by Robbie Busch, lettered by Todd Klein, covers by Dave McKean. Originally published in single magazine form as *The Sandman* #8–16, 1989–1990. New York: DC Comics/Vertigo, 1990. Print.

———. *The Sandman: Dream Country*. Vol. 3 of *The Sandman* series. Art by Kelley Jones, Charles Vess, Colleen Doran, and Malcolm Jones III, colors by Robbie Busch and Steve Oliff, lettered by Todd Klein, covers by Dave

McKean. Originally published in single magazine form as *The Sandman* #17–20, 1990. New York: DC Comics/Vertigo, 1991. Print.

——. *The Sandman: Fables and Reflections*. Vol. 6 of *The Sandman* series. Art by Bryan Talbot, Stan Woch, P. Craig Russell, Shawn McManus, John Watkiss, Jill Thompson, Duncan Eagleson, Kent Williams, Mark Buckingham, Vince Locke, and Dick Giordano, colors by Danny Vozzo and Lovern Kindzierski/Digital Chameleon, lettered by Todd Klein, covers by Dave McKean. Originally published in single magazine form as *The Sandman* #29–31, #38–40, #50, *Sandman Special* 1, and *Vertigo Preview*, 1991–1993. New York: DC Comics/Vertigo, 1993. Print.

——. *The Sandman: Preludes and Nocturnes*. Vol. 1 of *The Sandman* series. Art by Sam Kieth, Mike Dringenberg, and Malcolm Jones III, colors by Robbie Busch, lettered by Todd Klein, covers by Dave McKean. Originally published in single magazine form as *The Sandman* #1–8, 1988–1989. New York: DC Comics/Vertigo, 1991. Print.

——. *The Sandman: Season of Mists*. Vol. 4 of *The Sandman* series. Art by Kelley Jones, Mike Dringenberg, Malcolm Jones III, Matt Wagner, Dick Giordano, George Pratt, and P. Craig Russell, colors by Steve Oliff and Daniel Vozzo, lettered by Todd Klein, covers by Dave McKean. Originally published in single magazine form as *The Sandman* #21–28, 1990–1991. New York: DC Comics/Vertigo, 1992. Print.

——. *The Sandman: The Wake*. Vol. 10 of *The Sandman* series. Art by Michael Zulli, Jon J. Muth, and Charles Vess, colors by Daniel Vozzo and Jon J. Muth, lettered by Todd Klein, covers by Dave McKean. Originally published in single magazine form as *The Sandman* #70–75, 1995–1996. New York: DC Comics/Vertigo, 1997. Print.

Galloway, Dana, Kenneth McAlpine, and Paul Harris. "From Michael Moore to *JFK Reloaded*: Towards a Working Model of Interactive Documentary." *Journal of Media Practice* 8.3 (2007): 325–339. Print.

Game of Thrones. HBO, 2011– . Television.

Gardner, Jared. "Autography's Biography, 1972–2007." *Biography* 31.1 (2008): 1–26. Print.

——. *Projections: Comics and the History of Twenty-First-Century Storytelling*. Stanford: Stanford University Press, 2012. Print.

Gardner, Jared, and David Herman, eds. *Graphic Narratives and Narrative Theory*. Spec. issue *SubStance* 40.1 (2011). Print.

——. "Graphic Narratives and Narrative Theory: Introduction." *SubStance* 40.1 (2011): 3–13. Print.

Garnham, Alan. *Mental Models as Representations of Discourse and Text*. Chichester: Horwood, 1987. Print.

Gaudreault, André. *From Plato to Lumière: Narration and Monstration in Literature and Cinema*. Trans. Timothy Barnard. Toronto: University of Toronto Press, 2009. Print.

———. "Mimèsis, diégèsis et cinéma." *Recherches Semiotiques/Semiotic Inquiry* 5.1 (1985): 32–45. Print.

Gaudreault, André, and François Jost. "Enunciation and Narration." *A Companion to Film Theory*. Ed. Toby Miller and Robert Stam. Malden: Blackwell, 1999. 45–63. Print.

———. *Le récit cinématographique*. Paris: Nathan, 1990. Print.

Gaut, Berys. "Film Authorship and Collaboration." *Film Theory and Philosophy*. Ed. Richard Allen and Murray Smith. Oxford: Oxford University Press, 1997. 149–172. Print.

———. "The Philosophy of the Movies: Cinematic Narration." *The Blackwell Guide to Aesthetics*. Ed. Peter Kivy. Malden: Blackwell, 2004. 230–253. Print.

Gears of War. Epic Games/Microsoft, 2006. Xbox 360.

Genette, Gérard. *Fiction and Diction*. Trans. Catherine Porter. Ithaca NY: Cornell University Press, 1993. Print.

———. "Frontières du récit." *Communications* 8 (1966): 152–163. Print.

———. *Métalepse: De la figure à la fiction*. Paris: Éditions du Seuil, 2004. Print.

———. *Narrative Discourse: An Essay in Method*. Trans. Jane E. Lewin. Ithaca NY: Cornell University Press, 1980. Print.

———. *Narrative Discourse Revisited*. Trans. Jane E. Lewin. Ithaca NY: Cornell University Press, 1988. Print.

———. *Paratexts: Thresholds of Interpretation*. Trans. Jane E. Lewin. Cambridge: Cambridge University Press, 1997. Print.

Gernalzick, Nadja, and Gabriele Pisarz-Ramírez, eds. *Transmediality and Transculturality*. Heidelberg: Winter, 2013. Print.

Gerrig, Richard J. *Experiencing Narrative Worlds: On the Psychological Activities of Reading*. New Haven: Yale University Press, 1993. Print.

Gibbons, Alison. *Multimodality, Cognition, and Experimental Literature*. New York: Routledge, 2012. Print.

Gibson, James J. *The Ecological Approach to Visual Perception*. Boston: Houghton Mifflin, 1979. Print.

Gilbert, Margaret. *Joint Commitment: How We Make the Social World*. Oxford: Oxford University Press, 2014. Print.

———. *On Social Facts*. Princeton: Princeton University Press, 1992. Print.

———. *A Theory of Political Obligation*. Oxford: Oxford University Press, 2006. Print.

Gillan, Jennifer. *Television and New Media: Must-Click TV*. New York: Routledge, 2011. Print.

God of War. SCE Santa Monica Studio/Sony, 2005. PlayStation 2.

Goffman, Erving. *The Presentation of Self in Everyday Life*. New York: Anchor Books, 1959. Print.

Goldie, Peter. *The Emotions: A Philosophical Exploration*. Oxford: Oxford University Press, 2000. Print.

Goldman, Alvin I. "Interpretation Psychologized." *Mind and Language* 4.3 (1989): 161–185. Print.

———. *Simulating Minds: The Philosophy, Psychology, and Neuroscience of Mindreading*. Oxford: Oxford University Press, 2006. Print.

Gombrich, Ernst H. *Art and Illusion: A Study in the Psychology of Pictorial Representation*. New York: Pantheon, 1960. Print.

———. *The Image and the Eye: Further Studies in the Psychology of Pictorial Representation*. Oxford: Phaidon Press, 1982. Print.

Goodman, Nelson. *Languages of Art: An Approach to a Theory of Symbols*. Indianapolis: Bobbs-Merrill, 1968. Print.

———. *Ways of Worldmaking*. Indianapolis: Hackett, 1978. Print.

Gordon, Ian. "Comics, Creators, and Copyright: On the Ownership of Serial Narratives by Multiple Authors." *A Companion to Media Authorship*. Ed. Jonathan Gray and Derek Johnson. Chichester: Wiley-Blackwell, 2013. 221–236. Print.

Gordon, Robert M. "Folk Psychology as Simulation." *Mind and Language* 1.2 (1986): 158–171. Print.

———. "The Simulation Theory: Objections and Misconceptions." *Mind and Language* 7.1–2 (1992): 11–34. Print.

Gorman, David. "Fiction, Theories of." *The Routledge Encyclopedia of Narrative Theory*. Ed. David Herman, Manfred Jahn, and Marie-Laure Ryan. Abingdon: Routledge, 2005. 163–167. Print.

Grand Theft Auto IV. Rockstar North/Rockstar Games, 2008. PlayStation 3.

Grau, Oliver. *Virtual Art: From Illusion to Immersion*. Trans. Gloria Custance. Cambridge MA: MIT Press, 2003. Print.

Grau, Oliver, and Andreas Keil, eds. *Mediale Emotionen: Zur Lenkung von Gefühlen durch Bild und Sound*. Frankfurt am Main: Fischer, 2005. Print.

Gravett, Paul. *Graphic Novels: Stories to Change Your Life*. London: Aurum, 2005. Print.

Gray, Jonathan. *Show Sold Separately: Promos, Spoilers, and Other Media Paratexts*. New York: New York University Press, 2010. Print.

———. "When Is the Author?" *A Companion to Media Authorship*. Ed. Jonathan Gray and Derek Johnson. Chichester: Wiley-Blackwell, 2013. 88–111. Print.

Gray, Jonathan, and Derek Johnson, eds. *A Companion to Media Authorship*. Chichester: Wiley-Blackwell, 2013. Print.

Greimas, Algirdas J. "Eléments pour une théorie de l'interprétation du récit mythique." *Communications* 8 (1966): 28–59. Print.

———. *Structural Semantics: An Attempt at a Method*. Trans. Daniele McDowell, Ronald Schleifer, and Alan Velie. Lincoln: University of Nebraska Press, 1983. Print.

Grice, H. P. *Studies in the Way of Words*. Cambridge MA: Harvard University Press, 1989. Print.

Grodal, Torben. *Embodied Visions: Evolution, Emotion, Culture, and Film*. Oxford: Oxford University Press, 2009. Print.

———. "Film Narrative." *The Routledge Encyclopedia of Narrative Theory*. Ed. David Herman, Manfred Jahn, and Marie-Laure Ryan. Abingdon: Routledge, 2005. 168–172. Print.

———. *Moving Pictures: A New Theory of Film Genres, Feelings, and Cognition*. Oxford: Oxford University Press, 1997. Print.

Groensteen, Thierry. *Comics and Narration*. Trans. Ann Miller. Jackson: University Press of Mississippi, 2013. Print.

———. "The Monstrator, the Recitant and the Shadow of the Narrator." Trans. Laurence Grove. *European Comic Art* 3.1 (2010): 1–21. Print.

———. *The System of Comics*. Trans. Bart Beaty and Nick Nguyen. Jackson: University Press of Mississippi, 2007. Print.

Grünewald, Dietrich, ed. *Der dokumentarische Comic: Reportage und Biografie*. Bochum: Bachmann, 2013. Print.

Günzel, Stephan. *Egoshooter: Das Raumbild des Computerspiels*. Frankfurt am Main: Campus, 2012. Print.

Hague, Ian. *Comics and the Senses: A Multisensory Approach to Comics and Graphic Novels*. New York: Routledge, 2014. Print.

Half-Life. Valve/Sierra Entertainment, 1998. PC.

Half-Life 2. Valve/Sierra Entertainment, 2004. PC.

Hall, Stuart. "The Work of Representation." *Representation: Cultural Representation and Signifying Practices*. Ed. Stuart Hall. London: Sage, 1997. 13–74. Print.

Halo: Combat Evolved. Bungie/Gearbox/Microsoft, 2003. PC. [Originally published as *Halo: Combat Evolved*. Bungie/Microsoft, 2001. Xbox.]

Halo 2. Bungie/Microsoft, 2004. Xbox.

Hamburger, Käte. *The Logic of Literature*. Trans. Marilyn J. Rose. 2nd ed. Bloomington: Indiana University Press, 1993. Print.

Hammond, Michael, and Lucy Mazdon, eds. *The Contemporary Television Series*. Edinburgh: Edinburgh University Press, 2005. Print.

Hancock, Hugh. "Better Game Design through Cutscenes." *Gamasutra* April 2, 2002. Web. December 1, 2013.

Hanich, Julian. *Cinematic Emotion in Horror Films and Thrillers: The Aesthetic Paradox of Pleasurable Fear*. New York: Routledge, 2010. Print.

Hansen, Per Krogh. "Reconsidering the Unreliable Narrator." *Semiotica* 165 (2007): 227–246. Print.

Hansen, Per Krogh, Stefan Iversen, Henrik Skov Nielsen, and Rolf Reitan, eds. *Strange Voices in Narrative Fiction*. Berlin: De Gruyter, 2011. Print.

Harpold, Terry. "Screw the Grue: Mediality, Metalepsis, Recapture." *Game Studies* 7.1 (2007): n. pag. Web. December 1, 2013.

Harry Potter and the Philosopher's Stone. Dir. Chris Columbus. Warner Bros. Pictures, 2001. Film.

Hartley, John, ed. *Creative Industries*. Malden: Blackwell, 2005. Print.

Hartmann, Britta. *Aller Anfang: Zur Initialphase des Spielfilms*. Marburg: Schüren, 2009. Print.

Harvey, Colin B. "A Taxonomy of Transmedia Storytelling." *Storyworlds across Media: Toward a Media-Conscious Narratology*. Ed. Marie-Laure Ryan and Jan-Noël Thon. Lincoln: University of Nebraska Press, 2014. 278–294. Print.

Häsner, Bernd. "Metalepsen: Zur Genese, Systematik und Funktion transgressiver Erzählweisen." PhD thesis Free University Berlin, 2001. Web. December 1, 2013.

Hatfield, Charles. *Alternative Comics: An Emerging Literature*. Jackson: University Press of Mississippi, 2005. Print.

Hausken, Liv. "Coda: Textual Theory and Blind Spots in Media Studies." *Narrative across Media: The Languages of Storytelling*. Ed. Marie-Laure Ryan. Lincoln: University of Nebraska Press, 2004. 391–403. Print.

Heintz, John. "Reference and Inference in Fiction." *Poetics* 8.1–2 (1979): 85–99. Print.

Heinze, Carl. *Mittelalter Computer Spiele: Zur Darstellung und Modellierung von Geschichte im populären Computerspiel*. Bielefeld: transcript, 2012. Print.

Helbig, Jörg, ed. *"Camera doesn't lie": Spielarten erzählerischer Unzuverlässigkeit im Film*. Trier: Wissenschaftlicher Verlag Trier, 2006. Print.

———. "'Follow the White Rabbit!' Signale erzählerischer Unzuverlässigkeit im zeitgenössischen Spielfilm." *Was stimmt denn jetzt? Unzuverlässiges Erzählen in Literatur und Film.* Ed. Fabienne Liptay and Yvonne Wolf. München: edition text + kritik, 2005. 131–146. Print.

———, ed. *Intermedialität: Theorie und Praxis eines interdisziplinären Forschungsgebiets.* Berlin: Erich Schmidt, 1998. Print.

Hepp, Andreas. *Cultures of Mediatization.* Cambridge: Polity Press, 2012. Print.

Hepp, Andreas, and Friedrich Krotz, eds. *Mediatized Worlds: Culture and Society in a Media Age.* Basingstoke: Palgrave Macmillan, 2014. Print.

Herman, David. *Basic Elements of Narrative.* Chichester: Wiley-Blackwell, 2009. Print.

———, ed. *The Cambridge Companion to Narrative.* Cambridge: Cambridge University Press, 2007. Print.

———. "Histories of Narrative Theory (I): A Genealogy of Early Developments." *A Companion to Narrative Theory.* Ed. James Phelan and Peter J. Rabinowitz. Malden: Blackwell, 2005. 19–35. Print.

———. "Hypothetical Focalization." *Narrative* 2.3 (1994): 230–253. Print.

———. "Introduction." *Narrative Theory and the Cognitive Sciences.* Ed. David Herman. Stanford: CSLI, 2003. 1–30. Print.

———. "Introduction: Narratologies." *Narratologies: New Perspectives on Narrative Analysis.* Ed. David Herman. Columbus: Ohio State University Press, 1999. 1–30. Print.

———. "Narrative: Cognitive Approaches." *Encyclopedia of Language and Linguistics.* Vol. 8. 2nd ed. Ed. Catherine Emmott. Oxford: Elsevier, 2006. 452–459. Print.

———. "Scripts, Sequences, and Stories: Elements of a Postclassical Narratology." *PMLA* 112.5 (1997): 1046–1059. Print.

———. *Story Logic: Problems and Possibilities of Narrative.* Lincoln: University of Nebraska Press, 2002. Print.

———. *Storytelling and the Sciences of Mind.* Cambridge MA: MIT Press, 2013. Print.

———. "Toward a Formal Description of Narrative Metalepsis." *Journal of Literary Semantics* 26.2 (1997): 132–152. Print.

———. "Toward a Transmedial Narratology." *Narrative across Media: The Languages of Storytelling.* Ed. Marie-Laure Ryan. Lincoln: University of Nebraska Press, 2004. 47–75. Print.

———. "Word-Image/Utterance-Gesture: Case Studies in Multimodal Storytelling." *New Perspectives on Narrative and Multimodality.* Ed. Ruth Page. New York: Routledge, 2010. 78–98. Print.

Herman, David, Manfred Jahn, and Marie-Laure Ryan, eds. *Routledge Encyclopedia of Narrative Theory*. Abingdon: Routledge, 2005. Print.

Herman, Luc, and Bart Vervaeck. "Focalization between Classical and Postclassical Narratology." *The Dynamics of Narrative Form: Studies in Anglo-American Narratology*. Ed. John Pier. Berlin: De Gruyter, 2004. 115–138. Print.

———. *Handbook of Narrative Analysis*. Lincoln: University of Nebraska Press, 2005. Print.

Hernadi, Paul. *Beyond Genre: New Directions in Literary Classification*. Ithaca NY: Cornell University Press, 1972. Print.

Herriman, George. *Krazy Kat*. Syndicated newspaper comic strip. Original run October 28, 1913–June 25, 1944. Print.

Herrnstein Smith, Barbara. "Narrative Versions, Narrative Theories." *On Narrative*. Ed. W. J. T. Mitchell. Chicago: University of Chicago Press, 1981. 209–232. Print.

Hesmondhalgh, David, and Sarah Baker. *Creative Labour: Media Work in Three Cultural Industries*. Abingdon: Routledge, 2011. Print.

Hight, Craig. *Television Mockumentary: Reflexivity, Satire and a Call to Play*. Manchester: Manchester University Press, 2010. Print.

Hills, Matt. *Fan Cultures*. Abingdon: Routledge, 2002. Print.

———. *Triumph of a Time Lord: Regenerating* Doctor Who *in the Twenty-First Century*. London: I. B. Tauris, 2010. Print.

Hirsch, Marianne. "Family Pictures: *Maus*, Mourning, and Post-Memory." *Discourse: Journal for Theoretical Studies in Media and Culture* 15.2 (1992): 3–29. Print.

Hitman: Blood Money. IO Interactive/Eidos Interactive, 2006. PC.

Hjarvard, Stig. *The Mediatization of Culture and Society*. Abingdon: Routledge, 2013. Print.

Hoesterey, Ingeborg. "Introduction." *Neverending Stories: Toward a Critical Narratology*. Ed. Ann Fehn, Ingeborg Hoesterey, and Maria Tatar. Princeton: Princeton University Press, 1992. 3–14. Print.

Hogan, Patrick C. *Cognitive Science, Literature, and the Arts: A Guide for Humanists*. New York: Routledge, 2003. Print.

———. *Narrative Discourse: Authors and Narrators in Literature, Film, and Art*. Columbus: Ohio State University Press, 2013. Print.

———. *What Literature Teaches Us about Emotion*. Cambridge: Cambridge University Press, 2011. Print.

Holly, Werner. "Alte und neue Medien: Zur inneren Logik der Mediengeschichte." *Kommunikation und Lernen mit alten und neuen Medien: Beiträge zum Rahmenthema Schlagwort*

"Kommunikationsgesellschaft" der 26. Jahrestagung der Gesellschaft für Angewandte Linguistik GAL e.V. Ed. Bernd Rüschoff and Ulrich Schmitz. Frankfurt am Main: Peter Lang, 1996. 9–16. Print.

Horstkotte, Silke. "Zooming In and Out: Panels, Frames, Sequences, and the Building of Graphic Storyworlds." *From Comic Strips to Graphic Novels: Contributions to the Theory and History of Graphic Narrative*. 2nd ed. Ed. Daniel Stein and Jan-Noël Thon. Berlin: De Gruyter, 2015. 27–48. Print.

Horstkotte, Silke, and Nancy Pedri. "Focalization in Graphic Narrative." *Narrative* 19.3 (2011): 330–357. Print.

Hot Shots! Part Deux. Dir. Jim Abrahams. 20th Century Fox, 1993. Film.

Howell, Robert. "Fictional Objects: How They Are and How They Aren't." *Poetics* 8.1–2 (1979): 129–178. Print.

Hühn, Peter. "Event and Eventfulness." *Handbook of Narratology*. Ed. Peter Hühn, John Pier, Wolf Schmid, and Jörg Schönert. Berlin: De Gruyter, 2009. 80–97. Print.

———. "Functions and Forms of Eventfulness in Narrative Fiction." *Theorizing Narrativity*. Ed. John Pier and José Á. García Landa. Berlin: De Gruyter, 2008. 141–163. Print.

———. "Transgeneric Narratology: Application to Lyric Poetry." *The Dynamics of Narrative Form: Studies in Anglo-American Narratology*. Ed. John Pier. Berlin: De Gruyter, 2004. 139–158. Print.

Hühn, Peter, and Jens Kiefer, eds. *The Narratological Analysis of Lyric Poetry: Studies in English Poetry from the 16th to the 20th Century*. Berlin: De Gruyter, 2005. Print.

Hühn, Peter, John Pier, Wolf Schmid, and Jörg Schönert, eds. *Handbook of Narratology*. Berlin: De Gruyter, 2009. Print.

Hühn, Peter, Wolf Schmid, and Jörg Schönert, eds. *Point of View, Perspective, and Focalization: Modeling Mediation in Narrative*. Berlin: De Gruyter, 2009. Print.

Hühn, Peter, and Jörg Schönert. "Zur narratologischen Analyse von Lyrik." *Poetica* 34.3–4 (2002): 287–305. Print.

Hühn, Peter, and Roy Sommer. "Narration in Poetry and Drama." *Handbook of Narratology*. Ed. Peter Hühn, John Pier, Wolf Schmid, and Jörg Schönert. Berlin: De Gruyter, 2009. 228–241. Print.

Huizinga, Johan. *Homo Ludens: A Study of the Play-Element in Culture*. London: Routledge, 1949. Print.

Hünig, Wolfgang K. *Strukturen des Comic Strip: Ansätze zu einer textlinguistisch-semiotischen Analyse narrativer Comics*. Hildesheim: Olms, 1974. Print.

Hurst, Matthias. *Erzählsituationen in Literatur und Film: Ein Modell zur vergleichenden Analyse von literarischen Texten und filmischen Adaptionen*. Tübingen: Niemeyer, 1996. Print.

Hutcheon, Linda. *A Theory of Adaptation*. 2nd ed. Epilogue by Siobhan O'Flynn. Abingdon: Routledge, 2013. Print.

Identity. Dir. James Mangold. Columbia Pictures, 2003. Film.

Inception. Dir. Christopher Nolan. Warner Bros. Pictures, 2010. Film.

Indigo Prophecy. Quantic Dream/Atari, 2005. PC.

Irwin, William, ed. *The Death and Resurrection of the Author?* Westport: Greenwood Press, 2002. Print.

Iser, Wolfgang. *The Act of Reading: A Theory of Aesthetic Response*. Baltimore: Johns Hopkins University Press, 1978. Print.

———. *The Implied Reader: Patterns of Communication in Prose Fiction from Bunyan to Beckett*. Baltimore: Johns Hopkins University Press, 1974. Print.

———. "Indeterminacy and the Reader's Response in Prose Fiction." *Aspects of Narrative: Selected Papers from the English Institute*. Ed. J. Hillis Miller. New York: Columbia University Press, 1971. 1–45. Print.

Jacquenod, Claudine. *Contribution à une étude du concept de fiction*. Bern: Peter Lang, 1988. Print.

Jahn, Manfred. "Focalization." *The Cambridge Companion to Narrative*. Ed. David Herman. Cambridge: Cambridge University Press, 2007. 94–108. Print.

———. "More Aspects of Focalisation: Refinements and Applications." *GRAAT* 21 (1999): 85–110. Print.

———. "Narrative Voice and Agency in Drama: Aspects of a Narratology of Drama." *New Literary History* 32.3 (2001): 659–679. Print.

———. *Narratology: A Guide to the Theory of Narrative*. Cologne: University of Cologne, 2005. Web. December 1, 2013.

———. "Windows of Focalization: Deconstructing and Reconstructing a Narratological Concept." *Style* 30.2 (1996): 241–267. Print.

Jahn, Manfred, and Ansgar Nünning. "Briefings 7: Narratology." *European English Messenger* 2.2 (1993): 24–29. Print.

———. "Forum: A Survey of Narratological Models." *Literatur in Wissenschaft und Unterricht* 27.4 (1994): 283–303. Print.

Jancovich, Mark, and James Lyons, eds. *Quality Popular Television: Cult TV, the Industry and Fans*. London: British Film Institute, 2008. Print.

Janik, Dieter. *Die Kommunikationsstruktur des Erzählwerks: Ein semiologisches Modell*. Bebenhausen: Rotsch, 1973. Print.

Jannidis, Fotis. "Character." *Handbook of Narratology*. Ed. Peter Hühn, John Pier, Wolf Schmid, and Jörg Schönert. Berlin: De Gruyter, 2009. 14–29. Print.

———. "Event-Sequences, Plots and Narration in Computer Games." *The Aesthetics of Net Literature: Writing, Reading and Playing in Programmable Media*. Ed. Peter Gendolla and Jörgen Schäfer. Bielefeld: transcript, 2007. 281–305. Print.

———. *Figur und Person: Beitrag zu einer historischen Narratologie*. Berlin: De Gruyter, 2004. Print.

———. "Narratology and the Narrative." *What Is Narratology? Questions and Answers regarding the Status of a Theory*. Ed. Tom Kindt and Hans-Harald Müller. Berlin: De Gruyter, 2003. 35–54. Print.

———. "Wer sagt das? Erzählen mit Stimmverlust." *Stimme(n) im Text: Narratologische Positionsbestimmungen*. Ed. Andreas Blödorn, Daniela Langer, and Michael Scheffel. Berlin: De Gruyter, 2006. 151–164. Print.

Jannidis, Fotis, Gerhard Lauer, Matías Martínez, and Simone Winko, eds. *Rückkehr des Autors: Zur Erneuerung eines umstrittenen Begriffs*. Tübingen: Niemeyer, 1999. Print.

Järvinen, Aki. "Making and Breaking Games: A Typology of Rules." *Level Up: DiGRA Conference Proceedings 2003*. 68–79. Web. December 1, 2013.

———. "Understanding Video Games as Emotional Experiences." *The Video Game Theory Reader 2*. Ed. Bernard Perron and Mark J. P. Wolf. New York: Routledge, 2009. 85–108. Print.

Jauss, Hans R. "Literary History as a Challenge to Literary Theory." *Toward an Aesthetic of Reception*. Trans. Timothy Bahti. Minneapolis: University of Minnesota Press, 1982. 3–45. Print.

Jenkins, Henry. *Convergence Culture: Where Old and New Media Collide*. New York: New York University Press, 2006. Print.

———. "Game Design as Narrative Architecture." *FirstPerson: New Media as Story, Performance, and Game*. Ed. Noah Wardrip-Fruin and Pat Harrigan. Cambridge MA: MIT Press, 2004. 118–130. Print.

———. *Textual Poachers: Television Fans and Participatory Culture*. New York: Routledge, 1992. Print.

———. "Transmedia 202: Further Reflections." *Confessions of an Aca-Fan* August 1, 2011. Web. December 1, 2013.

———. "Transmedia Storytelling 101." *Confessions of an Aca-Fan* March 22, 2007. Web. December 1, 2013.

———. "*The Walking Dead*: Adapting Comics." *How to Watch Television*. Ed. Ethan Thompson and Jason Mittell. New York: New York University Press, 2013. 373–382. Print.

Jenkins, Henry, Sam Ford, and Joshua Green. *Spreadable Media: Creating Value and Meaning in a Networked Culture.* New York: New York University Press, 2013. Print.

Jesch, Tatjana, and Malte Stein. "Perspectivization and Focalization: Two Concepts—One Meaning? An Attempt at Conceptual Differentiation." *Point of View, Perspective, and Focalization: Modeling Mediation in Narrative.* Ed. Peter Hühn, Wolf Schmid, and Jörg Schönert. Berlin: De Gruyter, 2009. 59–77. Print.

La jetée. Dir. Chris Marker. Argos Films, 1962. Film.

Jewitt, Carey. "An Introduction to Multimodality." *The Routledge Handbook of Multimodal Analysis.* Ed. Carey Jewitt. London: Routledge, 2009. 14–27. Print.

JFK Reloaded. Traffic Games, 2004. PC.

Johnson, Derek. *Media Franchising: Creative License and Collaboration in the Culture Industries.* New York: New York University Press, 2013. Print.

Johnson, Derek, and Jonathan Gray. "Introduction: The Problem of Media Authorship." *A Companion to Media Authorship.* Ed. Jonathan Gray and Derek Johnson. Chichester: Wiley-Blackwell, 2013. 1–19. Print.

Johnson, Derek, Derek Kompare, and Avi Santo, eds. *Making Media Work: Cultures of Management in the Entertainment Industries.* New York: New York University Press, 2014. Print.

Johnson, Mark. *The Body in the Mind: The Bodily Basis of Meaning, Imagination, and Reason.* Chicago: University of Chicago Press, 1987. Print.

———. *The Meaning of the Body: Aesthetics of Human Understanding.* Chicago: University of Chicago Press, 2007. Print.

Johnson, Steven. *Everything Bad Is Good for You: How Popular Culture Is Making Us Smarter.* New York: Riverhead Books, 2006. Print.

Johnson-Laird, Philip N. *Mental Models: Towards a Cognitive Science of Language, Inference, and Consciousness.* Cambridge MA: Harvard University Press, 1983. Print.

Jørgensen, Kristine. *A Comprehensive Study of Sound in Computer Games: How Audio Affects Player Action.* Lewiston: Mellen Press, 2009. Print.

———. *Gameworld Interfaces.* Cambridge MA: MIT Press, 2013. Print.

Jost, François. "The Look: From Film to Novel: An Essay in Comparative Narratology." *A Companion to Literature and Film.* Ed. Robert Stam and Alessandra Raengo. Malden: Blackwell, 2004. 71–80. Print.

———. *L'oeil-caméra: Entre film et roman.* Lyon: Presses Universitaires de Lyon, 1987. Print.

———. "Le regard romanesque: Ocularisation et focalisation." *Hors Cadre* 2 (1984): 67–85. Print.
Juul, Jesper. *The Art of Failure: An Essay on the Pain of Playing Video Games.* Cambridge MA: MIT Press, 2013. Print.
———. *Half-Real: Video Games between Real Rules and Fictional Worlds.* Cambridge MA: MIT Press, 2005. Print.
Kablitz, Andreas. "Erzählperspektive—Point of View—Focalisation: Überlegungen zu einem Konzept der Erzähltheorie." *Zeitschrift für französische Sprache und Literatur* 98.3 (1988): 237–255. Print.
Kafalenos, Emma. *Narrative Causalities.* Columbus: Ohio State University Press, 2006. Print.
Kalinak, Kathryn. *Film Music: A Very Short Introduction.* Oxford: Oxford University Press, 2010. Print.
Kania, Andrew. "Against the Ubiquity of Fictional Narrators." *Journal of Aesthetics and Art Criticism* 63.1 (2005): 47–54. Print.
Kawin, Bruce. *Mindscreen: Bergman, Godard, and First-Person Film.* Princeton: Princeton University Press, 1978. Print.
Kayser, Wolfgang. "Wer erzählt den Roman?" *Texte zur Theorie der Autorschaft.* Ed. Fotis Jannidis, Gerhard Lauer, Matías Martínez, and Sabine Winko. Stuttgart: Reclam, 2000. 124–137. Print.
Keen, Suzanne. "Fast Tracks to Narrative Empathy: Anthropomorphism and Dehumanization in Graphic Narratives." *SubStance* 40.1 (2011): 135–155. Print.
Keller, James R. *V for Vendetta as Cultural Pastiche: A Critical Study of the Graphic Novel and Film.* Jefferson: McFarland, 2008. Print.
Kelleter, Frank. *Serial Agencies: The Wire and Its Readers.* Winchester: Zero Books, 2014. Print.
Kemp, Wolfgang, ed. *Der Betrachter ist im Bild: Kunstwissenschaft und Rezeptionsästhetik.* Berlin: Dietrich Reimer Verlag, 1992. Print.
———, ed. *Der Text des Bildes: Möglichkeiten und Mittel eigenständiger Bilderzählung.* München: edition text + kritik, 1989. Print.
Kessler, Frank. "Von der Filmologie zur Narratologie: Anmerkungen zum Begriff der Diegese." *montage AV* 16.2 (2007): 9–16. Print.
Khordoc, Catherine. "The Comic Book's Soundtrack: Visual Sound Effects in *Asterix*." *The Language of Comics: Word and Image.* Ed. Robin Varnum and Christina T. Gibbons. Jackson: University Press of Mississippi, 2001. 156–173. Print.
Kinder, Marsha. *Playing with Power in Movies, Television, and Video Games: From* Muppet Babies *to* Teenage Mutant Ninja Turtles. Berkeley: University of California Press, 1991. Print.

Kinder, Marsha, and Tara McPherson, eds. *Transmedia Frictions: The Digital, the Arts, and the Humanities*. Berkeley: University of California Press, 2014. Print.

Kindt, Tom. *Unzuverlässiges Erzählen und literarische Moderne: Eine Untersuchung der Romane von Ernst Weiß*. Tübingen: Niemeyer, 2008. Print.

Kindt, Tom, and Tilmann Köppe, eds. *Unreliable Narration*. Spec. issue *Journal of Literary Theory* 5.1 (2011). Print.

Kindt, Tom, and Hans-Harald Müller. *The Implied Author: Concept and Controversy*. Trans. Alastair Matthews. Berlin: De Gruyter, 2006. Print.

——. "Narrative Theory and/or/as Theory of Interpretation." *What Is Narratology? Questions and Answers regarding the Status of a Theory*. Ed. Tom Kindt and Hans-Harald Müller. Berlin: De Gruyter, 2003. 205–219. Print.

——. "Narratology and Interpretation: A Rejoinder to David Darby." *Poetics Today* 24.3 (2003): 413–421. Print.

Kiss Kiss Bang Bang. Dir. Shane Black. Warner Bros. Pictures, 2005. Film.

Klastrup, Lisbeth, and Susana P. Tosca. "*Game of Thrones*: Transmedial Worlds, Fandom, and Social Gaming." *Storyworlds across Media: Toward a Media-Conscious Narratology*. Ed. Marie-Laure Ryan and Jan-Noël Thon. Lincoln: University of Nebraska Press, 2014. 295–314. Print.

——. "Transmedial Worlds—Rethinking Cyberworld Design." *Proceedings of the International Conference on Cyberworlds 2004*. Web. December 1, 2013.

Klauk, Tobias, and Tilmann Köppe, eds. *Fiktionalität: Ein interdisziplinäres Handbuch*. Berlin: De Gruyter, 2014. Print.

——. "Reassessing Unnatural Narratology: Problems and Prospects." *Storyworlds: A Journal of Narrative Studies* 5 (2013): 77–100. Print.

Klein, Melanie. *The Psycho-Analysis of Children*. Trans. Alix Strachey. London: Hogarth Press, 1932. Print.

Klepper, Martin. *The Discovery of Point of View: Observation and Narration in the American Novel, 1790–1910*. Heidelberg: Winter, 2011. Print.

Klevjer, Rune. "In Defense of Cutscenes." *Proceedings of the Computer Games and Digital Cultures Conference*. Ed. Frans Mäyrä. Tampere: Tampere University Press, 2002. 191–202. Web. December 1, 2013.

——. "What Is the Avatar? Fiction and Embodiment in Avatar-Based Singleplayer Computer Games." PhD thesis University of Bergen, 2006. Web. December 1, 2013.

Klimek, Sonja. *Paradoxes Erzählen: Die Metalepse in der phantastischen Literatur*. Paderborn: mentis, 2010. Print.

Klimmt, Christoph. *Computerspielen als Handlung: Dimensionen und Determinanten des Erlebens interaktiver Unterhaltungsangebote*. Cologne: Herbert von Halem, 2006. Print.
Konrad, Eva-Maria. "Panfiktionalismus." *Fiktionalität: Ein interdisziplinäres Handbuch*. Ed. Tobias Klauk and Tilmann Köppe. Berlin: De Gruyter, 2014. 235–254. Print.
Köppe, Tilmann, and Jan Stühring. "Against Pan-Narrator Theories." *Journal of Literary Semantics* 40.1 (2011): 59–80. Print.
Korthals, Holger. *Zwischen Drama und Erzählung: Ein Beitrag zur Theorie geschehensdarstellender Literatur*. Berlin: Erich Schmidt, 2003. Print.
Korthals Altes, Liesbeth. *Ethos and Narrative Interpretation: The Negotiation of Values in Fiction*. Lincoln: University of Nebraska Press, 2014. Print.
Kozloff, Sarah. *Invisible Storytellers: Voice-Over Narration in American Fiction Film*. Berkeley: University of California Press, 1988. Print.
Kress, Gunther. *Multimodality: A Social Semiotic Approach to Contemporary Communication*. Abingdon: Routledge, 2010. Print.
———. "What Is Mode?" *The Routledge Handbook of Multimodal Analysis*. Ed. Carey Jewitt. London: Routledge, 2009. 54–67. Print.
Kress, Gunther, and Theo van Leeuwen. *Multimodal Discourse: The Modes and Media of Contemporary Communication*. London: Arnold, 2001. Print.
Krotz, Friedrich. *Mediatisierung: Fallstudien zum Wandel von Kommunikation*. Wiesbaden: VS Verlag für Sozialwissenschaften, 2007. Print.
Kuhlman, Martha B. "Teaching Paul Karasik's and David Mazzucchelli's Graphic Novel Adaptation of Paul Auster's *City of Glass*." *Teaching the Graphic Novel*. Ed. Stephen E. Tabachnick. New York: MLA, 2009. 120–128. Print.
Kuhlman, Martha B., and David M. Ball. "Introduction: Chris Ware and the 'Cult of Difficulty.'" *The Comics of Chris Ware: Drawing Is a Way of Thinking*. Ed. David M. Ball and Martha B. Kuhlman. Jackson: University Press of Mississippi, 2010. ix–xxiii. Print.
Kuhn, Markus. *Filmnarratologie: Ein erzähltheoretisches Analysemodell*. Berlin: De Gruyter, 2011. Print.
Kukkonen, Karin. "Comics as a Test Case for Transmedial Narratology." *SubStance* 40.1 (2011): 34–51. Print.
———. *Contemporary Comics Storytelling*. Lincoln: University of Nebraska Press, 2013. Print.
———. "Metalepsis in Comics and Graphic Novels." *Metalepsis in Popular Culture*. Ed. Karin Kukkonen and Sonja Klimek. Berlin: De Gruyter, 2011. 213–231. Print.

———. "Navigating Infinite Earths: Readers, Mental Models, and the Multiverse of Superhero Comics." *Storyworlds: A Journal of Narrative Studies* 2 (2010): 39–58. Print.

———. "Space, Time, and Causality in Graphic Narratives: An Embodied Approach." *From Comic Strips to Graphic Novels: Contributions to the Theory and History of Graphic Narrative*. 2nd ed. Ed. Daniel Stein and Jan-Noël Thon. Berlin: De Gruyter, 2015. 49–66. Print.

Kukkonen, Karin, and Sonja Klimek, eds. *Metalepsis in Popular Culture*. Berlin: De Gruyter, 2011. Print.

Kuma\War. Kuma Reality Games, 2004– . PC.

Kunzle, David. "The Voices of Silence: Willette, Steinlen and the Introduction of the Silent Strip in the *Chat Noir*, with a German Coda." *The Language of Comics: Word and Image*. Ed. Robin Varnum and Christina T. Gibbons. Jackson: University Press of Mississippi, 2001. 3–18. Print.

Kuper, Peter. *The System*. New York: DC Comics/Vertigo, 1997. Print.

Laass, Eva. *Broken Taboos, Subjective Truths: Forms and Functions of Unreliable Narration in Contemporary American Cinema*. Trier: Wissenschaftlicher Verlag Trier, 2008. Print.

Lahn, Silke, and Jan Christoph Meister. *Einführung in die Erzähltextanalyse*. Stuttgart: Metzler, 2008. Print.

Lakoff, George. "Cognitive Models and Prototype Theory." *Concepts: Core Readings*. Ed. Eric Margolis and Stephen Laurence. Cambridge MA: MIT Press, 1999. 391–421. Print.

———. *Women, Fire, and Dangerous Things: What Categories Reveal about the Mind*. Chicago: University of Chicago Press, 1987. Print.

Lakoff, George, and Mark Johnson. *Metaphors We Live By*. Chicago: University of Chicago Press, 1980. Print.

———. *Philosophy in the Flesh: The Embodied Mind and Its Challenge to Western Thought*. New York: Basic Books, 1999. Print.

Lamarque, Peter. "The Intentional Fallacy." *Literary Theory and Criticism: An Oxford Guide*. Ed. Patricia Waugh. Oxford: Oxford University Press, 2006. 177–188. Print.

Lamarque, Peter, and Stein Haugom Olsen. *Truth, Fiction, and Literature: A Philosophical Perspective*. Oxford: Oxford University Press, 1994. Print.

Lanser, Susan S. *Fictions of Authority: Women Writers and Narrative Voice*. Ithaca NY: Cornell University Press, 1992. Print.

———. *The Narrative Act: Point of View in Prose Fiction*. Princeton: Princeton University Press, 1981. Print.

Lara Croft: Tomb Raider. Dir. Simon West. Paramount Pictures, 2001. Film.

Laurence, Stephen, and Eric Margolis. "Concepts and Cognitive Science." *Concepts: Core Readings*. Ed. Eric Margolis and Stephen Laurence. Cambridge MA: MIT Press, 1999. 3–81. Print.

The League of Extraordinary Gentlemen. Dir. Stephen Norrington. 20th Century Fox, 2003. Film.

Lefèvre, Pascal. "Narration in Comics." *Image [&] Narrative* 1 (2000): n. pag. Web. December 1, 2013.

Lego Star Wars: The Video Game. Traveller's Tales/LucasArts, 2005. PC.

Lego Star Wars II: The Original Trilogy. Traveller's Tales/LucasArts, 2006. PC.

Lego The Lord of the Rings. Traveller's Tales/Warner Bros. Interactive, 2012. PC.

Leitch, Thomas. *What Stories Are: Narrative Theory and Interpretation*. University Park: Pennsylvania State University Press, 1986. Print.

Leschke, Rainer, and Henriette Heidbrink, eds. *Formen der Figur: Figurenkonzepte in Künsten und Medien*. Marburg: Schüren, 2010. Print.

Levinson, Jerrold. *The Pleasures of Aesthetics: Philosophical Essays*. Ithaca NY: Cornell University Press, 1996. Print.

Lévy, Pierre. *Collective Intelligence: Mankind's Emerging World in Cyberspace*. Trans. Robert Bononno. New York: Plenum Trade, 1997. Print.

Lewis, David. "Truth in Fiction." *American Philosophical Quarterly* 15.1 (1978): 37–46. Print.

Limoges, Jean-Marc. "Metalepsis in the Cartoons of *Tex Avery*: Expanding the Boundaries of Transgression." *Metalepsis in Popular Culture*. Ed. Karin Kukkonen and Sonja Klimek. Berlin: De Gruyter, 2011. 197–212. Print.

Lintvelt, Jaap. *Essai de typologie narrative: Le "point de vue": Théorie et analyse*. Paris: J. Corti, 1981. Print.

Liptay, Fabienne, and Yvonne Wolf, eds. *Was stimmt denn jetzt? Unzuverlässiges Erzählen in Literatur und Film*. München: edition text + kritik, 2005. Print.

Living in Oblivion. Dir. Tom DiCillo. Sony Pictures Classics, 1995. Film.

Livingston, Paisley. "Cinematic Authorship." *Film Theory and Philosophy*. Ed. Richard Allen and Murray Smith. Oxford: Oxford University Press, 1997. 132–148. Print.

Lorente, Joaquín Martínez. "Blurring Focalization: Psychological Expansions of Point of View and Modality." *Revista Alicantina de Estudios Ingleses* 9 (1996): 63–98. Print.

Löschnigg, Martin. "Narratological Perspectives on 'Fiction and Autobiography.'" *Fiction and Autobiography: Modes and Models of*

Interaction. Ed. Sabine Coelsch-Foisner and Wolfgang Görtschacher. Frankfurt am Main: Peter Lang, 2006. 1–12. Print.

———. "Postclassical Narratology and the Theory of Autobiography." *Postclassical Narratology: Approaches and Analyses.* Ed. Jan Alber and Monika Fludernik. Columbus: Ohio State University Press, 2010. 255–274. Print.

Lost. ABC, 2004–2010. Television.

Lost Highway. Dir. David Lynch. October Films, 1997. Film.

Lothe, Jakob. *Narrative in Fiction and Film: An Introduction.* Oxford: Oxford University Press, 2000. Print.

Lotz, Amanda D. *The Television Will Be Revolutionized.* New York: New York University Press, 2007. Print.

Lubbock, Percy. *The Craft of Fiction.* New York: Viking Press, 1957. Print.

Luhmann, Niklas. *The Reality of the Mass Media.* Trans. Kathleen Cross. Stanford: Stanford University Press, 2000. Print.

———. *Social Systems.* Trans. John Bednarz Jr., with Dirk Baecker. Stanford: Stanford University Press, 1995. Print.

Lundby, Knut, ed. *Mediatization: Concept, Changes, Consequences.* New York: Peter Lang, 2009. Print.

Lycan, William G. *Consciousness and Experience.* Cambridge MA: MIT Press, 1996. Print.

———. *Modality and Meaning.* Dordrecht: Kluwer, 1994. Print.

MacCabe, Colin, Kathleen Murray, and Rick Warner, eds. *True to the Spirit: Film Adaptation and the Question of Fidelity.* Oxford: Oxford University Press, 2011. Print.

Mahne, Nicole. *Transmediale Erzähltheorie: Eine Einführung.* Göttingen: Vandenhoeck und Ruprecht, 2007. Print.

Malina, Debra. *Breaking the Frame: Metalepsis and the Construction of the Subject.* Columbus: Ohio State University Press, 2002. Print.

Manovich, Lev. *The Language of New Media.* Cambridge MA: MIT Press, 2001. Print.

Margolin, Uri. "Characters and Their Versions." *Fiction Updated: Theories of Fictionality, Narratology, and Poetics.* Ed. Calin-Andrei Mihailescu and Walid Hamarneh. Toronto: University of Toronto Press, 1996. 113–132. Print.

———. "The Constitution of Story Worlds: Fictional and/or Otherwise." *Semiotica* 131.3–4 (2000): 327–357. Print.

———. "Focalization: Where Do We Go from Here?" *Point of View, Perspective, and Focalization: Modeling Mediation in Narrative.* Ed. Peter Hühn, Wolf Schmid, and Jörg Schönert. Berlin: De Gruyter, 2009. 41–57. Print.

———. "Individuals in Narrative Worlds: An Ontological Perspective." *Poetics Today* 11.4 (1990): 843–871. Print.
———. "Narrator." *Handbook of Narratology*. Ed. Peter Hühn, John Pier, Wolf Schmid, and Jörg Schönert. Berlin: De Gruyter, 2009. 351–369. Print.
———. "The Nature and Functioning of Fiction: Some Recent Views." *Canadian Review of Comparative Literature/Revue Canadienne de Littérature Comparée* 19.1–2 (1992): 101–117. Print.
———. "Text Worlds, Fictional Worlds, Narrative Fiction." *Canadian Review of Comparative Literature/Revue Canadienne de Littérature Comparée* 27.1–2 (2000): 256–273. Print.
———. "The What, the When, and the How of Being a Character in Literary Narrative." *Style* 24.3 (1990): 453–468. Print.
Marion, Philippe. *Traces en cases: Travail graphique, figuration narrative et participation du lecteur*. Louvain-la-Neuve: Bruylant-Academia, 1993. Print.
Marks, Lawrence E., Robin J. Hammeal, and Marc H. Bornstein. *Perceiving Similarity and Comprehending Metaphor*. Chicago: University of Chicago Press, 1987. Print.
Martínez, Matías. *Doppelte Welten: Struktur und Sinn zweideutigen Erzählens*. Göttingen: Vandenhoeck und Ruprecht, 1996. Print.
———, ed. *Handbuch Erzählliteratur: Theorie, Analyse, Geschichte*. Stuttgart: Metzler, 2011. Print.
Martínez, Matías, and Michael Scheffel. *Einführung in die Erzähltheorie*. München: C. H. Beck, 1999. Print.
———. "Narratology and Theory of Fiction: Remarks on a Complex Relationship." *What Is Narratology? Questions and Answers regarding the Status of a Theory*. Ed. Tom Kindt and Hans-Harald Müller. Berlin: De Gruyter, 2003. 221–237. Print.
Mathieu, Marc-Antoine. *L'origine*. Vol. 1 of the *Julius Corentin Acquefacques, prisonnier des rêves* series. Paris: Delcourt, 1990. Print.
The Matrix. Dir. Andy Wachowski and Lana Wachowski. Warner Bros. Pictures, 1999. Film.
Max Payne. Remedy Entertainment/Gathering of Developers, 2001. PC.
Max Payne 2: The Fall of Max Payne. Remedy Entertainment/Rockstar Games, 2003. PC.
Mayer, Vicki, Miranda J. Banks, and John T. Caldwell, eds. *Production Studies: Cultural Studies of Media Industries*. New York: Routledge, 2009. Print.
Mazzucchelli, David. *Asterios Polyp*. New York: Pantheon, 2009. Print.

McCabe, Janet, and Kim Akass. *Quality TV: Contemporary American Television and Beyond*. London: I. B. Tauris, 2007. Print.

McCloud, Scott. *Understanding Comics: The Invisible Art*. Northampton: Kitchen Sink Press, 1993. Print.

McFarlane, Brian. *Novel to Film: An Introduction to the Theory of Adaptation*. Oxford: Oxford University Press, 1996. Print.

McGinn, Colin. *Mindsight: Image, Dream, Meaning*. Cambridge MA: Harvard University Press, 2004. Print.

McGlothlin, Erin. "No Time Like the Present: Narrative and Time in Art Spiegelman's *Maus*." *Narrative* 11.2 (2003): 177–198. Print.

McGonigal, Jane. *Reality Is Broken: Why Games Make Us Better and How They Can Change the World*. London: Jonathan Cape, 2011. Print.

McHale, Brian. "Beginning to Think about Narrative in Poetry." *Narrative* 17.1 (2009): 11–27. Print.

———. "Narrative in Poetry." *Routledge Encyclopedia of Narrative Theory*. Ed. David Herman, Manfred Jahn, and Marie-Laure Ryan. Abingdon: Routledge, 2005. 356–358. Print.

———. *Postmodernist Fiction*. New York: Methuen, 1987. Print.

McKee, Robert. *Story: Substance, Structure, Style, and the Principles of Screenwriting*. New York: HarperCollins, 1997. Print.

McMahan, Alison. "Immersion, Engagement, and Presence: A Method for Analyzing 3-D Video Games." *The Video Game Theory Reader*. Ed. Mark J. P. Wolf and Bernard Perron. Abingdon: Routledge, 2003. 67–86. Print.

Meifert-Menhart, Felicitas. "Emergent Narrative, Collaborative Storytelling: Toward a Narratological Analysis of Alternate Reality Games." *Beyond Classical Narration: Transmedial and Unnatural Challenges*. Ed. Jan Alber and Per Krogh Hansen. Berlin: De Gruyter, 2014. 161–177. Print.

Meister, Jan Christoph. *Computing Action: A Narratological Approach*. Berlin: De Gruyter, 2003. Print.

———. "The *Metalepticon*: A Computational Approach to Metalepsis." 2003. Web. December 1, 2013.

———. "Narratology." *Handbook of Narratology*. Ed. Peter Hühn, John Pier, Wolf Schmid, and Jörg Schönert. Berlin: De Gruyter, 2009. 329–350. Print.

———, ed. *Narratology beyond Literary Criticism: Mediality, Disciplinarity*. Berlin: De Gruyter, 2005. Print.

———. "The Temporality Effect: Towards a Process Model of Narrative Time Construction." *Time: From Concept to Narrative Construct: A*

Reader. Ed. Jan Christoph Meister and Wilhelm Schernus. Berlin: De Gruyter, 2011. 171–216. Print.
Melville, Herman. *Moby-Dick; or, The Whale*. New York: Harper and Brothers, 1851. Print.
Memento. Dir. Christopher Nolan. Newmarket, 2000. Film.
Memoria. Daedalic Entertainment, 2013. PC.
Meskin, Aaron. "Authorship." *The Routledge Companion to Philosophy and Film*. Ed. Paisley Livingston and Carl Plantinga. Abingdon: Routledge, 2009. 12–28. Print.
Metal Gear Solid: Peace Walker. Kojima Productions/Konami, 2010. PlayStation 3.
Metal Gear Solid 4: Guns of the Patriots. Kojima Productions/Konami, 2008. PlayStation 3.
Metz, Christian. "Aural Objects." *Film Sound: Theory and Practice*. Ed. Elizabeth Weis and John Belton. New York: Columbia University Press, 1985. 154–161. Print.
———. "Current Problems of Film Theory." Trans. Diana Matias. *Screen* 14.1–2 (1973): 40–87. Print.
———. *L'ènonciation impersonelle, ou le site du film*. Paris: Méridiens Klincksieck, 1991. Print.
———. *Film Language: A Semiotics of the Cinema*. Trans. Michael Taylor. Chicago: University of Chicago Press, 1974. Print.
———. "The Impersonal Enunciation, or the Site of Film." Trans. Béatrice Durand-Sendrail and Kristen Brookes. *New Literary History* 22.3 (1991): 747–772. Print.
———. *Language and Cinema*. Trans. Donna Jean Umiker-Sebeok. The Hague: Mouton, 1974. Print.
———. "A Profile of Etienne Souriau." Trans. Howard Davis, Luli McCarroll, and Fabrice Ziolkowski. *On Film* 12 (1984): 5–8. Print.
Metzinger, Thomas. *Being No One: The Self-Model Theory of Subjectivity*. Cambridge MA: MIT Press, 2003. Print.
Meyer, Christina. "Un/Taming the Beast, or Graphic Novels (Re)Considered." *From Comic Strips to Graphic Novels: Contributions to the Theory and History of Graphic Narrative*. 2nd ed. Ed. Daniel Stein and Jan-Noël Thon. Berlin: De Gruyter, 2015. 271–299. Print.
Meyer, Urs. "Transmedialität (Intermedialität, Paramedialität, Metamedialität, Hypermedialität, Archimedialität): Das Beispiel der Werbung." *Transmedialität: Zur Ästhetik paraliterarischer Verfahren*. Ed. Urs Meyer, Roberto Simanowski, and Christoph Zeller. Göttingen: Wallstein, 2006. 110–130. Print.

Meyer, Urs, Roberto Simanowski, and Christoph Zeller, eds. *Transmedialität: Zur Ästhetik paraliterarischer Verfahren*. Göttingen: Wallstein, 2006. Print.

Mikkonen, Kai. "Focalization in Comics: From the Specificities of the Medium to Conceptual Reformulation." *Scandinavian Journal of Comic Art* 1.1 (2012): 70–95. Web. December 1, 2013.

———. "Graphic Narratives as a Challenge to Transmedial Narratology: The Question of Focalization." *Amerikastudien/American Studies* 56.4 (2011): 637–652. Print.

———. "Subjectivity and Style in Graphic Narratives." *From Comic Strips to Graphic Novels: Contributions to the Theory and History of Graphic Narrative*. 2nd ed. Ed. Daniel Stein and Jan-Noël Thon. Berlin: De Gruyter, 2015. 101–123. Print.

Mikos, Lothar. *Fern-Sehen: Bausteine zu einer Rezeptionsästhetik des Fernsehens*. Berlin: Vistas, 2001. Print.

Mikos, Lothar, Susanne Eichner, Elizabeth Prommer, and Michael Wedel. *Die "Herr der Ringe"-Trilogie: Attraktion und Faszination eines populärkulturellen Phänomens*. Konstanz: UVK, 2007. Print.

Miller, Ann. "Autobiography in *Bande Dessinée*." *Textual and Visual Selves: Photography, Film, and Comic Art in French Autobiography*. Ed. Natalie Edwards, Amy L. Hubbell, and Ann Miller. Lincoln: University of Nebraska Press, 2011. 235–262. Print.

Miller, Cynthia J., ed. *Too Bold for the Box Office: The Mockumentary from Big Screen to Small*. Lanham: Scarecrow Press, 2012. Print.

Miller, Frank. *300*. Colors by Lynn Varley. Originally published as *300* #1–5, 1998. Milwaukee: Dark Horse, 1999. Print.

———. *Batman: The Dark Knight Returns*. Art by Frank Miller and Klaus Janson, colors by Lynn Varley, lettered by John Costanza. Originally published in single magazine form as *Batman: The Dark Knight Returns* #1–4, 1986. New York: DC Comics, 2002. Print.

———. *Sin City: The Hard Goodbye*. Vol. 1 of the *Sin City* series. Originally published in *Dark Horse Presents* #51–62 and *Dark Horse Presents Fifth Anniversary Special*, 1991–1992. 2nd ed. Milwaukee: Dark Horse, 2005. Print.

———. *Sin City: Hell and Back*. Vol. 7 of the *Sin City* series. Originally published in single magazine form as *Sin City: Hell and Back* #1–9, 1999–2000. 2nd ed. Milwaukee: Dark Horse, 2005. Print.

Milligan, Peter. *Enigma*. Art by Duncan Fegredo, colors by Sherilyn van Valkenburgh, lettered by John Costanza. Originally published in single magazine form as *Enigma* #1–8, 1993. New York: DC Comics/Vertigo, 1993. Print.

Mitchell, W. J. T. *Iconology: Image, Text, Ideology*. Chicago: University of Chicago Press, 1987. Print.

Mitry, Jean. *The Aesthetics and Psychology of the Cinema*. Trans. Christopher King. Bloomington: Indiana University Press, 1997. Print.

Mittell, Jason. *Complex TV: The Poetics of Contemporary Television Storytelling*. New York: New York University Press, 2015. Print.

———. *Genre and Television: From Cop Shows to Cartoons in American Culture*. New York: Routledge, 2004. Print.

———. "Narrative Complexity in Contemporary American Television." *The Velvet Light Trap* 58 (2006): 29–40. Print.

———. "Strategies of Storytelling on Transmedia Television." *Storyworlds across Media: Toward a Media-Conscious Narratology*. Ed. Marie-Laure Ryan and Jan-Noël Thon. Lincoln: University of Nebraska Press, 2014. 253–277. Print.

Mock, Thomas. "Was ist ein Medium? Eine Unterscheidung kommunikations- und medienwissenschaftlicher Grundverständnisse eines zentralen Begriffs." *Publizistik* 51.2 (2006): 183–200. Print.

Montfort, Nick. *Twisty Little Passages: An Approach to Interactive Fiction*. Cambridge MA: MIT Press, 2003. Print.

Moore, Alan. *From Hell*. Art by Eddie Campbell. Originally published in single magazine form as *From Hell* #1–10, 1989–1996. Marietta: Top Shelf Productions, 1999. Print.

———. *The League of Extraordinary Gentlemen: Vol. 1*. Art by Kevin O'Neill, colors by Ben Dimagmaliw, lettered by Bill Oakley. Originally published in single magazine form as *The League of Extraordinary Gentlemen, Vol. 1*, #1–6, 1999–2000. London: Titan Books, 2002. Print.

———. *The League of Extraordinary Gentlemen: Vol. 2*. Art by Kevin O'Neill, colors by Ben Dimagmaliw, lettered by Bill Oakley. Originally published in single magazine form as *The League of Extraordinary Gentlemen, Vol. 2*, #1–6, 2002–2003. London: Titan Books, 2004. Print.

———. *Promethea*. Art by James H. Williams III and Mick Gray, colors by Jeromy Cox and José Villarrubia, lettered by Todd Klein. Vols. 1–5. 2001–2006. San Diego: DC Comics/Wildstorm. Print.

———. *Watchmen*. Illustrated and lettered by Dave Gibbons, colors by John Higgins. Originally published in single magazine form as *Watchmen* #1–12, 1986–1987. London: Titan Books, 2007. Print.

Morreall, John. "The Myth of the Omniscient Narrator." *Journal of Aesthetics and Art Criticism* 52.4 (1994): 429–435. Print.

Müller-Zettelmann, Eva. "Lyrik und Narratologie." *Erzähltheorie transgenerisch, intermedial, interdisziplinär*. Ed. Ansgar Nünning and

Vera Nünning. Trier: Wissenschaftlicher Verlag Trier, 2002. 129–153. Print.

Münker, Stefan, and Alexander Roesler, eds. *Was ist ein Medium?* Frankfurt am Main: Suhrkamp, 2008. Print.

Münsterberg, Hugo. *The Photoplay: A Psychological Study*. New York: D. Appleton, 1916. Print.

Murray, Janet H. *Hamlet on the Holodeck: The Future of Narrative in Cyberspace*. New York: Free Press, 1997. Print.

———. *Inventing the Medium: Principles of Interaction Design as a Cultural Practice*. Cambridge MA: MIT Press, 2012. Print.

Nagel, Thomas. *The View from Nowhere*. Oxford: Oxford University Press, 1986. Print.

———. "What Is It Like to Be a Bat?" *Philosophical Review* 83 (1974): 435–450. Print.

Nama, Adilifu. *Super Black: American Pop Culture and Black Superheroes*. Austin: University of Texas Press, 2011. Print.

Naremore, James, ed. *Film Adaptation*. New Brunswick NJ: Rutgers University Press, 2000. Print.

Nasar, Sylvia. *A Beautiful Mind: The Biography of John Forbes Nash, Jr., Winner of the Nobel Prize in Economics, 1994*. New York: Simon and Schuster, 1998. Print.

Nash, Kate, Craig Hight, Catherine Summerhayes, eds. *New Documentary Ecologies: Emerging Platforms, Practices and Discourses*. Basingstoke: Palgrave Macmillan, 2014. Print.

Neale, Steve. *Genre and Hollywood*. London: Routledge, 2000. Print.

Neitzel, Britta. "Gespielte Geschichten: Struktur- und prozessanalytische Untersuchungen der Narrativität von Videospielen." PhD thesis Bauhaus-University Weimar, 2000. Web. December 1, 2013.

———. "Levels of Play and Narration." *Narratology beyond Literary Criticism: Mediality, Disciplinarity*. Ed. Jan Christoph Meister. Berlin: De Gruyter, 2005. 45–64. Print.

———. "Medienrezeption und Spiel." *Game Over!? Perspektiven des Computerspiels*. Ed. Jan Distelmeyer, Christine Hanke, and Dieter Mersch. Bielefeld: transcript, 2008. 95–113. Print.

———. "Metacommunication in Play and in (Computer) Games." *Self-Reference in the Media*. Ed. Winfried Nöth and Nina Bishara. Berlin: De Gruyter, 2007. 237–252. Print.

———. "Narrativity in Computer Games." *Handbook of Computer Game Studies*. Ed. Joost Raessens and Jeffrey Goldstein. Cambridge MA: MIT Press, 2005. 227–245. Print.

———. "Point of View und Point of Action: Eine Perspektive auf die Perspektive in Computerspielen." *Computer/Spiel/Räume: Materialien zur Einführung in die Computer Game Studies.* Ed. Klaus Bartels and Jan-Noël Thon. Hamburg: University of Hamburg, 2007. 8–28. Print.

Nelles, William. *Frameworks: Narrative Levels and Embedded Narrative.* New York: Peter Lang, 1997. Print.

———. "Getting Focalization into Focus." *Poetics Today* 11.2 (1990): 365–382. Print.

Neverwinter Nights. Bioware/Atari, 2002. PC.

Nichols, Bill. *Blurred Boundaries: Questions of Meaning in Contemporary Culture.* Bloomington: Indiana University Press, 1994. Print.

———. *Representing Reality.* Bloomington: Indiana University Press, 1991. Print.

Niederhoff, Burkhard. "Focalization." *Handbook of Narratology.* Ed. Peter Hühn, John Pier, Wolf Schmid, and Jörg Schönert. Berlin: De Gruyter, 2009. 115–123. Print.

———. "Fokalisation und Perspektive: Ein Plädoyer für friedliche Koexistenz." *Poetica* 33.1–2 (2001): 1–21. Print.

———. "Perspective/Point of View." *Handbook of Narratology.* Ed. Peter Hühn, John Pier, Wolf Schmid, and Jörg Schönert. Berlin: De Gruyter, 2009. 384–397. Print.

Nielsen, Henrik Skov. "Fictional Voices? Strange Voices? Unnatural Voices?" *Strange Voices in Narrative Fiction.* Ed. Per Krogh Hansen, Stefan Iversen, Henrik Skov Nielsen, and Rolf Reitan. Berlin: De Gruyter, 2011. 55–82. Print.

———. "Natural Authors, Unnatural Narration." *Postclassical Narratology: Approaches and Analyses.* Ed. Jan Alber and Monika Fludernik. Columbus: Ohio State University Press, 2010. 275–301. Print.

Nielsen, Henrik Skov, James Phelan, and Richard Walsh. "Ten Theses about Fictionality." *Narrative* 23.1 (2015): 61–73. Print.

Nieragden, Göran. "Focalization and Narration: Theoretical and Terminological Refinements." *Poetics Today* 23.4 (2002): 685–697. Print.

Nitsche, Michael. *Video Game Spaces: Image, Play, and Structure in 3D Worlds.* Cambridge MA: MIT Press, 2008. Print.

Noë, Alva. *Action in Perception.* Cambridge MA: MIT Press, 2004. Print.

Nöth, Winfried. "Narrative Self-Reference in a Literary Comic: M.-A. Mathieu's *L'Origine.*" *Semiotica* 165 (2007): 173–190. Print.

Nöth, Winfried, Nina Bishara, and Britta Neitzel. *Mediale Selbstreferenz: Grundlagen und Fallstudien zu Werbung, Computerspiel und den Comics.* Cologne: Herbert von Halem, 2008. Print.

Nünning, Ansgar. *Grundzüge eines kommunikationstheoretischen Modells der erzählerischen Vermittlung: Die Funktionen der Erzählinstanz in den Romanen George Eliots*. Trier: Wissenschaftlicher Verlag Trier, 1989. Print.

———. "Mimesis des Erzählens: Prolegomena zu einer Wirkungsästhetik, Typologie und Funktionsgeschichte des Aktes des Erzählens und der Metanarration." *Erzählen und Erzähltheorie im 20. Jahrhundert: Festschrift für Wilhelm Füger*. Ed. Jörg Helbig. Heidelberg: Winter, 2001. 13–47. Print.

———. "Narratology or Narratologies? Taking Stock of Recent Developments, Critique and Modest Proposals for Future Usage of the Term." *What Is Narratology? Questions and Answers regarding the Status of a Theory*. Ed. Tom Kindt and Hans-Harald Müller. Berlin: De Gruyter, 2003. 239–275. Print.

———. "Renaissance eines anthropomorphisierten Passepartouts oder Nachruf auf ein literaturkritisches Phantom? Überlegungen und Alternativen zum Konzept des 'implied author.'" *Deutsche Vierteljahreszeitschrift für Literaturwissenschaft und Geistesgeschichte* 67 (1993): 1–25. Print.

———. "Surveying Contextualist and Cultural Narratologies: Towards an Outline of Approaches, Concepts and Potentials." *Narratology in the Age of Cross-Disciplinary Narrative Research*. Ed. Sandra Heinen and Ron Sommer. Berlin: De Gruyter, 2009. 48–70. Print.

———. "Unreliable, Compared to What? Towards a Cognitive Theory of Unreliable Narration: Prolegomena and Hypotheses." *Grenzüberschreitungen: Narratologie im Kontext/Transcending Boundaries: Narratology in Context*. Ed. Walter Grünzweig and Andreas Solbach. Tübingen: Narr, 1999. 53–73. Print.

———, ed. *Unreliable Narration: Studien zur Theorie und Praxis unglaubwürdigen Erzählens in der englischsprachigen Erzählliteratur*. Trier: Wissenschaftlicher Verlag Trier, 1998. Print.

Nünning, Ansgar, and Vera Nünning. "Von der strukturalistischen Narratologie zur 'postklassischen' Erzähltheorie: Ein Überblick über neue Ansätze und Entwicklungstendenzen." *Neue Ansätze in der Erzähltheorie*. Ed. Ansgar Nünning and Vera Nünning. Trier: Wissenschaftlicher Verlag Trier, 2002. 1–33. Print.

Nünning, Ansgar, and Ron Sommer. "Diegetic and Mimetic Narrativity: Some Further Steps towards a Narratology of Drama." *Theorizing Narrativity*. Ed. John Pier and José Á. García Landa. Berlin: De Gruyter, 2008. 331–354. Print.

———. "Drama und Narratologie: Die Entwicklung erzähltheoretischer Modelle und Kategorien für die Dramenanalyse." *Erzähltheorie transgenerisch, intermedial, interdisziplinär*. Ed. Ansgar Nünning and Vera Nünning. Trier: Wissenschaftlicher Verlag Trier, 2002. 105–128. Print.

Nussbaum, Martha. *Upheavals of Thought: The Intelligence of Emotions*. Cambridge: Cambridge University Press, 2001. Print.

Odin, Roger. *De la fiction*. Brussels: De Boeck, 2000. Print.

Ohler, Peter. *Kognitive Filmpsychologie: Verarbeitung und mentale Repräsentation narrativer Filme*. Münster: MAkS-Publikationen, 1994. Print.

Olson, Greta. "Reconsidering Unreliability: Fallible and Untrustworthy Narrators." *Narrative* 11.1 (2003): 93–109. Print.

Onega, Susana. "Structuralism and Narrative Poetics." *Literary Theory and Criticism: An Oxford Guide*. Ed. Patricia Waugh. Oxford: Oxford University Press, 2006. 259–279. Print.

Onega, Susana, and José Á. García Landa. "Introduction." *Narratology: An Introduction*. Ed. Susana Onega and José Á. García Landa. London: Longman, 1996. 1–41. Print.

On the Rain-Slick Precipice of Darkness: Episode One. Hothead Games, 2008. PC.

Orlean, Susan. *The Orchid Thief*. New York: Random House, 1998. Print.

Orth, Dominik. "Eine Frage der Perspektive: Greg Marcks' *11:14*, polyfokalisiertes Erzählen und das Problem der Fokalisierung im Film." *Probleme filmischen Erzählens*. Ed. Hannah Birr, Maike Sarah Reinerth, and Jan-Noël Thon. Münster: LIT, 2009. 111–130. Print.

The Others. Dir. Alejandro Amenábar. Miramax Films, 2001. Film.

Packard, Stephan. *Anatomie des Comics: Psychosemiotische Medienanalyse*. Göttingen: Wallstein, 2006. Print.

Paech, Joachim, ed. *Film, Fernsehen, Video und die Künste: Strategien der Intermedialität*. Stuttgart: Metzler, 1994. Print.

Paech, Joachim, and Jens Schröter, eds. *Intermedialität analog/digital: Theorien—Methoden—Analysen*. München: Fink, 2008. Print.

Page, Ruth. "Introduction." *New Perspectives on Narrative and Multimodality*. Ed. Ruth Page. New York: Routledge, 2010. 1–13. Print.

Paget, Derek. *No Other Way to Tell It: Dramadoc/Docudrama on Television*. Manchester: Manchester University Press, 1998. Print.

Painkiller. People Can Fly/DreamCatcher Interactive, 2004. PC.

Palahniuk, Chuck. *Fight Club*. New York: W. W. Norton, 1996. Print.

Palmer, Alan. "The Construction of Fictional Minds." *Narrative* 10.1 (2002): 28–46. Print.

———. *Fictional Minds*. Lincoln: University of Nebraska Press, 2004. Print.

———. *Social Minds in the Novel*. Columbus: Ohio State University Press, 2010. Print.
Paranormal Activity. Dir. Oren Peli. Paramount Pictures, 2007. Film.
Parody, Clare. "Franchising/Adaptation." *Adaptation* 4.2 (2011): 210–218. Print.
Parsons, Terence. *Nonexistent Objects*. New Haven: Yale University Press, 1980. Print.
Patron, Sylvie. *Le Narrateur: Introduction à la théorie narrative*. Paris: Armand Colin, 2009. Print.
Pavel, Thomas G. *The Feud of Language: A History of Structuralist Thought*. Oxford: Blackwell, 1989. Print.
———. *Fictional Worlds*. Cambridge MA: Harvard University Press, 1986. Print.
Pearson, Roberta, ed. *Reading* Lost: *Perspectives on a Hit Television Show*. London: I. B. Tauris, 2009. Print.
Pearson, Roberta, and Anthony N. Smith, eds. *Storytelling in the Media Convergence Age: Exploring Screen Narratives*. Basingstoke: Palgrave Macmillan, 2014. Print.
Pearson, Roberta, and William Uricchio, eds. *The Many Lives of the Batman: Critical Approaches to a Superhero and His Media*. New York: Routledge, 1991. Print.
Pedri, Nancy. "Graphic Memoir: Neither Fact nor Fiction." *From Comic Strips to Graphic Novels: Contributions to the Theory and History of Graphic Narrative*. 2nd ed. Ed. Daniel Stein and Jan-Noël Thon. Berlin: De Gruyter, 2015. 127–153. Print.
Peeters, Benoît. *Case, planche, récit: Comment lire une bande dessinée*. Tournai: Casterman, 1991. Print.
Perfume: The Story of a Murderer. Dir. Tom Tykwer. Paramount Pictures/DreamWorks Pictures, 2006. Film.
Perron, Bernard. "A Cognitive Psychological Approach to Gameplay Emotions." *Changing Views—Worlds in Play: DiGRA Conference Proceedings 2005*. Web. December 1, 2013.
———, ed. *Horror Video Games: Essays on the Fusion of Fear and Play*. Jefferson: McFarland, 2009. Print.
———. *Silent Hill: The Terror Engine*. Ann Arbor: University of Michigan Press, 2012. Print.
Persson, Per. *Understanding Cinema: A Psychological Theory of Moving Imagery*. Cambridge: Cambridge University Press, 2003. Print.
Petersen, Robert S. "The Acoustics of Manga: Narrative Erotics and the Visual Presence of Sound." *International Journal of Comic Art* 9.1 (2007): 578–590. Print.

Pfister, Manfred. *The Theory and Analysis of Drama*. Trans. John Halliday. Cambridge: Cambridge University Press, 1988. Print.

Phelan, James. "Estranging Unreliability, Bonding Unreliability, and the Ethics of *Lolita*." *Narrative* 15.2 (2007): 222–238. Print.

———. *Living to Tell about It: A Rhetoric and Ethics of Character Narration*. Ithaca NY: Cornell University Press, 2005. Print.

———. *Reading People, Reading Plots: Character, Progression, and the Interpretation of Narrative*. Chicago: University of Chicago Press, 1989. Print.

Phelan, James, and Peter J. Rabinowitz, eds. *A Companion to Narrative Theory*. Malden: Blackwell, 2005. Print.

Piaget, Jean. *Biology and Knowledge: An Essay on the Relations between Organic Regulations and Cognitive Processes*. Trans. Beatrix Walsh. Edinburgh: Edinburgh University Press, 1971. Print.

Pier, John. "After This, Therefore because of This." *Theorizing Narrativity*. Ed. John Pier and José Á. García Landa. Berlin: De Gruyter, 2008. 109–140. Print.

———. "Métalepse et hiérarchies narratives." *Métalepses: Entorses au pacte de la représentation*. Ed. John Pier and Jean-Marie Schaeffer. Paris: Éditions de l'École des Hautes Études en Sciences Sociales, 2005. 247–261. Print.

Pier, John, and José Á. García Landa, eds. *Theorizing Narrativity*. Berlin: De Gruyter, 2008. Print.

Pier, John, and Jean-Marie Schaeffer, eds. *Métalepses: Entorses au pacte de la représentation*. Paris: Éditions de l'École des Hautes Études en Sciences Sociales, 2005. Print.

Pitt, David. "Mental Representation." *The Stanford Encyclopedia of Philosophy*. Ed. Edward N. Zalta. Stanford: Stanford University, 2012. Web. December 1, 2013.

Plantinga, Carl. "Defining Documentary: Fiction, Non-fiction, and Projected Worlds." *Persistence of Vision* 5 (1987): 44–54. Print.

———. *Moving Viewers: American Film and the Spectator's Experience*. Berkeley: University of California Press, 2009. Print.

———. *Rhetoric and Representation in Nonfiction Film*. Cambridge: Cambridge University Press, 1997. Print.

Plantinga, Carl, and Greg M. Smith, eds. *Passionate Views: Film, Cognition, and Emotion*. Baltimore: Johns Hopkins University Press, 1999. Print.

Pochat, Götz. *Bild—Zeit: Zeitgestalt und Erzählstruktur in der bildenden Kunst von den Anfängen bis zur frühen Neuzeit*. Vienna: Böhlau, 1996. Print.

Pombo, Olga, and Alexander Gerner, eds. *Studies in Diagrammatology and Diagram Praxis*. London: College Publications, 2010. Print.

Ponech, Trevor. "What Is Non-fiction Cinema?" *Film Theory and Philosophy*. Ed. Richard Allen and Murray Smith. Oxford: Oxford University Press, 1997. 203–220. Print.

———. *What Is Non-fiction Cinema? On the Very Idea of Motion Picture Communication*. Boulder: Westview Press, 1999. Print.

Popper, Karl. *Objective Knowledge: An Evolutionary Approach*. Oxford: Oxford University Press, 1972. Print.

Poremba, Cindy. "Real|Unreal: Crafting Actuality in the Documentary Videogame." PhD thesis Concordia University, 2011. Web. December 1, 2013.

Portal. Valve, 2007. PC.

Postema, Barbara. *Narrative Structure in Comics: Making Sense of Fragments*. Rochester: RIT Press, 2013. Print.

Pratt, Henry John. "Medium Specificity and the Ethics of Narrative in Comics." *Storyworlds: A Journal of Narrative Studies* 1 (2009): 97–113. Print.

Pratt, Marie Louise. *Toward a Speech Act Theory of Literary Discourse*. Bloomington: Indiana University Press, 1977. Print.

Priest, Graham. *An Introduction to Non-classical Logic*. Cambridge: Cambridge University Press, 2001. Print.

———. "Sylvan's Box: A Short Story and Ten Morals." *Notre Dame Journal of Formal Logic* 38.4 (1997): 573–582. Print.

Prince, Gerald. *A Dictionary of Narratology*. Lincoln: University of Nebraska Press, 1987. Print.

———. *A Dictionary of Narratology*. Rev. ed. Lincoln: University of Nebraska Press, 2003. Print.

———. *A Grammar of Stories*. The Hague: Mouton, 1973. Print.

———. "Narrative Analysis and Narratology." *New Literary History* 13.2 (1982): 179–188. Print.

———. "Narrativehood, Narrativeness, Narrativity, Narratability." *Theorizing Narrativity*. Ed. John Pier and José Á. García Landa. Berlin: De Gruyter, 2008. 19–27. Print.

———. "Narratology." *The Cambridge History of Literary Criticism*. Vol. 8. Ed. Raman Selden. Cambridge: Cambridge University Press, 1995. 110–130. Print.

———. *Narratology: The Form and Functioning of Narrative*. Berlin: De Gruyter, 1982. Print.

———. "On a Postcolonial Narratology." *A Companion to Narrative Theory*. Ed. James Phelan and Peter J. Rabinowitz. Malden: Blackwell, 2005. 372–381. Print.

———. "A Point of View on Point of View or Refocusing Focalization." *New Perspectives on Narrative Perspective*. Ed. Willie van Peer and Seymour Chatman. Albany: State University of New York Press, 2001. 43–50. Print.

———. "Remarks on Narrativity." *Perspectives on Narratology: Papers from the Stockholm Symposium on Narratology*. Ed. Claes Wahlin. Frankfurt am Main: Peter Lang, 1996. 95–106. Print.

———. "Revisiting Narrativity." *Grenzüberschreitungen: Narratologie im Kontext/Transcending Boundaries: Narratology in Context*. Ed. Walter Grünzweig and Andreas Solbach. Tübingen: Narr, 1999. 43–51. Print.

———. "Surveying Narratology." *What Is Narratology? Questions and Answers regarding the Status of a Theory*. Ed. Tom Kindt and Hans-Harald Müller. Berlin: De Gruyter, 2003. 1–16. Print.

Prince of Persia: The Sands of Time. Ubisoft, 2003. PC.

Prince of Persia: The Sands of Time. Dir. Mike Newell. Walt Disney Studios Motion Pictures, 2010. Film.

Propp, Vladimir Y. *Morphology of the Folktale*. Trans. Laurence Scott. 2nd ed. Austin: University of Texas Press, 1968. Print.

Proudfoot, Diane. "Possible Worlds Semantics and Fiction." *Journal of Philosophical Logic* 35 (2006): 9–40. Print.

Psychonauts. Double Fine Productions/Majesco Entertainment, 2005. PC.

Pulp Fiction. Dir. Quentin Tarantino. Miramax Films, 1994. Film.

Punday, Daniel. *Five Strands of Fictionality: The Institutional Construction of Contemporary American Fiction*. Columbus: Ohio State University Press, 2010. Print.

———. "Seeing into the Worlds of Digital Fiction." *Analyzing Digital Fiction*. Ed. Alice Bell, Astrid Ensslin, and Hans Kristian Rustad. New York: Routledge, 2014. 57–72. Print.

The Queen. Dir. Stephen Frears. Miramax Films, 2006. Film.

Rabatel, Alain. *La construction textuelle du point de vue*. Lausanne: Delachaux et Niestlé, 1998. Print.

———. *Une histoire du point de vue*. Paris: Klincksieck, 1997. Print.

Rabinowitz, Peter. "Assertion and Assumption: Fictional Patterns and the External World." *PMLA* 96.3 (1981): 408–419. Print.

Raessens, Joost. "Reality Play: Documentary Computer Games beyond Fact and Fiction." *Popular Communication* 4.3 (2006): 213–224. Print.

Rajewsky, Irina O. "Border Talks: The Problematic Status of Media Borders in the Current Debate about Intermediality." *Media Borders, Multimodality and Intermediality*. Ed. Lars Elleström. Basingstoke: Palgrave Macmillan, 2010. 51–68. Print.

———. *Intermedialität*. Tübingen: Francke, 2002. Print.

———. "Intermediality, Intertextuality, and Remediation: A Literary Perspective on Intermediality." *Intermédialités* 6 (2005): 43–64. Print.

———. "Von Erzählern, die (nichts) vermitteln: Überlegungen zu grundlegenden Annahmen der Dramentheorie im Kontext einer transmedialen Narratologie." *Zeitschrift für französische Sprache und Literatur* 117.1 (2007): 25–68. Print.

Rapp, Bernhard. "Self-Reflexivity in Computer Games: Analyses of Selected Examples." *Self-Reference in the Media*. Ed. Winfried Nöth and Nina Bishara. Berlin: De Gruyter, 2007. 253–265. Print.

Rashomon. Dir. Akira Kurosawa. RKO Radio Pictures, 1951. Film. [Originally released in Japanese as *Rashōmon*. Daiei Film, 1950. Film.]

Rauscher, Andreas. *Spielerische Fiktionen: Transmediale Genrekonzepte in Videospielen*. Marburg: Schüren, 2012. Print.

Recettear: An Item Shop's Tale. EasyGameStation/Carpe Fulgur, 2010. PC.

Reinerth, Maike Sarah. "Intersubjective Subjectivity? Transdisciplinary Challenges in Analysing Cinematic Representations of Character Interiority." *Amsterdam International Electronic Journal for Cultural Narratology* 6 (2010/2011): n. pag. Web. December 1, 2013.

———. "Spulen, Speichern, Überspielen: Zur Darstellung von Erinnerung im Spielfilm." *Probleme filmischen Erzählens*. Ed. Hannah Birr, Maike Sarah Reinerth, and Jan-Noël Thon. Münster: LIT, 2009. 33–58. Print.

Remember Me. Dontnod Entertainment/Capcom, 2013. PC.

Renov, Michael, ed. *Theorizing Documentary*. New York: Routledge, 1993. Print.

Rescher, Nicholas. *Objectivity: The Obligations of Impersonal Reason*. Notre Dame: University of Notre Dame Press, 1997. Print.

Rescher, Nicholas, and Robert Brandom. *The Logic of Inconsistency: A Study in Non-standard Possible-World Semantics and Ontology*. Oxford: Blackwell, 1979. Print.

Restall, Greg. "Ways Things Can't Be." *Notre Dame Journal of Formal Logic* 38.4 (1997): 583–596. Print.

The Return of Ishtar. Namco, 1986. Arcade.

Rhodes, Gary Don, and John Parris Springer, eds. *Docufictions: Essays on the Intersection of Documentary and Fictional Filmmaking*. Jefferson: McFarland, 2006. Print.

Richardson, Alan. *Mental Imagery*. New York: Springer, 1969. Print.

Richardson, Brian. "Beyond Story and Discourse: Narrative Time in Postmodern and Nonmimetic Fiction." *Narrative Dynamics: Essays on Time, Plot, Closure, and Frames*. Ed. Brian Richardson. Columbus: Ohio State University Press, 2002. 47–63. Print.

———. "Drama and Narrative." *The Cambridge Companion to Narrative.* Ed. David Herman. Cambridge: Cambridge University Press, 2007. 142–155. Print.

———, ed. *The Implied Author.* Spec. issue of *Style* 45.1 (2011). Print.

———. "Recent Concepts of Narrative and the Narratives of Narrative Theory." *Style* 34.2 (2000): 168–175. Print.

———. *Unlikely Stories: Causality and the Nature of Modern Narrative.* Newark: University of Delaware Press, 1997. Print.

———. *Unnatural Voices: Extreme Narration in Modern and Contemporary Fiction.* Columbus: Ohio State University Press, 2006. Print.

———. "Voice and Narration in Postmodern Drama." *New Literary History* 32.3 (2001): 681–694. Print.

———. "What Is Unnatural Narrative Theory?" *Unnatural Narratives— Unnatural Narratology.* Ed. Jan Alber and Rüdiger Heinze. Berlin: De Gruyter, 2011. 23–40. Print.

Ricoeur, Paul. *Time and Narrative.* Vols. 1–3. Trans. Kathleen Blamey and David Pellauer. Chicago: University of Chicago Press, 1984–1988. Print.

Riffaterre, Michael. *Fictional Truth.* Baltimore: Johns Hopkins University Press, 1990. Print.

Rimmon-Kenan, Shlomith. *The Concept of Ambiguity: The Example of James.* Chicago: University of Chicago Press, 1977. Print.

———. *Narrative Fiction: Contemporary Poetics.* 2nd ed. London: Routledge, 2002. Print.

Rippl, Gabriele, and Lukas Etter. "Intermediality, Transmediality, and Graphic Narrative." *From Comic Strips to Graphic Novels: Contributions to the Theory and History of Graphic Narrative.* 2nd ed. Ed. Daniel Stein and Jan-Noël Thon. Berlin: De Gruyter, 2015. 191–217. Print.

Rogue Legacy. Cellar Door Games, 2013. PC.

Rollins, Mark. *Mental Imagery: On the Limits of Cognitive Psychology.* New Haven: Yale University Press, 1989. Print.

Ronen, Ruth. "Completing the Incompleteness of Fictional Entities." *Poetics Today* 9.3 (1988): 497–514. Print.

———. "Paradigm Shifts in Plot Models: An Outline of the History of Narratology." *Poetics Today* 11.4 (1990): 817–842. Print.

———. *Possible Worlds in Literary Theory.* Cambridge: Cambridge University Press, 1994. Print.

Rorty, Richard. *Objectivity, Relativism, and Truth: Philosophical Papers.* Cambridge: Cambridge University Press, 1991. Print.

Rosch, Eleanor. "Cognitive Representations of Semantic Categories." *Journal of Experimental Psychology* 104.3 (1975): 192–233. Print.

Roscoe, Jane, and Craig Hight. *Faking It: Mock-Documentary and the Subversion of Factuality.* Manchester: Manchester University Press, 2001. Print.

Round, Julia. "Visual Perspective and Narrative Voice in Comics: Redefining Literary Terminology." *International Journal of Comic Art* 9.2 (2007): 316–329. Print.

Rouse, Richard. *Game Design: Theory and Practice.* 2nd ed. Plano: Wordware, 2005. Print.

Roussin, Philippe. "Rhétorique de la métalepse, états de cause, typologie, récit." *Métalepses: Entorses au pacte de la représentation.* Ed. John Pier and Jean-Marie Schaeffer. Paris: Éditions de l'École des Hautes Études en Sciences Sociales, 2005. 37–58. Print.

Routley, Richard. "The Semantical Structure of Fictional Discourse." *Poetics* 8.1–2 (1979): 3–30. Print.

The Rules of Attraction. Dir. Roger Avary. Lionsgate, 2002. Film.

Run Lola Run. Dir. Tom Tykwer. Bavaria Film International, 1998. Film. [Originally released in German as *Lola rennt.* Prokino, 1998. Film.]

Ryan, Marie-Laure. *Avatars of Story.* Minneapolis: University of Minnesota Press, 2006. Print.

———. "Fiction, Non-factuals, and the Principle of Minimal Departure." *Poetics* 9.4 (1980): 403–422. Print.

———. "From Narrative Games to Playable Stories: Toward a Poetics of Interactive Narrative." *Storyworlds: A Journal of Narrative Studies* 1 (2009): 43–59. Print.

———. "Impossible Worlds." *The Routledge Companion to Experimental Literature.* Ed. Joe Bray, Alison Gibbons, and Brian McHale. Abingdon: Routledge, 2012. 368–379. Print.

———. "Introduction." *Narrative across Media: The Languages of Storytelling.* Ed. Marie-Laure Ryan. Lincoln: University of Nebraska Press, 2004. 1–40. Print.

———. "Narration in Various Media." *Handbook of Narratology.* Ed. Peter Hühn, John Pier, Wolf Schmid, and Jörg Schönert. Berlin: De Gruyter, 2009. 263–281. Print.

———, ed. *Narrative across Media: The Languages of Storytelling.* Lincoln: University of Nebraska Press, 2004. Print.

———. *Narrative as Virtual Reality: Immersion and Interactivity in Literature and Electronic Media.* Baltimore: Johns Hopkins University Press, 2001. Print.

———. "The Narratorial Functions: Breaking Down a Theoretical Primitive." *Narrative* 9.2 (2001): 146–152. Print.

———. "On the Theoretical Foundations of Transmedial Narratology." *Narratology beyond Literary Criticism: Mediality, Disciplinarity*. Ed. Jan Christoph Meister. Berlin: De Gruyter, 2005. 1–23. Print.

———. *Possible Worlds, Artificial Intelligence, and Narrative Theory*. Bloomington: Indiana University Press, 1991. Print.

———. "Postmodernism and the Doctrine of Panfictionality." *Narrative* 5.2 (1997): 165–187. Print.

———. "Space." *Handbook of Narratology*. Ed. Peter Hühn, John Pier, Wolf Schmid, and Jörg Schönert. Berlin: De Gruyter, 2009. 420–433. Print.

———. "Story/Worlds/Media: Tuning the Instruments of a Media-Conscious Narratology." *Storyworlds across Media: Toward a Media-Conscious Narratology*. Ed. Marie-Laure Ryan and Jan-Noël Thon. Lincoln: University of Nebraska Press, 2014. 25–49. Print.

———. "Toward a Definition of Narrative." *The Cambridge Companion to Narrative*. Ed. David Herman. Cambridge: Cambridge University Press, 2007. 22–35. Print.

———. "Transfictionality across Media." *Theorizing Narrativity*. Ed. John Pier and José Á. García Landa. Berlin: De Gruyter, 2008. 385–417. Print.

———. "Transmedial Storytelling and Transfictionality." *Poetics Today* 34.3 (2013): 362–388.

Ryan, Marie-Laure, and Ernst van Alphen. "Narratology." *Encyclopedia of Contemporary Literary Theory: Approaches, Scholars, Terms*. Ed. Irena R. Makaryk. Toronto: University of Toronto Press, 1993. 110–116. Print.

Ryan, Marie-Laure, and Jan-Noël Thon. "Storyworlds across Media: Introduction." *Storyworlds across Media: Toward a Media-Conscious Narratology*. Ed. Marie-Laure Ryan and Jan-Noël Thon. Lincoln: University of Nebraska Press, 2014. 1–21. Print.

Sacco, Joe. *Palestine*. Originally published as *Palestine* #1–9, 1993–1995. Seattle: Fantagraphics, 2001. Print.

———. *Safe Area Goražde*. Seattle: Fantagraphics, 2000. Print.

Sachs-Hombach, Klaus. *Das Bild als kommunikatives Medium: Elemente einer allgemeinen Bildwissenschaft*. Cologne: Herbert von Halem, 2003. Print.

Salen, Katie, and Eric Zimmerman. *Rules of Play: Game Design Fundamentals*. Cambridge MA: MIT Press, 2003. Print.

Salmon, Nathan. "Impossible Worlds." *Analysis* 44.3 (1984): 114–117. Print.

Sam and Max: The Devil's Playhouse. Telltale Games, 2010. PC.

Sarris, Andrew. "Notes on the *Auteur* Theory in 1962." *The Film Studies Reader*. Ed. Joane Hollows, Peter Hutchings, and Mark Jancovich. Oxford: Oxford University Press, 2000. 68–71. Print.

Satrapi, Marjane. *Persepolis*. Vols. 1–4. Paris: L'Association, 2000–2003. Print.

Saxer, Ulrich. "Der Forschungsgegenstand der Medienwissenschaft." *Medienwissenschaft: Ein Handbuch zur Entwicklung der Medien und Kommunikationsformen*. Ed. Joachim-Felix Leonhard. Berlin: De Gruyter, 1999. 1–14. Print.

Schaeffer, Jean-Marie. *Why Fiction?* Trans. Dorrit Cohn. Lincoln: University of Nebraska Press, 2010. Print.

Schaffrick, Matthias, and Marcus Willand, eds. *Theorien und Praktiken der Autorschaft*. Berlin: De Gruyter, 2014. Print.

Schatz, Thomas. *Hollywood Genres: Formulas, Filmmaking, and the Studio System*. New York: McGraw-Hill, 1981. Print.

Schell, Jesse. *The Art of Game Design: A Book of Lenses*. Burlington MA: Morgan Kaufmann, 2008. Print.

Schlickers, Sabine. "Focalization, Ocularization and Auricularization in Film and Literature." *Point of View, Perspective, and Focalization: Modeling Mediation in Narrative*. Ed. Peter Hühn, Wolf Schmid, and Jörg Schönert. Berlin: De Gruyter, 2009. 243–258. Print.

———. *Verfilmtes Erzählen: Narratologisch-komparative Untersuchung zu* El beso de la mujer araña *(Manuel Puig/Héctor Babenco) und* Crónica de una muerte anunciada *(Gabriel García Marquez/Fransesco Rosi)*. Frankfurt am Main: Vervuert, 1997. Print.

Schmid, Wolf. "Implied Author." *Handbook of Narratology*. Ed. Peter Hühn, John Pier, Wolf Schmid, and Jörg Schönert. Berlin: De Gruyter, 2009. 161–173. Print.

———. "Narrativity and Eventfulness." *What Is Narratology? Questions and Answers regarding the Status of a Theory*. Ed. Tom Kindt and Hans-Harald Müller. Berlin: De Gruyter, 2003. 17–33. Print.

———. *Narratology: An Introduction*. Trans. Alexander Starritt. Berlin: De Gruyter, 2010. Print.

Schmidt, Siegfried J. "The Fiction Is That Reality Exists: A Constructivist Model of Reality, Fiction, and Literature." Trans. Helmut Hauptmeier. *Poetics Today* 5.2 (1984): 253–274. Print.

———. *Kalte Faszination: Medien • Kultur • Wissenschaft in der Mediengesellschaft*. Weilerswist: Velbrück Wissenschaft, 2000. Print.

Schmitz-Emans, Monika. *Literatur-Comics: Adaptationen und Transformationen der Weltliteratur*. Berlin: De Gruyter, 2012. Print.

Schnackertz, Herman J. *Form und Funktion medialen Erzählens: Narrativität in Bildsequenz und Comicstrip*. München: Fink, 1980. Print.

Schneider, Christian W. *Framing Fear: The Gothic Mode in Graphic Literature*. Trier: Wissenschaftlicher Verlag Trier, 2014.

Schneider, Ralf. "Toward a Cognitive Theory of Literary Character: The Dynamics of Mental-Model Construction." *Style* 35.4 (2001): 607–639. Print.

Scholes, Robert. *Structuralism in Literature: An Introduction*. New Haven: Yale University Press, 1974. Print.

Schönert, Jörg, Peter Hühn, and Malte Stein, eds. *Lyrik und Narratologie: Text-Analysen zu deutschsprachigen Gedichten vom 16. bis zum 20. Jahrhundert*. Berlin: De Gruyter, 2007. Print.

Schrape, Niklas. *Die Rhetorik von Computerspielen: Wie politische Spiele überzeugen*. Frankfurt am Main: Campus Verlag, 2012. Print.

Schröter, Felix, and Jan-Noël Thon. "Simulierte Spielfiguren und/oder/als mediale Menschenbilder." *Medialität und Menschenbild*. Ed. Jens Eder, Joseph Imorde, and Maike Sarah Reinerth. Berlin: De Gruyter, 2013. 119–143. Print.

——. "Video Game Characters: Theory and Analysis." *Diegesis* 3.1 (2014): 40–77. Web. July 1, 2014.

Schuldiner, Michael. "Writer's Block and the Metaleptic Event in Art Spiegelman's Graphic Novel, *Maus*." *Studies in American Jewish Literature* 21 (2002): 108–115. Print.

Schulz, Charles M. *Peanuts*. Syndicated newspaper comic strip. Original run October 2, 1950–February 13, 2000. Print.

Schüwer, Martin. *Wie Comics erzählen: Grundriss einer intermedialen Erzähltheorie der grafischen Literatur*. Trier: Wissenschaftlicher Verlag Trier, 2008. Print.

Schwarz, Angela. "Game Studies und Geschichtswissenschaft." *Game Studies: Aktuelle Ansätze der Computerspielforschung*. Ed. Klaus Sachs-Hombach and Jan-Noël Thon. Cologne: Herbert von Halem, 2015. 398–447. Print.

Schweinitz, Jörg. "Die Ambivalenz des Augenscheins am Ende einer Affäre: Über Unzuverlässiges Erzählen, Doppelte Fokalisierung und die Kopräsenz narrativer Instanzen im Film." *Was stimmt denn jetzt? Unzuverlässiges Erzählen in Literatur und Film*. Ed. Fabienne Liptay and Yvonne Wolf. München: edition text + kritik, 2005. 89–106. Print.

——. "Multiple Logik filmischer Perspektivierung: Fokalisierung, narrative Instanz und wahnsinnige Liebe." *montage AV* 16.1 (2007): 83–100. Print.

——. "Totale Immersion und die Utopien von der virtuellen Realität: Ein Mediengründungsmythos zwischen Kino und Computerspiel." *Das Spiel* mit dem Medium: Partizipation—Immersion—Interaktion: Zur Teilhabe an den Medien von Kunst bis Computerspiel. Ed. Britta Neitzel and Rolf F. Nohr. Marburg: Schüren, 2006. 135-152. Print.

The Science of Sleep. Dir. Michel Gondry. Warner Independent Pictures, 2006. Film. [Originally released in French as *La science des rêves.* Gaumont, 2006. Film.]

Scolari, Carlos A. "Transmedia Storytelling: Implicit Consumers, Narrative Worlds, and Branding in Contemporary Media Production." *International Journal of Communication* 3 (2009): 586-606. Print.

Searle, John R. "Collective Intentions and Actions." *Intentions in Communication.* Ed. Philip R. Cohen, Jerry Morgan, and Martha E. Pollack. Cambridge MA: MIT Press, 1990. 401-415. Print.

———. *The Construction of Social Reality.* London: Penguin, 1995. Print.

———. "The Logical Status of Fictional Discourse." *New Literary History* 6.2 (1975): 319-332. Print.

———. *Mind, Language and Society: Doing Philosophy in the Real World.* London: Weidenfeld and Nicolson, 1999. Print.

The Secret Life of Walter Mitty. Dir. Ben Stiller. 20th Century Fox, 2013. Film.

Segal, Erwin M. "Narrative Comprehension and the Role of Deictic Shift Theory." *Deixis in Narrative: A Cognitive Science Perspective.* Ed. Judith F. Duchan, Gail A. Bruder, and Lynne E. Hewitt. Mahwah: Erlbaum, 1995. 3-17. Print.

Sellors, C. Paul. "Collective Authorship in Film." *Journal of Aesthetics and Art Criticism* 65.3 (2007): 263-271. Print.

Semino, Elena. *Language and World Creation in Poems and Other Texts.* London: Longman, 1997. Print.

Shame. Dir. Steve McQueen. Fox Searchlight Pictures, 2011. Film.

Sherlock. BBC, 2010- . Television.

Shklovsky, Viktor. *Theory of Prose.* Trans. Benjamin Sher. Normal: Dalkey Archive Press, 1990. Print.

Short Cuts. Dir. Robert Altman. Fine Line Features, 1993. Film.

Sicart, Miguel. *Beyond Choices: The Design of Ethical Gameplay.* Cambridge MA: MIT Press, 2013. Print.

Sigismondi, Paolo. *The Digital Glocalization of Entertainment: New Paradigms in the 21st Century Global Mediascape.* New York: Springer, 2012. Print.

Silent Hill 2. Konami, 2001. PlayStation 2.

Sin City. Dir. Frank Miller and Robert Rodriguez. Dimension Films, 2005. Film.

Singer, Jane B., Alfred Hermida, David Domingo, Ari Heinonen, Steve Paulussen, Thorsten Quandt, Zvi Reich, and Marina Vujnovic. *Participatory Journalism: Guarding Open Gates at Online Newspapers.* Chichester: Wiley-Blackwell, 2011. Print.
The Sixth Sense. Dir. M. Night Shyamalan. Buena Vista Pictures, 1999. Film.
Small, David. *Stitches: A Memoir.* New York: W. W. Norton, 2009. Print.
Smith, Greg M. *Film Structure and the Emotion System.* Cambridge: Cambridge University Press, 2003. Print.
———. "Local Emotions, Global Moods, and Film Structure." *Passionate Views: Film, Cognition, and Emotion.* Ed. Carl Plantinga and Greg M. Smith. Baltimore: Johns Hopkins University Press, 1999. 103–126. Print.
Smith, Jeff. *Bone.* Originally published in the black-and-white comic book series *Bone,* 1991–2004. Columbus: Cartoon Books, 2004. Print.
Smith, Murray. "Consciousness." *The Routledge Companion to Philosophy and Film.* Ed. Paisley Livingston and Carl Plantinga. Abingdon: Routledge, 2009. 39–51. Print.
———. *Engaging Characters: Fiction, Emotion, and the Cinema.* Oxford: Oxford University Press, 1995. Print.
———. "Triangulating Aesthetic Experience." *Aesthetic Science: Connecting Minds, Brains, and Experience.* Ed. Arthur P. Shimamura and Stephen E. Palmer. New York: Oxford University Press, 2014. 80–106. Print.
Sobchack, Vivian. *The Address of the Eye: A Phenomenology of Film Experience.* Princeton: Princeton University Press, 1992. Print.
The Social Network. Dir. David Fincher. Columbia Pictures, 2010. Film.
Sommer, Roy. "'Contextualism' Revisited: A Survey (and Defence) of Postcolonial and Intercultural Narratologies." *Journal of Literary Theory* 1.1 (2007): 61–79. Print.
———. "Drama and Narrative." *Routledge Encyclopedia of Narrative Theory.* Ed. David Herman, Manfred Jahn, and Marie-Laure Ryan. Abingdon: Routledge, 2005. 119–124. Print.
Souriau, Étienne. "La structure de l'univers filmique et le vocabulaire de la filmologie." *Revue Internationale de Filmologie* 2.7–8 (1951): 231–240. Print.
Spec Ops: The Line. Yager Development/2K Games, 2012. PC.
Sperber, Dan, and Deirdre Wilson. *Relevance: Communication and Cognition.* 2nd ed. Oxford: Blackwell, 1995. Print.
Spiegelman, Art. *The Complete Maus.* Originally published as *Maus,* vol. 1, 1986, and *Maus,* vol. 2, 1991. New York: Pantheon, 1996. Print.
———. "Maus." *MetaMaus: A Look inside a Modern Classic.* New York: Pantheon, 2011. 105–107. Print. [Originally published in 1972 as "Maus." *Funny Animals.* Ed. Terry Zwigoff. San Francisco: Apex Novelties. Print.]

———. *MetaMaus: A Look inside a Modern Classic*. New York: Pantheon, 2011. Print.

Spigel, Lynn, and Jan Olsson, eds. *Television after TV: Essays on a Medium in Transition*. Durham: Duke University Press, 2004. Print.

Spoerhase, Carlos. "Hypothetical Intentionalism." *Journal of Literary Theory* 1.1 (2007): 81–110. Print.

Spore. Maxis/Electronic Arts, 2008. PC.

Stage Fright. Dir. Alfred Hitchcock. Warner Bros. Pictures, 1950. Film.

Staiger, Janet. *Interpreting Films: Studies in the Historical Reception of American Cinema*. Princeton: Princeton University Press, 1992. Print.

Stam, Robert, Robert Burgoyne, and Sandy Flitterman-Lewis. *New Vocabularies in Film Semiotics: Structuralism, Post-Structuralism and Beyond*. London: Routledge, 1992. Print.

The Stanley Parable. Galactic Cafe, 2013. PC.

Stanzel, Franz K. *Narrative Situations in the Novel:* Tom Jones, Moby Dick, The Ambassadors, Ulysses. Trans. James P. Pusack. Bloomington: Indiana University Press, 1971. Print.

———. *A Theory of Narrative*. Trans. Charlotte Goedsche. Cambridge: Cambridge University Press, 1984. Print.

Star Wars: The Clone Wars. Dir. Dave Filoni. Warner Bros. Pictures, 2008. Film.

Star Wars: The Clone Wars. Cartoon Network/Netflix, 2008–2014. Television.

Star Wars: Dark Forces. LucasArts, 1995. PC.

Star Wars Episode I: The Phantom Menace. Dir. George Lucas. 20th Century Fox, 1999. Film.

Star Wars Episode II: Attack of the Clones. Dir. George Lucas. 20th Century Fox, 2002. Film.

Star Wars Episode III: Revenge of the Sith. Dir. George Lucas. 20th Century Fox, 2005. Film.

Star Wars Episode IV: A New Hope. Dir. George Lucas. 20th Century Fox, 1977. Film.

Star Wars Episode V: The Empire Strikes Back. Dir. Irvin Kershner. 20th Century Fox, 1980. Film.

Star Wars Episode VI: Return of the Jedi. Dir. Richard Marquand. 20th Century Fox, 1983. Film.

Star Wars Episode VII: The Force Awakens. Dir. J. J. Abrams. Walt Disney Studios Motion Pictures, 2015. Film.

Star Wars Episode VIII: The Last Jedi. Dir. Rian Johnson. Walt Disney Studios Motion Pictures, 2017. Film.

Stein, Daniel. "Superhero Comics and the Authorizing Functions of the Comic Book Paratext." *From Comic Strips to Graphic Novels: Contributions to the Theory and History of Graphic Narrative*. 2nd ed. Ed. Daniel Stein and Jan-Noël Thon. Berlin: De Gruyter, 2015. 155–189. Print.

Stein, Daniel, and Jan-Noël Thon, eds. *From Comic Strips to Graphic Novels: Contributions to the Theory and History of Graphic Narrative*. 2nd ed. Berlin: De Gruyter, 2015. Print.

———. "Introduction: From Comic Strips to Graphic Novels." *From Comic Strips to Graphic Novels: Contributions to the Theory and History of Graphic Narrative*. 2nd ed. Ed. Daniel Stein and Jan-Noël Thon. Berlin: De Gruyter, 2015. 1–23. Print.

Sternberg, Meir. *Expositional Modes and Temporal Ordering in Fiction*. Baltimore: Johns Hopkins University Press, 1978. Print.

———. "Omniscience in Narrative Construction: Old Challenges and New." *Poetics Today* 28.4 (2007): 683–794. Print.

Stingel-Voigt, Yvonne. *Soundtracks virtueller Welten: Musik in Videospielen*. Glückstadt: Verlag Werner Hülsbusch, 2014. Print.

Stranglehold. Midway Chicago/Midway Games, 2007. PC.

Super Columbine Massacre RPG! Danny Ledonne, 2005. PC.

Surdiacourt, Steven. "Can You Hear Me Drawing? 'Voice' and the Graphic Novel." *Travelling Concepts, Metaphors, and Narratives: Literary and Cultural Studies in an Age of Interdisciplinary Research*. Ed. Sibylle Baumbach, Beatrice Michaelis, and Ansgar Nünning. Trier: Wissenschaftlicher Verlag Trier, 2012. 165–178. Print.

Surkamp, Carola. "Perspective." *Routledge Encyclopedia of Narrative Theory*. Ed. David Herman, Manfred Jahn, and Marie-Laure Ryan. London: Abingdon, 2005. 423–425. Print.

———. *Die Perspektivenstruktur narrativer Texte: Zu ihrer Theorie und Geschichte im englischen Roman zwischen Viktorianismus und Moderne*. Trier: Wissenschaftlicher Verlag Trier, 2003. Print.

Süskind, Patrick. *Das Parfum: Die Geschichte eines Mörders*. Zürich: Diogenes, 1985. Print.

Sutton-Smith, Brian. *The Ambiguity of Play*. Cambridge MA: Harvard University Press, 1997. Print.

Swanson, Dorothy C. *The Story of Viewers for Quality Television: From Grassroots to Prime Time*. Syracuse: Syracuse University Press, 2000. Print.

Talbot, Bryan. *The Tale of One Bad Rat*. Originally published in single magazine form as *The Tale of One Bad Rat* #1–4, 1994–1995. Milwaukee: Dark Horse, 1995. Print.

Tammi, Pekka. "Against Narrative ('A Boring Story')." *Partial Answers: Journal of Literature and the History of Ideas* 4.2 (2006): 19–40. Print.

Tan, Ed. S. *Emotion and the Structure of Narrative Film: Film as an Emotion Machine*. Mahwah: Erlbaum, 1996. Print.

Tan, Shaun. *The Arrival*. New York: Arthur A. Levine Books, 2007. Print.

Tavinor, Grant. *The Art of Video Games*. Chichester: Wiley-Blackwell, 2009. Print.

Thomas, Nigel J. T. "Mental Imagery." *The Stanford Encyclopedia of Philosophy*. Ed. Edward N. Zalta. Stanford: Stanford University, 2012. Web. December 1, 2013.

Thompson, Craig. *Blankets*. Marietta: Top Shelf Productions, 2003. Print.

———. *Habibi*. New York: Pantheon, 2011. Print.

Thompson, Hunter S. *Fear and Loathing in Las Vegas: A Savage Journey to the Heart of the American Dream*. New York: Random House, 1972. Print.

Thompson, Kristin. *Breaking the Glass Armor: Neoformalist Film Analysis*. Princeton: Princeton University Press, 1988. Print.

———. *The Frodo Franchise:* The Lord of the Rings *and Modern Hollywood*. Berkeley: University of California Press, 2007. Print.

———. *Storytelling in the New Hollywood: Understanding Classical Narrative Technique*. Cambridge MA: Harvard University Press, 1999. Print.

Thomson-Jones, Katherine. *Aesthetics and Film*. London: Continuum, 2008. Print.

———. "Cinematic Narrators." *Philosophy Compass* 4.2 (2009): 296–311. Print.

———. "The Literary Origins of the Cinematic Narrator." *British Journal of Aesthetics* 47.1 (2007): 76–94. Print.

Thon, Jan-Noël. "Computer Games, Fictional Worlds, and Transmedial Storytelling: A Narratological Perspective." *Proceedings of the Philosophy of Computer Games Conference 2009*. Ed. John R. Sageng. Oslo: University of Oslo, 2009. 1–6. Web. December 1, 2013.

———. "Converging Worlds: From Transmedial Storyworlds to Transmedial Universes." *Storyworlds: A Journal of Narrative Studies* 7.2 (2015): 21–53. Print.

———. "Fiktionalität in Film- und Medienwissenschaft." *Fiktionalität: Ein interdisziplinäres Handbuch*. Ed. Tobias Klauk and Tilmann Köppe. Berlin: De Gruyter, 2014. 443–466. Print.

———. "Game Studies und Narratologie." *Game Studies: Aktuelle Ansätze der Computerspielforschung*. Ed. Klaus Sachs-Hombach and Jan-Noël Thon. Cologne: Herbert von Halem, 2015. 104–164. Print.

———. "Immersion Revisited: On the Value of a Contested Concept." *Extending Experiences: Structure, Analysis and Design of Computer Game Player Experience*. Ed. Olli Leino, Hanna Wirman, and Amyris Fernandez. Rovaniemi: Lapland University Press, 2008. 29–43. Print.

———. "Mediality." *The Johns Hopkins Guide to Digital Media*. Ed. Marie-Laure Ryan, Lori Emerson, and Benjamin J. Robertson. Baltimore: Johns Hopkins University Press, 2014. 334–337. Print.

———. "Mind-Bender: Zur Popularisierung komplexer narrativer Strukturen im amerikanischen Kino der 1990er Jahre." *Post-Coca-Colanization: Zurück zur Vielfalt?* Ed. Sophia Komor and Rebekka Rohleder. Frankfurt am Main: Peter Lang, 2009. 175–192. Print.

———. "Narratives across Media and the Outlines of a Media-Conscious Narratology." *Handbook of Intermediality: Literature—Image—Sound—Music*. Ed. Gabriele Rippl. Berlin: De Gruyter, 2015. 439–456. Print.

———. "Narrativity." *The Johns Hopkins Guide to Digital Media*. Ed. Marie-Laure Ryan, Lori Emerson, and Benjamin J. Robertson. Baltimore: Johns Hopkins University Press, 2014. 351–355. Print.

———. "Perspective in Contemporary Computer Games." *Point of View, Perspective, and Focalization: Modeling Mediation in Narrative*. Ed. Peter Hühn, Wolf Schmid, and Jörg Schönert. Berlin: De Gruyter, 2009. 279–299. Print.

———. "Subjectivity across Media: On Transmedial Strategies of Subjective Representation in Contemporary Feature Films, Graphic Novels, and Computer Games." *Storyworlds across Media: Toward a Media-Conscious Narratology*. Ed. Marie-Laure Ryan and Jan-Noël Thon. Lincoln: University of Nebraska Press, 2014. 67–102. Print.

———. "Toward a Transmedial Narratology: On Narrators in Contemporary Graphic Novels, Feature Films, and Computer Games." *Beyond Classical Narration: Transmedial and Unnatural Challenges*. Ed. Jan Alber and Per Krogh Hansen. Berlin: De Gruyter, 2014. 25–56. Print.

———. "Unendliche Weiten? Schauplätze, fiktionale Welten und soziale Räume heutiger Computerspiele." *Computer/Spiel/Räume: Materialien zur Einführung in die Computer Game Studies*. Ed. Klaus Bartels and Jan-Noël Thon. Hamburg: University of Hamburg, 2007. 29–60. Print.

———. "Who's Telling the Tale? Authors and Narrators in Graphic Narrative." *From Comic Strips to Graphic Novels: Contributions to the Theory and History of Graphic Narrative*. 2nd ed. Ed. Daniel Stein and Jan-Noël Thon. Berlin: De Gruyter, 2015. 67–99. Print.

———. "Zur Metalepse im Film." *Probleme filmischen Erzählens*. Ed. Hannah Birr, Maike Sarah Reinerth, and Jan-Noël Thon. Münster: LIT, 2009. 85–110. Print.

Thoss, Jeff. "Tell It Like a Game: *Scott Pilgrim* and Performative Media Rivalry." *Storyworlds across Media: Toward a Media-Conscious Narratology*. Ed. Marie-Laure Ryan and Jan-Noël Thon. Lincoln: University of Nebraska Press, 2014. 211–229. Print.

———. *When Storyworlds Collide: Metalepsis in Popular Fiction, Film and Comics*. Leiden: Brill | Rodopi, 2015. Print.

Time Shift. Saber Interactive/Sierra, 2007. PC.

Todorov, Tzvetan. "Les catégories du récit littéraire." *Communications* 8 (1966): 125–151. Print.

———. *The Fantastic: A Structural Approach to a Literary Genre*. Trans. Richard Howard. Ithaca NY: Cornell University Press, 1975. Print.

———. *Grammaire du Décaméron*. The Hague: Mouton, 1969. Print.

Tolmie, Jane, ed. *Drawing from Life: Memory and Subjectivity in Comic Art*. Jackson: University Press of Mississippi, 2013. Print.

Tomasello, Michael. *Why We Cooperate*. Cambridge MA: MIT Press, 2009. Print.

Tomb Raider. Crystal Dynamics/Square Enix, 2013. PC.

Tompkins, Jane P., ed. *Reader-Response Criticism: From Formalism to Post-Structuralism*. Baltimore: Johns Hopkins University Press, 1980. Print.

Transistor. Supergiant Games, 2014. PC.

Tröhler, Magrit. *Offene Welten ohne Helden: Plurale Figurenkonstellationen im Film*. Marburg: Schüren, 2007. Print.

Truffaut, François. "A Certain Tendency of the French Cinema." Trans. Bill Nichols. *Movies and Methods*. Vol. 1. Ed. Bill Nichols. Berkeley: University of California Press, 1976. 224–237. Print.

Tuomela, Raimo. *The Importance of Us: A Philosophical Study of Basic Social Notions*. Stanford: Stanford University Press, 1995. Print.

Turner, Mark. *Death Is the Mother of Beauty: Mind, Metaphor, Criticism*. Chicago: University of Chicago Press, 1987. Print.

Uidhir, Christy M. "Comics and Collective Authorship." *The Art of Comics: A Philosophical Approach*. Ed. Aaron Meskin and Roy T. Cook. Chichester: Wiley-Blackwell, 2012. 47–67. Print.

Ultima Underworld. Blue Sky Productions/Electronic Arts, 1992. PC.

Uncharted: Drake's Fortune. Naughty Dog/Sony, 2007. PlayStation 3.

Under Siege. Afkar Media/Dar al-Fikr, 2005. PC.

Uricchio, William. "Simulation, History, and Computer Games." *Handbook of Computer Game Studies*. Ed. Joost Raessens and Jeffrey Goldstein. Cambridge MA: MIT Press, 2005. 327–338. Print.

Uspensky, Boris. *A Poetics of Composition: The Structure of the Artistic Text and Typology of a Compositional Form*. Trans. Valentina Zavarin and Susan Wittig. Berkeley: University of California Press, 1973. Print.

The Usual Suspects. Dir. Bryan Singer. Gramercy Pictures, 1995. Film.

van Dijk, Teun A. *Macrostructures: An Interdisciplinary Study of Global Structures in Discourse, Interaction, and Cognition*. Hillsdale: Erlbaum, 1980. Print.

van Dijk, Teun A., and Walter Kintsch. *Strategies of Discourse Comprehension*. New York: Academic Press, 1983. Print.

van Leeuwen, Theo. *Introducing Social Semiotics*. Abingdon: Routledge, 2005. Print.

Vogel, Matthias. *Media of Reason: A Theory of Rationality*. Trans. Darrell Arnold. New York: Columbia University Press, 2012. Print.

Vogler, Christopher. *The Writer's Journey: Mythic Structure for Writers*. 3rd ed. Studio City: Michael Wiese Productions, 2007. Print.

Voss, Christiane. *Narrative Emotionen: Eine Untersuchung über Möglichkeiten und Grenzen philosophischer Emotionstheorien*. Berlin: De Gruyter, 2004. Print.

Waco Resurrection. C-level, 2003. PC.

Walker Rettberg, Jill. "Fiction and Interaction: How Clicking a Mouse Can Make You Part of a Fictional World." PhD thesis University of Bergen, 2003. Web. December 1, 2013.

The Walking Dead. AMC, 2010– . Television.

The Walking Dead: Season One. Telltale Games, 2012. PC.

The Walking Dead: Survival Instinct. Terminal Reality/Activision, 2013. PC.

Walsh, Richard. *The Rhetoric of Fictionality: Narrative Theory and the Idea of Fiction*. Columbus: Ohio State University Press, 2007. Print.

——— . "Who Is the Narrator?" *Poetics Today* 18.4 (1997): 495–513. Print.

Walton, Kendall L. *Mimesis as Make-Believe: On the Foundations of the Representational Arts*. Cambridge MA: Harvard University Press, 1990. Print.

Wanted. Dir. Timur Bekmambetov. Universal Pictures, 2008. Film.

Warcraft III: Reign of Chaos. Blizzard, 2002. PC.

Ware, Chris. *Jimmy Corrigan: The Smartest Kid on Earth*. New York: Pantheon, 2000. Print.

Warhol, Robyn R. *Gendered Interventions: Narrative Discourse in the Victorian Novel*. New Brunswick NJ: Rutgers University Press, 1989. Print.

Warhol, Robyn R., and Susan S. Lanser, eds. *Narrative Theory Unbound: Queer and Feminist Interventions*. Columbus: Ohio State University Press, 2015. Print.

Watchmen. Dir. Zack Snyder. Warner Bros. Pictures, 2009. Film.

Weaver, Tyler. *Comics for Film, Games, and Animation: Using Comics to Construct Your Transmedia Storyworld*. Burlington: Focal Press, 2013. Print.

Wedel, Michael. "Backbeat and Overlap: Time, Place, and Character Subjectivity in *Run Lola Run*." *Puzzle Films: Complex Storytelling in Contemporary Cinema*. Ed. Warren Buckland. Chichester: Wiley-Blackwell, 2009. 129–150. Print.

Weidle, Roland. "Organizing the Perspectives: Focalization and the Superordinate Narrative System in Drama and Theatre." *Point of View, Perspective, and Focalization: Modeling Mediation in Narrative*. Ed. Peter Hühn, Wolf Schmid, and Jörg Schönert. Berlin: De Gruyter, 2009. 221–242. Print.

Weiner, Stephen. "How the Graphic Novel Changed American Comics." *The Rise of the American Comics Artist: Creators and Contexts*. Ed. Paul Williams and James Lyons. Jackson: University Press of Mississippi, 2010. 3–13. Print.

Werth, Paul. *Text Worlds: Representing Conceptual Space in Discourse*. London: Longman, 1999. Print.

Whitlock, Gillian. "Autographics: The Seeing 'I' of the Comics." *Modern Fiction Studies* 52.4 (2006): 965–979. Print.

Williams, Paul, and James Lyons, eds. *The Rise of the American Comics Artist: Creators and Contexts*. Jackson: University Press of Mississippi, 2010. Print.

Williamson, Timothy. *Knowledge and Its Limits*. Oxford: Oxford University Press, 2000. Print.

Willingham, Bill. *Fables: Arabian Nights (and Days)*. Vol. 7. Art by Mark Buckingham, Jim Fern, Steve Leialoha, Jimmy Palmiotti, and Andrew J. Pepoy, colors by Daniel Vozzo, lettered by Todd Klein, covers by James Jean. Originally published in single magazine form as *Fables* #42–47, 2005–2006. New York: DC Comics/Vertigo, 2006. Print.

Wilson, George. "Elusive Narrators in Literature and Film." *Philosophical Studies* 135.1 (2007): 73–88. Print.

———. *Narration in Light: Studies in Cinematic Point of View*. Baltimore: Johns Hopkins University Press, 1986. Print.

———. "On Film Narrative and Narrative Meaning." *Film Theory and Philosophy*. Ed. Richard Allen and Murray Smith. Oxford: Oxford University Press, 1997. 221–238. Print.

———. "Transparency and Twist in Narrative Fiction Film." *Journal of Aesthetics and Art Criticism* 64.1 (2006): 81–96. Print.
Wimsatt, William K., and Monroe C. Beardsley. "The Intentional Fallacy." *Sewanee Review* 54.3 (1946): 468–488. Print.
Winko, Simone. *Kodierte Gefühle: Zu einer Poetik der Emotionen in lyrischen und poetologischen Texten um 1900*. Berlin: Erich Schmidt, 2003. Print.
Winston, Brian. *Claiming the Real: The Documentary Film Revisited*. London: British Film Institute, 1995. Print.
The Wire. HBO, 2002–2008. Television.
The Witcher 2: Assassins of Kings. CD Projekt RED/Atari, 2011. PC.
Wolf, Mark J. P. *Building Imaginary Worlds: The Theory and History of Subcreation*. New York: Routledge, 2012. Print.
Wolf, Werner. "'Cross the Border—Close that Gap': Towards an Intermedial Narratology." *European Journal of English Studies* 8.1 (2004): 81–103. Print.
———. "Das Problem der Narrativität in Literatur, bildender Kunst und Musik: Ein Beitrag zu einer intermedialen Erzähltheorie." *Erzähltheorie transgenerisch, intermedial, interdisziplinär*. Ed. Ansgar Nünning and Vera Nünning. Trier: Wissenschaftlicher Verlag Trier, 2002. 23–104. Print.
———. "Description as a Transmedial Mode of Representation: General Features and Possibilities of Realization in Painting, Fiction and Music." *Description in Literature and Other Media*. Ed. Werner Wolf and Walter Bernhart. Amsterdam: Rodopi, 2007. 1–87. Print.
———. "Framing Borders in Frame Stories." *Framing Borders in Literature and Other Media*. Ed. Werner Wolf and Walter Bernhart. Amsterdam: Rodopi, 2006. 179–206. Print.
———. "Intermediality Revisited: Reflections on Word and Music Relations in the Context of a General Typology of Intermediality." *Word and Music Studies: Essays in Honor of Steven Paul Scher on Cultural Identity and the Musical Stage*. Ed. Suzanne M. Lodato, Suzanne Aspden, and Walter Bernhart. Amsterdam: Rodopi, 2002. 13–34. Print.
———. "Is There a Metareferential Turn, and If So, How Can It Be Explained?" *The Metareferential Turn in Contemporary Arts and Media: Forms, Functions, Attempts at Explanation*. Ed. Werner Wolf. Amsterdam: Rodopi, 2011. 1–47. Print.
———. "Metalepsis as a Transgeneric and Transmedial Phenomenon: A Case Study of the Possibilities of 'Exporting' Narratological Concepts."

Narratology beyond Literary Criticism: Mediality, Disciplinarity. Ed. Jan Christoph Meister. Berlin: De Gruyter, 2005. 83–107. Print.

———. "Metareference across Media: The Concept, Its Transmedial Potentials and Problems, Main Forms and Functions." *Metareference across Media: Theory and Case Studies.* Ed. Werner Wolf. Amsterdam: Rodopi, 2009. 1–85. Print.

———. *The Musicalization of Fiction: A Study in the Theory and History of Intermediality.* Amsterdam: Rodopi, 1999. Print.

———. "Music and Narrative." *Routledge Encyclopedia of Narrative Theory.* Ed. David Herman, Manfred Jahn, and Marie-Laure Ryan. Abingdon: Routledge, 2005. 324–329. Print.

———. "Narrative and Narrativity: A Narratological Reconceptualization and Its Applicability to the Visual Arts." *Word and Image* 19.3 (2003): 180–197. Print.

———. "Narratology and Media(lity): The Transmedial Expansion of a Literary Discipline and Possible Consequences." *Current Trends in Narratology.* Ed. Greta Olson. Berlin: De Gruyter, 2011. 145–180. Print.

Wollen, Peter. *Signs and Meaning in the Cinema.* 3rd ed. Bloomington: Indiana University Press, 1972. Print.

Wollheim, Richard. *Art and Its Objects.* 2nd ed. Cambridge: Cambridge University Press, 1980. Print.

———. "On Pictorial Representation." *Journal of Aesthetics and Art Criticism* 56.3 (1998): 217–226. Print.

———. *Painting as an Art.* Princeton: Princeton University Press, 1987. Print.

Wolterstorff, Nicholas. *Works and Worlds of Art.* Oxford: Oxford University Press, 1980. Print.

Woo, Benjamin. "Reconsidering Comics Journalism: Information and Experience in Joe Sacco's *Palestine*." *The Rise and Reason of Comics and Graphic Literature: Critical Essays on the Form.* Ed. Joyce Goggin and Dan Hassler-Forest. Jefferson: McFarland, 2010. 166–177. Print.

Woods, John. *Paradox and Paraconsistency: Conflict Resolution in the Abstract Sciences.* Cambridge: Cambridge University Press, 2003. Print.

World of Warcraft. Blizzard, 2004– . PC.

Wulff, Hans Jürgen. *Darstellen und Mitteilen: Elemente einer Pragmasemiotik des Films.* Tübingen: Narr, 1999. Print.

Wuss, Peter. *Filmanalyse und Psychologie: Strukturen des Films im Wahrnehmungsprozess.* Berlin: Edition Sigma, 1993. Print.

XIII. Ubisoft, 2003. PC.

Yacobi, Tamar. "Fictional Reliability as a Communicative Problem." *Poetics Today* 2.2 (1981): 113–126. Print.

Yagisawa, Takashi. "Beyond Possible Worlds." *Philosophical Studies* 53.2 (1988): 175–204. Print.

Zerweck, Bruno. "Historicizing Unreliable Narration: Unreliability and Cultural Discourse in Narrative Fiction." *Style* 35.1 (2001): 151–178. Print.

Zierold, Kirsten. *Computerspielanalyse: Perspektivenstrukturen, Handlungsspielräume, moralische Implikationen*. Trier: Wissenschaftlicher Verlag Trier, 2011. Print.

Zipfel, Frank. "Fiction across Media: Toward a Transmedial Concept of Fictionality." *Storyworlds across Media: Toward a Media-Conscious Narratology*. Ed. Marie-Laure Ryan and Jan-Noël Thon. Lincoln: University of Nebraska Press, 2014. 103–125. Print.

———. *Fiktion, Fiktivität, Fiktionalität: Analysen zur Fiktion in der Literatur und zum Fiktionsbegriff in der Literaturwissenschaft*. Berlin: Erich Schmidt, 2001. Print.

Zunshine, Lisa. *Why We Read Fiction: Theory of Mind and the Novel*. Columbus: Ohio State University Press, 2006. Print.

Zwaan, Rolf A. "Situation Models: The Mental Leap into Imagined Worlds." *Current Directions in Psychological Science* 8.1 (1996): 15–18. Print.

Index

11:14 (film), 84, 362n8
12 Monkeys (film), xxi, 84, 262, 266–270, 277, 325, 263n8, 363n10, 413nn3–4
300 (comic), 86, 157
300 (film), 157, 308

Aarseth, Espen, 149–151, 339n23, 336n27, 377n14
Abbott, H. Porter, 4
Abrahams, Jim, 149
action-adventure (genre), 19, 86, 105, 113, 117, 208, 306, 308, 329, 342n33, 370n40, 420n33
actual world, 41, 58, 67, 69, 91, 93, 39, 351n24, 355n36, 357n44, 375n9, 382n40, 401n20
Aczel, Richard, 139–141, 144, 155
Adaptation. (film), xxi, 64, 66, 85, 88, 162, 168, 178–182, 206, 219, 265, 358n47, 363n10, 386n2, 387nn9–10, 390n19
adaptations, xvii–xxi, 145, 157, 178, 182, 277, 308, 328–330, 332, 333n2, 386n1, 390n19, 413n3, 414n11, 421n2, 422n3
adaptation studies, 333n2, 421n2
Adventure (video game), 396
affects, 404n34. *See also* desires; emotions; feelings; moods; subjectivity

Alan Wake (video game), xxi, 64, 85, 103, 105–106, 113, 117, 120, 253, 255, 262–263, 305, 313, 321–325, 370nn40–41, 390n19, 420n33
Alan Wake (video game series), 208, 306, 308
Alan Wake's American Nightmare (video game), 370nn40–41
Alber, Jan, 56–58, 60, 63, 66–67, 356n39, 356n41, 358n45
Alice's Adventures in Wonderland (novel), 416n16
Altman, Robert, 84, 362n8
The Amazing Spider-Man (comics series), 390n19
The Amazing Spider-Man (video game), 390n19
ambiguity, 55–60, 83, 97, 115, 355n34, 418n23
Amélie (film), 412n2
Amenábar, Alejandro, 412n2
American Beauty (film), 167
American McGee's Alice (video game), 311
American Splendor (comics series), 390
American Splendor (film), 390
Amnesia: The Dark Descent (video game), xxi, 311–313, 317, 320, 325, 419n31

anachrony, 345n2. *See also* analepsis; flashback; flash-forward; prolepsis

analepsis, 77–78, 95–98, 169, 171, 174–175, 180, 269, 282, 345n2, 394n31, 418n23. *See also* anachrony; flashback

analysis, xviii–xx, 1–11, 24–26, 30–31, 49–50, 52, 76–84, 91–104, 109–120, 145–146, 151, 165, 168–182, 184–206, 208–220, 227–229, 231–232, 239, 247–249, 253–255, 257, 263–264, 266–304, 307–325, 327–329, 331–332, 334nn5–6, 341n26, 354n31, 363n14, 385n46, 398n8, 402n22, 422n3. *See also* method

animation, 82, 88, 363n11, 368n32

Anodyne (video game), 321

Arjoranta, Jonne, 235–236

The Arrival (comic), xxi, 285–287, 325, 364n17, 378n17, 389n12, 417n20

art history, 4, 397n3, 400n18

The Artist (film), 87, 364n16

Assassin's Creed (video game), 368n33

Asterios Polyp (comic), 417n18

audience, 78–79, 154, 225, 331, 375n10. *See also* recipients

auricularization, 230, 399n12, 410n55. *See also* focalization; ocularization; perspective; point of audition; point of view; subjectivity

author, 40, 48, 53–54, 61, 74, 94, 115, 125–154, 156, 165, 171–172, 177–180, 185, 187, 193–195, 199, 200–202, 211, 227, 237, 331, 336nn10–11, 367n29, 373nn3–10, 376n12, 377nn14–17, 378nn20–21, 379nn25–26, 380nn28–29, 381n31, 384n42, 384n44, 386n3, 387n10, 389n13, 389n15, 390nn18–19, 391n21, 391n23, 392n27, 401n21, 405n35; actual, 125–127, 129–132, 134–137, 143–144, 147–148, 178–179, 204, 373n4, 374n7; as author function, 374n5; death of the, 374n5; hypothetical, 132–134, 137–138, 142, 147, 150–153, 156, 165, 171–172, 177, 187, 194–195, 211, 374n7, 380n26, 381n31, 384n44, 391n21; implied, 125–128, 131–133, 135, 138, 142, 143–145, 149–152, 156, 336n11, 373n3, 374nn6–8, 378nn20–21, 379nn25–26, 380nn28–29, 381n31, 384n42, 384n44. *See also* author collectives; author figure; authorship; characters: authoring

author collectives, 131–133, 135–138, 142, 147, 150–153, 156, 165, 171–172, 177, 187, 194–195, 211, 331, 373n4, 375n10, 376n12, 377n14, 381n31, 384n44, 391n21. *See also* author

author figure, 131, 134, 154, 171–172, 177, 185, 187, 200, 373n4, 375n9, 389n15. *See also* author; characters: authoring

authorship, xvii, 128, 131–133, 136–137, 150–151, 154, 178, 192–194, 200, 202, 204–206, 331, 373n4, 375n10, 376n12, 377n14, 378n21, 380n28, 386n3, 387n9, 392n27, 401n21. *See also* author; intentionalism

autobiography, 204, 365n18, 375n9. *See also* biography

Avary, Roger, 412n2

B., David, 68, 91

Bacharach, Sondra, 136

Backe, Hans-Joachim, 14
The Baconing (video game), 395n34
Baetens, Jan, 147, 380n26
Bal, Mieke, 4–5, 49–50, 74, 126, 227–228, 232, 235, 377n15, 409n45
Balázs, Bela, 257
Baldur's Gate (video game), 117, 207–208, 253, 396
Baldur's Gate (video game series), 371n42
Baldur's Gate II: Shadows of Amn (video game), 421n38
Balzer, Jens, 90
Banfield, Ann, 377n15
Banksy, 68
Baron Cohen, Sacha, 68
Barthes, Roland, 2, 21, 334n5
Bartkowiak, Andrzej, 329
Bastion (video game), xxi, 156, 164, 215–219, 305–306, 308, 393n30, 395n35, 395nn37–38, 420n33
Batman (comics series), 102
Batman (franchise), xvii–xix, 12, 329, 366n24, 420n35
Batman: Arkham Asylum (video game), xxi, 256, 261, 313–320, 325, 329, 420n34
Batman Begins (film), 329
Batman Begins (video game), 329
Batman: The Dark Knight Returns (comic), 94, 183–184, 256, 418n25
Batman: Whatever Happened to the Caped Crusader? (comic), 93, 164
Bazin, André, 257
Beardsley, Monroe C., 352n27, 374n7
A Beautiful Mind (biography), 414n11
A Beautiful Mind (film), xii, 77, 173, 256, 261, 273–277, 280, 325, 414nn11–14

Bechdel, Alison, 68
Beil, Benjamin, xiii, 236, 400n17
Being John Malkovich (film), 179
Bekmambetov, Timur, 308
beliefs, 67, 239, 243, 245, 248–249, 255, 374n7, 403n26, 407n37. *See also* knowledge; subjectivity
Big Fish (film), 382n34
The Big Lebowski (film), 156
biography, 204, 414n11. *See also* autobiography
BioShock (video game), 208
Black, David A., 160–162, 383n38
Black, Shane, 387n9
Black Hole (comic), xxi, 85, 256, 262, 296–304, 325
Blankets (comic), 68
Blomkamp, Neill, 68
Bogost, Ian, 69, 366n27
Bone (comic), 392n26
Booth, Wayne C., 125–126, 373n3, 374n6, 384n42
Borat (film), 68
Bordwell, David, 54, 78, 128–130, 144, 151–152, 226, 237, 342n32, 377n14, 378n21
bottom-up processes, 7, 43, 239–240, 247, 263. *See also* comprehension
Brandom, Robert, 62
Branigan, Edward, 14, 43–44, 67, 129–131, 133, 153, 225, 229, 236–237, 239–240, 246, 257–259, 261–262, 377n16, 399n10, 407n39
Braveheart (film), 157
Brazil (film), 412n2
Breaking Bad (television series), 328
Bremond, Claude, 2, 5, 21
Brinkmann, Christine N., 410n54
Burns, Charles, xxi, 85, 256, 296
Burton, Tim, 382n34

Index 495

Buscombe, Edward, 376n11
Bush, George W., 353n29

Cage, Nicolas, 88, 178–179
Call of Cthulhu: Dark Corners of the Earth (video game), 311
Call of Duty (video game), 419n29, 420n33
Call of Duty 2 (video game), 85
camera (in film), 83, 145, 272, 409n49. *See also* virtual camera (in video games)
Campbell, Eddie, 85
canon, 58, 125, 330, 334n6, 422n5
Caracciolo, Marco, 242
Carey, Mike, xxi, 64, 85, 102, 282, 372n47, 390n19
causality, 30, 43–44, 46–49, 54, 62, 71–72, 76, 79, 81–83, 85, 94, 96, 98, 100–101, 103–104, 113, 121, 240, 268, 343n36, 343n40, 350n19, 351n21, 362n6, 363n12, 392n27, 416n16
characters, xvii, 12, 22, 35–36, 41, 45–50, 52–53, 56, 64–66, 71–72, 77–81, 86–90, 95, 100–102, 105–107, 112, 115–120, 125–126, 129–130, 134, 138–139, 141–144, 146–147, 150–151, 153–155, 158–160, 165–173, 176, 178–181, 185, 193–194, 200–201, 204, 209–213, 223–232, 234–241, 244–253, 255–256, 259–265, 269–270, 283–284, 286, 288, 298, 306–312, 321–325, 328–329, 331, 337n15, 342n33, 344n1, 345n3, 350n19, 351n22, 353n28, 353n29, 354n30, 355n36, 362n8, 363n10, 366n25, 369n36, 371n43, 375n9, 377n16, 378n17, 379nn25–26, 385n45, 387nn8–9, 389n13, 389n15, 390n19, 393n30, 398nn8–9, 400n17, 401n19, 401n21, 402n24, 405nn35–36, 408n43, 409n49, 410n51, 411n59, 412n2, 414n8, 417n20, 418nn24–25, 419n27, 419nn30–31, 420nn33–34, 421n38; authoring, 134, 154–155, 178, 185, 193, 200–201, 204, 375n9, 378n17, 387n9, 389n15, 390n19; fictional, 178–180, 185; as ludic objects, 371n43; narrating, 50, 138–139, 141–144, 146–147, 150–151, 153–154, 160, 165–172, 185, 211, 286, 377n16, 378n17, 379nn25–26, 400n17, 405n35; nonfictional, 353n29; player-controlled, 110, 117, 118–120, 207–212, 215–217, 234, 305–312, 321, 368n33, 393nn29–30, 395n33, 395n35, 395nn37–38, 407n38, 419n30, 420nn33–34, 421n38. *See also* narrators; storyworlds; subjectivity
character speech, 86, 100, 252, 255, 278, 288, 411n56, 417n21. *See also* characters; narrators; voice
Charles, Larry, 68
Chatman, Seymour, 3–4, 8, 35–36, 38–39, 46, 126–127, 132, 141–146, 149, 152, 155, 160, 164, 225–227, 236–238, 336n7, 377n15, 378nn20–21, 379n23, 400n17, 406n36
Chion, Michel, 260, 407n39, 410n55
The Chronicles of Riddick: Assault on Dark Athena (video game), 421n38
The Chronicles of Riddick: Escape from Butcher Bay (video game), 421n38
Ciccoricco, David, 399n13

cinematic narrator, 141–146, 148, 151,
  372n2, 378nn20–21, 379n23.
  See also narrators
Clash of the Titans (film), 86
Cloverfield (film), 68
Clowes, David, 45
Coen, Ethan, 156
Coen, Joel, 156
cognitive theory, 8–10, 337n13,
  348n16. *See also* narratology:
  cognitive
Cohn, Dorrit, 252–256, 384n42,
  401n21, 407nn40–41
color, 82–84, 87, 97–99, 168, 185, 194,
  258–259, 265, 285, 295, 307, 309,
  312, 418n25, 420n33
Columbus, Chris, 89
comics, xvii–xviii, xx, 2–4, 6–7,
  14–17, 19–20, 22–23, 25, 27–28, 30,
  42–45, 58, 60, 64–65, 69–76, 85, 87,
  89–105, 107–108, 113, 116, 120–121,
  129, 131–135, 137–138, 140–141, 147–
  153, 155–166, 171, 182–207, 219, 229,
  231–236, 240, 245, 248–256, 260–
  264, 282–306, 308, 319, 321, 325,
  327–332, 338n22, 342n32, 343n40,
  354n32, 357n42, 358n47, 360n53,
  361n4, 362n7, 363n14, 364nn17–18,
  365nn20–25, 371nn46–47, 375n10,
  377n14, 378n17, 380n26, 381n32,
  382n35, 387n9, 389nn12–28, 399n11,
  400n16, 404n34, 409n47, 411n56,
  417nn18–26, 421nn1–3, 423n8.
  See also graphiator (in comics);
  graphic novel; monstrator
  (in comics); narration boxes
  (in comics); narrative
  representation: verbal-pictorial
  mode of; page layout (in comics);
  panels (in comics); speech
balloons (in comics); thought
  bubbles (in comics)
comics studies, xix, 20, 26, 31,
  68, 75–76, 138, 142, 145–147,
  149, 231, 233–234, 249, 252, 260,
  327–328, 333n2, 338n22, 342n32,
  398n2, 421n2, 423n8. *See also*
  narratology: comics
Command & Conquer (video game
  series), 306
communication, 13, 18, 39–40, 52, 68,
  72–73, 125–126, 131, 136, 138, 143,
  145–152, 158, 227, 341n28, 342n31,
  352n26, 355n34, 360n2, 361n5,
  363n15, 369n38, 377n15, 379n22,
  379n25, 381n32, 382n34, 395n38;
  extrafictional, 395n38; literary,
  40, 125, 146, 150–151, 355n34;
  metarepresentational, 361n5;
  narrative, 52, 125–126, 138, 143,
  145–147, 150–151, 363n15, 377n15,
  379n22, 379n25; visual, 360n2
communication studies, xiii, 12,
  337n16, 341n28
comprehension, 43–44, 47, 52, 54–55,
  67, 85, 93, 104, 116, 125, 128–130,
  132, 137, 171, 224–225, 237, 244, 268,
  302, 331, 346n5, 346n9, 352n25,
  354nn31–32, 357n44, 365n18,
  374n7, 376n16, 387n10, 397n5,
  401n21, 412n1, 414n9. *See also*
  interpretation; meaning; meaning
  making; representational
  correspondence; storyworlds: as
  intersubjective communicative
  constructs
computer games, 27, 339n23, 342n33.
  See also video games
computer-generated imagery (CGI),
  368n32, 369n35

consciousness, xx, 16, 30–31,
100, 115, 121, 128–129, 223–225,
228–229, 231–232, 238–249, 252,
259, 261, 263–264, 282, 296, 321,
332, 344n41, 353n28, 400n17,
401n19, 402nn24–25, 403nn27–28,
404n30, 404nn32–34, 408nn43–44,
410n52, 411n59, 419n26. See also
subjectivity
A Contract with God (comic), 94
contradiction, 55–56, 111, 161, 163,
254, 357n42, 357n44, 365n19,
366n24, 371n45, 393n30,
422n4
conventions, 21, 38, 53–54, 58, 61,
63–64, 70, 74, 85, 87, 89, 91, 94, 96,
97, 103, 105–106, 113, 117, 121, 137,
160, 165, 174, 177, 183–184, 217, 219,
225, 258–259, 262–263, 265–267,
274, 277, 283, 285, 287–288, 293,
297, 301, 307, 312–313, 316, 324,
342n31, 342n33, 358n45, 369n35,
369n38, 370n40, 372n47, 373n3,
391n25, 400n18, 407n39, 413nn6–7,
417n18, 418n23
Cooper, Chris, 178
Cox, Brian, 179
Crash (film), 84, 362n8
criterion of continuity, 7, 23–24, 130,
327, 400n18
criterion of neutrality, 7–8, 23, 26,
130, 327
Cronenberg, David, xxi, 64, 78, 265
Crowther, Will, 395n38
Cunningham, Merle, 217
Currie, Gregory, 51–53, 60, 88, 132,
154, 346n5, 347n12, 352n26, 363n15,
385n44, 398n8, 403n26
cut-scenes (in video games), 75,
105–111, 113–115, 117, 119–120,
207–215, 305, 311, 315, 317, 319,
321–322, 324–325, 368nn32–33,
369nn35–36, 370n40, 371n44,
395n33, 419n28, 421n36

The Dark Knight (film), 329
The Dark Knight Rises (film), 329
Das Parfum (novel), 386n1
DeathSpank (video game), xxi, 157,
208, 212, 219, 394n31, 395n38
DeathSpank (video game series),
212–213, 218, 305, 387n9
DeathSpank: Thongs of Virtue (video
game), 212–214, 355n33
de Crécy, Nicolas, 364n17
Defense Grid: The Awakening (video
game), 208
Deleyto, Celestino, 230
Dena, Christy, 423n8
de Saussure, Ferdinand, 74, 351n24
desires, 72, 239, 243, 403n26.
See also affects; emotions;
feelings; moods; subjectivity
Deus Ex: Human Revolution (video
game), 420n34
Diablo (video game), 112
Diablo (video game series),
369n37
dialogue, 45, 71–72, 105, 111, 115, 118,
167, 209, 213, 251, 270, 315, 369n36,
371n44
DiCillo, Tom, 390n19
diegesis (diégèse), 8, 150, 346n6.
See also storyworlds
diegetic levels, 38, 49–50, 63–64, 84,
94–95, 100–102, 116, 121, 139, 155,
157, 161–162, 169, 178–179, 262, 286,
346n7, 351nn22–23, 387n11, 392n27,
394n31, 411n59, 412n1. See also
storyworlds

digital games, 79–81, 150, 342n33, 380n30, 412n1. *See also* video games
discourse, 2–3, 22, 27, 35–38, 90, 155, 160, 232, 252, 335n5, 349n18, 358n48, 378n21, 383n38, 408n43. *See also* narrative representation; syuzhet
District 9 (film), 68
Doctor Who (franchise), xvii, 366n24
documentary film, 68, 359n52. *See also* film; nonfictionality
documentary game, 68–69. *See also* nonfictionality; video games
Doležel, Lubomír, 3, 6–7, 39–42, 55, 57–59, 68, 347n10, 349n18
Domsch, Sebastian, 14
Doom (film), 329
Doom (video game series), 306
Doom 3 (video game), 306, 329, 420nn32–33
Dragon Age (video game series), 371n42
Dragon Age II (video game), 208
Dragon Age: Origins (video game), xxi, 105, 112–113, 117–120, 156, 208–213, 218–219, 305, 308, 321, 368n33, 371n44, 395n38, 420n33
drama, 2, 28, 150, 409n49. *See also* theatrical performance
Dream (video game), 321
dreams, 42, 49–50, 64, 77, 84, 95–98, 100–103, 113–114, 116, 161, 229, 243, 245, 249, 255, 262–269, 283–285, 298–299, 301–302, 305–306, 313, 321–322, 324, 351n22, 365n22, 370n40, 391n24, 410n54, 411n58, 512n2, 413n5, 413n7, 417nn19–20, 421n38. *See also* subjectivity
Drucker, Johanna, 365n21

Eco, Umberto, 39, 59–60
Eder, Jens, xiii, 10–11, 49, 52–53, 131, 224–225, 237, 240, 247, 337n15, 353nn28–30, 397n5, 406n36, 410n52
Edminston, William F., 227
Eisner, Will, 94
Eliot, T. S., 168, 386n3
Elleström, Lars, 73
Emmott, Catherine, 348n15
emotions, 2, 29, 60, 72, 126, 158, 174, 244–245, 248–249, 255, 270, 328, 354n32, 404n34, 405n37, 408n43, 413n6. *See also* affects; desires; feelings; moods; subjectivity
Endo, Masanobu, 387n9
Enigma (comic), 157
Enter the Matrix (video game), 308
enunciation theory, 142–144, 146–148
Epileptic (comic), 68, 91
epitext, 127, 134. *See also* paratext; peritext
Erzählforschung, 338n22, 377n15. *See also* narratology
Eskelinen, Markku, 339n23
Eternal Darkness: Sanity's Requiem (video game), 311, 421n38
Eternal Sunshine of the Spotless Mind (film), 84, 262, 363n10, 412n2
eventfulness, 27, 46, 350n19. *See also* events; narrativity
events, 2, 22, 27, 29–30, 35–38, 45–49, 57, 69, 72, 75, 77–79, 81–82, 87, 89, 95, 100, 105–111, 114–117, 119–120, 126, 130, 142, 146, 150, 169–170, 172–173, 209–211, 214–216, 218,

events (cont.)
226, 243, 246–247, 266, 276, 282, 292–293, 298, 305, 307, 312–313, 317, 321, 323–325, 345nn2–3, 350nn19–21, 367n29, 367n31, 368n33, 369n36, 370n40, 373n3, 381n31, 387n10, 390n16, 394n32, 406n36, 409n49, 415n11, 419n28, 420n35. *See also* eventfulness; ludic events (in video games); scripted events (in video games); situations; storyworlds

eXistenZ (film), xxi, 64, 66, 78–82, 84, 265, 363n10, 366n23, 412n1

Exit through the Gift Shop (film), 68

experience, 10–11, 41, 44–45, 59–60, 69, 72, 81, 84, 95, 97–98, 105, 115, 117–118, 180, 189, 218, 220, 223–224, 239–244, 247–248, 268, 279, 302, 315–316, 322, 351n24, 354n32, 357n43, 363n13, 367n28, 382n35, 387n8, 392n27, 402n25, 403nn27–28, 404n31, 412n1, 413n5. *See also* subjectivity

experiencing I, 157–158, 173–176, 178, 187–190, 194–195, 198, 200, 209, 213, 215, 217, 254–255, 266, 270–273, 276–282, 291–293, 295, 298, 302–303, 305, 322, 370n40, 382n35, 387n8, 390n20, 391n22, 394n31, 400n17, 407n41, 413nn6–9, 416nn15–16, 417n19, 418n23, 419n27. *See also* characters; narrating I; narrators

Fables: Arabian Nights (and Days) (comic), 231–232

fabula, 35–36, 128, 228, 335n5. *See also* histoire; plot; story

The Fall (film), 421n2

Fallout 3 (video game), 420nn33–34

fantasies, 41, 50, 64, 97, 99, 103, 245, 249, 255, 262, 264–265, 269, 321, 370n40, 411n58, 413n7, 417nn19–20. *See also* imaginations; subjectivity

fantasy (genre), 19, 58, 356n41

Far Cry (video game), 208, 420nn32–33

Fear and Loathing in Las Vegas (film), xxi, 89, 255–256, 263, 277–282, 298, 325, 329, 382n36, 416nn15–17, 419n26

F.E.A.R.: First Encounter Assault Recon (video game), xxi, 307–313, 320, 325, 419n28, 419n30, 420nn32–33

feelings, 49, 231, 239, 244–245, 250, 392n27, 404n34, 408n43. *See also* affects; desires; emotions; moods; subjectivity

Ferenz, Volker, 384n42, 387n8

Ferrari, Simon, 69

fictionality, 39–40, 67–69, 105, 347n10, 352n25, 358nn48–49, 359n52, 375n9. *See also* markers of fictionality; nonfictionality

fictional recentering, 41, 56, 347n9, 348n15

fictional truth, 42, 61, 200, 206, 348n13, 349n17

fictional worlds, 22, 39–44, 51, 53, 56–58, 61, 105, 223, 226, 346n4, 347n10, 347nn12–13, 349n18, 355n36, 361n5, 372n2. *See also* storyworlds

Fight Club (film), xxi, 64, 66, 76, 84, 89, 164, 167–168, 171, 173–178, 180, 191, 206, 219, 253, 255, 261, 266, 270–277, 280, 325, 328, 358n47,

369n38, 386n2, 387n9, 390n20, 413n7, 414nn10–11, 415nn13–14
Fight Club (novel), 328, 386n1
film, xvii–xxi, 2–4, 6–9, 14, 16–17, 19–20, 22–23, 25–28, 30–31, 37, 42–45, 58, 60, 62, 64–65, 68–90, 100, 102–105, 107, 113, 116, 120–121, 128–138, 140–153, 155–160, 162–184, 191, 193, 206–207, 219, 229–231, 233–237, 239–240, 245, 247–282, 287–288, 305–306, 308, 319, 321, 325, 327–332, 335n6, 338n21, 342n32, 343n40, 354n32, 357n42, 358n47, 359n52, 362nn7–13, 363nn15–16, 372n47, 375nn10–12, 377n14, 377nn16–25, 382nn34–36, 383n38, 385n44, 386nn1–11, 389n13, 389n15, 390nn18–20, 391n25, 399n11–12, 400n16, 404nn34–35, 407nn39–40, 408nn43–44, 409nn47–60, 412nn1–17, 421nn1–3, 422nn5–6, 423n8. *See also* camera (in film); cinematic narrator; intertitles (in film); mise-en-scène (in film); montage (in film); narrative representation: audiovisual mode of; point-of-view shot (in film); shot (in film); slow motion (in film); zoom (in film)
film studies, 20, 26, 75–76, 79, 129, 135, 142, 145, 149, 225, 233, 237, 249, 252, 258, 260, 333n2, 338nn21–22, 342n32, 346n6, 353n28, 354n31, 364n16, 400n18, 413n3, 423n8
Final Fantasy (video game series), 112
Final Fantasy VII (video game), 112
Fincher, David, xxi, 64, 68, 84, 89, 164, 167, 173, 177, 253, 266, 270, 328, 369n38

first-person perspective (in video games), 234, 306. *See also* point of view (in video games)
first-person shooter (genre), 19, 105, 108–109, 111, 117, 207, 305–308, 311, 313, 329, 331, 342n33, 419n28, 420n33
flashback, 78, 176, 257–258, 345n2, 411n59. *See also* anachrony; analepsis
flash-forward, 345n2. *See also* anachrony; prolepsis
Fleishman, Avrom, 251–252, 407n40
Flückiger, Barbara, 410n55
Fludernik, Monika, 4–5, 27, 86, 343n39, 384n42, 408n44
focalization, 23, 129, 140, 223, 226–239, 246, 338n22, 377n16, 379n22, 397n4, 399nn9–12, 400n16, 400n18, 402n23, 406n36, 408n43, 409n45; character-bound, 232, 235; external, 129, 226–231, 234–236, 402n23; and the focalizing subject, 228, 232–233, 409n45; and the focalized object, 228, 232–233, 409n45; and the focalizer, 228, 230, 235, 406n36; internal, 129, 226–231, 234–236, 246, 402n23; multidimensional/multiaspectual models of, 232, 246, 397n5, 406n36; narratorial, 232, 233; zero, 226–227, 230, 234–236, 399n10. *See also* auricularization; ocularization; perspective; point of view; subjectivity
folk psychology, 239, 403n26
Forceville, Charles, 73, 360n2
Forrest Gump (film), 312n2
Foucault, Michel, 374n5

Frasca, Gonzalo, 339n23, 367n29, 381n31
Frears, Stephen, 412n2
From Hell (comic), 85
functions, 17, 42, 52, 112, 114, 128, 136, 139–141, 143–144, 148, 150–151, 153–155, 162, 182–183, 193, 199, 204, 206–209, 210, 213, 219–220, 232, 239, 248, 258, 291–292, 303, 305, 307–309, 311, 313, 320–321, 323–329, 344n41, 350n19, 359n52, 369n37, 371n43, 380n28, 385n46, 389n13, 391n25, 393n29, 395n38, 404n32, 407n38, 411n58, 419n30; authorial, 153, 162, 193, 220; ludic, 112, 114, 150, 183, 206–210, 213, 220, 303, 305, 307–308, 311, 313, 320–321, 323–326, 329, 369n37, 371n43, 385n46, 393n29, 395n38, 407n38, 419n30; narrative, 52, 128, 141, 199, 207, 209–210, 220, 248, 258, 291–292, 309, 311, 313, 320, 325–326, 344n41, 350n19, 385n46, 389n13, 395n38, 411n58; narratorial, 139–141, 143–144, 148, 154–155, 204
Fun Home (comic), 68
Funny Animals (comics series), 91

Gaiman, Neil, xxi, 64, 85, 90–91, 94, 100, 156, 164, 184, 187, 194–195, 253, 283, 321, 371n46
game (nondigital), 367n30. *See also* video games
Game of Thrones (television series), xix, 328
gameplay (in video games), 87, 105–109, 111–112, 114, 117, 119–120, 182, 207–208, 212–216, 218–219, 305–306, 308, 310–311, 313, 316–317, 320–325, 329, 367n29, 368nn32–33, 412n1, 421n38, 423n6
games of emergence (in video games), 116–117
games of progression (in video games), 117
game spaces (in video games), 107, 109–112, 207, 209, 213, 215, 234–235, 306, 311–313, 369nn37–38, 423n5. *See also* space
game studies, xix, 20, 26, 31, 68, 75–76, 138, 142, 145, 149, 235, 249, 252, 260, 327–328, 333n2, 339n23, 342nn32–33, 347n9, 381n31, 393n30, 396n2, 421n2, 423nn7–8. *See also* ludology
Gardner, Jared, 338n22
Gaudreault, André, 141–145
Gaut, Berys, 135–146, 376n12
Gears of War (video game), 420n33
Genette, Gérard, 3, 5–6, 14, 25, 38–39, 49–50, 64–65, 126–127, 139, 145, 155, 157, 220, 226–230, 232–235, 237, 246, 335n6, 345n2, 346nn6–7, 349n18, 351nn22–23, 358n46, 377n15, 381n32, 382n34, 399nn9–10, 302n23, 306n36
genre, 2, 5, 8, 19, 21, 53–54, 58, 85, 88, 91, 105, 111, 113–114, 117, 207, 211–212, 305, 309–311, 313, 342nn32–33, 349n17, 356n41, 371n42, 371n44, 372n47, 391n25
Gerrig, Richard J., 43–44, 51, 67, 347n9, 348nn14–15, 350n20
Ghost World (comic), 45
Gibbons, Alison, 73, 360n2
Gibbons, Dave, 157, 329, 371n46, 391n23, 392n26, 418n25

Gibson, James J., 402n25
Gibson, Mel, 157
Gilbert, Margaret, 136, 377n13
Gilliam, Terry, xxi, 89, 255, 262, 266, 277, 329, 362n8, 363n10, 382n36, 412nn2–3
goals (in video games), 107, 109–111, 207, 209, 213, 220, 307, 322, 324, 368n34, 393n29, 407n38
goals (of characters), 29, 48, 213, 223, 311, 407nn37–38
God of War (video game), 86, 306, 420n33
god's eye perspective (in video games), 234, 306. *See also* point of view (in video games)
Goffman, Erving, 373n3
Gondry, Michel, 84, 262, 363n10, 312n2
Gorman, David, 358n48
Grand Theft Auto IV (video game), 312
Grant, Cary, 363n15
graphiator (in comics), 146–147, 193, 380n26
graphic memoir, 68–69, 91, 200–202, 360n53. *See also* comics; nonfictionality
graphic novel, xxi, 19–20, 45, 86, 91, 94–95, 100, 104, 134, 183, 187–189, 194–195, 202, 204–207, 291–292, 296, 343n40, 354n32, 365n20, 371n46, 391nn25–28. *See also* comics
graphic user interface (in video games), 150, 322–323, 369n38, 393n29, 419nn30–31
Gray, Jonathan, 131, 333n1, 373n4, 375n10
Grice, H. P., 52, 346n8, 352n26

Groensteen, Thierry, 147–149, 365n21
Gross, Peter, xxi, 64, 85, 102, 282, 372n47, 390n19

Habibi (comic), xxi, 134, 187–195, 198, 200, 206, 219, 282, 390n17, 392n26, 417n19
Haggis, Paul, 84, 362n8
Half-Life (video game), 387n9, 419n28
Half-Life 2 (video game), 419n28
hallucinations, 50, 64, 173, 229, 245, 249, 255, 264, 268–270, 277–281, 291–296, 306, 309–310, 315–317, 319–320, 370n40, 414n9, 415n14, 416n16, 419n26. *See also* quasi-perception; subjectivity
Halo (video game), xxi, 105–111, 117, 120, 208, 305–306, 369n36, 420nn32–33
Halo (video game series), 306, 308
Halo 2 (video game), 85
Hamburger, Käte, 377n15
Hancock, Hugh, 108
Hansen, Per Krogh, 384n43
happenings, 36, 38–39, 48, 224, 237, 397n5. *See also* events
"Happy Together" (song), 182
Harry Potter (novel series), 103
Harry Potter and the Philosopher's Stone (film), 89
Hartmann, Britta, 163
Hausken, Liv, 15, 21
Hazanavicius, Michel, 87
Helbig, Jörg, 384n42
Herberger, Sepp, 168, 386n3
Herman, David, xiii, 4–5, 9–10, 14–15, 21–22, 37, 43–44, 47–48, 67, 335n3, 337n15, 338n22, 345nn3–4, 347n9

Index 503

Herriman, George, 90
Herrnstein Smith, Barbara, 8–9
hierarchy of knowledge, 129–130, 169, 205, 246–247, 269, 288. *See also* focalization; knowledge; subjectivity: structure of
histoire, 35–36, 335n5. *See also* fabula; plot; story
Hitchcock, Alfred, 173
Hitman: Blood Money (video game), 208
The Hobbit (film series), xix
Hoesterey, Ingeborg, 335n3
Hogan, Patrick C., 47, 55, 78
Holly, Werner, 342n31
Hollywood, 78, 179, 342n32, 343n40, 362n9, 376n11
horror (genre), 19, 113–114, 309, 312
Horstkotte, Silke, 232–233
Hot Shots! Part Deux (film), 159
Howard, Ron, xxi, 173, 256, 273
Hurst, Matthias, 14

Identity (film), 363n10
ideology, 1–2, 109, 232, 368n34, 384n42, 397n5, 400n14, 406n36, 423n7
images, 4, 40, 45, 71, 73, 126, 133, 141–143, 145, 148, 164, 257–258, 350n20, 359n52, 363n15, 365n21, 383n40, 402n23, 409n49. *See also* pictures
imaginations, 42, 47, 50–51, 53, 57, 59, 61, 70, 72, 81, 87, 90, 95–96, 98–99, 105, 127, 132, 137, 195, 241–242, 244, 274–277, 293, 316–318, 322, 349n17, 353n28, 354n30, 355n36, 363n13, 365n22, 402nn25–26, 412n2, 413n7, 415n12, 416n16, 419n26. *See also* fantasies; subjectivity

impossibility, 56–67, 116, 271, 356n37, 356nn40–42; logical, 56–64, 356nn40–42; physical, 57, 63, 67, 271, 356nn40–41; representational, 64–66, 116. *See also* metalepsis; narratology: unnatural
Inception (film), 84, 103, 321, 363n10, 412n2
Indiana Jones (video game series), xix
Indigo Prophecy (video game), 311
inferences, 38, 40, 44, 51–52, 89, 94, 109, 127, 132, 247, 262, 287, 346n8, 351n21, 352n26, 373n3. *See also* comprehension
intentional fallacy, 52, 132, 352n27. *See also* intentionalism
intentionalism, 51–53, 70, 131–134, 152, 352n27, 359n48, 374n7, 403n29; actual, 131–134, 152, 374n7; hypothetical, 52, 131–133, 352n27, 374n7, 403n29. *See also* authorship; intentional fallacy
intentionality (philosophy of mind), 243, 403n29. *See also* consciousness; subjectivity
interactive fiction, 16, 20, 400n13
interactivity (in video games), 19–20, 69, 73, 75–76, 104–107, 111, 116–117, 119–121, 149, 151, 153, 161, 165, 182–183, 193, 206–209, 212–218, 235, 252, 303, 305–306, 309–311, 313, 315–317, 319–322, 325–326, 362n7, 366n27, 367n31, 368nn32–33, 371n45, 378n17, 381n31, 383n39, 393n30, 410n52, 421n36, 421n38
intermediality, xvii–xxi, 2, 11–15, 328–329, 332, 333n2, 337nn17–18,

504 *Index*

338n20, 421n2. *See also* mediality; medium; transmediality
interpretation, 26, 54–55, 94, 132–133, 346n5, 352n27, 354n31, 363n12, 365n18, 374nn6–7. *See also* meaning: interpretative
intersubjective stability (in video games), 69, 111–112, 419n30. *See also* storyworlds: as intersubjective communicative constructs
intersubjectivity, 51–56, 61, 66, 70, 74, 77–78, 82, 85–86, 94, 104–106, 111, 121, 133, 137, 159, 162, 165, 168, 173–174, 220, 229, 239–242, 246–250, 254, 258–259, 261, 263, 271–272, 274, 287–288, 298, 307, 313–316, 344n41, 353nn29–30, 356n41, 361nn5–6, 364n17, 371n45, 373n3, 386n7, 401nn19–20, 414n8, 416n15, 417nn21–22, 418n24. *See also* objectivity; storyworlds: as intersubjective communicative constructs; subjectivity: and intersubjective representation; subjectivity: structure of
intertitles (in film), 78, 167–168, 170
intertitles (in video games), 395n38
intrigant (in video games), 149–151, 380n29, 381n31. *See also* narrators
Iser, Wolfgang, 38

Jackson, Peter, xix, 329
Jahn, Manfred, 5, 15
Jannidis, Fotis, 21–22, 27–28, 39, 139, 141, 337n15, 344nn1–2, 367n29, 381n31
Jenkins, Henry, 367n31, 423n8
La jetée (film), 413n3
Jeunet, Jean-Pierre, 412n2

JFK Reloaded (video game), 68
Jimmy Corrigan: The Smartest Kid on Earth (comic), xxi, 85, 94–101, 183, 185, 261, 283, 365n22, 369n38, 371n46, 417n18
Johnson, Derek, 131, 373n4
Johnson-Laird, Philip N., 348n14, 350n20
Jolie, Angelina, 329
Jonze, Spike, xxi, 64, 85, 162, 168, 178, 265, 363n10
Jost, François, 14, 141–145, 229–230, 235, 339n12, 410n55
Justice League (comics series), 102
Justice League of America (comics series), 102
Juul, Jesper, 105–106, 116–117, 339n34, 367nn30–31

Kablitz, Andreas, 227
Kasavin, Greg, 395n35
Kaufman, Charlie, xix, 64, 85, 88, 162, 168, 178–181, 265, 363n10, 390n19
Kawin, Bruce, 225, 257, 407n39, 410n51
Kayser, Wolfgang, 377n15
Kindt, Tom, 5, 7–8, 132–133, 336n11, 354n31, 374nn6–7, 380n29, 384n42
Kirkman, Robert, 330
Kiss Kiss Bang Bang (film), 162, 387nn9–10, 398n15, 392n27
knowledge, 41, 46, 56, 66, 80, 82–83, 85, 91, 93–94, 106, 121, 128, 129–130, 137, 169, 175–176, 205, 218, 226–227, 230, 237, 244–249, 255, 269, 288, 349n17, 351n21, 397n5, 404n33, 406n36, 413n6. *See also* hierarchy of knowledge
Kojima, Hideo, 85, 387n9

Köppe, Tilmann, 127, 139, 372nn2–3
Kozloff, Sarah, 159, 163, 250–252, 382n40, 407n40, 408n43
Krazy Kat (comic strip), 90
Kress, Gunther, 73
Kuhlman, Martha B., 365n21
Kuhn, Markus, 14, 145–146, 149, 152, 162–163, 251–252, 379nn23–24, 407n40, 410n52
Kukkonen, Karin, 14, 231–232, 338n22
Kuma\War (video game), 68
Kuper, Peter, 364n17
Kurosawa, Akira, 173

Laass, Eva, 384n42
Lahn, Silke, 4
Lamarque, Peter, 374n7
Lanser, Susan S., 8, 127–130, 139, 157–158, 224, 377n16
Lara Croft: Tomb Raider (film), 329
LaRoche, John, 178
law of excluded middle, 56, 356n37, 356n40. *See also* impossibility; law of noncontradiction; storyworlds: incompleteness of
law of noncontradiction, 57, 59–60, 62–64, 357n42, 357n44. *See also* contradiction; impossibility; law of excluded middle
The League of Extraordinary Gentlemen (comic), xix, 94, 162, 184–186, 195, 198, 200, 206, 282, 287–291, 325, 328, 358n47, 364n17, 366n25, 371n46, 389nn14–15, 392n27, 417nn21–22, 420n34
The League of Extraordinary Gentlemen (film), 328
Ledonne, Danny, 68
Lee, Stan, 390n19

Lego (franchise), 423n6
The Lego Movie (film), 423n6
Lego Star Wars (video game), 330, 423n6
Lego Star Wars II: The Original Trilogy (video game), 330, 423n6
Lego The Lord of the Rings (video game), 329–330
Leitch, Thomas, 8
Leterrier, Louis, 86
Levinson, Jerrold, 374n7
linguistics, 1, 39, 49, 72, 355n34
literary studies, xviii, 1–2, 9, 333n2, 338n21, 342n32
literary texts, 3, 4, 14, 16, 22, 29, 31, 41, 43, 45, 52, 60, 102, 125, 127, 132–135, 138–143, 146, 148–151, 153, 229, 233, 235–236, 239, 246, 249, 252, 328, 330, 336n11, 338n21, 341n26, 344n41, 347n10, 351n21, 352n27, 354n31, 366n16, 377n15, 379n25, 398n6, 408n42
Living in Oblivion (film), 390n19
Livingston, Paisley, 136–137, 376n12
logic, 39–40, 49, 56–57, 139, 216, 351n23, 356n37, 357n44, 377n16, 387n10
The Lord of the Rings (film series), xix, 329
The Lord of the Rings (franchise), xvii, xix, 366n24
L'origine (comic), 85
Lost (franchise), xvii
Lost (television series), 328
Lost Highway (film), 82
Lothe, Jakob, 4, 14
ludic events (in video games), 107, 108, 117, 214–216. *See also* events

ludology, 339n23, 367n30. *See also* game studies; narratology: vs. ludology
Lynch, David, 82

Mahne, Nicole, 15–16
Mangold, James, 363n10
Marcks, Greg, 84, 362n8
Margolin, Uri, 40, 42, 50–51, 153–154
Marion, Philippe, 146–147, 380n26
Marker, Chris, 413n3
markers of fictionality, 67, 359n49. *See also* fictionality; nonfictionality
markers of subjectivity, 84, 97–99, 232, 258–259, 261–269, 279–280, 283–288, 292–293, 298, 301–302, 307–308, 312–313, 316–317, 324–325, 412n60, 413n4, 416nn15–16, 418n23; a posteriori, 262, 266–269, 283–285, 288, 301, 313, 324, 413n4; a priori, 262, 265, 268, 280, 284, 286, 288, 293, 302, 313, 316–317, 413n4, 416n16; content, 84, 97, 99, 261, 263, 265–269, 280, 283–288, 293, 298, 301–302, 316–317, 324–325, 413n4, 416n16; contextual, 84, 262–263, 265–269, 279–280, 283–286, 288, 293, 298, 301–302, 313, 316–317, 324–325, 413n4, 416n16; narratorial, 263, 279–280, 293, 298, 325, 413n4; representational, 84, 97, 259, 261, 263, 265–266, 268–269, 280, 283–284, 288, 292–293, 298, 301, 307–308, 312–313, 315–316, 325, 413n4, 418n23; simultaneous, 262–263, 266, 268–269, 279–280, 283–284, 287–288, 292–293, 298, 301, 307–308, 312, 315, 325, 416n16, 418n23. *See also* subjectivity; transparency
Martínez, Matías, 4
Mass Effect (video game series), 371n42
massively multiplayer role-playing game (genre), 342n33, 371n45
materiality, 17, 90
Mathieu, Marc-Antoine, 85
The Matrix (film), 308
The Matrix (film series), 363n10
The Matrix (franchise), xvii
Maus (comic), xxi, 68, 91–94, 134, 162, 200–206, 219, 282, 365n18, 371n46, 390n19, 392n27
"Maus" (comic), 91–92
Max Payne (video game), 108–109, 262, 370n40, 420n33, 421n36
Max Payne (video game series), 208, 421n36
Max Payne 2: The Fall of Max Payne (video game), 370n40, 421n36
Mazzucchelli, David, 417n18
McKee, Robert, 179
McQuarrie, Christopher, 172
McQueen, Steve, 89
meaning, xvii, xx, 15, 40, 51–56, 61, 72–75, 94, 104, 126, 131–132, 134, 331, 346n8, 351n24, 352n26, 353n28, 354n32, 355n33, 362n6, 371n45, 375n10, 401n20; interpretative, 54, 355n33; perceptual, 53; referential, 53–55, 75, 94, 104, 354n32, 355n33, 362n6; transmedial, xvii, 331, 375n10. *See also* comprehension; interpretation; meaning making
meaning making, xx, 51–56, 61, 75, 132, 134, 331–332, 346n8, 351n24, 353n28, 355n33, 371n45,

meaning making (cont.)
401n20. *See also* comprehension;
interpretation; meaning
mechanics (in video games), 107,
109, 110, 114, 207, 209, 216–217,
220, 311–312, 318–319, 323–324,
368n34, 370n40, 395n38, 423n6
media blindness, 20–23
media convergence, xvii, xix, 333n1,
362n7
media culture, xvii–xx, 12, 16, 19, 28,
30, 62, 64, 76, 131, 134, 244, 282,
327, 331, 334n6, 343n40, 393n30,
421n1
mediality, xviii, 2, 7, 12, 14–19, 25,
38, 69–70, 72–73, 105–106, 167,
182, 193, 219, 327, 332, 338n22,
342n32, 362n7, 365n18, 387n9,
411n57. *See also* intermediality;
medium; medium specificity;
transmediality
media studies, xiii, xvii–xviii, 12, 15,
17, 20, 31, 68, 72–73, 334n6, 337n14,
337n18, 373n4, 375n9, 423n8
medium, xvii–xxi, 2–8, 10–31, 35,
38, 42–43, 45–46, 55–56, 58, 61–62,
64–65, 68–73, 75–76, 86–87, 94,
102–104, 108, 121, 129–134, 136–137,
139–140, 146, 151–156, 158, 160–162,
164–165, 177–178, 180, 182–183, 193,
199–200, 206, 213, 219, 225, 230,
237–240, 242–244, 246, 253–254,
256, 260, 263–264, 282, 285,
326–327, 331–332, 333n1, 334n5,
336n10, 338nn19–20, 339n23,
340n25, 341nn27–33, 343n38,
344n1, 347nn10–11, 349n17, 350n19,
352n26, 354n32, 357n42, 361n4,
362n7, 365n21, 372n47, 373n3,
375n10, 377n16, 379n25, 382n35,
383n29, 385n44, 387n10, 391n25,
399n13, 404n34, 408n42, 411n56,
413n6, 417n17. *See also* mediality;
medium specificity
medium specificity, xix–xx, 6–7, 15,
17, 19, 21–23, 24–26, 31, 45, 53–54,
65, 68, 70–71, 75–76, 78, 85–87,
90–91, 94, 105–106, 111, 121, 145,
147, 164–167, 182–183, 205, 208,
212–214, 219, 231, 233–236, 248,
258, 262, 264, 282, 284–285, 297,
306–308, 310, 325–328, 337n17,
338nn21–22, 342n32, 343n34,
345n2, 349n17, 354n32, 356n41,
362n6, 367n29, 371n43, 372n47,
391n25, 395n36, 395n38, 396n2,
407n38, 417n18, 419n31. *See also*
mediality; medium
Meister, Jan-Christoph, xiii, 1–2, 4,
8–9, 29, 181–182, 336n8, 351n21,
388n11
Melville, Herman, 104
Memento (film), 84, 362n8
Memoria (video game), 85
memories, 44, 64, 77–78, 81, 95–96,
115, 161–162, 229, 245, 249, 255, 262,
264, 269–271, 276–277, 282, 286–
287, 292–293, 298, 309–311, 313, 317,
321, 365n22, 370n40, 411nn58–59,
412n2, 413nn7–8, 417nn19–20,
418n23. *See also* subjectivity
Mendes, Sam, 167
mental imagery, 74, 245, 402n25.
See also quasi-perception;
subjectivity
mental model, 44, 47, 51, 53, 62, 74,
348n14, 350n20, 353n29, 362n6.
See also mental representation
(vs. medial representation);
situation model

mental representation (vs. medial representation), 37, 40–42, 44–45, 51–53, 70, 74–75, 103, 105–106, 242–244, 348n16, 350n20, 351n24, 353n28, 402n25. *See also* mental model; narrative representation

metalepsis, 50, 64–66, 79–85, 94, 101–104, 113, 115–116, 121, 171, 174–175, 176–182, 206, 207, 272, 319, 323–324, 366n23, 388n11, 393n30, 395n38; autopoietic, 66, 115, 180–182, 323–324; epistemic, 66, 82–83, 175, 272; metaleptic effects, 66, 79–80, 82, 94, 101–106, 319; ontological, 66, 79–82, 102–104, 174. *See also* impossibility: representational; metareferentiality; mise en abyme

Metal Gear Solid 4: Guns of the Patriots (video game), 85

Metal Gear Solid: Peace Walker (video game), 387n9

metaphor, 44, 91–93, 145, 148, 200–201, 246, 260, 293, 337n13, 347n9, 348n15, 365n18, 369n35, 392n27, 397n5, 408n44, 410n53, 413n6, 416n16

metareferentiality, 30, 47, 64–65, 104, 180, 182, 191, 200, 205, 215, 342n33, 387n10, 392n27

method, xviii–xx, 5–7, 9–11, 16, 20, 26, 30–31, 263, 327–329, 331–332, 336n10. *See also* analysis; methodology; theory

methodology, xvii, 1–2, 6–7, 20, 46, 332, 336n10, 352n27. *See also* method; theoretical frame; theory

Metz, Christian, 257, 260

Metzinger, Thomas, 403n28

Mikkonen, Kai, 232–233, 338n22

Miller, Frank, xxi, 85–86, 94, 134, 183, 255–256, 291, 328, 371n46, 390n20, 418n25, 420n34

Milligan, Peter, 157

mind-bender, 76, 78, 277, 343n40, 386n6

minds, 26, 41, 51, 84, 96, 154–155, 238–245, 248–250, 253, 255, 262–264, 270, 272, 276–277, 279–280, 292–294, 298, 305, 209, 322, 324–325, 363n13, 399n13, 400n17, 401n19, 402n24, 403nn29–30, 404nn32–33, 406nn36–37, 407n39, 410n51, 413nn6–7, 414n11, 416n16, 417n18, 419n27. *See also* consciousness; subjectivity

mise en abyme, 388n11. *See also* metalepsis; metareferentiality

mise-en-scène (in film), 75–76, 78

Mitry, Jean, 257, 402n23, 409n49

Moby-Dick (novel), 104

Mock, Thomas, 341n28, 342n31

monologue, 250–256, 407n40, 408nn42–43

monstrator (in comics), 146–150, 380n26

montage (in film), 75–76, 277

moods, 191, 244–245, 248–249, 255, 404nn34–35. *See also* affects; desires; emotions; feelings; subjectivity

Moore, Alan, xxi, 85, 94, 157, 162, 184–185, 187, 282, 287, 328–329, 364n17, 366n25, 371n46, 389n15, 391n23, 392n26, 418n25, 420n34

motivations, 48, 223, 244–245, 247–249, 255, 351n21, 385n45. *See also* goals (of characters); subjectivity

Müller, Hans-Harald, 5, 7–8, 132–133, 336n11, 354n31, 374nn6–7, 380n29
multimodality, 5–6, 70, 71–73, 75–76, 108, 134, 137–140, 146, 151–153, 155, 158, 161–162, 164–165, 180, 200, 232, 253–254, 256, 260, 282, 357n42, 360n2, 361n4, 369n36, 378n42, 379n25, 382n3, 385n44, 387n10, 398n8, 408nn42–43, 413n6. *See also* narrative representation
Münsterberg, Hugo, 257
music, 2–3, 28, 71–73, 143, 315, 418n43, 421n37. *See also* point of audition; sound; voice
mutual belief principle, 42, 348n13. *See also* actual world; principle of minimal departure; reality principle; storyworlds

Nagel, Thomas, 241–242, 401n20
narrating I, 157–158, 173–176, 178, 187–189, 195, 200, 205, 209, 213, 215, 218–219, 254, 270, 277–280, 291–292, 295–296, 298, 303, 322, 382n35, 387n8, 387n10, 392n27, 394n31, 395n33, 400n17, 407n41, 414n9, 416n15. *See also* characters; experiencing I; narrators
narrating instance, 138, 142–152, 162, 224, 229, 252, 379n23, 379n25, 389n39. *See also* narrators
narrating situation, 156, 158, 187, 189, 214, 217, 292, 381n33, 382nn36–37, 387n10, 389n13, 390n16, 394n31. *See also* narrators
narration, 21, 27–28, 35–36, 48, 58–59, 83, 89, 103–104, 108–109, 125, 127–130, 139–144, 146–147, 149–153, 156–178, 180, 182–187, 189, 191, 193–195, 198–205, 207–211, 215–218, 225–226, 237, 247, 250–255, 258, 270, 291–292, 295, 298, 301–303, 345n2, 367n29, 369n36, 377n16, 379n24, 381n32, 382n34, 383nn38–40, 384nn42–43, 385n45, 386n2, 386n5, 387nn9–10, 389nn12–13, 390nn16–17, 390nn20–23, 391n25, 393nn28–33, 395nn35–38, 398n8, 408n42, 413n6, 414n9, 414n11, 416n15, 417n18, 417n22, 418n25, 422n3. *See also* narrative representation; narrators; subjectivity
narration boxes (in comics), 89, 183–185, 189, 194–195, 250, 291–292, 295, 298, 301–303, 381n32, 389n13, 391n22, 417n18, 417n22, 418n25. *See also* narrators
narrative. *See* narrative representation; narrative works; narrativity
narrative complexity, 30, 47, 69, 76–80, 82, 94, 100, 102–106, 113, 116, 121, 134, 163–165, 168, 171, 179–180, 194, 202, 208, 217, 219, 247, 249, 253, 270–271, 277, 288, 291, 293, 296, 306, 310, 313, 321, 327–330, 340n25, 342n33, 343n40, 354n32, 365n20, 370n40, 371nn46–47, 386n6, 422n3. *See also* narrativity
narrative representation, xviii–xxii, 2–3, 5–14, 16–17, 20, 22–31, 35, 37–38, 40–56, 58–77, 82–85, 87, 94–95, 101, 103, 107–108, 113, 116–117, 120–122, 126, 128–131, 153–155, 168, 180, 182, 200, 207, 219–220, 223–225, 228–229, 231–232, 236, 238–242, 244, 246–248, 253, 259, 261, 264,

282–283, 327–328, 331–332, 334nn5–6, 336n10, 338n22, 341n26, 344n41, 345n3, 349nn17–20, 351n22, 351nn24–26, 353nn28–29, 354nn31–32, 355n35, 356n41, 357n44, 358n48, 361nn5–7, 364n16, 367n29, 367nn31–33, 370n40, 373n3, 374n7, 378n17, 383n39, 389n13, 391n23, 381n25, 401nn19–20, 404n33, 406n36, 411n58, 412nn1–2, 416n15, 421n1; audiovisual mode of, 14, 19–20, 73, 75–77, 83, 87–89, 121, 141–146, 153, 160–161, 165, 167–179, 182, 191, 193, 207, 210, 225, 229–230, 252, 256–258, 260, 266, 270–271, 276, 278–279, 312, 361n4, 362n7, 364n16, 368n32, 371n44, 372n47, 378n17, 378n20, 379n24, 383nn38–39, 386n5, 387nn9–10, 409n48, 410nn51–52, 413n4, 414n11, 416n16; auditive mode of, 151, 183, 265, 313, 364n16, 368n32, 379n23, 386n5, 409n48, 411n56, 415n12; intentional-pragmatic account of, 51–54, 70, 358n48; interactive mode of, 19–20, 69, 73, 75–76, 106–107, 111, 117, 119–121, 153, 161, 165, 182, 193, 207, 209, 212–218, 252, 303, 305, 309–311, 313, 316–317, 319–322, 325, 362n7, 367n31, 368nn32–33, 378n17, 381n31, 383n39, 393n30, 410n52, 421n36, 421n38; oral mode of, 27–28, 35, 49, 154–155; pictorial mode of, 60, 74–75, 82, 86–90, 97, 100, 108, 121, 148, 151, 191, 205, 256–261, 265, 274, 286, 288, 291, 298, 313, 357n43, 360nn3–4, 364nn16–17, 365n22, 379nn23–24, 381n32, 386n5, 389n12, 397n3,
400n18, 409n48, 411n56, 417n18; verbal mode of, 3–5, 18, 23, 27–28, 45, 60, 74–75, 86, 96–97, 103–104, 108–109, 121, 139–141, 143–145, 148–151, 153, 155, 157–162, 164–165, 167, 169–176, 178, 180, 182–185, 187, 189, 191, 193–195, 199, 201–205, 207–212, 215–218, 231, 270, 291–292, 298, 301–303, 335n6, 347n10, 348n15, 357n42, 360n3, 361n4, 364n17, 369n36, 378n17, 381n32, 382n34, 383nn38–39, 385n45, 386n5, 387n9, 389nn12–13, 390n17, 390nn20–21, 392n26, 393nn29–31, 395n33, 395n36, 395n38, 397n5, 408nn42–43, 413n6, 414n9, 416n15, 417n18, 417n22, 422n3; verbal-pictorial mode of, 73, 75–76, 87, 90–91, 94, 96, 100, 103, 109, 121, 146–149, 153, 161, 165, 182, 188–189, 191, 193–194, 198–199, 201, 204–205, 207, 252, 284, 288, 291, 293, 302, 362n7, 368n32, 378n17, 383n39, 387n9, 390n17, 392n26, 410n52; written mode of, 28, 35, 49, 73, 155, 158–159, 167–168, 180, 172–173, 179–180, 182–183, 190–192, 207, 210–211, 215, 217, 219, 266, 313, 361n4, 364n17, 382n36, 389n12, 391n23, 395n38, 411n56, 422n3. *See also* narrators; storyworlds; subjectivity

narrative works, xvii–xix, xxi, 9, 13, 25, 27, 30, 36, 42, 51, 55, 58–64, 66, 86, 94, 101–102, 104, 113, 121, 125, 127–128, 130–139, 151–154, 158, 163, 165, 200–202, 224, 240, 247–248, 253–254, 263–264, 269, 325–326, 328, 330–331, 334n6, 349n17, 353n28, 354n32, 357n42, 358n48,

Index 511

narrative works (cont.)
360n53, 361n5, 363n14, 365n19,
373n3, 374nn6–7, 375n10, 382n37,
383n39, 384n42, 388n11, 389n13,
390n19, 391n25, 392n26,
404nn34–35, 408n42, 413n3,
422n4

narrative worlds, 40, 44–45, 67.
See also storyworlds

narrativity, xviii, 13, 26–29, 68,
105, 223, 335n6, 339n23, 342n33,
343n35, 347n10, 389n13, 419n28.
See also narrative representation;
narrators; subjectivity

narratology, xviii–xxi, 1–11, 13–17,
20–31, 35–39, 43–47, 49, 51, 54,
57, 63, 65, 67–68, 71–72, 74–76,
125–133, 137–138, 140, 142,
145–152, 162, 164–165, 223–224,
228, 231–234, 237, 246, 239, 251,
256–258, 260, 327–328, 332, 335n3,
335n5, 336n7, 336nn9–10, 337n13,
337n17, 338nn21–23, 341n26,
345n3, 349nn18–20, 354n31,
355n33, 356n38, 356n41, 358n47,
361n4, 372n2, 375n10, 379n24,
381n31, 396nn2–3, 398n6, 398n8,
399n10, 399n12, 405n34, 406n36,
407n39, 409n48, 421n1, 423n7;
classical, 1–5, 21, 35, 37, 39, 46,
49, 74, 127–128, 131, 138, 246,
335n3, 336nn9–10, 345n3, 350n19,
354n31, 397n3, 406n36; cognitive,
2, 8–11, 39, 43–47, 51, 67, 130, 133,
137, 337n13, 350n20; comics, 14,
146–149, 231–233, 338n22, 361n4,
381n31, 423n7; contextual, 2, 8–9,
355n33; discourse-oriented, 3; film,
xix, 4, 9, 14, 31, 74, 128, 130, 138,
142, 145–146, 149, 162, 231, 233–234,
249, 251, 256–257, 327–328, 336n7,
337n13, 338nn21–22, 341n26,
375n24, 381n31, 396n2, 399n12,
400n16, 405n34, 407n39, 409n48,
423n7; intermedial, 14, 337n17;
literary, xix, 14, 31, 125–128,
130, 138, 140, 145, 149, 165, 228,
231, 233–234, 237, 249, 327–328,
336n7, 338n21, 341n26, 381n31,
396n2, 400n16, 405n35, 423n7;
vs. ludology, 14, 149–151, 339n23,
381n31, 423n7; media-conscious,
31, 75, 337n17; medium-specific,
337n17, 338n21; neoclassical, 4–5,
9–10, 46, 49, 74, 128, 137, 336nn9–10,
350n19, 354n31; postclassical, 1, 4,
35, 39, 131, 138, 335n3, 336nn9–10,
345n3, 397n3; story-oriented, 3,
349n18; transmedial, xviii–xxi,
2–3, 10–11, 13–17, 20–31, 65, 71, 75,
129, 132, 137–138, 152, 258, 260, 317,
332, 336n7, 337n17, 338n22, 355n33,
356n41, 358n47, 372n2, 375n10,
398n8, 421n1, 423n7; unnatural,
57, 63, 356n38; visual, 4, 74, 228

narrators, xx–xxi, 11, 16, 20–21,
23, 27, 30–31, 49–50, 64–65, 78,
82, 95, 100–101, 113, 121, 125–131,
133–134, 138–220, 223–227, 231–233,
237, 239, 244–258, 263–266, 270,
273, 277–282, 286, 288, 291–293,
295–298, 301–305, 310–311, 313,
321–325, 328–329, 332, 336n10,
344n41, 363n10, 365n18, 369n36,
370n40, 372nn1–3, 375n9,
377nn15–16, 378n20, 379nn25–26,
380n28, 380n30, 381nn32–40,
384n42, 384nn43–46, 386nn2–6,
387nn8–10, 389nn12–13, 390n16,
390nn20–23, 391nn25–27,

393nn30–38, 398nn8–9, 400n17, 401n21, 405nn41–44, 407n39, 407nn41–44, 409n47, 411n59, 412n2, 413nn6–7, 414n9, 414n11, 416n15, 417n17, 417n20, 417n22, 418n25, 419n27, 422n3; covert, 127, 153, 155–156, 170, 172, 185, 187, 194–195, 207, 386n5, 391n21, 395n38, 414n11; extradiegetic, 49, 64–65, 82, 95, 113, 139, 155, 160, 162, 167–170, 172–178, 182–189, 194–195, 200, 202, 205, 207–212, 214, 217–219, 251, 253–254, 266, 270, 273, 277–279, 291–293, 295–296, 298, 301, 303, 322, 370n40, 383n38, 387n10, 389n13, 390n20, 391n23, 392n27, 393n30, 408n43, 414n11, 416n15, 417n17, 419n27; framing, 78, 83, 113, 159–161, 165, 167, 169, 171–173, 175, 179–180, 188, 200, 202, 208–209, 211, 215, 219, 286, 322, 363n10, 391n23, 394n31, 414n11, 417n20, 422n3; heterodiegetic, 139, 157, 167–170, 172, 182, 184, 186–188, 190, 194–195, 199, 207–210, 217–219, 250, 253, 282n34, 390n17, 393n30; homodiegetic, 139, 157, 160–161, 164, 167, 170–173, 178, 182, 187–189, 194–195, 198, 200, 202–204, 207–211, 213–214, 218–219, 250–251, 253–254, 256, 266, 270, 273, 277–279, 286, 291, 296, 298, 303, 305, 322, 369n36, 382nn34–35, 387n10, 390n20, 394n32, 408n43, 414n11, 416n15, 417n17, 417n20, 419n27; hypodiegetic, 50, 173, 195, 213, 381n33, 386n4, 395n33; intradiegetic, 49, 64, 78, 83, 139, 155–163, 167–169, 172, 173, 175, 178, 182–184, 187–190, 194–195, 198–200, 202–204, 207–214, 219, 250, 253–254, 256, 278–279, 286, 292, 298, 302–305, 313, 369n36, 378n17, 381n33, 382n34, 382nn36–37, 387n10, 389nn12–13, 390n17, 390nn19–20, 391n23, 393n29, 394n31, 395n33, 414n11, 416n15, 417n17, 417n20; and narratorial representation, xx–xxi, 16, 20, 30–31, 101, 121, 151, 153–155, 158–168, 171, 175, 177–178, 182–183, 187, 191, 197, 199–200, 206–208, 211–216, 218–220, 250, 255–256, 291–293, 296–298, 301–303, 305, 313, 322, 324–325, 329, 332, 344n41, 365n18, 382n35, 382n37, 383nn39–40, 385n44, 386n5, 387nn9–10, 391n30, 395n35, 395n37, 400n17, 408n44, 411n59, 412n2, 413nn6–7, 414n9, 414n11, 416n15, 417n17, 417n22, 418n25, 422n3; nonframing, 159–160, 165, 167, 169, 202–203, 209, 211, 219; and nonnarratorial representation, 152–153, 155, 158–166, 171–172, 175, 177, 180, 183, 187, 191, 194–195, 199, 211–213, 215, 218–220, 250, 252–254, 256, 258, 260–263, 265–271, 274, 276, 282–287, 313–316, 319–322, 324–325, 382n35, 383nn39–40, 385nn44–45, 387nn9–10, 391n21, 392n26, 407n39, 408n44, 409n46, 410n52, 411n59, 412nn1–2, 413n7, 414n11, 416n16, 417nn19–20, 417n22, 418nn25–26; overt, 142, 155–156, 167, 187, 195, 204, 213, 217. *See also* characters: narrating; experiencing I; narrating I; narrating situation; subjectivity; voice-over

Nasar, Sylvia, 414n11
Nash, John Forbes, Jr., 274–277, 414n11, 415n13
Neitzel, Britta, 150, 234–236, 339n23, 380n28, 381n32
Nelles, William, 227
Neverwinter Nights (video game), 108, 117, 207–208
Neverwinter Nights (video game series), 371n42
Newell, Gabe, 387n9
Newell, Mike, 328
Niederhoff, Burkhard, 223, 397n4
Nitsche, Michael, 235–236
Nolan, Christopher, 84–85, 103, 321, 329, 362nn9–10, 412n2
nonfictionality, 12, 52, 56, 67–69, 91, 93, 154, 161, 169, 171, 193, 200, 218–219, 353n29, 359n52, 382n37, 391n23, 394n31, 395n38, 401n20, 411n59. *See also* characters: nonfictional; documentary film; documentary game; fictionality; markers of fictionality
nonlinearity (in video games), 69, 75, 104–106, 116–121, 149, 183, 206, 208, 210–215, 219, 355n35, 366n27, 371n42, 371nn44–45, 393nn30–31, 395n33, 395n37
norms, 53–54, 70, 109, 245, 247–249, 255, 354n30, 384n42, 404n33, 405nn35–36, 407n38, 423n8. *See also* values
Norrington, Stephen, 328
Norton, Edward, 173, 178
novel, xvii–xviii, 4, 16, 35, 39, 103, 134, 178–179, 254–255, 277–278, 328–329, 373n3, 386n1, 399n13, 407n41, 413n3, 414n11

Nünning, Ansgar, 1–2, 5, 8, 15, 140, 150, 165, 336n9, 380n29
Nünning, Vera, 5

objectivity, 229–230, 240, 401n20, 417n22. *See also* intersubjectivity; subjectivity: and objective representation; subjectivity: structure of
ocularization, 230, 235, 399n12. *See also* auricularization; focalization; perspective; point of view; subjectivity
Olson, Greta, 384n43
omniscience, 399n10, 408n43. *See also* knowledge; narrators
O'Neill, Kevin, xxi, 162, 184–185, 282, 287, 328, 364n17, 366n25, 371n46, 389n15, 420n34
On the Rain-Slick Precipice of Darkness (video game), 393n30
optional-narrator theories, 127, 381n32. *See also* narrators
The Orchid Thief (novel), 178–181
Orlean, Susan, 178–179
The Others (film), 412n2

Paetsch, Hans, 168
Page, Ruth, 73, 360n2
page layout (in comics), 75, 89, 96, 188, 286, 338n22
Painkiller (video game), 308
paintings, 2–3, 42, 74
Palahniuk, Chuck, 328, 386n1, 414n11
Palestine (comic), 201, 360n53
Palmer, Alan, 39–40, 239
panels (in comics), 17, 45, 75, 89, 96–99, 101, 182–183, 189, 202, 231,

285–288, 291–293, 298, 301–302, 338n22, 365n22, 417n18, 417n22
panfictionalism, 68, 352n25. *See also* fictionality
pan-narrator theories, 127. *See also* narrators
Paranormal Activity (film), 68
paratext, 67, 93, 127, 134, 137, 154, 195. *See also* epitext; peritext
Pavel, Thomas, 11, 39
Peanuts (comic strip), 90
Pedri, Nancy, 232–233
Peirce, Charles S., 351n24
Pekar, Harvey, 390n19
Peli, Oren, 68
perception, 43–44, 49, 53, 74–76, 97, 130, 171, 174, 227–232, 241–249, 253, 255, 257–266, 270–276, 278–282, 287–288, 291–293, 295–298, 305–309, 312–313, 315–318, 320–322, 325, 341n28, 342n31, 354n32, 360n3, 385n45, 397n5, 399n9, 401n19, 402nn25–27, 404n33, 405n35, 406nn36–37, 409n49, 410n52, 410n54, 412n2, 413n6, 414n8, 415n12, 418n24, 419nn26–27, 419nn29–30, 420n34. *See also* quasi-perception; subjectivity
Perfume: The Story of a Murderer (film), 167, 253
peritext, 127, 134, 137, 185, 204, 389n15, 392n27. *See also* epitext; paratext
Persepolis (comic), 68
perspective, 23, 45, 77–78, 99, 109, 223–226, 231–238, 240, 244–248, 259, 267–268, 298, 306, 311, 396nn1–6, 399n9, 400n14, 400n16, 400n18,
401n21, 403n28, 406n36, 407n38; emotional, 244, 247; epistemic, 244, 246–247; evaluative/ideological, 109, 244, 247, 368n34, 397n5, 400n14, 407n38; linguistic, 397n5; motivational, 244, 247; multidimensional/multiaspectual models of, 246, 397n5, 406n36; perceptual, 244, 397n5; spatial, 306, 311, 397n5, 400n14, 400n18; temporal, 397n5. *See also* focalization; perspective structure; point of view; subjectivity
perspective structure, 225, 246–248, 368n34, 398n6, 407n38; emotional, 247–248; epistemic, 246–247; evaluative/ideological, 247–248, 368n34, 407n38; motivational, 247–248. *See also* hierarchy of knowledge; perspective
Persson, Per, 53–54, 75, 239, 407n37
Pfister, Manfred, 398n6
Phelan, James, 384n43
phenomenology, 357n44, 404n31, 404n34
philosophy, 1, 26, 39–40, 51–52, 68, 82, 168, 240–243, 338n21, 347n12, 351n24, 353n28, 361n5, 370n39, 374n7, 403n29, 404nn33–34, 407n39
photography, 69, 74, 359n52, 363n15
pictures, 17, 20, 28, 60, 71–72, 75, 78, 82–83, 87–90, 96, 108, 110, 147, 168–170, 174, 176–177, 189, 211, 230, 266, 270, 285, 312, 316, 338n22, 360n3, 363n11, 381n32, 387n10, 389n12, 392n26, 397n3. *See also* narrative representation: pictorial mode of

Index 515

plausibilization, 62–63, 66, 79, 80–82, 103–104, 116, 156, 268, 284, 358n45, 366n23, 386n9. *See also* metalepsis

players, 10–11, 75, 81, 87, 105–113, 116–120, 131, 133, 141, 150, 207–213, 215–218, 235, 306–313, 315, 317, 319, 321–324, 367nn28–29, 367n31, 368nn33–34, 369nn36–37, 371n42, 371n44, 380n28, 381nn31–32, 393nn29–31, 395nn35–38, 407n38, 412n1. *See also* recipients

playthrough (in video games), 82, 111, 116–118, 120, 355n35, 371n45, 395n37

plot, 35–36, 38–39, 54, 62, 77–78, 94–96, 100, 102–103, 113–114, 116, 119, 121, 180–181, 189, 210, 224, 246, 266, 269, 286, 309, 311, 328, 343n40, 345n2, 370n41, 372n47, 387n10, 422n3. *See also* fabula; histoire; story

plural subject theory, 136. *See also* author collectives; authorship

poetics, 6, 19, 336n11, 342n32, 360n2, 365n21; antimimetic, 58; mimetic, 58; nonmimetic, 58; particularistic, 6, 19, 342n32; universalistic, 6, 19, 342n32

poetry, 2

point-and-click adventure (genre), 330, 342n33, 393n30

point of action (in video games), 235, 370n40, 380n28, 400n15. *See also* point of view (in video games); possibilities of interaction (in video games)

point of audition, 260, 278, 309, 313, 315, 317–318, 410n55, 419n29.

See also auricularization; music; sound; subjectivity

point of view, 23, 223–226, 229–231, 233–238, 246, 257–262, 265, 274, 276, 278, 280, 282, 287–289, 291, 293, 297, 305–313, 315–316, 325, 368n34, 396nn2–5, 398nn8–9, 400n14, 400n16, 400n18, 401n21, 406n36, 409n50, 415n12, 417n22, 418n24, 419n26, 419nn29–30, 420n34; evaluative/ideological, 368n34, 397n5, 400n14, 406n36; linguistic, 397n5, 406n36; multidimensional/multiaspectual models of, 246, 406n36; perceptual, 259–262, 274, 276, 278, 280, 282, 287–289, 291, 293, 297, 306–310, 312, 315–316, 325, 397n5, 406n36, 415n12, 418n24, 419n26, 419nn29–30, 420n34; spatial, 259–260, 262, 265, 274, 280, 282, 287–288, 293, 297, 305–307, 311–313, 325, 397n5, 400n14, 406n36, 417n22, 416n26, 419n29, 420n34; temporal, 397n5, 406n36. *See also* focalization; perspective; point of view (in video games); point-of-view shot (in film); subjectivity

point of view (in video games), 234–235, 306, 370n40. *See also* point of action (in video games); point of view; point-of-view shot (in film)

point-of-view shot (in film), 225–226, 229, 257–259, 400n18, 410n52. *See also* point of view; point of view (in video games)

politique des auteurs, 135, 376n11. *See also* author; authorship

Popper, Karl, 353n28

Portal (video game), 208
possibilities of interaction (in video games), 107, 110, 312, 323. *See also* point of action (in video games)
possible worlds, 39–41, 53, 56–57, 62, 65, 346n4, 347n12, 355n36, 356n37, 361n5. *See also* storyworlds
Pratt, Marie Louise, 8
presentation (vs. representation), 60, 90–91, 94, 315, 365n21. *See also* narrative representation; representational correspondence
Priest, Graham, 59, 357n42
Prince, Gerald, 3, 5, 28
Prince of Persia: The Sands of Time (film), 328
Prince of Persia: The Sands of Time (video game), xxi, 214–217, 219, 305, 321, 328, 393n30, 395n38
principle of charity, 61, 63, 70, 76, 85–88, 90–91, 106, 111, 121, 349n17, 395n36. *See also* representational correspondence; silly questions
principle of minimal departure, 41–42, 75, 83, 85, 121, 345n3, 348n13, 349n17, 366n23. *See also* actual world; mutual belief principle; reality principle; storyworlds
"Prisoner on the Hell Planet" (comic), 390n19
production culture studies, 134, 152, 373n4, 421n1
prolepsis, 77, 170, 345n2. *See also* anachrony; flash-forward
Promethea (comic), 85
propositions, 71–72, 74–75, 350n20, 357n42, 361n5, 404n33
Prosopopus (comic), 364n17
psychoanalysis, 146, 404n34, 411n57

psychology, 26, 39, 44, 74, 241, 337n13, 348n16, 404nn33–34
psycho-narration, 252–255, 407n41. *See also* narrators; subjectivity: and narratorial strategies of subjective representation
Psychonauts (video game), 64, 85, 321
Pulp Fiction (film), xxi, 76–78, 81, 84, 95, 167, 265
Punday, Daniel, xiii, 369n38

quasi-perception, 74, 245–249, 253, 255, 259, 260–262, 254–266, 270–276, 278–282, 287–288, 291–293, 295–298, 305–309, 312–313, 315–318, 320–322, 325, 401n19, 402n25, 404n33, 405n35, 406n36, 409n49, 410n52, 412n2, 413n6, 414n8, 415n12, 418n24, 419nn26–27, 419nn29–30, 420n34. *See also* mental imagery; perception; subjectivity
The Queen (film), 412n2
quotations, 59–60, 103, 125, 168, 252–256, 278, 333n1, 334n2, 386n3, 407n40

radio, 16, 115, 314, 342n31
Rajewsky, Irina O., 12–14, 18–19, 338n19, 341n29
Rashomon (film), 173, 386n2
Ravenscroft, Ian, 403n26
reader-response theory, 44, 337n14. *See also* reception theory
readers, 10–11, 37, 39–40, 44, 47, 51, 63, 87, 90–91, 93, 95–96, 98–100, 104, 125–127, 129, 131, 133, 140–141, 147, 187, 195, 204, 227, 287–288, 291–292, 337n14, 364n17, 365n21,

Index 517

readers (cont.)
373n3, 384n43, 390n20, 396n2, 417n18, 418n23, 418n25. *See also* recipients
realism, 58, 67, 89
reality principle, 42, 348n13. *See also* actual world; mutual belief principle; principle of minimal departure; storyworlds
real-time strategy (genre), 19, 111, 306, 342n33
reception theory, 1–2, 10–11, 38, 337nn14–15, 353n28. *See also* reader-response theory
Recettear: An Item Shop's Tale (video game), 369n37
recipients, 9, 30, 38, 41–42, 45–46, 48, 51–54, 56, 60–63, 66, 69–70, 74, 76, 78, 80, 82, 89, 103, 113, 121, 130–131, 133–134, 136–137, 151–153, 157, 159–160, 162, 165, 182, 220, 238–240, 245, 247, 264, 266, 269, 286, 328, 337n15, 344n41, 345n3, 351n24, 353nn28–29, 354n32, 356n41, 362n6, 375n6, 375n10, 384n43, 386n7, 404nn34–35, 407n39, 410n55, 411n58, 414n8
Reeves, Matt, 62
Reinerth, Maike Sarah, xiii, 242, 413n4
relevance theory, 38, 352n26
Remember Me (video game), 85, 321
representational correspondence, 60–61, 70, 85–88, 90–91, 94, 106, 113, 121, 204, 364n17, 369nn37–38; and external explanations, 61–63, 88, 111–112; and internal explanations, 61–63, 65–66, 81–84, 101–102, 112, 284, 356n41, 366n23, 369n37, 387n10. *See also* narrative representation; principle of charity; representation-by-origin; representation-by-use
representation-by-origin, 88–89, 363nn15–16. *See also* narrative representation; representational correspondence
representation-by-use, 88–89, 363nn15–16. *See also* narrative representation; representational correspondence
represented worlds, 37, 39, 46–47, 51, 65, 125, 237, 346n6. *See also* storyworlds
Rescher, Nicholas, 62
retelling, xix, 330, 423n6. *See also* adaptations
The Return of Ishtar (video game), 387n9
Rezeptionsästhetik, 337n14. *See also* reader-response theory; reception theory
rhetoric, 1, 336n11, 368n34, 399n10
Richardson, Brian, 58, 60, 334n5, 356n41, 375n8
Rimmon-Kenan, Shlomith, 4–5, 49–50, 126, 232, 237, 351n23, 377n15, 397n5, 406n36
Rodriguez, Robert, 328
Rogue Legacy (video game), 87
role-playing game (genre), 19, 87, 105, 108, 112, 117, 207–208, 211–212, 215, 308, 342n33, 368n33, 369n37, 371n42, 371n45, 393nn29–30, 395n38, 420n33
Ronen, Ruth, 39, 58
Rouse, Richard, 367n31
rules (in video games), 105, 107, 109, 111–112, 117, 215, 367n29

The Rules of Attraction (film), 412n2
rules of representation (in video games), 107, 234. *See also* point of view (in video games)
Run Lola Run (film), xxi, 82–84, 87–88, 90, 156, 167–171, 206, 219, 265, 363n12, 372n47
Ryan, Marie-Laure, xiii, 3, 5–6, 15, 17–18, 20–22, 27, 29–30, 37, 39–44, 50, 55–57, 60–61, 71–72, 75, 85, 105, 154–155, 337n17, 343nn34–35, 343n37, 345nn3–4, 347nn9–10, 348n13, 348n15, 349nn17–18, 355nn35–36, 356n39, 361n4, 421n2

Sacco, Joe, 201, 360n53
Safe Area Goražde (comic), 360n53
Sam and Max: The Devil's Playhouse (video game), 85, 393n30
The Sandman (comics series, 1974–1976), 102
The Sandman (comics series, 1989–1996), 64, 85, 90–91, 94, 100–104, 194, 206, 219, 255, 283, 321, 371n46, 391n21
The Sandman: Dream Country (comic), 101
The Sandman: Fables and Reflections (comic), 101
The Sandman: Preludes and Nocturnes (comic), xxi, 156, 184–187, 194–198, 253, 262, 283, 389n14, 392n26
The Sandman: The Doll's House (comic), 102
The Sandman: The Season of Mists (comic), 283–285, 292, 298, 325
The Sandman: The Wake (comic), 101

sanity meter (in video games), 311–312, 419n31. *See also* hallucinations; subjectivity
Sarris, Andrew, 135
Satrapi, Marjane, 68
Scheffel, Michael, 4
Schlickers, Sabine, 14, 145, 152, 260, 379n22
Schmid, Wolf, 4–5, 14, 27, 36–40, 46–47, 50, 125, 133, 140, 145, 223–224, 227, 237, 247, 345n3, 377n15, 397n5, 401n21, 406n36
Schmidt, Siegfried J., 17–18, 359n50
Schulz, Charles M., 90
Schüwer, Martin, 14, 90, 231–232, 381n32
Schweizer, Bobby, 69
science fiction (genre), 19, 58, 356n41
The Science of Sleep (film), 412n2
scripted events (in video games), 75, 107, 109–111, 114, 117, 119, 211, 305, 312–313, 317, 321, 323–325, 368n33, 370n40, 395n35, 419n28. *See also* events; ludic events (in video games)
Searle, John R., 136, 242–243, 359n50, 402n25, 403n27, 403nn29–30
The Secret Life of Walter Mitty (film), 412n2
Segal, Erwin M., 348n15
Sellors, Paul, 136, 376n12
seriality, 91, 102, 121, 366n25, 370n41, 371nn46–47, 421n1
setting, 46, 71, 86, 88, 114, 126, 357n41, 366n25, 415n14. *See also* space; storyworlds
Shakespeare, William, 86
Shame (film), 89
Sherlock (television series), 328
Short Cuts (film), 84, 362n8

shot (in film), 43, 78, 83–84, 89, 159, 182, 225–226, 229, 257–262, 277, 387n8, 400n18, 410nn52–53, 411n57
Shyamalan, M. Night, 173, 412n2
Silent Hill 2 (video game), 159
silly questions, 93, 112, 365n19, 369nn37–39. *See also* principle of charity; representational correspondence
simulation (in video games), 75, 106–107, 112, 117, 119–120, 182, 207, 209, 213–215, 308, 321, 367n29, 367n31, 368n33, 371n43, 381n31. *See also* gameplay (in video games); narrative representation: interactive mode of
Sin City (comics series), 87, 94, 134, 328, 371n46, 390n20
Sin City (film), 328
Sin City: Hell and Back (comic), xxi, 85, 87, 255–256, 261, 263, 291–298, 325, 418n24, 420n34
Sin City: The Hard Goodbye (comic), 390n20
Singer, Bryan, xxi, 167, 172, 265, 363n10
Singh, Tarsem, 412n2
singleplayer mode (in video games), xviii, 19, 105, 110–111
situation model, 44, 47, 51, 53, 74, 348n14, 350n20. *See also* mental model
situations, 36, 43–44, 46–49, 53–54, 59–65, 69, 75–79, 81–85, 89, 94–101, 103–104, 106, 113–115, 121, 156–158, 161, 167–170, 172, 176, 178, 180–181, 187–189, 194–195, 204, 208, 214–215, 217–218, 220, 223, 225, 239, 263, 268, 270, 278, 283, 285, 292, 298, 302, 325, 339n23, 350n20, 357n42, 362n6, 381nn33–34, 382nn36–37, 386n4, 387n10, 389n13, 390n16, 392n27, 394n31, 395n38, 416n16. *See also* diegetic levels; narrating situation; storyworlds
The Sixth Sense (film), 77, 173, 412n2
slow motion (in film), 258, 266, 308, 413n4
slow motion (in video games), 308, 311, 313, 413n4
Small, David, 68, 159, 201
Smith, Greg M., 404n34
Smith, Jeff, 392n26
Smith, Murray, 241, 247, 404nn31–32
Snyder, Zack, 157, 308, 329
The Social Network (film), 68
A Song of Ice and Fire (franchise), xvii, xix
sound, 72–73, 75–76, 89–90, 142, 174, 230, 250, 257, 260–261, 361n4, 364nn16–17, 386n32, 407n39, 409n48, 410nn55–56, 419n29. *See also* auricularization; music; point of audition; voice
Souriau, Anna, 346n6
Souriau, Etienne, 346n6
space, 35, 43–48, 54, 69, 71, 75–76, 79, 88–89, 94, 96, 98, 100–101, 103–104, 107–113, 121, 167, 172, 183, 189, 207, 209, 213, 215, 234–245, 259–262, 265, 268, 274, 280, 287–288, 293, 297, 305–307, 311–313, 325, 342n33, 350n19, 362n6, 364n16, 369nn37–38, 392n27, 397n5, 400n14, 400n18, 406n36, 416n16, 417n22, 418n24, 419n26, 419nn29–30, 420n34, 423n6. *See also* setting; storyworlds; subjectivity: spatial point-of-view sequences

Spec Ops: The Line (video game), 261, 420n33
spectators, 10–11, 43, 77–81, 87, 90, 128–131, 133, 141–142, 168, 170–172, 178, 180, 246, 266, 268–271, 276, 282, 359n52, 386n7, 387n10, 407n37, 415n13. *See also* recipients
Spector, Warren, 387n9
speech balloons (in comics), 45, 89, 183, 189, 195, 285, 302, 364n17. *See also* character speech
Sperber, Dan, 38, 52, 352n26
Spiegelman, Art, xxi, 68, 91–94, 134, 162, 200–206, 282, 371n46, 390n19, 392nn27–28
Spiegelman, Vladek, 93, 202–206, 392nn27–28
Spore (video game), 387n9
Springer Berman, Shari, 390n19
Stage Fright (film), 173, 386n2
Staiger, Janet, 342n32, 377n14
The Stanley Parable (video game), 393n30
Stanzel, Franz K., 398n7
Star Wars (comics series), 330
Star Wars (film series), 330, 423n6
Star Wars (franchise), xvii–xix, 12, 330, 366n24, 422nn5–6
Star Wars: Dark Forces (video game), 208
Star Wars: Knights of the Old Republic (video game series), 330, 371n42
Star Wars: The Clone Wars (film), 422n5
Star Wars: The Clone Wars (television series), 422n5
Stein, Daniel, xiii, 334n1, 338n22
Stein, Malte, 227
Stiller, Ben, 412n2
Stitches (comic), 68, 159, 201
story, xvii, xix, 2–4, 9–12, 15, 22, 27, 30, 35–38, 45–48, 50, 52, 61–62, 72, 77–78, 86, 94–96, 100–104, 108–110, 113, 117, 138, 142, 146–147, 150, 154–160, 163, 168, 178, 180–181, 187–189, 191, 194, 202, 204–205, 207, 209, 212–213, 215, 217–218, 220, 223, 232, 266, 271, 278, 283, 286, 309, 312, 321, 323, 328–330, 335n5, 339n23, 342n33, 343n40, 345nn2–5, 357n42, 367n31, 370nn40–41, 378n17, 378nn20–21, 382n34, 382n36, 385n44, 386n7, 392n26, 393nn30–31, 406n36, 413n6, 417n22, 422n3, 423n6. *See also* fabula; histoire; plot
storyworlds, xvii–xxii, 9, 12, 16, 20, 22, 30, 35, 37–59, 61–72, 74–85, 87, 89–91, 94–117, 119–122, 137, 139, 141, 143–144, 146–148, 151, 155–162, 164–165, 167–176, 178–180, 187–189, 195, 202, 204–205, 207–209, 211, 213, 215–216, 218–220, 223–225, 239–241, 247–248, 254–255, 259–262, 264, 266, 269–271, 278, 283–284, 286, 288, 292–293, 295, 298, 305, 309, 313, 315–316, 320–322, 328–332, 338n22, 342n33, 344n41, 344n1, 345nn3–5, 347n10, 348n15, 349n18, 351nn23–24, 353nn28–30, 354nn32–33, 356n39, 356nn41–42, 357n44, 361nn5–6, 363nn10–11, 364nn16–17, 365n22, 366nn24–25, 367n29, 369nn36–37, 370nn40–41, 371n45, 372n47, 373n3, 378n17, 381nn33–34, 383n38, 386n7, 387n10, 389n15, 391nn23–24,

Index 521

storyworlds (cont.)
392n27, 394n31, 395n33, 395nn37–38, 401nn19–20, 409n48, 411n56, 412n2, 414n8, 417n20, 418nn23–24, 419nn29–30, 421n36, 421nn1–2, 422n4; accessibility of, 57–58, 79, 356n39; arrangement of virtual, 120–121, 371n45; "factual domain" of, 41, 101–103, 255, 261–262, 270, 278, 283–284, 288, 295, 298, 309, 313, 316, 320, 363n10, 391n24, 401n19, 412n2, 413nn7–8, 418n24; incompleteness of, 40, 46, 56, 66, 105–106, 355n36, 356n40; as intersubjective communicative constructs, 54–56, 61, 66, 70, 77, 82, 106, 121, 133, 137, 159, 162, 168, 344n41, 353nn29–30, 356n41, 361nn5–6, 364n17, 386n7, 401n20; and ontologically disconnected subworlds, 38, 49, 64–66, 76, 80, 82, 95–96, 100–104, 363n12, 392n27; transmedial, xvii, xix, 12, 330–331, 422n4; and transmedial universes, xviii, 330–331, 422n4; work-specific, 330–331, 422n4. *See also* characters; comprehension; diegetic levels; meaning: referential; narrative representation; narrators; situations; story; subjectivity

Stranglehold (video game), 368n33

Streep, Meryl, 178

structuralism, 1–3, 21, 35, 37, 39, 46, 53, 350n19

Stühring, Jan, 127, 139, 372nn2–3

subjectivity, xx–xxi, 16, 20, 30–31, 51, 53, 78, 95–100, 121, 140, 161, 173, 183–185, 220, 223, 225–226, 228–229, 231–266, 268, 270–272, 273–274, 277–285, 287–288, 291–293, 295–298, 300–301, 303, 305–308, 310–312, 315, 319–321, 324–326, 328–329, 332, 344n41, 363n10, 385n45, 389n12, 391n22, 397n5, 400n15, 400n17, 401n20, 402n23, 403n28, 405nn35–36, 407n39, 407n41, 408nn43–47, 409n49, 410nn51–52, 410nn54–56, 411nn59–60, 412nn1–4, 413nn6–8, 416nn15–18, 417nn22–25, 419nn30–31; and "direct access" to a character's consciousness, xx, 30–31, 121, 238–239, 245, 247, 252–253, 264, 270, 279, 291, 298, 322, 332, 400n17, 401n19, 404n33, 405n35, 409n45, 413n6, 417n18, 419n27; and intersubjective representation, 239–240, 247–248, 287–288, 298, 313–314, 316, 414n8, 417n22; and narratorial strategies of subjective representation, 249–256, 270, 296, 313, 407n39, 407n41, 408n43, 409n47, 418n25; and objective representation, 240–241, 247, 249, 254, 263, 401n21, 402n23, 409n49; and (quasi-)perceptual overlay, 261–262, 265–266, 270–276, 278–282, 287, 291, 293, 295, 297, 305, 308, 313, 315–317, 320, 325, 411n57, 412n2, 414n8, 415n12, 419n26, 419n30, 420n34; and (quasi-)perceptual point-of-view sequences, 259–262, 274, 276, 278, 280, 282, 287–288, 291, 293, 297, 306–309, 312, 315, 415n12, 418n24, 419n26, 419nn29–30, 420n34; and the representation of internal worlds, 262, 265–266, 269, 271, 274, 283, 285–286,

292, 297–298, 310, 313, 315, 320, 324–325, 409n46, 411n59, 412nn1–2, 416n16; and spatial point-of-view sequences, 259–260, 262, 265, 274, 280, 297, 305–307, 311–313, 325, 417n22, 419n26, 420n34; structure of, 240, 248–249, 254, 263, 268, 270, 273–274, 277, 291, 296, 298, 306, 310, 325. *See also* affects; beliefs; consciousness; desires; dreams; emotions; experience; fantasies; feelings; focalization; hallucinations; imaginations; markers of subjectivity; memories; mental imagery; minds; moods; motivations; perception; perspective; point of view; quasi-perception; wishes

Super Columbine Massacre RPG! (video game), 68

superhero (genre), 19

Surdiacourt, Steven, 147, 380n26

Süskind, Patrick, 386n1

Swamp Thing (comics series), 102

The System (comic), 364n17

syuzhet, 35–36, 128, 335n5. *See also* discourse; narrative representation

Talbot, Bryan, 91

The Tale of One Bad Rat (comic), 91

Tan, Shaun, xxi, 285, 364n17, 378n17, 389n12

Tarantino, Quentin, xxi, 76, 167, 265

television, xvii–xviii, 16, 20, 102, 115, 327–328, 330–331, 340nn25–26, 342n31, 343nn40–41, 375n10, 421n1, 422n5

television studies, 328, 342n32

terminology, 3, 6, 13–14, 35–36, 46, 49–50, 129, 140–141, 148, 224, 226, 229–230, 233–238, 243, 252, 257, 337n14, 351nn23–24, 379nn24–25, 380n28, 385n44, 398n8, 399n10, 404n34, 407n41, 410n51. *See also* method; methodology; theoretical frame

text adventure (genre), 149, 395n38

text worlds, 348n15. *See also* storyworlds

theatrical performance, 16, 328, 330, 341n26, 344n41. *See also* drama

theoretical frame, xix–xx, 6–7, 31, 39, 327. *See also* methodology; terminology; theory

theory, xvii, xix–xx, 1–2, 5–11, 14–15, 21, 26, 28, 31, 35, 38–40, 42–44, 46, 51–52, 56–58, 60, 68, 72–73, 105, 127, 129–130, 132, 135–136, 142, 145–148, 152, 204, 256–257, 259, 288, 327, 332, 336n11, 337nn13–15, 337nn22–23, 341nn30–31, 342n33, 344n1, 345n3, 346n6, 346nn8–9, 347nn11–12, 348nn15–16, 352nn26–28, 354nn32–34, 355nn36–37, 359n52, 360n2, 361n5, 365n19, 366n27, 370n39, 374nn5–7, 375nn9–11, 380n28, 381n32, 397n3, 402nn24–26, 403n29, 407n39, 408n43, 409n48. *See also* cognitive theory; enunciation theory; method; methodology; plural subject theory; reader-response theory; reception theory; relevance theory; theoretical frame

third-person perspective (in video games), 234. *See also* point of view (in video games)

Index 523

third-person shooter (genre), 208, 370, 413n4, 420n33
Thompson, Craig, xxi, 68, 134, 187, 282
Thompson, Hunter S., 277–278, 329
Thompson, Kristin, 342n32, 377n14
Thomson-Jones, Katherine, 141, 144, 372n2
Thoss, Jeff, 358n47
thought bubbles (in comics), 89, 96, 183, 195, 231, 285, 302, 417n18
time, 29, 35, 38, 43–48, 54, 71–72, 76, 79, 81–85, 87, 89–90, 94, 96, 98, 100–101, 103–104, 112–113, 121, 160, 167–172, 174, 179–180, 184, 187, 209, 213, 217, 240, 246–247, 264, 266–269, 278, 284, 292, 308, 342n33, 343n40, 345n2, 350nn19–20, 362n6, 368n33, 383n38, 392n27, 394n31, 395n37, 397n5, 406n36, 416n16, 418n23, 419n30. *See also* anachrony; storyworlds
Time Shift (video game), 308
time travel, 82–84, 112, 217, 266–269, 395n37
Todorov, Tzvetan, 5
Tollefsen, Deborah, 136
Tomb Raider (franchise), xvii, 366n24
Tomb Raider (video game), 368n33, 420n33
top-down processes, 7, 43. *See also* comprehension
transfictionality, 102, 366n24, 421n2. *See also* storyworlds: transmedial; storyworlds: and transmedial universes; transmedial entertainment franchises
Transistor (video game), 395n35

transmedial entertainment franchises, xvii–xi, 12, 330–332, 363n14, 366n24, 421n2, 422n4, 423n8. *See also* media convergence; storyworlds: transmedial; storyworlds: and transmedial universes
transmediality, xvii–xxii, 1–3, 6–8, 10–17, 19–27, 29–31, 41–46, 52, 58, 60, 65, 70–71, 75–76, 84–87, 91, 120–121, 129–132, 136–138, 158, 165–166, 182, 199, 219–220, 229, 233, 236–239, 252, 255, 257–260, 264, 269, 283–284, 306, 310, 321, 325, 327–328, 330–332, 337n17, 338nn19–20, 341n26, 343n34, 344nn1–2, 347n10, 349n18, 351n24, 354n31, 356n41, 362n7, 363n14, 366n24, 369n38, 371n46, 377n16, 399n13, 421n2, 422n4, 423n6, 423n8. *See also* intermediality; mediality; medium; narratology: transmedial; storyworlds: transmedial; storyworlds: and transmedial universes
transparency, 45, 103, 147, 254–255, 262–263, 265–266, 270, 274–275, 277, 279, 325, 365n21, 412n2, 414n8. *See also* markers of subjectivity; narrators; unreliability; subjectivity; twist
Truffaut, François, 135
twist, 156, 173, 177, 213, 218, 271, 274, 276, 381n33, 387n10, 415n13. *See also* unreliability; markers of subjectivity; narrators; subjectivity; transparency
Tykwer, Tom, xxi, 82–83, 156, 167, 171, 253, 265, 372n47

Ultima Underworld (video game), 387n9
Uncharted: Drake's Fortune (video game), 368n33
Under Siege (video game), 68
unreliability, 95, 158, 161–165, 171–174, 182, 205–206, 208, 211, 216–217, 219–220, 270, 315, 325–326, 328, 384nn42–45, 386n2, 386nn6–7, 391n25, 393n30, 412n2; evaluative, 164–165, 328, 384nn42–44; ludic, 216–217, 393n30; narrative, 95, 163–164, 171–174, 205, 219–220, 270, 315, 325–326, 384n42, 385nn44–45, 386n6, 391n25, 412n2; narratorial, 158, 161, 163–165, 171–174, 182, 206, 208, 211, 217, 219, 270, 384nn42–43, 385n44, 386n2, 386nn6–7; representational, 164–165, 171–174, 217, 325–326, 384n42, 385nn44–45, 386n6, 391n25. *See also* narrators; subjectivity
The Unwritten (comics series), 64, 85, 102–104, 282, 358n47, 390n19
The Unwritten: Dead Man's Knock (comic), 372n47
The Unwritten: Leviathan (comic), xxi, 104
The Unwritten: Tommy Taylor and the Bogus Identity (comic), 102–103
Uricchio, William, 69
Uspensky, Boris, 397n5, 406n36
The Usual Suspects (film), xxi, 167–168, 171–173, 178, 206, 219, 265, 363n10, 386n2, 386n7

values, 109, 223, 245, 247–249, 255, 404n33, 405nn35–36, 407n38. *See also* norms

van Dijk, Teun A., 348n16
van Leeuwen, Theo, 73
video games, xvii–xix, 2, 6–7, 16–17, 19–20, 22–23, 25, 28, 30, 43, 58, 60, 62, 64–65, 69–76, 85–87, 102–122, 131–135, 137–138, 140–141, 148–153, 155–160, 162–166, 171, 182–183, 191, 193, 206–220, 229, 231, 233–236, 240, 245, 248–256, 260–264, 282, 303, 305–330, 332, 339n23, 342nn32–33, 343n40, 347n9, 347n11, 354n32, 355n35, 357n42, 360n54, 362n7, 363n12, 366nn26–45, 372n47, 375n10, 377n14, 378n17, 380nn27–32, 382n35, 385n46, 387n9, 390nn18–19, 393nn29–38, 399n11, 399nn13–16, 404nn34–36, 407n38, 309n47, 411n56, 419nn28–38, 421nn1–2, 423n6, 423n8. *See also* action-adventure (genre); computer games; cut-scenes (in video games); digital games; first-person perspective (in video games); first-person shooter (genre); gameplay (in video games); games of emergence (in video games); games of progression (in video games); game spaces (in video games); goals (in video games); god's eye perspective (in video games); graphic user interface (in video games); interactivity (in video games); intersubjective stability (in video games); intertitles (in video games); intrigant (in video games); ludic events (in video games); massively multiplayer role-playing game (genre); mechanics (in video

video games (cont.) games); narrative representation: interactive mode of; nonlinearity (in video games); playthrough (in video games); point of action (in video games); point of view (in video games); possibilities of interaction (in video games); real-time strategy (genre); role-playing game (genre); rules (in video games); rules of representation (in video games); sanity meter (in video games); scripted events (in video games); simulation (in video games); singleplayer mode (in video games); slow motion (in video games); third-person perspective (in video games); third-person shooter (genre); virtual camera (in video games)

virtual camera (in video games), 110, 136, 368n33, 369n35. *See also* camera (in film)

virtual worlds, 79, 363n10. *See also* storyworlds

Vogel, Matthias, 341n30

voice, 88, 97, 113, 116, 126–128, 140–143, 149, 151, 156, 158–160, 163, 167–168, 173, 178–179, 184, 194, 211, 213, 217, 250–252, 254–256, 260, 277–279, 282, 292–293, 295, 301–303, 309, 313–315, 322, 324–325, 328, 373n3, 377n16, 381n32, 383n38, 389n13, 390n20, 391n22, 392n27, 394n31, 395n38, 407n39, 409n47, 411n56, 413n6, 414nn11–12, 417n22, 418n25, 420n32; authorial, 127–128, 141, 328, 373n3, 377n16, 392n27; extrafictional, 127–128, 395n38; internal, 159, 174, 184, 194, 250–252, 256, 260, 276–277, 279, 282, 292–293, 295, 301–303, 309, 313–314, 322, 325, 389n13, 390n20, 391n22, 407n39, 409n47, 411n56, 413n6, 415n12, 418n25, 420n32; narratorial, 113, 126–128, 140–141, 156, 158, 163, 179, 184, 194, 211, 217, 250–252, 254–256, 277–279, 295, 322, 377n16, 381n32, 383n38, 389n13, 390n20, 394n31, 409n47, 414n11, 417n22. *See also* character speech; narrators; sound; subjectivity; voice-over

voice-over, 82, 143, 147, 156, 159, 160, 163, 167–168, 172, 174, 177–178, 181–182, 208, 214, 250–251, 278–279, 322, 383n38, 386n2, 389n13, 410n54, 422n3. *See also* narrators; voice

Wachowski, Andy, 308, 363n10
Wachowski, Lana, 308, 363n10
Waco Resurrection (video game), 68
The Walking Dead (comics series), 330
The Walking Dead (franchise), xvii, xix, 330
The Walking Dead (television series), 328, 330
The Walking Dead: Season One (video game series), 330
The Walking Dead: Survival Instinct (video game), 331
Walsh, Richard, 51–53, 125, 138–141, 352nn25–26
Walton, Kendall L., 40–42, 51, 61, 74, 76, 85–86, 90, 345n3, 347nn11–13, 349n17, 355n36, 360n3, 361n5, 365n19, 370n39
Wanted (film), 308

Warcraft (franchise), xvii, xix, 12
Warcraft (video game series), 306
Warcraft III: Reign of Chaos (video game), 108, 111, 370n39
Ware, Chris, xxi, 85, 94–96, 183, 261, 283, 365n21, 369n38, 371n46, 417n18
Watchmen (comic), 94, 157, 329, 371n46, 391n23, 392n26, 418n25, 422n3
Watchmen (film), 308, 329, 422n3
Werth, Paul, 348n15, 350n20
West, Simon, 329
Willingham, Bill, 231–232
Wilson, Deirdre, 38, 52, 352n26
Wilson, George, 226, 258–259, 261–262, 407n39
Wimsatt, William K., 352n27, 374n7
The Wire (television series), 328
wishes, 41, 244–245, 248–249, 255. *See also* goals (of characters); motivations

The Witcher 2: Assassins of Kings (video game), 208
Wolf, Werner, xiii, 5, 12–14, 18, 23–24, 27–28, 30, 48, 65, 337nn18–20, 340n24, 343n39, 388n11
Wollheim, Richard, 60, 357n43
Wolterstorff, Nicholas, 39
World of Warcraft (video game), 312
Wreden, Davey, 393n30
Wright, Will, 387n9

XIII (video game), 108

Yacobi, Tamar, 62–63

Zemeckis, Robert, 412n2
Zierold, Kirsten, 150, 380nn29–31
Zipfel, Frank, 39
zoom (in film), 83, 263, 265
Zunshine, Lisa, 239

IN THE FRONTIERS OF NARRATIVE SERIES:

Unnatural Narrative: Impossible Worlds in Fiction and Drama
by Jan Alber

*Useful Fictions:
Evolution, Anxiety, and
the Origins of Literature*
by Michael Austin

*Possible Worlds Theory and
Contemporary Narratology*
edited by Alice Bell and
Marie-Laure Ryan

*Stories and Minds:
Cognitive Approaches
to Literary Narrative*
edited by Lars Bernaerts, Dirk
De Geest, Luc Herman, and
Bart Vervaeck

*Telling Children's Stories:
Narrative Theory and
Children's Literature*
edited by Mike Cadden

*Strange Narrators in Contemporary
Fiction: Explorations in Readers'
Engagement with Characters*
by Marco Caracciolo

*Refiguring Minds in
Narrative Media*
by David Ciccoricco

*Coincidence and Counterfactuality:
Plotting Time and Space in
Narrative Fiction*
by Hilary P. Dannenberg

*The Emergence of Mind:
Representations of Consciousness
in Narrative Discourse in English*
edited by David Herman

*Story Logic: Problems and
Possibilities of Narrative*
by David Herman

Handbook of Narrative Analysis
by Luc Herman and Bart Vervaeck

*Affective Narratology:
The Emotional Structure of Stories*
by Patrick Colm Hogan

*Imagining Kashmir:
Emplotment and Colonialism*
by Patrick Colm Hogan

*Spaces of the Mind: Narrative
and Community in the
American West*
by Elaine A. Jahner

*The Storyworld Accord:
Econarratology and
Postcolonial Narratives*
by Erin James

*Talk Fiction: Literature
and the Talk Explosion*
by Irene Kacandes

*Ethos and Narrative Interpretation:
The Negotiation of Values in Fiction*
by Liesbeth Korthals Altes

Contemporary Comics Storytelling
by Karin Kukkonen

The Cruft of Fiction: Mega-Novels and the Science of Paying Attention
by David Letzler

The Imagined Moment: Time, Narrative, and Computation
by Inderjeet Mani

Storying Domestic Violence: Constructions and Stereotypes of Abuse in the Discourse of General Practitioners
by Jarmila Mildorf

New Narratives: Stories and Storytelling in the Digital Age
edited by Ruth Page and Bronwen Thomas

Fictional Minds
by Alan Palmer

Writing at the Limit: The Novel in the New Media Ecology
by Daniel Punday

Narrative Beginnings: Theories and Practices
edited by Brian Richardson

Opening Acts: Narrative Beginnings in Twentieth-Century Feminist Fiction
by Catherine Romagnolo

Narrative across Media: The Languages of Storytelling
edited by Marie-Laure Ryan

Storyworlds across Media: Toward a Media-Conscious Narratology
edited by Marie-Laure Ryan and Jan-Noël Thon

Fictional Dialogue: Speech and Conversation in the Modern and Postmodern Novel
by Bronwen Thomas

Transmedial Narratology and Contemporary Media Culture
by Jan-Noël Thon

The Story of "Me": Contemporary American Autofiction
by Marjorie Worthington

To order or obtain more information on these or other University of Nebraska Press titles, visit nebraskapress.unl.edu.

www.ingramcontent.com/pod-product-compliance
Lightning Source LLC
Chambersburg PA
CBHW030558230426
43661CB00053B/1768